D0397075

RANDOM HOUSE WEBSTER'S

SPELL CHECKER

RANDOM HOUSE WEBSTER'S

SPELL CHECKER

Second Edition

RANDOM HOUSE
NEW YORK

Random House Webster's Spell Checker, 2nd Edition
Copyright © 1998 by Random House, Inc.

This is a revised and updated edition of the *Random House Spell Checker* first published in 1992.

The Random House Living Dictionary Database™, the *Random House Living Database Dictionary*™, and the *Random House Living Dictionary Project*™, are trademarks of Random House, Inc. Random House and the house design are registered trademarks of Random House, Inc.

Trademarks

This book is available for special purchases in bulk by organizations and institutions, not for resale, at special discounts. Please direct your inquiries to the Random House Special Sales Department, toll-free 888-591-1200 or fax 212-572-4961.

Please address inquiries about electronic licensing of this division's products, for use on a network or in software or on CD-ROM, to the Subsidiary Rights Department, Random House Reference & Information Publishing, fax 212-940-7370.

Library of Congress Cataloging-in-Publication Data
Random House Webster's spell checker. — 2nd ed.
    p.   cm.
  ISBN 0-375-40390-6 (hardcover)
   1. English language—Syllabification. 2. Spellers.
PE1168.R36   1998
428.1—dc21
                                         98-28868
                                           CIP

Visit the Random House Web site at www.randomhouse.com
Typeset and printed in the United States of America.

Second Edition

0 9 8 7 6 5 4 3 2 1
August 1998

ISBN: 0-375-40390-6
New   York   Toronto   London   Sydney   Auckland

CONTENTS

STAFF

Project Editor: Enid Pearsons
Contributing Editor: Chris Reid
Support Staff: Erika Illyes, Marina Padakis,
   Aaron Tichenor, Jessica Erace
Database Associate: Diane Joao
Database Manager: Constance A. Baboukis
Director of Production: Patricia W. Ehresmann
Managing Editor: Andrew Ambraziejus
Editorial Director: Wendalyn Nichols
Associate Publisher: Page Edmunds
Publisher: Charles M. Levine

HOW TO USE THIS BOOK

WHY A SPELL CHECKER?

Dictionaries are most commonly used to look up spellings. But a dictionary offers a great wealth of information—meanings, pronunciations, syllable divisions, word origins, parts of speech, usage notes, and, frequently, illustrations, maps, tables, and charts. For exploring words in depth, nothing can take the place of a dictionary.

There are times, however, when a dictionary's very virtues, its richness, size, and complexity, make it a less than convenient reference choice. For looking up a spelling quickly or determining where to hyphenate a word, it is an advantage to be able to reach for something small and streamlined—a "speller-divider." *The Random House Webster's Spell Checker* offers that advantage.

CONTENTS OF THIS BOOK

In a single alphabetical list, this spell checker shows some 50,000 entries—common vocabulary words, names and places, and terms frequently encountered in the workplace, including the vocabularies of business and finance and the world of personal computers. Abbreviations and acronyms are also included in the list. Abbreviations shown for states are those recommended for use with ZIP codes.

The entry list also provides short definitions to distinguish between words that sound alike or look alike, or whose meanings are often confused. Each shows only its own definition, and you can look nearby to find the entry with which it is being compared.

WORD DIVISION

In addition to dividing words into syllables, this book distinguishes between those syllable divisions that can appropriately be used for end-of-line hyphenation and those that cannot. Here are some general guidelines about word division:

➤ Do not divide a one-syllable word. This includes past tenses like *walked* and *dreamed*, which should never be split before the *-ed* ending.

➤ Do not divide a word so that a single letter is left at the end of a line, as in *a∘bout*, or so that a single letter starts the following line, as in *cit∘y*.

➤ Hyphenated compounds should preferably be divided only after the hyphen. If the first portion of the compound is a single letter, however, as in *D-day*, the word should not be divided.

➤ Word segments like *-ceous, -scious, -sial, -tion, -tious* should not be divided.

➤ The portion of a word left at the end of a line should not encourage a misleading pronunciation, as would be the case if *acetate*, a three-syllable word, were divided after the first *e*.

SYMBOLS USED IN THIS BOOK

All syllable divisions recommended for use as end-of-line hyphenation points are marked with a bold, centered dot, or bullet (•). This symbol is the one used most frequently in dictionaries to mark word divisions.

The mark used in this book to divide syllables where end-of-line hyphenation is NOT recommended is a hollow bullet (∘).

WORDS COMMONLY MISSPELLED

We have listed here some of the words that have traditionally proved difficult to spell. The list includes not only "exceptions," words that defy common spelling rules, but some that pose problems even while adhering to these conventions.

aberrant
abscess
absence
absorption
abundance
accede
acceptance
accessible
accidentally
accommodate
according
accordion
accumulate
accustom
achievement
acknowledge
acknowledgment
acoustics
acquaintanc
acquiesce
acquire
acquittal
across
address

adequate
adherent
adjourn
admittance
adolescence
adolescent
advantageous
advertisement
affidavit
against
aggravate
aggression
aging
aisle
all right
alien
allegiance
almost
although
always
amateur
analysis
analytical
analyze

anesthetic
annual
anoint
anonymous
answer
antarctic
antecedent
anticipation
antihistamine
anxiety
aperitif
apocryphal
apostasy
apparent
appearance
appetite
appreciate
appropriate
approximate
apropos
arctic
arguing
argument
arouse

arrangement
arthritis
article
artificial
asked
assassin
assess
asthma
athlete
athletic
attorneys
author
authoritative
auxiliary

bachelor
balance
bankruptcy
barbiturate
barrette
basically
basis
beggar
beginning
belief
believable
believe
beneficial
beneficiary
benefit
benefited
blizzard
bludgeon
bologna
bookkeeping
bouillon

boundaries
breathe
brief
brilliant
broccoli
bronchial
brutality
bulletin
buoy
buoyant
bureau
bureaucracy
burglary
business

cafeteria
caffeine
calisthenics
camaraderie
camouflage
campaign
cancel
cancellation
candidate
cantaloupe
capacity
cappuccino
carburetor
career
careful
carriage
carrying
casserole
category
caterpillar
cavalry

ceiling
cellar
cemetery
census
certain
challenge
chandelier
changeable
changing
characteristic
chief
choir
choose
cinnamon
circuit
civilized
clothes
codeine
collateral
colloquial
colonel
colossal
column
coming
commemorate
commission
commitment
committed
committee
comparative
comparison
competition
competitive
complaint
concede
conceivable

conceive
condemn
condescend
conferred
confidential
congratulate
conscience
conscientious
conscious
consensus
consequently
consistent
consummate
continuous
control
controlled
controversy
convalesce
convenience
coolly
copyright
cornucopia
corollary
corporation
correlate
correspondence
correspondent
counselor
counterfeit
courageous
courteous
crisis
criticism
criticize
culinary
curiosity

curriculum
cylinder

debt
debtor
deceive
decide
decision
decisive
defendant
definite
definitely
dependent
de rigueur
descend
descendant
description
desiccate
desirable
despair
desperate
destroy
develop
development
diabetes
diaphragm
different
dilemma
dining
diocese
diphtheria
disappear
disappearance
disappoint
disastrous
discipline

disease
dissatisfied
dissident
dissipate
distinguish
divide
divine
doesn't
dormitory
duly
dumbbell
during

easier
easily
ecstasy
effervescent
efficacy
efficiency
efficient
eighth
eightieth
electrician
eligibility
eligible
eliminate
ellipsis
embarrass
encouraging
endurance
energetic
enforceable
enthusiasm
environment
equipped
erroneous

especially
esteemed
exacerbate
exaggerate
exceed
excel
excellent
except
exceptionally
excessive
executive
exercise
exhibition
exhilarate
existence
expense
experience
experiment
explanation
exquisite
extemporaneous
extraordinary
extremely

facilities
fallacy
familiar
fascinate
fascism
feasible
February
fictitious
fiend
fierce
fiftieth
finagle

finally
financial
foliage
forcible
forehead
foreign
forfeit
formally
forte
fortieth
fortunately
forty
fourth
friend
frieze
fundamental
furniture

galoshes
gauge
genealogy
generally
gnash
government
governor
graffiti
grammar
grateful
grievance
grievous
guarantee
guard
guidance

handkerchief
haphazard

harass
harebrained
hazard height
hemorrhage
hemorrhoid
hereditary
heroes
hierarchy
hindrance
hoping
hors d'oeuvres
huge
humorous
hundredth
hydraulic
hygiene
hygienist
hypocisy

icicle
identification
idiosyncrasy
imaginary
immediately
immense
impresario
inalienable
incident
incidentally
inconvenience
incredible
indelible
independent
indestructible
indictment
indigestible

indispensable
inevitable
inferred
influential
initial
initiative
innocuous
innuendo
inoculation
inscrutable
installation
instantaneous
intellectual
intelligence
intercede
interest
interfere
intermittent
intimate
inveigle
irrelevant
irresistible
island

jealous
jeopardize
journal
judgment
judicial

khaki
kindergarten
knowledge

laboratory
laid

larynx
leery
leisure
length
liable
liaison
libel
library
license
lieutenant
likelihood
liquefy
liqueur
literature
livelihood
loneliness
losing
lovable

magazine
maintenance
manageable
management
maneuver
manufacturer
maraschino
marital
marriage
marriageable
mathematics
mayonnaise
meant
medicine
medieval
memento
mileage

millennium
miniature
minuet
miscellaneous
mischievous
misspell
mistletoe
moccasin
molasses
molecule
monotonous
mortgage
murmur
muscle
mutual
mysterious

naive
naturally
necessarily
necessary
necessity
neighbor
neither
nickel
niece
ninetieth
ninety
ninth
noticeable
notoriety
nuptial

obbligato
occasion
occasionally

occurred
occurrence
offense
official
omission
omit
omitted
oneself
ophthalmology
opinion
opportunity
optimism
optimist
ordinarily
origin
original
outrageous

paean
pageant
paid
pamphlet
paradise
parakeet
parallel
paralysis
paralyze
paraphernalia
parimutuel
parliament
partial
participate
particularly
pasteurize
pastime
pavilion

peaceable
peasant
peculiar
penicillin
perceive
perform
performance
peril
permanent
permissible
perpendicular
perseverance
persistent
personnel
perspiration
persuade
persuasion
persuasive
petition
philosophy
physician
piccolo
plaited
plateau
plausible
playwright
pleasant
plebeian
pneumonia
poinsettia
politician
pomegranate
possess
possession
possibility
possible

practically
practice
precede
precedence
precisely
predecessor
preference
preferred
prejudice
preparatory
prescription
prevalent
primitive
prior
privilege
probability
probably
procedure
proceed
professor
proffer
pronounce
pronunciation
propagate
protégé
psychiatry
psychology
pursuant
pursue
pursuit
putrefy

quantity
questionnaire
queue

rarefy
recede
receipt
receivable
receive
recipe
reciprocal
recognize
recommend
reference
referred
reign
relegate
relevant
relieve
religious
remembrance
reminisce
remiss
remittance
rendezvous
repetition
replaceable
representative
requisition
resistance
responsibility
restaurant
restaurateur
resuscitate
reticence
reveille
rhyme
rhythm
riddance
ridiculous

rococo
roommate

sacrifice
sacrilegious
safety
salary
sandwich
sarsaparilla
sassafras
satisfaction
scarcity
scene
scenery
schedule
scheme
scholarly
scissors
secede
secrecy
secretary
seize
seizure
separate
separately
sergeant
serviceable
seventieth
several
sheik
shepherd
sheriff
shining
shoulder
shrapnel
siege

sieve
significance
silhouette
similar
simultaneity
simultaneous
sincerely
sixtieth
skiing
socially
society
solemn
soliloquy
sophomore
sorority
sovereign
spaghetti
spatial
special
specifically
specimen
speech
sponsor
spontaneous
statistics
statute
stevedore
stiletto
stopped
stopping
strength
strictly
studying
stupefy
submitted
substantial

subtle
subtly
succeed
successful
succession
successive
sufficient
superintendent
supersede
supplement
suppress
surprise
surveillance
susceptible
suspicion
sustenance
syllable
symmetrical
sympathize
sympathy
synchronous
synonym
syphilis
systematically

tariff
temperament
temperature
temporarily
tendency
tentative
terrestrial
therefore
thirtieth
thorough

thought
thousandth
through
till
titillate
together
tonight
tournament
tourniquet
tragedy
tragically
transferred
transient
tries
truly
twelfth
twentieth
typical
tyranny

unanimous
undoubtedly
unique
unison
unmanageable
unnecessary
until
upholsterer
usable
usage
using
usually
utilize

vacancy

vacuum
vague
valuable
variety
vegetable
veil
vengeance
vermilion
veterinarian
vichyssoise
village
villain

warrant
Wednesday
weird
wherever
whim
wholly
whose
wield
woolen
wretched
writing
written
wrote
wrought

xylophone

yacht
yield

zealous
zucchini

A

A-○bomb (atom bomb)
a cap•pel•la
a for•ti•o•ri
A-○frame
à la carte
à la king
à la mode
a pos•te•ri•o•ri
a pri•o•ri
a○a○na
aard•vark
a○back
ab○a•cus or ab○a•ci
  n., pl. ab○a•cus○es.
a○baft
ab○a•lo○ne
a○ban•don v.,
  a○ban•doned,
  a○ban•don•ing.
a○ban•don•ment
a○base v., a○based,
  a○bas•ing.
a○bash
a○bashed
a○bate v., a○bat○ed,
  a○bat•ing.
a○bate•ment Business.
ab•at•toir
ab○bé
ab○bess
ab○bey n., pl. ab•
  beys.
ab○bot
ab•bre•vi•ate v., ab•
  bre•vi○at○ed, ab•
  bre•vi•at•ing.
ab•di•cate v., ab•di•
  cat○ed, ab•di•cat•
  ing. (to renounce: cf.
  ADJURE)
ab•di•ca•tion
ab•do•men

ab•dom○i•nal
ab•duct
ab•duc•tion
ab•duc•tor
a○beam
a○bed
ab•er•rance or ab•
  er•ran○cy
ab•er•rant
ab•er•ra•tion
a○bet v., a○bet•ted,
  a○bet•ting.
a○bet•tor or a○bet•
  ter
a○bey•ance
ab•hor v., ab•horred,
  ab•hor•ring.
ab•hor•rence
ab•hor•rent
a○bide or a○bode, v.,
  a○bid○ed, a○bid•
  ing.
a○bil○i○ty n., pl.
  a○bil○i•ties.
ab•ject
ab•ject○ly
ab•ject•ness
ab•ju•ra•tion
ab•jure v., ab•jured,
  ab•jur•ing.
ab•la•tive
a○blaze
a○ble adj., a○bler,
  a○blest.
a○ble-bod○ied
a○ble•ism
a○bloom
ab•lu•tion
a○bly
ab•ne•gate v., ab•
  ne•gat○ed, ab•ne•
  gat•ing.
ab•ne•ga•tion

ab•nor•mal
ab•nor•mal○i•ty n.,
  pl. ab•nor•mal○i•
  ties.
ab•nor•mal○ly
a○board
a○bode
a○bol•ish v., a○bol•
  ished, a○bol•ish•
  ing.
ab○o•li•tion
ab○o•li•tion•ism
ab○o•li•tion•ist
a○bom○i•na•ble
a○bom○i•na•bly
a○bom○i•na•tion
ab○o•rig○i•nal
aboriginal cost
ab○o•rig○i○ne
a○born•ing
a○bort v., a○bort○ed,
  a○bort•ing.
a○bor•tion
a○bor•tion•ist
a○bor•tive
a○bound v.,
  a○bound○ed,
  a○bound•ing.
a○bout
a○bout-face
a○bove
a○bove-the-line Busi-
  ness.
a○bove•board
a○bove•ground
a○bove•men•tioned
ab•ra•ca•dab○ra
a○brade v.,
  a○brad○ed,
  a○brad•ing.
Ab•ra•ham
a○bra•sion
a○bra•sive

ab•re•ac•tion
a•breast
a•bridge v.,
  a•bridged,
  a•bridg•ing.
a•bridg•ment or
  a•bridge•ment
a•broad
ab•ro•gate v., ab•ro•
  gat•ed, ab•ro•gat•
  ing.
ab•ro•ga•tion
ab•rupt
ab•scess
ab•scessed
ab•scis•sa or ab•scis•
  sas n., pl. ab•scis•
  sae.
ab•scond v., ab•
  scond•ed, ab•
  scond•ing.
ab•scond•er
ab•sence
ab•sent v., ab•
  sent•ed, ab•sent•
  ing.
ab•sent-mind•ed
ab•sen•tee Business.
absentee bal•lot
absentee man•age•
  ment
ab•sen•tee•ism Busi-
  ness.
ab•sinthe
ab•so•lute
absolute ze•ro
ab•so•lute•ly
ab•so•lu•tion
ab•so•lut•ism
ab•so•lut•ist
ab•solve v., ab•
  solved, ab•solv•ing.
ab•sorb v., ab•
  sorbed, ab•sorb•ing.
ab•sorb•a•ble
absorbable risk
ab•sorb•en•cy

ab•sorb•ent
ab•sorp•tion
ab•sorp•tive
ab•stain v., ab•
  stained, ab•stain•
  ing.
ab•stain•er
ab•ste•mi•ous
ab•ste•mi•ous•ness
ab•sten•tion
ab•sti•nence
ab•sti•nent
ab•stract v., ab•
  stract•ed, ab•stract•
  ing.
abstract ex•pres•
  sion•ism
abstract of ti•tle Busi-
  ness.
ab•stract•ed
ab•strac•tion
ab•strac•tion•ism
ab•strac•tion•ist
ab•struse
ab•surd
ab•surd•i•ty n., pl.
  ab•surd•i•ties.
a•bun•dance
a•bun•dant
a•buse v. a•bused,
  a•bus•ing.
a•bus•er
a•bu•sive
a•but v., a•but•ted,
  a•but•ting.
a•but•ment
a•bys•mal
a•byss
a•ca•cia
ac•a•deme
ac•a•de•mi•a
ac•a•dem•ic
ac•a•dem•i•cal•ly
ac•a•de•mi•cian
ac•a•dem•i•cism

a•cad•e•my n., pl.
  a•cad•e•mies.
a•can•thus or a•can•
  thus•es n., pl.
  a•can•thi.
ac•cede v., ac•
  ced•ed, ac•ced•ing.
  (to consent: cf. EXCEED)
ac•cel•er•ant
ac•cel•er•ate v., ac•
  cel•er•at•ed, ac•
  cel•er•at•ing.
accelerated de•pre•
  ci•a•tion Business.
ac•cel•er•o•a•tion
acceleration clause
  Business.
ac•cel•er•o•a•tive
ac•cel•er•o•a•tor
accelerator board
  Computers.
ac•cel•er•om•e•ter
ac•cent v., ac•
  cent•ed, ac•cent•
  ing.
ac•cen•tu•al
ac•cen•tu•ate v., ac•
  cen•tu•at•ed, ac•
  cen•tu•at•ing.
ac•cen•tu•a•tion
ac•cept v., ac•
  cept•ed, ac•cept•
  ing. (to receive: cf. EX-
  CEPT)
ac•cept•a•bil•i•ty
ac•cept•a•ble
ac•cept•a•bly
ac•cept•ance
ac•cep•ta•tion
ac•cept•ed
ac•cess v., ac•cessed,
  ac•cess•ing. (ap-
  proach; to gain access
  to: cf. EXCESS)
ac•ces•si•bil•i•ty
ac•ces•si•ble
ac•ces•sion

ac•ces•so•ry *n., pl.* ac•ces•so•ries.

access time *Computers.*

ac•ci•dence

ac•ci•dent

accident in•sur•ance *Business.*

ac•ci•dent-prone

ac•ci•den•tal

ac•ci•den•tal•ly

ac•claim *v.,* ac•claimed, ac•claim•ing.

ac•cla•ma•tion

ac•cli•mate *v.,* ac•cli•mat•ed, ac•cli•mat•ing.

ac•cli•ma•ti•za•tion

ac•cli•ma•tize *v.,* ac•cli•ma•tized, ac•cli•ma•tiz•ing.

ac•cliv•i•ty *n., pl.* ac•cliv•i•ties.

ac•co•lade

ac•com•mo•date *v.,* ac•com•mo•dat•ed, ac•com•mo•dat•ing.

ac•com•mo•da•tion

ac•com•pa•ni•ment

ac•com•pa•nist

ac•com•pa•ny *v.,* ac•com•pa•nied, ac•com•pa•ny•ing.

ac•com•plice

ac•com•plish

ac•com•plished

ac•com•plish•ment

ac•cord *v.,* ac•cord•ed, ac•cord•ing.

ac•cord•ance

ac•cord•ing

ac•cord•ing•ly

ac•cor•di•on

ac•cor•di•on•ist

ac•cost *v.,* ac•cost•ed, ac•cost•ing.

ac•count *v.,* ac•count•ed, ac•count•ing.

account debt•or

account ex•ec•u•tive *Business.*

ac•count•a•bil•i•ty

ac•count•a•ble

ac•count•an•cy *Business.*

ac•count•ant *Business.*

ac•count•ing *Business.*

ac•counts pay•a•ble *Business.*

accounts re•ceiv•a•ble *Business.*

ac•cou•ter•ment or ac•cou•tre•ment

ac•cred•it *v.,* ac•cred•it•ed, ac•cred•it•ing.

ac•cred•i•ta•tion

ac•cre•tion

ac•cru•al *Business.*

ac•crue *v.,* ac•crued, ac•cru•ing.

accrued in•come *Business.*

accrued li•a•bil•i•ty *Business.*

ac•cul•tur•ate *v.,* ac•cul•tur•at•ed, ac•cul•tur•at•ing.

ac•cul•tur•a•tion

ac•cu•mu•late *v.,* ac•cu•mu•lat•ed, ac•cu•mu•lat•ing.

ac•cu•mu•la•tion

ac•cu•mu•la•tive

ac•cu•mu•la•tor

ac•cu•ra•cy

ac•cu•rate

ac•cu•rate•ly

ac•curs•ed

ac•cu•sa•tion

ac•cu•sa•tive

ac•cu•sa•to•ry

ac•cuse *v.,* ac•cused, ac•cus•ing.

ac•cus•er

ac•cus•tom *v.,* ac•cus•tomed, ac•cus•tom•ing.

ac•cus•tomed

ace *n., v.,* aced, ac•ing, *adj.*

a•cer•bic

a•cer•bi•ty

ac•et•al•de•hyde

a•ce•ta•min•o•phen

ac•e•tate

a•ce•tic (of vinegar: cf. ASCETIC)

ac•e•tone

a•cet•y•lene

ache *v.,* ached, ach•ing, *n.*

a•chene

a•chieve *v.,* a•chieved, a•chiev•ing.

a•chieve•ment

a•chiev•er

A•chil•les heel

Achilles ten•don

ach•ro•mat•ic

ac•id

acid rain

acid test

a•cid•ic

a•cid•i•fi•ca•tion

a•cid•i•fy *v.,* a•cid•i•fied, a•cid•i•fy•ing.

a•cid•i•ty

ac•i•do•sis

a•cid•u•la•tion

a•cid•u•lous

ack-ack

ac•knowl•edge *v.,*

ac•knowl•edged, ac•knowl•edg•ing.
ac•knowl•edg•ment or ac•knowl•edge•ment
acme (highest point)
acne (skin eruption)
ac•o•lyte
ac•o•nite
a•corn
acorn squash
a•cous•tic or a•cous•ti•cal
acoustic coup•ler Computers.
a•cous•ti•cal•ly
ac•ous•ti•cian
a•cous•tics
ac•quaint v., ac•quaint•ed, ac•quaint•ing.
ac•quaint•ance
acquaintance rape
ac•qui•esce v., ac•qui•esced, ac•qui•esc•ing.
ac•qui•es•cence
ac•qui•es•cent
ac•quire v., ac•quired, ac•quir•ing.
ac•quire•ment
ac•qui•si•tion
ac•quis•i•tive
ac•quit v., ac•quit•ted, ac•quit•ting.
ac•quit•tal
a•cre
a•cre•age
ac•rid
a•crid•i•ty
ac•ri•mo•ni•ous
ac•ri•mo•ni•ous•ly
ac•ri•mo•ni•ous•ness
ac•ri•mo•ny
ac•ro•bat

ac•ro•bat•ic
ac•ro•bat•ics
ac•ro•lect
ac•ro•lec•tal
ac•ro•nym
ac•ro•nym•ic or a•cron•y•mous
ac•ro•pho•bi•a
ac•ro•pho•bic
a•crop•o•lis
a•cross
a•cross-the-board
a•cros•tic
a•cryl•ic
act v., act•ed, act•ing.
act•ing
ac•tin•ic
ac•tin•i•um
ac•tion
ac•tion•a•ble
ac•ti•vate v., ac•ti•vat•ed, ac•ti•vat•ing.
ac•ti•va•tion
ac•ti•va•tor
ac•tive
ac•tive•ly
ac•tiv•ism
ac•tiv•ist
ac•tiv•i•ty n., pl. ac•tiv•i•ties.
activity ra•ti•o Business.
ac•tor
ac•tress
acts (deeds: cf. AXE; ASK)
ac•tu•al
ac•tu•al•i•ty n., pl. ac•tu•al•i•ties.
ac•tu•al•ize v., ac•tu•al•ized, ac•tu•al•iz•ing.
ac•tu•al•ly
ac•tu•ar•i•al Business.

ac•tu•ar•y n., pl. ac•tu•ar•ies. Business.
ac•tu•ate v., ac•tu•at•ed, ac•tu•at•ing.
a•cu•i•ty
a•cu•men
ac•u•punc•ture
a•cute
a•cute•ly
a•cute•ness
ad (advertisement: cf. ADD)
ad ho•mi•nem
ad in•fi•ni•tum
ad-lib v., ad-•libbed, ad-lib•bing.
ad-lib•ber
ad nau•se•am
ad va•lo•rem Business.
ad•age
a•da•gio n., pl. a•da•gios.
Ad•am
ad•a•mant
ad•a•man•tine
Ad•am's ap•ple
a•dapt v., a•dapt•ed, a•dapt•ing. (to modify: cf. ADEPT; ADOPT)
a•dapt•a•bil•i•ty
a•dapt•a•ble
ad•ap•ta•tion
a•dapt•er or a•dap•tor
a•dap•tive
add v., add•ed, add•ing. (to increase: cf. AD)
add-in
add-in pro•gram Computers.
add-on Computers.
ad•dend
ad•den•dum n., pl. ad•den•da.

add•er¹ (one that adds)
ad•der² (snake)
ad•dict
ad•dict•ed
ad•dic•tion
ad•dic•tive
ad•di•tion (an adding: cf. EDITION)
ad•di•tion•al
ad•di•tion•al•ly
ad•di•tive
ad•dle v., ad•dled, ad•dling.
ad•dress v., ad•dressed, ad•dress•ing.
ad•dress•a•ble
ad•dress•ee
ad•duce v., ad•duced, ad•duc•ing. (to put evidence forward: cf. EDUCE)
ad•e•o•nine
ad•e•noid
ad•e•noi•dal
a•dept¹ (skilled: cf. ADAPT; ADOPT)
ad•ept² (an expert)
a•dept•ly
a•dept•ness
ad•e•qua•cy
ad•e•quate
ad•e•quate•ly
ad•here v., ad•hered, ad•her•ing.
ad•her•ence
ad•her•ent
ad•he•sion
ad•he•sive
ad•he•sive•ness
ad hoc
a•dieu n., pl. a•dieus, a•dieux. (good-bye: cf. ADO)
ad•i•os
ad•i•pose

ad•i•pos•i•ty
ad•ja•cen•cy
ad•ja•cent
ad•jec•ti•val
ad•jec•ti•val•ly
ad•jec•tive
ad•join
ad•join•ing
ad•journ v., ad•journed, ad•journ•ing.
ad•journ•ment
ad•judge v., ad•judged, ad•judg•ing.
ad•ju•di•cate v., ad•ju•di•cat•ed, ad•ju•di•cat•ing.
ad•ju•di•ca•tion
ad•ju•di•ca•tor
ad•junct
ad•ju•ra•tion
ad•jure v., ad•jured, ad•jur•ing. (to request: cf. ABJURE)
ad•just v., ad•just•ed, ad•just•ing.
ad•just•a•ble
ad•just•a•ble-rate Business.
ad•just•ed gross income Business.
ad•just•er or ad•jus•tor
ad•just•ing en•try Business.
ad•just•ment
ad•ju•tant
ad•man n., pl. ad•men. Business.
ad•min•is•ter v., ad•min•is•tered, ad•min•is•ter•ing.
ad•min•is•trate v., ad•min•is•trat•ed, ad•min•is•trat•ing.
ad•min•is•tra•tion

ad•min•is•tra•tive
ad•min•is•tra•tor
ad•mi•ra•ble
ad•mi•ra•bly
ad•mi•ral
ad•mi•ral•ty n., pl. ad•mi•ral•ties.
ad•mi•ra•tion
ad•mire v., ad•mired, ad•mir•ing.
ad•mir•er
ad•mir•ing•ly
ad•mis•si•bil•i•ty
ad•mis•si•ble
ad•mis•si•bly
ad•mis•sion
ad•mit v., ad•mit•ted, ad•mit•ting.
ad•mit•tance
ad•mit•ted•ly
ad•mix or ad•mixed v., ad•mixt, ad•mix•ing.
ad•mix•ture
ad•mon•ish v., ad•mon•ished, ad•mon•ish•ing.
ad•mon•ish•ment
ad•mo•ni•tion
ad•mon•i•to•ry
a•do (fuss: cf. ADIEU)
a•do•be
ad•o•les•cence
ad•o•les•cent
a•dopt v., a•dopt•ed, a•dopt•ing. (to take as one's own: cf. ADAPT; ADEPT)
a•dopt•ee
a•dop•tion
a•dop•tive
a•dor•a•ble
ad•o•ra•tion
a•dore v., a•dored, a•dor•ing.
a•dor•ing•ly

a•dorn *v.*, a•dorned,
   a•dorn•ing.
a•dorn•ment
ADP *Computers.* (automatic data processing)
ad•re•nal
a•dren•a•line
a•drift
a•droit
a•droit•ly
a•droit•ness
ad•sorb *v.*, ad•
   sorbed, ad•sorb•ing.
   (to gather on a sur-
   face: cf. ABSORB)
ad•sorb•ent
ad•sorp•tion
ad•u•late *v.*, ad•u•
   lat•ed, ad•u•lat•
   ing.
ad•u•la•tion
ad•u•la•to•ry
a•dult
a•dul•ter•ant
a•dul•ter•ate *v.*,
   a•dul•ter•at•ed,
   a•dul•ter•at•ing.
a•dul•ter•a•tion
a•dul•ter•er
a•dul•ter•ess
a•dul•ter•ous
a•dul•ter•y *n.*, *pl.*
   a•dul•ter•ies.
a•dult•hood
ad•um•brate *v.*, ad•
   um•brat•ed, ad•
   um•brat•ing.
ad•um•bra•tion
ad•vance *v.*, ad•
   vanced, ad•vanc•
   ing.
ad•vance•ment
ad•van•tage
ad•van•taged
ad•van•ta•geous
ad•van•ta•geous•ly
ad•vent

ad•ven•ti•tious
ad•ven•ture *v.*, ad•
   ven•tured, ad•ven•
   tur•ing.
ad•ven•tur•er
ad•ven•ture•some
ad•ven•tur•ess
ad•ven•tur•ous
ad•verb
ad•ver•bi•al
ad•ver•bi•al•ly
ad•ver•sar•y *n.*, *pl.*
   ad•ver•sar•ies.
ad•verse (opposing, as
   in "adverse opinions":
   cf. AVERSE)
adverse pos•ses•sion
   Business.
ad•verse•ly
ad•ver•si•ty *n.*, *pl.*
   ad•ver•si•ties.
ad•vert
ad•ver•tise *v.*, ad•
   ver•tised, ad•ver•
   tis•ing. *Business.*
ad•ver•tise•ment
   Business.
ad•ver•tis•er *Busi-
   ness.*
ad•ver•tor•i•al
ad•vice (an opinion of-
   fered: cf. ADVISE)
ad•vis•a•bil•i•ty
ad•vis•a•ble
ad•vise *v.*, ad•vised,
   ad•vis•ing. (to offer
   an opinion: cf. ADVICE)
ad•vis•ed•ly
ad•vise•ment
ad•vis•er or ad•vi•
   sor
ad•vi•so•ry *n.*, *pl.*
   ad•vi•sories.
ad•vo•ca•cy
ad•vo•cate *v.*, ad•
   vo•cat•ed, ad•vo•
   cat•ing.

ae•gis
ae•on
aer•ate *v.*, aer•at•ed,
   aer•at•ing.
aer•a•tion
aer•a•tor
aer•i•al
aer•i•al•ist
aer•ie (bird's nest: cf.
   AIRY)
aer•o•bat•ic
aer•o•bat•ics
aer•obe
aer•o•bic
aer•o•bics
aer•o•dy•nam•ic
aer•o•dy•nam•ics
aer•o•naut
aer•o•nau•ti•cal or
   aer•o•nau•tic
aer•o•nau•tics
aer•o•sol
aer•o•space
aes•thete or es•thete
aes•thet•ic or es•
   thet•ic
aes•thet•i•cal•ly or
   es•thet•i•cal•ly
aes•thet•ics or es•
   thet•ics
aes•ti•vate *v.*, aes•
   ti•vat•ed, aes•ti•
   vat•ing.
aes•ti•va•tion
a•far
af•fa•bil•i•ty
af•fa•ble
af•fa•bly
af•fair
af•fect *v.*, af•fect•ed,
   af•fect•ing. (to act
   on: cf. EFFECT)
af•fec•ta•tion
af•fect•ed
af•fect•ing
af•fect•ing•ly

af•fec•tion
af•fec•tion•ate
af•fer•ent
af•fi•ance v., af•fi•
  anced, af•fi•anc•
  ing.
af•fi•da•vit
af•fil•i•ate v., af•fil•
  i•at•ed, af•fil•i•at•
  ing.
af•fil•i•a•tion
af•fin•i•ty n., pl. af•
  fin•i•ties.
af•firm v., af•firmed,
  af•firm•ing.
af•fir•ma•tion
af•firm•a•tive
af•fix v., af•fixed, af•
  fix•ing.
af•fix•a•tion
af•fla•tus
af•flict v., af•flict•ed,
  af•flict•ing.
af•flic•tion
af•flu•ence
af•flu•ent (rich: cf. EF-
  FLUENT)
af•ford v., af•
  ford•ed, af•ford•
  ing.
af•ford•a•ble
af•fray v., af•frayed,
  af•fray•ing.
af•fright
af•front v., af•
  front•ed, af•front•
  ing.
af•ghan
Af•ghan•i•stan
a•fi•cio•na•do n., pl.
  a•fi•cio•na•dos.
a•field
a•fire
AFL-CIO Business. (la-
  bor union)
a•flame
a•float

a•flut•ter
a•foot
a•fore
a•fore•men•tioned
a•fore•said
a•fore•thought
a•foul
a•fraid
a•fresh
Af•ri•ca
Af•ri•can
Af•ri•can-
  A•mer•i•can
African vi•o•let
Af•ri•kaans
Af•ro n., pl. Af•ros.
Af•ro-A•mer•i•can
Af•ro-cen•tric
af•ter
af•ter cost
af•ter-hours
af•ter•birth
af•ter•burn•er
af•ter•care
af•ter•deck
af•ter•ef•fect
af•ter•glow
af•ter•life
af•ter•mar•ket
af•ter•math
af•ter•noon
af•ter•shave
af•ter•shock
af•ter•taste
af•ter•tax
af•ter•thought
af•ter•ward or
  af•ter•wards
af•ter•world
a•gain
a•gainst
a•gape
a•gar
ag•ate
a•ga•ve
a•gaze

age v., aged, ag•ing,
  age•ing. (to grow
  older)
age-old
a•ged adj. (elderly)
age•ism
age•ist
age•less
a•gen•cy n., pl.
  a•gen•cies.
a•gen•da or a•gen•
  das n., pl. a•gen•da.
a•gen•dum or
  a•gen•da n., pl.
  a•gen•dums.
a•gent
ag•er•a•tum
ag•glom•er•ate v.,
  ag•glom•er•at•ed,
  ag•glom•er•at•ing.
ag•glom•er•a•tion
ag•glu•ti•nate v.,
  ag•glu•ti•nat•ed,
  ag•glu•ti•nat•ing.
ag•glu•ti•na•tion
ag•gran•dize v., ag•
  gran•dized, ag•
  gran•diz•ing.
ag•gran•dize•ment
ag•gra•vate v., ag•
  gra•vat•ed, ag•gra•
  vat•ing.
ag•gra•va•tion
ag•gre•gate
aggregate de•mand
  Business.
aggregate sup•ply
  Business.
ag•gre•ga•tion
ag•gres•sion
ag•gres•sive
ag•gres•sive•ly
ag•gres•sive•ness
ag•gres•sor
ag•grieve v., ag•
  grieved, ag•griev•
  ing.

a•ghast
ag•ile
a•gil•i•ty
ag•i•tate v., ag•i•
  tat•ed, ag•i•tat•
  ing.
ag•i•ta•tion
ag•i•ta•tor
a•gleam
a•glim•mer
a•glit•ter
a•glow
ag•nos•tic
ag•nos•ti•cism
a•go
a•gog
ag•o•nize v., ag•o•
  nized, ag•o•niz•ing.
ag•o•niz•ing•ly
ag•o•ny n., pl. ag•o•
  nies.
ag•o•ra n., pl. ag•o•
  rae.
ag•o•ra•pho•bi•a
ag•o•ra•pho•bic
a•gou•ti or a•gou•tis
  n., pl. a•gou•ties.
a•grar•i•an
a•gree v., a•greed,
  a•gree•ing.
a•gree•a•ble
a•gree•a•bly
a•gree•ment
ag•ri•busi•ness
ag•ri•cul•tur•al
ag•ri•cul•ture
ag•ri•cul•tur•ist
ag•ro-e•co•no•mic
  Business.
ag•ro-in•dus•tri•al
  Business.
ag•ro•nom•ic
ag•ro•nom•ics
a•gron•o•mist
a•gron•o•my
a•ground

a•gue
a•head
a•hold
a•hoy
AI Computers. (artificial
  intelligence)
aid (to help)
aide (a helper)
aide-de-camp n., pl.
  aides-•de-•camp.
AIDS (acquired immune
  deficiency syndrome)
ai•grette
ail v., ailed, ail•ing.
  (to be ill: cf. ALE)
ai•ler•on
ail•ment
aim•less
air v., aired, air•ing.
  (atmosphere; to air: cf.
  E'ER; ERE; ERR; HEIR)
air bag
air-con•di•tion
air con•di•tion•er
air-cool v., air-•
  cooled, air-•cool
air force
air kiss
air pock•et
air-to-air
air-to-sur•face
air•borne
air•brush
air•bus
air•craft n., pl. air•
  craft.
aircraft car•ri•er
air•drome
air•drop v., air•
  dropped, air•drop•
  ping.
Aire•dale
air•field
air•flow
air•foil
air•glow

air•head
air•lift
air•line
air•lin•er
air•mail v., air•
  mailed, air•mail•ing.
air•man n., pl. air•
  men.
air•plane
air•port
air•ship
air•sick
air•sick•ness
air•space
air•speed
air•stream
air•strip
air•tight
air•waves
air•way
air•wor•thi•ness
air•wor•thy
air•y adj., air•i•er,
  air•i•est. (like air: cf.
  AERIE)
aisle (passage: cf. I'LL;
  ISLE)
a•jar
AK (Alaska)
a•kim•bo
a•kin
AL (Alabama)
al den•te
Al•a•bam•a (AL)
al•a•bam•i•an
al•a•bas•ter
a•lac•ri•ty
a•larm v., a•larmed,
  a•larm•ing.
a•larm•ing
a•larm•ist
a•las
A•las•ka (AK)
A•las•kan
alb
al•ba•core

Al•ba•ni•a
Al•ba•ni•an
al•ba•tross
Al•be•it
Al•ber•ta
Al•ber•tan
al•bi•nism
al•bi•no n., pl. al•bi•nos.
al•bum
al•bu•men (egg white)
al•bu•min (protein)
al•che•mist
al•che•my
al•co•hol
al•co•hol•ic
al•co•hol•ism
al•cove
al•de•hyde
al•der
al•der•man n., pl. al•der•men.
ale (a beverage: cf. AIL)
a•le•a•to•ry
a•lee
ale•house n., pl. ale•hous•es.
a•lert v., a•lert•ed, a•lert•ing.
ale•wife n., pl. ale•wives.
al•ex•an•drine
a•lex•i•a
al•fal•fa
al•fres•co
a•lga n., pl. al•gae.
al•gal
al•ge•bra
al•ge•bra•ic
Al•ge•ri•a
Al•ge•ri•an
ALGOL Computers. (programming language)
al•go•rithm Computers.

al•go•rith•mic Computers.
a•li•as
a•li•as•ing Computers.
al•i•bi
al•ien
alien cor•po•ra•tion Business.
al•ien•a•ble
al•ien•ate v., al•ien•at•ed, al•ien•at•ing.
al•ien•a•tion
al•ien•ist
a•light or a•lit, v., a•light•ed, a•light•ing.
a•lign v., a•ligned, a•lign•ing.
a•lign•ment
a•like
al•i•ment
al•i•men•ta•ry (digestive: cf. ELEMENTARY)
al•i•men•ta•tion
al•i•mo•ny n., pl. al•i•mo•nies.
al•i•quot
a•live
al•ka•li or al•ka•lis n., pl. al•ka•lies.
al•ka•line
al•ka•lin•i•ty
al•ka•loid
al•kyd
al•kyl
all (whole: cf. AWL)
all-A•mer•i•can
all-a•round
all-im•por•tant
all-in•clu•sive
all-out
all-pow•er•ful
all-pur•pose

all read•y (entirely ready: cf. ALREADY)
all right
all-round
all-star
all-time
all to•geth•er (completely together: cf. ALTOGETHER)
Al•lah
al•lay v., al•layed, al•lay•ing.
al•le•ga•tion
al•lege v., al•leged, al•leg•ing.
al•leg•ed•ly
al•le•giance
al•le•gor•i•cal
al•le•go•ry n., pl. al•le•go•ries.
al•le•gret•to n., pl. al•le•gret•tos.
al•le•gro n., pl. al•le•gros.
al•lele
al•le•lu•ia
al•ler•gen
al•ler•gen•ic
al•ler•gic
al•ler•gist
al•ler•gy n., pl. al•ler•gies.
al•le•vi•ate v., al•le•vi•at•ed, al•le•vi•at•ing.
al•le•vi•a•tion
al•le•vi•a•tor
al•ley n., pl. al•leys. (street: cf. ALLY)
al•ley cat
al•ley•way
al•li•ance
al•lied
al•li•ga•tor
al•lit•er•ate v., al•lit•er•at•ed, al•lit•er•at•ing.

al•lit•er•a•tion
al•lit•er•a•tive
al•lo•cate v., al•lo•cat•ed, al•lo•cat•ing.
al•lo•ca•tion
al•lo•morph
al•lo•mor•phic
al•lo•path•ic
al•lop•a•thy
al•lo•phone
al•lo•phon•ic
al•lot v., al•lot•ted, al•lot•ting.
al•lot•ment
all•o•ver
al•low v., al•lowed, al•low•ing.
al•low•a•ble
al•low•ance
al•lowed (permitted: cf. ALOUD)
al•loy
all•spice
al•lude v., al•lud•ed, al•lud•ing. (to refer: cf. ELUDE)
al•lure v., al•lured, al•lur•ing.
al•lure•ment
al•lu•sion (reference. cf. ILLUSION)
al•lu•sive (suggestive: cf. ELUSIVE; ILLUSIVE)
al•lu•vi•al
al•lu•vi•um or al•lu•vi•ums n., pl. al•lu•vi•a.
al•ly¹ n., pl. al•lies. (friend: cf. ALLEY)
al•ly² v., al•lied, al•ly•ing. (to unite)
al•ma ma•ter
al•ma•nac
al•might•y
al•mond
al•mon•er

al•most
alms•house
al•ni•co
al•oe n., pl. al•oes.
a•loft
a•lo•ha
a•lone
a•long
a•long•shore
a•long•side
a•loof
a•loof•ness
a•loud (with the voice: cf. ALLOWED)
al•pac•a
al•pen•horn
al•pen•stock
al•pha
al•pha rhythm
al•pha•bet
al•pha•bet•i•cal
al•pha•bet•i•cal•ly
al•pha•bet•ize v., al•pha•bet•ized, al•pha•bet•iz•ing.
al•pha•mer•ic
al•pha•nu•mer•ic Computers.
al•pha•nu•mer•i•cal•ly Computers.
al•pine
al•read•y (previously: cf. ALL READY)
al•so
al•so-ran
al•tar (platform for worship)
al•ter v., al•tered, al•ter•ing. (to change)
alter e•go
al•ter•a•tion
al•ter•ca•tion
al•ter•nate v., al•ter•nat•ed, al•ter•nat•ing.
al•ter•nate•ly

al•ter•na•tion
al•ter•na•tive
al•ter•na•tive•ly
al•ter•na•tor
al•though
al•tim•e•ter
al•ti•tude (height: cf. ATTITUDE)
al•to n., pl. al•tos.
al•to•geth•er (wholly: cf. ALL TO-GETHER)
al•tru•ism
al•tru•ist
al•tru•is•tic
ALU Computers. (arithmetic logic unit)
al•um
a•lu•mi•na
a•lu•min•i•um Brit.
a•lu•mi•num
a•lum•na n., pl. a•lum•nae.
a•lum•nus n., pl. a•lum•ni.
al•ve•o•lar
al•ve•o•lus n., pl. al•ve•o•li.
al•ways
a•lys•sum
Alz•hei•mer's dis•ease
a•mah
a•main
a•mal•gam
a•mal•ga•mate v., a•mal•ga•mat•ed, a•mal•ga•mat•ing.
a•mal•ga•ma•tion
a•mal•ga•ma•tor
a•man•u•en•sis n., pl. a•man•u•en•ses.
am•a•ranth
am•a•ret•to
am•a•ryl•lis
a•mass

am•a•teur
am•a•teur•ish
am•a•teur•ism
am•a•to•ry
a•maze v., a•mazed, a•maz•ing.
a•maze•ment
a•maz•ing•ly
Am•a•zon
Am•a•zo•ni•an
am•bas•sa•dor
am•bas•sa•do•ri•al
am•bas•sa•dress
am•ber
am•ber•gris
aes•thete or es•thete
am•bi•dex•trous
am•bi•ent
am•bi•gu•i•ty n., pl. am•bi•gu•i•ties.
am•big•u•ous (unclear: cf. AMBIVALENT)
am•bi•tion
am•bi•tious
am•biv•a•lence
am•biv•a•lent (uncertain: cf. AMBIGUOUS)
am•ble v., am•bled, am•bling.
am•bly•o•pi•a
am•bro•sia
am•bro•sial
am•bu•lance
am•bu•lant
am•bu•la•to•ry
am•bu•lette
am•bush v., am•bushed, am•bush•ing.
a•me•ba n., pl. a•me•bas, a•me•bae.
a•me•bic or a•moe•bic
a•mel•io•rate v.,

a•mel•io•rat•ed, a•mel•io•rat•ing.
a•mel•io•ra•tion
a•mel•io•ra•tive
a•me•na•ble
a•mend v., a•mend•ed, a•mend•ing. (to revise: cf. EMEND)
a•mend•ment
a•mends
a•men•oi•ty n., pl. a•men•oi•ties.
A•mer•i•ca
A•mer•i•can
American In•di•an
A•mer•i•ca•na
A•mer•i•can•ism
A•mer•i•can•i•za•tion
A•mer•i•can•ize v., A•mer•i•can•ized, A•mer•i•can•iz•ing.
am•er•oi•ci•um
am•er•ind
am•e•thyst
AMEX Business. (American Stock Exchange)
a•mi•a•bil•i•ty
a•mi•a•ble (good-natured: cf. AMICABLE)
a•mi•a•bly
am•i•ca•bil•i•ty
am•i•ca•ble (peaceable: cf. AMIABLE)
am•i•ca•bly
a•mid
a•mide
a•mid•ships
a•midst
a•mi•go n., pl. a•mi•gos.
a•mi•no, n., pl. am•ni•os.
A•mish
a•miss

am•oi•ty (friendship: cf. ENMITY)
am•me•ter
am•mo
am•mo•nia
am•mo•nite
am•mo•ni•um
am•mu•ni•tion
am•ne•sia
am•ne•si•ac
am•nes•ty n., pl. am•nes•ties. v., am•nes•tied, am•nes•ty•ing.
am•ni•o
am•ni•o•cen•te•sis
am•ni•on or am•ni•ons n., pl. am•ni•a.
am•ni•ot•ic
a•moe•ba or a•moe•bas n., pl. a•moe•bae.
a•moe•bic
a•mok
a•mong
a•mongst
a•mon•til•la•do
a•mor•al (without moral standards: cf. IMMORAL; IMMORTAL)
a•mo•ral•i•ty
am•o•rous
am•o•rous•ly
a•mor•phous
a•mor•phous•ness
am•or•ti•za•tion Business.
am•or•tize v., am•or•tized, am•or•tiz•ing. Business.
a•mount v., a•mount•ed, a•mount•ing.
a•mour
a•mour-pro•pre
am•per•age
am•pere

am•pere-hour
am•per•sand
am•phet•a•mine
am•phib•i•an
am•phib•i•ous
am•phi•the•a•ter
am•pho•ra or am•
pho•rae n., pl. am•
pho•ras.
am•ple adj., am•pler,
am•plest.
am•pli•fi•ca•tion
am•pli•fi•er
am•pli•fy v., am•pli•
fied, am•pli•fy•ing.
am•pli•tude
am•ply
aes•thete or es•thete
am•pu•tate v., am•
pu•tat•ed, am•pu•
tat•ing.
am•pu•ta•tion
am•pu•tee
Am•trak
a•muck
a•mu•let
a•muse v., a•mused,
a•mus•ing.
a•muse•ment
amusement park
amusement tax Busi-
ness.
a•mus•ing•ly
am•yl
am•yl•ase
an•a•bol•ic
a•nach•ro•nism
a•nach•ro•nis•tic
an•a•con•da
a•nae•mi•a
a•nae•mic
an•aer•obe
an•aer•o•bic
an•aes•the•sia
an•aes•the•si•ol•oo•
gist

an•aes•the•si•
ol•oo•gy
an•aes•thet•ic
an•aes•the•tist
an•aes•the•tize v.,
an•aes•the•tized,
an•aes•the•tiz•ing.
an•a•gram
a•nal
an•al•ge•si•a
an•al•ge•sic
an•a•log
analog com•put•er
Computers.
analog mon•i•tor
Computers.
an•a•log•i•cal
a•nal•oo•gous
an•a•logue
a•nal•oo•gy n., pl.
a•nal•o•gies.
a•nal•y•sand
a•nal•y•sis n., pl.
a•nal•y•ses.
an•a•lyst (one who
analyzes: cf. ANNALIST)
an•a•lyt•ic or an•a•
lyt•i•cal
an•a•lyze v., an•a•
lyzed, an•a•lyz•ing.
an•a•pest
an•a•phy•lac•tic
an•a•phy•lax•is
an•ar•chic
an•ar•chism
an•ar•chist
an•ar•chis•tic
an•ar•chy n., pl. an•
ar•chies.
an•as•tig•mat•ic
a•nath•e•ma n., pl.
a•nath•e•mas.
a•nath•e•ma•tize v.,
a•nath•e•ma•tized,
a•nath•e•ma•tiz•
ing.

an•a•tom•i•cal or
an•a•tom•ic
a•nat•oo•mist
a•nat•oo•mize v.,
a•nat•oo•mized,
a•nat•oo•miz•ing.
a•nat•oo•my n., pl.
a•nat•oo•mies.
an•ces•tor
an•ces•tral
an•ces•try n., pl. an•
ces•tries.
an•chor v., an•
chored, an•chor•ing.
anchor store Business.
an•chor•age
an•cho•rite
an•chor•man n., pl.
an•chor•men.
an•chor•per•son
an•chor•wom•an n.,
pl. an•chor•
wom•en.
an•cho•vy n., pl. an•
cho•vies.
an•cient
an•cil•lar•y
and/••or
an•dan•te
and•i•ron
an•dro•gen
an•dro•gen•ic
an•drog•y•nous
an•droid
an•ec•dot•al
an•ec•dote (short nar-
rative: cf. ANTIDOTE)
a•ne•mi•a
a•ne•mic
an•e•mom•e•ter
a•nem•oo•ne
a•nent
an•er•oid
an•es•the•sia or an•
aes•the•sia
an•es•the•si•ol•oo•

gist or an•aes•the•
si•ol•o•gist
an•es•the•si•
ol•o•gy or an•aes•
the•si•ol•o•gy
an•es•thet•ic or an•
aes•thet•ic
an•es•the•tist or an•
aes•the•tist
an•es•the•tize or
an•aes•the•tize v.,
an•es•the•tized,
an•es•the•tiz•ing.
an•eu•rysm
a•new
an•gel (heavenly spirit:
cf. ANGLE)
an•gel•fish n., pl. an•
gel•fish or an•gel•
fish•es.
an•gel•ic
An•ge•lus
an•ger v., an•gered,
an•ger•ing.
an•gi•na pec•to•ris
an•gi•o•gram
an•gi•o•plas•ty
an•gi•o•sperm
an•gle[1] (projecting cor-
ner; to angle: cf. AN-
GEL)
an•gle[2] v., an•gled,
an•gling. (to fish: cf.
ANGEL)
an•gler
an•gle•worm
An•gli•can
An•gli•can•ism
An•gli•cism
An•gli•ci•za•tion
An•gli•cize v., An•
gli•cized, An•gli•
ciz•ing.
an•gling
An•glo n., pl. An•
glos.
An•glo-A•mer•i•can

An•glo-Sax•on
An•glo•phile
An•glo•phil•i•a
An•glo•phobe
An•glo•pho•bi•a
An•glo•phone
An•go•ra
an•gri•ly
an•gry v., an•gri•er,
an•gri•est.
angst
ang•strom
an•guish v., an•
guished, an•guish•
ing.
an•gu•lar
an•gu•lar•i•ty n., pl.
an•gu•lar•i•ties.
an•hy•dride
an•hy•drite
an•hy•drous
an•i•line
an•i•mad•ver•sion
an•i•mad•vert
an•i•mal
animal rights
an•i•mal•cule
an•i•mal•ism
an•i•mal•like
an•i•mate v., an•i•
mat•ed, an•i•mat•
ing.
an•i•mat•ed•ly
an•i•ma•tion
an•i•ma•tor
an•i•ma•tron•ics
an•i•mism
an•i•mist
an•i•mis•tic
an•i•mos•i•ty n., pl.
an•i•mos•i•ties.
an•i•mus
an•i•on
an•i•on•ic
an•ise
an•i•seed

an•i•sette
ankh
an•kle
an•kle•bone
an•klet
an•nal•ist (historian:
cf. ANALYST)
an•nals
an•neal v., an•
nealed, an•neal•ing.
an•ne•lid
an•nex v., an•nexed,
an•nex•ing.
an•nex•a•tion
an•ni•hi•late v., an•
ni•hi•lat•ed, an•ni•
hi•lat•ing.
an•ni•hi•la•tion
an•ni•hi•la•tor
an•ni•ver•sa•ry n.,
pl. an•ni•ver•sa•
ries.
an•no Dom•i•ni
an•no•tate v., an•
no•tat•ed, an•no•
tat•ing.
an•no•ta•tion
an•no•ta•tor
an•nounce v., an•
nounced, an•nounc•
ing.
an•nounce•ment
an•nounc•er
an•noy v., an•noyed,
an•noy•ing.
an•noy•ance
an•noyed
an•noy•ing
an•noy•ing•ly
an•nu•al
annual re•port Busi-
ness.
an•nu•al•ize v., an•
nu•al•ized, an•nu•
al•iz•ing.
an•nu•al•ly

an•nu•i•tant *Business.*

an•nu•i•ty *n., pl.* an•
nu•i•ties. *Business.*

an•nul *v.,* an•nulled,
an•nul•ling.

an•nu•lar

an•nul•la•ble

an•nul•ment

an•nun•ci•a•tion
(announcement: cf.
ENUNCIATION)

an•nun•ci•a•tor

an•ode

an•o•dize *v.,* an•o•
dized, an•o•diz•ing.

an•o•dyne

a•noint *v.,*
a•noint•ed,
a•noint•ing.

a•nom•a•lis•tic

a•nom•a•lous

a•nom•a•ly *n., pl.*
a•nom•a•lies.

a•non

an•o•nym•i•ty

a•non•y•mous

a•noph•e•les

an•o•rak

an•o•rec•tic

an•o•rex•i•a

an•o•rex•ic

an•oth•er

an•ox•i•a

an•ox•ic

ANSI *Computers.*
(American National
Standards Institute)

an•swer *v.,* an•
swered, an•swer•
ing.

an•swer-on•ly mo•
dem *Computers.*

an•swer•a•ble

an•swer•ing ma•
chine

ant (the insect: cf.
AUNT)

ant•ac•id

an•tag•o•nism

an•tag•o•nist

an•tag•o•nis•tic

an•tag•o•nize *v.,* an•
tag•o•nized, an•
tag•o•niz•ing.

ant•arc•tic

Ant•arc•ti•ca

an•te *v.,* (to pay: cf.
ANTI)

an•te- (before: cf.
ANTI-)

an•te me•rid•i•em

ant•eat•er

an•te•bel•lum

an•te•ced•ent

an•te•cham•ber

an•te•date *v.,* an•te•
dat•ed, an•te•dat•
ing.

an•te•di•lu•vi•an

an•te•lope *n., pl.* an•
te•lopes, an•te•
lope.

an•te•na *n., pl.* an•
ten•nas, an•ten•
nae.

an•te•pe•nult

an•te•pe•nul•ti•
mate

an•te•ri•or

an•te•room

an•them

ant•hill

an•thol•o•gist

an•thol•o•gy *n., pl.*
an•thol•o•gies.

an•thra•cite

an•thrax

an•thro•po•cen•tric

an•thro•po•cen•
trism

an•thro•poid

an•thro•poi•dal

an•thro•po•log•i•cal

an•thro•pol•o•gist

an•thro•pol•o•gy

an•thro•po•met•ric

an•thro•pom•e•try

an•thro•po•mor•
phic

an•thro•po•mor•
phism

an•ti *n., pl.* an•tis.
(one who is opposed:
cf. ANTE)

an•ti- (against: cf.
ANTE-)

an•ti•a•bor•tion

an•ti•air•craft

an•ti•a•li•as•ing
Computers.

an•ti•bac•te•ri•al

an•ti•bal•lis•tic

an•ti•bi•ot•ic

an•ti•bod•y *n., pl.*
an•ti•bod•ies.

an•tic

an•ti•choice

An•ti•christ

an•tic•i•pate *v.,* an•
tic•i•pat•ed, an•
tic•i•pat•ing.

an•tic•i•pa•tion

an•tic•i•pa•tor

an•tic•i•pa•to•ry

an•ti•cler•i•cal

an•ti•cler•i•cal•ism

an•ti•cli•mac•tic

an•ti•cli•max

an•ti•co•ag•u•lant

an•ti•cy•clone

an•ti•de•pres•sant

an•ti•dote (remedy:
cf. ANECDOTE)

an•ti•dump•ing

an•ti•freeze

an•ti•gen

an•ti•gen•ic

an•ti•ge•nic•i•ty

an•ti•ges•ta•tion•al drug
an•ti•his•ta•mine
an•ti-in•tel•lec•tu•al
an•ti-in•tel•lec•tu•al•ism
an•ti•knock
an•ti•lock brake
an•ti•log•a•rithm
an•ti•ma•cas•sar
an•ti•mag•net•ic
an•ti•mat•ter
an•ti•mis•sile
an•ti•moo•ny
an•ti•neu•tri•no n., pl. an•ti•neu•tri•nos.
an•ti•nu•cle•ar
an•ti•ox•i•dant
an•ti•par•ti•cle
an•ti•pas•to
an•ti•pa•thet•ic
an•tip•a•thy n., pl. an•tip•a•thies.
an•ti•per•son•nel
an•ti•per•spi•rant
an•ti•phon
an•tiph•o•nal
an•tiph•o•ny n., pl. an•tiph•o•nies.
an•tip•o•dal
an•tip•o•des
an•ti•pol•lu•tion
an•ti•pro•ton
an•ti•py•ret•ic
an•ti•quar•i•an
an•ti•quar•y n., pl. an•ti•quar•ies.
an•tique v., an•tiqued, an•tiqu•ing.
an•tiq•ui•ty n., pl. an•tiq•ui•ties.
an•ti-Sem•ite
an•ti-Se•mit•ic
an•ti-Sem•i•tism

an•ti•sense
an•ti•sep•sis
an•ti•sep•tic
an•ti•sep•ti•cal•ly
an•ti•slav•er•y
an•ti•so•cial
an•ti•stat•ic
an•tith•e•sis n., pl. an•tith•e•ses.
an•ti•thet•i•cal
an•ti•tox•in
an•ti•trust
an•ti•ven•in
an•ti•vi•rus pro•gram Computers.
ant•ler
ant•lered
an•to•nym
an•ton•y•mous
an•u•re•sis
an•u•ret•ic
a•nus
an•vil
anx•i•e•ty n., pl. anx•i•e•ties.
anx•ious
an•y
an•y•bod•y
an•y•how
an•y•more
an•y•one
an•y•place
an•y•thing
an•y•time
an•y•way
an•y•where
an•y•wise
a•or•ta n., pl. a•or•tas, a•or•tae.
a•or•tic
a•pace
A•pach•e
a•part
a•part•heid
a•part•ment
ap•a•thet•ic

ap•a•thet•i•cal•ly
ap•a•thy
ape n., v., aped, ap•ing.
a•pé•ri•tif
ap•er•ture
a•pex n., pl. a•pex•es, a•pi•ces.
a•pha•sia
a•pha•sic
a•phe•li•on n., pl. a•phe•li•a.
a•phid
aph•o•rism
aph•o•ris•tic
aph•ro•dis•i•ac
a•pi•ar•y n., pl. a•pi•ar•ies.
a•pi•cal
a•piece
a•plen•ty
a•plomb
ap•ne•a
a•poc•a•lypse
a•poc•a•lyp•tic
a•poc•ry•pha
a•poc•ry•phal
ap•o•ge•an
ap•o•gee
a•po•lit•i•cal
a•pol•o•get•ic
a•pol•o•get•i•cal•ly
a•po•lo•gi•a
a•pol•o•gist
a•pol•o•gize v., a•pol•o•gized, a•pol•o•giz•ing.
a•pol•o•gy n., pl. a•pol•o•gies.
ap•o•plec•tic
ap•o•plex•y
a•port
a•pos•ta•sy n., pl. a•pos•ta•sies.
a•pos•tate

a•pos•tle
a•pos•to•late
ap•os•tol•ic
a•pos•tro•phe
a•pos•tro•phize v.,
  a•pos•tro•phized,
  a•pos•tro•phiz•ing.
a•poth•e•car•y n., pl.
  a•poth•e•car•ies.
ap•o•thegm (saying)
ap•o•them (geometric
  line)
a•poth•e•o•sis n., pl.
  a•poth•e•o•ses.
Ap•pa•la•chi•an
ap•pall v., ap•palled,
  ap•pall•ing.
ap•palled
ap•pall•ing
ap•pall•ing•ly
ap•pa•rat•us n., pl.
  ap•pa•rat•us•es.
ap•pa•rel v., ap•par•
  eled, ap•par•elled,
  ap•par•el•ing, ap•
  par•el•ling.
ap•par•ent
ap•par•ent•ly
ap•pa•ri•tion
ap•peal v., ap•
  pealed,
  ap•peal•ing.
ap•peal•ing
ap•pear v., ap•
  peared,
  ap•pear•ing.
ap•pear•ance
ap•pease v., ap•
  peased,
  ap•peas•ing.
ap•pease•ment
ap•peas•er
ap•pel•lant
ap•pel•late
ap•pel•la•tion
ap•pel•lee
ap•pend v., ap•

pend○ed,
  ap•pend•ing.
ap•pend•age
ap•pen•dec•to•my
  n., pl. ap•pen•dec•
  to•mies.
ap•pen•di•ci•tis
ap•pen•dix n., pl. ap•
  pen•dix•es, ap•
  pen•di•ces.
ap•per•cep•tion
ap•per•tain v., ap•
  per•tained, ap•per•
  tain•ing.
ap•pe•stat
ap•pe•tite
ap•pe•tiz•er
ap•pe•tiz•ing
ap•pe•tiz•ing•ly
ap•plaud v., ap•
  plaud○ed, ap•
  plaud•ing.
ap•plause
ap•ple
ap○ple•jack
ap○ple•sauce
ap•pli•ance
appliance ga•rage
ap•pli•anced
ap•pli•ca•bil○i○ty
ap•pli•ca•ble
ap•pli•cant
ap•pli•ca•tion
applications soft•
  ware Computers.
ap•pli•ca•tor
ap•plied
applied cost Business.
applied o○ver•head
  Business.
ap•pli•qué
ap•ply v., ap•plied,
  ap•ply•ing.
ap•point v., ap•
  point○ed,
  ap•point•ing.
ap•point○ee

ap•poin•tive
ap•point•ment
ap•por•tion v., ap•
  por•tioned, ap•por•
  tion•ing.
ap•por•tion•ment
ap•po•site (suitable:
  cf. OPPOSITE)
ap•po•si•tion
ap•prais○al
ap•praise v., ap•
  praised,
  ap•prais•ing. (to
  evaluate: cf. APPRISE)
ap•prais○er
ap•pre•ci•a•ble
ap•pre•ci•a•bly
ap•pre•ci•ate v., ap•
  pre•ci•at○ed, ap•
  pre•ci•at•ing.
ap•pre•ci•a•tion
ap•pre•cia•tive
ap•pre•hend v., ap•
  pre•hend○ed, ap•
  pre•hend•ing.
ap•pre•hen•sion
ap•pre•hen•sive
ap•pren•tice v., ap•
  pren•ticed, ap•
  pren•tic•ing.
ap•pren•tice•ship
ap•prise v., ap•
  prised, ap•pris•ing.
  (to inform: cf. AP-
  PRAISE)
ap•proach v., ap•
  proached, ap•
  proach•ing.
ap•proach•a•bil○i○ty
ap•proach•a•ble
ap•pro•ba•tion
ap•pro•pri•ate v.,
  ap•pro•pri•at○ed,
  ap•pro•pri•at•ing.
ap•pro•pri•ate•ly
ap•pro•pri•ate•ness
ap•pro•pri•a•tion

ap•pro•pri•a•tor
ap•prov•al
ap•prove v., ap•
 proved,
 ap•prov•ing.
ap•prox∘i•mate v.,
 ap•prox∘i•mat∘ed,
 ap•prox∘i•mat•ing.
ap•prox∘i•mate∘ly
ap•prox∘i•ma•tion
ap•pur•te•nance
ap•pur•te•nant
ap•ri•cot
A∘pril
a∘pron
ap•ro•pos
apse
apt
ap•ti•tude
apt∘ly
apt•ness
aq∘ua
Aq∘ua-lung
aq∘ua•cade
aq•ua•cul•ture
aq∘ua•ma•rine
aq∘ua•naut
aq•ua•plane v., aq•
 ua•planed, aq•ua•
 plan•ing.
a∘quar•i•um n., pl.
 a∘quar•i•ums or
 a∘quar•i∘a.
a∘quat∘ic
aq∘ua•tint
naq•ua•vit
aq•ue•duct
a∘que•ous
aq•ui•line
a∘quiv∘er
AR (Arkansas)
Ar∘ab
ar∘a•besque
A∘ra•bi∘an
A∘ra•bic
ar•a∘ble

a∘rach•nid
Ar∘a•ma∘ic
ar•bi•tra•ble
ar•bi•trage v., ar•bi•
 traged, ar•bi•trag•
 ing. Business.
ar•bi•trag∘er or ar•
 bi•tra•geur Business.
ar•bi•trar∘i∘ly
ar•bi•trar∘i•ness
ar•bi•trar∘y
ar•bi•trate v., ar•bi•
 trat∘ed, ar•bi•trat•
 ing.
ar•bi•tra•tion
ar•bi•tra•tor Business.
ar•bor
ar•bo•re∘al
ar•bo•re•tum n., pl.
 ar•bo•re•tums, ar•
 bo•re∘ta.
ar•bor•vi•tae
ar•bu•tus
arc v., arced, arcked,
 arc•ing, arck•ing.
 (curve; to arc: cf. ARK
 BOAT)
ar•cade
ar•cane
ar•chae•o•log∘i•cal
 or ar•che•o•log∘i•
 cal
ar•chae•ol•o∘gist
ar•chae•ol•o∘gy
ar•chae•op•ter∘yx
ar•cha∘ic
ar•cha•i•cal∘ly
ar•cha•ism
arch•an∘gel
arch•bish∘op
arch•dea•con
arch•di•oc∘e•san
arch•di•o•cese
arch•duch•ess
arch•duke

arch•en∘e•my n., pl.
 arch•en∘e•mies.
ar•che•o•log∘i•cal
ar•che•ol•o∘gist
ar•che•ol•o∘gy
arch∘er
arch•er∘y
ar•che•type
arch•fiend
ar•chi•pel•a∘go n.,
 pl. ar•chi•pel∘a•
 gos, ar•chi•pel∘a•
 goes.
ar•chi•tect
ar•chi•tec•ton∘ic
ar•chi•tec•ton∘ics
ar•chi•tec•tur∘al
ar•chi•tec•tur•al∘ly
ar•chi•tec•ture
ar•chi•trave
ar•chi•val
ar•chive
ar•chi•vist
arch∘ly
arch•ness
arch•way
arc•tic
ar•dent
ar•dor
ar•du∘ous
ar∘e∘a (space: cf. ARIA)
ar∘e∘a code
ar∘e∘a•way
a∘re∘na n., pl. a∘re•
 nas.
ar•en∘a•vi•rus
aren't (are not)
Ar•gen•ti∘na
Ar•gen•tine
ar•gon
ar•go∘sy n., pl. ar•
 go∘sies.
ar•got
ar•gu•a•ble
ar•gu•a•bly

ar•gue *v.*, ar•gued,
  ar•gu•ing.
ar•gu•ment
ar•gu•men•ta•tion
ar•gu•men•ta•tive
ar•gyle
a•ri•a (song: cf. AREA)
ar•id
a•rid•i•ty
a•right
a•rise *v.*, a•rose,
  a•ris•en,
  a•ris•ing.
ar•is•toc•ra•cy *n.*, *pl.*
  ar•is•toc•ra•cies.
a•ris•to•crat
a•ris•to•crat•ic
a•rith•me•tic[1] *n.*
ar•ith•met•ic or ar•
  ith•met•i•cal[2] *adj.*
arithmetic log•ic u•
  nit (ALU) *Computers.*
Ar•i•zo•na (AZ)
Ar•i•zo•nan
ark (boat: cf. ARC)
Ar•kan•san
Ar•kan•sas (AR)
arm
ar•ma•da
ar•ma•dil•lo *n.*, *pl.*
  ar•ma•dil•los.
Ar•ma•ged•don
ar•ma•ment
ar•ma•ture
arm•band
arm•chair
Ar•me•ni•a
Ar•me•ni•an
arm•ful *n.*, *pl.* arm•
  fuls.
arm•hole
arm•i•stice
arm•let
arm•load
ar•moire
ar•mor

ar•mored
ar•mor•er
ar•mo•ri•al
ar•mor•y *n.*, *pl.* ar•
  mor•ies.
arm•pit
arm•rest
ar•my *n.*, *pl.* ar•mies.
ar•ni•ca
a•ro•ma *n.*, *pl.* a•ro•
  mas.
a•ro•ma•ther•a•py
ar•o•mat•ic
ar•o•mat•i•cal•ly
a•round
a•rous•al
a•rouse *v.*, a•roused,
  a•rous•ing.
ARPANET *Computers.*
  (the computer net•
  work)
ar•peg•gi•o *n.*, *pl.*
  ar•peg•gi•os.
ar•raign
ar•raign•ment
ar•range *v.*, ar•
  ranged, ar•rang•ing.
ar•range•ment
ar•rang•er
ar•rant
ar•ras
ar•ray *v.*, ar•rayed,
  ar•ray•ing.
ar•rears *Business.*
ar•rest *v.*, ar•rest•ed,
  ar•rest•ing.
ar•rest•ing
ar•rhyth•mi•a
ar•ri•val
arrival rate *Business.*
ar•rive *v.*, ar•rived,
  ar•riv•ing.
ar•ro•gance
ar•ro•gant
ar•ro•gate *v.*, ar•ro•

gat•ed, ar•ro•gat•
  ing.
ar•row
arrow key *Computers.*
ar•row•head
ar•row•root
ar•roy•o *n.*, *pl.* ar•
  roy•os.
ar•se•nal
ar•se•nic[1] *n.*
ar•sen•ic[2] *adj.*
ar•son
ar•son•ist
art
art dec•o
ar•te•ri•al
ar•te•ri•o•gram
ar•te•ri•ole
ar•te•ri•o•scle•ro•
  sis
ar•ter•y *n.*, *pl.* ar•
  ter•ies.
ar•te•sian
art•ful
art•ful•ly
ar•thrit•ic
ar•thri•tis
ar•thro•pod
ar•ti•choke
ar•ti•cle
ar•tic•u•late *v.*, ar•
  tic•u•lat•ed, ar•
  tic•u•lat•ing.
ar•tic•u•late•ly
ar•tic•u•la•tion
ar•tic•u•la•to•ry
ar•ti•fact
ar•ti•fice
ar•ti•fi•cial
artificial in•tel•li•
  gence (AI) *Computers.*
ar•ti•fi•cial res•
  pi•ra•tion
ar•ti•fi•ci•al•i•ty
ar•ti•fi•cial•ly
ar•til•ler•y

ar•ti•san
artisan's lien *Business.*
art•ist
ar•tiste
ar•tis•tic
ar•tis•ti•cal•ly
art•ist•ory
art•less
art•work
art•y *adj.,* art•i•er,
 art•i•est.
ar-um
Ar•y•an
as•bes•tos
as•bes•to•sis
as•cend *v.,* as•
 cend•ed, as•cend•
 ing.
as•cend•an•cy or as•
 cend•en•cy
as•cend•ant or as•
 cend•ent
as•cen•sion
as•cent (climb: cf. AS-
 SENT)
as•cer•tain *v.,* as•
 cer•tained, as•cer•
 tain•ing.
as•cer•tain•a•ble
as•cet•ic (austere: cf.
 ACETIC)
as•cet•i•cism
ASCII *Computers.*
 (American Standard
 Code for International
 Interchange)
ASCII file *Computers.*
a•scor•bic
as•cot
as•crib•a•ble
as•cribe *v.,* as•cribed,
 as•crib•ing.
as•crip•tion
a•sea
a•sep•sis
a•sep•tic

a•sex•u•al
a•shamed
a•sham•ed•ly
ash•can
ash•en
a•shore
ash•ram
ash•tray
A•sia-dol•lar *Busi-
 ness.*
A•sian
A•si•at•ic
a•side
as•i•nine
as•i•nin•i•ty
ask *v.,* asked, ask•ing.
 (to inquire: cf. ACTS;
 AXE)
a•skance
a•skew
ask•ing price *Business.*
a•slant
a•sleep
a•slope
a•so•cial
as•par•a•gus
as•par•tame
as•pect
as•pen
as•per•i•ty
as•perse *v.,* as•
 persed, as•pers•ing.
as•per•sion
as•phalt
as•pho•del
as•phyx•i•a
as•phyx•i•ate *v.,* as•
 phyx•i•at•ed, as•
 phyx•i•at•ing.
as•phyx•i•a•tion
as•phyx•i•a•tor
as•pic
as•pi•dis•tra
as•pir•ant
as•pi•rate *v.,* as•pi•

rat•ed, as•pi•rat•
 ing.
as•pi•ra•tion
as•pire *v.,* as•pired,
 as•pir•ing.
as•pi•rin
as•sail *v.,* as•sailed,
 as•sail•ing.
as•sail•a•ble
as•sail•ant
as•sas•sin
as•sas•si•nate *v.,* as•
 sas•si•nat•ed, as•
 sas•si•nat•ing.
as•sas•si•na•tion
as•sault
as•say *v.,* as•sayed,
 as•say•ing. (to evalu-
 ate: cf. ESSAY)
as•sem•blage
as•sem•ble *v.,* as•
 sem•bled, as•sem•
 bling.
assemble to or•der
 Business.
as•sem•bler *Comput-
 ers.*
as•sem•bly *n., pl.* as•
 sem•blies.
assembly lan•guage
 Computers.
as•sem•bly•man *n.,
 pl.* as•sem•bly•men.
as•sem•bly•wom•an
 n., pl. as•sem•bly•
 wom•en.
as•sent (agreement: cf.
 ASCENT)
as•sert *v.,* as•sert•ed,
 as•sert•ing.
as•ser•tion
as•ser•tive
as•sess *v.,* as•sessed,
 as•sess•ing.
as•sess•ment
as•ses•sor *Business.*
as•set

as•sev•er•ate *v.*, as•sev•er•at•ed, as•sev•er•at•ing.
as•sev•er•a•tion
as•si•du•i•ty
as•sid•u•ous
as•sign *v.*, as•signed, as•sign•ing.
as•sig•na•tion
as•sign◦ee *Business.*
as•sign•ment
as•sign◦or *Business.*
as•sim◦i•la•ble
as•sim◦i•late *v.*, as•sim◦i•lat◦ed, as•sim◦i•lat•ing.
as•sim◦i•la•tion
as•sist *v.*, as•sist◦ed, as•sist•ing.
as•sis•tance (help: cf. ASSISTANTS)
as•sis•tant
as•sizes
as•so•ci•ate *v.*, as•so•ci•at◦ed, as•so•ci•at•ing.
as•so•ci•a•tion
as•so•ci•a•tive
as•so•nance
as•so•nant
as•sort *v.*, as•sort◦ed, as•sort•ing.
as•sort◦ed
as•sort•ment
assortment plan *Business.*
as•suage *v.*, as•suaged, as•suag•ing.
as•suage•ment
as•sume *v.*, as•sumed, as•sum•ing.
as•sump•tion
as•sur•ance
as•sure *v.*, as•sured, as•sur•ing.
as•sur•ed◦ly

as•ta•tine
as•ter
as•ter•isk
as•ter•ism
a◦stern
as•ter•oid
asth◦ma
asth•mat◦ic
as•tig•mat◦ic
a◦stig•ma•tism
a◦stir
as•ton•ish *v.*, as•ton•ished, as•ton•ish•ing.
as•ton•ish•ing
as•ton•ish•ment
as•tound *v.*, as•tound◦ed, as•tound•ing.
as•tound•ing
a◦strad•dle
as•tra•khan
as•tral
a◦stray
a◦stride
as•trin•gent
as•tro•dome
as•tro•labe
as•trol◦o•ger
as•tro•log◦i•cal
as•trol◦o•gist
as•trol◦o•gy
as•tro•naut
as•tro•nau•ti•cal
as•tro•nau•tics
as•tron◦o•mer
as•tro•nom◦i•cal or as•tro•nom◦ic
as•tron◦o•my
as•tro•phys◦i•cist
as•tro•phys◦ics
As•tro•turf
as•tute
a◦sun•der
a◦sy•lum

a◦sym•met•ric or a◦sym•met•ri•cal
a◦sym•me•try
a◦syn•chro•nous
at par
at-the-mar◦ket
at◦a•vism
at◦a•vis•tic
ate (did eat: cf. EIGHT)
at•el•ier
a◦the•ism
a◦the•ist
a◦the•is•tic
ath◦er◦o◦scle•ro◦sis
ath◦er◦o◦scle•rot◦ic
a◦thirst
ath•lete
ath•let◦ic
ath•let◦i•cal◦ly
ath•let◦i•cism
ath•let◦ics
a◦thwart
a◦tilt
a◦tin•gle
At•lan•tic
at•las
ATM *Business.* (automated teller machine)
at•mos•phere
at•mos•pher◦ic
at•mos•pher◦i•cal◦ly
at◦oll
at◦om
a◦tom◦ic
at•om•ize *v.*, at•om•ized, at•om•iz•ing.
at•om•iz◦er
a◦ton•al
a◦to•nal◦i◦ty
a◦ton•al◦ly
a◦tone *v.*, a◦toned, a◦ton•ing.
a◦tone•ment
a◦top
a◦trem•ble

a•tri•um or a•tri•a n., pl. a•tri•ums.

a•tro•cious

a•troc•i•ty n., pl. a•troc•i•ties.

at•ro•phy v., at•ro•phied, at•ro•phy•ing.

at•ro•pine

at•tach v., at•tached, at•tach•ing. (to fasten)

at•ta•ché (embassy official)

at•tached

at•tach•ment

at•tack v., at•tacked, at•tack•ing.

at•tack•er

at•tain v., at•tained, at•tain•ing.

at•tain•a•ble

at•tain•der

at•tain•ment

at•taint

at•tar

at•tempt v., at•tempt•ed, at•tempt•ing.

at•tend v., at•tend•ed, at•tend•ing.

at•tend•ance

at•tend•ant

at•ten•tion

at•ten•tive

at•ten•u•ate v., at•ten•u•at•ed, at•ten•u•at•ing.

at•ten•u•a•tion

at•test v., at•test•ed, at•test•ing.

at•tes•ta•tion

at•tic

at•tire v., at•tired, at•tir•ing.

at•ti•tude (manner: cf. ALTITUDE)

at•ti•tu•di•nize v., at•ti•tu•di•nized, at•ti•tu•di•niz•ing.

at•tor•ney n., pl. at•tor•neys.

at•tor•ney-at-law n., pl. at•tor•neys-•at-•law.

at•tract v., at•tract•ed, at•tract•ing.

at•trac•tion

at•trac•tive

at•trib•ut•a•ble

at•trib•ute[1] v., at•trib•ut•ed, at•trib•ut•ing.

at•tri•bute[2] n.

at•tri•bu•tion

at•trib•u•tive

at•tri•tion

at•tune v., at•tuned, at•tun•ing.

a•typ•i•cal

a•typ•i•cal•ly

au cou•rant

au pair

au re•voir

au•burn

auc•tion v., auc•tioned, auc•tion•ing.

auc•tion•eer

au•da•cious

au•dac•i•ty

au•di•bil•i•ty

au•di•ble

au•di•bly

au•di•ence

au•di•o

au•di•ol•o•gist

au•di•ol•o•gy

au•di•om•e•ter

au•di•o•phile

au•di•o•tape

au•di•o•vis•u•al

au•dit v., au•dit•ed, au•dit•ing.

audit com•mit•tee

audit o•pin•ion

audit trail

au•di•tion v., au•di•tioned, au•di•tion•ing.

au•di•tor

au•di•to•ri•um n., pl. au•di•to•ri•ums, au•di•to•ri•a.

au•di•to•ry

au•ger (a drill: cf. AUGUR)

aught (zero: cf. OUGHT)

aug•ment

aug•men•ta•tion

au•gur v., au•gured, au•gur•ing. (to predict: cf. AUGER)

au•gu•ry n., pl. au•gu•ries.

au•gust (majestic)

Au•gust (the month)

aunt (the relative: cf. ANT)

au•ra n., pl. au•ras, au•rae.

au•ral (of hearing: cf. ORAL)

au•re•ate

au•re•ole

Au•re•o•my•cin

au•ri•cle (outer ear: cf. ORACLE)

au•ric•u•lar

au•rif•er•ous

au•ro•ra aus•tra•lis

aurora bo•re•al•is

aus•cul•ta•tion

aus•pic•es

aus•pi•cious

aus•tere

aus•ter•i•ty
aus•tral
Aus•tral•ia
Aus•tral•ian
Aus•tri•a
Aus•tri•an
au•then•tic
au•then•ti•cal•ly
au•then•ti•cate v., au•then•ti•cat•ed, au•then•ti•cat•ing.
au•then•ti•ca•tion
au•then•tic•i•ty
au•thor v., au•thored, au•thor•ing.
au•tho•ri•al
au•thor•i•tar•i•an
au•thor•i•tar•i•an•ism
au•thor•i•ta•tive
au•thor•i•ty n., pl. au•thor•i•ties.
au•thor•i•za•tion
au•thor•ize v., au•thor•ized, au•thor•iz•ing.
authorized deal•er•ship
au•thor•ship
au•tism
au•tis•tic
au•to n., pl. au•tos.
au•to•an•swer Computers.
au•to•bahn
au•to•bi•og•ra•pher
au•to•bi•o•graph•i•cal or au•to•bi•o•graph•ic
au•to•bi•og•ra•phy n., pl. au•to•bi•og•ra•phies.
au•to•chang•er Computers.
au•toch•tho•nous
au•to•clave

au•toc•ra•cy, n., pl. au•toc•ra•cies.
au•to•crat
au•to•crat•ic
au•to•crat•i•cal•ly
au•to•di•al•ing Computers.
au•to•di•dact
au•to•e•rot•ic as•phyx•ia
au•to•gi•ro n., pl. au•to•gi•ros.
au•to•graph v., au•to•graphed, au•to•graph•ing.
Au•to•harp
au•to•im•mune
au•to•in•tox•i•ca•tion
au•to•mate v., au•to•mat•ed, au•to•mat•ing.
au•to•mat•ed-tell•er ma•chine (ATM)
au•to•mat•ic
au•to•mat•ic da•ta proc•ess•ing (ADP) Computers.
automatic head park•ing
automatic mark•down Business.
au•to•mat•ic-tell•er ma•chine
au•to•mat•i•cal•ly
au•to•ma•tion (automatic operation)
au•tom•a•tize v., au•tom•a•tized, au•tom•a•tiz•ing.
au•tom•a•ton n., pl. au•tom•a•tons, au•tom•a•ta. (robot)
au•to•mo•bile
au•to•mo•bil•ist
au•to•mo•tive
au•to•nom•ic

au•ton•o•mous
au•ton•o•my
au•top•sy n., pl. au•top•sies.
au•to•re•peat Computers.
au•to•siz•ing Computers.
au•to•start
au•to•stra•da
au•to•sug•ges•tion
au•to•trace
au•tumn
au•tum•nal
aux•il•ia•ry n., pl. aux•il•ia•ries.
a•vail v., a•vailed, a•vail•ing.
a•vail•a•bil•i•ty
a•vail•a•ble
av•a•lanche
a•vant-garde
av•a•rice
av•a•ri•cious
a•vast
av•a•tar
a•venge v., a•venged, a•veng•ing.
a•veng•er
av•e•nue
a•ver v., a•verred, a•ver•ring.
av•er•age v., av•er•aged, av•er•ag•ing.
average cost Business.
a•verse (unwilling, as in "not averse to doing something": cf. AD-VERSE)
a•ver•sion
a•ver•sive
a•vert v., a•vert•ed, a•vert•ing.
a•vi•an
a•vi•ar•y n., pl. a•vi•ar•ies.

a•vi•a•tion
a•vi•a•tor
a•vi•a•trix
av•oid
a•vid•i•ty
av•id•ly
a•vi•on•ic
a•vi•on•ics
av•o•ca•do n., pl.
  av•o•ca•dos.
av•o•ca•tion (hobby:
  cf. VOCATION)
av•o•cet
a•void v., a•void•ed,
  a•void•ing. (to shun:
  cf. EVADE)
a•void•a•ble
a•void•a•bly
a•void•ance
av•oir•du•pois
a•vouch v.,
  a•vouched,
  a•vouch•ing.
a•vow v., a•vowed,
  a•vow•ing.
a•vow•al
a•vowed

a•vun•cu•lar
a•wait v., a•wait•ed,
  a•wait•ing.
a•wake v., a•woke,
  a•waked, a•wak•
  ing.
a•wak•en v., a•wak•
  ened, a•wak•en•
  ing.
a•wak•en•ing
a•ward
a•ware
a•ware•ness
a•wash
a•way (apart: cf.
  AWEIGH)
a•weigh (raised: cf.
  AWAY)
awe•some
awe•struck or awe•
  strick•en
aw•ful (very bad: cf.
  OFFAL)
aw•ful•ly
a•while
a•whirl
awk•ward

awl (drill: cf. ALL)
awn•ing
a•wry
ax or axe n., pl.
  ax•es,. v., axed, ax•
  ing. (the tool: cf. ACTS;
  ASK)
ax•i•al
ax•i•om
ax•i•o•mat•ic
ax•is n., pl. ax•es.
ax•le
ax•le•tree
ax•on
a•ya•tol•lah
aye (yes: cf. IANDEYE)
AZ (Arizona)
a•zal•ea
az•i•muth
A•zor•es
AZT Trademark. (the
  drug azidothymidine)
Az•tec
az•ure
az•ur•ite

B

B.A. (bachelor of arts)
baa v., baaed, baa•
  ing.
Ba•al n., pl. Ba•al•im.
Bab•bitt
Bab•bitt•ry
bab•ble v., bab•bled,
  bab•bling.
babe
Ba•bel
ba•boon
ba•boon•er•y
ba•bush•ka n., pl.
  ba•bush•kas.
ba•by n., pl. ba•bies;

v., ba•bied, ba•by•
  ing.
baby boom
baby bust
baby grand
ba•by-sit or ba•by•sit
  v., ba•by-sat,
  ba•by-sit•ting.
ba•by-sit•ter or ba•
  by•sit•ter
ba•by•hood
ba•by•ish
ba•by•ish•ness
ba•by•like
Bab•y•lon
Bab•y•lo•ni•a

Bab•y•lo•ni•an
ba•by's-breath
bac•ca•lau•re•ate
bac•ca•rat or bac•
  ca•ra
bac•cha•nal
Bac•cha•na•li•a n.,
  pl. Bac•cha•na•li•a,
  Bac•cha•na•li•as.
bac•cha•na•li•an
Bac•chic
Bac•chus
Bach
bach•e•lor
bach•e•lor•hood
bach•e•lor's-but•ton

ba•cil•lus *n., pl.* ba•cil•li.

back

back-haul allowance *Business.*

back of•fice *n. Business.*

back-of•fice *adj. Business.*

back or•der *n. Business.*

back-or•der *v. Business.*

back-ped•al *v.,* back-ped•aled or back-ped•alled, back-ped•al•ing or back-ped•al•ling.

back•ache

back•beat

back•bite *v.,* back•bit, back•bit•ten, back•bit•ing.

back•bit•er

back•board

back•bone

back•break•er

back•break•ing

back•date *v.,* back•dat•ed, back•dat•ing.

back•drop *v.,* back•dropped, back•drop•ping.

back•er

back•field

back•fire *v.,* back•fired, back•fir•ing.

back•gam•mon

back•ground

back•ground•er

back•hand

back•hand•ed

back•ing

back•lash

back•less

back•log *v.,* back•logged, back•log•ging.

back•pack

back•pack•er

back•rest

back•seat driv•er

back•side

back•slap•per

back•slap•ping

back•slash

back•slide *v.,* back•slid, back•slid•ing.

back•slid•er

back•space *v.,* back•spaced, back•spac•ing.

back•spin

back•stage

back•stairs or back•stair

back•stop *v.,* back•stopped, back•stop•ping.

back•stretch

back•stroke *v.,* back•stroked, back•strok•ing.

back•swept

back•swing

back talk *n.*

back-talk *v.*

back•track

back•up

backup stock *Business.*

back•ward

back•ward-com•pat•i•ble

backward in•te•gra•tion *Business.*

backward sched•ul•ing *Business.*

back•ward•ly

back•ward•ness

back•wash

back•wa•ter

back•woods

back•yard

ba•con

bac•te•ri•a *n., pl.* bac•te•ri•um.

bac•te•ri•al

bac•te•ri•cid•al

bac•te•ri•cide

bac•te•ri•o•log•i•cal

bac•te•ri•ol•o•gist

bac•te•ri•ol•o•gy

bad *adj.,* worse, worst; bad•der, bad•dest. (not good: cf. BADE)

bad-mouth or bad-mouth, *v.,* bad-mouthed, bad-mouth•ing or bad-mouth•ing.

bade

badge

badg•er *v.,* badg•ered, badg•er•ing.

bad•i•nage

bad•lands

bad•ly *adj.,* worse, worst.

bad•min•ton

baf•fle, *v.,* baf•fled, baf•fling, *n.*

baf•fle•ment

baf•fling•ly

bag *v.,* bagged, bag•ging.

bag•a•telle

ba•gel

bag•gage

bag•gi•ly

bag•gi•ness

bag•gy *adj.,* bag•gi•er, bag•gi•est.

Bagh•dad or Bag•dad

bag la•dy

bag•man *n., pl.* bag•men.

bag•pipe

bag•pip•er

ba•guette
bah
Ba•ha•mas *n., pl.*
Ba•ha•mi•an
Bah•rain or Bah•rein
Bah•rain•i or Bah•
rein•i
bail (security money:
cf. BALE)
bail•iff
bail•i•wick
bail•ment
bail•out *Business.*
bail•out pe•ri•od
bails•man
bait (lure: cf. BATE)
bait•er
baize
bake *v.,* baked bak•
ing.
bak•er
Ba•kers•field
bak•er•y *n., pl.* bak•
er•ies.
bak•ing pow•der
baking so•da
bal•a•lai•ka *n., pl.*
bal•a•lai•kas.
bal•ance *v.,* bal•
anced, bal•anc•ing.
balance beam
balance of pay•ments
Business.
balance sheet *Busi-
ness.*
bal•co•nied
bal•co•ny *n., pl.* bal•
co•nies.
bald (hairless: cf.
BALLED; BAWLED)
bal•der•dash
bald•ish
bald•ly
bald•ness
bale *v.,* baled, bal•
ing. (bundle: cf. BAIL)

bale•ful
bale•ful•ly
bale•ful•ness
Ba•li
Ba•li•nese *n., pl.* Ba•
li•nese.
balk
Bal•kan
balk•i•ly
balk•i•ness
balk•y *adj.,* balk•ier,
balk•iest.
ball (sphere: cf. BAWL)
bal•lad (narrative
poem: cf. BALLET; BAL-
LOT)
bal•lad•eer
bal•lad•like
bal•lad•ry
bal•last *v.,* bal•
last•ed, bal•last•
ing.
balled (shaped into a
ball: cf. BALD; BAWLED)
ball•er
bal•le•ri•o•na *n., pl.*
bal•le•ri•nas.
bal•let (dance form: cf.
BALLAD; BALLOT)
bal•let•o•ic
bal•lis•tic
bal•lis•tics
bal•loon *v.,* bal•
looned, bal•loon•
ing.
balloon pay•ment
Business.
bal•lot (vote: cf. BAL-
LAD; BALLET)
bal•lot•er
ball•park
ballpark pric•ing *Busi-
ness.*
ball•point
ball•room
bal•ly•hoo *v.,* bal•ly•

hoos, bal•ly•hooed,
bal•ly•hoo•ing.
balm (ointment: cf.
BOMB)
balm•i•ness
balm•y *v.,* balm•ier,
balm•i•est.
ba•lo•ney (nonsense:
cf. BOLOGNA; Bologna)
bal•sa
bal•sam
bal•sam•ic
balsamic vin•e•gar
Bal•tic
Bal•ti•more
bal•us•ter
bal•us•trade
Bal•zac
bam•boo *n., pl.* bam•
boos.
bam•boo•zle *v.,*
bam•boo•zled,
bam•boo•zling.
bam•boo•zle•ment
ban *v.,* banned, ban•
ning.
ba•nal
ba•nal•i•ty
ba•nal•ly
ba•nan•a *n., pl.* ba•
nan•as.
band (strip; group: cf.
BANNED)
Band-Aid *Trademark.*
band•age *v.,* band•
aged, band•ag•ing.
ban•dan•na or ban•
dan•a *n., pl.* ban•
dan•nas or ban•
dan•as.
ban•dan•naed
ban•di•ness
ban•dit *n., pl.* ban•
dits, ban•dit•ti.
ban•di•to•ry
band•lead•er

ban•do•leer or ban•do•lier
ban•do•lier
bands (groups: cf. BANNS; BANS)
band•stand
band•wag•on
band•width
ban•dy n., pl. ban•died, ban•dy•ing.
ban•dy-leg∘ged
bane
bane•ful
bang v., banged, bang•ing.
Bang•kok
Ban•gla•desh
Ban•gla•desh∘i
ban•gle
Ban•gui
bang-up
ban•ish v., ban•ished, ban•ish•ing.
ban•ish•ment
ban•is•ter or ban•nis•ter
ban•jo n., pl. ban•jos, ban•joes.
ban•jo•ist
Ban•jul
bank v., banked, bank•ing.
bank account Business.
bank card Business.
bank draft Business.
bank•a∘ble
bank•book Business.
bank∘er
bank∘er's ac•cept•ance Business.
bank•note Business.
bank∘roll
bank∘roll∘er
bank•rupt v., bank•rupt∘ed, bank•rupt•ing. Business.

bank•rupt∘cy n., pl. bank•rupt∘cies. Business.
ban•na•ble
banned (barred: cf. BAND)
ban•ner
banns (marriage notice: cf. BANDS; BANS)
ban•quet
ban•quet∘er or ban•que•teer
ban•quette
bans (prohibits: cf. BANDS; BANNS)
ban•shee
ban•tam
bantam store
ban∘tam•weight
ban•ter v., ban•tered, ban•ter•ing.
ban•ter•ing∘ly
Ban∘tu n., pl. Ban•tus, Ban•tu.
ban•yan
ban•zai
ba•o•bab
bap•tism
bap•tis•mal
Bap•tist
bap•tis•ter∘y, n., pl. bap•tis•ter•ies.
bap•tize v., bap•tized, bap•tiz•ing.
bar v., barred, bar•ring.
bar code Business.
bar mitz•vah
barb
Bar•ba•di•an
Bar•ba•dos
bar•bar•i•an
bar•bar∘ic
bar•bar•i•cal∘ly
bar•ba•rism

bar•bar•i•ty n., pl bar•bar•i∘ties.
bar•ba•rous
bar•ba•rous∘ly
bar•be•cue or bar•be•que v., bar•be•cued or bar•be•qued, bar•be•cu•ing or bar•be•qu•ing
barbed
bar•bel
bar•bell
bar•ber
bar•ber∘ry, n., pl. bar•ber•ries.
bar•bi•tu•rate
Bar•ce•lo∘na
bard (poet: cf. BARRED)
bard∘ic
bare adj., bar∘er, bar•est; v., bare, bared, bar•ing. (uncovered; to bare: cf. BEAR)
bare•back or bare•backed
bare•faced
bare•foot or bare•foot∘ed
bare•hand∘ed
bare∘ly
bare•ness
bar•gain v., bar•gained, bar•gain•ing.
bar•gain∘er
bar•gain•ing u∘nit Business.
barge v., barged, barg•ing.
bar∘i•tone
bar∘i•um
bark[1] n. (tree covering; dog's cry: cf. BARQUE)
bark[2] v., barked, bark•ing.
bark∘er

baton

bark•less
bar•ley
barn
bar•na•cle
bar•na•cled
barn•like
barn•storm
barn•storm•er
barn•yard
ba•rom•e•ter
bar•o•met•ric
bar•on (nobleman: cf. BARREN)
bar•on•ess
bar•on•et
ba•ro•ni•al
ba•roque (ornate)
barque (ship: cf. BARK)
bar•racks
bar•ra•cu•da n., pl. bar•ra•cu•da, bar•ra•cu•das.
bar•rage
barred (stopped: cf. BARD)
bar•rel v., bar•reled or bar•relled, bar•rel•ing or bar•rel•ling.
bar•ren (empty: cf. BARON)
bar•ren•ness
bar•rette (hair clasp: cf. BERET)
bar•ri•cade v., bar•ri•cad•ed, bar•ri•cad•ing.
bar•ri•er
bar•ring
bar•ris•ter
bar•room
bar•row
bar•tend•er
bar•tend•ing
bar•ter
Bar•tók

bar•y•on
bar•y•on•ic
bas-re•lief
ba•sal
ba•salt
ba•sal•tic
base[1] v., based, bas•ing.
base[2] adj., bas•er, bas•est. (vile: cf. BASS)
base pay Business.
base-point pric•ing Business.
base-stock meth•od Business.
base•ball
base•band
base•board
base•less
base•less•ness
base•line or base line
base•ly
base•ment
base•ness
bash v., bashed, bash•ing.
bash•er
bash•ful
bash•ful•ly
bash•ful•ness
BASIC Computers. (programming language)
ba•sic
ba•si•cal•ly
bas•il
ba•sil•i•ca n., pl. ba•sil•i•cas.
ba•sin
ba•sis n., pl. ba•ses.
bask
bas•ket
basket pur•chase Business.
bas•ket•ball
bas•ket•work

Basque
Bas•ra
bass n., pl. bass or bass•es. (male singers; fish: cf. BASE)
bas•set hound
bas•si•net
bass•ist
bas•so n., pl. bas•sos, bas•si.
bas•soon
bas•soon•ist
bast
bas•tard
bas•tard•i•za•tion
bas•tard•ize v., bas•tard•ized.
bas•tard•ly
baste v., bast•ed, bast•ing.
bas•tille
bas•tion
bat v., bat•ted, bat•ting.
bat mitz•vah
batch
batch proc•ess•ing Computers.
batch file Computers.
bate v., bat•ed, bat•ing.
bath n., pl. baths.
bathe v., bathed, bath•ing.
bath•er
ba•thet•ic
bath•house
ba•thos (anticlimax: cf. PATHOS)
bath•robe
bath•room
bath•tub
ba•tik
ba•tiste
bat•like
ba•ton

Bat∘on Rouge

bat•tal•ion

bat•ten v., bat•tened, bat•ten•ing.

bat•ter v., bat•tered, bat•ter•ing.

bat•ter∘er

bat•ter∘y n., pl. bat•ter•ies.

bat•ting

bat•tle v., bat•tled, bat•tling.

bat•tle-ax or bat•tle-axe

bat∘tle•field

bat∘tle•ment

bat•tler

bat∘tle•ship

bat∘ty v., bat•ti∘er, bat•ti∘est.

bau•ble (trinket: cf. BABBLE; BUBBLE)

baud n., pl. baud. Computers.

baux•ite

Ba•var•i∘a

Ba•var•i∘an

bawd∘i∘ly

bawd∘i•ness

bawd∘y adj., bawd•i∘er, bawd•i∘est.

bawl (to wail: cf. BALL)

bawled (cried: cf. BALD; BALLED)

bay

bay•ber∘ry n., pl. bay•ber•ries.

bay•o∘net v., bay•o∘net∘ed or bay•o∘net•ted, bay•o∘net•ing or bay•o∘net•ting.

bay∘ou n., pl. bay•ous.

ba•zaar (marketplace: cf. BIZARRE)

ba•zoo∘ka n., pl. ba•zoo∘kas.

BBB Business. (Better Business Bureau)

BBS Computers. (bulletin board system)

be v., am, are, is, are; was, were; been, be∘ing.

beach¹ n. (shore: cf. BEECH)

beach² v., beached, beach•ing.

beach•comb∘er

beach•head

bea•con

bead

bead∘ed

bea•dle

bea•gle

beak

beaked

beak∘er

beam

bean (the vegetable: cf. BEEN; BIN)

bear¹ n., pl. bears or bear. (the animal: cf. BARE)

bear² v., bore, borne or born, bear•ing. (to carry: cf. BARE)

bear mar•ket Business.

bear•a∘ble

beard

bear∘er bond Business.

bear•ing

bear•ish Business.

bear•like

beast

beast•li•ness

beast∘ly adj., beast•li∘er, beast•li∘est.

beat v., beat, beat∘en, beat•ing. (to strike: cf. BEET)

beat-up

beat•a∘ble

be•a•tif∘ic

be•a•tif∘i∘cal∘ly

be•at∘i•fi•ca•tion

be•at∘i∘fy v., be•at∘i•fied, be•at∘i•fy•ing. (to make happy: cf. BEAUTIFY)

beat•ing

be•at∘i•tude

beat•nik

beau n., pl. beaus or beaux. (sweetheart: cf. BOW)

Beau•mont

beaut

beau•te•ous

beau•ti•cian

beau•ti•fi•ca•tion

beau•ti•ful

beau•ti•ful∘ly

beau•ti∘fy v., beau•ti•fied, beau•ti•fy•ing. (to make beautiful: cf. BEATIFY)

beau•ty n., pl. beau•ties.

bea•ver n., pl. bea•vers or bea•ver.

be•calm

be•calmed

be•cause

beck and call

beck∘on v., beck•oned, beck∘on•ing.

be•cloud v., be•cloud∘ed, be•cloud•ing.

be•come v., be•came, be•come, be•com•ing.

be•com•ing∘ly

bed v., bed•ded, bed•ding.

be•daub

be•daz•zle v., be•

daz•zled, be•daz•zling

bed•bug or bed bug

bed•clothes

bed•ding

be•deck

be•dev•il v., be•dev•iled or be•dev•illed, be•dev•il•ing or be•dev•il•ling.

be•dev•il•ment

bed•fel•low

be•diz•en, v., be•diz•ened, be•diz•en•ing.

bed•lam

Bed•ling•ton ter•ri•er

Bed•ou•in or Bed•u•in n., pl. Bed•ou•ins or Bed•ou•in.

bed•pan

bed•post

be•drag•gle v., be•drag•gled, be•drag•gling.

bed•rid•den

bed•rock

bed•roll

bed•room

bed•side

bed•sore

bed•spread

bed•spring

bed•stead

bed•time

bee

beech (the tree: cf. BEACH)

beef n., pl. beeves or beefs;. v., beefed, beef•ing.

beef•burg•er

beef•cake

beef•i•ness

beef•steak

beef•y adj., beef•i•er, beef•i•est.

bee•hive

bee•keep•er

bee•keep•ing

bee•line

Be•el•ze•bub

been (existed: cf. BEAN; BIN)

beep

beep•er

beer (the beverage: cf. BIER)

bees•wax

beet (the vegetable: cf. BEAT)

Bee•tho•ven

bee•tle v., bee•tled, bee•tling.

bee•tle-browed

be•fall v., be•fell, be•fall•en, be•fall•ing.

be•fit v., be•fit•ted, be•fit•ting.

be•fog v., be•fogged, be•fog•ging.

be•fore

be•fore•hand

be•foul v., be•fouled, be•foul•ing.

be•friend v., be•friend•ed, be•friend•ing.

be•fud•dle v., be•fud•dled, be•fud•dling.

be•fud•dle•ment

beg v., begged, beg•ging.

be•gan

be•get v., be•got, be•got•ten, be•get•ting.

be•get•ter

beg•gar

beg•gar•ly

be•gin v., be•gan, be•gun, be•gin•ning.

be•gin•ner

be•gone

be•go•nia n , pl. be•go•nias.

be•grimed

be•grudge v., be•grudged, be•grudg•ing.

be•guile v., be•guiled, be•guil•ing.

be•gun

be•half

be•have v., be•haved, be•hav•ing.

be•hav•ior

be•hav•ior•al

be•head

be•held

be•he•moth

be•hest

be•hind

be•hind•hand

be•hold v., be•held, be•hold•ing.

be•hold•en

be•hold•er

be•hoove v., be•hooved, be•hoov•ing.

beige

Bei•jing or Pe•king

be•ing

Bei•rut

be•jew•eled or be•jew•elled

bel can•to

be•la•bor v., be•la•bored, be•la•bor•ing.

Be•la•rus

be•lat•ed

be•lat•ed•ly

be•lay v., be•layed, be•lay•ing.

belch v., belched, belch•ing.
be•lea•guer
Bel•fast
bel•fry n., pl. bel•fries.
Bel•gian
Bel•gium
Bel•grade
be•lie v., be•lied, be•ly•ing.
be•lief
be•liev•a•bil•i•ty
be•liev•a•ble
be•liev•a•ble•ness
be•liev•a•bly
be•lieve v., be•lieved, be•liev•ing.
be•liev•er
be•lit•tle v., be•lit•tled, be•lit•tling.
Be•lize
Be•li•ze•an
bell (ringing instrument)
bell-bot•tom
bell-less
bel•la•don•na
bell•boy
belle (charming woman)
belles-let•tres
bell•hop
bel•li•cose
bel•li•cos•i•ty or bel•li•cose•ness
bel•lig•er•ent
bel•lig•er•ent•ly
bel•low (to roar: cf. BE-LOW)
bel•lows
bell•weth•er
bel•ly n., pl. bel•lies;. v., bel•lied, bel•ly•ing.
bel•ly•ache v.,

bel•ly•ached, bel•ly•ach•ing.
bel•ly•ach•er
bel•ly•but•ton or bel•ly but•ton
bel•ly•ful n., pl. bel•ly•fuls.
be•long, v., be•longed, be•long•ing.
Be•lo•rus•sia or Bye•lo•rus•sia
Be•lo•rus•sian or Bye•lo•rus•sian
be•lov•ed or be•loved adj.
be•low
be•low-the-line
belt v., belt•ed, belt•ing.
belt bag
belt•less
belt•way
be•moan v., be•moaned, be•moan•ing.
be•mused
be•muse•ment
bench v., benched, bench•ing.
bench press n.
bench-press v., bench-•pressed, bench-•press•ing.
bench•mark or bench mark
bend v., bent, bend•ing.
bend•a•ble
bend•er
be•neath
ben•e•dic•tion
ben•e•dic•to•ry
ben•e•fac•tion
ben•e•fac•tor
ben•e•fac•tress
ben•e•fice

be•nef•i•cence
be•nef•i•cent
ben•e•fi•cial
beneficial in•ter•est Business.
ben•e•fi•cial•ly
ben•e•fi•ci•ar•y n., pl. ben•e•fi•ci•ar•ies.
ben•e•fit v., ben•e•fit•ed, ben•e•fit•ing.
be•nev•o•lence
be•nev•o•lent
be•nev•o•lent•ly
Ben•gal
be•night•ed
be•nign
be•nig•nant
be•nig•nant•ly
be•nig•ni•ty
be•nign•ly
Be•nin
Be•ni•nese n., pl. Be•ni•nese.
bent
be•numb v., be•numbed, be•numb•ing.
ben•zene (chemical compound)
ben•zine (hydrocarbon mixture)
be•queath v., be•queathed, be•queath•ing.
be•queath•al or be•queath•ment
be•quest
be•rate v., be•rat•ed, be•rat•ing.
Ber•ber
be•reave adj., be•reaved or be•reft;. v., be•reav•ing.
be•reave•ment

be•ret (soft hat: cf. BARRETTE)
berg
ber•oi•ber•oi
Ber•ing Strait
Berke•ley
ber•ke•li∘um
Ber•lin
Ber•mu•da
Ber•mu•dan or Ber•mu•di∘an
Bern or Berne
Ber•noul∘li drive *Computers.*
ber∘ry n., pl. ber•ries. (small fruit: cf. BURY)
ber•serk
berth (sleeping place: cf. BIRTH)
ber∘yl
ber•yl•ine
be•ryl•li∘um
be•seech v., be•sought or be•seeched, be•seech•ing.
be•seech•ing∘ly
be•set v., be•set, be•set•ting. *(to attack: cf.* BESOT)
be•side (near)
be•sides (moreover)
be•siege v., be•sieged, be•sieg•ing.
be•sieg∘er
be•smear v., be•smeared, be•smear•ing.
be•smirch v., be•smirched, be•smirch•ing.
be•som
be•sot (to stupefy: cf. BESET)
be•sot•ted
be•sought
be•spat•ter

be•speak v., be•spoke, be•spo•ken, be•speak•ing.
be•spec•ta•cled
best
best-sell∘ing
bes•tial
bes•ti•a•l∘i∘ty
bes•tial∘ly
bes•ti•ar∘y n., pl. bes•ti•ar•ies.
be•stir v., be•stirred, be•stir•ring.
be•stow v., be•stowed, be•stow•ing.
be•stow∘al
be•stride v., be•strode or be•strid, be•strid•den, be•strid•ing.
best•sell∘er
best•sell•er•dom
bet v., bet or bet•ted, bet•ting.
be∘ta n., pl. be•tas.
beta fac∘tor *Business.*
beta test *Computers.*
be•take v., be•took, be•tak∘en, be•tak•ing.
bête noire n., pl. bêtes noires.
be•tel
be•think v., be•thought, be•think•ing.
Beth•le•hem
be•tide
be•times
be•to•ken v., be•to•kened, be•to•ken•ing.
be•tray v., be•trayed, be•tray•ing.
be•tray∘al
be•tray∘er

be•troth v., be•trothed, be•troth•ing.
be•troth∘al
bet•ter (superior)
bet•ter•ment
bet•tor or bet•ter (one who bets)
be•tween
be•twixt
bev∘el v., bev•eled or bev•elled, bev•el•ing or bev•el•ling.
bev•er•age
bev∘y n., pl. bev•ies.
be•wail v., be•wailed, be•wail•ing.
be•ware
be•wigged
be•wil•der v., be•wil•dered, be•wil•der•ing.
be•wil•der•ing∘ly
be•wil•der•ment
be•witch v., be•witched, be•witch•ing.
be•witch•ing∘ly
be•witch•ment
bey n., pl. beys.
be•yond
bez∘el
Bho•pal
Bhu•tan
Bhu•tan•ese n., pl. Bhu•tan•ese.
bi n., pl. bis.
bi•a∘ly n., pl. bi•a•lies.
bi•an•nu∘al (twice a year: cf. BIENNIAL)
bi•an•nu•al∘ly
bi∘as v., bi•ased or bi•assed, bi•as•ing or bi•as•sing.
bi•ath•lon
bib

Bi•ble
Bib•li•cal
Bib•li•cal•ly
bib•li•og•ra•pher
bib•li•o•graph•ic or
  bib•li•o•graph•i•
  cal
bib•li•o•graph•i•
  cal•ly
bib•li•og•ra•phy n.,
  pl. bib•li•og•ra•
  phies.
bib•li•o•phile
bib•u•lous
bi•cam•er•al
bi•car•bo•nate
bi•cen•ten•ni•al
bi•ceps n., pl. bi•ceps
  or bi•ceps•es.
bick•er v., bick•ered,
  bick•er•ing.
bi•con•cave
bi•con•vex
bi•cul•tur•al
bi•cul•tur•al•ism
bi•cus•pid
bi•cy•cle v., bi•cy•
  cled, bi•cy•cling.
bi•cy•cler or bi•cy•
  clist
bid v., bade or bid,
  bid•den or bid, bid•
  ding.
bid and asked Busi-
  ness.
bid•der
bid•dy n., pl. bid•
  dies.
bide v., bid•ed or
  bode, bid•ed, bid•
  ing.
bi•det
bi•en•ni•al
bi•en•ni•al•ly
bier (coffin: cf. BEER)
bi•fo•cal
bi•fur•cate v., bi•

fur•cat•ed, bi•fur•
  cat•ing.
bi•fur•ca•tion
big v., big•ger, big•
  gest.
big bang theo•ry
Big Board Business.
big busi•ness Busi-
  ness.
big-tick•et Business.
big•a•mist
big•a•mous
big•a•my n., pl.
  big•a•mies.
big•gie or big•gy, n.,
  pl. big•gies.
big•gish
big•heart•ed
big•heart•ed•ness
big•horn n., pl. big•
  horns or big•horn.
bight (loop: cf. BITE;
  BYTE)
big•mouth n., pl. big•
  mouths or big•
  mouth.
big•ness
big•ot
big•wig
bike v., biked, bik•
  ing.
bik•er
bike•way
bi•ki•ni n., pl. bi•ki•
  nis.
bi•ki•nied
bi•lat•er•al
bi•lat•er•al•ism
bile
bilge
bi•lin•gual
bi•lin•gual•ism
bi•lin•gual•ly
bil•ious
bil•ious•ly
bil•ious•ness

bilk v., bilked, bilk•
  ing.
bill v., billed, bill•ing.
bill of ex•change
  Business.
bill of lad•ing Busi-
  ness.
bill of sale Business.
bill•board
bil•let
bil•let-doux n., pl.
  bil•lets-doux.
bill•fold
bil•liard
bil•liards
bill•ing
bil•lings•gate
bil•lion n., pl. bil•
  lions or bil•lion.
bil•lion•aire
bil•lionth
bil•low v., bil•lowed,
  bil•low•ing.
bil•ly n., pl. bil•lies.
bim•bo n., pl. bim•
  bos or bim•boes.
bi•month•ly n., pl.
  bi•month•lies.
bin (box: cf. BEAN; BEEN)
bi•na•ry n., pl. bi•
  na•ries.
bind v., bound, bind•
  ing.
bind•er•y n., pl.
  bind•er•ies.
bind•ing
binge v., binged,
  bing•ing.
bin•go
bin•go card
bin•na•cle
bin•oc•u•lar
bin•oc•u•lar•i•ty
bi•no•mi•al
bi•o n., pl. bi•os.
bi•o•chem•i•cal

bi•o•chem•oi•cal•ly
bi•o•chem•ist
bi•o•chem•is•try
bi•o•chip
bi•o•cid•al
bi•o•cide
bi•o•de•grad•a•bil•oi•ty
bi•o•de•grad•a•ble
bi•o•di•ver•si•ty
bi•o•eth•ics
bi•o•feed•back
bi•og•ra•pher
bi•o•graph•i•cal
bi•og•ra•phy n., pl. bi•og•ra•phies.
bi•o•log•i•cal
bi•o•log•i•cal•ly
bi•ol•o•gist
bi•ol•o•gy
bi•o•mass
bi•o•med•i•cal
bi•o•med•i•cine
bi•on•ic
bi•o•phys•i•cal
bi•o•phys•i•cal•ly
bi•o•phys•i•cist
bi•o•phys•ics
bi•op•sy n., pl. bi•op•sies,. v., bi•op•sied, bi•op•sy•ing.
bi•o•rhythm
BIOS Computers. (basic input/output system)
bi•o•sci•ence
bi•o•sci•en•tist
bi•o•sphere
bi•o•tech•ni•cal
bi•o•tech•no•log•i•cal
bi•o•tech•nol•o•gist
bi•o•tech•nol•o•gy
bi•ot•ic
bi•o•tin
bi•par•ti•san
bi•par•ti•san•ship

bi•par•tite
bi•ped
bi•plane
bi•po•lar
bi•po•lar•oi•ty
bi•po•lar•oi•za•tion
bi•po•lar•ize v., bi•po•lar•ized, bi•po•lar•iz•ing.
bi•ra•cial
birch
bird
bird-brained or bird•brained
bird•bath
bird•brain
bird•cage
bird•er
bird•house
bird•ie v., bird•ied, bird•ie•ing.
bird•like
bird•lime v., bird•limed, bird•lim•ing.
bird's-eye n., pl. bird's-•eyes.
bird•seed
bi•ret•o•ta n., pl. bi•ret•tas.
Bir•ming•ham
birth¹ (act of being born: cf. BERTH)
birth² v., birthed, birth•ing.
birth•day
birth•mark
birth•place
birth•rate
birth•right
birth•stone
bis•cuit
bi•sect
bi•sec•tion
bi•sex•u•al
bi•sex•u•al•oi•ty
bi•sex•u•al•ly

bish•op
bish•op•ric
Bis•marck
bis•muth
bi•son n., pl. bi•son.
bisque
Bis•sau
bis•tro n., pl. bis•tros.
bit
bit map
bit-mapped Computers.
bitch
bitch•i•ness
bitch•y adj., bitch•i•er, bitch•i•est.
bite v., bit, bit•ten, bit•ing. (to cut with teeth: cf. BIGHT; BYTE)
bit•ing
bit•ing•ly
bit•ter v., bit•ter•er, bit•ter•est.
bit•ter•ly
bit•tern
bit•ter•ness
bit•ters
bit•ter•sweet
bit•ter•sweet•ness
bi•tu•men
bi•tu•mi•nous
bi•va•lence or bi•va•len•cy
bi•va•lent
bi•valve
biv•ou•ac
bi•week•ly n., pl. bi•week•lies.
bi•year•ly
bi•zarre (strange: cf. BAZAAR)
bi•zarre•ly
bi•zarre•ness
Bi•zet
blab or blab•ber v., blabbed or blab•

bered, blab•bing or
blab•ber•ing.
blab○ber•mouth
black *adj.*, black○er,
black•est.
black-and-blue
black-eyed Su•san
black mar•ket
black tie *n.*
black-tie *adj.*,
black•ball *v.*, black•
balled, black•ball•
ing.
black•ber○ry *n., pl.*
black•ber•ries.
black•bird
black•board
black○en
black•ened
black•guard
black•head
black•ish
black•jack
black•list *v.*, black•
list○ed, black•list•
ing.
black•mail *v.*, black•
mailed, black•mail•
ing.
black•mail•er
black•out
black•smith
black•thorn
black•top *v.*, black•
topped, black•top•
ping.
blad•der
blade
blam•a○ble or blame•
a○ble
blame *v.*, blamed,
blam•ing.
blame•less
blame•less•ness
blame•wor•thy
blanch *v.*, blanched,
blanch•ing.

bland *adj.*, bland○er,
bland•est.
blan•dish *v.*, blan•
dished, blan•dish•
ing.
blan•dish•ment
bland○ly
bland•ness
blank *adj.*, blank○er,
blank•est.
blank check *Business.*
blank en•dorse•ment
Business.
blan•ket *v.*, blan•
ket○ed, blan•ket•
ing.
blanket lien *Business.*
blank○ly
blank•ness
blare *v.*, blared, blar•
ing.
blar•ney
bla○sé
blas•pheme *v.*, blas•
phemed, blas•
phem•ing.
blas•phem○er
blas•phe•mous
blas•phe•mous○ly
blas•phe•my *n., pl.*
blas•phe•mies.
blast *v.*, blast○ed,
blast•ing.
blast○er
blast•off
bla•tant
bla•tant○ly
blath○er *v.*, blath•
ered, blath•er•ing.
blaze *v.*, blazed, blaz•
ing.
blaz○er
bla•zon *v.*, bla•
zoned, bla•zon•ing.
bleach *v.*, bleached,
bleach•ing.
bleach•a○ble

bleach○er
bleak *adj.*, bleak○er,
bleak•est.
bleak○ly
bleak•ness
blear○i○ly
blear○i•ness
blear○y *adj.*, blear•
i○er, blear•i•est.
bleat *v.*, bleat○ed,
bleat•ing.
bleed *v.*, bled, bleed•
ing.
bleed○er
bleep *v.*, bleeped,
bleep•ing.
blem•ish *v.*, blem•
ished, blem•ish•ing.
blench *v.*, blenched,
blench•ing.
blend *v.*, blend○ed,
blend•ing.
blend○er
bless *v.*, blessed or
blest, bless•ing.
bless○ed
bless•ed○ly
bless•ed•ness
bless•ing
blew (did blow: cf.
BLUE)
blight *v.*, blight○ed,
blight•ing.
blimp
blind *adj.*, blind○er,
blind•est;. *v.*,
blind○ed, blind•ing.
blind check *Business.*
blind trust *Business.*
blind•fold *v.*, blind•
fold○ed, blind•fold•
ing.
blind•ing○ly
blind○ly
blind•ness
blind•side *v.*, blind•

sid○ed, blind•sid•ing.
blink v., blinked, blink•ing.
blink○er
blintz
blip v., blipped, blip•ping.
bliss
bliss•ful
bliss•ful○ly
blis•ter v., blis•tered, blis•ter•ing.
blithe adj., blith•er, blith•est.
blithe○ly
blithe•ness
blitz v., blitzed, blitz•ing.
blitz○er
blitz•krieg
bliz•zard
bloat v., bloat○ed, bloat•ing.
blob
bloc (political group)
block (solid mass; to obstruct)
block•a○ble
block•ade v., block•ad○ed, block•ad•ing.
block•ad○er
block•age
block•bust○er
block•bust•ing
block○er
block•head
block•head○ed
block•house
bloke
blond adj., blond○er, blond•est.
blond•ish
blond•ness
blood

blood•bath
blood•cur•dling
blood○ed
blood•hound
blood○i○ly
blood○i•ness
blood•less
blood•less○ly
blood•less•ness
blood•like
blood•line
blood•mo•bile
blood•shed
blood•shot
blood•stream
blood•suck○er
blood•suck•ing
blood•thirst○i•ness
blood•thirst○y
blood○y v., blood•ied, blood•y•ing; adj., blood•i○er, blood•i•est.
bloom v., bloomed, bloom•ing.
bloom○er (one that blooms; blunder)
bloo•mers (loose trousers)
bloom•ing
bloop○er
blos•som
blot v., blot•ted, blot•ting.
blotch○y adj., blotch•i○er, blotch•i•est.
blot•ter
blouse v., bloused, blous•ing.
blouse•like
blous○on
blow v., blew, blown, blow•ing.
blow-by-blow
blow-dry v., blow-•

dried, blow-•dry•ing, blow-•dries.
blow fly or blow•fly
blow○er
blow•gun
blow•out
blow•torch
blow○up
blow○y adj., blow•i○er, blow•i•est.
blowz•i○i•ly or blows•i○ly
blowz○y or blows○y, adj., blowz•i○er, blowz•i•est.
BLS Business. (Bureau of Labor Statistics)
blub•ber
bludg•eon v., bludg•eoned, bludg•eon•ing.
blue adj., blu○er, blu•est; v., blued, blu•ing or blue•ing. (the color; to make blue: cf. BLEW)
blue-blood○ed
blue chip n. Business.
blue-chip adj. Business.
blue-col○lar
blue-pen○cil v., blue-pen○ciled or blue-pen○cilled, blue-pen○cil○ing or blue-pen○cil○ling.
blue-rinse or blue-rinsed
blue-sky law Business.
blue•bell
blue•ber○ry n., pl. blue•ber•ries.
blue•bird
blue•gill
blue•grass
blue•jack○et
blue•ness
blue•nose

blue•point
blue•print
blues
blue•stock•ing
blu∘et
bluff *adj.*, bluff∘er, bluff•est.
bluff•a∘ble
bluff∘er
bluff∘ly
bluff•ness
blu•ing or blue•ing
blu•ish or blue•ish
blun•der *v.*, blun•dered, blun•der•ing.
blun•der•buss
blun•der∘er
blun•der•ing∘ly
blunt *adj.*, blunt∘er, blunt•est.
blunt∘ly
blunt•ness
blur *v.*, blurred, blur•ring.
blurb
blur•red•ness
blur∘ry *adj.*, blur•ri∘er, blur•ri∘est.
blurt *v.*, blurt∘ed, blurt•ing.
blush *v.*, blushed, blush•ing.
blush∘er
blush•ing∘ly
blush wine
blus•ter *v.*, blus•tered, blus•ter•ing.
blus•ter∘er
blus•ter•ing∘ly
blus•ter∘y
bo∘a *n.*, *pl.* bo∘as.
boar (male swine: cf. BORE)
board (lumber; to en-ter: cf. BORED)

board of di•rec•tors *Business.*
board∘er (lodger: cf. BORDER)
boarder ba∘by
board•ing•house or board•ing house
board•walk
boast *v.*, boast∘ed, boast•ing.
boast∘er
boast•ful
boast•ful∘ly
boast•ful•ness
boast•ing∘ly
boat
boat∘el
boat∘er
boat•swain or bo's'n
bob *v.*, bobbed, bob•bing.
bob•bin
bob•ble *v.*, bob•bled, bob•bling.
bob•by *n.*, *pl.* bob•bies.
bobby pin
bob∘by•socks or bob∘by•sox *n.*, *pl.*
bob∘by•sox∘er or bobby sox∘er
bob•cat *n.*, *pl.* bob•cats, bob•cat.
bob•sled *v.*, bob•sled•ded, bob•sled•ding.
bob•sled•der
bob•tail
bob•white
Boc•cac•ci∘o
boc•cie or boc∘ci
bock beer
bode *v.*, bod∘ed, bod•ing.
bod•ice
bod•i∘ly

bod•kin
bod∘y *n.*, *pl.* bod•ies;. *v.*, bod•ied, bod•y•ing.
bod∘y•build∘er or bod∘y-build∘er
bod∘y•build∘ing or bod∘y-build∘ing
bod∘y•guard
Boer
bog *v.*, bogged, bog•ging.
bo•gey *n.*, *pl.* bo•geys; *v.*, bo•geyed, bo•gey•ing. (golf score; to bogey: cf. BOGGY; BOGY)
bo•gey•man *n.*, *pl.* bogey•men.
bog•gle *v.*, bog•gled, bog•gling.
bog∘gy (of a bog)
Bo•go∘tá
bo•gus
bo∘gy *n.*, *pl.* bo•gies. (hobgoblin)
Bo•he•mi∘a
Bo•he•mi∘an
Bo•he•mi•an•ism
boil *v.*, boiled, boil•ing.
boil∘er
bois d'arc
Boi•se
bois•ter•ous
bois•ter•ous∘ly
bois•ter•ous•ness
bo∘la, *n.*, *pl.* bo•las.
bold *adj.*, bold∘er, bold•est. (brave: cf. BOWLED)
bold∘er (braver: cf. BOULDER)
bold•face or bold•faced
bold∘ly
bold•ness

bole (tree trunk: cf. BOLE; BOWL)
bo•le•ro *n., pl.* **bo•le•ros.**
bol•i•var or **bo•lívar** *n., pl.* **bol•i•vars** or **bo•li•va•res.**
Bol•i•var
Bo•liv•i•a
Bo•liv•i•an
boll (seed pod)
boll wee•vil
bo•lo *n., pl.* **bo•los.**
bo•lo•gna (cold cut sausage: cf. BALONEY)
Bol•she•vik *n., pl.* **Bol•she•viks, Bol•she•vik•i.**
Bol•she•vism
Bol•she•vist
bol•ster
bolt *v.,* **bolt•ed, bolt•ing.**
bolt•er
bo•lus *n., pl.* **bo•lus•es.**
bomb *v.,* **bombed, bomb•ing.** (explosive device; to bomb: cf. BALM)
bom•bard *v.,* **bom•bard•ed, bom•bard•ing.**
bom•bar•dier
bom•bard•ment
bom•bast
Bom•bay
bomb•er
bomb•shell
bon ap•pe•tit
bon mot *n., pl.* **bons mots.**
bon vi•vant *n., pl.* **bons vi•vants.**
bon vo•yage
bo•na fide or **bo•na-fide**

bo•nan•za *n., pl.* **bo•nan•zas.**
Bo•na•parte
bon•bon
bond *v.,* **bond•ed, bond•ing.**
bond rat•ing *Business.*
bond•a•ble *Business.*
bond•age
bond•ed ware•house *Business.*
bond•hold•er *Business.*
bond•hold•ing *Business.*
bond•ing com•pa•ny *Business.*
bond•man *n., pl.* **bond•men.**
bonds•man *n., pl.* **bonds•men.** *Business.*
bonds•wom•an *n., pl.* **bonds•wom•en.** *Business.*
bond•wom•an *n., pl.* **bond•wom•en.**
bone *v.,* **boned, bon•ing.**
bone-dry
bone meal or **bone•meal**
bone•head
bone•head•ed•ness
bone•less
bon•er
bon•fire
bong
bon•go *n., pl.* **bon•gos, bon•goes.**
bon•i•ness
bo•ni•to *n., pl.* **bo•ni•to, bo•ni•tos.**
bon•jour
bon•kers
Bonn
bon•net *v.,* **bon•**

net•ed, bon•net•ing.
bon•ny *adj.,* **bon•ni•er, bon•ni•est.**
bon•ny•clab•ber or **bon•ny•clap•per**
bon•sai *n., pl.* **bon•sai.**
bon•soir
bo•nus *n., pl.* **bo•nus•es.**
bonus meth•od *Business.*
bon•y *adj.,* **bon•i•er, bon•i•est.**
boo *n., pl.* **boos;.** *v.,* **booed, boo•ing.**
boo-boo *n., pl.* **boo-•boos.**
boob tube
boo•by trap *n.*
boo•by-trap *v.*
boo•dle
boog•ie *v.,* **boog•ied, boog•ie•ing.**
book *v.,* **booked, book•ing.**
book in•ven•to•ry *Business.*
book val•ue *Business.*
book•case
book•end
book•ie
book•ing
book•ish
book•ish•ness
book•keep•er *Business.*
book•keep•ing *Business.*
book•let
book•mak•er
book•mak•ing
book•mark
book•mo•bile
book•sell•er
book•sell•ing

book•shelf n., pl.
book•shelves.
book•store
book•worm
Bool•e◦an log◦ic
Computers.
boom v., boomed,
boom•ing.
boom town or boom•
town
boo•mer•ang
boon
boon•docks
boon•dog•gle
boon•dog•gler
boor
boor•ish
boor•ish◦ly
boost v., boost◦ed,
boost•ing.
boost◦er
boost•er•ism
boot v., boot◦ed,
boot•ing.
boot•black
boot◦ee or boot◦ie
(baby shoe: cf. BOOTY)
booth n., pl. booths.
boot•leg v., boot•
legged, boot•leg•·
ging.
boot•leg•ger
boot•less
boot•less•ness
boot•lick◦er
boo◦ty (plunder: cf.
BOOTEE or BOOTIE)
booze v., boozed,
booz•ing.
booz◦er
bop v., bopped, bop•
ping.
bo•rax
Bor•deaux n., pl. Bor•
deaux.
bor•del◦lo n., pl. bor•
del•los.

bor•der¹ n. (edge: cf.
BOARDER)
bor•der² v., bor•
dered, bor•der•ing.
bor◦der•land
bor◦der•line
bore v., bored, bor•
ing. (dull person; to
drill: cf. BOAR)
bo•re◦al
bored (weary: cf.
BOARD)
bore•dom
bo•ric ac◦id
bor•ing
bor•ing◦ly
bork
born (brought forth by
birth)
born-a◦gain
borne (supported)
Bor•ne◦an
Bor•ne◦o
bo•ron
bor•ough (municipal-
ity: cf. BUREAU; BURRO;
BURROW)
bor•row v., bor•
rowed, bor•row•
ing.
bor•row◦er
borscht or borsch
bor•zoi n., pl. bor•
zois.
bosh
bo's'n (boatswain)
bos◦om
bos•om◦y
bo◦son
boss v., bossed, boss•
ing.
bos◦sa no◦va n., pl.
bos◦sa no◦vas.
boss◦i◦ly
boss◦i•ness
boss•ism

boss◦y adj., boss•
i◦er, boss•i•est.
Bos•ton
Bos•to•ni◦an
bo•sun
bo•tan◦i•cal or bo•
tan◦ic
bot◦a•nist
bot◦a•ny
botch
both
both◦er
both◦er•some
Bot•swa◦na
Bot•ti•cel◦li
bot•tle v., bot•tled,
bot•tling.
bot◦tle•neck
bot•tler
bot•tom v., bot•
tomed, bot•tom•
ing.
bottom line n. Busi-
ness.
bot◦tom-line adj. Busi-
ness.
bot•tom man•age•
ment Business.
bot•tom•less
bot◦u•lism
bou•doir
bouf•fant
bou•gain•vil•le◦a n.,
pl. bou•gain•vil•
le◦as.
bough (tree branch: cf.
BOW)
bought
bouil•la•baisse
bouil•lon (broth: cf.
BULLION)
boul•der (large rock:
cf. BOLDER)
boul◦e•vard
bounce v., bounced,
bounc•ing.
bounc◦er

bounc•ing
bounc◦y
bound
bound◦a◦ry n., pl. bound◦a•ries.
bound◦en
bound◦er
bound•less
boun•te•ous
boun•ti•ful
boun•ti•ful◦ly
boun•ti•ful•ness
boun◦ty n., pl. boun•ties.
bou•quet
Bour•bon
bour•geois n., pl. bour•geois.
bour•geoi•sie
bourse Business.
bout
bou•tique
bou•ton•niere
bo•vine
bow[1] (to bend: cf. BOUGH)
bow[2] (curve: cf. BEAU)
bowd•ler◦i•za•tion
bowd•ler•ize v., bowd•ler•ized, bowd•ler•iz•ing.
bowd•ler•iz◦er
bow◦el
bow◦er
bow◦ie knife
bow•knot
bowl (dish: cf. BOLE; BOLL)
bowled (did bowl: cf. BOLD)
bow•leg
bow•leg•ged
bow•leg•ged•ness
bowl◦er
bowl•ing

bow•man n., pl. bow•men.
bow•sprit
box v., boxed, box•ing.
box of•fice n.
box-of•fice adj.
box•car
box◦er
box•like
boy (male child: cf. BUOY)
boy scout
boy toy
boy•cott v., boy•cott◦ed, boy•cott•ing.
boy•cott◦er
boy•friend
boy•sen•ber◦ry n., pl. boy•sen•ber•ries.
bps Computers. (bits per second)
bra
brace v., braced, brac•ing.
brace•let
brack◦en
brack◦et v., brack•et◦ed, brack•et•ing.
bracket creep Business.
brack•ish
brack•ish•ness
bract
brac•te◦al
brac•te•ate
bract◦ed
bract•less
brad v., brad•ded, brad•ding.
brag v., bragged, brag•ging.
brag•ga•do•ci◦o n., pl. brag•ga•do•ci◦os.
brag•gart

Brah◦ma
Brah•man n., pl. Brah•mans. (Hindu priest; cattle breed)
Brah•min (cultured person)
Brahms
braid v., braid◦ed, braid•ing.
Braille
brain v., brained, brain•ing.
brain-dead or brain dead
brain•child n., pl. brain•chil•dren.
brain◦i•ness
brain•storm
brain•storm◦er
brain•storm•ing
brain•teas◦er
brain•wash
brain•wash◦er
brain•wash•ing
brain◦y adj., brain•i◦er, brain•i•est.
braise v., braised, brais•ing. (to cook by simmering: cf. BRAYS; BRAZE)
brake v., braked, brak•ing. (device for stopping; to stop: cf. BREAK)
brake•man n., pl. brake•men.
bra•less
bram•ble
bram•bly
bran
branch v., branched, branch•ing.
branch•less
brand v., brand◦ed, brand•ing.
brand a◦ware•ness Business.

brand im•age *Business.*

brand name *Business.*

brand-new

brand switch•ing *Business.*

bran•dish *v.,* bran•dished, bran•dish•ing.

bran•dy *n., pl.* bran•dies.

brash *adj.,* brash∘er, brash•est.

brash∘ly

brash•ness

Bra•síl∘ia

brass

bras•siere (woman's undergarment: cf. BRA-ZIER)

brat

Bra•ti•sla∘va

brat•tish *or* brat∘ty

brat•wurst

Braun•schwei•ger

bra•va∘do

brave *v.,* braved, brav•ing; *adj.,* brav∘er, brav•est.

brave∘ly

brav•er∘y

bra∘vo *n., pl.* bra•vos, bra•voes; *v.,* bra•voed, bra•vo•ing.

bra•vu∘ra *n., pl.* bra•vu•ras.

brawl *v.,* brawled, brawl•ing.

brawl∘er

brawn

brawn∘y *adj.,* brawn•i∘er, brawn•i•est.

bray *v.,* brayed, bray•ing.

braze *v.,* brazed, braz•ing. (to make of brass: cf. BRAISE; BRAYS)

bra•zen

bra•zen∘ly

bra•zen•ness

bra•zier *or* bra•sier (one who makes brass articles: cf. BRASSIERE)

Bra•zil

Bra•zil∘i•an

Braz•za•ville

breach *v.,* breached, breach•ing. (infraction; to breach: cf. BREECH)

bread (baked dough: cf. BRED)

bread•bas•ket

bread•board

bread•crumb

bread∘ed

bread•fruit

breadth (width: cf. BREATH; BREATHE)

bread•win•ner

bread•win•ning

break *v.,* broke, bro•ken, break•ing. (to shatter: cf. BRAKE)

break-e∘ven point *Business.*

break-in

break•a∘ble

break•age

break•down

break∘er

break•fast *v.,* break•fast∘ed, break•fast•ing.

break•fast∘er

break•front

break•neck

break•out

break•through

break∘up

break•wa•ter

breast *v.,* breast∘ed, breast•ing.

breast-feed *v.,* breast--fed, breast--feed∘ing.

breast•bone

breast•plate

breast•stroke

breast•strok∘er

breast•work

breath (air inhaled and exhaled: cf. BREADTH)

breathe *v.,* breathed, breath•ing. (to inhale and exhale: cf. BREADTH)

breath∘er

breath∘i∘ly

breath•less

breath•less∘ly

breath•tak•ing

breath•tak•ing∘ly

breath∘y *adj.,* breath•i∘er, breath∘i•est.

Brecht

Brecht•i∘an

bred (raised: cf. BREAD)

breech (rear part: cf. BREACH)

breech•cloth *or* breech•clout

breech∘es

breed *v.,* bred, breed•ing.

breed∘er

breed•ing

breeze *v.,* breezed, breez•ing.

breeze•less

breeze•way

Brem∘en

breth•ren

breve

bre•vet *v.,* bre•vet•ted *or* bre•vet∘ed, bre•vet•ting *or* bre•vet•ing.

bre•vi•ar∘y *n., pl.* bre•vi•ar•ies.

brev•i•ty

brew *v.*, brewed, brew•ing.

brewed (did brew: cf. BROOD)

brew•er

brew•er•y *n., pl.* brew•er•ies.

brews (makes beer: cf. BRUISE)

Brezh•nev

bri•ar

bri•ar•y or bri•er•y

brib•a•ble or bribe•a•ble

bribe *v.*, bribed, brib•ing.

brib•er

brib•er•y *n., pl.* brib•er•ies.

bric-a-brac or bric-à-brac

brick

brick•bat

bricked

brick•lay•er

brick•lay•ing

brid•al (of a wedding: cf. BRIDLE)

bride

bride•groom

brides•maid

bridge *v.*, bridged, bridg•ing.

bridge loan *Business.*

bridge•a•ble

bridge•head

Bridge•port

bridge•work

bri•dle *v.*, bri•dled, bri•dling. (harness; to restrain: cf. BRIDAL)

Brie

brief *adj.*, brief•er, brief•est.

brief•case

brief•ing

brief•ly

brief•ness

bri•er or bri•ar

bri•er•y or bri•ar•y

brig

bri•gade *v.*, bri•gad•ed, bri•gad•ing.

brig•a•dier

brig•and

brig•and•age

brig•an•tine

bright *v.*, bright•er, bright•est.

bright•en *v.*, bright•ened, bright•en•ing.

bright•en•er

bright•ly

bright•ness

bril•liance

bril•lian•cy

bril•liant

bril•lian•tine

bril•liant•ly

brim *v.*, brimmed, brim•ming.

brim•ful

brim•stone

brin•dled

brine *v.*, brined, brin•ing.

bring *v.*, brought, bring•ing.

bring•er

brin•i•ness

brink

brink•man•ship or brinks•man•ship

brin•y *adj.*, brin•i•er, brin•i•est.

bri•oche

bri•quette or bri•quet *v.*, bri•quet•ted, bri•quet•ting.

Bris•bane

brisk *adj.*, brisk•er, brisk•est.

bris•ket

brisk•ly

brisk•ness

bris•ling

bris•tle *v.*, bris•tled, bris•tling.

bris•tle•cone pine

bris•tly *adj.*, bris•tli•er, bris•tli•est.

Bris•tol

Brit

Brit•ain

britch•es

Brit•i•cism

Brit•ish

Brit•ish•ness

Brit•on

brit•tle *adj.*, brit•tler, brit•tlest.

brit•tle•ness

bro or Bro *n., pl.* bros or Bros.

broach *v.*, broached, broach•ing. (to mention: cf. BROOCH)

broad *adj.*, broad•er, broad•est.

broad-form in•sur•ance *Business.*

broad jump *n.*

broad-jump *v.*, broad-•jumped, broad-•jump•ing.

broad-mind•ed

broad-mind•ed•ly

broad-mind•ed•ness

broad-spec•trum

broad•band *Computers.*

broad•cast *v.*, broad•cast or broad•cast•ed, broad•cast•ing.

broad•cast•er

broad•cloth

broad•en v., broad•
ened, broad•en•ing.
broad•ish
broad•loom
broad•ly
broad•ness
broad•side v., broad•
sid•ed, broad•sid•
ing.
broad•sword
broad•tail
Broad•way
bro•cade v., bro•
cad•ed, bro•cad•
ing.
broc•co•li
bro•chette
bro•chure
bro•gan
brogue
broil v., broiled, broil•
ing.
broil•er
broil•ing•ly
broke
bro•ken
bro•ken-down
broken lot *Business.*
bro•ken•heart•ed
bro•ken•heart•ed•ly
bro•ken•heart•ed•
ness
bro•ken•ly
bro•ker *Business.*
bro•ker•age *Business.*
bro•mide
bro•mine
bron•chi•al
bron•chi•tis
bron•chus n., pl.
bron•chi.
bron•co, n., pl. bron•
cos.
bron•co•bust•er
bron•co•bust•ing
Bron•të

bron•to•saur
Bronx
bronze v., bronzed,
bronz•ing.
brooch (ornamental
pin: cf. BROACH)
brood v., brood•ed,
brood•ing. (offspring;
to worry: cf. BREWED)
brood•er
brood•mare
brook
Brook•lyn
broom•stick
broth
broth•el
broth•er n., pl. broth•
ers, breth•ren.
broth•er-in-law n., pl.
broth•ers-•in-•law.
broth•er•hood
brought
brou•ha•ha n , pl.
brou•ha•has.
brow
brow•beat v., brow•
beat, brow•beat•en,
brow•beat•ing.
brow•beat•er
brown adj., brown•er,
brown•est.
brown-bag v.,
brown-•bagged,
brown-•bag•ging.
brown-bag•ger
brown•ie
Brown•ing
brown•ish
brown•ness
brown•out
brown•stone
Browns•ville
brows (foreheads)
browse v., browsed,
brows•ing. (to read
casually)
brows•er

bru•in
bruise v., bruised,
bruis•ing. (to injure:
cf. BREWS)
bruis•er
bruit v., bruit•ed,
bruit•ing. (to rumor:
cf. BRUT; BRUTE)
brunch
Bru•nei
Bru•nei•an
bru•nette
brunt
brush v., brushed,
brush•ing.
brush-off
brush•wood
brusque
brusque•ly
brusque•ness
Brus•sels
brut (dry: cf. BRUIT;
BRUTE)
bru•tal
bru•tal•i•za•tion
bru•tal•ize v., bru•
tal•ized, bru•tal•iz•
ing.
bru•tal•ly
brute (beast: cf. BRUIT;
BRUT)
brut•ish
brut•ish•ness
bub•ble v., bub•bled,
bub•bling. (globule
of gas contained in a
liquid: cf. BABBLE; BAU-
BLE)
bubble mem•o•ry
Computers.
bub•ble•gum
bub•ble•top or
bub•ble-top
bub•bling•ly
bu•bo n., pl. bu•boes.
bu•bon•ic plague
buc•ca•neer

Bu•chan○an
Bu•cha•rest
buck v., bucked, buck•ing.
buck•board
buck○et
bucket shop Business.
buck•eye n., pl. buck•eyes.
buck○le v., buck•led, buck•ling.
buck•ler
buck•ram
buck•saw
buck•shot
buck•skin
buck•tooth n. pl. buck•teeth.
buck•toothed
buck•wheat
bu•col○ic
bud v., bud•ded, bud•ding.
Bu•da•pest
Bud•dha n., pl. Bud•dhas.
Bud•dha•hood
Bud•dhism
Bud•dhist
bud○dy n., pl. bud•dies;. v., bud•died, bud•dy•ing.
budge v., budged, budg•ing.
budg•er○i•gar
budg○et v., budg•et○ed, budg•et•ing. Business.
budg•et•ar○y Business.
budg•et○er Business.
budg○ie
Bue○nos Ai•res
buff v., buffed, buff•ing.
buf•fa○lo n., pl. buf•fa•loes, buf•fa•los,

buf•fa○lo; v., buffa•loed, buffa•lo○ing.
buff○er v., buff•ered, buff•er•ing.
buffer stock Business.
buf•fet[1] (self-service meal)
buff○et[2] (strike repeatedly)
buf•foon
buf•foon•er○y
buf•foon•ish
bug v., bugged, bug•ging.
bug-eyed
bug-free Computers.
bug○a•boo, n., pl bug○a•boos.
bug•bear
bug○gy n., pl. bug•gies.
bu•gle n., v., bu•gled, bu•gling.
bu•gler
build v., built, build•ing.
build○er
build•ing
building and loan as•so○ci•a•tion Business.
build○up or build-up
built-in
built-up
Bu•jum•bu○ra
bulb
Bul•gar•i○a
Bul•gar•i○an
bulge v., bulged, bulg•ing.
bulg○y adj., bulg•i○er, bulg•i•est.
bu•lim•i○a
bulk v., bulked, bulk•ing.
bulk dis•count Business.

bulk freight Business.
bulk•head
bulk○y adj., bulk○i○er, bulk•i•est.
bull v., bulled, bull•ing.
bull-like
bull mar•ket Business.
bull•dog v., bull•dogged, bull•dog•ging.
bull•doze v., bull•dozed, bull•doz•ing.
bull•doz○er
bul•let
bul•le•tin
bulletin board
bul○let•proof
bull•fight
bull•fight○er
bull•fight•ing
bull•finch
bull•frog
bull•head○ed
bull•head•ed○ly
bull•head•ed•ness
bull•horn or bull horn
bul•lion (gold or silver ingots: cf. BOUILLON)
bull•ish Business.
bul•lock
bull pen or bull•pen
bull•ring
bull's-eye n., pl. bull's-eyes.
bul○ly n., pl. bul•lies; v., bul•lied, bul•ly•ing.
bul•rush
bul•wark
bum v., bummed, bum•ming.
bum-rush, v., bum-rushed, bum-rushing.
bum•ble v., bum•bled, bum•bling.

bum•ble•bee or
bum•ble bee
bum•bler
bum•mer
bump v., bumped,
bump•ing.
bump∘er
bump•kin
bump•tious
bump•tious•ness
bump∘y adj., bump•
i∘er, bump•i•est.
bun
bunch v., bunched,
bunch•ing.
bun•dle v., bun•dled,
bun•dling.
bung v., bunged,
bung•ing.
bun•ga•low
bun•gee cord
bung•hole
bun•gle v., bun•gled,
bun•gling.
bun•gler
bun•ion
bunk¹ (nonsense)
bunk² v., bunked,
bunk•ing. (bed; to
bed down)
bun•ker
bunk•house
bun∘ko or bun∘co, n.,
pl. bun∘kos or bun•
cos.
bun•kum or bun•
combe
bun∘ny n., pl. bun•
nies.
Bun•sen burn∘er
bunt v., bunt∘ed,
bunt•ing.
bunt∘er
bun•ting
bu∘oy (floating marker:
cf. BOY)
buoy•an∘cy

buoy•ant
buoy•ant∘ly
bup∘py, n., pl. bup•
pies.
bur•den v., bur•
dened, bur•den•ing.
bur•dock
bu•reau n., pl. bu•
reaus, bu•reaux.
(government depart-
ment; chest of
drawers: cf. BOROUGH)
bu•reauc•ra∘cy n., pl.
bu•reauc•ra•cies.
bu•reau•crat
bu•reau•crat∘ic
bu•reau•crat∘i•cal∘ly
bu•reauc•ra•ti•za•
tion
bu•reauc•ra•tize v.,
bu•reauc•ra•tized,
bu•reauc•ra•tiz•
ing.
bu•rette or bu•ret
burg
bur•geon
burg∘er (hamburger)
burgh∘er (townsper-
son)
bur•glar
bur•glar•ize v., bur•
glar•ized, bur•glar•
iz•ing.
bur•gla∘ry n., pl.
bur•gla•ries.
bur•gle v., bur•gled,
bur•gling.
bur•go•mas•ter
Bur•gun∘dy n., pl.
Bur•gun•dies.
bur•i∘al
Bur•ki∘na Fa∘so
bur•lap
bur•lesque v., bur•
lesqued, bur•les•
quing.
bur•li•ness

bur•ly adj., bur•li∘er,
bur•li•est.
Bur∘ma
Bur•mese n., pl. Bur•
mese.
burn v., burned or
burnt, burn•ing.
burn-in n. Computers.
burn•a∘ble
burn∘er
bur•nish
bur•noose or bur•
nous
bur•noosed or bur•
noused
burn out
burn rate Business.
burnt
burp v., burped,
burp•ing.
burr
bur∘ro n., pl. bur•ros.
(donkey)
bur•row v., bur•
rowed, bur•row•
ing. (hole; to dig)
bur∘sa n., pl. bur•sae,
bur•sas.
bur•sal
bur•sar Business.
bur•si•tis
burst v., burst, burst•
ing.
Bu•run∘di
Bu•run•di∘an
bur∘y v., bur•ied,
bur•y•ing. (to con-
ceal: cf. BERRY)
bus n., pl. bus∘es or
bus•ses; v., bused or
bussed, bus•ing or
bus•sing. (the vehi-
cle: cf. BUSS)
bus mouse Computers.
bus to•pol∘o∘gy Com-
puters.
bus•boy or bus boy

bus∘by *n., pl.* bus•
  bies.
bush
bushed
bush∘el
bush•ing
bush•man *n., pl.*
  bush•men.
bush•mas•ter
bush∘y *adj.,* bush•
  i∘er, bush•i•est.
bus•i∘ly
busi∘ness *Business.*
business col•lege
  Business.
business cy•cle *Busi-*
  ness.
busi•ness•like
busi•ness•man *n., pl.*
  busi•ness•men. *Busi-*
  ness.
busi•ness•per•son
  Business.
busi•ness•wo•man
  n., pl. busi•ness•
  wo•men. *Business.*
bus•kin
buss *v.,* bussed, buss•
  ing. (the kiss: cf. BUS)
bust *v.,* bust∘ed,
  bust•ing.
bus•tle *v.,* bus•tled,
  bus•tling.
bus∘y *v.,* bus•ied,
  bus•y•ing; *adj.,*
  bus•i∘er, bus•i•est.
bus∘y•bod∘y *n., pl.*
  bus∘y•bod∘ies.
bus∘y•ness
bus∘y•work
but (on the contrary: cf.
  BUTT)
bu•tane

butch
butch∘er
butch•er∘y
but•ler
butt (end; to push: cf.
  BUT)
butte (hill)
but•ter *v.,* but•tered,
  but•ter•ing.
but∘ter•cup
but∘ter•fat
but∘ter•fin•gered
but∘ter•fin•gers *n.,*
  pl. but∘ter•fin•gers.
but∘ter•fish *n., pl.*
  but∘ter•fish∘es,
  but∘ter•fish.
but∘ter•fly *n., pl.*
  but∘ter•flies.
but•ter•fly ef•fect
but∘ter•less
but∘ter•milk
but∘ter•nut
but∘ter•scotch
but•ter∘y
but•tock
but•ton *v.,* but•
  toned, but•ton•ing.
but∘ton-down
but∘ton•hole *v.,*
  but∘ton•holed,
  but∘ton•hol•ing.
but∘ton•less
but•tress *v.,* but•
  tressed, but•tress•
  ing.
bub∘ba
bux∘om
bux•om•ness
buy *v.,* bought, buy•
  ing. *Business.* (to purchase: cf. BY; BYE)
buy•back *Business.*

buy∘er *Business.*
buy•ers' mar•ket
  Business.
buy•ing pow∘er *Busi-*
  ness.
buy•out *Business.*
buzz *v.,* buzzed,
  buzz•ing.
buz•zard
buzz∘er
buzz•word
by (near: cf. BUY; BYE)
by-and-by
by-elec•tion
by-path *or* by•path,
  n., pl. by-paths.
by-prod•uct
by-road *or* by•road
bye (good-bye: cf. BUY;
  BY)
bye-bye
Bye•lo•rus•sia
Bye•lo•rus•sian (Bye-
  lorussia)
by•gones
by•law
by•line *or* by-line *v.,*
  by•lined, by•lin•ing
  or by•lin•ing.
by•pass *or* by-pass *v.,*
  by•passed, by•
  pass•ing *or* by•
  pass•ing.
by•play *or* by-play
By•ron
By•ron∘ic
by•stand∘er
byte *Computers.* (com-
  puter unit: cf. BIGHT;
  BITE)
by•way
by•word
Byz•an•tine

C

C/o or c/o
C-o•sec•tion
CA (California)
cab v., cabbed, cab•bing.
ca•bal v., ca•balled, ca•bal•ling.
cab•a•la or cab•ba•la n., pl. cab•a•las.
ca•bal•le•ro n., pl. ca•bal•le•ros.
ca•ban•a n., pl. ca•ban•as.
cab•a•ret
cab•bage
cab•by or cab•bie, n., pl. cab•bies.
cab•in
cab•i•net
cab•i•net•mak•er
cab•i•net•mak•ing
cab•i•net•work
ca•ble v., ca•bled, ca•bling.
cable car or ca•ble•car
ca•ble-read•y
ca•ble•cast v., ca•ble•cast, ca•ble•cast•ed, ca•ble•cast•ing.
ca•ble•gram
cab•oo•chon
ca•boo•dle
ca•boose
cab•ri•o•let
ca•ca•o n., pl. ca•ca•os.
cac•cia•to•re
cache v., cached, cach•ing. (hiding place; computer accel-

erator; to cache: cf. CASH)
ca•chet
cack•le v., cack•led, cack•ling.
ca•coph•o•nous
ca•coph•o•nous•ly
ca•coph•o•ny n., pl. ca•coph•o•nies.
cad
CAD (computer-aided design)
CAD/CAM (computer-aided design/computer-aided manufacturing)
ca•dav•er
ca•dav•er•ous
cad•die v., cad•died, cad•dy•ing. (golf attendant; to caddie)
cad•dy n., pl. cad•dies. (container)
ca•den•za n., pl. ca•den•zas.
ca•det
Ca•dette
cadge v., cadged, cadg•ing.
cad•mi•um
ca•dre
ca•du•ce•ous n., pl. ca•du•ce•i.
Cae•sar
Cae•sar•e•an or Cae•sar•i•an
cae•su•ra or ce•su•ra n., pl. cae•su•ras or ce•su•ras or cae•su•rae.

ca•fé or ca•fe n., pl. ca•fés or ca•fes.
café au lait
caf•e•te•ri•a n., pl. caf•e•te•ri•as.
cafeteria plan Business.
caf•feine
caf•tan or kaf•tan
cage v., caged, cag•ing.
cag•ey or cag•y, adj., cag•i•er, cag•i•est.
cag•i•ly
cag•i•ness
ca•hoots
CAI (computer-assisted instruction)
Cain
cairn
Cai•ro
cais•son
ca•jole v., ca•joled, ca•jol•ing.
ca•jol•er•y
Ca•jun
cake v., caked, cak•ing.
cal•a•bash
cal•a•boose
cal•a•mine
ca•lam•i•tous
ca•lam•i•tous•ly
ca•lam•i•ty n., pl. ca•lam•i•ties.
cal•car•e•ous
cal•cif•er•ous
cal•ci•fi•ca•tion
cal•ci•fy v., cal•ci•fied, cal•ci•fy•ing.
cal•ci•mine or Kal•so•mine v., cal•ci•

mined, cal•ci•min•ing.

cal•cine *v.*, cal•cined, cal•cin•ing.

cal•cite

cal•ci•um

cal•cu•la•ble

cal•cu•late *v.*, cal•cu•lat∘ed, cal•cu•lat•ing.

cal•cu•la•tion

cal•cu•la•tor

cal•cu•lus *n.*, *pl.* cal•cu∘li or cal•cu•lus∘es.

Cal•cut∘ta

Cal•der

cal•dron

cal•en•dar (table of dates: cf. COLANDER)

cal•en•der (pressing machine)

calf *n.*, *pl.* calves.

calf•less

calf•like

calf•skin

Cal•ga∘ry

cal∘i•ber

cal∘i•brate *v.*, cal∘i•brat∘ed, cal∘i•brat•ing.

cal∘i•bra•tion

cal∘i•co *n.*, *pl.* cal∘i•coes or cal∘i•cos.

Cal∘i•for•nia (CA)

Cal∘i•for•nian

cal∘i•for•ni∘um

cal∘i•per or cal•li•per

ca•liph or ca•lif

cal•is•then•ic

cal•is•then•ics or cal•lis•then•ics

calk *v.*, calked, calk•ing.

call *v.*, called, call•ing.

call girl

call op•tion *Business.*

call-up

cal∘la *n.*, *pl.* cal•las.

call•a∘ble bond *Business.*

call•back or call-back, *Business.*

call∘er

cal•ler ID

cal•lig•ra•pher

cal•li•graph∘ic

cal•lig•ra•phy

call•ing

cal•li•o∘pe

cal•lous (insensitive: cf. CALLUS)

cal•lous•ly

cal•lous•ness

cal•low

cal•low•ness

cal•lus *n.*, *pl.* cal•lus∘es. (hardened skin: cf. CALLOUS)

calm *adj.*, calm∘er, calm•est; *v.*, calmed, calm•ing. (still; to make calm: cf. CAM)

calm•ly

calm•ness

ca•lor∘ic

cal∘o•rie or cal∘o∘ry *n.*, *pl.* cal∘o•ries.

cal∘o•rif∘ic

cal∘u•met

ca•lum•ni•ate *v.*, ca•lum•ni•at∘ed, ca•lum•ni•at•ing.

ca•lum•ni•a•tion

ca•lum•ni•a•tor

ca•lum•ni•ous

cal•um∘ny *n.*, *pl.* cal•um•nies.

Cal•va∘ry (biblical place: cf. CAVALRY)

calve *v.*, calved, calv•ing.

calves

Cal•vin

Cal•vin•ism

Cal•vin•ist

Cal•vin•is•tic

Ca•lyp∘so *n.*, *vl.* Ca•lyp•sos.

ca•lyx *n.*, *pl.* ca•lyx∘es or cal•y∘ces.

cam (round machine part: cf. CALM)

CAM (computer-aided manufacturing)

ca•ma•ra•de•rie

cam•ber

cam•bi∘um *n.*, *pl.* cam•bi•ums or cam•bi∘a.

Cam•bo•di∘a

Cam•bo•di∘an

Cam•bri∘an

cam•bric

Cam•bridge

cam•cord∘er

came

cam∘el

ca•mel•lia *n.*, *pl.* ca•mel•lias.

Cam•em•bert

cam•e∘o *n.*, *pl.* cam•e∘os.

cam•er∘a *n.*, *pl.* cam•er∘as.

cam•er∘a•man *n.*, *pl.* cam•er∘a•men.

Cam•e∘roon

cam∘i•sole

cam∘o *n.*, *pl.* cam∘os.

cam•o•mile

cam•ou•flage *v.*, cam•ou•flaged, cam•ou•flag•ing.

camp *v.*, camped, camp•ing.

cam•paign

cam•paign∘er

cam•pa•ni∘le

camp•er
camp•fire
cam•phor
camp•site or camp-
site
cam•pus *n., pl.* cam•
pus•es.
camp•y *adj.,* camp•
i•er, camp•i•est.
cam•shaft
Ca•mus
can¹ *v.,* could. (be able
to)
can² *v.,* canned, can•
ning. (preserve)
Ca•naan
Can•a•da
Ca•na•di•an
Canadian ba•con
Ca•na•di•an•ism
ca•nal
can•a•pé *n., pl.*
can•a•pés. (appe-
tizer: cf. CANOPY)
ca•nard
ca•nar•y *n., pl.* ca•
nar•ies.
ca•nas•ta
Can•ber•ra
can•can
can•cel *v.,* can•celed
or can•celled, can•
cel•ing or can•cel•
ling.
can•cel•a•ble
can•cel•la•tion
can•cer (malignant tu-
mor: cf. CANKER)
can•cer•ous
Can•cún
can•de•la•bra *n., pl.*
can•de•la•bras.
can•de•la•brum *n.,*
pl. can•de•la•bra or
can•de•la•brums.
can•did (frank: cf. CAN-
DIED)

can•di•da•cy
can•di•date
can•did•ly
can•did•ness
can•died (sugared: cf.
CANDID)
can•dle
can•dle•stick
can•dor
can•dy *n., pl.* can•
dies; *v.,* can•died,
can•dy•ing.
candy strip•er
can•dy•like
cane *v.,* caned, can•
ing.
cane•brake
ca•nine
can•is•ter
can•ker (ulcerous sore:
cf. CANCER)
can•ker•ous
can•na•bis
canned
can•ner•y *n., pl.* can•
ner•ies.
can•ni•bal
can•ni•bal•ism
can•ni•bal•is•tic
can•ni•bal•ize *v.,*
can•ni•bal•ized,
can•ni•bal•iz•ing.
can•ni•ly
can•ni•ness
can•non *n., pl.* can•
nons or can•non.
(mounted gun: cf. CA-
NON; CANYON)
can•non•ade *v.,* can•
non•ad•ed, can•
non•ad•ing.
can•not
can•ny *adj.,* can•
ni•er, can•ni•est.
ca•noe *v.,* ca•noed,
ca•noe•ing.
ca•noe•ist

can•on (law: cf. CAN-
NON; canyon)
ca•ñon (canyon)
ca•non•i•cal or ca•
non•ic
can•on•i•za•tion
can•on•ize *v.,* can•
on•ized, can•on•iz•
ing.
can•o•py *n., pl.*
can•o•pies. (awning:
cf. CANAPÉ)
cant (jargon; angle)
can't (cannot)
can•ta•bi•le
can•ta•loupe or can•
ta•loup
can•tan•ker•ous
can•tan•ker•ous•
ness
can•ta•ta *n., pl.* can•
ta•tas.
can•teen
can•ter *v.,* can•tered,
can•ter•ing. (slow
gallop: cf. CANTOR)
can•ti•cle
can•ti•le•ver
can•to *n., pl.* can•tos.
can•ton
can•ton•al
Can•ton•ese *n., pl.*
Can•ton•ese.
can•tor (singer: cf.
CANTER)
can•to•ri•al
can•vas (cloth)
can•vas•back *n., pl.*
can•vas•backs or
can•vas•back.
can•vass *v.,* can•
vassed, can•vass•
ing. (to solicit)
can•vass•er
can•yon (valley: cf.
CANNON; CANON)

cap v., capped, cap•ping.

ca•pa•bil•i•ty

ca•pa•ble

ca•pa•bly

ca•pa•cious

ca•pa•cious•ly

ca•pa•cious•ness

ca•pac•i•tance

ca•pac•i•tor

ca•pac•i•ty n., pl. ca•pac•i•ties.

ca•par•i•son v., ca•par•i•soned, ca•par•i•son•ing.

cape

Cape Verde

caped

ca•per v., ca•pered, ca•per•ing.

cape•skin

cap•il•lar•i•ty

cap•il•lar•y n., pl. cap•il•lar•ies.

cap•i•tal (principal; official city: cf. CAPITOL)

capital as•set *Business.*

capital gain *Business.*

capital goods *Business.*

cap•i•tal-in•ten•sive *Business.*

capital stock *Business.*

cap•i•tal•ism *Business.*

cap•i•tal•ist *Business.*

cap•i•tal•is•tic

cap•i•tal•i•za•tion

capitalization rate *Business.*

cap•i•tal•ize v., cap•i•tal•ized, cap•i•tal•iz•ing.

Cap•i•tol (building: cf. CAPITAL)

ca•pit•u•late v., ca•pit•u•lat•ed, ca•pit•u•lat•ing.

ca•pit•u•la•tion

cap•let

ca•pon

cap•puc•ci•no

ca•pric•ci•o n., pl. ca•pric•ci•os or ca•pric•ci.

ca•price

ca•pri•cious

ca•pri•cious•ly

ca•pri•cious•ness

Cap•ri•corn

caps

cap•siz•a•ble

cap•size v., cap•sized, cap•siz•ing.

cap•stan

cap•stone

cap•su•lar

cap•sule

cap•tain

cap•tain•cy

cap•tion v., cap•tioned, cap•tion•ing.

cap•tious

cap•tious•ly

cap•tious•ness

cap•ti•vate v., cap•ti•vat•ed, cap•ti•vat•ing.

cap•ti•va•tion

cap•tive

cap•tiv•i•ty

cap•tor

cap•ture v., cap•tured, cap•tur•ing.

car

car wash or car•wash

Ca•ra•cas

car•a•cul

ca•rafe

car•a•mel

car•a•mel•ize v.,

car•a•mel•ized, car•a•mel•iz•ing.

car•a•pace

car•at (gem weight: cf. CARET; CARROT; KARAT)

car•a•van v., car•a•vaned or car•a•vanned, car•a•van•ing or car•a•van•ning.

car•a•van•sa•ry or car•a•van•se•rai n., pl. car•a•van•sa•ries or car•a•van•se•rais.

car•a•way

car•bide

car•bine

car•bo, n., pl. car•bos.

car•bo-load•ing

car•bo•hy•drate

car•bol•ic ac•id

car•bon

carbon 14

car•bon-date

carbon di•ox•ide

carbon mon•ox•ide

carbon tet•ra•chlo•ride

car•bon•ate v., car•bon•at•ed, car•bon•at•ing.

car•bon•a•tion

Car•bon•if•er•ous

Car•bo•run•dum *Trademark.*

car•boy

car•bun•cle

car•bu•re•tor

car•cass

car•cin•o•gen

car•cin•o•gen•ic

car•ci•no•ge•nic•i•ty

car•ci•no•ma n., pl.

car•ci•no•mas or
car•ci•no•ma•ta.
card
card-car•ry•ing
card•board
car•di•ac
car•di•gan
car•di•nal
car•di•o•gram
car•di•o•graph
car•di•o•graph•ic
car•di•og•ra•phy
car•di•o•log•i•cal
car•di•ol•o•gist
car•di•ol•o•gy
car•di•o•pul•mo•
nar•y
car•di•o•vas•cu•lar
card•sharp or card•
sharp•er
care v., cared, car•ing.
CARE (Cooperative for
American Relief Every-
where)
ca•reen v., ca•reened,
ca•reen•ing.
ca•reer v., ca•reered,
ca•reer•ing.
care•free
care•ful
care•ful•ly
care•ful•ness
care•giv•er
care•less
care•less•ly
care•less•ness
ca•ress n.,v., ca•
ressed, ca•ress•ing.
car•et
care•tak•er
care•worn
car•fare
car•go n., pl. car•
goes or car•gos.
car•hop
Car•ib•be•an Sea

car•i•bou n., pl.
car•i•bous or car•i•
bou.
car•i•ca•ture v.,
car•i•ca•tured,
car•i•ca•tur•ing.
car•i•ca•tur•ist
car•ies n., pl. car•ies.
(decay: cf. CARRIES)
car•il•lon
car•i•ous
car•jack•ing
car•load
carload lot Business.
car•mine
car•nel•ian
car•nage
car•nal
car•na•tion
car•ni•val
car•ni•vore
car•niv•o•rous
car•ny n., pl. car•nie.
car•ol v., car•oled or
car•olled, car•ol•ing
or car•ol•ling. 1.
(song; to carol: cf. CAR-
REL) 2.
car•ol•er or car•ol•
ler
car•om v., car•omed,
car•om•ing.
car•o•tene
ca•rot•id
ca•rous•al
ca•rouse v., ca•
roused, ca•rous•ing.
car•ou•sel or car•
rou•sel
carp¹ v., carped, carp•
ing.
carp² v., carp or carps.
car•pal (of the wrist)
carpal tun•nel syn•
drome
car•pel (flower part)
car•pen•ter

car•pen•try
car•pet v., car•
pet•ed, car•pet•ing.
car•pet•bag
car•pet•bag•ger
car•pet•ing
car•pool v., car•
pooled, car•pool•
ing.
car•port
car•pus n., pl. car•pi.
car•rel (study nook: cf.
CAROL)
car•riage
carriage re•turn
car•ri•er
carrier pig•eon
car•ri•er's lien Busi-
ness.
car•ries (does carry: cf.
CARIES)
car•ri•on
Car•roll
car•rot (the vegetable:
cf. CARAT; CARET; KARAT)
car•rou•sel
car•ry n., pl. car•ries;.
v., car•ried, car•ry•
ing.
car•ry-back Business.
car•ry-for•ward Busi-
ness.
car•ry-on
car•ry•all
car•ry•ing charge Busi-
ness.
car•ry•o•ver
car•sick
car•sick•ness
Car•son Cit•y
cart v., cart•ed, cart•
ing.
cart•age Business.
carte blanche n., pl.
cartes blanches.
car•tel Business.

cart∘er
Car•ter
Car•te•sian
car•ti•lage
car•ti•lag∘i•nous
car•tog•ra•pher
car•to•graph∘ic
car•tog•ra•phy
car•ton
car•toon
car•toon•ist
car•tridge
cart•wheel
carve v., carved, carv•
   ing.
carv∘er
Car•ver
car•y•at∘id n., pl.
   car•y•at•ids or car•
   y•at∘i•des.
ca•sa∘ba or cas•
   sa∘ba n., pl. ca•sa•
   bas or cas•sa•bas.
Cas∘a•blan∘ca
Cas∘a•no∘va
cas•cade v., cas•
   cad∘ed, cas•cad•
   ing.
cascading men∘u
cas•car∘a
case v., cased, cas•
   ing.
case•hard∘en
ca•sein
case•load
case•ment
case•work
case•work∘er
cash v., cashed, cash•
   ing. (money; to cash:
   cf. CACHE)
cash ac•count•ing
   Business.
cash-and-car∘ry Busi-
   ness.
cash budg∘et Business.

cash cow Business.
cash flow Business.
cash machine Business.
cash reg•is•ter Busi-
   ness.
cash•book Business.
cash∘ew
cash•ier Business.
cashier's check Busi-
   ness.
cash•less
cash•mere or kash•
   mir
cash•point Business.
cas•ing
ca•si∘no n., pl. ca•si•
   nos. (amusement hall:
   cf. CASSINO)
cask (container)
cas•ket (coffin: cf. GAS-
   KET)
Cas•pi∘an Sea
casque (helmet)
cas•sa∘ba
Cas•san•dra n., pl.
   Cas•san•dras.
cas•sa∘va n., pl. cas•
   sa•vas.
cas•se•role
cas•sette
cas•sia n., pl. cas•sias.
cas•sin•gle
cas•si∘no (card game:
   cf. CASINO)
cas•sock
cas•so•war∘y n., pl.
   cas•so•war•ies.
cast v., cast, cast•ing.
   (to throw)
cast iron n.
cast-i∘ron adj.
cas•ta•net
cast•a•way
caste (social class)
cast∘er
cas•ti•gate v., cas•ti•

gat∘ed, cas•ti•gat•
   ing.
cas•ti•ga•tion
cas•tle
cast•off
cas•tor oil
cas•trate v., cas•
   trat∘ed, cas•trat•
   ing.
cas•tra•tion
Cas•tro
cas•u∘al (offhand: cf.
   CAUSAL)
cas•u•al∘ly
cas•u•al•ness
cas•u•al∘ty n., pl.
   cas•u•al•ties.
cas•u•ist
cas•u•ist∘ry
cat
CAT (computerized ax-
   ial tomography)
cat box
cat-o'-nine-tails n., pl.
   cat-o'-nine-tails.
CAT scan (computer-
   ized axial tomography
   scan)
CAT scan•ner
cat∘a•clysm
cat∘a•clys•mic
cat∘a•comb
cat∘a•falque
cat∘a•lep∘sy
cat∘a•lep•tic
cat∘a•log or cat∘a•
   logue v., cat∘a•
   loged or cat∘a•
   logued, cat∘a•log•
   ing or cat∘a•logu•
   ing.
ca•tal∘pa n., pl. ca•
   tal∘pas.
ca•tal∘y•sis, n., pl.
   ca•tal∘y•ses.
cat∘a•lyst
cat∘a•lyt∘ic

cat○a•lyze *v.*, cat○a•lyzed, cat○a•lyz•ing.
cat○a•ma•ran
cat○a•pult *v.*, cat○a•pult○ed, cat○a•pult•ing.
cat○a•ract
ca•tarrh
ca•tas•tro•phe
cat○a•stroph○ic
cat○a•to•ni○a
cat○a•ton○ic
cat•bird
cat•boat
cat•call
catch *v.*, caught, catch•ing.
Catch-22 *n.*, *pl.* Catch-•22s or Catch-•22's.
catch•all
catch○er
catch○i○ness
catch•ing
catch•ment
catch•up
catch•word
catch○y *adj.*, catch•i○er, catch•i•est.
cat○e•chism
cat○e•chist
cat○e•chize *v.*, cat○e•chized, cat○e•chiz•ing.
cat○e•gor○i•cal
cat○e•gor○i•cal○ly
cat○e•go•rize *v.*, cat○e•go•rized, cat○e•go•riz•ing.
cat○e•go○ry *n.*, *pl.* cat○e•go•ries.
ca•ter *v.*, ca•tered, ca•ter•ing.
cat○er-cor•nered or cat○er-cor○ner
cat•er•pil•lar
cat•er•waul *v.*, cat•er•wauled, cat•er•waul•ing.
cat•fish *n.*, *pl.* cat•fish or cat•fish○es.
cat•gut
ca•thar•sis *n.*, *pl.* ca•thar•ses.
ca•thar•tic
ca•the•dral
cath○e•ter
cath○e•ter•ize *v.*, cath○e•ter•ized, cath○e•ter•iz•ing.
cath•ode
cath•ode-ray tube
cath○o•lic
Cath○o•lic
Ca•thol○i•cism
cath○o•lic○i•ty
cat•i○on
cat•nap *v.*, cat•napped, cat•nap•ping.
cat•nip
cat's-paw or cats•paw
Cats•kill Moun•tains
cat•sup (ketchup)
cat•tail
cat•ti○ly
cat•ti•ness
cat•tle
cat•tle•man *n.*, *pl.* cat•tle•men.
cat○ty *adj.*, cat•ti○er, cat•ti•est.
cat○ty-cor•nered or cat○ty-cor○ner
CATV (community antenna television)
cat•walk
Cau•ca•sian
Cau•ca•sus, the
cau•cus *n.*, *pl.* cau•cus○es.
cau•dal
caught

caul•dron or cal•dron
cau•li•flow○er
caulk or calk *v.*, caulked or calked, caulk•ing or calk•ing.
caus○al (of a cause: cf. CASUAL)
caus•al○i○ty
cau•sa•tion
caus○a•tive
cause *v.*, caused, caus•ing.
cause ce•le•bre, *n.*, *pl.* causes ce•le•bres.
cau•se•rie
cause•way
caus•tic
caus•ti•cal○ly
cau•ter○i•za•tion
cau•ter•ize *v.*, cau•ter•ized, cau•ter•iz•ing.
cau•tion *v.*, cau•tioned, cau•tion•ing.
cau•tion•ar○y
cau•tious
cau•tious○ly
cau•tious•ness
cav•al•cade
cav○a•lier
cav○a•lier○ly
cav•al○ry *n.*, *pl.* cav•al•ries (troops on horseback: cf. CAL-VARY)
cav•al•ry•man *n.*, *pl.* cav•al•ry•men.
cave *v.*, caved, cav•ing.
cave-in
cave man
ca•ve○at
caveat emp•tor *Business.*

caveat ven•di•tor *Business.*

cav•ern

cav•ern•ous

cav•i•ar or **cav•i•are**

cav•il v., **cav•iled** or **cav•illed, cav•il•ing** or **cav•il•ling.**

cav•i•ty n., pl. **cav•i•ties.**

ca•vort v., **ca•vort•ed, ca•vort•ing.**

caw v., **cawed, caw•ing.**

cay (island: cf. KEY; QUAY)

cay•enne

cay•use

CD (compact disc)

CD (certificate of deposit)

CD-ROM (compact disc read-only memory)

cease v., **ceased, ceas•ing.**

cease-fire

cease•less

cease•less•ly

ce•cum or **cae•cum** n., pl. **ce•ca** or **cae•ca.**

ce•dar

cede v., **ced•ed, ced•ing.** (to give up: cf. SEED)

ce•dil•la n., pl. **ce•dil•las.**

ce•ru•le•an

ceil•ing (top of room: cf. SEALING)

cel•e•brant

cel•e•brate v., **cel•e•brat•ed, cel•e•brat•ing.**

cel•e•brat•ed

cel•e•bra•tion

ce•leb•ri•ty n., pl. **ce•leb•ri•ties.**

ce•leb•ou•tante

ce•ler•i•ty

cel•er•y

ce•les•ta or **ce•les•te** n., pl. **ce•les•tas** or **ce•les•tes.**

ce•les•tial

cel•i•ba•cy

cel•i•bate

cell (small compartment: cf. SELL)

cel•lar (basement: cf. SELLER)

cell•block

celled

Cel•li•ni

cel•list

cel•lo n., pl. **cel•los.**

cel•lo•phane

cel•lu•lar

cellular phone

cel•lu•lite

cel•lu•loid

cel•lu•lose

Cel•si•us

Celt or **Kelt**

Celt•ic or **Kelt•ic**

ce•ment v., **ce•ment•ed, ce•ment•ing.**

cem•e•ter•y n., pl. **cem•e•ter•ies.**

ce•no•bite or **coe•no•bite**

cen•o•taph

Ce•no•zo•ic

cen•ser (container for incense)

cen•sor (official overseer)

cen•so•ri•ous

cen•sor•ship

cen•sur•a•ble

cen•sure v., **cen•**
sured, cen•sur•ing. (disapproval)

cen•sus n., pl. **cen•sus•es.** (population count: cf. SENSES)

cent (penny: cf. SCENT; SENT)

cen•taur

cen•ta•vo n., pl. **cen•ta•vos.**

cen•te•nar•i•an

cen•ten•ar•y n., pl. **cen•ten•ar•ies.**

cen•ten•ni•al

cen•ter v., **cen•tered, cen•ter•ing.**

cen•ter•board

cen•ter•fold

cen•ter•piece

cen•ti•grade

cen•ti•gram

cen•time n., pl. **cen•times.**

cen•ti•me•ter

cen•ti•me•ter-gram-sec•ond

cen•ti•pede

cen•tral

central proc•ess•ing u•nit (CPU) *Computers.*

cen•tral•i•ty

cen•tral•i•za•tion

cen•tral•ize v., **cen•tral•ized, cen•tral•iz•ing.**

cen•tral•ly

cen•tre v., **cen•tred, cen•tring.**

cen•trif•u•gal

cen•trif•u•gal•ly

cen•tri•fuge v., **cen•tri•fuged, cen•tri•fug•ing.**

cen•trip•e•tal

cen•trip•e•tal•ly

cen•trist

cents (pennies: cf. SCENTS; SENSE)

cents-off *Business.*

cen•tu•ri•on

cen•tu•ry *n., pl.* cen•tu•ries.

CEO *or* C.E.O. *Business.* (chief executive officer)

ce•phal•ic

ce•ram•ic

ce•ram•ics

ce•ram•ist

ce•re•al (grain: cf. SERIAL)

cer•e•bel•lum *n., pl.* cer•e•bel•lums *or* cer•e•bel•la.

ce•re•bral

cer•e•bra•tion

ce•re•brum *n., pl.* ce•re•brums *or* ce•re•bra.

cer•e•mo•ni•al

cer•e•mo•ni•ous

cer•e•mo•ni•ous•ly

cer•e•mo•ny *n., pl.* cer•e•mo•nies.

ce•rise

ce•ri•um

cer•met

cer•tain

cer•tain•ly

cer•tain•ty *n., pl.* cer•tain•ties.

cer•ti•fi•a•ble

cer•tif•i•cate *v.,* cer•tif•i•cat•ed, cer•tif•i•cat•ing.

certificate of de•pos•it (CD)

cer•ti•fi•ca•tion

cer•ti•fied check

certified pub•lic ac•count•ant (CPA) *Business.*

cer•ti•fy *v.,* cer•ti•fied, cer•ti•fy•ing.

cer•ti•tude

Cer•van•tes

cer•vi•cal

cer•vix *n., pl.* cer•vix•es *or* cer•vi•ces.

Ce•sar•e•an

ce•si•um

ces•sa•tion

ces•sion (yielding: cf. SESSION)

cess•pool

ce•ta•cean

ce•ta•ceous

Cey•lon

Cey•lon•ese *n., pl.* Cey•lon•ese.

Cé•zanne

CFO *or* C.F.O. *Business.* (chief financial officer)

cha-cha *n., pl.* cha-•chas;. *v.,* cha-•chaed, cha-•cha•ing.

Cha•blis

Chad

Chad•i•an

chafe *v.,* chafed, chaf•ing. (to rub)

chaff *v.,* chaffed, chaff•ing. (husks; to chaff)

chaf•finch

chaff•ing•ly

Cha•gall

cha•grin

cha•grined *or* cha•grinned

chain

chain-re•act *v.,* chain-•re•act•ed, chain-•re•act•ing.

chain saw *n.*

chain-saw *v.,* chain-•sawed, chain-•saw•ing.

chain-smoke *v.,*

chain-•smoked, chain-•smok•ing.

chain store *Business.*

chair *v.,* chaired, chair•ing.

chair•lift

chair•man *n., pl.* chair•men.

chairman of the board *Business.*

chair•man•ship

chair•per•son

chair•per•son•ship

chair•wom•an *n., pl.* chair•wom•en.

chair•wom•an•ship

chaise longue *n., pl.* chaise longues *or* chaises longues.

chal•ced•o•ny

cha•let

chal•ice (wine cup: cf. CHALLIS)

chalk *v.,* chalked, chalk•ing.

chalk•board

chal•lah

chal•lenge *v.,* chal•lenged, chal•leng•ing.

chal•lenged

chal•leng•er

chal•lis (the fabric: cf. CHALICE)

cham•ber

chamber of commerce *Business.*

cham•bered

cham•ber•lain

cham•ber•maid

cha•me•le•on

cham•ois *n., pl.* cham•ois.

cham•o•mile *or* cam•o•mile

champ *or* chomp[1] *v.,* champed, champ•

ing or **chomped,
chomp•ing.** (chew)
champ[2] (champion)
cham•pagne
cham•pi•on v., **cham•
pi•oned, cham•pi•
on•ing.**
chance v., **chanced,
chanc•ing.**
chan•cel
chan•cel•ler•oy n., pl.
chan•cel•ler•ies.
chan•cel•lor
chan•cel•lor•ship
chan•cer•oy n., pl.
chan•cer•ies.
chanc•i•ness
chan•cre
chan•croid
chanc•y
chan•de•lier
chan•dler
change v., **changed,
chang•ing.**
changea•ble
change•less
change•ling
change•o•over
chang•er
chan•nel v., **chan•
neled** or **chan•
nelled, chan•nel•ing**
or **chan•nel•ling.**
chan•nel-surf, v.
**chan•nel-surfed,
chan•nel-surf•ing.**
chan•nel•ize v.,
**chan•nel•ized,
chan•nel•iz•ing.**
chan•son n., pl. **chan•
sons.**
chant v., **chant•ed,
chant•ing.**
chan•teuse n., pl.
chan•teuses.
chan•tey (sailor's
song: cf. SHANTY)

Cha•nu•kah (Hanuk-
kah)
cha•os
cha•ot•ic
chap[1] v., **chapped,
chap•ping.**
chap[2]
chap•ar•ral
cha•peau n., pl. **cha•
peaux** or **cha•peaus.**
chap•el
chap•er•on or **chap•
er•one** v., **chap•er•
oned, chap•er•on•
ing.**
chap•fall•en or **chop•
fall•en**
chap•lain
chap•lain•cy
chap•lain•ship
chap•let
Chap•lin
chap•ter
Chapter 11 Business.
char v., **charred, char•
ring.**
char•ac•ter
char•ac•ter-based
character string
char•ac•ter•is•tic
**char•ac•ter•is•ti•
cal•ly**
char•ac•ter•oi•za•tion
char•ac•ter•ize v.,
**char•ac•ter•ized,
char•ac•ter•iz•ing.**
cha•rade
char•broil v., **char•
broiled, char•broil•
ing.**
char•coal
chard
Char•don•nay
charge v., **charged,
charg•ing.**
charge account Busi-
ness.

charge card Business.
char•gé d'af•faires n.,
pl. **char•gés d'af•
faires.**
charge•a•ble
charg•er
char•i•ot
cha•ris•oma n., pl.
cha•ris•ma•ta.
char•is•mat•ic
char•oi•ta•ble
char•oi•ta•ble•ness
char•oi•ta•bly
char•i•ty n., pl. **char•
i•ties.**
char•la•tan
Char•le•magne
Charles•ton[1] n. (the
city)
Charles•ton[2] n., v.,
**Charles•toned,
Charles•ton•ing.** (the
dance; to do the
Charleston)
char•ley horse
char•lotte russe
Char•lotte•town
charm v., **charmed,
charm•ing.**
charm•er
charm•ing
charm•ing•ly
char•nel
Char•on
chart v., **chart•ed,
chart•ing.**
char•ter[1] v., **char•
tered, char•ter•ing.**
(to authorize)
chart•er[2] (one who
charts)
char•treuse Trade-
mark.
char•wom•an n., pl.
char•wom•en.
char•y adj., **char•i•er,**

char•i•est. (cautious:
cf. CHERRY)
chase v., chased,
chas•ing. (pursued:
cf. CHASTE)
chas•er
chasm
chas•sis n., pl. chas•
sis.
chaste (pure: cf.
CHASED)
chaste•ly
chas•ten v., chas•
tened, chas•ten•ing.
chas•tise v., chas•
tised, chas•tis•ing.
chas•tise•ment
chas•ti•ty
chas•u•ble
chat v., chat•ted,
chat•ting.
châ•teau or cha•teau
n., pl. châ•teaus or
cha•teaux.
chat•e•laine
Chat•ta•noo•ga
chat•tel
chattel mort•gage
Business.
chat•ter v., chat•
tered, chat•ter•ing.
chat•ter•box
chat•ter•ing class
chat•ti•ness
chat•ty adj., chat•
ti•er, chat•ti•est.
Chau•cer
chauf•feur
chau•vin•ism
chau•vin•ist
chau•vin•is•tic
cheap adj., cheap•er,
cheap•est. (inexpen-
sive: cf. CHEAP)
cheap•en
cheap•ly
cheap•ness

cheap•skate
cheat v., cheat•ed,
cheat•ing.
cheat•er
check v., checked,
check•ing. Business.
(cf. CZECH)
check•book Business.
checkbook jour•nal•
ism
check•er
check•er•board
check•ing ac•count
Business.
check•list
check•mate v., check•
mat•ed, check•mat•
ing.
check•off Business.
check•out or check-
out
check•point
check•room
check•sum
check•up
check•writ•er Busi-
ness.
ched•dar
cheek
cheek•bone
cheek•i•ness
cheek•y adj., cheek•
i•er, cheek•i•est.
cheep v., cheeped,
cheep•ing. (chirp; to
cheep: cf. CHEAP)
cheer v., cheered,
cheer•ing.
cheer•ful
cheer•ful•ly
cheer•ful•ness
cheer•i•ly
cheer•i•ness
cheer•i•o
cheer•lead•er
cheer•less

cheer•less•ly
cheer•less•ness
cheer•y adj., cheer•
i•er, cheer•i•est.
cheese
cheese•burg•er
cheese•cake
cheese•cloth
chees•y adj., chees•
i•er, chees•i•est.
chee•tah
chef
Che•khov
Che•kho•vi•an
chem
chem•i•cal
chem•i•cal•ly
che•mise
chem•ist
chem•is•try
che•mo•ther•a•py
chem•ur•gy
che•nille
cheque
cher•ish v., cher•
ished, cher•ish•ing.
Cher•o•kee n., pl.
Cher•o•kees or
Cher•o•kee.
che•root
cher•ry n., pl. cher•
ries. (the fruit: cf.
CHARY)
cher•ry•stone
chert
cher•ub n., pl. cher•
ubs or cher•u•bim.
che•ru•bic
cher•vil
Ches•a•peake
chess
chess•board
chess•man n., pl.
chess•men.
chest
ches•ter•field

chest•nut

chev○a•lier

Che•va•lier

chev•ron

chew *v.*, chewed, chew•ing.

chews (masticates: cf. CHOOSE)

chew○y *adj.*, chew•i○er, chew•i•est.

Chey•enne *n.*, *pl.* Chey•ennes or Chey•enne.

Chi•an○ti

chi•a•ro•scu○ro *n.*, *pl.* chi•a•ro•scu•ros.

chic (stylish: cf. CHICK; SHEIK)

Chi•ca○go

Chi•ca○na

chi•can•er○y *n.*, *pl.* chi•can•er•ies.

Chi•ca○no *n.*, *pl.* Chi•ca•nos.

chi•chi

chick (baby chicken: cf. CHIC; SHEIK)

chick○a•dee

Chick○a•saw *n.*, *pl.* Chick○a•saws or Chick○a•saw.

chick○en

chicken feed

chick•en-heart○ed

chick•en•pox or chick○en pox

chick•pea

chic○le

chic○o○ry *n.*, *pl.* chic○o•ries.

chide *v.*, chid○ed, chid, chid•ing.

chief

chief ex○ec○u•tive of•fi•cer (CEO) *Business.*

chief fi•nan•cial offi•cer (CFO) *Business.*

chief op•er•at•ing officer (COO) *Business.*

chief○ly

chief•tain

chif•fon

chig•ger

chi•gnon

Chi•hua•hua

chil•blain

child *n.*, *pl.* chil•dren.

child•bear•ing

child•birth

child•hood

child•ish

child•ish○ly

child•ish•ness

child•less

child•like

chil•dren

Chil○e (the country)

Chil•e○an

chil○i or chil•e, *n.*, *pl.* chil•ies or chil○es. (pepper)

chili con car○ne

chill *v.*, chilled, chill•ing.

chill•er

chill○i•ness

chill•ing ef•fect

chill○y *adj.*, chill•i○er, chill•i•est. (cold)

chi•me○ra

chi•mer○i•cal or chi•mer○ic

chim•ney *n.*, *pl.* chim•neys.

chimp

chim•pan•zee

chin *v.*, chinned, chin•ning.

chi○na

chinch bug

chin•chil○la *n.*, *pl.* chin•chil•las.

Chi•nese *n.*, *pl.* Chi•nese.

chink *v.*, chinked, chink•ing.

chi○no *n.*, *pl.* chi•nos.

Chi•nook *n.*, *pl.* Chi•nooks or Chi•nook.

chintz

chintz○y *adj.*, chintz•i○er, chintz•i•est.

chip *v.*, chipped, chip•ping.

chip•munk

chip•per

Chip•pe○wa *n.*, *pl.* Chip•pe•was or Chip•pe○wa.

chi•rog•ra•phy

chi•rop○o•dist

chi•rop○o○dy

chi○ro•prac•tic

chi○ro•prac•tor

chirp *v.*, chirped, chirp•ing.

chir•rup *v.*, chir•ruped, chir•rup•ing.

chis•el *v.*, chis•eled or chis•elled, chis•el•ing or chis•el•ling.

chis•el○er or chis•el•ler

chit

chit•chat

chi•tin

chit•ter•lings or chit•lings

chiv•al•rous

chiv•al•rous○ly

chiv•al○ry

chive

chlo○ral

chlo•ride

chlo•ri•nate *v.*, chlo•

ri•nat•ed, chlo•ri•
nat•ing.
chlo•ri•na•tion
chlo•rine
chlo•ro•form
chlo•ro•phyll
chock
chock-full
choc○o•hol○ic
choc○o•late
Choc•taw
choice adj., choic○er,
choic○est.
choir (chorus: cf. QUIRE)
choke v., choked,
chok○ing.
choke•point
chok○er
chol○er (anger: cf. COL-
LAR; COLOR)
chol•er○a
chol•er○ic
cho•les•ter•ol
chomp v., chomped,
chomp•ing.
Chong•qing or
Chung•king
choose v., chose, cho•
sen, choos•ing. (to
select: cf. CHEWS)
choos○er
choos○i•ness
choos○y adj., choos•
i○er, choos•i•est.
chop v., chopped,
chop•ping.
chop su○ey
chop•house
Cho•pin
chop•per
chop•pi•ness
chop○py adj., chop•
pi○er, chop•pi•est.
chop•stick
cho•ral (of a chorus:
cf. CORAL; CORRAL)

cho•rale (hymn)
chord (musical tones:
cf. CORD)
chor•date
chore
cho•re•a
cho•re○o•graph v.,
cho•re○o•graphed,
cho•re○o•graph•
ing.
cho•re•og•ra•pher
cho•re○o•graph○ic
cho•re•og•ra•phy
cho•roid
chor•tle v., chor•tled,
chor•tling.
cho•rus n., pl. cho•
rus○es.
chose
cho•sen
chow
chow mein
chow•der
chrism
Christ
chris•ten v., chris•
tened, chris•ten•ing.
Chris•ten•dom
chris•ten•ing
Chris•tian
Chris•ti•an○i•ty
Chris•tian•ize v.,
Chris•tian•ized,
Chris•tian•iz•ing.
Christ•mas
chro•mat○ic
chro•mat○i•cal○ly
chrome
chro•mi○um
chro○mo•so•mal
chro○mo•some
chron○ic
chronic fa•tigue syn•
drome
chron○i•cal○ly
chron○i•cle v.,

chron○i•cled,
chron○i•cling.
chron○i•cler
chron○o•log○i•cal
chron○o•log○i•cal○ly
chro•nol○o○gy n., pl.
chro•nol○o○gies.
chro•nom○e•ter
chrys○a•lis n., pl.
chrys○a•lis○es or
chry•sal○i•des.
chry•san•the•mum
chub•bi•ness
chub○by adj., chub•
bi○er, chub•bi•est.
chuck
chuck○le v., chuck•
led, chuck•ling.
chug v., chugged,
chug•ging.
chuk○ka boot
chum v., chummed,
chum•ming.
chum○my adj., chum•
mi○er, chum•mi•est.
chump
Chung•king
chunk
chunk○i•ness
chunk○y adj., chunk•
i○er, chunk•i•est.
church
church•go○er
Church•ill
church•man n., pl.
church•men.
church•ward○en
church•wom○an n.,
pl. church•wom○en.
church•yard
churl
churl•ish
churn v., churned,
churn•ing.
chute (inclined chan-
nel: cf. SHOOT)
chut•ney

chutz○pa or chutz•
pah
CIA or **C.I.A.** (Central
Intelligence Agency)
ciao
ci•ca○da n., pl. ci•ca•
das or ci•ca•dae.
cic○a•trix or cic○a•
trice n., pl. cic○a•tri•
ces.
Cic○e○ro
ci•der
Cie. or **cie.** *Business.*
(company)
CIF *Business.* (cost, insurance, and freight
included)
ci•gar
cig○a•rette or cig○a•
ret
cig○a•ril○lo n., pl.
cig○a•ril•los.
cil•i○a n., pl. cil•i○um.
cinch
cin•cho○na
Cin•cin•nat○i
cinc•ture
cin•der
cin○e○ma n., pl.
cin○e•mas.
cin○e○ma vé•ri○té
cin○e•mat○ic
cin○e○ma•tog•ra•
pher
cin○e○ma•tog•ra•
phy
cin•na•bar
cin•na•mon
ci•pher v., ci•phered,
ci•pher•ing.
cir○ca
cir•ca•di○an
cir•cle v., cir•cled,
cir•cling.
cir•clet
cir•cuit
circuit board

cir○cuit-switched
cir•cu•i•tous
cir•cu•i•tous○ly
cir•cu•i•tous•ness
cir•cuit○ry
cir•cu•lar
cir•cu•lar○i○ty
cir•cu•late v., cir•cu•
lat○ed, cir•cu•lat•
ing.
cir•cu•la•tion
cir•cu•la•to○ry
cir○cum•cise v.,
cir○cum•cised,
cir○cum•cis•ing.
cir○cum•ci•sion
cir○cum•fer•ence
cir○cum•flex
cir○cum•lo•cu•tion
cir○cum•nav○i•gate
v., cir○cum•nav○i•
gat○ed, cir○cum•
nav○i•gat•ing.
cir○cum•nav○i•ga•
tion
cir○cum•scribe v.,
cir○cum•scribed,
cir○cum•scrib•ing.
cir○cum•scrip•tion
cir○cum•spect
cir○cum•spec•tion
cir○cum•stance
cir○cum•stan•tial
cir○cum•vent v., cir•
cum•vent○ed, cir•
cum•vent•ing.
cir○cum•ven•tion
cir•cus n., pl. cir•
cus○es.
cir•rho•sis
cir•rus n., pl. cir○ri.
CISC (complex instruction set computer)
cis•tern
cit○a•del
ci•ta•tion
cite v., cit○ed, cit•ing.

(to refer to: cf. SIGHT;
SITE)
cit○i•fied or cit○y•
fied
cit○i•zen
cit○i•zen○ry
cit○i•zen•ship
cit•ric ac○id
cit•ron
cit•ron•el○la
cit•rus fruit
cit○y n., pl. cit•ies.
cit○y-state
civ○et
civ○ic
civ•ics
civ•il
ci•vil•ian
ci•vil•i○ty n., pl. ci•
vil○i•ties.
civ•i•li•za•tion
civ○i•lize v., civ○i•
lized, civ○i•liz•ing.
civ•vies or civ•ies
clack (to make a sharp
sound: cf. CLAQUE)
clad
claim v., claimed,
claim•ing.
claim•ant
clair•voy•ance
clair•voy•ant
clam v., clammed,
clam•ming.
clam•bake
clam•ber v., clam•
bered, clam•ber•ing.
clam•mi•ness
clam○my adj., clam•
mi○er, clam•mi•est.
clam○or v., clam•
ored, clam•or•ing.
clam•or•ous
clamp v., clamped,
clamp•ing.

clam•shell com•
put•er

clan

clan•des•tine

clan•des•tine•ly

clang *v.*, clanged,
clang•ing.

clang•or

clank *v.*, clanked,
clank•ing.

clan•nish

clan•nish•ness

clans•man *n., pl.*
clans•men.

clans•wom•an *n., pl.*
clans•wom•en.

clap *v.*, clapped, clap•
ping.

clap•board

clap•per

clap•trap

claque (hired audience:
cf. CLACK)

clar•et

clar•i•fi•ca•tion

clar•i•fy *v.*, clar•i•
fied, clar•i•fy•ing.

clar•i•net

clar•i•net•ist

clar•i•net•tist

clar•i•on call

clar•i•ty

clash *v.*, clashed,
clash•ing.

clasp *v.*, clasped,
clasp•ing.

class *v.*, classed, class•
ing.

clas•sic

clas•si•cal

clas•si•cism

clas•si•fi•ca•tion

clas•si•fied ad

classified ad•ver•tis•
ing

clas•si•fy *v.*, clas•si•
fied, clas•si•fy•ing.

class•less

class•mate

class•room

class•y *adj.*, class•
i•er, class•i•est.

clat•ter *v.*, clat•tered,
clat•ter•ing.

clause (part of sen-
tence: cf. CLAWS)

claus•tro•pho•bi•a

claus•tro•pho•bic

clav•i•chord

clav•i•cle

cla•vier

claw *v.*, clawed, claw•
ing.

claws (animal nails: cf.
CLAUSE)

clay

Clay•ma•tion

clean *adj.*, clean•er,
clean•est;. *v.*,
cleaned, clean•ing.

clean-cut

clean•er

clean•li•ness

clean•ly *adj.*, clean•
li•er, clean•li•est.

clean•ness

cleanse *v.*, cleansed,
cleans•ing.

cleans•er

clean•up

clear *adj.*, clear•er,
clear•est; *v.*, cleared,
clear•ing.

clear-cut

clear•ance

clear•ing

clearing ac•count
Business.

clear•ing•house or
clear•ing house *n., pl.* clear•ing•
hous•es. *Business.*

clear•ly

clear•ness

cleat

cleav•age

cleave *v.*, cleft or
cleaved, clove or
clo•ven, cleav•ing.

cleav•er

clef

cleft

clem•a•tis

clem•en•cy

Clem•ens

clem•ent

clench *v.*, clenched,
clench•ing. (to close
tightly: cf. CLINCH)

Cle•o•pa•tra

clere•sto•ry, *n., pl.*
clere•sto•ries.

cler•gy

cler•gy•man *n., pl.*
cler•gy•men.

cler•gy•wom•an *n.,
pl.* cler•gy•wom•en.

cler•ic

cler•i•cal

cler•i•cal•ism

clerk

Cleve•land

clev•er *adj.*, clev•
er•er, clev•er•est.

clev•er•ly

clev•er•ness

clev•is

clew é

cli•ché éd

cli•chéd

click *v.*, clicked, click•
ing. (sharp sound; to
click: cf. CLIQUE)

cli•ent

cli•ent/•serv•er

cli•en•tele

cliff

cliff-hang∘er or **cliff∙hang∘er**

cli∙mac∙ter∘ic

cli∙mac∙tic (of a climax)

cli∙mate

cli∙mat∘ic (of climate)

cli∙max

climb v., climbed, **climb∙ing.** (to ascend)

climb∙a∘ble

climb∘er

clime (climate)

clinch v., clinched, **clinch∙ing.** (to settle: cf. CLENCH)

clinch∘er

cling v., clung, **cling∙ing.**

clin∘ic

clin∘i∙cal

clin∘i∙cal∘ly

cli∙ni∙cian

clink v., clinked, **clink∙ing.**

clink∘er

Clin∙ton

cli∙o∙met∙rics *Business.*

clip v., clipped, **clip∙ping.**

clip art

clip∙board

clip∙per

clip∙ping

clique (exclusive group: cf. CLICK)

cli∙quish

clit∘o∙ral

clit∘o∙ris n., pl. **clit∘o∙ris∘es** or **cli∙to∙ri∙des.**

cloak, v., cloaked, **cloak∙ing.**

cloak-and-dag∙ger

cloak∙room

clob∙ber v., clob∙bered, clob∙ber∙ing.

cloche

clock v., clocked, **clock∙ing.**

clock speed

clock∙wise

clock∙work

clod

clod∙dish

clod∙hop∙per

clog v., clogged, **clog∙ging.**

cloi∙son∙né

clois∙ter

clomp v., clomped, **clomp∙ing.**

clone v., cloned, **clon∙ing.**

clop v., clopped, **clop∙ping.**

close v., closed, **clos∙ing;.** adj., **clos∘er, clos∙est. 1.** (to shut: cf. CLOTHES; CLOTHS) **2.**

close-fit∘ting

close-knit

closed-cap∘tioned

closed-cir∘cuit

closed cor∙po∙ra∙tion *Business.*

closed dis∙play *Business.*

closed-end *Business.*

close∙fist∘ed

close∘ly

close∙mouthed

close∙ness

close∙out *Business.*

clos∙et v., clos∙et∘ed, clos∙et∙ing.

close∙up

clo∙sure

clot v., clot∙ted, **clot∙ting.**

cloth

clothe v., clothed, clad, cloth∙ing.

clothes (garments: cf. CLOSE; CLOTHS)

clothes∙horse

clothes∙line

clothes∙pin

cloth∙ier

cloth∙ing

cloths (pieces of fabric)

clo∙ture

cloud v., cloud∙ed, **cloud∙ing.**

cloud∙burst

cloud∙less

cloud∘y adj., cloud∙i∘er, cloud∙i∙est.

clout

clove

clo∙ven

clo∙ver n., pl. clo∙vers or clo∙ver.

clo∙ver∙leaf n., pl. clo∙ver∙leafs or clo∙ver∙lea ves.

Clo∙vis

clown v., clowned, **clown∙ing.**

clown∙ish

clown∙ish∘ly

cloy v., cloyed, **cloy∙ing.**

club v., clubbed, **club∙bing.**

club∙foot n., pl. club∙feet.

club∙foot∘ed

club∙house n., pl. club∙hous∘es.

cluck v., clucked, **cluck∙ing.**

clue v., clued, **clu∙ing.**

clump v., clumped, **clump∙ing.**

clum∙si∘ly

clum∙si∙ness

clum•sy *adj.*, clum•
si•er, clum•si•est.

clung

clunk•er

clunk•y *adj.*, clunk•
i•er, clunk•i•est.

clus•ter *v.*, clus•tered,
clus•ter•ing.

clutch *v.*, clutched,
clutch•ing.

clut•ter *v.*, clut•tered,
clut•ter•ing.

CMOS (complementary
metal oxide semicon-
ductor)

cni•dar•i•an

CO (Colorado)

Co. *Business.* (com-
pany)

co-op *n., v.*, co-•oped,
co-op•ing. (coopera-
tive enterprise)

co-opt *v.*, co-•opt∘ed,
co-•opt•ing.

coach *v.*, coached,
coach•ing.

coach•man *n., pl.*
coach•men.

co•ad•ju•tor

co•ag•u•lant

co•ag•u•late *v.*, co•
ag•u•lat∘ed, co•
ag•u•lat•ing.

co•ag•u•la•tion

coal (the mineral: cf.
KOHL)

co•a•lesce *v.*, co•a•
lesced, co•a•lesc•
ing.

co•a•les•cence

co•a•les•cent

co•a•li•tion

coarse *adj.*, coars∘er,
coars•est. (rough: cf.
COURSE)

coarse•ly

coars∘en *v.*, coars•
ened, coars•en•ing.

coarse•ness

coars∘er

coast

coast•al

coast∘er

coast•line

coat (outer garment: cf.
COTE)

coat•tail

co•au•thor

coax

co•ax•i•al

coax•ing•ly

cob

co•balt

cob•ble *v.*, cob•bled,
cob•bling.

cob•bler

cob•ble•stone

COBOL *Computers.*
(programming lan-
guage)

co•bra *n., pl.* co•bras.

cob•web

cob•webbed

co•caine

coc•cus *n., pl.* coc∘ci.

coc•cyx *n., pl.* coc•cy•
ges.

coch∘i•neal

coch•le•a *n., pl.*
coch•le•ae, coch•
le•as.

coch•le•ar

cock

cock-and-bull sto∘ry

cock•ade

cock∘a•ma•mie or
cock∘a•ma∘my

cock∘a•too *n., pl.*
cock∘a•toos.

cock∘a•trice

cock•crow

cock∘er span•iel

cock•er∘el

cock•eyed

cock•fight

cock•fight•ing

cock•horse

cock•i∘ly

cock∘i•ness

cock∘le

cock•le•shell

cock•ney *n., pl.* cock•
neys.

cock•pit

cock•roach

cocks•comb

cock•sure

cock•tail

cock∘y *adj.*, cock•i∘er,
cock•i•est.

co•coa

co•co•nut or co•coa•
nut

co•coon

co•coon•ing

cod *n., pl.* cod or cods.

C.O.D. or c.o.d. *Busi-
ness.* (cash on deliv-
ery)

co∘da *n., pl.* co•das.

cod•dle *v.*, cod•dled,
cod•dling.

code *v.*, cod∘ed, cod•
ing.

co•deine

co•de•pend•ent

co•dex *n., pl.* co•di•
ces.

cod•fish *n., pl.* cod•
fish or cod•fish∘es.

codg∘er

cod∘i•cil

cod∘i•fi•ca•tion

cod∘i•fy *v.*, cod∘i•
fied, cod∘i•fy•ing.

co•don

co∘ed or co-ed

co•ed∘u•ca•tion

co•ed○u•ca•tion○al
co•ef•fi•cient
coe•len•ter•ate
co•e○qual○ly
co•erce v., co•erced, co•erc○ing.
co•er•cive
co•e○val
co•ex•ist v., co•ex•ist○ed, co•ex•ist•ing.
co•ex•ist•ence
co•ex•ist•ent
co•ex•ten•sive
cof•fee
cof○fee•cake
cof○fee•house n., pl. cof○fee•hous○es.
cof○fee•pot
cof•fer
cof•fin
cog
c.o.g. (customer-owned goods)
co•gen○cy
co•gent
co•gent○ly
cog○i○tate v., cog○i○tat○ed, cog○i•tat•ing.
cog○i○ta•tion
cog○i○ta•tor
co•gnac
cog•nate
cog•ni•tion
cog•ni•za•ble
cog•ni•zance
cog•ni•zant
cog•no•men n., pl. cog•no•mens or cog•nom○i○na.
co•gno•scen○ti n., pl. co•gno•scen○te.
cog•wheel
co•hab○it v., co•hab•

it○ed, co•hab•it○ing.
co•hab•it○ant
co•hab○i○ta•tion
co•heir
co•here v., co•hered, co•her○ing.
co•her•ence
co•her•ent
co•her•ent○ly
co•he•sion
co•he•sive
co•hort
coif v., coifed, coif•ing. (hair style: cf. QUAFF)
coif•feur (hairdresser)
coif•fure (hair style)
coil v., coiled, coil•ing.
coin v., coined, coin•ing.
coin•age
co•in○cide v., co•in○cid○ed, co•in•cid•ing.
co•in○ci•dence
co•in○ci•den•tal
co•in○ci•den•tal○ly
co•i•tal
co•i•tus
coke v., coked, cok•ing.
COLA n., pl. COLAs or COLA's. Business. (cost of living adjustment: cf. COLA or kola)
col•an•der (strainer: cf. CALENDAR; CALENDER)
cold adj., cold○er, cold○est.
cold-blood○ed or cold•blood○ed
cold boot Computers.
cold call Business.
cold fu•sion
cold shoul•der n.

cold-shoul○er v.
cold-tur○key adj.
cold○ly
cold•ness
cole•slaw
co•le○us n., pl. co•le•us○es.
col○ic
col•ick○y
col○i•se○um (stadium: cf. COLOSSEUM)
co•li•tis
col•lab○o○rate v., col•lab○o○rat○ed, col•lab○o○rat•ing.
col•lab○o○ra•tion
col•lab○o○ra•tor
col•lage (art form: cf. COLLEGE)
col•lag•ist
col•lapse v., col•lapsed, col•laps•ing.
col•laps•i○ble
col•lar v., col•lared, col•lar•ing. (neck of garment: cf. CHOLER; COLOR)
col•lar•bone
col•lard
col•lar•less
col•late v., col•lat○ed, col•lat•ing.
col•lat•er○al Business.
col•la•tion
col•la•tor
col•league
col•lect v., col•lect○ed, col•lect•ing.
col•lect•a○ble or col•lect•i○ble
col•lect○ed
col•lec•tion
col•lec•tive Business.
collective bar•gain•ing
col•lec•tive○ly

col•lec•tiv•ism
col•lec•tiv•ist
col•lec•ti•vi•za•tion
col•lec•ti•vize v.,
  col•lec•ti•vized,
  col•lec•ti•viz•ing.
col•lec•tor
col•leen
col•lege (school: cf.
  COLLAGE)
Col•lege Sta•tion
col•le•gial
col•le•gi•al•i•ty
col•le•gian
col•le•giate
col•lide v., col•lid∘ed,
  col•lid•ing.
col•lie
col•lier
col•lier∘y n., pl. col•
  lier•ies.
col•li•sion (crash: cf.
  COLLUSION)
col•lo•cate v., col•lo•
  cat∘ed, col•lo•cat•
  ing.
col•lo•ca•tion
col•loid
col•loi•dal
col•lo•qui•al
col•lo•qui•al•ism
col•lo•qui•al•ly
col•lo•qui•um n., pl.
  col•lo•qui•ums or
  col•lo•qui∘a.
col•lo•quy n., pl. col•
  lo•quies.
col•lude v., col•
  lud∘ed, col•lud•ing.
col•lu•sion (conspir-
  acy: cf. COLLISION)
col•lu•sive
co•logne
Co•lom•bi∘a
Co•lom•bi•an (of the
  country Colombia: cf.
  COLUMBIAN)

Co•lom∘bo
co•lon n., pl. co•lons.
co•lo•nel (military offi-
  cer: cf. KERNEL)
co•lo•ni∘al
co•lo•ni•al•ism
co•lo•ni•al•ist
col∘o•nist
col∘o•ni•za•tion
col∘o•nize v., col∘o•
  nized, col∘o•niz•
  ing.
col∘o•niz∘er
col•on•nade
col•on•nad∘ed
col∘o•ny n., pl.
  col∘o•nies.
col∘o•phon
col•or v., col•ored,
  col•or•ing. (hue; to
  color: cf. CHOLER; COL-
  LAR)
col∘or-blind
col∘or mon∘i•tor
Col∘o•rad∘an
Col∘o•rad∘o (CO)
col•or•ant
col•or•a•tion
col∘o•ra•tu∘ra n., pl.
  col∘o•ra•tu•ras.
col∘or•cast v., col∘or•
  cast, col∘or•cast•
  ing.
co∘lo•rec•tal
col∘ored
col∘or•fast
col∘or•ful
col∘or•ful•ly
col∘or•ful•ness
col•or•ing
col•or∘i•za•tion
col•or•ize v., col•or•
  ized, col•or•iz•ing.
col•or•less
col•or•less∘ly
col•or•less•ness

co•los•sal
co•los•sal•ly
Col•os•se∘um (Roman
  amphitheater: cf. COLI-
  SEUM)
co•los•sus n., pl. co•
  los∘si or co•los•
  sus∘es.
co•los•to∘my n., pl.
  co•los•to•mies.
co•los•trum
col•our v., col•oured,
  col•our•ing.
colt
colt•ish
Co•lum•bi∘a
Co•lum•bi•an (of the
  explorer Columbus: cf.
  COLOMBIAN)
col•um•bine
Co•lum•bus
col•umn
co•lum•nar
col•um•nist
co∘ma n., pl. co•mas.
  (unconscious state: cf.
  COMMA)
co•mak∘er Business.
Co•man•che
com∘a•tose
comb v., combed,
  comb•ing.
com•bat v., com•
  bat∘ed, com•bat•
  ing, com•bat•ted,
  com•bat•ting.
com•bat•ant
com•bat•ive
com•bi•na•tion
com•bine v., com•
  bined, com•bin•ing.
comb•ings
com∘bo n., pl. com•
  bos.
com•bus•ti•bil∘i•ty
com•bus•ti•ble
com•bus•tion

come *v.*, came, come, com•ing.
come-on *n.*
come•back
co•me•di•an
co•me•di•enne
come•down
com∘e∘dy *n., pl.* com∘e•dies.
come•li•ness
come∘ly *adj.*, come•li∘er, come•li•est.
com∘er
co•mes•ti•ble
com∘et
com•et•ar∘y
come•up•pance
COMEX *Business.* (Commodity Exchange, New York)
com•fort *v.*, com•fort∘ed, com•fort•ing.
comfort let•ter *Business.*
com•fort•a∘ble
com•fort∘er
com∘fy *adj.*, com•fi∘er, com•fi•est.
com∘ic (funny: cf. KARMIC)
com∘i•cal
com∘i•cal∘ly
com•ing
com∘i•ty *n., pl.* com∘i•ties.
com∘ma *n., pl.* com•mas. (punctuation mark: cf. COMA)
com•mand (to order: cf. COMMENT)
command driv∘en
command e∘con∘o∘my
command shell
com•man•dant
com•man•deer *v.*,

com•man•deered, com•man•deer•ing.
com•mand∘er
com•mand•ment
com•man∘do *n., pl.* com•man•dos or com•man•does.
com•mem∘o•rate *v.*, com•mem∘o•rat∘ed, com•mem∘o•rat•ing.
com•mem∘o•ra•tion
com•mem∘o•ra•tive
com•mence *v.*, com•menced, com•menc•ing.
com•mence•ment
com•mend *v.*, com•mend∘ed, com•mend•ing. (to recommend: cf. COMMAND)
com•mend∘a•ble
com•mend∘a•bly
com•men•da•tion (praise: cf. CONDEMNATION)
com•mend∘a•to∘ry
com•men•su•ra•bil∘i∘ty
com•men•su•ra•ble
com•men•su•rate
com•ment *v.*, com•ment∘ed, com•ment•ing.
com•men•tar∘y *n., pl.* com•men•tar•ies.
com•men•ta•tor
com•merce *Business.*
com•mer•cial
commercial bank *Business.*
commercial pa•per *Business.*
com•mer•cial•ism
com•mer•cial∘i•za•tion
com•mer•cial•ize *v.*,

com•mer•cial•ized, com•mer•cial•iz•ing.
com•mer•cial∘ly
com•min•gle *v.*, com•min•gled, com•min•gling.
com•mis•er•ate *v.*, com•mis•er•at∘ed, com•mis•er•at•ing.
com•mis•er•a•tion
com•mis•sar
com•mis•sar•i∘at
com•mis•sar∘y *n., pl.* com•mis•sar•ies.
com•mis•sion *v.*, com•mis•sioned, com•mis•sion•ing.
com•mis•sion∘er
com•mit *v.*, com•mit•ted, com•mit•ting.
com•mit•ment
com•mit•tee
com•mit•tee•man *n., pl.* com•mit•tee•men.
com•mit•tee•wom∘an *n., pl.* com•mit•tee•wom∘en.
com•mode
com•mo•di∘ous
com•mod∘i∘ty *n., pl.* com•mod∘i•ties. *Business.*
commodity ex•change *Business.*
com•mo•dore
com•mon *adj.*, com•mon∘er, com•mon•est.
common car•ri∘er *Business.*
Common Mar•ket *Business.*
common sense *n.*
com∘mon-size state•ment *Business.*

com•mon•al•ty n., pl.
com•mon•al•ties.
com•mon•er
com•mon•ly
com•mon•place
com•mon•sense adj.,
com•mon•sen•si•cal
common stock Busi-
ness.
com•mon•weal or
com•monweal
com•mon•wealth
com•mo•tion
com•mu•nal
com•mune v., com•
muned, com•mun•
ing.
com•mu•ni•ca•
bil•i•ty
com•mu•ni•ca•ble
com•mu•ni•cant
com•mu•ni•cate v.,
com•mu•ni•cat•ed,
com•mu•ni•cat•ing.
com•mu•ni•ca•tion
communications pro•
to•col
com•mu•ni•ca•tive
com•mu•ni•ca•tor
com•mun•ion
com•mu•ni•qué
com•mu•nism
com•mu•nist
com•mu•ni•ty n., pl.
com•mu•ni•ties.
community chest Busi-
ness.
com•mu•ta•tion
com•mu•ta•tive
com•mute v., com•
mut•ed, com•mut•
ing.
com•mut•er
Com•o•ros
comp
com•pact v., com•

pact•ed, com•pact•
ing.
com•pact disc (CD)
com•pact•ly
com•pact•ness
com•pac•tor
com•pan•ion
com•pan•ion•a•ble
com•pan•ion•ship
com•pan•ion•way
com•pa•ny n., pl.
com•pa•nies.
company loan Busi-
ness.
com•pa•ra•bil•i•ty
com•pa•ra•ble
com•pa•ra•bly
com•par•a•tive
com•par•a•tive•ly
com•pare v., com•
pared, com•par•ing.
com•par•i•son
com•part•ment v.,
com•part•ment•ed,
com•part•ment•ing.
com•part•men•tal
com•part•men•tal•i•
za•tion
com•part•men•tal•
ize v., com•part•
men•tal•ized, com•
part•men•tal•iz•
ing.
com•pass v., com•
passed, com•pass•
ing.
com•pas•sion
com•pas•sion•ate
com•pas•sion•ate•ly
com•pat•i•bil•i•ty
com•pat•i•ble
com•pat•i•ble•ness
com•pa•tri•ot
com•peer
com•pel v., com•
pelled, com•pel•
ling.

com•pen•di•um n.,
pl. com•pen•di•ums
or com•pen•di•a.
com•pen•sate v.,
com•pen•sat•ed,
com•pen•sat•ing.
com•pen•sa•tion
com•pen•sa•to•ry
com•pete v., com•
pet•ed, com•pet•
ing.
com•pe•tence
com•pe•tent
com•pe•tent•ly
com•pe•ti•tion
com•pet•i•tive
competitive mar•ket
Business.
com•pet•i•tor
com•pi•la•tion
com•pile v., com•
piled, com•pil•ing.
com•pile-time er•ror
com•pil•er
com•pla•cen•cy or
com•pla•cence
com•pla•cent (self-
satisfied: cf. COMPLAI-
SANT)
com•plain v., com•
plained, com•plain•
ing.
com•plain•ant
com•plain•er
com•plaint
com•plai•sance
com•plai•sant (agree-
able: cf. COMPLACENT)
com•plai•sant•ly
com•pleat
com•plect•ed
com•ple•ment v.,
com•ple•ment•ed,
com•ple•ment•ing.
(completing part: cf.
COMPLIMENT)
com•ple•men•ta•ry

com•plete v., com•
plet∘ed, com•plet•
ing.
com•plete∘ly
com•plete•ness
com•ple•tion
com•plex
com•plex•ion
com•plex•i∘ty
com•pli•ance
com•pli•ant
com•pli•cate v., com•
pli•cat∘ed, com•pli•
cat•ing.
com•pli•ca•tion
com•plic∘i∘ty
com•pli•ment v.,
com•pli•ment∘ed,
com•pli•ment•ing.
(praise: cf. COMPLE-
MENT)
com•pli•men•ta∘ry
com•ply v., com•
plied, com•ply•ing.
com•po•nent
com•port v., com•
port∘ed, com•port•
ing.
com•port•ment
com•pose v., com•
posed, com•pos•ing.
(to make up: cf. COM-
PRISE)
com•posed
com•pos•ed∘ly
com•pos∘er
com•pos•ite
com•po•si•tion
com•pos∘i∘tor
com•post v., com•
post∘ed, com•post•
ing.
com•po•sure
com•pote
com•pound v., com•
pound∘ed, com•
pound•ing.

compound in•ter•est
Business.
com•pre•hend v.,
com•pre•hend∘ed,
com•pre•hend•ing.
com•pre•hen•si∘ble
(intelligible)
com•pre•hen•sion
com•pre•hen•sive
Business. (inclusive)
comprehensive in•
sur•ance
com•pre•hen•sive∘ly
com•pre•hen•sive•
ness
com•press v., com•
pressed, com•press•
ing.
com•pres•sion
com•prise v., com•
prised, com•pris•
ing. (to contain: cf.
COMPOSE)
com•pro•mise v.,
com•pro•mised,
com•pro•mis•ing.
comp•trol•ler *Busi-
ness.*
com•pul•sion (coer-
cion)
com•pul•sive
com•pul•sive∘ly
com•pul•sive•ness
com•pul•so∘ry
compulsory ar•bi•
tra•tion *Business.*
com•punc•tion (re-
morse)
com•pu•ta•tion
com•pute v., com•
put∘ed, com•put•
ing.
com•put∘er
com∘put∘er-aid∘ed
computer graph•ics
Computers.

computer lan•guage
Computers.
computer lit•er∘a∘cy
Computers.
computer vi•rus *Com-
puters.*
computer worm *Com-
puters.*
com•put•er•ese
com•put•er∘i•za•
tion *Computers.*
com•put•er•ize v.,
com•put•er•ized,
com•put•er•iz•ing.
Computers.
com•put•er•ized ax•
i∘al to•mog•ra•phy
(CAT)
com•put∘er•ma•ni∘a
Computers.
com•put∘er•pho•
bi∘a *Computers.*
com•rade
com•rade•ship
con v., conned, con•
ning.
con•cat∘e•nate v.,
con•cat∘e•nat∘ed,
con•cat∘e•nat•ing.
con•cat∘e•na•tion
con•cave (curved in-
ward: cf. CONVEX)
con•ceal v., con•
cealed, con•ceal•
ing.
con•ceal∘er
con•ceal•ment
con•cede v., con•
ced∘ed, con•ced•
ing.
con•ceit
con•ceit∘ed
con•ceiv•a∘ble
con•ceiv•a∘bly
con•ceive v., con•
ceived, con•ceiv•
ing.

con•cen•trate *v.*,
con•cen•trat•ed,
con•cen•trat•ing.
con•cen•tra•tion
con•cen•tric
con•cept
con•cep•tion
con•cep•tu○al
con•cep•tu•al•i•za•
tion
con•cep•tu•al•ize *v.*,
con•cep•tu•al•ized,
con•cep•tu•al•iz•
ing.
con•cep•tu•al○ly
con•cern
con•cerned
con•cern•ing
con•cert
con•cert○ed
con•cert•ed○ly
con○cer•ti•na
con○cert•mas•ter
con•cer○to *n., pl.*
con•cer•tos or con•
cer○ti.
con•ces•sion
con•ces•sion•aire or
con•ces•sion○er
conch *n., pl.* conchs or
con•ches. (marine
mollusk: cf. CONK)
con•cierge *n., pl.* con•
cierges.
con•cil•i•ate *v.*, con•
cil•i•at○ed, con•cil•
i•at•ing.
con•cil•i•a•tion
con•cil•i•a•tor
con•cil•i•a•to○ry
con•cise
con•cise○ly
con•cise○ness
con•clave
con•clude *v.*, con•
clud○ed, con•clud•
ing.

con•clu•sion
con•clu•sive
con•clu•sive○ly
con•clu•sive•ness
con•coct *v.*, con•
coct○ed, con•coct•
ing.
con•coc•tion
con•com○i•tant
con•cord
con•cord•ance
con•cord•ant
con•cor•dat
con•course
con•crete
con•crete○ly
con•crete•ness
con•cu•bine
con•cu•pis•cence
con•cu•pis•cent
con•cur *v.*, con•
curred, con•cur•
ring.
con•cur•rence
con•cur•rent
con•cur•rent○ly
con•cus•sion
con•demn *v.*, con•
demned, con•demn•
ing. (to censure: cf.
CONTEMN)
con•dem•na•tion (de-
nunciation: cf. COM-
MENDATION)
con•dem•na•to○ry
con•den•sa•tion
con•dense *v.*, con•
densed, con•dens•
ing.
con•dens○er
con•de•scend *v.*,
con•de•scend○ed,
con•de•scend•ing.
con•de•scend•ing○ly
con•de•scen•sion
con•dign

con•di•ment
con•di•tion *v.*, con•
di•tioned, con•di•
tion•ing.
con•di•tion○al
conditional sale *Busi-
ness.*
con•di•tion•al○ly
con•di•tioned
con•di•tion○er
con○do *n., pl.* con•
dos.
con•dole *v.*, con•
doled, con•dol•ing.
con•do•lence
con•dom
con•do•min•i•um
con•done *v.*, con•
doned, con•don•
ing.
con•dor
con•duce *v.*, con•
duced, con•duc•ing.
con•du•cive
con•duct *v.*, con•
duct○ed, con•duct•
ing.
con•duct•ance
con•duc•tion
con•duc•tive
con•duc•tiv○i•ty *n.,
pl.* con•duc•tiv•i•
ties.
con•duc•tor
con•duit
cone *v.*, coned, con•
ing.
co•ney *n., pl.* co•
neys.
con•fab *v.*, con•
fabbed, con•fab•
bing.
con•fab○u•late *v.*,
con•fab○u•lat○ed,
con•fab○u•lat•ing.
con•fab○u•la•tion
con•fec•tion

con•fec•tion•er

con•fec•tion•er•y *n.,*
pl. con•fec•tion•er•
ies.

con•fed•er•a•cy *n.,*
pl. con•fed•er•a•
cies.

con•fed•er•ate *v.,*
con•fed•er•at•ed,
con•fed•er•at•ing.

con•fed•er•a•tion

con•fer *v.,* con•
ferred, con•fer•ring.

con•fer•ee

con•fer•ence *v.,* con•
fer•enced, con•fer•
enc•ing.

con•fer•ment

con•fess *v.,* con•
fessed, con•fess•
ing.

con•fess•ed•ly

con•fes•sion

con•fes•sion•al

con•fes•sor

con•fet•ti

con•fi•dant or con•
fi•dante

con•fide *v.,* con•
fid•ed, con•fid•ing.

con•fi•dence

con•fi•dent

con•fi•den•tial

con•fi•den•ti•al•i•ty

con•fi•den•tial•ly

con•fi•dent•ly

con•fig•u•ra•tion

con•fig•ure, *v.,* con•
fig•ured, con•fig•
ur•ing.

con•fine *v.,* con•
fined, con•fin•ing.

con•fine•ment

con•firm *v.,* con•
firmed, con•firm•
ing.

con•fir•ma•tion

con•firmed

con•fis•cate *v.,* con•
fis•cat•ed, con•fis•
cat•ing.

con•fis•ca•tion

con•fis•ca•to•ry

con•fla•gra•tion

con•flate *v.,* con•
flat•ed, con•flat•
ing.

con•fla•tion

con•flict *v.,* con•
flict•ed, con•flict•
ing.

conflict of in•ter•est
Business.

con•flic•to•ry

con•flu•ence

con•flu•ent

con•form *v.,* con•
formed, con•form•
ing.

con•form•a•ble

con•for•ma•tion

con•form•er

con•form•ism

con•form•ist

con•form•i•ty *n.,* pl.
con•form•i•ties.

con•found *v.,* con•
found•ed, con•
found•ing.

con•fra•ter•ni•ty *n.,*
pl. con•fra•ter•ni•
ties.

con•frere

con•front *v.,* con•
front•ed, con•
front•ing.

con•fron•ta•tion

con•fron•ta•tion•al

Con•fu•cian

Con•fu•cian•ism

Con•fu•cius

con•fuse *v.,* con•
fused, con•fus•ing.

con•fus•ed•ly

con•fus•ing•ly

con•fu•sion

con•fute *v.,* con•
fut•ed, con•fut•ing.

con•ga *n.,* pl. con•
gas;. *v.,* con•gaed,
con•ga•ing.

con•geal *v.,* con•
gealed, con•geal•
ing.

con•geal•ment

con•gen•ial

con•ge•ni•al•i•ty

con•gen•ial•ly

con•gen•i•tal

con•gen•i•tal•ly

con•ger

con•ge•ries

con•gest

con•gest•ed

con•ges•tion

con•ges•tive

con•glom•er•ate *v.,*
con•glom•er•at•ed,
con•glom•er•at•
ing.

con•glom•er•a•tion

Con•go

con•grat•u•late *v.,*
con•grat•u•lat•ed,
con•grat•u•lat•ing.

con•grat•u•la•tion

con•grat•u•la•to•ry

con•gre•gate *v.,* con•
gre•gat•ed, con•
gre•gat•ing.

con•gre•ga•tion

con•gre•ga•tion•al

con•gre•ga•tion•al•
ism

con•gre•ga•tion•al•
ist

con•gress

con•gres•sion•al

con•gress•man *n.,* pl.
con•gress•men.

con•gress•per•son

con•gress•wom•an
n., pl. con•gress•
wom•en.
con•gru•ence
con•gru•ent
con•gru•i•ty
con•gru•ous
con•ic or con•i•cal
con•i•cal•ly
co•ni•fer
co•nif•er•ous
con•jec•tur•al
con•jec•ture v., con•
jec•tured, con•jec•
tur•ing.
con•join v., con•
joined, con•join•ing.
con•joint
con•ju•gal
con•ju•gate v., con•
ju•gat•ed, con•ju•
gat•ing.
con•ju•ga•tion
con•junc•tion
con•junc•ti•va n., pl.
con•junc•ti•vas or
con•junc•ti•vae.
con•junc•ti•vi•tis
con•jur•a•tion
con•jure v., con•
jured, con•jur•ing.
con•jur•er or con•ju•
ror
conk v., conked,
conk•ing. (to hit on
the head: cf. CONCH)
con•nect v., con•
nect•ed, con•nect•
ing.
Con•nect•i•cut (CT)
con•nec•tion
con•nec•tive
con•nip•tion
con•niv•ance
con•nive v., con•
nived, con•niv•ing.
con•niv•er

con•nois•seur
con•no•ta•tion
con•no•ta•tive
con•note v., con•
not•ed, con•not•
ing.
con•nu•bi•al
con•quer v., con•
quered, con•quer•
ing.
con•quer•a•ble
con•quer•or
con•quest
con•quis•ta•dor n.,
pl. con•quis•ta•dors
or con•qu is•ta•do•
res.
Con•rad
con•san•guin•e•ous
or con•san•guine
con•san•guin•i•ty
con•science
con•science•less
con•sci•en•tious (me-
ticulous)
conscientious ob•jec•
tor
con•sci•en•tious•ly
con•sci•en•tious•
ness
con•scious (aware)
con•scious•ly
con•scious•ness
con•script v., con•
script•ed, con•
script•ing.
con•scrip•tion
con•se•crate v., con•
se•crat•ed, con•se•
crat•ing.
con•se•cra•tion
con•sec•u•tive
con•sec•u•tive•ly
con•sen•sus
con•sent v., con•
sent•ed, con•sent•
ing.

consent or•der Busi-
ness.
con•se•quence
con•se•quent
con•se•quen•tial
con•se•quent•ly
con•serv•an•cy n., pl.
con•serv•an•cies.
con•ser•va•tion
con•ser•va•tion•ist
con•serv•a•tism
con•serv•a•tive
con•serv•a•tive•ly
con•serv•a•tor
con•serv•a•to•ry n.,
pl. con•serv•a•to•
ries.
con•serve v., con•
served, con•serv•
ing.
con•sid•er v., con•
sid•ered, con•sid•
er•ing.
con•sid•er•a•ble
con•sid•er•a•bly
con•sid•er•ate
con•sid•er•ate•ly
con•sid•er•a•tion
con•sid•er•ing
con•sign v., con•
signed, con•sign•
ing.
con•sign•ee Business.
con•sign•ment Busi-
ness.
con•sign•or Business.
con•sist v., con•
sist•ed, con•sist•
ing.
con•sist•en•cy or
con•sist•ence n., pl.
con•sist•en•cies.
con•sist•ent
con•sist•ent•ly
con•sis•to•ry n., pl.
con•sis•to•ries.
con•so•la•tion

con•sol•a•to•ry
con•sole v., con•
soled, con•sol•ing.
con•sol•i•date v.,
con•sol•i•dat•ed,
con•sol•i•dat•ing.
con•sol•i•da•tion
con•sol•ing•ly
con•som•mé
con•so•nance
con•so•nant
con•so•nan•tal
con•so•nant•ly
con•sort v., con•
sort•ed, con•sort•
ing.
con•sor•ti•um n., pl.
con•sor•ti•a. Busi-
ness.
con•spec•tus, n., pl.
con•spec•tus•us.
con•spic•u•ous
con•spic•u•ous•ly
con•spic•u•ous•ness
con•spir•a•cy n., pl.
con•spir•a•cies.
con•spir•a•tor or
con•spir•er
con•spir•a•to•ri•al
con•spire v., con•
spired, con•spir•ing.
con•sta•ble
con•stan•cy
con•stant
constant dol•lars Busi-
ness.
Con•stan•ti•no•ple
con•stant•ly
con•stel•la•tion
con•ster•na•tion
con•sti•pate v., con•
sti•pat•ed, con•sti•
pat•ing.
con•sti•pa•tion
con•stit•u•en•cy n.,
pl. con•stit•u•en•
cies.

con•stit•u•ent
con•sti•tute v., con•
sti•tut•ed, con•sti•
tut•ing.
con•sti•tu•tion
con•sti•tu•tion•al
con•sti•tu•tion•
al•i•ty
con•sti•tu•tion•al•ly
con•strain v., con•
strained, con•strain•
ing.
con•straint
con•strict v., con•
strict•ed, con•strict•
ing.
con•stric•tion
con•stric•tive
con•stric•tor
con•stru•a•ble
con•struct v., con•
struct•ed, con•
struct•ing.
con•struc•tion
con•struc•tion•ist
con•struc•tive
con•struc•tive•ly
con•strue v., con•
strued, con•stru•
ing.
con•sub•stan•ti•a•
tion
con•sul (diplomat: cf.
COUNCIL; COUNSEL)
con•su•lar
con•su•late
con•sult v., con•
sult•ed, con•sult•
ing.
con•sult•ant
con•sul•ta•tion
con•sum•a•ble
con•sume v., con•
sumed, con•sum•
ing.
con•sum•er Business.

consumer cred•it Busi-
ness.
consumer price index
(CPI) Business.
con•sum•er•ism Busi-
ness.
con•sum•mate v.,
con•sum•mat•ed,
con•sum•mat•ing.
con•sum•mate•ly
con•sum•ma•tion
con•sump•tion
con•sump•tive
con•tact v., con•
tact•ed, con•tact•
ing.
con•ta•gion
con•ta•gious
con•ta•gious•ly
con•ta•gious•ness
con•tain v., con•
tained, con•tain•
ing.
con•tain•er
con•tain•er•i•za•
tion Business.
con•tain•er•ize v.,
con•tain•er•ized,
con•tain•er•iz•ing.
Business.
con•tain•er•ship Busi-
ness.
con•tain•ment
con•tam•i•nant
con•tam•i•nate v.,
con•tam•i•nat•ed,
con•tam•i•nat•ing.
con•tam•i•na•tion
con•temn v., con•
temned, con•temn•
ing. (to despise: cf.
CONDEMN)
con•tem•plate v.,
con•tem•plat•ed,
con•tem•plat•ing.
con•tem•pla•tion
con•tem•pla•tive

con•tem•po•ra•ne•ous

con•tem•po•rar•y n., pl. con•tem•po•rar•ies.

con•tempt•i•ble

con•tempt•i•bly

con•temp•tu•ous

con•temp•tu•ous•ly

con•tend v., con•tend•ed, con•tend•ing.

con•tend•er

con•tent

con•tent•ed

con•tent•ed•ly

con•ten•tion

con•ten•tious

con•tent•ment

con•ter•mi•nus

con•test v., con•test•ed, con•test•ing.

con•test•a•ble

con•test•ant

con•text

con•text-sen•si•tive *Computers.*

con•tex•tu•al

con•ti•gu•i•ty

con•tig•u•ous

con•ti•nence

con•ti•nent

con•ti•nen•tal

con•tin•gen•cy n., pl. con•tin•gen•cies.

con•tin•gent *Business.*

contingent li•a•bil•i•ty

con•tin•u•al (intermittent: cf. CONTINUOUS)

con•tin•u•al•ly

con•tin•u•ance

con•tin•u•a•tion

con•tin•ue v., con•tin•ued, con•tin•u•ing.

con•ti•nu•i•ty

con•tin•u•ous (uninterrupted: cf. CONTINUAL)

continuous speech sys•tem *Computers.*

con•tin•u•ous•ly

con•tin•u•um n., pl. con•tin•u•a.

con•tort

con•tor•tion

con•tor•tion•ist

con•tour

con•tra n., pl. con•tras.

contra ac•count *Business.*

con•tra•band

con•tra•cep•tion

con•tra•cep•tive

con•tract v., con•tract•ed, con•tract•ing.

contract car•ri•er *Business.*

con•trac•tile

con•trac•tion

con•trac•tor *Business.*

con•trac•tu•al

con•tra•dict v., con•tra•dict•ed, con•tra•dict•ing.

con•tra•dic•tion

con•tra•dic•to•ry

con•tra•dis•tinc•tion

con•trail

con•tra•in•di•cate v., con•tra•in•di•cat•ed, con•tra•in•di•cat•ing.

con•tra•in•di•ca•tion

con•tral•to n., pl. con•tral•tos.

con•trap•tion

con•tra•pun•tal

con•trar•i•ness

con•trar•i•wise

con•trar•y n., pl. con•trar•ies.

con•trast v., con•trast•ed, con•trast•ing.

con•tra•vene v., con•tra•vened, con•tra•ven•ing.

con•tra•ven•tion

con•tre•temps n., pl. con•tre•temps.

con•trib•ute v., con•trib•ut•ed, con•trib•ut•ing.

con•tri•bu•tion

con•trib•u•tor

con•trib•u•to•ry

con•trite

con•trite•ly

con•tri•tion or con•trite•ness

con•triv•ance

con•trive v., con•trived, con•triv•ing.

con•trol v., con•trolled, con•trol•ling.

control char•ac•ter *Computers.*

con•trol•la•ble

con•trol•ler

controller board *Computers.*

con•tro•ver•sial

con•tro•ver•sy n., pl. con•tro•ver•sies.

con•tro•vert v., con•tro•vert•ed, con•tro•vert•ing.

con•tu•ma•cious

con•tu•ma•cy

con•tu•me•li•ous

con•tu•me•ly

con•tuse *v.*, con•
tused, con•tus•ing.
con•tu•sion
co•nun•drum
con•ur•ba•tion
con•va•lesce *v.*, con•
va•lesced, con•va•
lesc•ing.
con•va•les•cence
con•va•les•cent
con•vec•tion
con•vene *v.*, con•
vened, con•ven•ing.
con•ven•ience
convenience goods
  Business.
con•ven•ient
con•ven•ient•ly
con•vent
con•ven•ti•cle
con•ven•tion
con•ven•tion•al
conventional
  mem•o•ry *Comput-
  ers.*
con•ven•tion•al•i•ty
con•ven•tion•al•ly
con•verge *v.*, con•
verged, con•verg•
ing.
con•ver•gence
con•ver•gent
con•ver•sant
con•ver•sa•tion
con•ver•sa•tion•al
con•ver•sa•tion•al•
ist
con•verse¹ *adj., n.*
con•verse² *v.*, con•
versed, con•vers•
ing.
con•verse•ly
con•ver•sion
con•vert *v.*, con•
vert•ed, con•vert•
ing.
con•vert•er

con•vert•i•ble
convertible bond *Busi-
ness.*
con•vex (curved out-
ward: cf. CONCAVE)
con•vex•i•ty
con•vey *v.*, con•
veyed, con•vey•ing.
con•vey•ance
con•vey•er or con•
vey•or
con•vict *v.*, con•
vict•ed, con•vict•
ing.
con•vic•tion
con•vince *v.*, con•
vinced, con•vinc•
ing.
con•vinc•ing
con•vinc•ing•ly
con•viv•i•al
con•viv•i•al•i•ty
con•vo•ca•tion
con•voke *v.*, con•
voked, con•vok•ing.
con•vo•lut•ed
con•vo•lu•tion
con•voy *v.*, con•
voyed, con•voy•ing.
con•vulse *v.*, con•
vulsed, con•vuls•
ing.
con•vul•sion
con•vul•sive
con•vul•sive•ly
coo *v.*, cooed, coo•
ing.
COO *Business.* (chief
operating officer)
cook *v.*, cooked,
cook•ing.
cook•book
cook•er
cook•er•y *n., pl.*
cook•er•ies.
cook∘ie or cook∘y, *n.,*

pl. cook•ies. (flat
cake: cf. KOOKY)
cook•out
cool *adj.*, cool•er,
cool•est; *v.*, cooled,
cool•ing.
cool•ant
cool•er
Cool•idge
coo•lie (laborer: cf.
COOLLY; COULEE)
cool∘ing-off law *Busi-
ness.*
cooling-off pe•ri•od
Business.
cool•ly (calmly)
cool•ness
coon
coon•hound
coon•skin
coop (enclosure: cf.
COUP; COUPE)
coop•er
Coo•per
co•op•er•ate or
co-op•er•ate *v.*, co•
op•er•at•ed or co-•
op•er∘at•ed, co•
op•er•at•ing or
co-•op•er•at•ing.
co•op•er•a•tion or
co-op•er•a•tion
co•op•er•a•tive or
co-op•er•a•tive
co•or•di•nate or co•
or•di•nate *v.*, co•
or•di•nat•ed or co-•
or•di•nat•ed, co•
or•di•nat•ing or
co•or•di•nat•ing.
co•or•di•na•tion or
co-or•di•na•tion
co•or•di•na•tor or
co-or•di•na•tor
coot
coot∘ie

cop *v.*, copped, cop•ping.

cop-out

cope *v.*, coped, cop•ing.

Co•pen•ha•gen

Co•per•ni•can

Co•per•ni•cus

cop•i•er

co•pi•lot

cop•ing

co•pi•ous

co•pi•ous•ly

co•pi•ous•ness

Cop•land

co•pol•y•mer

cop•per

cop•per•head

cop•per•y

cop•ra

co•proc•es•sor *Computers.*

copse or cop•pice

cop•ter

cop•u•la *n.*, pl. cop•u•las or cop•u•lae.

cop•u•late *v.*, cop•u•lat•ed, cop•u•lat•ing.

cop•u•la•tion

cop•u•la•tive

cop•y *n.*, pl. cop•ies; *v.*, cop•ied, cop•y•ing.

copy pro•tec•tion *Computers.*

cop•y•board scan•ner *Computers.*

cop•y•book

cop•y•cat

cop•y•ed•it or cop•y-ed•it *v.*, cop•y•ed•it•ed or cop•y-ed•it•ed, cop•y•ed•it•ing or cop•y-ed•it•ing.

cop•y•ed•i•tor

cop•y•right *v.*, cop•y•right•ed, cop•y•right•ing.

cop•y•writ•er

co•quet *v.*, co•quet•ted, co•quet•ting.

co•quet•ry

co•quette

co•quet•tish

cor•al (marine skeleton: cf. CHORAL; CHORALE; CORRAL)

cor•bel

cord (string: cf. CHORD)

cor•dial

cor•dial•i•ty

cor•dial•ly

cor•dil•le•ra

cord•ite

cord•less

cor•don *v.*, cor•doned, cor•don•ing.

Cor•do•van

cor•du•roy

core *v.*, cored, cor•ing. (center; to remove the core of: cf. CORPS; CORPSE)

co•re•spond•ent (joint defendant: cf. CORRESPONDENT)

co•ri•an•der

Co•rin•thi•an

cork

cork•er

cork•screw

corm

cor•mo•rant

corn

corn bread or corn•bread

corn pone

corn•ball

corn•cob

cor•ne•a *n.*, pl. cor•ne•as.

cor•ne•al

corned

cor•ner *v.*, cor•nered, cor•ner•ing.

cor•ner•stone

cor•net

corn•flow•er

cor•nice

corn•meal

corn•row

corn•starch

cor•nu•co•pi•a *n.*, pl. cor•nu•co•pi•as.

corn•y *adj.*, corn•i•er, corn•i•est.

co•rol•la *n.*, pl. co•rol•las.

cor•ol•lar•y *n.*, pl. cor•ol•lar•ies.

co•ro•na *n.*, pl. co•ro•nas or co•ro•nae.

cor•o•nar•y *n.*, pl. cor•o•nar•ies.

cor•o•na•tion

cor•o•ner

cor•o•net

Corp. *Business.* (corporation)

cor•po•ra

cor•po•ral (of the body; military officer)

cor•po•rate *Business.*

corporate bond *Business.*

corporate raid•er *Business.*

cor•po•ra•tion *Business.*

cor•po•re•al (material)

corps *n.*, pl. corps. (organization: cf. CORE)

corpse (dead body)

corps•man *n.*, *pl.* corps•men.

cor•pu•lence

cor•pu•lent

cor•pus *n.*, *pl.* cor•po•ra or cor•pus•es.

Cor•pus Chris•ti

corpus de•lic•ti *n.*, *pl.* cor•po•ra de•lic•ti.

cor•pus•cle

cor•ral *v.*, cor•ralled, cor•ral•ling. (enclosure; to corral: cf. CHORAL; CHORALE; CORAL)

cor•rect *v.*, cor•rect•ed, cor•rect•ing.

cor•rec•tion

cor•rec•tion•al

cor•rec•tive

cor•rect•ly

cor•rect•ness

cor•re•late *v.*, cor•re•lat•ed, cor•re•lat•ing.

cor•re•la•tion

cor•re•la•tive

cor•re•spond *v.*, cor•re•spond•ed, cor•re•spond•ing.

cor•re•spond•ence

cor•re•spond•ent (writer: cf. CORESPONDENT)

correspondent bank *Business.*

cor•re•spond•ing•ly

cor•ri•dor

cor•rob•o•rate *v.*, cor•rob•o•rat•ed, cor•rob•o•rat•ing.

cor•rob•o•ra•tion

cor•rob•o•ra•tive

cor•rob•o•ra•tor

cor•rode *v.*, cor•rod•ed, cor•rod•ing.

cor•ro•sion

cor•ro•sive

cor•ru•gate *v.*, cor•ru•gat•ed, cor•ru•gat•ing.

cor•ru•ga•tion

cor•rupt *v.*, cor•rupt•ed, cor•rupt•ing.

cor•rupt•i•ble

cor•rup•tion

cor•rupt•ly

cor•sage

cor•sair

cor•set *v.*, cor•set•ed, cor•set•ing.

cor•tege or cor•tège

cor•tex *n.*, *pl.* cor•ti•ces.

cor•ti•cal

cor•ti•sone

co•run•dum

cor•us•ca•tion

cor•vette

co•sign *v.*, co•signed, co•sign•ing. *Business.*

co•sign•er *Business.*

cos•met•ic

cos•met•i•cal•ly

cos•me•tol•o•gist

cos•me•tol•o•gy

cos•mic

cos•mog•o•o•ny *n.*, *pl.* cos•mog•o•o•nies.

cos•mo•log•i•cal

cos•mol•o•o•gy

cos•mo•naut

cos•mo•pol•i•tan

cos•mo•pol•i•tan•ism

cos•mos *n.*, *pl.* cos•mos or cos•mos•es.

Cos•sack

cos•set, *v.*, cos•set•ed cos•set•ing.

cost *v.*, cost, cost○ed, cost○ing.

cost ac•count•ing *Business.*

cost-ben•e•fit a•nal•y•sis *Business.*

cost-ef•fec•tive *Business.*

cost of liv•ing *Business.*

cost o•ver•run *Business.*

cost-plus *Business.*

cost-push *Business.*

Cos•ta Ri•ca

Cos•ta Ri•can

co•star or co-•star, *v.*, co•starred or co-•starred, co••star•ring or co•star•ring.

cos•tive

cost•li•ness

cost○ly *adj.*, cost•li•er, cost•li•est.

cos•tume *v.*, cos•tumed, co•tum•ing.

cos•tum○er

co○sy *n.*, *pl.* co•sies; *v.*, co•sied, co•sy•ing; *adj.*, co•si○er, co•si•est.

cot

cote (coop: cf. COAT)

Côte d'I○voire

co•te•rie

co•ter•mi•nous or co•ter•mi•nal

co•til•lion

cot•tage

cottage in•dus•try

cot•ter pin

cot•ton

cot○ton•mouth *n.*, *pl.* cot○ton•mouths.

cot○ton•seed *n.*, *pl.* cot○ton•seeds or cot○ton•seed.

cot·ton·tail

cot·y·le·don

couch *v.*, couched, couch·ing.

cou·gar *n., pl.* cou·gars or cou·gar.

cough *v.*, coughed, cough·ing.

could

cou·lee (ravine: cf. COOLIE; COOLLY)

cou·lomb

coun·cil (assembly: cf. CONSUL; COUNSEL)

coun·cil·man *n., pl.* coun·cil·men.

coun·ci·lor or coun·cil·lor (member of a council).

coun·cil·per·son

coun·cil·wom·an *n., pl.* coun·cil·wom·en.

coun·sel *n., pl.* coun·sel; *v.*, coun·seled or coun·selled, coun·sel·ing or coun·sel·ling. (advice; to advise: cf. CONSUL; COUNCIL)

coun·se·lor (adviser)

count *v.*, count·ed, count·ing.

count·down

coun·te·nance *v.*, coun·te·nanced, coun·te·nanc·ing.

count·er¹ (one who counts)

count·er² (long, narrow table)

coun·ter³ (against)

coun·ter·act *v.*, coun·ter·act·ed, coun·ter·act·ing.

coun·ter·ac·tion

coun·ter·at·tack *v.*,

coun·ter·tacked, coun·ter·tack·ing.

coun·ter·bal·ance *v.*, coun·ter·bal·anced, coun·ter·bal·anc·ing.

coun·ter·claim *v.*, coun·ter·claimed, coun·ter·claim·ing.

coun·ter·clock·wise

coun·ter·cul·ture

coun·ter·es·pi·o·nage

coun·ter·feit, *v.*, coun·ter·feit·ed, coun·ter·feit·ing.

coun·ter·feit·er

coun·ter·in·sur·gen·cy *n., pl.* coun·ter·in·sur·gen·cies.

coun·ter·in·tel·li·gence

count·er·man *n., pl.* count·er·men.

coun·ter·mand *v.*, coun·ter·mand·ed, coun·ter·mand·ing.

coun·ter·meas·ure

coun·ter·of·fen·sive

coun·ter·pane

coun·ter·part

coun·ter·point

coun·ter·poise

coun·ter·pro·duc·tive

coun·ter·rev·o·lu·tion

coun·ter·rev·o·lu·tion·ar·y

coun·ter·sign *v.*, coun·ter·signed, coun·ter·sign·ing.

coun·ter·sink *v.*, coun·ter·sank, coun·ter·sunk, coun·ter·sink·ing.

coun·ter·spy *n., pl.* coun·ter·spies.

coun·ter·ten·or

coun·ter·vail *v.*, coun·ter·vailed, coun·ter·vail·ing.

coun·ter·weight

count·ess

count·ing house *Business.*

count·less

coun·tri·fied

coun·try *n., pl.* coun·tries.

coun·try-and-west·ern

coun·try·man *n., pl.* coun·try·men.

coun·try·side

coun·try·wom·an *n., pl.* coun·try·wom·en.

coun·ty *n., pl.* coun·ties.

coup *n., pl.* coups. (daring act: cf. CO-OP; COOP; COUPE)

coup de grâce *n., pl.* coups de grâce.

coup d'é·tat *n., pl.* coups d'é·tat.

cou·pé

coupe (two-door car)

cou·ple *v.*, cou·pled, cou·pling.

cou·plet

cou·pling

cou·pon

coupon bond *Business.*

coupon rate *Business.*

cou·pon·ing *Business.*

cour·age

cou·ra·geous

cou·ra·geous·ly

cour·i·er

course *v.*, coursed, cours·ing. (class;

route; to course: cf. COARSE).

course•ware Computers.

court v., court•ed, court•ing.

court-mar•tial n., pl. courts-•mar•tial or court-•mar•tials;. v., court-•mar•tialed or court-•mar•tialled, court-•mar•tialing or court-•mar•tial○ling.

cour•te•ous

cour•te•ous•ly

cour•te•san

cour•te•sy (politeness: cf. CURTSY)

court•house n., pl. court•hous•es.

cour•ti○er

court•li•ness

court○ly adj., court•li○er, court•li•est.

court•room

court•ship

court•yard

cous•cous

cous○in

cou•ture

cou•tu•ri○er or cou•tu•ri•ère

cove

cov○en

cov○e○nant

Cov•en•try

cov○er v., cov•ered, cov•er○ing.

cov○er-up

cov•er•age

cov•er•all

cov•er•let

co•vert

co•vert○ly

cov○et v., cov•et○ed, cov•et•ing.

cov•et•ous

cov•et•ous•ness

cov○ey n., pl. cov•eys.

cow v., cowed, cow•ing.

cow•ard (one who lacks courage: cf. COW-ERED).

cow•ard•ice

cow•ard•li•ness

cow•ard○ly

cow•bird

cow•boy or cow•girl

cow○er

cow○ered v., cow•ered, cow•er○ing. (crouched: cf. COWARD)

cow•hand

cow•hide

cowl

cow•lick

cowl•ing

co•work○er

cow•poke

cow•pox

cow•punch○er

cow•slip

cox•comb

cox•swain

coy adj., coy○er, coy•est.

coy○ly

coy•ness

coy•o○te n., pl. coy•o○tes or coy•o○te.

coz○en, v., coz•ened, coz•en•ing.

co•zi○ly

co•zi•ness

co○zy n., pl. co•zies; v. co•zied, co•zy•ing; adj., co•zi○er, co•zi•est.

CPA or C.P.A. Business. (certified public accountant)

CPI Business. (consumer price index)

CPU Computers. (central processing unit)

CR Computers. (carriage return)

crab v., crabbed, crab•bing.

crab•bed

crab○by

crack v., cracked, crack•ing.

crack•down

cracked

crack○er

crack•er•jack

crack•head

crack•house

crack○le v., crack•led, crack•ling.

crack•pot

crack○up

cra•dle v., cra•dled, cra•dling.

craft n., pl. crafts or craft; v., craft○ed, craft•ing.

craft un•ion Business.

crafts•man n., pl. crafts•men.

crafts•man•ship

crafts•wom○an n., pl. crafts•wom○en.

crafts•wom•an•ship

craft○y adj., craft•i○er, craft•i•est.

crag

crag○gy adj., crag•gi○er, crag•gi•est.

cram v., crammed, cram•ming.

cramp

cramped

cran•ber○ry n., pl. cran•ber•ries.

crane v., craned, cran•ing.

cra•ni○al

cra•ni•um *n., pl.* cra•
ni•ums *or* cra•ni•a.

crank *v.,* cranked,
crank•ing.

crank•case

crank∘i•ness

crank•shaft

crank∘y *adj.,* crank•
i∘er, crank•i•est.

cran∘ny *n., pl.* cran•
nies.

crap *v.,* crapped,
crap•ping.

crape

crap∘py *adj.,* crap•
pi∘er, crap•pi•est.

craps

crap•shoot∘er

crash *v.,* crashed,
crash•ing.

crash-land[1]

crash-land[2] *v.,* crash-•
land∘ed, crash-•
land∘ing.

crass

crass∘ly

crass•ness

crate *v.,* crat∘ed, crat•
ing.

Cra•ter

cra•ter[1] (depression)

crat∘er[2] (one who
crates)

cra•vat

crave *v.,* craved, crav•
ing.

cra•ven

cra•ven∘ly

crav•ing

craw

craw•fish *n., pl.*
craw•fish *or* craw•
fish∘es.

crawl *v.,* crawled,
crawl•ing.

crawl∘er

crawl•space *or* crawl
space

cray•fish *or* craw•fish
n., pl. cray•fish *or*
craw•fish∘es.

cray∘on

craze

crazed

cra•zi∘ly

cra•zi•ness

cra∘zy *n., pl.* cra•zies;
adj., cra•zi∘er, cra•
zi•est.

creak *v.,* creaked,
creak•ing. (to squeak:
cf. CREEK)

creak∘y *adj.,* creak•
i∘er, creak•i•est.

cream *v.,* creamed,
cream•ing.

cream∘er

cream•er∘y *n., pl.*
cream•er•ies.

cream∘i•ness

cream∘y *adj.,* cream•
i∘er, cream•i•est.

crease *v.,* creased,
creas•ing.

crease•less

cre•ate *v.,* cre•at∘ed,
cre•at•ing.

cre•a•tion

cre•a•tion•ism

cre•a•tion•ist

cre•a•tive

cre•a•tive∘ly

cre•a•tiv∘i•ty

cre•a•tor

crea•ture

crèche

cre•dence

cre•den•tial

cre•den∘za *n., pl.*
cre•den•zas.

cred•i•bil∘i•ty

cred•i•ble (trust-
worthy)

cred•i•bly

cred∘it *v.,* cred•it∘ed,
cred•it•ing.

credit card *Business.*

credit rat∘ing *Busi-
ness.*

credit un∘ion *Business.*

cred•it•a•ble (praise-
worthy)

cred•it•a•bly

cred∘i•tor *Business.*

cred•it•wor•thy *Busi-
ness.*

cre•do *n., pl.* cre•dos.

cre•du•li∘ty

cred∘u•lous

cred∘u•lous∘ly

Cree *n., pl.* Crees *or*
Cree.

creed

Creek *n., pl.* Creeks *or*
Creek.

creek (stream: cf.
CREAK)

creel

creep *v.,* crept *or*
creeped, creep•ing.

creep∘er

creep∘i∘ly

creep∘i•ness

creep∘y *adj.,* creep•
i∘er, creep•i•est.

cre•mate *v.,* cre•
mat∘ed, cre•mat•
ing.

cre•ma•tion

cre•ma•to∘do *n., pl.*
cre•ma•to•dos *or*
cre•ma•to•di; *v.,*
cre•ma•to•doed.

cre•ma•to∘ry *or* cre•
ma•to•ri∘um *n., pl.*
cre•ma•to•ries *or*
cre•ma•to•ri•ums.

crème de menthe

cren•el∘a•tion

Cre•ole

cre•o•sote

crepe

crept

cre•pus•cu•lar

cres•cent

cress

crest *v.*, crest∘ed, crest•ing.

crest•fall∘en

Cre•ta•ceous

Cre•tan (of Crete)

Crete

cre•tin (deformed person)

cre•tin•ism

cre•tonne

cre•vasse

crev•ice

crew

crew∘el (yarn: cf. CRUEL)

crew•el•work

crew•man *n.*, *pl.* crew•men.

crews (groups: cf. CRUISE; CRUSE)

crib *v.*, cribbed, crib•bing.

crib•bage

crick

crick∘et

crick•et∘er

cried

cri∘er

crime

Cri•me∘a

Cri•me∘an

crim∘i•nal

crim∘i•nal∘i∘ty

crim∘i•nal∘ly

crim∘i•nol∘o•gist

crim∘i•nol∘o∘gy

crimp *v.*, crimped, crimp•ing.

crim•son

cringe *v.*, cringed, cring•ing.

crin•kle *v.*, crin•kled, crin•kling.

crin•kly *adj.*, crin•kli∘er, crin•kli•est.

crin∘o•line

crip•ple *v.*, crip•pled, crip•pling.

cri•sis *n.*, *pl.* cri•ses.

crisp *v.*, crisped, crisp•ing; *adj.*, crisp∘er, crisp•est.

crisp∘ly

crisp•ness

crisp∘y *adj.*, crisp∘i∘er, crisp•i•est.

criss•cross *v.*, criss•crossed, criss•cross•ing.

cri•te•ri∘on *n.*, *pl.* cri•te•ri∘a or cri•te•ri∘ons.

crit∘ic (one who evaluates: cf. CRITIQUE)

crit∘i•cal

critical path *Business.*

crit∘i•cal∘ly

crit∘i•cism

crit∘i•cize *v.*, crit∘i•cized, crit∘i•ciz•ing.

crit∘i•ciz∘er

cri•tique *v.*, cri•tiqued, cri•ti•quing. (review: cf. CRITIC)

crit•ter

croak *v.*, croaked, croak•ing.

Cro•a•tia

cro•chet *v.*, cro•cheted, cro•chet•ing. (needlework: cf. CROTCHET)

crock

crocked

crock•er∘y

Crock•pot *Trademark.*

croc∘o•dile

cro•cus *n.*, *pl.* cro•cus∘es.

crois•sant *n.*, *pl.* crois•sants.

Crom•well

crone

cro∘ny *n.*, *pl.* cro•nies

crook

crooked[1] (did bend)

crook∘ed[2] (not straight)

crook•ed∘ly

crook•ed•ness

crook•neck

croon *v.*, crooned, croon•ing.

croon∘er

crop *v.*, cropped, crop•ping.

crop-dust *v.*, crop-•dust∘ed, crop-•dust•ing.

crop-dust∘er

crop•land

crop•per

cro•quet (the game)

cro•quette (ball of minced food)

cro•sier

cross *v.*, crossed, cross•ing; *adj.*, cross∘er, cross•est.

cross-coun∘try

cross-e∘las∘tic∘i∘ty *Business.*

cross-ex∘am∘i∘na∘tion

cross-ex∘am•ine *v.*, cross-•ex∘am∘ined, cross-•ex∘am∘in∘ing.

cross-eye

cross-eyed

cross fire or cross•fire

cross-pol∘li∘nate *v.*, cross-•

pol○li○nat○ed,
cross-●
pol○li○nat○ing.

cross-pol○li○na○tion

cross-sec○tion○al

cross●bar

cross●beam

cross●bones

cross●bow

cross●breed v., cross●
bred, cross●breed●
ing.

cross●cut v., cross●
cut, cross●cut●ting.

cross●hatch v., cross●
hatched, cross●
hatch●ing.

cross●ing

cross○ly

cross○o○ver

cross●piece

cross●road

cross●ruff

crossruff pro●mo●tion
Business.

cross●town

cross●walk

cross●wise or cross●
ways

cross●word puz●zle

crotch

crotch○et (whim: cf.
CROCHET)

crotch●et○y

crouch v., crouched,
crouch●ing.

croup

crou●pi○er

croup○y adj., croup●
i○er, croup●i●est.

crou●ton

crow v., crowed or
crew, crowed, crow●
ing. (did crow)

crow●bar

crowd (large group)

crowd○ed

crow●foot n., pl.
crow●foots or crow●
feet.

crown v., crowned,
crown●ing.

crow's-foot n., pl.
crow's-feet.

crow's-nest or crow's
nest

CRT (cathode-ray tube)

cru●cial

cru●cial○ly

cru●ci●ble

cru●ci●fix

cru●ci●fix○ion

cru●ci●form

cru●ci●fy v., cru●ci●
fied, cru●ci●fy○ing.

crude adj., crud○er,
crud○est.

crude○ly

crude●ness

cru●di●tés (raw vege-
tables)

crud○i○ty (crudeness)

cru●el adj., cru●el○er,
cru●el●est. (causing
pain: cf. CREWEL)

cru●el○ly

cru●el○ty

cru○et

cruise v., cruised,
cruis●ing. (to sail: cf.
CREWS; CRUSE)

cruis○er

crul●ler

crumb

crum●ble v., crum●
bled, crum●bling.

crum●bly adj., crum●
bli○er, crum●bli●est.
(full of crumbs: cf.
CRUMMY)

crum○my adj., crum●
mi○er, crum●mi●est.

(shabby; worthless: cf.
CRUMBY)

crum●pet

crum●ple v., crum●
pled, crum●pling.

crunch v., crunched,
crunch●ing.

crunch○y v., crunch●
i○er, crunch●i●est.

crup●per

cru●sade v., cru●
sad○ed, cru●sad●
ing.

cru●sad○er

cruse (earthen con-
tainer: cf. CREWS;
CRUISE)

crush v., crushed,
crush●ing.

crust v., crust○ed,
crust●ing.

crus●ta●cean

crust○y adj., crust●
i○er, crust●i●est.

crutch

crux n., pl. crux○es or
cru●ces.

cry n., pl. cries;. v.,
cried, cry●ing.

cry●ba○by n., pl. cry●
ba●bies.

cry○o○gen○ic

cry○o○gen●ics

cry○o○sur●ger○y

crypt

cryp●tic

cryp●ti○cal○ly

cryp○to○gram

cryp●tog●ra●pher

cryp●tog●ra●phy

crys●tal

crys●tal○line

crys●tal○li○za○tion

crys●tal●lize v., crys●
tal●lized, crys●tal●
liz○ing.

crys●tal●log●ra●phy

CT (Connecticut)
cten∘o•phore
cub
cub scout
Cu∘ba
Cu•ban
cub∘by•hole
cube *v.*, cubed, cub•ing.
cu•bic
cu∘bic zir•co•ni∘a
cu•bi•cle
cub•ism
cub•ist
cu•bit
cuck•old
cuck∘oo *n., pl.* cuck•oos; *v.*, cuck•ooed, cuck•oo•ing.
cu•cum•ber
cud
cud•dle *v.*, cud•dled, cud•dling.
cud•dle•some
cud•dly *adj.*, cud•dli∘er, cud•dli•est.
cudg∘el *v.*, cudg•eled or cudg•elled, cudg•el•ing or cudg•el•ling.
cue *v.*, cued, cu•ing. (signal: cf. QUEUE)
cuff *v.*, cuffed, cuff•ing.
cuff link or cuff•link
Cui∘si∘nart *Trademark.*
cui•sine
cul-de-sac *n., pl.* culs-∘de-∘sac.
cu•li•nar∘y
cull *v.*, culled, cull•ing.
cul•mi•nate *v.*, cul•mi•nat∘ed, cul•mi•nat•ing.
cul•mi•na•tion

cu•lottes or cu•lotte
cul•pa•bil•i∘ty
cul•pa•ble
cul•pa•bly
cul•prit
cult
cult•ist
cul•ti•va•ble or cul•ti•vat•a∘ble
cul•ti•vate *v.*, cul•ti•vat∘ed, cul•ti•vat•ing.
cul•ti•va•tion
cul•tur∘al
cul•tur•al∘ly
cul•ture *v.*, cul•tured, cul•tur•ing.
cul•vert
cum div∘i•dend *Business.*
cum•ber, *v.*, cum•ber•ing.
cum•ber•some
cum∘in
cum•mer•bund
cu•mu•la•tive
cu•mu•la•tive∘ly
cu•mu•lus *n., pl.* cu•mu∘li.
cu•ne•i•form
cun•ning
cun•ning∘ly
cup *v.*, cupped, cup•ping.
cup•board
cup•cake
cup•ful *n., pl.* cup•fuls.
Cu•pid
cu•pid∘i∘ty
cu•po∘la *n., pl.* cu•po•las.
cur
cur•a∘ble
cu•ra∘re
cu•rate

cur∘a•tive
cu•ra∘tor
curb *v.*, curbed, curb•ing.
curd (cheese: cf. KURD)
cur•dle *v.*, cur•dled, cur•dling.
cu∘ré *n., pl.* cu•rés.
cure *v.*, cured, cur•ing.
cure-all
cu•ret•tage
cu•rette *v.*, cu•ret•ted, cu•ret•ting.
cur•few
cu•ri∘a *n., pl.* cu•ri∘ae.
cu•rie
cu•ri∘o *n., pl.* cu•ri∘os.
cu•ri•os∘i∘ty *n., pl.* cu•ri•os∘i•ties.
cu•ri•ous
cu•ri•ous∘ly
cu•ri∘um
curl *v.*, curled, curl•ing.
curl∘er
cur•lew
curl∘i•cue
curl∘y *adj.*, curl•i∘er, curl•i•est.
cur•mudg•eon
cur•rant (the fruit)
cur•ren∘cy *n., pl.* cur•ren•cies.
currency ex•change *Business.*
cur•rent (present; flow)
current val∘ue *Business.*
cur•rent∘ly
cur•ric∘u•lar
cur•ric∘u•lum *n., pl.* cur•ric∘u•la or cur•ric∘u•lums.

cur•ry n., pl. cur•ries; v., cur•ried, cur•ry•ing.

cur•ry•comb

curse v., cursed, curs•ing. (did curse)

curs•ed (deserving a curse)

cur•sive

cur•sor Computers.

cursor con•trol mode Computers.

cur•so•ri•ly

cur•so•ry

curt adj., curt•er, curt•est.

cur•tail v., cur•tailed, cur•tail•ing.

cur•tail•ment

cur•tain

cur•tained

curt•ly

curt•ness

curt•sy n., pl. curt•sies; v., curt•sied, curt•sy•ing. (bow: cf. COURTESY)

cur•va•ceous

cur•va•ture

curve v., curved, curv•ing.

curv•y adj., curv•i•er, curv•i•est.

cush•ion v., cush•ioned, cush•ion•ing.

cush•y adj., cush•i•er, cush•i•est.

cusp

cus•pid

cus•pi•dor

cuss v., cussed, cuss•ing.

cus•tard

Cus•ter

cus•to•di•an

cus•to•dy

cus•tom

cus•tom-built

cus•tom-made

cus•tom•ar•i•ly

cus•tom•ar•y

cus•tom•er Business.

customer serv•ice Business.

cus•tom•er's man Business.

cus•tom•house n., pl. cus•tom•hous•es. Business.

cus•tom•i•za•tion

cus•tom•ize v., cus•tom•ized, cus•tom•iz•ing.

cus•toms un•ion Business.

cut v., cut, cut•ting.

cut-and-dried

cut-rate

cut-sheet feed•er Computers.

cu•ta•ne•ous

cut•a•way

cut•back

cute adj., cut•er, cut•est.

cute•ness

cute•sy

cu•ti•cle

cut•ie

cut•lass

cut•ler•y

cut•let

cut•off

cutoff test Business.

cut•out

cut•ter

cut•throat

cut•ting

cut•ting•ly

cut•tle•fish n., pl. cut•tle•fish or cut•tle•fish•es.

CVP Business. (cost-volume-profit analysis)

cy•a•nide

cy•ber•na•tion Computers.

cy•ber•net•ics Computers.

cy•ber•punk Computers.

cy•ber•space Computers.

cy•cla•men

cy•cle v., cy•cled, cy•cling.

cycle bill•ing Business.

cy•clic•al or cy•clic Business.

cyclical un•em•ploy•ment

cy•cli•cal•ly

cy•clist or cy•cler

cy•clom•e•ter

cy•clone

cy•clon•ic

Cy•clops

cy•clo•spo•rine or cy•clo•spo•rin

cy•clo•tron

cyg•net (young swan· cf. SIGNET)

cyl•in•der

cy•lin•dri•cal

cym•bal (percussion instrument: cf. SYMBOL)

cym•bal•ist

cyn•ic

cyn•i•cal

cyn•i•cal•ly

cyn•i•cism

cy•no•sure

cy•pher

cy•press (the tree)

Cyp•ri•ot

Cy•prus (the country)

cyst

cys•tic fi•bro•sis

cy•tol∘o∘gy
cy•to•plasm
cy•to•sine

czar or tsar
cza∘ri∘na or tsa•ri∘na
n., pl. cza•ri∘nas.

Czech (the people and
language: cf. CHECK)

Czech Re•pub•lic

D

D and C (dilation and
curetage, uterine sur-
gery)
D-∘day or D-∘Day
da Vin∘ci
dab *v.,* dabbed, dab•
bing.
dab•ble *v.,* dab•bled,
dab•bling.
dab•bler
Dac∘ca
da•cha
dachs•hund
Da•cron *Trademark.*
dac•tyl
dad
da∘da
da•da•ism
da•da•ist
dad∘dy *n., pl.* dad•
dies.
dad∘dy-long∘legs or
dad∘dy long∘legs *n.,
pl.* dad∘dy•
long∘legs or
dad∘dy•long•legs.
da∘do *n., pl.* da•does,
da•dos.
dae•mon
dae•mon∘ic
daf•fi•ness
daf•fo•dil
daf∘fy *adj.,* daf•fi∘er,
daf•fi∘est.
daft
dag•ger
da•guerre•o•type
dahl∘ia *n., pl.* dahl•
ias.

Da•ho•man or Da•
ho•me∘an
Da•ho•mey
dai∘ly *n., pl.* dai•lies.
dain•ties
dain•ti∘ly
dain•ti•ness
dain∘ty *adj.,* dain•
ti∘er, dain•ti•est.
dai•qui∘ri *n., pl.* dai•
qui•ris.
dair∘y *n., pl.* dair•ies.
(milk farm: cf. diary)
dair•y•ing
dair∘y•maid
dair∘y•man or
dair∘y•wom∘an *n.,
pl.* dair∘y•men or
dair∘y•wom∘en.
da∘is
dai∘sy *n., pl.* dai•sies.
dai∘sy-wheel print∘er
Computers.
Da•kar
Da•ko∘ta *n., pl.* Da•
ko•tas, Da•ko∘ta.
Da•ko∘tan
dale
Da∘li
Da•li•esque
Dal•las
dal•li•ance
dal∘ly *v.,* dal•lied,
dal•ly•ing.
Dal•ma•tian
dam *v.,* dammed,
dam•ming. (obstruct:
cf. damn)
dam∘age *v.,* dam•
aged, dam•ag•ing.

dam•age con•trol *n.*
dam∘age-con∘trol *adj.*
Da•mas•cus
dam•ask
dame
damn *v.,* damned,
damn∘ing. (to con-
demn: cf. dam)
dam•na•ble
dam•na•bly
dam•na•tion
damned *adj.,*
damned•est or
damnd•est.
Dam∘o∘cles
damp *adj.,* damp∘er,
damp•est.
damp-dry *v.,* damp-
dried, damp-dry∘ing.
damp∘en *v.,* damp•
ened, damp•en•ing.
damp•en∘er
damp∘er
damp•ness
dam•sel
dam•sel•fly *n., pl.*
dam•sel•flies.
dam•son
dance *v.,* danced,
danc•ing.
danc∘er
danc•er•cise
dan•de•li∘on
dan•der
dan•dle *v.,* dan•dled,
dan•dling.
dan•druff
dan∘dy *n., pl.* dan•
dies; *adj.,* dan•di∘
est.

dan•dy•ish
Dane
dan•ger
dan•ger•ous
dan•ger•ous•ly
dan•gle v., dan•gled, dan•gling.
Dan•iel
Dan•ish
dank
dank∘ly
dan•seur
dan•seuse n., pl. dan• seuses.
Dan•te
Dan•ube
Dan∘u•bi∘an
dap•per
dap•pled
Dar•da•nelles
dare n., pl. dares or dare; v., dared, dar• ing.
dare•dev∘il
dare•dev•il∘ry or dare•dev•il•try
dar•ing
dar•ing∘ly
dark adj., dark∘er, dark•est.
dark mat•ter
dark∘en v., dark• ened, dark•en•ing.
dark∘ly
dark•ness
dark•room
dar•ling
darn v., darned, darn• ing.
darned
dart v., dart∘ed, dart• ing.
dart•ing∘ly
Dar•von Trademark.
Dar•win
Dar•win•ism

dash v., dashed, dash•ing.
dash•board
da•shi∘ki n., pl. da• shi•kis.
dash•ing
dash•ing∘ly
das•tard
das•tard∘ly
DAT Computers. (digital audiotape)
da∘ta Computers.
data bank or da∘ta• bank Computers.
da∘ta bus Computers.
data com•pres•sion Computers.
data high•way Com-puters.
data proc∘ess•ing Computers.
data proc•es•sor Computers.
data type Computers.
da∘ta•base or da∘ta base Computers.
da•ta•base man• age∘ment sys∘tem (DBMS) Computers.
database serv∘er Com-puters.
date v., dat∘ed, dat• ing.
date rape
dat•ed•ness
date•line
date•lined
da•tive
da•tum n., pl. da∘ta, da•tums.
daub v., daubed, daub•ing.
daub∘er
daugh•ter
daugh∘ter-in-law n., pl. daugh∘ters-in-law.

daugh∘ter•board Computers.
daunt v., daunt∘ed, daunt•ing.
daunt•ing∘ly
daunt•less
daunt•less∘ly
daunt•less•ness
dau•phin
dav•en•port
Da•vid
Da•vis
dav•it
daw•dle v., daw• dled, daw•dling.
daw•dler
dawn v., dawned, dawn•ing.
day
day care n.
day-care adj.
Day-Glo Trademark.
day-to-day
day•bed
day•break
day•dream v., day• dreamed, day• dream•ing.
day•dream∘er
day•light
day∘light-sav∘ing time or day•light sav∘ing time (DST)
day•time
Day•ton
Day•to∘na Beach
daze
dazed
daz•ed∘ly
daz•zle v., daz•zled, daz•zling.
daz•zler
d/b/a Business. (doing business as)
DBMS Computers. (da-

tabase management
system)

DC (District of Columbia)

DDT (insecticide)

DE (Delaware)

de-em∘pha∘sis

de-em∘pha∘size v., de-em∘pha∘sized, de-em∘pha∘siz∘ing.

de-es∘ca∘late or de-es∘ca∘late v., de-es∘ca∘lat∘ed, de-es∘ca∘lat∘ing, or de-es∘ca∘lat∘ing.

de-es∘ca∘la∘tion

de fac∘to

de Gaulle

de-ic∘er or de∘ic∘er

dea∘con

de-ac∘ti∘vate v., de∘ac∘ti∘vat∘ed, de∘ac∘ti∘vat∘ing.

de-ac∘ti∘va∘tion

dead adj., dead∘er, dead∘est.

dead end n.

dead-end adj.

dead∘beat

dead∘bolt

dead∘en v., dead∘ened, dead∘en∘ing.

dead∘line

dead∘li∘ness

dead∘lock v., dead∘locked, dead∘lock∘ing.

dead∘ly adj., dead∘li∘er, dead∘li∘est.

dead∘pan v., dead∘panned, dead∘pan∘ning.

dead∘wood

deaf adj., deaf∘er, deaf∘est.

deaf-mute

deaf∘en v., deaf∘ened, deaf∘en∘ing.

deaf∘ness

deal v., dealt, deal∘ing.

deal∘er

dealer tie-in Business.

deal∘er∘ship

dean

dear adj., dear∘er, dear∘est. (beloved: cf. DEER)

dear∘ly

dear∘ness

dearth

death

death ben∘e∘fit Business.

death∘bed

death∘blow

death∘less

death∘like

death∘ly

death∘trap

deb

de∘ba∘cle

de∘bar v., de∘barred, de∘bar∘ring.

de∘bark v., de∘barked, de∘bark∘ing.

de∘bar∘ka∘tion

de∘bar∘ment

de∘base v., de∘based, de∘bas∘ing.

de∘base∘ment

de∘bat∘a∘ble

de∘bate v., de∘bat∘ed, de∘bat∘ing.

de∘bat∘er

de∘bauch v., de∘bauched, de∘bauch∘ing.

deb∘au∘chee

de∘bauch∘er∘y

de∘ben∘ture Business.

de∘bil∘i∘tate v., de∘bil∘i∘tat∘ed, de∘bil∘i∘tat∘ing.

de∘bil∘i∘ta∘tion

de∘bil∘i∘ty

deb∘it[1] n. Business. (bookkeeping entry: cf. DEBT)

debit[2] v., deb∘it∘ed, deb∘it∘ing.

debit bal∘ance Business.

debit card Business.

deb∘o∘nair

de∘brief v., de∘briefed, de∘brief∘ing.

de∘bris or dé∘bris

debt (obligation: cf. DEBIT)

debt-eq∘ui∘ty Business.

deb∘tor Business.

de∘bug v., de∘bugged, de∘bug∘ging. Computers.

de∘bug∘ger Computers.

de∘bunk v., de∘bunked, de∘bunk∘ing.

De∘bus∘sy

de∘but or dé∘but v., de∘buted, de∘but∘ing.

deb∘u∘tante or déb∘u∘tante

dec∘ade

dec∘a∘dence

de∘caf∘fein∘at∘ed

de∘cal

Dec∘a∘logue or Dec∘a∘log

de∘camp v., de∘camped, de∘camp∘ing.

de∘cant v., de∘

cant∘ed, de•cant•
ing.
de•cant∘er
de•cap•i•tal•ize *Busi-
ness.*
de•cap∘i•tate *v.,* de•
cap∘i•tat∘ed, de•
cap∘i•tat•ing.
de•cap∘i•ta•tion
de•cath∘lon
de•cay *v.,* de•cayed,
de•cay•ing.
de•cease *v.,* de•
ceased, de•ceas•ing.
de•ceased (dead: cf.
DISEASED)
de•ce•dent
de•ceit
de•ceit•ful
de•ceit•ful∘ly
de•ceit•ful•ness
de•ceive *v.,* de•
ceived, de•ceiv•ing.
de•ceiv∘er
de•ceiv•ing∘ly
de•cel•er•ate *v.,* de•
cel•er•at∘ed, de•
cel•er•at•ing.
de•cel•er•a•tion
de•cel•er∘a•tor
De•cem•ber
de•cen∘cy *n., pl.* de•
cen•cies.
de•cen•ni∘al
de•cen•ni∘al∘ly
de•cent (proper: cf. DE-
SCENT; DISSENT)
de•cent∘ly
de•cen•tral∘i•za•
tion
de•cen•ize *v.,* de•
cen•ized, de•cen•
iz•ing.
de•cep•tion
de•cep•tive
de•cer•ti•fi•ca•tion
Business.

dec∘i•bel
de•cide *v.,* de•cid∘ed,
de•cid•ing.
de•cid•ed∘ly
de•cid∘u•ous
dec∘i•li•ter
dec∘i•mal
dec∘i•mate *v.,* dec∘i•
mat∘ed, dec∘i•mat•
ing.
dec∘i•ma•tion
de•ci•pher *v.,* dec∘i•
phered, dec∘i•pher•
ing.
de•ci•pher•a∘ble
de•ci•sion
decision mak•ing *n.*
decision-mak•ing *adj.*
de•ci•sive
de•ci•sive∘ly
de•ci•sive•ness
deck *v.,* decked, deck•
ing.
de•claim *v.,* de•
claimed, de•claim•
ing.
dec•la•ma•tion
de•clam∘a•to•ry
de•clar∘a∘ble
dec•la•ra•tion
de•clar∘a•tive
de•clare *v.,* de•clared,
de•clar•ing.
de•clas•si•fy *v.,* de•
clas•si•fied, de•
clas•si•fy•ing.
de•clen•sion
dec•li•na•tion
de•cline *v.,* de•clined,
de•clin•ing.
de•clin•ing bal•ance
Business.
de•cliv∘i•ty *n., pl.*
de•cliv∘i•ties.
de•code *v.,* de•
cod∘ed, de•cod•ing.

de•coi•bel
de•col•le•tage or
de•col•le•tage
dé•col•le•té or de•
col•le∘te
de•col∘o•ni•za•tion
de•col∘o•nize *v.,* de•
col∘o•nized, de•
col∘o•niz•ing.
de•com•mis•sion *v.,*
de•com•mis•sioned,
de•com•mis•sion•
ing.
de•com•pose *v.,* de•
com•posed, de•
com•pos•ing.
de•com•po•si•tion
de•com•press *v.,* de•
com•pressed, de•
com•press•ing.
de•com•pres•sion
de•con•ges•tant
de•con•struct *v.,* de•
con•struct∘ed, de•
con•struct•ing.
de•con•struc•tion
de•con•tam∘i•nate
v., de•con•tam∘i•
nat∘ed, de•con•
tam∘i•nat•ing.
de•con•tam∘i•na•
tion
dé•cor or de•cor
dec∘o•rate *v.,* dec∘o•
rat∘ed, dec∘o•rat•
ing.
dec∘o•ra•tion
dec∘o•ra•tive
dec∘o•ra•tor
dec∘o•rous
dec∘o•rous∘ly
de•co•rum
de•cou•page or dé•
cou•page
de•coy *v.,* de•coyed,
de•coy•ing.
de•crease *v.,* de•

creased, de•creas•ing.

de•cree[1] (law: cf. DE-GREE)

de•cree[2] v., de•creed, de•cree•ing.

de•crep•it

de•crep•i•tude

de•cre•scen•do n., pl. de•cre•scen•dos, de•cre•scen•di.

de•crim•i•nal•ize v., de•crim•i•nal•ized, de•crim•i•nal•iz•ing.

de•cry v., de•cried, de•cry•ing.

de•cryp•tion

ded•i•cate v., ded•i•cat•ed, ded•i•cat•ing.

dedicated serv•er Computers.

de•duce v., de•duced, de•duc•ing.

de•duc•i•ble

de•duct v., de•duct•ed, de•duct•ing.

de•duct•i•ble Business.

de•duc•tion

de•duc•tive

deed v., deed•ed, deed•ing.

deed of trust Business

dee•jay

deem v., deemed, deem•ing.

deep adj., deep•er, deep•est.

deep e•col•o•gy

deep freeze n.

deep-freeze v., deep-freezed or deep-froze, deep-freezed

or deep-fro•zen, deep-freez•ing.

deep-fry v., deep-fried, deep-fry•ing.

deep pock•ets

deep-root•ed

deep-sea

deep-seat•ed

deep six n.

deep-six v., deep-sixed, deep-six•ing.

deep space n.

deep-space adj.

deep•en v., deep•ened, deep•en•ing.

deep•ly

deep•ness

deer n., pl. deer, deers. (animal: cf. DEAR)

def

de•face v., de•faced, de•fac•ing.

de•face•ment

de•fal•ca•tion

def•a•ma•tion

de•fame v., de•famed, de•fam•ing.

de•fault v., de•fault•ed, de•fault•ing.

de•fault•er

de•feat v., de•feat•ed, de•feat•ing.

de•feat•ism

de•feat•ist

def•e•cate v., def•e•cat•ed, def•e•cat•ing.

def•e•ca•tion

de•fect v., de•fect•ed, de•fect•ing.

de•fec•tion

de•fec•tive

de•fend v., de•fend•ed, de•fend•ing.

de•fend•ant

de•fend•er

de•fense

de•fense•less

de•fen•si•ble

de•fen•sive

de•fer v., de•ferred, de•fer•ring. (to postpone: cf. DIFFER)

def•er•ence (respect: cf. DIFFERENCE)

def•er•en•tial

de•fer•ment

de•ferred an•nu•i•ty Business.

deferred com•pen•sa•tion Business.

de•fi•ance

de•fi•ant

de•fi•ant•ly

de•fi•cien•cy

de•fi•cient

def•i•cit

deficit spend•ing Business.

de•file v., de•filed, de•fil•ing.

de•file•ment

de•fine v., de•fined, de•fin•ing.

de•fin•er

def•i•nite (precise: cf. DEFINITIVE)

def•i•nite•ly

def•i•nite•ness

def•i•ni•tion

de•fin•i•tive (final: cf. DEFINITE)

de•flate v., de•flat•ed, de•flat•ing.

de•fla•tion Business.

de•fla•tion•ar•y Business.

de•flect v., de•

flect○ed, de•flect•
ing.
de•flec•tion
de•flec•tor
De•foe
de•fog v., de•fogged,
de•fog•ging.
de•fog•ger
de•fo•li•ant
de•fo•li•ate v., de•
fo•li•at○ed, de•fo•
li•at•ing.
de•fo•li•a•tion
de•for•est v., de•
for•est○ed, de•for•
est•ing.
de•for•est•a•tion
de•form v., de•
formed, de•form•
ing.
de•for•ma•tion
de•formed
de•form○i•ty n., pl.
de•form○i•ties.
de•frag•ment Com-
puters.
de•frag•men•ta•tion
Computers.
de•fraud v., de•
fraud○ed, de•fraud•
ing.
de•fray v., de•frayed,
de•fray•ing.
de•frost v., de•
frost○ed, de•frost•
ing.
de•frost○er
deft adj., deft○er,
deft○est.
deft○ly
de•funct
de•fuse v., de•fused,
de•fus•ing. (to make
harmless: cf. DIFFUSE)
de○fy n., pl. de•fies;
v., de•fied, de•fy•
ing.

De•gas
de•gas v., de•gassed,
de•gas•sing.
de•gen•er○a•cy
de•gen•er•ate v.,
de•gen•er•at○ed,
de•gen•er•at•ing.
de•gen•er○a•tion
de•gen•er○a•tive
de•grade v., de•
grad○ed, de•grad•
ing.
de•gree (step; aca-
demic title: cf. DECREE)
de•hire Business.
de•hu•man○i•za•
tion
de•hu•man•ize v.,
de•hu•man•ized,
de•hu•man•iz•ing.
de•hu•mid○i•fi○er
de•hu•mid○i•fy v.,
de•hu•mid○i•fied,
de•hu•mid○i•fy•
ing.
de•hy•drate v., de•
hy•drat○ed, de•hy•
drat•ing.
de•hy•dra•tion
de•hy•dra•tor
de•hy•dro•gen•ate
v., de•hy•dro•gen•
at○ed, de•hy•dro•
gen•at•ing.
de•ice or de-ice v.,
de•iced, de•ic•ing.
de•i•fi•ca•tion
de•i○fy v., de•i•fied,
de•i•fy•ing.
deign v., deigned,
deign•ing.
de•ism
de•i○ty n., pl. de•i•
ties.
dé○jà vu
de•ject○ed
de•jec•tion

Del○a•ware (DE) n.,
pl. Del○a•wares,
Del○a•ware.
Del○a•war•e○an
de•lay v., de•layed,
de•lay•ing.
de•lec•ta•ble
de•lec•ta•tion
del○e•gate v., del○e•
gat○ed, del○e•gat•
ing.
del○e•ga•tion
de•lete v., de•let○ed,
de•let•ing.
del○e•te•ri•ous
de•le•tion
delft (pottery)
Delft (the city)
Del○hi
del○i n., pl. del○is.
de•lib•er•ate v., de•
lib•er•at○ed, de•
lib•er•at•ing.
de•lib•er•ate○ly
de•lib•er○a•tion
del○i•ca○cy n., pl.
del○i•ca•cies.
del○i•cate
del○i•cate○ly
del○i•cate•ness
del○i•ca•tes•sen
de•li•cious
de•li•cious○ly
de•li•cious•ness
de•light v., de•
light○ed, de•light•
ing.
de•light○ed
de•light•ful
de•light•ful○ly
de•lim○it v., de•lim•
it○ed, de•lim•it•ing.
de•lim○i•ta•tion
de•lim○i•ta•tive
de•lim○it○er Comput-
ers.

de•lin•e•ate v., de•lin•e•at•ed, de•lin•e•at•ing.
de•lin•e•a•tion
de•lin•quen•cy
de•lin•quent
del•i•quesce v., del•i•quesced, del•i•quesc•ing
del•i•ques•cent
de•lir•i•ous
de•lir•i•ous•ly
de•lir•i•ous•ness
de•lir•i•um n., pl. de•lir•i•ums, de•lir•i•a.
de•list v., de•list•ed, de•list•ing. Business.
de•liv•er v., de•liv•ered, de•liv•er•ing.
de•liv•er•ance
de•liv•ered cost Business.
de•liv•er•y n., pl. de•liv•er•ies.
dell
Del•phi
del•phin•i•um n., pl. del•phin•i•ums, del•phin•i•a.
del•ta n., pl. del•tas.
del•toid
delts n., pl.
de•lude v., de•lud•ed, de•lud•ing.
del•uge v., del•uged, del•ug•ing.
de•lu•sion
de•lu•sive
de•luxe or de luxe
delve v., delved, delv•ing.
delv•er
de•mag•net•i•za•tion
de•mag•net•ize v.,

de•mag•net•ized, de•mag•net•iz•ing.
dem•a•gogue
dem•a•gogu•er•y
dem•a•go•gy
de•mand v., de•mand•ed, de•mand•ing.
demand curve Business.
demand de•pos•it Business.
demand loan Business.
demand note Business.
de•mand-pull Business.
de•mand-side Business.
de•mand•ing•ly
de•mar•cate v., de•mar•cat•ed, de•mar•cat•ing.
de•mar•ca•tion
de•mean v., de•meaned, de•mean•ing.
de•mean•or
de•ment•ed
de•men•tia
de•mer•it
de•mesne
De•me•ter
dem•i•god
dem•i•john
de•mil•i•ta•rize v., de•mil•i•ta•rized, de•mil•i•ta•riz•ing.
dem•i•mon•daine
dem•i•monde
de•mise v., de•mised, de•mis•ing.
dem•i•tasse
dem•o n., pl. dem•os.
de•mo•bi•li•za•tion
de•mo•bi•lize v., de•mo•bi•lized, de•mo•bi•liz•ing.

de•moc•ra•cy n., pl. de•moc•ra•cies.
dem•o•crat
dem•o•crat•ic
Dem•o•crat•ic Par•ty
dem•o•crat•i•cal•ly
de•moc•ra•ti•za•tion
de•moc•ra•tize v., de•moc•ra•tized, de•moc•ra•tiz•ing.
de•mod•u•late v., de•mod•u•lat•ed, de•mod•u•lat•ing.
de•mod•u•la•tion
de•mod•u•la•tor
dem•o•graph•ic
dem•o•graph•ics n., pl.
de•mol•ish v., de•mol•ished, de•mol•ish•ing.
dem•o•li•tion
de•mon
de•mon•e•tize v., de•mon•e•tized, de•mon•e•tiz•ing. Business.
de•mo•ni•ac or de•mo•ni•a•cal
de•mo•ni•a•cal•ly
de•mon•ic
de•mon•stra•ble
de•mon•stra•bly
dem•on•strate v., dem•on•strat•ed, dem•on•strat•ing.
dem•on•stra•tion
de•mon•stra•tive
dem•on•stra•tor
de•mor•al•i•za•tion
de•mor•al•ize v., de•mor•al•ized, de•mor•al•iz•ing.
dem•os¹ (demonstrations)
de•mos² (populace)

De•mos•the•nes
de•mote v., de•
mot∘ed, de•mot•
ing.
de•mo•tion
de•mul•cent
de•mur v., de•
murred, de•mur•
ring. (to object)
de•mure adj., de•
mur∘er, de•mur•est.
de•mure•ly
de•mur•rage Business.
de•mur•rer
den
de•na•tured
den•drite
Deng Xiao•ping
de•ni•a•bil•i•ty
de•ni•a•ble
de•ni•al
de•nier¹ (weight unit)
de•ni•er² (one who de•
nies)
den∘i•grate v.,
den∘i•grat∘ed,
den∘i•grat•ing.
den∘i•gra•tion
den∘im
den∘i•zen
Den•mark
de•nom∘i•nate v.,
de•nom∘i•nat∘ed,
de•nom∘i•nat•ing.
de•nom∘i•na•tion
de•nom∘i•na•tion∘al
de•nom∘i•na•tor
de•no•ta•tion
de•note v., de•
not∘ed, de•not•ing.
de•noue•ment or dé•
noue•ment
de•nounce v., de•
nounced, de•nounc•
ing.
dense adj., dens∘er,
dens•est.

dense•ly
dense•ness
den•si∘ty n., pl. den•
si•ties.
dent v., dent∘ed,
dent•ing.
den•tal
dental floss
den•ti•frice
den•tin or den•tine
den•tist
den•tis•to∘ry
den•ture
de•nu•cle•ar•ized
de•nude v., de•
nud∘ed, de•nud•
ing.
de•nun•ci•a•tion
Den•ver
de∘ny v., de•nied,
de•ny•ing.
de•o•dor•ant
de•o•dor•ize v., de•
o•dor∘ized, de•o•
dor•iz•ing.
de•o•dor•iz∘er
de•ox∘y•ri•bo•
nu•cle∘ic ac∘id
de•part v., de•
part∘ed, de•part•
ing.
de•part•ment
department store
Business.
de•part•men•tal
de•part•men•tal∘i•
za•tion
de•part•men•tal•ize
v., de•part•men•
tal∘ized, de•part•
men•tal•iz•ing.
de•par•ture
de•pend v., de•
pend∘ed, de•pend•
ing.
de•pend•a•bil•i•ty
de•pend•a•ble

de•pend•ence
de•pend•en∘cy n., pl.
de•pend•en•cies.
de•pend•ent
de•per•son•al•ize v.,
de•per•son•al•ized,
de•per•son•al•iz•
ing.
de•pict v., de•
pict∘ed, de•pict•ing.
de•pic•tion
de•pil∘a•to∘ry n., pl.
de•pil∘a•to•ries.
de•plane v., de•
planed, de•plan•ing.
de•plete v., de•
plet∘ed, de•plet•
ing.
de•ple•tion
depletion al•low•
ance Business.
de•plor∘a•ble
de•plore v., de•
plored, de•plor•ing.
de•ploy v , de•
ployed, de•ploy•ing.
de•ploy•ment
de•po•lar∘i•za•tion
de•po•lar•ize v., de•
po•lar•ized, de•po•
lar•iz•ing.
de•po•lit∘i•cize v.,
de•po•lit∘i•cized,
de•po•lit∘i•ciz•ing.
de•po•nent
de•pop•u•late v.,
de•pop∘u•lat∘ed,
de•pop∘u•lat•ing.
de•pop∘u•la•tion
de•port v., de•
port∘ed, de•port•
ing.
de•por•ta•tion
de•port•ment
de•pose v., de•posed,
de•pos•ing.
de•pos•it v., de•pos•

it∘ed, de•pos•it•ing.

dep∘o•si•tion (testimony: cf. DISPOSITION)

de•pos∘i•tor Business.

de•pos∘i•to∘ry n., pl. de•pos∘i•to•ries.

de•pot

de•praved (corrupt: cf. DEPRIVED)

de•prav•i∘ty

dep•re•cate v., dep•re•cat∘ed, dep•re•cat•ing. (to belittle: cf. DEPRECIATE)

dep•re•ca•tion

dep•re•ca•to∘ry

de•pre•ci•a•ble Business.

de•pre•ci•ate v., de•pre•ci•at∘ed, de•pre•ci•at•ing. Business. (to lessen in value: cf. DEPRECATE)

de•pre•ci•a•tion Business.

dep•ri•va•tion

de•prive v., de•prived, de•priv•ing.

de•prived (lacking necessities: cf. DEPRAVED)

de•pro•gram v., de•pro•grammed or de•pro•gramed, de•pro•gram•ming or de•pro•gram•ing.

de•pro•gram∘er or de•pro•gram•mer

dept. (department)

depth

de•pou•ta•tion

de•pute v., de•put∘ed, de•put•ing.

de•pou•tize v., de•pou•tized, de•pou•tiz•ing.

de•pou∘ty n., pl. de•pou•ties.

de•rail v., de•railed, de•rail•ing.

de•rail•leur

de•rail•ment

de•range v., de•ranged, de•rang•ing.

de•range•ment

der∘by n., pl. der•bies.

de•reg∘u•late v., de•reg∘u•lat∘ed, de•reg∘u•lat•ing. Business.

de•reg∘u•la•tion Business.

der∘e•lict

der∘e•lic•tion

de•ride v., de•rid∘ed, de•rid•ing.

de•ri•sion

de•ri•sive

de•ri•sive∘ly

der∘i•va•tion

de•riv∘a•tive

de•rive v., de•rived, de•riv•ing.

derived de•mand Business.

der•ma•ti•tis

der•ma•to•log∘i•cal

der•ma•tol∘o∘gist

der•ma•tol∘o∘gy

der•mis

der∘o•gate v., der∘o•gat∘ed, der∘o•gat•ing.

der∘o•ga•tion

de•rog∘a•to∘ry

der•rick

der•ri•ère or der•ri•ere

der•rin•ger

der•vish

DES (diethylstilbestrol)

Des Moines

de•sal∘i•nate v., de•sal∘i•nat∘ed, de•sal∘i•nat•ing.

de•sal∘i•na•tion

de•salt, v., de•salt∘ed, de•salt•ing.

des•cant or dis•cant v., des•cant∘ed, des•cant•ing.

Des•cartes

de•scend v., de•scend∘ed, de•scend•ing.

de•scend•ant (offspring)

de•scend•ent (falling)

de•scend∘er (part of lowercase letter)

de•scent (downward movement: cf. DECENT; DISSENT)

de•scribe v., de•scribed, de•scrib•ing.

de•scrip•tion

de•scrip•tive

de•scry v., de•scried, de•scry•ing.

des∘e•crate v., des∘e•crat∘ed, des∘e•crat•ing.

des∘e•cra•tion

de•seg•re•gate v., de•seg•re•gat∘ed, de•seg•re•gat•ing.

de•seg•re•ga•tion

de•sen•si•ti•za•tion

de•sen•si•tize v., de•

sen•si•tized, de•
sen•si•tiz•ing.

des•ert[1] (dry place)

de•sert[2] v., de•
sert∘ed, de•sert•
ing. (to run away: cf.
DESSERT)

de•sert∘er

de•serve v., de•
served, de•serv•ing.

de•serv•ed•ly

des•ha•bille

des•ic•cate v., des•
ic•cat∘ed, des•ic•
cat•ing.

des•ic•ca•tion

de•sid•er•a∘tum n.,
pl. de•sid•er•a∘ta.

de•sign v., de•signed,
de•sign•ing.

des•ig•nate v., des•
ig•nat∘ed, des•ig•
nat•ing.

des•ig•na•tion

de•sign∘er

de•sign•ing

de•sir•a•bil•i∘ty

de•sir•a∘ble

de•sir•a•bly

de•sire v., de•sired,
de•sir•ing.

Ie•sir∘ous

Ie•sist v., de•sist∘ed,
de•sist•ing.

desk

desk•top

desktop com•put∘er`
Computers.

desktop con•fig∘u•
ra•tion *Computers.*

desktop pub•lish∘er
Computers.

desktop pub•lish•ing
(DTP) *Computers.*

des∘o•late (forlorn: cf.
DISSOLUTE)

des∘o•lat∘ed

des∘o•late•ly

des∘o•la•tion

de•spair v., de•
spaired, de•spair•
ing.

des•patch v., des•
patched, des•patch•
ing.

des•per∘a∘do n., pl.
des•per∘a•does,
des•per∘a•dos.

des•per•ate (hopeless:
cf. DISPARATE)

des•per•ate•ly

des•per∘a•tion

des•pi∘ca∘ble

de•spise v., de•
spised, de•spis•ing.

de•spite

de•spoil v., de•
spoiled, de•spoil•
ing.

de•spond•en∘cy or
de•spond•ence

de•spond•ent

des•pot

des•pot∘ic

des•pot∘i•cal∘ly

des•pot•ism

des•sert (sweet food:
cf. DESERT)

des•ti•na•tion

destination di•rec•
to∘ry *Computers.*

des•tine v., des•
tined, des•tin•ing.

des•ti∘ny n., pl. des•
ti•nies.

des•ti•tute

des•ti•tut∘ed

des•ti•tu•tion

de•stroy v., de•
stroyed, de•stroy•
ing.

de•stroy∘er

de•struct v., de•

struct∘ed, de•
struct•ing.

de•struc•tion

de•struc•tive

de•struc•tive•ly

de•struc•tive•ness

des•ue•tude

des•ul•to∘ry

de•tach v., de•
tached, de•tach•ing.

de•tach•a∘ble

de•tached

de•tach•ment

de•tail v., de•tailed,
de•tail•ing.

de•tain v., de•tained,
de•tain•ing.

de•tect v., de•
tect∘ed, de•tect•
ing.

de•tect•a∘ble or
de•tect•i∘ble

de•tec•tion

de•tec•tive

de•tec•tor

dé•tente or de•tente

de•ten•tion

de•ter v., de•terred,
de•ter•ring.

de•ter•gent

de•te•ri•o•rate v.,
de•te•ri•o•rat∘ed,
de•te•ri•o•rat•ing.

de•ter•i•o•ra•tion

de•ter•mi•na∘ble

de•ter•mi•nant

de•ter•mi•nate

de•ter•mi•na•tion

de•ter•mine v., de•
ter•mined, de•ter•
min•ing.

de•ter•rence

de•ter•rent

de•test v., de•
test∘ed, de•test•
ing.

de•test•a∘ble

de•tes•ta•tion
de•throne *v.*, de•throned, de•thron•ing.
det•o•nate *v.*, det•o•nat•ed, det•o•nat•ing.
det•o•na•tion
det•o•na•tor
de•tour *v.*, de•toured, de•tour•ing.
de•tox *v.*, de•toxed, de•tox•ing.
de•tox•i•fi•ca•tion
de•tox•i•fy *v.*, de•tox•i•fied, de•tox•i•fy•ing.
de•tract *v.*, de•tract•ed, de•tract•ing. (to take away: cf. DISTRACT)
de•trac•tion
de•trac•tor
det•ri•ment
det•ri•men•tal
de•tri•tus
De•troit
deuce
deu•te•ri•um
Deut•sche mark
de•val•u•a•tion *Business.*
de•val•ue *v.*, de•val•ued, de•val•u•ing.
dev•as•tate *v.*, dev•as•tat•ed, dev•as•tat•ing.
dev•as•ta•tion
de•vel•op *v.*, de•vel•oped, de•vel•op•ing.
de•vel•op•er
de•vel•op•ment
de•vi•ance
de•vi•ant
de•vi•ate *v.*, de•vi•at•ed, de•vi•at•ing.

de•vi•a•tion
de•vi•a•tor
de•vice (contrivance: cf. DEVISE)
de•vice-de•pend•ent *Computers.*
device driv•er *Computers.*
dev•il *v.*, dev•iled or dev•illed, dev•il•ing or dev•il•ling.
dev•il-may-care
dev•il•ish
dev•il•ment
dev•il•try *n.*, *pl.* dev•il•tries.
de•vi•ous
de•vi•ous•ness
de•vise *v.*, de•vised, de•vis•ing. (to work out: cf. DEVICE)
de•vi•see *Business.*
de•vi•sor *Business.*
de•vi•tal•ize *v.*, de•vi•tal•ized, de•vi•tal•iz•ing.
de•void
de•volve *v.*, de•volved, de•volv•ing.
de•vote *v.*, de•vot•ed, de•vot•ing.
de•vot•ed•ly
dev•o•tee
de•vo•tion
de•vo•tion•al
de•vour *v.*, de•voured, de•vour•ing.
de•vout *adj.*, de•vout•er, de•vout•est.
de•vout•ly
dew (moisture: cf. DO; DUE)
dew•ber•ry, *n.*, *pl.* dew•ber•ries.
dew•claw

dew•drop
dew•lap
dew•y *adj.*, dew•i•er, dew•i•est.
dex•ter•i•ty
dex•ter•ous
dex•trose
Dha•ka or Dac•ca
dho•ti *n.*, *pl.* dho•tis.
di•a•be•tes
di•a•bet•ic
di•a•bol•ic or di•a•bol•i•cal
di•a•bol•i•cal•ly
di•a•crit•ic
di•a•dem
di•ag•nose *n.*, *pl.* di•ag•nos•es; *v.*, di•ag•nosed, di•ag•nos•ing.
di•ag•no•sis *n.*, *pl.* di•ag•no•ses.
di•ag•nos•tic
di•ag•nos•ti•cian
di•ag•o•nal
di•ag•o•nal•ly
di•a•gram *v.*, di•a•gramed or di•a•grammed, di•a•gram•ing or di•a•gram•ming.
di•al *v.*, di•aled or di•alled, di•al•ing or di•al•ling.
di•a•lect
di•a•lec•tal (of a dialect)
di•a•lec•tic (logical debate)
di•a•lec•ti•cal
di•a•logue or di•a•log
dialogue box *Computers.*
di•al•y•sis *n.*, *pl.* di•al•y•ses.
di•am•e•ter

di•a•met•ri•cal or
 di•a•met•ric
di•a•met•ri•cal•ly
dia•mond
dia•mond•back
Di•an•a
di•a•pa•son
dia•per v., dia•pered,
 dia•per•ing.
di•aph•a•nous
di•a•phragm
di•a•phrag•mat•ic
di•a•rist
di•ar•rhe•a or di•ar•
 rhoe•a
di•a•ry n., pl. di•a•
 ries. (journal: cf.
 DAIRY)
Di•as•po•ra
di•as•to•le
di•as•tol•ic
di•a•tom
di•a•ton•ic
di•a•tribe
di•az•o•e•pam
dib•ble, n., v., dib•
 bled, dib•bling.
dice n., pl. die; v.,
 diced, dic•ing.
di•chot•o•my n., pl.
 di•chot•o•mies.
dick
Dick•ens
dick•er v., dick•ered,
 dick•er•ing.
Dick•in•son
di•cot•y•le•don
di•cot•y•le•don•ous
Dic•ta•phone Trade-
 mark.
dic•tate v., dic•
 tat•ed, dic•tat•ing.
dic•ta•tion
dic•ta•tor
dic•ta•to•ri•al
dic•ta•tor•ship

dic•tion
dic•tion•ar•y n., pl.
 dic•tion•ar•ies.
dic•tum n., pl. dic•ta,
 dic•tums.
did
di•dac•tic
did•dle v., did•dled,
 did•dling.
di•o•do n., pl. di•dos,
 di•does.
die[1] n., pl. dice. (cube)
die[2] n., pl. dies. (device
 for forming or cutting
 material)
die[3] v., died, dy•ing.
 (to cease living: cf.
 DYE)
die-hard or die•hard
di•e•lec•tric
di•er•o•e•sis or di•
 aer•o•e•sis n., pl. di•
 er•o•e•ses.
di•e•o•ret•ic (of a diere-
 sis: cf. DIURETIC)
die•sel
di•o•et v., di•et•ed, di•
 et•ing.
di•e•tar•y
di•et•er
di•e•tet•ic
di•eth•yl•stil•bes•
 trol (DES)
di•e•ti•tian or di•
 e•ti•cian
dif•fer v., dif•fered,
 dif•fer•ing. (to disa-
 gree: cf. DEFER)
dif•fer•ence (unlike-
 ness: cf. DEFERENCE)
dif•fer•ent
dif•fer•en•tial
differential cost Busi-
 ness.
dif•fer•en•ti•ate v.,
 dif•fer•en•ti•at•ed,

dif•fer•en•ti•at•
 ing.
dif•fer•en•ti•a•tion
dif•fer•ent•ly
dif•fi•cult
dif•fi•cul•ty n., pl.
 dif•fi•cul•ties.
dif•fi•dence
dif•fi•dent
dif•frac•tion
dif•fuse[1] v., dif•
 fused, dif•fus•ing.
dif•fuse[2] (widely
 spread: cf. DEFUSE)
dif•fuse•ly
dif•fuse•ness
dif•fu•sion
dig v., dug, dig•ging.
di•gest v., di•
 gest•ed, di•gest•
 ing.
di•gest•i•ble
di•ges•tion
di•ges•tive
dig•ger
dig•it
dig•it•al Computers.
digital au•di•o•tape
 (DAT)
digital com•put•er
 Computers.
digital mon•i•tor
 Computers.
dig•i•tal•is
dig•it•al•ly
dig•i•tize v., dig•i•
 tized, dig•i•tiz•ing.
 Computers.
dig•i•tiz•er Comput-
 ers.
dig•i•tiz•ing tab•let
 Computers.
dig•ni•fied
dig•ni•fy v., dig•ni•
 fied, dig•ni•fy•ing.
dig•ni•tar•y n., pl.
 dig•ni•tar•ies.

dig•ni•ty *n., pl.* dig•ni•ties.

di•graph

di•gress *v.,* di•gressed, di•gress•ing.

di•gres•sion

dike

di•lap•i•dat•ed

di•lap•i•da•tion

di•late *v.,* di•lat•ed, di•lat•ing.

di•la•tion

dil•a•to•ry

di•lem•ma *n., pl.* di•lem•mas.

dil•et•tante *n., pl.* dil•et•tantes or dil•et•tan•ti.

dil•et•tant•ism

dil•i•gence

dil•i•gent

dil•i•gent•ly

dill

dil•ly *n., pl.* dil•lies.

dil•ly•dal•ly *v.,* dil•ly•dal•lied, dil•ly•dal•ly•ing.

di•lute *v.,* di•lut•ed, di•lut•ing.

di•lu•tion

dim *v.,* dimmed, dim•ming; *adj.,* dim•mer, dim•mest.

dime

di•men•sion

di•men•sion•al

di•min•ish *v.,* di•min•ished, di•min•ish•ing.

di•min•u•en•do *n., pl.* di•min•u•en•does.

dim•i•nu•tion

di•min•u•tive

dim•i•ty

dim•ly

dim•mer

dim•ness

dim•ple *v.,* dim•pled, dim•pling.

dim sum

dim•wit

dim•wit•ted

din *v.,* dinned, din•ning.

di•nar

dine *v.,* dined, din•ing.

din•er (person eating: cf. DINNER)

di•nette

ding *v.,* dinged, ding•ing.

ding-a-ling

din•ghy *n., pl.* din•ghies. (boat: cf. DINGY)

din•gi•ness

din•go *n., pl.* din•goes.

ding•us, *n., pl.* ding•us•es.

din•gy *adj.,* din•gi•er, din•gi•est. (dull: cf. DINGHY)

dink•y

din•ner (meal: cf. DINER)

din•ner•ware

di•no•saur

dint

di•oc•e•san

di•o•cese

di•ode

Di•og•e•nes

Di•o•ny•sus or Di•o•ny•sos

di•o•ram•a *n., pl.* di•o•ram•as.

di•ox•in

dip *v.,* dipped, dip•ping.

DIP switch *Computers.*

(dual in-line package switch)

diph•the•ri•a

diph•thong

dip•loid

di•plo•ma *n., pl.* di•plo•mas.

di•plo•ma•cy

dip•lo•mat

dip•lo•mat•ic

dip•lo•mat•i•cal•ly

dip•ole

dip•per

dip•py *v.,* dip•pi•er, dip•pi•est.

dip•so•ma•ni•a

dip•so•ma•ni•ac

dip•stick

dip•tych

dire

di•rect *v.,* di•rect•ed, di•rect•ing.

di•rect-con•nect mo•dem *Computers.*

direct cost *Business.*

direct cost•ing *Business.*

direct de•pos•it *Business.*

direct mail *Business.*

direct mar•ket•ing *Business.*

direct mem•o•ry ac•cess (DMA) *Computers.*

direct tax *Business.*

di•rec•tion

di•rec•tion•al

di•rec•tive

di•rect•ly

di•rect•ness

di•rec•tor

di•rec•to•rate

di•rec•tor•ship

di•rec•to•ry *n., pl.* di•rec•to•ries.

dirge

dir•i•gi•ble

dirk

dirn•dl

dirt

dirt-cheap

dirt•i•ness

dirt•y *v.*, dirt•ied, dirt•y•ing;. *adj.*, dirt•i•er dirt•i•est.

dis, *n., v.,* dissed, dis• ing.

dis•a•bil•i•ty *n., pl.* dis•a•bil•i•ties.

disability ben•e•fit *Business.*

disability in•sur•ance *Business.*

dis•a•ble *v.*, dis• a•bled, dis•a•bling.

dis•a•buse *v.*, dis• a•bused, dis•a•bus• ing.

dis•ad•van•tage

dis•ad•van•taged

dis•ad•van•ta•geous

dis•af•fect•ed

dis•af•fec•tion

dis•af•fil•i•ate *v.*, dis•af•fil•i•at•ed, dis•af•fil•i•at•ing.

dis•af•fil•i•a•tion

dis•a•gree *v.*, dis• a•greed, dis• a•gree•ing.

dis•a•gree•a•ble

dis•a•gree•a•bly

dis•a•gree•ment

dis•al•low *v.*, dis•al• lowed, dis•al•low• ing.

dis•ap•pear *v.*, dis• ap•peared, dis•ap• pear•ing.

dis•ap•pear•ance

dis•ap•point *v.*, dis•

ap•point•ed, dis• ap•point•ing.

dis•ap•point•ment

dis•ap•pro•ba•tion

dis•ap•prov•al

dis•ap•prove *v.*, dis• ap•proved, dis•ap• prov•ing. (to con- demn: cf. DISPROVE)

dis•ap•prov•ing•ly

dis•arm *v.*, dis• armed, dis•arm•ing.

dis•ar•ma•ment

dis•arm•ing

dis•arm•ing•ly

dis•ar•range *v.*, dis• ar•ranged, dis•ar• rang•ing.

dis•ar•range•ment

dis•ar•ray

dis•as•sem•ble *v.*, dis•as•sem•bled, dis•as•sem•bling. (to take apart: cf. DIS- SEMBLE)

dis•as•so•ci•ate *v.*, dis•as•so•ci•at•ed, dis•as•so•ci•at•ing.

dis•as•ter

dis•as•trous

dis•a•vow *v.*, dis• a•vowed, dis• a•vow•ing.

dis•a•vow•al

dis•band *v.*, dis• band•ed, dis•band• ing.

dis•bar *v.*, dis•barred, dis•bar•ring.

dis•bar•ment

dis•be•lief

dis•be•lieve *v.*, dis• be•lieved, dis•be• liev•ing.

dis•burse *v.*, dis• bursed, dis•burs•

ing. (to pay out: cf. DISPERSE)

dis•burse•ment

disc or disk

dis•card *v.*, dis• card•ed, dis•card• ing.

dis•cern *v.*, dis• cerned, dis•cern• ing.

dis•cern•a•ble or dis•cern•i•ble

dis•cern•ment

dis•charge *v.*, dis• charged, dis•charg• ing.

dis•ci•ple

dis•ci•pli•nar•i•an

dis•ci•pli•nar•y

dis•ci•pline *v.*, dis•ci• plined, dis•ci•plin• ing.

dis•claim *v.*, dis• claimed, dis•claim• ing.

dis•claim•er

dis•close *v.*, dis• closed, dis•clos•ing.

dis•clo•sure

disclosure a•gree• ment *Business.*

dis•co *n., pl.* dis•cos; *v.*, dis•coed, dis•co• ing.

dis•col•or *v.*, dis•col• ored, dis•col•or• ing.

dis•col•or•a•tion

dis•com•bob•u•late, *v.*, dis•com•bob•u• lat•ed, dis•com• bob•u•lat•ing.

dis•com•fit *v.*, dis• com•fit•ed, dis• com•fit•ing. (to frus- trate)

dis•com•fort (uneasi-
ness)
dis•com•mode v.,
dis•com•mod•ed,
dis•com•mod•ing.
dis•com•pose v., dis•
com•posed, dis•
com•pos•ing.
dis•com•po•sure
dis•con•cert v., dis•
con•cert•ed, dis•
con•cert•ing.
dis•con•nect v., dis•
con•nect•ed, dis•
con•nect•ing.
dis•con•nec•tion
dis•con•so•late
dis•con•so•late•ly
dis•con•tent v., dis•
con•tent•ed, dis•
con•tent•ing.
dis•con•tent•ed
dis•con•tin•u•ance
dis•con•tin•u•a•tion
dis•con•tin•ue v.,
dis•con•tin•ued,
dis•con•tin•u•ing.
dis•con•ti•nu•i•ty
n., pl. dis•con•ti•
nu•i•ties.
dis•cord
dis•cord•ant
dis•co•thèque or dis•
co•thèque
dis•count v., dis•
count•ed, dis•
count•ing.
discount house Busi-
ness.
discount store Busi-
ness.
dis•coun•te•nance v.,
dis•coun•te•nanced,
dis•coun•te•nanc•
ing.
dis•cour•age v., dis•

cour•aged, dis•
cour•ag•ing.
dis•cour•age•ment
dis•cour•ag•ing•ly
dis•course v., dis•
coursed, dis•cours•
ing.
dis•cour•te•ous
dis•cour•te•sy n., pl.
dis•cour•te•sies.
dis•cov•er v., dis•
cov•ered, dis•cov•
er•ing.
dis•cov•er•er
dis•cov•er•y n., pl.
dis•cov•er•ies.
dis•cred•it v., dis•
cred•it•ed, dis•
cred•it•ing.
dis•cred•it•a•ble
dis•creet (prudent: cf.
DISCRETE)
dis•creet•ly
dis•crep•an•cy n., pl.
dis•crep•an•cies.
dis•crep•ant
dis•crete (separate: cf.
DISCREET)
discrete speech sys•
tem Computers.
dis•cre•tion
dis•cre•tion•ar•y
discretionary ac•
count Business.
dis•crim•i•nate v.,
dis•crim•i•nat•ed,
dis•crim•i•nat•ing.
dis•crim•i•nat•ing
dis•crim•i•na•tion
dis•crim•i•na•tor•y
dis•cur•sive
dis•cus n., pl. dis•
cus•es.
dis•cuss v., dis•
cussed, dis•cuss•ing.
dis•cus•sant
dis•cus•sion

dis•dain v., dis•
dained, dis•dain•
ing.
dis•dain•ful
dis•ease
dis•eased (sick: cf. DE-
CEASED)
dis•em•bark v., dis•
em•barked, dis•em•
bark•ing.
dis•em•bar•ka•tion
dis•em•bod•ied
dis•em•bod•i•ment
dis•em•bod•y, v.,
dis•em•bod•ied,
dis•em•bod•y•ing.
dis•em•bow•el v.,
dis•em•bow•eled or
dis•em•bow•elled,
dis•em•bow•el•ing
or dis•em•bow•el•
ling.
dis•en•chant v., dis•
en•chant•ed, dis•
en•chant•ing.
dis•en•chant•ment
dis•en•cum•ber v.,
dis•en•cum•bered,
dis•en•cum•ber•
ing.
dis•en•gage v., dis•
en•gaged, dis•en•
gag•ing.
dis•en•gage•ment
dis•en•tan•gle v.,
dis•en•tan•gled,
dis•en•tan•gling.
dis•es•tab•lish v.,
dis•es•tab•lished,
dis•es•tab•lish•ing.
dis•es•tab•lish•ment
dis•es•teem, v., dis•
es•teemed, dis•es•
teem•ing.
dis•fa•vor v., dis•fa•
vored, dis•fa•vor•
ing.

dis•fig•ure v., dis•
fig•ured, dis•fig•
ur•ing.
dis•fig•ure•ment
dis•fran•chise or dis•
en•fran•chise v.,
dis•fran•chised, dis•
fran•chis•ing.
dis•fran•chise•ment
dis•gorge v., dis•
gorged, dis•gorg•
ing.
dis•grace v., dis•
graced, dis•grac•
ing.
dis•grace•ful
dis•grace•ful•ly
dis•grun•tled
dis•guise v., dis•
guised, dis•guis•ing.
dis•gust
dis•gust•ed
dis•gust•ing
dish v., dished, dish•
ing.
dis•ha•bille or des•
ha•bille
dis•har•mo•ny n., pl.
dis•har•mo•nies.
dish•cloth
dis•heart•en v., dis•
heart•ened, dis•
heart•en•ing.
di•shev•eled or di•
shev•elled
di•shev•el•ment
dis•hon•est
dis•hon•est•ly
dis•hon•es•ty
dis•hon•or v., dis•
heart•ored, dis•
heart•or•ing.
dis•hon•or•a•ble
dish•pan
dish•rag
dish•tow•el
dish•wash•er

dis•il•lu•sion v., dis•
il•lusioned, dis•il•
lu•sion•ing.
dis•il•lu•sion•ment
dis•in•clined
dis•in•fect v., dis•in•
fect•ed, dis•in•fect•
ing.
dis•in•fect•ant
dis•in•flate v., dis•
in•flat•ed, dis•in•
flat•ing. Business.
dis•in•fla•tion Busi-
ness.
dis•in•gen•u•ous
dis•in•her•it v., dis•
in•her•it•ed, dis•
in•her•it•ing.
dis•in•te•grate v.,
dis•in•te•grat•ed,
dis•in•te•grat•ing.
dis•in•te•gra•tion
dis•in•ter v., dis•in•
terred, dis•in•ter•
ring.
dis•in•ter•est•ed
dis•in•vest•ment
Business.
dis•joint•ed
disk Computers.
disk cache Computers.
disk crash Computers.
disk drive Computers.
disk jock•ey (DJ)
disk op•er•at•ing
sys•tem (DOS) Com-
puters.
disk op•ti•miz•er
Computers.
disk pack Computers.
disk•ette
dis•like v., dis•liked,
dis•lik•ing.
dis•lo•cate v., dis•lo•
cat•ed, dis•lo•cat•
ing.
dis•lo•ca•tion

dis•lodge v., dis•
lodged, dis•lodg•
ing.
dis•loy•al
dis•loy•al•ty
dis•mal
dis•mal•ly
dis•man•tle v., dis•
man•tled, dis•man•
tling.
dis•may v., dis•
mayed, dis•may•
ing.
dis•mem•ber v., dis•
mem•bered, dis•
mem•ber•ing.
dis•mem•ber•ment
dis•miss v., dis•
missed, dis•miss•
ing.
dis•miss•al
dis•mount v., dis•
mount•ed, dis•
mount•ing.
Dis•ney
dis•o•be•di•ence
dis•o•be•di•ent
dis•o•bey v., dis•
o•beyed, dis•
o•bey•ing.
dis•o•blige v., dis•
o•bliged, dis•
o•blig•ing.
dis•or•der v., dis•or•
dered, dis•or•der•
ing.
dis•or•der•li•ness
dis•or•der•ly
dis•or•gan•i•za•tion
dis•or•gan•ize v.,
dis•or•gan•ized,
dis•or•gan•iz•ing.
dis•o•ri•ent v., dis•
o•ri•ent•ed, dis•
o•ri•ent•ing.
dis•o•ri•en•ta•tion
dis•own v., dis•

owned, dis•own•
ing.

dis•par•age v., dis•
par•aged, dis•par•
ag•ing.

dis•par•age•ment

dis•par•ag•ing

dis•pa•rate (different:
cf. DESPERATE)

dis•par•i•ty

dis•pas•sion•ate

dis•pas•sion•ate•ly

dis•patch v., dis•
patched, dis•patch•
ing.

dis•patch∘er Business.

dis•pel v., dis•pelled,
dis•pel•ling.

dis•pen•sa•ble

dis•pen•sa∘ry n., pl.
dis•pen•sa•ries.

dis•pen•sa•tion

dis•pense v., dis•
pensed, dis•pens•
ing.

dis•pens∘er

dis•per•sal

dis•perse v., dis•
persed, dis•pers•
ing. (to scatter: cf. DIS-
BURSE)

dis•per•sion

dis•pir•it∘ed

dis•pir•it•ing

dis•place v., dis•
placed, dis•plac•ing.

dis•place•ment

dis•play v., dis•
played, dis•play•
ing.

display ad Business.

dis•please v., dis•
pleased, dis•pleas•
ing.

dis•pleas•ure

dis•port v., dis•

port∘ed, dis•port•
ing.

dis•pos•a•bil•i•ty

dis•pos•a•ble

disposable in•come
Business.

dis•pos∘al

dis•pose v., dis•
posed, dis•pos•ing.

dis•po•si•tion (tem-
perament: cf. DEPOSI-
TION)

dis•pos•sess v., dis•
pos•sessed, dis•
pos•sess•ing.

dis•pro•por•tion

dis•pro•por•tion•ate

dis•pro•por•tioned

dis•prov•a•ble

dis•prove v., dis•
proved, dis•prov•
ing. (to refute: cf. DIS-
APPROVE)

dis•put•a•ble

dis•pu•tant

dis•pu•ta•tion

dis•pu•ta•tious or
dis•put∘a•tive

dis•pu•ta•tious•ly

dis•pute v., dis•
put∘ed, dis•put•ing.

dis•qual•i•fi•ca•tion

dis•qual•i•fy v., dis•
qual•i•fied, dis•
qual•i•fy•ing.

dis•qui•et v., dis•
qui•et∘ed, dis•qui•
et•ing.

dis•qui•si•tion

dis•re•gard v., dis•
re•gard∘ed, dis•re•
gard•ing.

dis•re•pair

dis•rep∘u•ta•ble

dis•re•pute

dis•re•spect v., dis•

re•spect∘ed, dis•re•
spect•ing.

dis•re•spect•ful

dis•robe v., dis•
robed, dis•rob•ing.

dis•rupt v., dis•
rupt∘ed, dis•rupt•
ing.

dis•rup•tion

dis•rup•tive

dis•sat•is•fac•tion

dis•sat•is•fied

dis•sat•is•fy, v., dis•
sat•is•fied, dis•sat•
is•fy•ing.

dis•sect v., dis•
sect∘ed, dis•sect•
ing.

dis•sec•tion

dis•sem•ble v., dis•
sem•bled, dis•sem•
bling. (to disguise: cf.
DISASSEMBLE)

dis•sem•bler

dis•sem∘i•nate v.,
dis•sem•nat∘ed,
dis•sem•nat•ing.

dis•sem∘i•na•tion

dis•sen•sion

dis•sent[1] (disagree-
ment: cf. DECENT; DE-
SCENT)

dis•sent[2] v., dis•
sent∘ed, dis•sent•
ing.

dis•sent∘er

dis•ser•ta•tion

dis•serv•ice

dis•sev∘er, v., dis•
sev•ered, dis•sev•
er•ing.

dis•si•dence

dis•si•dent

dis•sim∘i•lar

dis•si•mil∘i•tude

dis•sim∘u•late v.,

dis•sim•u•lat•ed,
dis•sim•u•lat•ing.
dis•sim•u•la•tion
dis•si•pate v., dis•si•
pat•ed, dis•si•pat•
ing.
dis•si•pa•tion
dis•so•ci•ate v., dis•
so•ci•at•ed, dis•so•
ci•at•ing.
dis•so•ci•a•tion
dis•so•lute (immoral:
cf. DESOLATE)
dis•so•lute•ness
dis•so•lu•tion
dis•solve v., dis•
solved, dis•solv•ing.
dis•so•nance
dis•so•nant
dis•suade v., dis•
suad•ed, dis•suad•
ing.
dis•taff
dis•tal
dis•tance v., dis•
tanced, dis•tanc•
ing.
dis•tant
dis•tant•ly
dis•taste
dis•taste•ful
dis•tem•per
dis•tend v., dis•
tend•ed, dis•tend•
ing.
dis•ten•tion
dis•till v., dis•tilled,
dis•till•ing.
dis•til•late
dis•til•la•tion
dis•till•er
dis•till•er•y n., pl.
dis•till•er•ies.
dis•tinct
dis•tinc•tion
dis•tinc•tive
dis•tinc•tive•ly

dis•tinc•tive•ness
dis•tinct•ly
dis•tin•guish v., dis•
tin•guished, dis•
tin•guish•ing.
dis•tin•guish•a•ble
dis•tin•guished
dis•tort v., dis•
tort•ed, dis•tort•
ing.
dis•tor•tion
dis•tract v., dis•
tract•ed, dis•tract•
ing. (to divert: cf. DE-
TRACT)
dis•trac•tion
dis•trait
dis•traught
dis•tress v., dis•
tressed, dis•tress•
ing.
distress sale Business.
dis•trib•ute v., dis•
trib•ut•ed, dis•trib•
ut•ing.
distributed da•ta•
base Computers.
distributed proc•ess•
ing Computers.
dis•tri•bu•tion
dis•trib•u•tor
dis•trict
Dis•trict of Co•lum•
bi•a (D.C.)
dis•trust v., dis•
trust•ed, dis•trust•
ing.
dis•trust•ful
dis•turb v., dis•
turbed, dis•turb•
ing.
dis•turb•ance
dis•u•nite v., dis•
u•nit•ed, dis•u•nit•
ing.
dis•u•ni•ty
dis•use

ditch v., ditched,
ditch•ing.
dith•er v., dith•ered,
dith•er•ing.
dit•to n., pl. dit•tos;
v., dit•toed, dit•to•
ing.
dit•ty n., pl. dit•ties.
ditz
di•u•ret•ic (increasing
urine volume: cf. DIE-
RETIC)
di•ur•nal
di•ur•nal•ly
di•va n., pl. di•vas.
di•va•lent
di•van
dive n., pl. dives; v.,
dived or dove, dived,
div•ing. (plunges)
div•er
di•verge v., di•
verged, di•verg•ing.
di•ver•gence
di•ver•gent
di•vers (several)
di•verse (unlike)
di•verse•ly
di•ver•si•fi•ca•tion
di•ver•si•fy v., di•
ver•si•fied, di•ver•
si•fy•ing.
di•ver•sion
di•ver•sion•ar•y
di•ver•si•ty
di•vert v., di•vert•ed,
di•vert•ing.
di•ver•tic•u•li•tis
Di•ves (rich man)
di•vest v., di•vest•ed,
di•vest•ing.
di•vest•i•ture Busi-
ness.
di•vid•a•ble
di•vide v., di•vid•ed,
di•vid•ing.
div•i•dend Business.

di•vid•er

div•i•na•tion

di•vine v., di•vined, di•vin•ing;. adj., di•vin•er di•vin•est.

di•vine•ly

di•vin•er

di•vin•ing rod

di•vin•i•ty n., pl. di•vin•i•ties.

di•vis•i•bil•i•ty

di•vis•i•ble

di•vi•sion

di•vi•sion•al

di•vi•sive

di•vi•sive•ly

di•vi•sive•ness

di•vi•sor

di•vorce v., di•vorced, di•vorc•ing. (dissolution of marriage)

di•vor•cé (divorced man)

di•vor•cée or di•vor•cee (divorced woman).

div•ot

di•vulge v., di•vulged, di•vulg•ing.

div•vy n., pl. div•vies; v., div•vied, div•vy•ing.

Dix•ie

Dix•ie•land

diz•zi•ly

diz•zi•ness

diz•zy adj., diz•zi•er, diz•zi•est.

diz•zy•ing

D.J. (disk jockey)

djel•la•bah or djel•la•ba n., pl. djel•la•bahs or djel•la•bas.

Dji•bou•ti

DMA Computers. (direct memory access)

DNA (carrier of genes)

DNA fin•ger•print•ing

Dnie•per or Dne•pr

do¹ v., did, done, do•ing, does. (to act: cf. DEW; DUE).

do² n., pl. dos, do's. (party)

do³ n., pl. dos. (musical tone: cf. DOE; DOUGH)

do-good•er

do-it-your•self

do-it-your•self•er

do•a•ble

Do•ber•man pin•scher

doc

do•cent

doc•ile

do•cil•i•ty

dock v., docked, dock•ing.

dock•et v., dock•et•ed, dock•et•ing.

dock•o•min•i•um

dock•yard

doc•tor v., doc•tored, doc•tor•ing.

doc•tor•al

doc•tor•ate

doc•tri•naire

doc•tri•nal

doc•trine

doc•u•dra•ma

doc•u•ment v., doc•u•ment•ed, doc•u•ment•ing.

doc•u•men•ta•ry n., pl. doc•u•men•ta•ries.

doc•u•men•ta•tion

dod•der•ing

dodge v., dodged, dodg•ing.

Dodg•ers

DNA (carrier of genes)

do•do n., pl. do•dos, do•does.

doe n., pl. does, doe. (deer: cf. DO; DOUGH)

do•er

does

doe•skin

does•n't

doff v., doffed, doff•ing.

dog v., dogged, dog•ging. (did dog)

dog-tired

dog•catch•er

dog•eared

dog•fight

dog•fish n., pl. dog•fish or dog•fish•es.

dog•ged (stubborn)

dog•ged•ly

dog•ger•el

dog•gone adj., dog•gon•est.

dog•goned

dog•gy or dog•gie, n., pl. dog•gies. (small dog)

doggy bag

dog•house n., pl. dog•hous•es.

do•gie or do•gey, n., pl. dog•gies or dog•geys. (motherless calf)

dog•leg

dog•ma n., pl. dog•mas.

dog•mat•ic or dog•mat•i•cal

dog•mat•i•cal•ly

dog•ma•tism

dog•trot v., dog•trot•ted, dog•trot•ting.

dog•wood

doi•ly n., pl. doi•lies.

do•ing

Dol•by Trademark.

dol•drums *n.*, *pl.* dol•
drums.

dole *v.*, doled, dol•
ing.

dole•ful

dole•ful•ly

doll

dol•lar

dol•lar-a-year man
Business.

dol•lar•i•za•tion

dol•lop

dol•ly *n.*, *pl.* dol•lies;
v., dol•lied, dol•ly•
ing.

dol•men

do•lo•mite

do•lor•ous

do•lor•ous•ly

dol•phin

dolt

dolt•ish

do•main

dome

do•mes•tic

domestic cor•po•ra•
tion *Business.*

do•mes•ti•cal•ly

do•mes•ti•cate *v.*,
do•mes•ti•cat•ed,
do•mes•ti•cat•ing.

do•mes•ti•ca•tion

do•mes•tic•i•ty

dom•i•cile

dom•i•nance

dom•i•nant

dom•i•nate *v.*,
dom•i•nat•ed,
dom•i•nat•ing.

dom•i•na•tion

dom•i•neer

dom•i•neer•ing

Dom•i•ni•ca

Do•min•i•can Re•
pub•lic

do•min•ion

dom•i•no *n.*, *pl.*
dom•i•noes.

don *v.*, donned, don•
ning.

Don Quix•o•te

do•ña *n.*, *pl.* do•ñas.

do•ña *n.*, *pl.* do•ñas.

do•nate *v.*, do•
nat•ed, do•nat•ing.

do•na•tion

done (finished: cf. DUN)

don•key *n.*, *pl.* don•
keys.

Donne

don•ny•brook

do•nor

don't

do•nut

doo•dad

doo•dle *v.*, doo•dled,
doo•dling.

doo•fus, *n.*, *pl.* doo•
fus•es.

doom *v.*, doomed,
doom•ing.

dooms•day

door

door•bell

door•man *n.*, *pl.*
door•men.

door•mat

door•step

door•way

door•yard

dope *v.*, doped, dop•
ing.

dope•y or dop•y *adj.*,
dop•i•er, dop•i•est.

Dor•ic

dorm

dor•man•cy

dor•mant

dor•mer

dor•mi•to•ry *n.*, *pl.*
dor•mi•to•ries.

dor•mouse *n.*, *pl.*
dor•mice.

dor•sal

do•ry *n.*, *pl.* do•ries.

DOS *Computers.* (disk
operating system)

dos and don'ts

dos•age

dose *v.*, dosed, dos•
ing.

do•sim•e•ter

dos•si•er

dost

Dos•to•ev•sky or
Dos•to•yev•sky

dot *v.*, dot•ted, dot•
ting.

dot-ma•trix print•er
Computers.

dot•age

dote *v.*, dot•ed, dot•
ing.

doth

dot•ing

dot•ing•ly

dot pitch *Computers.*

dot•ty *adj.*, dot•ti•er,
dot•ti•est.

Dou•ay Bi•ble

dou•ble *v.*, dou•bled,
dou•bling.

dou•ble-bar•reled

dou•ble-blind

dou•ble-breast•ed

dou•ble-breast•ing

dou•ble-click *Comput-
ers.*

dou•ble-cross *v.*,
dou•ble-crossed,
dou•ble-cross•ing.

dou•ble-cross•er

double date *n.*

dou•ble-date *v.*,
dou•ble-dat•ed,
dou•ble-dat•ing.

dou•ble-deal•ing

dou•ble-deck•er

dou○ble-den○si○ty *Computers.*
dou○ble-dip○ping
double en○ten○dre *n.,* *pl.* double en○ten○dres.
dou○ble-en○try *Business.*
double in○dem○ni○ty *Business.*
dou○ble-joint○ed
double knit *n.*
dou○ble-knit *adj.*
dou○ble-•pre○ci○sion *Computers.*
dou○ble-reed
dou○ble-sid○ed *Computers.*
dou○ble-space *v.,* dou○ble-spaced, dou○ble-spac○ing.
dou○ble-talk
double tax•a•tion *Business.*
dou○ble•head○er
dou•blet
dou•bloon
dou•bly
doubt *v.,* doubt○ed, doubt•ing.
doubt○er
doubt•ful
doubt•ful○ly
doubt•less
doubt•less○ly
douche *v.,* douched, douch•ing.
dough (bread mixture: cf. DO; DOE)
dough•nut or do•nut
dough○ty *adj.,* dough•ti○er, dough•ti○est.
Doug○las fir
dour
dour•ness
douse or dowse *v.,*

doused or dowsed, dous○ing or dows•ing.
dove
Do•ver
dove•tail *v.,* dove•tailed, dove•tail○ing.
Dow Jones *Business.*
dow○a•ger
dow•di•ness
dow○dy *adj.,* dow•di○er, dow•di○est.
dow○el
dow•eled or dow•elled
dow○er *v.,* dow•ered, dow•er•ing.
down[1]
down[2] *v.,* downed, down•ing.
down-and-dirt○y
down-home
down pay•ment *Business.*
down-to-earth
down•beat
down•cast
down○er
down•fall
down•grade *v.,* down•grad○ed, down•grad•ing.
down•heart○ed
down•hill
down•load *Computers.*
down•load•a○ble *Computers.*
down•mar○ket *Business.*
down•pour
down•right
Down's syn•drome
down•scale *v.,* down•scaled, down•scal•ing. *Business.*

down•size, *v.,* down•sized, down•siz○ing.
down•stage
down•stairs
down•state
down•stream
down•swing
down•tick *Business.*
down•town
down•trod•den
down•turn
down•ward
down•ward-com○pat○i○ble *Computers.*
down•wind
down○y *adj.,* down•i○er, down•i○est.
dow○ry *n., pl.* dow•ries.
dowse *v.,* dowsed, dows•ing.
dox•ol○o○gy *n., pl.* dox•ol○o○gies.
doy○en *n., pl.* doy•ens.
doze *v.,* dozed, doz•ing.
doz○en *n., pl.* doz•ens, doz○en.
dpi *Computers.* (dots per inch)
Dr. *n., pl.* Drs. (doctor)
drab *adj.,* drab•ber, drab•best.
drab•ness
drach○ma *n., pl.* drach•mas drach•mae.
draft[1] (plan: cf. DRAUGHT; DROUGHT)
draft[2] *v.,* draft○ed, draft•ing.
draft mode *Computers.*
draft○ee
draft○i•ness

drafts•man *n.*, *pl.* drafts•men.

drafts•man•ship

draft◦y *adj.*, draft•i◦er, draft•i•est.

drag *v.*, dragged, drag•ging.

drag◦gy *adj.*, drag•gi◦er, drag•gi•est.

drag•net

drag◦o•man *n.*, *pl.* drag◦o•mans, drag◦o•men.

drag◦on

drag•on•fly *n.*, *pl.* drag•on•flies.

dra•goon *v.*, dra•gooned, dra•goon•ing.

drain *v.*, drained, drain•ing.

drain•age

drain◦er

drain•pipe

drake

DRAM *Computers.* (dynamic random access memory)

dram

dra◦ma *n.*, *pl.* dra•mas.

Dram◦a•mine *Trademark.*

dra•mat◦ic

dra•mat•ics

dram◦a•tist

dram◦a•ti•za•tion

dram◦a•tize *v.*, dram◦a•tized, dram◦a•tiz◦ing.

dra•me◦dy, *n.*, *pl.* dra•me•dies.

drank

drape *v.*, draped, drap•ing.

drap◦er

dra•per◦y *n.*, *pl.* dra•per◦ies.

dras•tic

dras•ti•cal◦ly

draught (drink: cf. DRAFT; DROUGHT)

draw *v.*, drew, drawn, draw•ing.

draw pro•gram *Computers.*

draw•back

draw•bridge

draw◦ee *Business.*

draw◦er

draw•ing

drawing ac•count *Business.*

drawl *v.*, drawled, drawl•ing.

drawn

draw•string or draw string

dray

dread *v.*, dread◦ed, dread•ing.

dread•ful

dread•locks *n.*, *pl.*

dread•nought or dread•naught

dream *v.*, dreamed or dreamt, dream•ing.

dream◦er

dream•i◦ly

dream•land

dream•less

dream•like

dream◦y *adj.*, dream•i◦er, dream•i•est.

dredge *v.*, dredged, dredg•ing.

dregs *n.*, *pl.*

Drei•ser

drench *v.*, drenched, drench•ing.

Dres•den

dress *v.*, dressed, dress•ing.

dres•sage

dress◦er

dress◦i•ness

dress•ing

dress◦ing-down

dress•mak◦er

dress•mak•ing

dress◦y *adj.*, dress•i◦er, dress•i•est.

drew

drib•ble *v.*, drib•bled, drib•bling.

drib•bler

drib•let

dried

dri◦er

dri◦est

drift *v.*, drift◦ed, drift•ing.

drift◦er

drift•wood

drill *v.*, drilled, drill•ing.

drill•mas•ter

dri◦ly

drink *v.*, drank, drunk, drink•ing.

drink•a◦ble

drink◦er

drip *v.*, dripped, drip•ping.

drip-dry *n.*, *pl.* drip-dries; *v.*, drip-dried, drip-dry◦ing.

drip•ping

drive *v.*, drove, driv◦en, driv•ing.

drive-in

driv◦el *v.*, driv•eled or driv•elled, driv•el•ing or driv•el•ling.

driv◦er

drive•way

driz•zle *v.*, driz•zled, driz•zling.

driz•zly

drogue

droll *adj.*, droll∘er, droll•est.

droll•er∘y *n.*, *pl.* droll•er∘ies.

drom∘e•da∘ry *n.*, *pl.* drom∘e•dar∘ies.

drone *v.*, droned, dron∘ing.

drool *v.*, drooled, drool•ing.

droop *v.*, drooped, droop•ing.

droop∘i•ness

droop∘y *adj.*, droop∘i∘er, droop•i•est.

drop *v.*, dropped, drop•ping.

drop kick *n.*

drop-kick *v.*, drop-kicked, drop-kick∘ing.

drop-kick∘er

drop-off

drop ship•per *Business.*

drop•let

drop∘out or drop-out

drop•per

drop•si•cal

drop∘sy

dross

drought (dry period: cf. DRAFT; DRAUGHT)

drove

drown *v.*, drowned, drown•ing.

drowse *v.*, drowsed, drows∘ing.

drow∘si•ness

drow∘sy *adj.*, drow∘si∘er, drow•si•est.

drub *v.*, drubbed, drub•bing.

drudge *v.*, drudged, drudg•ing.

drudg•er∘y

drug *v.*, drugged, drug•ging.

drug•gie or drug∘gy *n.*, *pl.* drug•gies.

drug•gist

drug•store or drug store

dru∘id

dru∘id•ism

drum *n.*, *pl.* drums; *v.*, drummed, drum• ming.

drum ma•jor•ette

drum•mer

drum•stick

drunk

drunk•ard

drunk∘en

drunk•en∘ly

drunk•en•ness

dry *n.*, *pl.* drys or dries; *v.*, dried, dry• ing; *adj.*, dri∘er, dri• est.

dry-clean *v.*, dry-cleaned, dry-clean• ing.

dry∘ad

dry∘er

dry∘ly

dry•ness

DST or D.S.T. (daylight-saving time).

DTP *Computers.* (desktop publishing)

du jour

du∘al (double: cf. DUEL)

du•al•ism

du•al∘i∘ty

dub *v.*, dubbed, dub• bing.

Du•bai

dub•ber

dub•bin

du•bi∘e•ty, *n.*, *pl.* du•bi∘e•ties.

du•bi•ous

du•bi•ous∘ly

Dub•lin

du•cal

duc∘at

duch•ess

duch∘y *n.*, *pl.* duch• ies.

duck[1] *n.*, *pl.* ducks or duck.

duck[2] *v.*, ducked, duck•ing.

duck•bill

duck•ling

duck∘y *adj.*, duck• i∘er, duck•i•est.

duct

duc•tile

duc•til∘i∘ty

duct•less

dud

dude

dudg•eon (indignation: cf. DUNGEON)

due (owed: cf. DEW; DO)

due bill *Business.*

due date *Business.*

du∘el *v.*, du•eled or du•elled, du•el∘ing or du•el•ling. (fight: cf. DUAL)

du•el•ist

du∘et

duf•fel bag

duff∘er

du∘fus, *n.*, *pl.* du• fus∘es.

dug

dug•out

duke

duke•dom

dul•cet

dul•ci•mer

dull *v.*, dulled, dull• ing; *adj.*, dull∘er, dull•est.

dull•ard

dull•ness
dul•ly
Du•luth
du•ly
Du•mas
dumb *adj.*, dumb•er, dumb•est.
dumb ter•mi•nal *Computers.*
dumb•bell
dumb•found *v.*, dumb•found•ed, dumb•found•ing.
dumb•ly
dumb•ness
dumb•wait•er
dum•dum
dum•my *n., pl.* dum•mies; *v.*, dum•mied, dum•my•ing.
dump *v.*, dumped, dump•ing.
dump•ling
dumps *n., pl.*
Dump•ster *Trademark.*
dump•y *adj.*, dump•i•er, dump•i•est.
dun *v.*, dunned, dun•ning. (to demand payment: cf. DONE)
dunce
dune
dung
dun•ga•ree
dun•geon (prison: cf. DUDGEON)
dung•hill
dunk *v.*, dunked, dunk•ing.
Dun•kirk
du•o *n., pl.* du•os.
du•o•de•nal
du•o•de•num *n., pl.* du•o•de•na, du•o•de•nums.
du•op•o•ly *n., pl.*

du•op•o•lies. *Business.*
dupe *v.*, duped, dup•ing.
du•ple
du•plex
du•pli•cate *v.*, du•pli•cat•ed, du•pli•cat•ing.
du•pli•ca•tion
du•pli•ca•tor
du•plic•i•ty *n., pl.* du•plic•i•ties.
du•ra ma•ter
du•ra•bil•i•ty
du•ra•ble
durable goods *Business.*
du•ra•bly
dur•ance
du•ra•tion
Dur•ban
du•ress
Dur•ham
dur•ing
du•rum wheat
dusk
dusk•y *adj.*, dusk•i•er, dusk•i•est.
Düs•sel•dorf
dust *v.*, dust•ed, dust•ing.
dust•er
dust•i•ness
dust•pan
dust•y *adj.*, dust•i•er, dust•i•est.
Dutch
Dutch auc•tion *Business.*
du•te•ous
du•ti•a•ble *Business.*
du•ti•ful
du•ti•ful•ly
du•ty *n., pl.* du•ties.
du•ty-free *Business.*

du•vet
Dvo• rvak (the composer)
Dvo•rak (keyboard)
Dvo•rák (the composer)
dwarf *n., pl.* dwarfs or dwarves; *v.*, dwarfed, dwarf•ing.
dwarf•ish
dwarf•ism
dweeb
dwell *v.*, dwelt or dwelled, dwell•ing.
dwell•er
dwell•ing
DWI (driving while intoxicated)
dwin•dle *v.*, dwin•dled, dwin•dling.
dyb•buk
dye *v.*, dyed, dye•ing. (to color: cf. DIE)
dyed-in-the-wool
dye•stuff
dy•ing
dy•na•book *Computers.*
dy•nam•ic
dy•nam•i•cal•ly
dy•nam•ics
dy•na•mism
dy•na•mite *v.*, dy•na•mit•ed, dy•na•mit•ing.
dy•na•mo *n., pl.* dy•na•mos.
dy•nas•tic
dy•nas•ty *n., pl.* dy•nas•ties.
dys•en•ter•y
dys•func•tion
dys•lex•i•a
dys•lex•ic
dys•pep•sia
dys•pep•tic

E-○mail or e-○mail
Computers.

e plu•ri•bus u○num

each

each oth○er

ea•ger

ea•ger○ly

ea•ger•ness

ea•gle

ea○gle-eyed

ea•glet

ear

ear can○dy

ear•ache

ear•drum

ear•flap

Ear•hart

earl

earl•dom

ear•less

ear•li•ness

ear•lobe or ear lobe

ear○ly *adj.*, ear•li○er,
ear•li•est.

early re•tire•ment

ear•mark *v.*, ear•
marked, ear•mark•
ing.

ear•muff

earn *v.*, earned, earn•
ing. (to gain: cf. URN)

earned in•come

earn○er

ear•nest

ear•nest○ly

ear•nest•ness

earn•ings *n., pl.*

earnings per share
(EPS) *Business*

ear•phone

ear•plug

ear•ring

ear•shot

ear•split•ting

earth *v.*, earthed,
earth•ing.

earth○en

earth•en•ware

earth○i•ness

earth•li•ness

earth•ling

earth○ly

earth•quake

earth•shak•ing

earth•ward

earth•work

earth•worm

earth○y *adj.*, earth•
i○er, earth•i•est.

ear•wax

ear•wig

ease *v.*, eased, eas•
ing.

ea•sel

ease•ment

eas○i○ly

eas○i•ness

east

Eas•ter

east•er○ly *n., pl.*
east•er•lies.

east•ern

east•ern○er

east•ward

eas○y *adj.*, eas•i○er,
eas•i•est.

eas○y chair

eas○y•go•ing

eat *v.*, ate, eat○en,
eat•ing.

eat•er○y *n., pl.* eat•
er•ies.

eats *n., pl.*

eau de Co•logne

eave

eaves•drop *v.*, eaves•

dropped, eaves•
drop•ping.

eaves•drop•per

ebb *v.*, ebbed, ebb•
ing.

EBCDIC *Computers.* (Ex-
tended Binary-Coded
Decimal Interchange
Code)

eb•on○y

e○bul•lience

e○bul•lient

e○bul•lient○ly

eb•ul•li•tion

EC *Business.* (European
Community)

ec•cen•tric

ec•cen•tri•cal○ly

ec•cen•tric○i○ty

Ec•cle•si•as•tes

ec•cle•si•as•tic

ec•cle•si•as•ti•cal

ECG (electrocardiogram;
electrocardiograph)

ech○e•lon

ech○o *n., pl.* ech•oes;
v., ech•oed, ech•o•
ing.

e○cho○ic

ech○o•lo•ca•tion

é○clair

é○clat

ec•lec•tic

ec•lec•ti•cal○ly

ec•lec•ti•cism

e○clipse *v.*, e○clipsed,
e○clips•ing.

e○clip•tic

ec•logue

ec○o•cide

ec○o•log○i•cal

ec○o•log○i•cal○ly

e○col○o•gist

e•col•o•o•gy
e•con•o•o•met•rics *Business.*
ec•o•nom•ic
economic in•di•ca•tor *Business.*
economic rent *Business.*
ec•o•nom•o•i•cal
ec•o•nom•o•i•cal•ly
ec•o•nom•ics *Business.*
e•con•o•o•mist *Business.*
e•con•o•o•mize v., e•con•o•o•mized, e•con•o•o•miz•ing.
e•con•o•o•my n., pl. e•con•o•o•mies.
economy of scale *Business.*
ec•o•o•sys•tem
ec•o•o•tage
ec•o•o•ter•ror•ist
ec•o•ru or éc•o•ru
ec•sta•o•sy n., pl. ec•sta•sies.
ec•stat•o•ic
ec•stat•o•i•cal•o•ly
ec•to•plasm
ECU *Business.* (currency of European Community)
Ec•ua•dor
Ec•ua•do•ran or Ec•ua•do•re•an or Ec•ua•do•ri•an
ec•o•u•men•o•i•cal or ec•o•u•men•o•ic
ec•o•u•men•o•i•cal•o•ly
ec•o•u•men•ism or ec•o•u•men•i•cism
ec•o•u•men•ist
ec•ze•ma
E•dam
ed•dy n., pl. ed•dies;

v., ed•died, ed•dy•ing.
e•del•weiss
e•de•ma n., pl. e•de•mas, e•de•ma•ta.
E•den
E•den•ic
edge v., edged, edg•ing.
edge con•nec•tor *Computers.*
edg•er
edge•wise or edge•ways
edg•i•ness
edg•ing
edg•y adj., edg•i•er, edg•i•est.
ed•i•bil•i•ty
ed•i•ble
ed•i•ble•ness
e•dict
ed•i•fi•ca•tion
ed•i•fice
ed•i•fy v., ed•i•fied, ed•i•fy•ing.
Ed•in•burgh
Ed•i•son
ed•it v., ed•it•ed, ed•it•ing.
e•di•tion (a printing: cf. ADDITION)
ed•i•tor
ed•i•to•ri•al
ed•i•to•ri•al•ize v., ed•i•to•ri•al•ized, ed•i•to•ri•al•iz•ing.
Ed•mon•ton
EDP *Computers.* (electronic data processing)
EDT or E.D.T. (Eastern daylight-saving time)
ed•u•ca•bil•i•ty
ed•u•ca•ble or ed•u•cat•a•ble
ed•u•cate v., ed•u•

cat•ed, ed•u•cat•ing.
ed•u•ca•tion
ed•u•ca•tion•al
ed•u•ca•tor
e•duce v., e•duced, e•duc•ing. (to draw out: cf. ADDUCE)
Ed•ward•i•an
Ed•ward•i•an•ism
EEC *Business.* (European Economic Community)
EEG (electroencephalo-gram)
eel n., pl. eel, eels.
EEPROM *Computers.* (electrical erasable programmable read-only memory)
e'er (ever: cf. AIR; ERE; HEIR)
ee•rie adj., ee•ri•er, ee•ri•est. (ghostly cf. EIRE; ERIE)
ee•ri•ly
ee•ri•ness
ef•face v., ef•faced, ef•fac•ing.
ef•face•ment
ef•fect v., ef•fect•ed, ef•fect•ing. (a result; to bring about: cf. AF-FECT)
ef•fec•tive
ef•fec•tive•ly
ef•fec•tive•ness
ef•fects n., pl.
ef•fec•tu•al
ef•fec•tu•al•ly
ef•fec•tu•ate v., ef•fec•tu•at•ed, ef•fec•tu•at•ing.
ef•fem•i•na•cy
ef•fem•i•nate
ef•fen•di, n., pl. ef•fen•dis.

ef•fer•ent
ef•fer•vesce *v.*, ef•
fer•vesced, ef•fer•
vesc•ing.
ef•fer•ves•cence
ef•fer•ves•cent
ef•fete
ef•fete•ness
ef•fi•ca•cious
ef•fi•ca•cious•ly
ef•fi•ca•cy
ef•fi•cien•cy
efficiency ex•pert
 Business.
ef•fi•cient
ef•fi•cient•ly
ef•fi•gy *n., pl.* ef•fi•
gies.
ef•flo•res•cence
ef•flo•res•cent
ef•flu•ence
ef•flu•ent (flowing: cf.
 AFFLUENT)
ef•flu•vi•um *n., pl.*
ef•flu•vi•a, ef•flu•
vi•ums.
ef•fort
ef•fort•less
ef•fort•less•ly
ef•fron•ter•y
ef•ful•gence
ef•ful•gent
ef•fu•sion
ef•fu•sive
ef•fu•sive•ly
ef•fu•sive•ness
eft
EFT *Business.* (electronic
 funds transfer)
e.g. (for example: cf.
 I.E.)
e•gad or e•gads
e•gal•i•tar•i•an
e•gal•i•tar•i•an•ism
egg *v.*, egged, egg•
ing.

egg foo yung or egg
 fu yung
egg•beat•er
egg•head
egg•nog
egg•plant
egg•shell
e•gis
eg•lan•tine
e•go *n., pl.* e•gos.
 (self: cf. ERGO)
e•go-trip•per
e•go•cen•tric
e•go•cen•tric•i•ty
e•go•ism
e•go•ist
e•go•is•tic
e•go•tism
e•go•tist
e•go•tis•tic
e•go•tis•ti•cal
e•go•tis•ti•cal•ly
e•go trip
e•gre•gious
e•gre•gious•ly
e•gre•gious•ness
e•gress
e•gret
E•gypt
E•gyp•tian
eh
ei•der•down
eight (number: cf. ATE)
eight•ball
eight•een
eight•eenth
eighth
eight•i•eth
eight•y *n., pl.*
Ein•stein
Ein•stein•i•an
ein•stein•i•um
Eir•e (Ireland: cf. EERIE;
 ERIE)
Ei•sen•how•er

ei•ther (one of two: cf.
 ETHER)
e•jac•u•late *v.*,
 e•jac•u•lat•ed,
 e•jac•u•lat•ing.
e•jac•u•la•tion
e•jac•u•la•to•ry
e•ject *v.*, e•ject•ed,
 e•ject•ing.
e•jec•tion
eke *v.*, eked, ek•ing.
EKG (electrocardiogram;
 electrocardiograph)
El Do•ra•do
El Gre•co
El Ni•ño
El Pas•o
El Sal•va•dor
e•lab•o•rate *v.*,
 e•lab•o•rat•ed,
 e•lab•o•rat•ing.
e•lab•o•rate•ly
e•lab•o•rate•ness
e•lab•o•ra•tion
é•lan
e•land *n., pl.* e•lands,
 e•land.
e•lapse *v.*, e•lapsed,
 e•laps•ing. (to pass:
 cf. LAPSE)
e•las•tic
e•las•tic•i•ty
e•las•ti•cize *v.*,
 e•las•ti•cized,
 e•las•ti•ciz•ing.
e•lat•ed
e•la•tion
el•bow *v.*, el•bowed,
 el•bow•ing.
el•bow•room
ELD *Computers.* (elec-
 troluminescent dis-
 play)
eld•er¹ (older person;
 older: cf. OLDER)
el•der² (tree)

el•der•ber•ry *n.*, *pl.*
el•der•ber•ries.
eld•er•ly
eld•est
e•lect *v.*, e•lect•ed,
e•lect•ing.
e•lec•tion (selection
by vote: cf. ELOCUTION)
e•lec•tion•eer *v.*,
e•lec•tion•eered,
e•lec•tion•eer•ing.
e•lec•tive
e•lec•tor
e•lec•tor•al
e•lec•tor•ate
e•lec•tric
e•lec•tri•cal•ly
e•lec•tri•cian
e•lec•tric•i•ty
e•lec•tri•fi•ca•tion
e•lec•tri•fi•er
e•lec•tri•fy *v.*, e•lec•
tri•fied, e•lec•tri•
fy•ing.
e•lec•tro•car•di•o•
gram (ECG; EKG)
e•lec•tro•car•di•o•
graph (ECG; EKG)
e•lec•tro•con•vul•
sive ther•apy
e•lec•tro•cute *v.*,
e•lec•tro•cut•ed,
e•lec•tro•cut•ing.
e•lec•tro•cu•tion
e•lec•trode
e•lec•tro•
en•ceph•a•lo•gram
(EEG)
e•lec•tro•
en•ceph•a•lo•graph
e•lec•trol•o•gist
e•lec•trol•y•sis
e•lec•tro•lyte
e•lec•tro•lyt•ic
e•lec•tro•mag•net
e•lec•tro•mag•net•ic

e•lec•tro•mag•
net•i•cal•ly
e•lec•tro•mag•net•
ism
e•lec•tro•mo•tive
e•lec•tron
electron mi•cro•scope
e•lec•tron•ic
electronic bank•ing
Business.
electronic da•ta proc•
essing (EDP) *Comput-
ers.*
electronic mail *Com-
puters.*
electronic mail•box
Computers.
electronic tab•let
Computers.
e•lec•tron•i•cal•ly
e•lec•tron•ics
e•lec•tro•plate *v.*,
e•lec•tro•plat•ed,
e•lec•tro•plat•ing.
e•lec•tro•scope
e•lec•tro•scop•ic
e•lec•tro•shock
e•lec•tro•stat•ic
e•lec•tro•stat•ics
e•lec•tro•type *v.*,
e•lec•tro•typed,
e•lec•tro•typ•ing.
el•ee•mos•y•nar•y
el•e•gance
el•e•gant
el•e•gant•ly
el•e•gi•ac
el•e•gy *n.*, *pl.* el•e•
gies. (poem of lament:
cf. EULOGY)
el•e•ment
el•e•men•tal
el•e•men•ta•ry (ba-
sic: cf. ALIMENTARY)
el•e•phant *n.*, *pl.*
el•e•phants, el•e•
phant.

el•e•phan•ti•a•sis
el•e•phan•tine
el•e•vate *v.*, el•e•
vat•ed, el•e•vat•
ing.
el•e•va•tion
el•e•va•tor
el•e•va•tor mu•sic
el•ev•en
el•ev•enth
elf *n.*, *pl.* elves.
ELF or elf (extremely
low frequency)
e•lic•it *v.*, e•lic•
it•ed, e•lic•it•ing.
(to bring forth: cf. IL-
LICIT)
e•lic•i•ta•tion
e•lide *v.*, e•lid•ed,
e•lid•ing.
el•i•gi•bil•i•ty
el•i•gi•ble (qualified:
cf. ILLEGIBLE)
E•li•jah
e•lim•i•nate *v.*,
e•lim•i•nat•ed,
e•lim•i•nat•ing.
e•lim•i•na•tion
El•i•ot
e•li•sion
e•lite or é•lite
e•lit•ism
e•lit•ist
e•lix•ir
E•liz•a•beth
E•liz•a•be•than
elk *n.*, *pl.* elks, elk.
ell
el•lipse *n.*, *pl.* el•
lips•es. (curve)
el•lip•sis *n.*, *pl.* el•
lip•ses. (omission of
word)
el•lip•ti•cal or el•lip•
tic
el•lip•ti•cal•ly
elm

el•o•cu•tion (public speaking: cf. ELECTION)

e•lon•gate v., e•lon•gat•ed, e•lon•gat•ing.

e•lon•ga•tion

e•lope v., e•loped, e•lop•ing.

e•lope•ment

el•o•quence

el•o•quent

el•o•quent•ly

else

else•where

e•lu•ci•date v., e•lu•ci•dat•ed, e•lu•ci•dat•ing.

e•lu•ci•da•tion

e•lude v., e•lud•ed, e•lud•ing. (to avoid: cf. ALLUDE)

e•lu•sive (evasive: cf. ALLUSIVE; ILLUSIVE)

e•lu•sive•ness

el•ver

elves

E•ly•sian

E•ly•si•um

e•ma•ci•at•ed

e•ma•ci•a•tion

em•a•nate v., em•a•nat•ed, em•a•nat•ing.

em•a•na•tion

e•man•ci•pate v., e•man•ci•pat•ed, e•man•ci•pat•ing.

e•man•ci•pa•tion

e•man•ci•pa•tor

e•mas•cu•late v., e•mas•cu•lat•ed, e•mas•cu•lat•ing.

e•mas•cu•la•tion

em•balm v., em•balmed, em•balm•ing.

em•balm•er

em•bank•ment

em•bar•go n., pl. em•bar•goes; v., em•bar•goed, em•bar•go•ing. Business.

em•bark v., em•barked, em•bark•ing.

em•bar•ka•tion

em•bar•rass v., em•bar•rassed, em•bar•rass•ing.

em•bar•rass•ing•ly

em•bar•rass•ment

em•bas•sy n., pl. em•bas•sies.

em•bat•tled

em•bed v., em•bed•ded, em•bed•ding.

embedded com•mand Computers.

em•bel•lish v., em•bel•lished, em•bel•lish•ing.

em•bel•lish•ment

em•ber

em•bez•zle v., em•bez•zled, em•bez•zling. Business.

em•bez•zle•ment Business.

em•bez•zler Business.

em•bit•ter v., em•bit•tered, em•bit•ter•ing.

em•bla•zoned

em•blem

em•blem•at•ic

em•bod•i•ment

em•bod•y v., em•bod•ied, em•bod•y•ing.

em•bold•en v., em•bold•ened, em•bold•en•ing.

em•bo•lism

em•boss v., em•bossed, em•boss•ing.

em•bou•chure

em•brace v., em•braced, em•brac•ing.

em•brace•a•ble

em•bra•sure

em•bro•ca•tion

em•broi•der v., em•broi•dered, em•broi•der•ing.

em•broi•der•y n., pl. em•broi•der•ies.

em•broil v., em•broiled, em•broil•ing.

em•broil•ment

em•bry•o n., pl. em•bry•os.

em•bry•o•log•i•cal

em•bry•ol•o•gist

em•bry•ol•o•gy

em•bry•on•ic

em•cee v., em•ceed, em•cee•ing.

e•mend v., e•mend•ed, e•mend•ing.

e•men•da•tion

em•er•ald

e•merge v., e•merged, e•merg•ing.

e•mer•gence

e•mer•gen•cy n., pl. e•mer•gen•cies.

e•mer•gent

e•mer•gi•cen•ter

e•mer•i•tus n., pl. e•mer•i•ti.

Em•er•son

em•er•y

e•met•ic

em•i•grant

em•i•grate v., em•i•grat•ed, em•i•grat•

ing. (to leave one's country: cf. IMMIGRATE)

em•i•gra•tion

é•mi•gré

em•i•nence

em•i•nent (renowned: cf. IMMANENT; IMMINENT)

e•mir

em•ir•ate

em•is•sar•y n., pl. em•is•sar•ies.

e•mis•sion

e•mit v., e•mit•ted, e•mit•ting.

e•mit•ter

e•mol•lient (softening)

e•mol•u•ment (salary)

e•mote v., e•mot•ed, e•mot•ing.

e•mo•ti•con

e•mo•tion

e•mo•tion•al

e•mo•tion•al•ism

e•mo•tion•al•ly

em•path•ic (sharing another's feelings: cf. EMPHATIC)

em•pa•thize v., em•pa•thized, em•pa•thiz•ing.

em•pa•thy

em•per•or

em•pha•sis n., pl. em•pha•ses.

em•pha•size v., em•pha•sized, em•pha•siz•ing.

em•phat•ic (uttered strongly: cf. EMPATHIC)

em•phat•i•cal•ly

em•phy•se•ma

em•pire (domain: cf. UMPIRE)

em•pir•i•cal

em•pir•i•cal•ly

em•pir•i•cism

em•pir•i•cist

em•place•ment

em•ploy v., em•ployed, em•ploy•ing.

em•ploy•a•ble

em•ploy•ee Business.

em•ploy•er Business.

em•ploy•ment Business.

employment a•gen•cy

em•po•ri•um n., pl. em•po•ri•ums, em•po•ri•a.

em•pow•er v., em•pow•ered, em•pow•er•ing.

em•pow•er•ment

em•press

emp•ti•ly

emp•ti•ness

emp•ty n., pl. emp•ties; v., emp•tied, emp•ty•ing; adj., emp•ti•er, emp•ti•est.

emp•ty-hand•ed

empty nest•er

em•py•re•an

e•mu n., pl. e•mus.

em•u•late v., em•u•lat•ed, em•u•lat•ing.

em•u•la•tion

em•u•la•tive

em•u•la•tor

e•mul•si•fi•ca•tion

e•mul•si•fy v., e•mul•si•fied, e•mul•si•fy•ing.

e•mul•sion

en bloc

en masse

en route

en•a•ble v., en•

a•bled, en•a•bling. (to give power: cf. UN•ABLE)

en•a•bler

en•act v., en•act•ed, en•act•ing.

en•act•ment

e•nam•el v., e•nam•eled or e•nam•elled, e•nam•el•ing or e•nam•el•ling.

e•nam•el•ware

en•am•or v., en•am•ored, en•am•or•ing.

en•camp v., en•camped, en•camp•ing.

en•camp•ment

en•cap•su•late v., en•cap•su•lat•ed, en•cap•su•lat•ing.

en•cap•su•la•tion

en•case v., en•cased, en•cas•ing.

en•ceph•a•lit•ic

en•ceph•a•li•tis

en•ceph•a•lo•my•e•li•tis

en•ceph•a•lon n., pl. en•ceph•a•lons, en•ceph•a•la.

en•chain v., en•chained, en•chain•ing.

en•chant v., en•chant•ed, en•chant•ing.

en•chant•ing•ly

en•chant•ment

en•chi•la•da n., pl. en•chi•la•das.

en•ci•pher v., en•ci•phered, en•ci•pher•ing.

en•ci•pher•ment

en•cir•cle v., en•cir•cled, en•cir•cling.

en•cir•cle•ment
en•clave
en•close v., en•closed, en•clos•ing.
en•clo•sure
en•code v., en•cod•ed, en•cod•ing.
en•co•mi•um n., pl. en•co•mi•ums, en•co•mi•a.
en•com•pass v., en•com•passed, en•com•pass•ing.
en•core v., en•cored, en•cor•ing.
en•coun•ter v., en•coun•tered, en•coun•ter•ing.
en•cour•age v., en•cour•aged, en•cour•ag•ing.
en•cour•age•ment
en•cour•ag•ing•ly
en•croach v., en•croached, en•croach•ing.
en•croach•ment
en•crust v., en•crust•ed, en•crust•ing.
en•crus•ta•tion
en•cryp•tion Computers.
en•cum•ber v., en•cum•bered, en•cum•ber•ing.
en•cum•brance
en•cyc•li•cal
en•cy•clo•pe•di•a or en•cy•clo•pae•di•a
en•cy•clo•pe•dic
en•cyst v., en•cyst•ed, en•cyst•ing.
end v., end•ed, end•ing.

end-of-file (EOF) Computers.
end-of-line (EOL) Computers.
end us•er Computers.
en•dan•ger v., en•dan•gered, en•dan•ger•ing.
endangered spe•cies
en•dan•ger•ment
en•dear v., en•deared, en•dear•ing.
en•dear•ing•ly
en•dear•ment
en•deav•or v., en•deav•ored, en•deav•or•ing.
en•dem•ic
end•ing
ending in•ven•to•ry Business.
en•dive
end•less
end•less•ly
end•less•ness
end•most
en•do•crine
en•do•cri•nol•o•gist
en•do•cri•nol•o•gy
en•dog•e•nous
en•dorse v., en•dorsed, en•dors•ing.
en•dorse•ment
en•dors•er
en•do•scope
en•do•scop•ic
en•dos•co•py
en•do•ther•mic or en•do•ther•mal
en•dow v., en•dowed, en•dow•ing.
en•dow•ment Business.
endowment in•sur•ance

en•due v., en•dued, en•du•ing. (to provide cf. UNDO; UNDUE)
en•dur•a•ble
en•dur•ance
en•dure v., en•dured, en•dur•ing.
en•dur•ing•ly
end•ways or end•wise
en•o•e•ma n., pl. en•e•mas.
en•e•my n., pl. en•e•mies.
en•er•get•ic
en•er•get•i•cal•ly
en•er•gize v., en•er•gized, en•er•giz•ing.
en•er•giz•er
en•er•gy n., pl. en•er•gies.
en•er•vate v., en•er•vat•ed, en•er•vat•ing. (to weaken: cf. INNERVATE)
en•er•va•tion
en•er•va•tor
en•fee•ble v., en•fee•bled, en•fee•bling.
en•fee•ble•ment
en•fi•lade v., en•fi•lad•ed, en•fi•lad•ing.
en•fold v., en•fold•ed, en•fold•ing. (to wrap: cf. UNFOLD)
en•force v., en•forced, en•forc•ing.
en•force•a•ble
en•force•ment
en•forc•er
en•fran•chise v., en•fran•chised, en•fran•chis•ing.

en•fran•chise•ment

en•gage v., en•gaged, en•gag•ing.

en•gage•ment

en•gag•ing

en•gag•ing•ly

En•gels

en•gen•der v., en•gen•dered, en•gen•der•ing.

en•gine

en•gi•neer v., en•gi•neered, en•gi•neer•ing.

Eng•land

Eng•lish

Eng○lish•man or Eng○lish•wom○an n., pl. Eng○lish•men or Eng○lish•wom○en.

en•gorge v., en•gorged, en•gorg•ing.

en•gram

en•grave v., en•graved, en•grav•ing.

en•grav○er

en•grav•ing

en•gross v., en•grossed, en•gross•ing.

en•gross•ing

en•gulf v., en•gulfed, en•gulf•ing.

en•hance v., en•hanced, en•hanc•ing.

enhanced key•board Computers.

en•hance•ment

e○nig○ma

en•ig•mat○ic

en•jamb•ment or en•jambement

en•join v., en•joined, en•join•ing.

en•joy v., en•joyed, en•joy•ing.

en•joy•a○ble

en•joy•ment

en•large v., en•larged, en•larg•ing.

en•large•ment

en•larg○er v.,

en•light○en v., en•light•ened, en•light•en•ing.

en•light•en•ment

en•list v., en•list○ed, en•list•ing.

en•list○ee

en•list•ment

en•liv○en v., en•liv•ened, en•liv•en•ing.

en•mesh v., en•meshed, en•mesh•ing.

en•mi○ty n., pl. en•mi•ties. (hostility: cf. AMITY)

en•no•ble v., en•no•bled, en•no•bling.

en•no•ble•ment

en•nui

e○nor•mi○ty n., pl. e○nor•mi•ties.

e○nor•mous

e○nor•mous○ly

e○nor•mous•ness

e○nough

en•plane or emplane, v., en•planed, en•plan•ing.

en•quire v., en•quired, en•quir•ing.

en•quir○y n., pl. en•quir•ies.

en•rage v., en•raged, en•rag•ing.

en•rap•ture v., en•

rap•tured, en•rap•tur•ing.

en•rich v., en•riched, en•rich•ing.

en•rich•ment

en•roll or en•rol v., en•rolled, en•roll•ing or en•rol•ling. (to enlist: cf. UNROLL)

en•roll•ment

en•sconced

en•sem•ble

en•shrine v., en•shrined, en•shrin•ing.

en•shroud v., en•shroud○ed, en•shroud•ing.

en•sign

en•si•lage

en•sile, v., en•siled, en•sil•ing.

en•slave v., en•slaved, en•slav•ing.

en•slave•ment

en•snare v., en•snared, en•snar•ing.

en•sue v., en•sued, en•su•ing.

en•sure v., en•sured, en•sur•ing.

en•tail v., en•tailed, en•tail•ing.

en•tail•ment

en•tan•gle v., en•tan•gled, en•tan•gling.

en•tan•gle•ment

en•tente

en•ter v., en•tered, en•ter•ing.

En•ter key Computers.

en•ter○i•tis

en•ter•prise

en•ter•pris•ing

en•ter•tain v., en•

ter•tained, en•ter•
tain•ing.
en•ter•tain•er
en•ter•tain•ment
en•thrall v., en•
thralled, en•thrall•
ing.
en•throne v., en•
throned, en•thron•
ing.
en•throne•ment
en•thuse v., en•
thused, en•thus•ing.
en•thu•si•asm
en•thu•si•ast
en•thu•si•as•tic
en•thu•si•as•ti•
cal•ly
en•tice v., en•ticed,
en•tic•ing.
en•tice•ment
en•tic•ing•ly
en•tire
en•tire•ly
en•tire•ty
en•ti•tle v., en•ti•
tled, en•ti•tling.
en•ti•tle•ment
en•ti•ty n., pl. en•ti•
ties.
en•tomb v., en•
tombed, en•tomb•
ing.
en•to•mol•o•gist
en•to•mol•o•gy
(study of insects: cf.
ETYMOLOGY)
en•tou•rage
en•tr'acte
en•trails n., pl.
en•train v., en•
trained, en•train•
ing.
en•trance[1] n.
en•trance[2] v., en•
tranced, en•tranc•
ing.

en•tranc•ing•ly
en•trant
en•trap v., en•
trapped, en•trap•
ping.
en•trap•ment
en•treat v., en•
treat•ed, en•treat•
ing.
en•treat•ing•ly
en•treat•y n., pl. en•
treat•ies.
en•trée or en•tree
en•trench v., en•
trenched, en•
trench•ing.
en•trench•ment
en•tre•pre•neur Busi-
ness.
en•tre•pre•neur•i•al
Business.
en•tro•py
en•trust v., en•
trust•ed, en•trust•
ing.
en•try n., pl. en•tries.
entry lev•el Business.
entry val•ue Business.
en•twine v., en•
twined, en•twin•
ing.
e•nu•mer•ate v.,
e•nu•mer•at•ed,
e•nu•mer•at•ing.
e•nu•mer•a•tion
e•nun•ci•ate v.,
e•nun•ci•at•ed,
e•nun•ci•at•ing.
e•nun•ci•a•tion (dic-
tion: cf. ANNUNCIATION)
en•u•re•sis
en•vel•op v., en•vel•
oped, en•vel•op•
ing. (to wrap)
en•ve•lope (covering)
en•vel•op•ment
en•ven•om v., en•

ven•omed, en•ven•
om•ing.
en•vi•a•ble
en•vi•a•bly
en•vi•ous
en•vi•ous•ly
en•vi•ous•ness
en•vi•ron•ment
en•vi•ron•men•tal
en•vi•ron•men•tal•
ism
en•vi•ron•men•tal•
ist
en•vi•ron•men•
tal•ly
en•vi•rons n., pl.
en•vis•age v., en•
vis•aged, en•vis•
ag•ing.
en•vi•sion v., en•vi•
sioned, en•vi•sion•
ing.
en•voy
en•vy n., pl. en•vies;
v., en•vied, en•vy•
ing.
en•zyme
EO Computers. (erasable
optical disk)
Eo•cene
EOF Computers. (end-of-
file)
EOL Computers. (end-of-
line)
Eo•li•an
e.o.m. or **E.O.M.** (end-
of-month)
e.o.m. dat•ing Busi-
ness.
e•on or ae•on
EPA Business. (Environ-
mental Protection
Agency)
ep•au•let or ep•au•
lette
é•pée or e•pee
e•phed•rine

e•ophem•er•o•a n., pl.
  e•ophem•er•o•as.
e•ophem•er•al
ep•ic (heroic poem: cf.
  EPOCH)
ep•oi•cene
ep•oi•cen•ter
ep•oi•cure
ep•oi•cu•re•an
Ep•oi•cu•rus
ep•oi•dem•oic
ep•oi•de•mi•ol•o•o•
  gist
ep•oi•de•mi•ol•o•o•gy
ep•oi•der•mal or
  ep•oi•der•mic
ep•oi•der•mis
ep•oi•glot•tis n., pl.
  ep•oi•glot•tis•es,
  ep•oi•glot•ti•des.
ep•oi•gram (pointed
  statement: cf. EPI-
  GRAPH)
ep•oi•gram•mat•ic
ep•oi•graph (motto: cf.
  EPIGRAM)
ep•oi•lep•o•sy
ep•oi•lep•tic
ep•oi•logue or ep•oi•
  log
ep•oi•neph•rine or
  ep•oi•neph•rin
e•opiph•o•a•ny n., pl
  e•opiph•o•a•nies.
e•opis•co•pa•cy n., pl.
  e•opis•co•pa•cies.
e•opis•co•pal
E•opis•co•pa•lian
e•opis•co•pate
ep•oi•sode
ep•oi•sod•ic
e•opis•te•mol•o•o•gy
e•opis•tle
e•opis•to•lar•oy
ep•oi•taph (inscription:
  cf. EPITHET)
ep•oi•the•li•o•al

ep•oi•the•li•um n., pl.
  ep•oi•the•li•ums,
  ep•oi•the•li•a.
ep•oi•thet (curse: cf.
  EPITAPH)
e•opit•o•ome
e•opit•o•mize v.,
  e•opit•o•mized,
  e•opit•o•miz•ing.
ep•och (era: cf. EPIC)
ep•och•al
ep•ox•oy n., pl. ep•
  ox•ies.
EPROM Computers.
  (erasable programma-
  ble read-only memory)
ep•si•lon
Ep•som salt
Ep•stein-Barr vi•rus
eq•ua•ble (uniform:
  cf. EQUITABLE)
eq•ua•bly
e•oqual v., e•oqualed or
  e•oqualled, e•oqual•
  ing or e•oqual•ling.
e•oqual•i•oty
e•oqual•i•za•tion
e•oqual•ize v.,
  e•oqual•ized,
  e•oqual•iz•ing.
e•oqual•iz•oer
e•oqual•ly
e•oqua•nim•oi•ty
e•oquat•a•oble
e•oquate v.,
  e•oquat•ed,
  e•oquat•ing.
e•oqua•tion
e•oqua•tor
E•oqua•to•ri•al
  Guin•ea
eq•uer•or•y n., pl. eq•
  uer•ries.
e•oques•tri•an
e•oques•tri•enne
e•oqui•dis•tant
e•oqui•lat•er•al

e•oqui•lib•ri•um n.,
  pl. e•oqui•lib•ri•ums,
  e•oqui•lib•ri•a.
e•oquine
e•oqui•noc•tial
e•oqui•nox
e•oquip v., e•oquipped,
  e•oquip•ping.
eq•ui•page
e•oquip•ment
e•oqui•poise v.,
  e•oqui•poised,
  e•oqui•pois•ing.
eq•ui•ta•ble (just: cf.
  EQUABLE)
eq•ui•ta•bly
eq•ui•oty n., pl. eq•
  ui•ties.
equity cap•i•tal
e•oquiv•o•a•lence or
  e•oquiv•o•a•len•cy
e•oquiv•o•a•lent
e•oquiv•o•o•cal
e•oquiv•o•o•cal•oy
e•oquiv•o•o•cate v.,
  e•oquiv•o•o•cat•ed,
  e•oquiv•o•o•cat•ing.
e•oquiv•o•o•ca•tion
e•oquiv•o•o•ca•tor
e•ora n., pl. e•oras. (age:
  cf. ERROR)
e•orad•oi•ca•ble
e•orad•oi•cate v.,
  e•orad•oi•cat•ed,
  e•orad•oi•cat•ing.
e•orad•oi•ca•tion
e•orad•oi•ca•tor
e•oras•a•oble (remova-
  ble: cf. IRASCIBLE)
erasable op•ti•cal
  disk (EO) Computers.
e•orase v., e•orased,
  e•oras•ing.
e•oras•oer
E•oras•mus
e•ora•sure
er•bi•um

ere (before: cf. AIR; E'ER; HEIR)

e•rect *v.*, e•rect•ed, e•rect•ing. (to build cf. ERUCT)

e•rec•tile

e•rec•tion

e•rect•ly

e•rect•ness

e•rec•tor

ere•long

er•e•mite

erg

er•go (therefore: cf. EGO)

er•go•nom•ic

er•go•nom•i•cal•ly

er•go•nom•ics

er•gos•ter•ol

er•got

E•rie *n.*, *pl.* E•ries, E•rie. (member of American Indian people: cf. EERIE; EIRE)

Er•in

ERISA *Business.* (Employee Retirement Income Security Act)

er•mine *n.*, *pl.* er•mines, er•mine.

e•rode *v.*, e•rod•ed, e•rod•ing.

e•rog•e•nous

E•ros

e•ro•sion

e•ro•sive

e•rot•ic (sexy: cf. ER-RATIC)

e•rot•i•ca

e•rot•i•cal•ly

e•rot•i•cism

err *v.*, erred, err•ing.

er•rand (excursion for a task)

er•rant (roving)

er•rat•ic (unpredictable: cf. EROTIC)

er•rat•i•cal•ly

er•ra•tum *n.*, *pl.* er•ra•ta.

er•ro•ne•ous

er•ro•ne•ous•ly

er•ror (mistake: cf. ERA)

error de•tec•tion *Computers.*

er•ror•less

er•satz

erst

erst•while

ERT (estrogen replacement therapy)

e•ruct *v.*, e•ruct•ed, e•ruct•ing. (to belch: cf. ERECT)

e•ruc•ta•tion

er•u•dite

er•u•dite•ly

er•u•di•tion

e•rupt *v.*, e•rupt•ed, e•rupt•ing.

e•rup•tion

e•rup•tive

er•y•sip•e•las

e•ryth•ro•cyte

es•ca•late *v.*, es•ca•lat•ed, es•ca•lat•ing.

es•ca•la•tion

es•ca•la•tor

escalator clause *Business.*

es•cal•lop *v.*, es•cal•loped, es•cal•lop•ing.

es•ca•pade

es•cape *v.*, es•caped, es•cap•ing.

escape char•ac•ter *Computers.*

escape clause *Business.*

escape se•quence *Computers.*

es•cap•ee

es•cape•ment

es•cap•ism

es•cap•ist

es•ca•role

es•carp•ment

es•chew *v.*, es•chewed, es•chew•ing.

es•cort *v.*, es•cort•ed, es•cort•ing.

es•cri•toire

es•crow *v.*, es•crowed, es•crow•ing. *Business.*

es•cu•do *n.*, *pl.* es•cu•dos.

es•cutch•eon

Es•ki•mo *n.*, *pl.* Es•ki•mos, Es•ki•mo.

ESL (English as a second language)

ESOP *Business.* (employee stock ownership plan)

e•soph•a•ge•al

e•soph•a•gus *n.*, *pl.* e•soph•a•gi.

es•o•ter•ic

es•o•ter•i•cal•ly

es•pa•drille

es•pal•ier

es•pe•cial

es•pe•cial•ly

Es•pe•ran•to

es•pi•o•nage

es•pla•nade

es•pous•al

es•pouse *v.*, es•poused, es•pous•ing.

es•pres•so

es•prit

es•prit de corps

es•py *v.*, es•pied, es•py•ing.

Esq. or Esqr. (esquire)

es•quire

es•say *v.*, es•sayed, es•say•ing. (to try; composition: 〔f. ASSAY)
es•say•ist
es•sence
Es•sene
es•sen•tial
es•sen•tial•ly
EST or E.S.T. (Eastern Standard Time)
es•tab•lish *v.*, es•tab•lished, es•tab•lish•ing.
es•tab•lish•ment
es•tate
estate tax *Business.*
es•teem *v.*, es•teemed, es•teem•ing.
es•ter
es•thete
es•thet•ic
es•thet•ics
es•ti•ma•ble
es•ti•mate *v.*, es•ti•mat•ed, es•ti•mat•ing.
es•ti•ma•tion
Es•to•ni•a
Es•to•ni•an
es•trange *v.*, es•tranged, es•trang•ing.
es•trange•ment
es•tro•gen
estrogen re•place•ment ther•a•py (ERT)
es•trous
es•trus
es•tu•ar•y *n.*, *pl.* es•tu•ar•ies.
et al. (and others)
ETA or E.T.A. (esti•mated time of arrival)
é•ota•gère or e•ota•gere

etc. et cetera)
et cet•er•a
etch *v.*, etched, etch•ing.
etch•er
etch•ing
e•ter•nal
e•ter•nal•ly
e•ter•ni•ty *n.*, *pl.* e•ter•ni•ties.
eth•ane
eth•a•nol
e•ther (anesthetic; drug: cf. EITHER)
e•the•re•al
e•the•re•al•ly
eth•ic (principle: cf. ETHNIC)
eth•i•cal
ethical pric•ing *Busi•ness.*
eth•i•cal•ly
eth•ics
E•thi•o•pi•a
E•thi•o•pi•an
eth•nic (cultural: cf. ETHIC)
eth•ni•cal•ly
eth•nic•i•ty
eth•no•cen•tric
eth•no•cen•trism
eth•no•log•i•cal
eth•nol•o•gist
eth•nol•o•gy
e•tho•log•i•cal
e•thol•o•gist
e•thol•o•gy
e•thos
eth•yl
eth•yl•ene
e•ti•ol•o•gy *n.*, *pl.* e•ti•ol•o•gies.
et•i•quette
Et•na
E•tru•ri•a
E•trus•can

é•tude
ETV (educational televi•sion)
et•y•mo•log•i•cal
et•y•mol•o•gist
et•y•mol•o•gy *n.*, *pl.* et•y•mol•o•gies. (study of words: 〔f. ENTOMOLOGY)
eu•ca•lyp•tus *n.*, *pl.* eu•ca•lyp•ti, eu•ca•lyp•tus•es.
Eu•cha•rist
Eu•cha•ris•tic
eu•chre *v.*, eu•chred, eu•chring.
Eu•clid
Eu•clid•e•an or Eu•clid•i•an
Eu•gene
eu•gen•ic
eu•gen•i•cal•ly
eu•gen•ics
eu•lo•gist
eu•lo•gis•tic
eu•lo•gize *v.*, eu•lo•gized, eu•lo•giz•ing.
eu•lo•gy *n.*, *pl.* eu•lo•gies. (speech of praise: cf. ELEGY)
eu•nuch
eu•phe•mism (mild substitution for offen•sive expression: cf. EU•PHUISM)
eu•phe•mis•tic
eu•phe•mis•ti•cal•ly
eu•pho•ni•ous
eu•pho•ni•ous•ly
eu•pho•ny *n.*, *pl.* eu•pho•nies.
eu•pho•ri•a
eu•phor•ic
Eu•phra•tes
eu•phu•ism (affected

literary style: cf. EUPHE-
MISM)
Eur•a○sia
Eur•a○sian
eu•re○ka
Eu•rip○i•des
Eu•ro•bond *Business.*
Eu•ro•cur•ren○cy *n.,*
pl. **Eu•ro•cur•ren•
cies.** *Business.*
Eu•ro•dol•lar *Busi-
ness.*
Eu•rope
Eu•ro•pe○an
**European Ec○o•
nom○ic Com•mu•
ni○ty (EEC).**
EU (European Union)
eu•ro•pi○um
Eu•sta•chian tube
eu•tha•na•sia
eu•then•ics
eu•tro•phic
eu•troph○i•ca•tion
e○vac○u•ate *v.,*
**e○vac○u•at○ed,
e○vac○u•at•ing.**
e○vac•u•a•tion
e○vac•u○ee
e○vade *v.,* **e○vad○ed,
e○vad•ing.** (to elude:
cf. AVOID)
e○vad○er
e○val○u•ate *v.,*
**e○val○u•at○ed,
e○val○u•at•ing.**
e○val•u•a•tion
e○val•u•a•tor
ev○a•nes•cence
ev○a•nes•cent
e○van•gel○i•cal
e○van•gel○i•cal•ism
e○van•ge•lism
e○van•ge•list
e○van•ge•lis•tic
e○van•ge•lize, *v.,*

**e○van•ge•lized,
e○van•ge•liz•ing.**
Ev•ans•ville
e○vap○o•rate *v.,*
**e○vap○o•rat○ed,
e○vap○o•rat•ing.**
e○vap○o•ra•tion
e○va•sion
e○va•sive
e○va•sive○ly
e○va•sive•ness
eve
e○ven *v.,* **e○vened,
e○ven•ing.** (making
even)
even foot○er *Comput-
ers.*
e○ven-tem○pered
e○ven•hand○ed
e○ven•hand•ed○ly
e○ven•hand•ed•ness
eve•ning (night)
e○ven○ly
e○ven•ness
E○ven•song
e○vent
event-driv○en *Computers.*
e○vent•ful
e○vent•ful○ly
e○ven•tide
e○ven•tu○al
e○ven•tu•al○i○ty *n.,*
pl. **e○ven•tu•al○i•
ties.**
e○ven•tu•al○ly
e○ven•tu•ate *v.,*
**e○ven•tu•at○ed,
e○ven•tu•at•ing.**
ev○er
Ev•er•est
Ev○er•glades
ev○er•green
ev○er•last•ing
ev○er•last•ing○ly
ev○er•more

eve○ry
eve○ry•bod○y
eve○ry•day
eve○ry•one
eve○ry•place
eve○ry•thing
eve○ry•where
e○vict *v.,* **e○vict○ed,
e○vict•ing.**
e○vic•tion
ev○i•dence *v.,* **ev○i•
denced, ev○i•denc•
ing.**
ev○i•dent
ev○i•dent○ly
e○vil
e○vil-mind○ed
e○vil-do○er
e○vil-do○ing
e○vil○ly
e○vince *v.,* **e○vinced,
e○vinc•ing.**
e○vis•cer•ate *v.,*
**e○vis•cer•at○ed,
e○vis•cer•at•ing.**
e○vis•cer○a•tion
ev○o•ca•tion
e○voc○a•tive
e○voc○a•tive○ly
e○voc○a•tive•ness
e○voke *v.,* **e○voked,
e○vok•ing.**
ev○o•lu•tion
ev○o•lu•tion•ar○y
ev○o•lu•tion•ism
ev○o•lu•tion•ist
e○volve *v.,* **e○volved,
e○volv•ing.**
ewe (female sheep: cf.
YEW; YOU)
ew○er
ex
ex div○i•dend *Busi-
ness.*
ex of•fi•ci○o
ex post fac○to

ex•ac•er•bate v., ex•ac•er•bat•ed, ex•ac•er•bat•ing.

ex•ac•er•ba•tion

ex•act v., ex•act•ed, ex•act•ing.

ex•act•ing•ly

ex•ac•tion

ex•ac•ti•tude

ex•act•ly

ex•act•ness

ex•ag•ger•ate v., ex•ag•ger•at•ed, ex•ag•ger•at•ing.

ex•ag•ger•at•ed•ly

ex•ag•ger•a•tion

ex•alt v., ex•alt•ed, ex•alt•ing. (glorify: cf. EXULT)

ex•al•ta•tion

ex•am

ex•am•i•na•tion

ex•am•ine v., ex•am•ined, ex•am•in•ing.

ex•am•in•er

ex•am•ple v., ex•am•pled, ex•am•pling.

ex•as•per•ate v., ex•as•per•at•ed, ex•as•per•at•ing.

ex•as•per•a•tion

ex•ca•vate v., ex•ca•vat•ed, ex•ca•vat•ing.

ex•ca•va•tion

ex•ca•va•tor

ex•ceed v., ex•ceed•ed, ex•ceed•ing. (to surpass: cf. ACCEDE)

ex•ceed•ing•ly

ex•cel v., ex•celled, ex•cel•ling.

ex•cel•lence

Ex•cel•len•cy n., pl. Ex•cel•len•cies.

ex•cel•lent

ex•cel•lent•ly

ex•cel•si•or

ex•cept v., ex•cept•ed, ex•cept•ing. (to exclude: cf. ACCEPT)

ex•cep•tion

ex•cep•tion•a•ble (objectionable)

ex•cep•tion•al (outstanding)

ex•cep•tion•al•ly

ex•cerpt v., ex•cerpt•ed, ex•cerpt•ing.

ex•cess (surplus: cf. ACCESS)

ex•ces•sive

ex•ces•sive•ly

ex•change v., ex•changed, ex•chang•ing.

exchange con•trol *Business.*

exchange rate *Business.*

ex•change•a•ble

ex•cheq•uer *Business.*

ex•cis•a•ble

ex•cise v., ex•cised, ex•cis•ing.

excise tax *Business.*

ex•ci•sion

ex•cit•a•bil•i•ty

ex•cit•a•ble

ex•ci•ta•tion

ex•cite v., ex•cit•ed, ex•cit•ing.

ex•cit•ed•ly

ex•cite•ment

ex•cit•ing

ex•cit•ing•ly

ex•claim v., ex•claimed, ex•claim•ing.

ex•cla•ma•tion

ex•clam•a•to•ry

ex•clude v., ex•clud•ed, ex•clud•ing.

ex•clu•sion

ex•clu•sive

ex•clu•sive•ly

ex•clu•sive•ness

ex•clu•siv•i•ty

ex•com•mu•ni•cate v., ex•com•mu•ni•cat•ed, ex•com•mu•ni•cat•ing.

ex•com•mu•ni•ca•tion

ex•co•ri•ate v., ex•co•ri•at•ed, ex•co•ri•at•ing.

ex•co•ri•a•tion

ex•cre•ment

ex•cre•men•tal

ex•cres•cence

ex•cres•cent

ex•cre•ta

ex•crete v., ex•cret•ed, ex•cret•ing.

ex•cre•tion

ex•cre•to•ry

ex•cru•ci•at•ing

ex•cru•ci•at•ing•ly

ex•cul•pate v., ex•cul•pat•ed, ex•cul•pat•ing.

ex•cul•pa•tion

ex•cur•sion

ex•cur•sive

ex•cur•sus, n., pl. ex•cur•sus•es, ex•cur•sus.

ex•cus•a•ble

ex•cus•a•bly

ex•cuse v., ex•cused, ex•cus•ing.

ex∘e∙cra∙ble

ex∘e∙crate v., ex∘e∙crat∘ed, ex∘e∙crat∙ing.

ex∘e∙cra∙tion

ex∘e∙cut∙a∘ble file Computers.

ex∘e∙cute v., ex∘e∙cut∘ed, ex∘e∙cut∙ing.

ex∘e∙cu∙tion

ex∘e∙cu∙tion∘er

ex•ec∘u∙tive Business.

executive of∙fi∙cer Business.

executive sec∙re∙tar∘y Business.

ex•ec∘u∙tor

ex•ec∘u∙trix n., pl. ex•ec∘u∙trix∘es, ex•ec∘u∙trix∘es.

ex∘e∙ge∙sis n., pl. ex∘e∙ge∙ses.

ex∘e∙get∘ic

ex•em∙plar

ex•em∙pla∘ry

ex•em∙pli∙fi∙ca∙tion

ex•em∙pli∘fy v., ex•em∙pli∘fied, ex•em∙pli∘fy∙ing.

ex•empt v., ex•empt∘ed, ex•empt∙ing.

exempt per∙son∙nel Business.

ex•emp∙tion

ex•er∙cise v., ex•er∙cised, ex•er∙cis∙ing. (to use; activity: cf. EXORCISE)

ex•er∙cis∘er

ex•ert v., ex•ert∘ed, ex•ert∙ing.

ex•er∙tion

ex•ha∙la∙tion

ex•hale v., ex•haled, ex•hal∙ing.

ex•haust v., ex•haust∘ed, ex•haust∙ing.

ex•haus∙tion

ex•haus∙tive

ex•hib∘it v., ex•hib∘it∘ed, ex•hib∙it•ing.

ex•hi•bi∙tion

ex•hi•bi∙tion•ism

ex•hi•bi∙tion•ist

ex•hi•bi∙tion•is•tic

ex•hib∘i∙tor

ex•hil∘a∙rate v., ex•hil∘a∙rat∘ed, ex•hil∘a∙rat∙ing.

ex•hil∘a∙rat∙ing•ly

ex•hil∘a∙ra∙tion

ex•hort v., ex•hort∘ed, ex•hort∙ing.

ex•hor∙ta∙tion

ex•hu∙ma∙tion

ex•hume v., ex•humed, ex•hum∙ing.

ex∘i∙gen∙cy n., pl. ex∘i∙gen∙cies.

ex∘i∙gent

ex•ile v., ex•iled, ex•il∙ing.

ex•ist v., ex•ist∘ed, ex•ist∙ing.

ex•ist∙ence

ex•ist∙ent

ex•is•ten∙tial

ex•is•ten∙tial•ism

ex•is•ten∙tial•ist

ex•is•ten∙tial•ly

ex∘it v., ex•it∘ed, ex•it∙ing.

ex∘o•bi∙ol∘o∙gy

ex∘o•crine

ex∘o•dus

ex•og∘e•nous

ex•on•er∙ate v., ex•on•er∙at∘ed, ex•on•er∙at∙ing.

ex•on•er∙a∙tion

ex•or•bi∙tance

ex•or•bi∙tant

ex•or•bi∙tant•ly

ex•or•cise v., ex•or•cised, ex•or•cis∙ing. (to expel: cf. EXERCISE)

ex•or•cism

ex•or•cist

ex∘o•sphere

ex∘o•ther•mic

ex∘ot∘ic

ex∘ot∘i•cism

ex•pand v., ex•pand∘ed, ex•pand∙ing. (to increase: cf. EXPEND)

expanded mem∘o∘ry Computers.

ex•panse

ex•pan•si∙ble

ex•pan•sion

expansion board Computers.

expansion bus Computers.

expansion card Computers.

expansion slot Computers.

ex•pan•sion•ism

ex•pan•sion•ist

ex•pan•sive (extensive: cf. EXPENSIVE)

ex•pan•sive•ly

ex•pan•sive•ness

ex par∘te

ex•pa∙ti∙ate v., ex•pa∙ti∙at∘ed, ex•pa∙ti∙at∙ing.

ex•pa∙ti∙a∙tion

ex•pa∙tri∙ate

ex•pa∙tri∙a∙tion

ex•pect v., ex•pect∘ed, ex•pect∙ing.

ex•pect•an•cy n., pl.
ex•pect•an•cies.
ex•pect•ant
ex•pect•ant•ly
ex•pec•ta•tion
ex•pect•ed yield Busi-
ness.
ex•pec•to•rant
ex•pec•to•rate v.,
ex•pec•to•rat•ed,
ex•pec•to•rat•ing.
ex•pec•to•ra•tion
ex•pe•di•en•cy
ex•pe•di•ent
ex•pe•dite v., ex•pe•
dit•ed, ex•pe•dit•
ing.
ex•pe•dit•er or ex•
pe•di•tor
ex•pe•di•tion
ex•pe•di•tion•ar•y
ex•pe•di•tious
ex•pe•di•tious•ly
ex•pe•di•tious•ness
ex•pe•di•tor
ex•pel v., ex•pelled,
ex•pel•ling.
ex•pend v., ex•
pend•ed, ex•pend•
ing. (to use up: cf. EX-
PAND)
ex•pend•a•ble
ex•pend•i•ture
ex•pense v., ex•
pensed, ex•pens•
ing.
expense ac•count
Business.
ex•pen•sive (costly:
cf. EXPANSIVE)
ex•pen•sive•ly
ex•pe•ri•ence v., ex•
pe•ri•enced, ex•pe•
ri•enc•ing.
ex•per•i•ment v.,
ex•per•i•ment•ed,
ex•per•i•ment•ing.

ex•per•i•men•tal
ex•per•i•men•tal•ly
ex•per•i•men•ta•
tion
ex•per•i•ment•er
ex•pert
expert sys•tem Com-
puters.
ex•per•tise
ex•pert•ly
ex•pert•ness
ex•pi•ate v., ex•pi•
at•ed, ex•pi•at•ing.
ex•pi•a•tion
ex•pi•ra•tion
ex•pire v., ex•pired,
ex•pir•ing.
ex•plain v., ex•
plained, ex•plain•
ing.
ex•pla•na•tion
ex•plan•a•to•ry
ex•ple•tive
ex•pli•ca•ble
ex•pli•cate v., ex•
pli•cat•ed, ex•pli•
cat•ing.
ex•pli•ca•tion
ex•plic•it
ex•plic•it•ly
ex•plic•it•ness
ex•plode v., ex•
plod•ed, ex•plod•
ing.
ex•ploit v., ex•
ploit•ed, ex•ploit•
ing.
ex•ploi•ta•tion
ex•ploit•a•tive or
ex•ploit•ive
ex•ploit•er
ex•plo•ra•tion
ex•plor•a•to•ry
ex•plore v., ex•
plored, ex•plor•ing.
ex•plor•er
ex•plo•sion

ex•plo•sive
ex•plo•sive•ly
ex•plo•sive•ness
ex•po n., pl. ex•pos.
ex•po•nent
ex•po•nen•tial
ex•po•nen•tial•ly
ex•port v., ex•
port•ed, ex•port•
ing. Business.
ex•por•ta•tion Busi-
ness.
ex•port•er Business.
ex•pose v., ex•posed,
ex•pos•ing. (to un-
cover)
ex•po•sé (public dis-
closure)
ex•po•si•tion
ex•pos•i•tor
ex•pos•i•to•ry
ex•pos•tu•late v.,
ex•pos•tu•lat•ed,
ex•pos•tu•lat•ing.
ex•pos•tu•la•tion
ex•po•sure
ex•pound v., ex•
pound•ed, ex•
pound•ing.
ex•pound•er
ex•press v., ex•
pressed, ex•press•
ing.
express war•ran•ty
Business.
ex•press•age Busi-
ness.
ex•press•i•ble
ex•pres•sion
ex•pres•sion•ism
ex•pres•sion•ist
ex•pres•sion•is•tic
ex•pres•sion•less
ex•pres•sive
ex•pres•sive•ly
ex•pres•sive•ness
ex•press•ly

ex•press•way
ex•pro•pri•ate *v.*,
  ex•pro•pri•at∘ed,
  ex•pro•pri•at•ing.
ex•pro•pri•a•tion
ex•pul•sion
ex•punge *v.*, ex•
  punged, ex•pung•
  ing.
ex•pur•gate *v.*, ex•
  pur•gat∘ed, ex•
  pur•gat•ing.
ex•pur•ga•tion
ex•quis•ite
ex•quis•ite∘ly
ex•quis•ite•ness
ex•tant (existing: cf.
  EXTENT).
ex•tem•po•ra•ne•
  ous
ex•tem•po∘re
ex•tem•po•rize *v.*,
  ex•tem•po•rized,
  ex•tem•po•riz•ing.
ex•tend *v.*, ex•
  tend∘ed, ex•tend•
  ing.
extended ASCII *Com-
  puters.*
extended fam∘i•ly
extended mem∘o∘ry
  Computers.
ex•tend∘er
ex•ten•si•ble
ex•ten•sion
ex•ten•sive
ex•ten•sive∘ly
ex•tent (scope: cf. EX-
  TANT)
ex•ten•u•ate *v.*, ex•
  ten•u•at∘ed, ex•
  ten•u•at•ing.
ex•ten•u•a•tion
ex•te•ri∘or
ex•ter•mi•nate *v.*,
  ex•ter•mi•nat∘ed,
  ex•ter•mi•nat•ing.

ex•ter•mi•na•tion
ex•ter•mi•na•tor
ex•tern
ex•ter•nal
external au∘di•tor
  Business.
external com•mand
  Computers.
external mo∘dem
  Computers.
ex•ter•nal∘ly
ex•tinct
ex•tinc•tion
ex•tin•guish *v.*, ex•
  tin•guished, ex•tin•
  guish•ing.
ex•tin•guish∘er
ex•tir•pate *v.*, ex•tir•
  pat∘ed, ex•tir•pat•
  ing.
ex•tir•pa•tion
ex•tol *v.*, ex•tolled,
  ex•tol•ling.
ex•tort *v.*, ex•
  tort∘ed, ex•tort•
  ing.
ex•tor•tion•ate
ex•tra *n.*, *pl.* ex•tras.
extra div∘i•dend *Busi-
  ness.*
ex∘tra-high-den∘si∘ty
  Computers.
ex•tract *v.*, ex•
  tract∘ed, ex•tract•
  ing.
ex•trac•tion
ex•trac•tor
ex•tra•cur•ric∘u•lar
ex•tra•dit∘a•ble
ex•tra•dite *v.*, ex•
  tra•dit∘ed, ex•tra•
  dit•ing.
ex•tra•di•tion
ex•tra•le∘gal
ex•tra•mar∘i•tal
ex•tra•mu•ral
ex•tra•ne•ous

ex•tra•ne•ous∘ly
ex•traor•di•nar∘i∘ly
ex•traor•di•nar∘y
extraordinary i∘tem
  Business.
extraordinary re•pair
  Business.
ex•trap∘o∘late *v.*,
  ex•trap∘o∘lat∘ed,
  ex•trap∘o∘lat•ing.
ex•trap∘o∘la•tion
ex•tra•sen•so∘ry
ex∘tra•ter•res•tri∘al
ex∘tra•ter•ri•to•ri∘al
ex∘tra•ter•ri•to•ri•a
  l•i∘ty
ex•trav∘a•gance
ex•trav∘a•gant
ex•trav∘a•gant∘ly
ex•trav∘a•gan∘za *n.*,
  pl. ex•trav∘a•gan•
  zas.
ex∘tra•ve∘hic∘u•lar
ex∘tra•vert
ex•treme
ex•treme∘ly
ex•trem•ism
ex•trem•ist
ex•trem∘i∘ty *n.*, *pl.*
  ex•trem∘i•ties.
ex•tri•cate *v.*, ex•tri•
  cat∘ed, ex•tri•cat•
  ing.
ex•tri•ca•tion
ex•trin•sic
ex•trin•si•cal∘ly
ex•tro•ver•sion
ex•tro•vert
ex•trude *v.*, ex•
  trud∘ed, ex•trud•
  ing.
ex•tru•sion
ex•tru•sive
ex∘u•ber•ance
ex∘u•ber•ant
ex∘u•ber•ant∘ly

ex•u•da•tion
ex•ude v., ex•ud•ed, ex•ud•ing.
ex•ult v., ex•ult•ed, ex•ult•ing. (rejoice: cf. EXALT)
ex•ult•ant
ex•ul•ta•tion
ex•ult•ing•ly
ex•ur•ban
ex•ur•ban•ite
ex•ur•bi•a
eye¹ n., (organ of sight: cf. AYE; I)
eye² v., eyed, ey•ing or eye•ing.
eye-catch•ing

eye shad•ow
eye•ball v., eye•balled, eye•ball•ing.
eye•brow
eyed
eye•drop•per
eye•ful n., pl. eye•fuls.
eye•glass
eye•lash
eye•less
eye•let (small hole: cf. ISLET)
eye•lid
eye•lin•er
eye••o•pen•er
eye••o•pen•ing

eye•piece
eye•shade
eye•sight
eye•sore
eye•strain
eye•tooth n., pl. eye•teeth.
eye•wash
eye•wit•ness v., eye•wit•nessed, eye•wit•ness•ing.
ey•rie or ey•ory, n., pl. ey•ries.
E•ze•ki•el

F

f-•num•ber
fa•ble
fa•bled
fab•ric
fab•ri•cate v., fab•ri•cat•ed, fab•ri•cat•ing.
fab•ri•ca•tion
fab•ri•ca•tor
fab•u•lous
fab•u•lous•ly
fa•cade or fa•çade
face v., faced, fac•ing.
face-lift
face-off
face-sav•ing
faced
face•less
fac•et (gem surface: cf. FAUCET)
fa•ce•tious
fa•ce•tious•ly
fa•ce•tious•ness
fa•cial
fac•ile
fac•ile•ly

fa•cil•i•tate v., fa•cil•i•tat•ed, fa•cil•i•tat•ing.
fa•cil•i•ta•tion
fa•cil•i•ta•tor
fa•cil•i•ty n., pl. fa•cil•i•ties. (ease: cf. FELICITY)
fac•ing
fac•sim•i•le v., fac•sim•i•led, fac•sim•i•le•ing.
fact
fact sheet Business.
fac•tion
fac•tion•al
fac•tion•al•ism
fac•tious (contentious: cf. FACTITIOUS; FICTI•TIOUS)
fac•tious•ness
fac•ti•tious (artificial: cf. FACTIOUS; FICTITIOUS)
fac•tor v., fac•tored, fac•tor•ing.
fac•tor•age Business.

fac•to•ry n., pl. fac•to•ries. Business.
fac•to•tum
fac•tu•al
fac•tu•al•ly
fac•ul•ty n., pl fac•ul•ties.
fad
fad•dish
fad•dist
fade v., fad•ed, fad•ing.
fae•cal
fae•ces
fa•er•ie or fa•er•y n., pl. fa•er•ies.
fag•got (disparaging term for homosexual)
fag•ot (bundle of twigs)
fag•ot•ing
Fahr•en•heit
fa•ience or fa•ïence
fail v., failed, fail•ing.
fail-safe

faille (ribbed fabric: cf. FILE)
fail•ure
fain
faint[1] adj., faint∘er, faint•est.
faint[2] v., faint∘ed, faint•ing. (to lose consciousness: cf. FEINT)
faint•heart∘ed
faint∘ly
faint•ness
fair adj., fair∘er, fair•est. (impartial: cf. FARE)
fair em•ploy•ment Business.
fair-haired
fair mar•ket val∘ue Business.
fair∘ground
fair∘ly
fair•ness
fair trade n. Business.
fair-trade adj. Business.
fair∘way
fair∘y n., pl. fair•ies.
fair∘y tale
fair∘y•land
fait ac•com•pli n., pl. faits ac•com•plis.
faith
faith•ful
faith•ful∘ly
faith•ful•ness
faith•less
faith•less∘ly
faith•less•ness
fa•ji•tas
fake v., faked, fak•ing.
fak∘er (one who pretends)
fa•kir (Muslim or Hindu monk)

fal•con
fal•con∘er
fal•con∘ry
fall v., fell, fall∘en, fall∘ing.
fal•la•cious
fal•la•cious∘ly
fal•la∘cy n., pl. fal•la•cies.
fal•li•bil∘i∘ty
fal•li•ble
fall∘ing-out n., pl. fall∘ings-out.
fall∘off
fal•lo•pi∘an or Fal•lo•pi∘an
fall•out or fall-out
fal∘low
false adj., fals∘er, fals•est.
false drop Computers.
false∘hood
false∘ly
false•ness
fal•set∘to n., pl. fal•set•tos.
fals∘ie
fal•si•fi•ca•tion
fal•si∘fy v., fal•si•fied, fal•si•fy•ing.
fal•si∘ty
fal•ter v., fal•tered, fal•ter•ing.
fal•ter•ing∘ly
fame
famed
fa•mil•ial
fa•mil•iar
fa•mil∘i•ar∘i∘ty n., pl. fa•mil∘i•ar∘i•ties.
fa•mil•iar•ize v., fa•mil•iar•ized, fa•mil•iar•iz•ing.
fa•mil•iar∘ly

fam∘i∘ly n., pl. fam∘i•lies.
fam•ine
fam•ish v., fam•ished, fam•ish•ing.
fa•mous
fa•mous∘ly
fan v., fanned, fan•ning.
fa•nat•ic
fa•nat∘i•cal∘ly
fa•nat∘i•cism
fan•ci∘er
fan•ci•ful
fan•ci•ful∘ly
fan∘cy n., pl. fan•cies; v., fan•cied, fan•cy•ing; adj., fan•ci∘er, fan•ci•est.
fan∘cy-free
fan∘cy•work
fan•dan∘go n., pl. fan•dan•gos.
fan•dom
fan•fare
fang
fanged
fan•jet or fan jet
fan•light
Fan•nie Mae Business. (Federal National Mortgage Association)
fan∘ny n., pl. fan•nies.
fan∘ny pack
fan•tail
fan•ta•sia n., pl. fan•ta•sias.
fan•ta•size v., fan•ta•sized, fan•ta•siz•ing.
fan•tas•tic
fan•tas•ti•cal∘ly
fan•ta∘sy or phan•ta∘sy n., pl. fan•ta•sies; v., fan•ta•sied, fan•ta•sy•ing.

far *adj.*, far•ther or fur•ther, far•thest or fur•thest.

far-fetched or far•fetched

far-flung

far-off

far-out

far-reach•ing

far○ad

far○a•way

farce

fare *v.*, fared, far•ing. (transportation charge; food: cf. FARE)

fare•well

fa•ri○na

far○i•na•ceous

farm *v.*, farmed, farm•ing.

Far•mer

farm•hand or farm hand

farm•house *n.*, *pl.* farm•hous○es.

farm•land

farm•stead

farm•yard

far○o

far•ra○go *n.*, *pl.* far•ra•goes.

far•row

far•sight○ed

far•sight○ed•ness

far•ther (to a greater distance: cf. FURTHER)

far•ther•most

far•thest

far•thing

F.A.S. *Business.* (free alongside ship)

fas•ci○cle

fas•ci•nate *v.*, fas•ci•nat○ed, fas•ci•nat•ing.

fas•ci•na•tion

fas•cism

fas•cist

fa•scis•tic

fash•ion *v.*, fash•ioned, fash•ion•ing.

fash•ion•a○ble

fash•ion•a•bly

fast[1] *adj.*, fast○er, fast•est.

fast[2] *v.*, fast○ed, fast•ing.

fast food *n.*

fast-food *adj.*

fast-talk *v.*, fast○talked, fast○talk•ing

fast•back

fas•ten *v.*, fast•tened, fast•ten•ing.

fas•ten○er

fas•tid○i•ous

fas•tid○i•ous○ly

fas•tid○i•ous•ness

fast•ness

FAT *Computers.* (file allocation table)

fa•tal

fatal er•ror *Computers.*

fa•tal•ism

fa•tal•ist

fa•tal•is•tic

fa•tal○i•ty *n.*, *pl.* fa•tal○i•ties.

fa•tal○ly

fat•back

fate (destiny: cf. FETE or FÊTE)

fat○ed

fate•ful

fate•ful○ly

fat•head

fat•head○ed

fa•ther *v.*, fa•thered, fa•ther•ing.

fa○ther-in-law *n.*, *pl.* fa○thers-in-law.

fa•ther•hood

fa•ther•land

fa•ther•less

fa•ther○ly

fath○om *n.*, *pl.* fath○oms or fath○om; *v.*, fath○omed, fath○om•ing.

fa•tigue *v.*, fa•tigued, fa•ti•guing.

fat•ness

fat•ten *v.*, fat•tened, fat•ten•ing.

fat•ti•ness

fat○ty *n.*, *pl.* fat•ties; *adj.*, fat•ti○er, fat•ti•est.

fa•tu○i•ty

fat○u•ous

fat○u•ous○ly

fat○u•ous•ness

fau•cet (flow control valve: cf. FACET)

Faulk•ner

fault *v.*, fault○ed, fault•ing.

fault-find•ing

fault○i○ly

fault•less

fault•less○ly

fault○y *adj.*, fault•i○er, fault•i•est.

faun (satyr: cf. FAWN)

fau○na *n.*, *pl.* fau•nas, fau•nae.

Faust or Faus•tus

Faus•ti○an

Fauve

Fauv•ism

faux pas *n.*, *pl.* faux pas.

fa•vor *v.*, fa•vored, fa•vor•ing.

fa•vor•a○ble

fa•vor•a•bly

fa•vor•ite

fa•vor•it•ism
fawn (cf. FAUN)
fawn•ing∘ly
fax *v.*, faxed, fax•ing. *Business.*
fay
faze *v.*, fazed, faz•ing. (young deer; to disconcert: cf. PHASE)
FBI (Federal Bureau of Investigation)
FCC *Business.* (Federal Communications Commission)
FDA (Food and Drug Administration)
FDIC *Business.* (Federal Deposit Insurance Corporation)
fe•al∘ty
fear *v.*, feared, fear•ing.
fear•ful
fear•ful∘ly
fear•ful•ness
fear•less
fear•less∘ly
fear•less•ness
fear•some
fea•si•bil•i•ty
fea•si∘ble
feast *v.*, feast∘ed, feast•ing.
feat
feath∘er *v.*, feath•ered, feath•er•ing.
feath∘er•bed∘ding *Business.*
feath•ered
feath∘er•weight
feath∘er∘y
fea•ture *v.*, fea•tured, fea•tur•ing.
fea•ture•less
feb•ri•fuge
fe•brile
Feb•ru•ar∘y

fe•cal
fe•ces
feck•less
feck•less∘ly
fe•cund
fe•cun•date, *v.*, fe•cun•dat∘ed, fe•cun•dat•ing.
fe•cun•di∘ty
fed
fe•da•yeen *n.*, *pl.*
fed•er∘al
Fed•er•al Re•serve *Business.*
fed•er•al•ism
fed•er•al•ist
fed•er•al•ize *v.*, fed•er•al•ized, fed•er•al•iz•ing.
fed•er•ate *v.*, fed•er•at∘ed, fed•er•at•ing.
fed•er∘a•tion
fe•do∘ra *n.*, *pl.* fe•do•ras.
fee
fee•ble *adj.*, fee•bler, fee•blest.
fee•ble-mind∘ed
fee•ble-mind∘ed∘ness
fee•ble•ness
fee•bly
feed *v.*, fed, feed•ing.
feed•back
feed∘er
feed•ing fren∘zy
feed•stuff
feel *v.*, felt, feel•ing.
feel-good
feel∘er
feel•ing
feel•ing∘ly
feet
feign *v.*, feigned, feign•ing.

feint *v.*, feint∘ed, feint•ing. (to deceive: cf. FAINT)
feist∘y *adj.*, feist•i∘er, feist•i•est.
feld•spar
fe•lic∘i•tate *v.*, fe•lic∘i•tat∘ed, fe•lic∘i•tat•ing.
fe•lic∘i•ta•tion
fe•lic∘i•ta•tor
fe•lic∘i•tous
fe•lic∘i•tous∘ly
fe•lic∘i∘ty (happiness: cf. FACILITY)
fe•line
fell *v.*, felled, fell•ing.
fel•lah *n.*, *pl.* fel•lahs, fel•la•hin,,fel•la•heen. (Arabic peasant)
fel•la•ti∘o or fel•la•tion
fel•low (man or boy)
fel•low•man or fel•low man *n.*, *pl.* fel•low•men or fel•lowmen.
fel•low•ship
fel∘on
fe•lo•ni•ous
fel∘o•ny *n.*, *pl.* fel•o•nies.
felt
fe•male
fem∘i•nine
fem∘i•nin∘i∘ty
fem∘i•nism
fem∘i•nist
femme fa•tale *n.*, *pl.* femmes fa•tales.
fem∘o•ral
fe•mur *n.*, *pl.* fe•murs, fem•o∘ra.
fen
fence *v.*, fenced, fenc•ing.
fenc∘er

fend *v.*, fend∘ed, fend•ing.

fend∘er

fen•es•tra•tion

fen•nel

fe•ral

fer•ment *v.*, fer•ment∘ed, fer•ment•ing. (to change to alcohol: cf. FOMENT)

fer•men•ta•tion

fer∘mi

fer•mi∘um

fern

fern bar

fe•ro•cious

fe•ro•cious∘ly

fe•roc•i∘ty or fe•ro•cious•ness

fer•ret *v.*, fer•ret∘ed, fer•ret•ing.

fer•ric

Fer•ris wheel

fer∘ro•mag•net∘ic

fer∘ro•mag•ne•tism

fer•rous

fer•rule (metal ring: cf. FERULE)

fer∘ry *n.*, *pl.* fer•ries; *v.*, fer•ried, fer•ry•ing.

fer∘ry•boat

fer•tile

fer•til∘i∘ty

fer•ti•li•za•tion

fer•ti•lize *v.*, fer•ti•lized, fer•ti•liz•ing.

fer•ti•liz∘er

fer•ule (rod: cf. FERRULE)

fer•ven∘cy

fer•vent

fer•vent∘ly

fer•vid

fer•vid∘ly

fer•vor

fes•cue

fes•tal

fes•ter *v.*, fes•tered, fes•ter•ing.

fes•ti•val

fes•tive

fes•tive∘ly

fes•tive•ness (festive quality)

fes•tiv∘i∘ty *n.*, *pl.* fes•tiv∘i•ties. (celebration)

fes•toon *v.*, fes•tooned, fes•toon•ing.

fet∘a

fe•tal or foe•tal

fetch *v.*, fetched, fetch•ing.

fetch•ing∘ly

fete or fête (celebration: cf. FATE)

fet∘id

fet•ish

fet•ish•ism

fet•ish•ist

fet•lock

fet•ter *v.*, fet•tered, fet•ter•ing.

fet•tle

fet•tuc•ci∘one or fet•tuc•ci∘oni

fe•tus or foe•tus *n.*, *pl.* fe•tus∘es.

feud *v.*, feud∘ed, feud•ing.

feu•dal

feu•dal•ism

feu•dal•is•tic

fe•ver *v.*, fe•vered, fe•ver•ing.

fe•ver•ish

fe•ver•ish∘ly

few *adj.*, few∘er, few∘est.

fey

fez *n.*, *pl.* fez∘zes.

FHA *Business.* (Federal Housing Administration)

fi•an∘cé (engaged man)

fi•an∘cée (engaged woman)

fi•as∘co *n.*, *pl.* fi•as•cos, fi•as•coes.

fi∘at

fib *v.*, fibbed, fib•bing.

fib•ber

fi∘ber

fi∘ber op•tics or fi∘ber-op•t ics

fi∘ber•board

fi∘ber•fill

fi∘ber•glass or fi∘ber glass

fi∘ber•op∘tic

fi•bril

fi•bril•late *v.*, fi•bril•lat∘ed, fi•bril•lat•ing.

fi•bril•la•tion

fi•brin

fi•brin∘o•gen

fi•broid

fi•brous

fib•u∘la *n.*, *pl.* fib•u•lae, fib•u•las.

fib•u•lar

FICA or **F.I.C.A.** (Federal Insurance Contributions Act).

fiche

fick∘le

fick•le•ness

fic•tion

fic•tion∘al

fic•tion•al•i•za•tion

fic•tion•al•ize *v.*, fic•tion•al•ized, fic•tion•al•iz•ing.

fic•ti•tious (imaginary: cf. FACTIOUS; FACTITIOUS)

finally

fic•ti•tious•ly

fic•tive

fid•dle *v.*, fid•dled, fid•dling.

fid•dler

fid•dle•sticks

fi•del•i•ty

fidelity bond *Business.*

fidg•et *v.*, fidg•et•ed, fidg•et•ing.

fidg•et•y

fi•du•ci•ar•y *n.*, *pl.* fi•du•ci•ar•ies. *Business.*

fie

fief

fief•dom

field *v.*, field•ed, field•ing.

field test *n.*

field-test *v.*

field ware•hous•ing *Business.*

field•er

field•work or field work

field•work•er

fiend (demon: cf. FRIEND)

fiend•ish

fiend•ish•ly

fierce *adj.*, fierc•er, fierc•est.

fierce•ly

fierce•ness

fier•i•ness

fier•y *adj.*, fier•i•er, fier•i•est.

fi•es•ta

fife

FIFO *Business.* (first-in, first-out)

fif•teen

fif•teenth

fifth

fifth•ly

fif•ti•eth

fif•ty *n.*, *pl.* fif•ties.

fif•ty-fif•ty or 50-•50

fig

fight *v.*, fought, fight•ing.

fight•er

fig•ment

fig•u•ra•tion

fig•ur•a•tive

fig•ur•a•tive•ly

fig•ure *v.*, fig•ured, fig•ur•ing.

fig•ure•head

fig•ur•ine

Fi•ji

Fi•ji•an

fil•a•ment

fil•bert

filch *v.*, filched, filch•ing.

file¹ (folder; tool: cf. FAILLE)

file² *v.*, filed, fil•ing.

file al•lo•ca•tion ta•ble (FAT) *Computers.*

file lock•ing *Computers.*

file man•ag•er *Computers.*

file serv•er *Computers.*

file•name *Computers.*

filename ex•ten•sion *Computers.*

fi•let (netting: cf. FIL-LET)

fi•let mi•gnon

fil•i•al

fil•i•bus•ter *v.*, fil•i•bus•tered, fil•i•bus•ter•ing.

fil•i•gree *v.*, fil•i•greed, fil•i•gree•ing.

fil•ings *n.*, *pl.*

Fil•i•pi•no *n.*, *pl.* Fil•i•pi•nos.

fill *v.*, filled, fill•ing.

fill-in

fill•a•ble

fill•er

fil•let *v.*, fil•let•ed, fil•leted, fi•let•ing. *(boneless strip, as fish; to debone: cf.* FILET*)*

fill•ing

fil•lip

Fill•more

fil•ly *n.*, *pl.* fil•lies.

film *v.*, filmed, film•ing.

film•i•ness

film•strip

film•y *adj.*, film•i•er, film•i•est.

Fi•lo•fax *Trademark.*

fil•ter¹ (strainer: cf. PHILTER)

fil•ter² *v.*, fil•tered, fil•ter•ing.

fil•ter•a•ble

filth

filth•i•ness

filth•y *adj.*, filth•i•er, filth•i•est.

fil•tra•ble

fil•tra•tion

fin

fin-de-siè•cle

fi•na•gle *v.*, fi•na•gled, fi•na•gling.

fi•na•gler

fi•nal

fi•na•le (last part: cf. FINALLY; FINELY)

fi•nal•ist

fi•nal•i•ty

fi•na•li•za•tion

fi•na•lize *v.*, fi•na•lized, fi•na•liz•ing.

fi•nal•ly (at last: cf. FI-NALE; FINELY)

fi•nance v., fi•
nanced, fi•nanc•ing.

finance com•pa•ny
Business.

fi•nan•cial

financial lease

fi•nan•cial state•
ment

fi•nan•cial•ly

fin•an•cier

finch

find v., found, find•
ing. (to locate: cf.
FINED)

find•a•ble

find•er

find•er's fee *Business.*

find•ing

fine v., fined, fin•ing;.
adj., fin•er, fin•est.

fine-tune v., fine-
tuned, fine-tun•ing.

fined (penalized: cf.
FIND)

fine•ly (delicately: cf.
FINALE; FINALLY)

fine•ness (thinness: cf.
FINESSE)

fin•er•y

fine•spun or fine-
spun

fi•nesse¹ (delicacy: cf.
FINENESS)

fi•nesse² v., fi•
nessed, fi•ness•ing.

fin•ger v., fin•gered,
fin•ger•ing.

fin•ger•board

fin•ger•ing

fin•ger•ling

fin•ger•nail

fin•ger•print v.,
fin•ger•print•ed,
fin•ger•print•ing.

fin•ger•tip

fin•i•al

fin•ick•y

fin•is (the end)

fin•ish v., fin•ished,
fin•ish•ing. (end; to
end)

fin•ished goods *Busi-
ness.*

fin•ish•er

fi•nite

fink

Fin•land

Finn

fin•nan had•die

finned

Finn•ish

fin•ny adj., fin•ni•er,
fin•ni•est.

F.I.O. *Business.* (free in
and out)

fiord

fir (tree: cf. FUR)

fire v., fired, fir•ing.

fire•arm

fire•ball

fire•bomb v., fire•
bombed, fire•bomb•
ing.

fire•box

fire•brand

fire•break

fire•brick

fire•bug

fire•crack•er

fire•damp

fire•fight

fire•fight•er or fire
fight•er

fire•fight•ing

fire•fly n., pl. fire•
flies.

fire•house n., pl. fire•
hous•es.

fire•less

fire•man n., pl. fire•
men.

fire•place

fire•plug

fire•pow•er or fire
pow•er

fire•proof v., fire•
proofed, fire•proof•
ing.

fire•side

fire•storm or fire
storm

fire•trap

fire•wa•ter

fire•wood

fire•work

firm v., firmed, firm•
ing;. adj., firm•er,
firm•est.

firm or•der *Business.*

fir•ma•ment

firm•ly

firm•ness

firm•ware *Computers.*

first

first aid n.

first-aid adj.

first class n.

first-class adj.

first-in first-out (FIFO)
Business.

first la•dy

first-night•er

first-rate

first-string

first-string•er

first•born

first•hand or first-
hand

first•ly

firth

fis•cal *Business.* (financial: cf. PHYSICAL)

fis•cal year *Business.*

fish n., pl. fish or
fish•es;. v., fished,
fish•ing.

fish•bowl or fish
bowl

fish•er

fish•er•man *n., pl.*
fish•er•men.
fish•er•y *n., pl.* fish•
er•ies.
fish•hook
fish∘i∘ly
fish∘i•ness
fish•ing
fish•wife *n., pl.* fish•
wives.
fish∘y *adj.,* fish•i∘er,
fish•i•est.
fis•sile
fis•sion *v.,* fis•sioned,
fis•sion•ing.
fis•sion•a∘ble
fis•sure *v.,* fis•sured,
fis•sur•ing.
fist
fist•ful *n., pl.* fist•
fuls.
fist∘i•cuff
fis•tu•la *n., pl.* fis•
tu•las, fis•tu•lae.
fit *v.,* fit•ted or fit,
fit•ting; *adj.,* fit•ter,
fit•test.
fit•ful
fit•ful∘ly
fit•ful•ness
fit∘ly
fit•ness
fit•ter
fit•ting
fit•ting∘ly
Fitz•ger•ald
five
five-and-ten
fix *v.,* fixed, fix•ing.
fix•at∘ed
fix•a•tion
fix•a•tive
fixed
fixed as•set *Business.*
fixed charge *Business.*
fixed cost *Business.*

fixed-length field
Computers.
fixed pitch *Computers.*
fix•ed∘ly
fix∘er
fix•ing
fix∘i∘ty
fix•ture
fizz *v.,* fizzed, fizz•
ing.
fiz•zle *v.,* fiz•zled,
fiz•zling.
fjord or fiord
FL (Florida)
fl. oz. (fluid ounce)
flab
flab•ber•gast∘ed
flab•bi•ness
flab∘by *adj.,* flab•
bi∘er, flab•bi•est.
flac∘cid
flack
flac∘on
flag *v.,* flagged, flag•
ging.
flag•el•late, *v.,* flag•
el•lat∘ed, flag•el•
lat∘ing. *adj., n.*
flag•el•la•tion
flag•pole
fla•grant (glaring: cf.
FRAGRANT)
fla•gran•te de•lic∘to
fla•grant∘ly
flag•ship
flag•stone
flail *v.,* flailed, flail•
ing.
flair (aptitude: cf. FLARE)
flak
flake *v.,* flaked, flak•
ing.
flak∘y *adj.,* flak•i∘er,
flak•i•est.
flam∘bé *v.,* flam•
béed, flam•bé∘ing.

flam•boy•ance
flam•boy•ant
flam•boy•ant∘ly
flame *v.,* flamed,
flam•ing.
flame-out
fla•men•co *n., pl.* fla•
men•cos.
flame•throw∘er
fla•min•go *n., pl.* fla•
min•gos, fla•min•
goes.
flam•ma•bil∘i∘ty
flam•ma•ble
Flan•ders
flange
flank *v.,* flanked,
flank•ing.
flan•nel
flan•nel∘et or flan•
nel•ette
flap *v.,* flapped, flap•
ping.
flap•jack
flap•per
flare *v.,* flared, flar•
ing. (to flame: cf.
FLAIR)
flare∘up
flash *v.,* flashed,
flash•ing.
flash-for∘ward
flash point or flash•
point
flash•back
flash•bulb or flash
bulb
flash•card or flash
card
flash•cube
flash∘er
flash•gun
flash∘i•ly
flash∘i•ness
flash•ing
flash•light

flash○y *adj.*, flash•
i○er, flash•i•est.

flask

flat *v.*, flat•ted, flat•
ting; *adj.*, flat•ter,
flat•test.

flat-file

flat-file da○ta•base
Computers.

flat-out

flat-screen dis•play
Computers.

flat tech•nol○o○gy
mon○i•tor Comput-
ers.

flat•bed

flatbed scan•ner *Com-
puters.*

flat•boat

flat•car

flat•fish *n.*, *pl.* flat•
fish, flat•fish○es.

flat•foot *n.*, *pl.* flat•
feet, flat•foots.

flat•foot○ed

flat•i○ron

flat○ly

flat•ness

flat•ten *v.*, flat•
tened, flat•ten•ing.

flat•ter *v.*, flat•tered,
flat•ter•ing.

flat•ter○er

flat•ter•ing○ly

flat•ter○y

flat•tish

flat•top

flato•u•lence

flato•u•lent

fla•tus, *n.*, *pl* fla•
tus○es.

flat•ware

Flau•bert

flaunt *v.*, flaunt○ed,
flaunt•ing. (to dis-
play boldly: cf. FLOUT)

flau•tist

fla•vor

fla•vor of the month

fla•vored

fla•vor•ful

fla•vor•ing

fla•vor•less

flaw

flawed

flaw•less

flaw•less○ly

flax

flax○en

flay *v.*, flayed, flay•
ing.

flea (small insect: cf.
FLEE)

flea-bit•ten

flea-bag

fleck

fledg•ling

flee *v.*, fled, flee•ing.
(to run away: cf. FLEA)

fleece *v.*, fleeced,
fleec○ing.

fleec○y *adj.*, fleec•
i○er, fleec•i•est.

fleer *v.*, fleered, fleer•
ing.

fleer•ing○ly

fleet[1]

fleet[2] *adj.*, fleet○er,
fleet•est.

fleet•ing

fleet•ing○ly

fleet○ly

fleet•ness

Flem•ing

Flem•ish

flesh *v.*, fleshed,
flesh•ing.

flesh○ly, *adj.*, flesh•
li○er, flesh•li•est.

flesh•pots *n.*, *pl.*

flesh○y *adj.*, flesh•
i○er, flesh•i•est.

fleur-de-lis *n.*, *pl.*
fleur-de-lis.

flew (did fly: cf. FLU;
FLUE)

flex *v.*, flexed, flex•
ing.

flex•i•bil•i○ty

flex•i○ble

flex○i○ble-rate mort•
gage Business.

flex•time or
flex○i•time *Business.*

flex•ure

flib•ber•ti•gib•bet

flick *v.*, flicked, flick•
ing.

flick○er *v.*, flick•ered,
flick•er•ing.

flied

fli○er or fly○er

flight

flight○i•ness

flight•ing *Business.*

flight•less

flight○y *adj.*, flight•
i○er, flight•i•est.

flim•flam

flim•si•ness

flim○sy *n.*, *pl.* flim•
sies; *adj.*, flim•si○er,
flim•si•est.

flinch *v.*, flinched,
flinch•ing.

fling *v.*, flung, fling•
ing.

flint

flint•lock

flint○y *adj.*, flint•i○er,
flint•i•est.

flip *v.*, flipped, flip•
ping; *adj.*, flip•per,
flip•pest.

flip-flop *v.*, flip-
flopped,
flip-flop○ping.

flip•pan○cy

flip•pant

flung

flip•pant•ly

flip•per

flirt *v.*, flirt∘ed, flirt•ing.

flir•ta•tion

flir•ta•tious

flir•ta•tious•ly

flit *v.*, flit•ted, flit•ting.

flit•ter

fliv•ver

float *v.*, float∘ed, float•ing.

float∘er

float∘ing-point num•ber *Computers.*

float∘ing-point u∘nit (FPU) *Computers.*

float∘ing-rate *Computers.*

flock *v.*, flocked, flock•ing.

flocks (groups: cf. PHLOX)

floe (floating ice: cf. FLOW)

flog *v.*, flogged, flog•ging.

flood *v.*, flood∘ed, flood•ing.

flood plain or flood•plain

flood•gate

flood•light *v.*, flood•light∘ed or flood•lit, flood•light•ing.

floor *v.*, floored, floor•ing.

floor•board

floor•ing

floor•walk∘er

floo∘zy or floo•zie *n.*, *pl.* floo•zies.

flop *v.*, flopped, flop•ping.

flop•house *n.*, *pl.* flop•hous∘es.

flop•py *n.*, *pl.* flop•pies; *adj.*, flop•pi∘er, flop•pi•est.

floppy disk *Computers.*

floppy drive *Computers.*

Flop•ti•cal disk *Computers.*

flo∘ra *n.*, *pl.* flo∘ras, flo•rae.

flo•ral

Flor•ence

Flor•en•tine

flo•res•cence (bloom: cf. FLUORESCENCE)

flo•ret

flor∘id

Flor∘i•da (FL)

Flor∘i•dan or Flo•rid∘i∘an

flor∘in

flo•rist

floss *v.*, flossed, floss•ing.

floss∘y *adj.*, floss•i∘er, floss•i•est.

flo•ta•tion or floa•ta•tion

flo•til∘la

flot•sam

flounce *v.*, flounced, flounc•ing.

floun•der *n.*, *pl.* floun•der or floun•ders; *v.*, floun•dered, floun•der•ing. (the fish; to struggle: cf. FOUNDER[1]; FOUNDER[2])

flour *v.*, floured, flour•ing. (fine meal; to coat with flour: cf. FLOWER)

flour•ish *v.*, flour•ished, flour•ish•ing.

flour•ish•ing∘ly

flour∘y

flout *v.*, flout∘ed, flout•ing. (to scoff at: cf. FLAUNT)

flow *v.*, flowed, flow•ing. (to stream: cf. FLOE)

flow chart or flow•chart

flow∘er *v.*, flow•ered, flow•er•ing. (blossom; to blosson: cf. FLOUR)

flow•er•pot

flow•er∘y *adj.*, flow•er•i∘er, flow•er•i•est.

flown

flu (influenza: cf. FLEW; FLUE)

flub *v.*, flubbed, flub•bing.

fluc•tu•ate *v.*, fluc•tu•at∘ed, fluc•tu•at•ing.

fluc•tu•a•tion

flue (chimney duct: cf. FLEW; FLU)

flu•en∘cy

flu•ent

flu•ent∘ly

fluff *v.*, fluffed, fluff•ing.

fluff∘i•ness

fluff∘y *adj.*, fluff•i∘er, fluff•i•est.

flu∘id

fluid ounce (fl. oz.)

flu•id∘i∘ty

flu•id∘ly

fluke

fluk∘y *adj.*, fluk•i∘er, fluk•i•est.

flum•mox *v.*, flum•moxed, flum•mox•ing.

flung

flunk *v.*, flunked, flunk•ing.

flun•ky or flun•key *n.*, *pl.* flun•kies, flun•keys.

fluo•resce *v.*, fluo•resced, fluo•resc•ing.

fluo•res•cence (light: cf. FLORESCENCE)

fluo•res•cent

fluor•oi•date *v.*, fluor•oi•dat•ed, fluor•oi•dat•ing.

fluor•oi•da•tion

fluor•ide

fluor•ine

fluo•rite

fluor•o•car•bon

fluor•o•scope *v.*, fluor•o•scoped, fluor•o•scop•ing.

flur•ry *n.*, *pl.* flur•ries; *v.*, flur•ried, flur•ry•ing.

flush *v.*, flushed, flush•ing.

flus•ter *v.*, flus•tered, flus•ter•ing.

flute

flut•ed

flut•ing

flut•ist or flautist

flut•ter *v.*, flut•tered, flut•ter•ing.

flut•ter•y

flux

fly[1] *n.*, *pl.* flies. (insect)

fly[2] *v.*, flew, flown, fly•ing. (to move through the air with wings)

fly-by-night

fly•blown

fly•by or fly-by *n.*, *pl.* fly•bys.

fly•catch•er

fly•er

fly•leaf *n.*, *pl.* fly•leaves.

fly•pa•per

fly•speck

fly•specked

fly•way

fly•weight

fly•wheel

FM (frequency modulation)

FNMA *Business.* (Federal National Mortgage Association)

foal *v.*, foaled, foal•ing.

foam *v.*, foamed, foam•ing.

foam•y *adj.*, foam•i•er, foam•i•est.

fob or f.o.b.[1] *Business.* (free on board).

fob[2] *v.*, fobbed, fob•bing.

fo•cac•cia

fo•cal

fo'c's'le (forecastle)

fo•cus *n.*, *pl.* fo•cus•es, fo•ci; *v.*, fo•cused or fo•cussed, fo•cus•ing or fo•cus•sing.

fod•der

foe

foe•tal

foe•tus *n.*, *pl.* foe•tus•es.

fog *v.*, fogged, fog•ging.

fog•gy *adj.*, fog•gi•er, fog•gi•est. (misty: cf. FOGY or FO•GEY)

fog•horn

fo•gy or fo•gey, *n.*, *pl.* fo•gies or fo•geys. (old-fashioned person: cf. FOGGY)

fo•gy•ish

foi•ble

foil *v.*, foiled, foil•ing.

foist *v.*, foist•ed, foist•ing.

fold *v.*, fold•ed, fold•ing.

fold•a•way

fold•er

fold•out or fold-out

fo•li•age

fo•li•at•ed

fo•lic ac•id

fo•li•o *n.*, *pl.* fo•li•os.

folk

folk•lore

folk•lor•ic

folk•lor•ist

folk•si•ness

folk•sy *adj.*, folk•si•er, folk•si•est.

folk•way

fol•li•cle

fol•low *v.*, folk•lowed, folk•low•ing.

fol•low-up

fol•low•er

fol•low•ing

fo•ly *n.*, *pl.* fol•lies.

fo•ment *v.*, fo•ment•ed, fo•ment•ing. (to instigate: cf. FERMENT)

fond *adj.*, fond•er, fond•est.

fon•dant

fon•dle *v.*, fon•dled, fon•dling.

fon•dling (caressing: cf. FOUNDLING)

fond•ly

fond•ness

foreman

fon•due
font *Computers.*
font card *Computers.*
font car•tridge *Computers.*
font fam•i•ly *Computers.*
food
food chain
food poi•son•ing
food proc•es•sor
food○ie
food•stuff
fool *v.,* fooled, fool•ing.
fool•er○y *n., pl.* fool•er•ies.
fool•har•di•ness
fool•har○dy
fool•ish
fool•ish○ly
fool•ish•ness
fool•proof
fools•cap
foot *n., pl.* feet.
foot-and-mouth dis-ease
foot-can○dle
foot-pound
foot•age
foot•ball
foot•board
foot•bridge
foot○er
foot•fall
foot•hill
foot•hold
foot•ing
foot•less
foot•light
foot•lock○er
foot•loose
foot•man *n., pl.* foot•men.
foot•note *v.,* foot•

not○ed, foot•not•ing.
foot•path *n., pl.* foot•paths.
foot•print
foot•rest
foot•sore
foot•step
foot•stool
foot•wear
foot•work
fop
fop•per○y
fop•pish
for (in favor of: cf. FORE; FOUR)
for•age *v.,* for•aged, for•ag•ing.
for•ag○er
for•as•much as
for○ay
for•bear *v.,* for•bore, for•borne, for•bear•ing. (to abstain: cf. FOREBEAR)
for•bear•ance
for•bid *v.,* for•bade or for•bad or for•bid, for•bid•den, for•bid•ding.
for•bid•ding
for•bid•ding○ly
force *v.,* forced, forc•ing.
force-feed *v.,* force-fed, force-feed○ing.
force•ful (powerful: cf. FORCIBLE)
force•ful○ly
force•ful•ness
for•ceps *n., pl.* for•ceps or for•ci•pes.
for•ci•ble (done by force: cf. FORCEFUL)
for•ci•bly
ford *v.,* ford○ed, ford•ing.

fore (front: cf. FOR; FOUR)
fore-and-aft
fore•arm
fore•armed
fore•bear (ancestor: cf. FORBEAR)
fore•bod•ing
fore•cast *v.,* fore•cast or fore•cast○ed, fore•cast•ing.
fore•cast○er
fore•cas•tle or fo'c's'l e
fore•close *v.,* fore•closed, fore•clos•ing.
fore•clo•sure *Business.*
fore•doom *v.,* fore•doomed, fore•doom•ing.
fore•fa•ther
fore•fin•ger
fore•foot *n., pl.* fore•feet.
fore•front
fore○go, *v.,* fore•went, fore•go•ing.
fore•go•ing
fore•gone
fore•ground
fore•hand
fore•head
for•eign
foreign cor•po•ra•tion *Business.*
foreign ex•change (FX) *Business.*
for•eign○er
for•eign•ness
fore•knowl•edge
fore•leg
fore•limb
fore•lock
fore•man *n., pl.* fore•men.

fore•mast
fore•most
fore•name
fore•noon
fo•ren•sic
fore•or•dain v., fore•
 or•dained, fore•or•
 dain•ing.
fore•part
fore•per•son
fore•play
fore•quar•ter
fore•run•ner
fore•sail
fore•see v., fore•saw,
 fore•seen, fore•
 see•ing.
fore•see•a•ble
fore•shad•ow v.,
 fore•shad•owed,
 fore•shad•ow•ing.
fore•short•en v.,
 fore•short•ened,
 fore•short•en•ing.
fore•sight
fore•sight•ed
fore•sight•ed•ness
fore•skin
for•est v., for•est•ed,
 for•est•ing.
fore•stall v., fore•
 stalled, fore•stall•
 ing.
for•est•a•tion
for•est•ed
for•est•er
for•est•ry
fore•taste v., fore•
 tast•ed, fore•tast•
 ing.
fore•tell v., fore•told,
 fore•tell•ing.
fore•thought
for•ev•er
for•ev•er•more
fore•warn v., fore•

warned, fore•warn•
 ing.
fore•wom•an n., pl.
 fore•wom•en.
fore•word (preface: cf.
 FORWARD)
for•feit v., for•
 feit•ed, for•feit•ing.
for•fei•ture
for•fend v., for•
 fend•ed, for•fend•
 ing.
for•gath•er v., for•
 gath•ered, for•
 gath•er•ing.
for•gave
forge v., forged, forg•
 ing.
forg•er
for•ger•y n., pl. for•
 ger•ies.
for•get v., for•got,
 for•get•ting.
for•get-me-not
for•get•ful
for•get•ful•ly
for•get•ful•ness
for•get•ta•ble
forg•ing
for•giv•a•ble
for•give v., for•gave,
 for•giv•en, for•giv•
 ing.
for•give•ness
for•giv•ing
for•go, v., for•went,
 for•gone, for•go•
 ing.
fork v., forked, fork•
 ing.
fork•ful n., pl. fork•
 fuls.
fork•lift
for•lorn
for•lorn•ly
form v., formed,
 form•ing.

form feed Computers.
for•mal
form•al•de•hyde
form•al•ism
form•al•ist
for•mal•i•ty n., pl.
 for•mal•i•ties.
for•mal•ize v., for•
 mal•ized, for•mal•
 iz•ing.
for•mal•ly (ceremoni-
 ally: cf. FORMERLY)
for•mat v., for•mat•
 ted, for•mat•ting.
for•ma•tion
form•a•tive
form•er¹ (one that
 forms)
for•mer² (earlier)
for•mer•ly (previ-
 ously: cf. FORMALLY)
form-fit•ting
for•mic
For•mi•ca Trademark.
for•mi•da•ble
for•mi•da•bly
form•less
form•less•ness
For•mo•sa
for•mu•la n., pl. for•
 mu•las, for•mu•lae.
for•mu•la•ic
for•mu•late v., for•
 mu•lat•ed, for•mu•
 lat•ing.
for•mu•la•tion
for•ni•cate v., for•
 ni•cat•ed, for•ni•
 cat•ing.
for•ni•ca•tion
for•ni•ca•tor
for•sake v., for•sook,
 for•sak•en, for•
 sak•ing.
for•sooth
for•swear v., for•

swore, for•sworn,
for•swearing.
for•syth•i•a *n., pl.*
for•syth•i•as.
fort (army post)
Fort Lau•der•dale
Fort Wayne
Fort Worth
forte¹ (specialty)
for•te² (loud; loudly)
FORTH *Computers.* (programming language)
forth•com•ing
forth•right
forth•right•ness
forth•with
for•ti•eth
for•ti•fi•a•ble
for•ti•fi•ca•tion
for•ti•fy *v.,* for•ti•fied, for•ti•fy•ing.
for•tis•si•mo
for•ti•tude
fort•night
fort•night•ly
FORTRAN *Computers.* (programming language)
for•tress
for•tu•i•tous (accidental)
for•tu•i•ty, *n., pl.* for•tu•i•ties.
for•tu•nate (lucky)
for•tu•nate•ly
for•tune
for•tune-tell•er
for•tune-tell•ing
for•ty *n., pl.* for•ties.
for•ty-five
for•ty-nin•er
fo•rum
for•ward¹ *v.,* for•ward•ed, for•ward•ing.

for•ward² (to the front: cf. FOREWORD)
for•ward•er
for•ward•ness
for•went
fos•sil
fos•sil•i•za•tion
fos•sil•ize *v.,* fos•sil•ized, fos•sil•iz•ing.
fos•ter *v.,* fos•tered, fos•ter•ing.
fought
foul¹ *v.,* fouled, foul•ing.
foul² *adj.,* foul•er, foul•est. (offensive: cf. FOWL)
foul-up
fou•lard
foul•ly
foul-mouthed
foul•ness
found *v.,* found•ed, found•ing.
foun•da•tion
foun•der¹ *v.,* foun•dered, foun•der•ing. (to sink: cf. FLOUNDER)
found•er² (one who founds: cf. FLOUNDER)
found•ling (abandoned infant: cf. FONDLING)
found•ry *n., pl.* found•ries.
fount
foun•tain
foun•tain•head
four (number: cf. FOR; FORE)
four-flush•er
four-flush•ing
four-in-hand
four-o'•clock
four-wheel or four-wheeled
four•fold

four•post•er
four•score
four•some
four•square
four•teen
four•teenth
fourth (next after third: cf. FORTH)
fourth class *n.*
fourth-class *adj.*
fowl *n., pl.* fowls or fowl. (poultry: cf. FOUL)
fowl•ing piece
fox *n., pl.* fox•es or fox; *v.,* foxed, fox•ing.
fox trot *n.*
fox•fire
fox•glove
fox•hole
fox•hound
fox•y *adj.,* fox•i•er, fox•i•est.
foy•er
FPT *Business.* (freight pass-through)
FPU *Computers.* (floating-point unit)
fra•cas
frac•tion
frac•tion•al
frac•tious
frac•tious•ness
frac•ture *v.,* frac•tured, frac•tur•ing.
frag•ile
fra•gil•i•ty
frag•ment *v.,* frag•ment•ed, frag•ment•ing.
frag•men•tar•y
frag•men•ta•tion
fra•grance
fra•grant (scented: cf. FLAGRANT)

frail *adj.*, frail•er,
frail•est.

frail•ly

frail•ty *n.*, *pl.* frail•
ties.

frame *v.*, framed,
fram•ing.

frame-up

fram•er

frame•work

franc (coin: cf. FRANK)

France

fran•chise *v.*, fran•
chised, fran•chis•
ing. *Business.*

fran•chi•see *n.*, *pl.*
fran•chi•sees. *Busi-
ness.*

fran•chis•er *Business.*

Fran•cis of As•si•si

Fran•cis•can

fran•ci•um

Franck

Fran•co

fran•gi•ble

frank *adj.*, frank•er,
frank•est. (candid: cf.
FRANC)

Frank•en•stein

Frank•fort

Frank•furt

frank•furt•er

frank•in•cense

Frank•ish

Frank•lin

frank•ly

frank•ness

fran•tic

fran•ti•cal•ly

frappe or frap•pé

fra•ter•nal

fra•ter•nal•ly

fra•ter•ni•ty *n.*, *pl.*
fra•ter•ni•ties.

frat•er•ni•za•tion

frat•er•nize *v.*, frat•

er•nized, frat•er•
niz•ing.

frat•ri•cid•al

frat•ri•cide

Frau *n.*, *pl.* Frau•en or
Fraus.

fraud

fraud•u•lence

fraud•u•lent

fraud•u•lent•ly

fraught

Fräu•lein *n.*, *pl.* Fräu•
leins or Fräu•lein.

fray *v.*, frayed, fray•
ing.

fraz•zle *v.*, fraz•zled,
fraz•zling.

freak *v.*, freaked,
freak•ing.

freak-out or freak•out

freak•ish

freak•y

freck•le *v.*, freck•led,
freck•ling.

freck•led

Fred•die Mac *Business.*
(Federal Home Loan
Mortgage Corporation)

free *v.*, freed, free•
ing; *adj.*, fre•er,
fre•est.

free-for-all

free mar•ket *Business.*

free on board *Busi-
ness.*

free port *Business.*

free trade *Business.*

free trad•er *Business.*

free•base or free-base
v., free•based, free•
bas•ing or free•bas•
ing.

free•bie

free•board

free•boot•er

free•born

freed•man *n.*, *pl.*
freed•men.

free•dom

freed•wom•an *n.*, *pl.*
freed•wom•en.

free hand *n.*

free•hand *adj.*

free•hold

free•hold•er

free•lance or free-
lance *v.*, free•lanced,
free•lanc•ing or
free-lanced, free-
lanc•ing.

free•load•er

free•ly

free•man *n.*, *pl.* free•
men.

Free•ma•son

Free•ma•son•ry

free•ness

free•stand•ing

free•stone

free•think•er

free•think•ing

Free•town

free•ware *Computers.*

free•way

free•wheel•ing

free will *n.*

free•will *adj.*

freez•a•ble

freeze *v.*, froze, fro•
zen, freez•ing. (to
harden into ice: cf.
FRIEZE)

freeze-dry *v.*, freeze-
dried, freeze-dry•
ing.

freez•er

freight *v.*, freight•ed,
freight•ing.

freight for•ward•er
Business.

freight•age *Business.*

freight•er

Fre•mont

French
French fries *n., pl.*
French-fry *v.*, French-fried, French-fry•ing.
French Gui•an•a
French•man *n., pl.* French•men.
French•wom•an *n., pl.* French•wom•en.
fre•net•ic
fren•zied
fren•zy *n., pl.* fren•zies.
Fre•on *Trademark.*
fre•quen•cy *n., pl.* fre•quen•cies.
fre•quent *v.*, fre•quent•ed, fre•quent•ing.
fre•quent fli•er
fre•quent•ly
fres•co *n., pl.* fres•coes, fres•cos;. *v.*, fres•coed, fres•co•ing.
fresh *adj.*, fresh•er, fresh•est.
fresh•en *v.*, fresh•ened, fresh•en•ing.
fresh•en•er
fresh•et
fresh•ly
fresh•man *n., pl.* fresh•men.
fresh•ness
fresh•wa•ter or fresh-wa•ter
Fres•no
fret *v.*, fret•ted, fret•ting.
fret•ful
fret•ful•ly
fret•ful•ness
fret•work
Freud
fri•a•ble

fri•ar (monk: cf. FRYER or FRIER)
fri•ar•y, *n., pl.* fri•ar•ies.
fric•as•see *v.*, fric•as•seed, fric•as•see•ing.
fric•a•tive
fric•tion
fric•tion•al
frictional un•em•ploy•ment *Business.*
fric•tion feed *Computers.*
Fri•day
fried
friend (comrade: cf. FIEND)
friend•less
friend•li•ness
friend•ly *n., pl.* friend•lies; *adj.*, friend•li•er, friend•li•est.
friend•ship
frieze (decorative band: cf. FREEZE)
frig•ate
fright
fright•en *v.*, fright•ened, fright•en•ing.
fright•en•ing•ly
fright•ful
fright•ful•ly
frig•id
fri•gid•i•ty
frill
frill•i•ness
frill•y *adj.*, frill•i•er, frill•i•est.
fringe
fringe ben•e•fit *Business.*
fringed
fring•ing
frip•per•y *n., pl.* frip•per•ies.

Fris•bee *Trademark.*
Fri•sian
frisk *v.*, frisked, frisk•ing.
frisk•i•ly
frisk•i•ness
frisk•y *adj.*, frisk•i•er, frisk•i•est.
frit•ter *v.*, frit•tered, frit•ter•ing.
fri•vol•i•ty
friv•o•lous
friv•o•lous•ly
frizz *v.*, frizzed, frizz•ing.
friz•zle *v.*, friz•zled, friz•zling.
frizz•y *adj.*, frizz•i•er, frizz•i•est.
fro
frock
frog
frog•man *n., pl.* frog•men.
frol•ic *v.*, frol•icked, frol•ick•ing.
frol•ic•some
from
frond
front *v.*, front•ed, front•ing.
front-end load *Business.*
front-run•ner or front-run•ner
front•age
fron•tal
fron•tier
fron•tiers•man *n., pl.* fron•tiers•men.
fron•tis•piece
frost *v.*, frost•ed, frost•ing.
frost•bite
frost•bit•ten
frost•i•ness

frost•ing
frost∘y adj., frost•i∘er, frost•i•est.
froth v., frothed, froth•ing.
froth∘y adj., froth•i∘er, froth•i•est.
frou-frou
fro•ward
frown v., frowned, frown•ing.
frown•ing∘ly
frowz∘y adj., frowz•i∘er, frowz•i•est.
froze
fro•zen
fruc•ti∘fy v., fruc•ti•fied, fruc•ti•fy•ing.
fruc•tose
fru•gal
fru•gal∘i∘ty
fru•gal∘ly
fruit n., pl. fruits or fruit.
fruit fly
fruit•cake
fruit∘ed
fruit•ful
fruit•ful∘ly
fruit•ful•ness
fruit∘i•ness
fru•i•tion
fruit•less
fruit•less∘ly
fruit•less•ness
fruit∘y adj., fruit•i∘er, fruit•i•est.
frump
frump∘y
frus•trate v., frus•trat∘ed, frus•trat•ing.
frus•trat•ing∘ly
frus•tra•tion
frus•tum n., pl. frus•tums, frus∘ta.

fry¹ n., pl. fries. (dish of fried food)
fry² v., fried, fry•ing. (to cook with fat or oil over direct heat)
fry³ n., pl. fry. (young of fish)
fry∘er or fri∘er (chicken: cf. FRIAR).
FSLIC Business. (Federal Savings and Loan Insurance Corporation)
FTC Business. (Federal Trade Commission)
fuch•sia n., pl. fuch•sias.
fud∘dy-dud∘dy n., pl. fud∘dy-dud∘dies.
fudge v., fudged, fudg•ing.
fu∘el v., fu•eled or fu•elled, fu•el•ing or fu•el•ling.
fu∘gal
fu•gi•tive
fugue
Füh•rer
Fu∘ji
ful•crum n., pl. ful•crums or ful•cra.
ful•fill or ful•fil v., ful•filled, ful•fill•ing.
ful•fill•ment
full adj., full∘er, full•est.
full-blood∘ed
full-blown
full-bod∘ied
full cost•ing Business.
full-du∘plex mode Computers.
full em•ploy•ment Business.
full-fledged
full-fron•tal

full-height drive Computers.
full-scale
full-screen ed∘i•tor Computers.
full serv•ice a∘gen•cy Business.
full-time
full-tim∘er
full war•ran∘ty Business.
full•back
full∘er
Full•er
full•ness
ful∘ly
ful•mi•nate v., ful•mi•nat∘ed, ful•mi•nat•ing.
ful•mi•na•tion
ful•some
Ful•ton
fum•ble v., fum•bled, fum•bling.
fum•bling∘ly
fume v., fumed, fum•ing.
fu•mi•gant
fu•mi•gate v. fu•mi•gat∘ed, fu•mi•gat•ing.
fu•mi•ga•tion
fun
func•tion v., func•tioned, func•tion•ing.
func•tion key Computers.
func•tion∘al
func•tion•al•ism
func•tion•al∘i∘ty
func•tion•al∘ly
func•tion•ar∘y n., pl. func•tion•ar•ies.
fund v., fund∘ed, fund•ing.
fun•da•men•tal

fun•da•men•tal•ism
fun•da•men•tal•ist
fun•da•men•tal•ly
fund•ing *Business.*
fu•ner•al (ceremony for the dead)
fu•ner•ar•y
fu•ne•re•al (mournful)
fun•gal
fun•gi•ble goods *Business.*
fun•gi•cide
fun•gous
fun•gus *n., pl.* fun•gi, fun•gus•es.
fu•nic•u•lar
funk•i•ness
funk•y *adj.,* funk•i•er, funk•i•est.
fun•nel *v.,* fun•neled or fun•nelled, fun•nel•ing or fun•nel•ling.
fun•nies *n., pl.*
fun•ni•ly
fun•ni•ness
fun•ning
fun•ny *adj.,* fun•ni•er, fun•ni•est.
fur (hairy animal skin: cf. FIR)
fur•be•low
fur•bish *v.,* fur•bished, fur•bish•ing.
fu•ri•ous
fu•ri•ous•ness
furl *v.,* furled, furl•ing.

fur•long
fur•lough *v.,* fur•loughed, fur•lough•ing.
fur•nace
fur•nish *v.,* fur•nished, fur•nish•ing.
fur•ni•ture
fu•ror
furred
fur•ri•er
fur•ri•ness
fur•row *v.,* fur•rowed, fur•row•ing.
fur•ry *adj.,* fur•ri•er, fur•ri•est. (having fur: cf. FURY)
fur•ther¹ *v.,* fur•thered, fur•ther•ing.
fur•ther² *adv., adj.* (to a greater extent: cf. FARTHER)
fur•ther•ance
fur•ther•more
fur•ther•most
fur•thest
fur•tive
fur•tive•ly
fur•tive•ness
fu•ry *n., pl.* fu•ries. (rage: cf. FURRY)
furze
fuse *v.,* fused, fus•ing.
fu•se•lage
fuse•less
fu•si•ble
fu•sil•lade *v.,* fu•sil•

lad•ed, fu•sil•lad•ing.
fu•sion
fuss *v.,* fussed, fuss•ing.
fuss•budg•et
fuss•i•ly
fuss•i•ness
fuss•y *adj.,* fuss•i•er, fuss•i•est.
fus•tian
fus•ty
fu•tile
fu•tile•ly
fu•til•i•ty
fu•ton
fu•ture
future shock
fu•tures trad•ing *Business.*
fu•tur•ism
fu•tur•ist
fu•tur•is•tic
fu•tu•ri•ty *n., pl.* fu•tu•ri•ties.
fu•tur•ol•o•gist
fu•tur•ol•o•gy
futz *v.,* futzed, futz•ing.
fuzz *n., pl.* fuzz, fuzz•es; *v.,* fuzzed, fuzz•ing.
fuzz•i•ly
fuzz•i•ness
fuzz•y *adj.,* fuzzi•er, fuzzi•est.
FX *Business.* (foreign exchange)

G

GA (Georgia)
GAAP *Business.* (generally accepted accounting principles)

gab *v.,* gabbed, gab•bing.
gab•ar•dine
gab•bi•ness

gab•ble *v.,* gab•bled, gab•bling.
gab•by *adj.,* gab•bi•er, gab•bi•est.

ga•ble

ga•bled

Ga•bon

Ga•bo•ro•ne

Ga•bri•el

gad v., gad•ded, gad•ding.

gad•a•bout

gad•fly n., pl. gad•flies.

gadg•et

gadg•et•ry

gad•o•lin•i•um

Gael•ic

gaff v., gaffed, gaff•ing. (hook)

gaffe (blunder)

gaf•fer

gag v., gagged, gag•ging.

gage (challenge: cf. GAUGE; GOUGE)

gag•gle

gai•e•ty n., pl. gai•e•ties.

gai•ly

gain v., gained, gain•ing.

gain•ful

gain•ful•ly

gain•say v., gain•said, gain•say•ing.

gain•say•er

gait (walk: cf. GATE)

ga•la

ga•lac•tic

ga•lac•tose

Gal•a•had

gal•ax•y n., pl. gal•ax•ies.

gale

ga•le•na

Gal•i•lee

Gal•i•le•o

gall (audacity: cf. GAUL)

gal•lant

gal•lant•ly

gal•lant•ry n., pl. gal•lant•ries.

gall•blad•der or gall blad•der

gal•le•on (sailing ship: cf. GALLION)

gal•ler•y n., pl. gal•ler•ies. (raised area)

gal•ley n., pl. gal•leys. (kitchen)

Gal•lic

Gal•li•cism

gal•li•mau•fry, n., pl. gal•li•mau•fries.

gall•ing

gal•li•um

gal•li•vant v., gal•li•vant•ed, gal•li•vant•ing.

gal•lon (unit of measure: cf. GALLEON)

gal•lop v., gal•loped, gal•lop•ing.

gal•lows n., pl. gal•lows, gal•lows•es.

gall•stone

ga•lore

ga•losh

gal•van•ic

gal•va•nism

gal•va•nize v., gal•va•nized, gal•va•niz•ing.

gal•va•nom•e•ter

Ga•ma

Gam•bi•a

Gam•bi•an

gam•bit

gam•ble v., gam•bled, gam•bling. (to bet: cf. GAMBOL)

gam•bler

gam•bol v., gam•boled or gam•bolled, gam•bol•ing or gam•bol•ling. (to frolic: cf. GAMBLE)

gam•brel roof

game v., gamed, gam•ing; adj., gam•er, gam•est.

game•cock

game•keep•er

game•ly

game•ness

games•man•ship

game•ster

gam•ete

gam•in

gam•ine

gam•i•ness

gam•ma n., pl. gam•mas.

gam•ma glob•u•lin

gam•ut

gam•y or gam•ey, adj., gam•i•er, gam•i•est.

gan•der

Gan•dhi

Gan•dhi•an

gang v., ganged, gang•ing.

Gan•ges

gang•land

gan•gling

gan•gli•on n., pl. gan•gli•a, gan•gli•ons.

gang•plank

gan•grene

gan•gre•nous

gang•ster

gang•way

gant•let

gan•try n., pl. gan•tries.

Gantt chart Business.

gap v., gapped, gap•ping.

gape v., gaped, gap•ing.

gar n., pl. gar or gars.

ga•rage v., ga•raged, ga•rag•ing.

garb v., garbed, garb•ing.

gar•bage

gar•ban•zo, n., pl. gar•ban•zos.

gar•ble v., gar•bled, gar•bling.

gar•çon

gar•den v., gar•dened, gar•den•ing.

gar•den-va∘ri∘e∘ty

gar•de•nia n., pl. gar•de•nias.

Gar•field

gar•fish n., pl. gar•fish or gar•fish•es.

gar•gan•tu∘an

gar•gle v., gar•gled, gar•gling.

gar•goyle

Gar∘i•bal∘di

gar•ish

gar•ish∘ly

gar•ish•ness

gar•land v., gar•land∘ed, gar•land•ing.

gar•lic

gar•lick∘y

gar•ment

gar•ner v., gar•nered, gar•ner•ing.

gar•net

gar•nish v., gar•nished, gar•nish•ing.

gar•nish∘ee v., gar•nish•eed, gar•nish•ee•ing. *Business.*

gar•ret

gar•ri•son v., gar•ri•

soned, gar•ri•son•ing.

gar•rote v., gar•rot∘ed or gar•rot•ted, gar•rot•ing or gar•rot•ting.

gar•ru•li∘ty

gar•ru•lous

gar•ru•lous•ness

gar•ter v., gar•tered, gar•ter•ing.

Gar∘y

gas n., pl. gas•ses, gas∘es; v., gassed, gas•sing. (does gas)

gas cham•ber

gas-guz•zler tax

gas-plas∘ma display *Computers.*

gas sta•tion

gas∘e•ous

gash v., gashed, gash•ing.

gas•ket (sealing ring: cf. CASKET)

gas•light

gas∘o•hol

gas∘o•line

gasp v., gasped, gasp•ing.

gas∘sy adj., gas•si∘er, gas•si∘est.

gas•tric

gas•tri•tis

gas∘tro•in∘tes•ti•nal

gas∘tro•nom∘ic

gas•tron∘o•my

gas∘tro•pod

gas•works, n., gas•works.

gate (hinged barrier: cf. GAIT)

gate-crash∘er

gate•fold

gate•post

gate•way

gateway drug

gath∘er v., gath•ered, gath•er•ing.

gath•er∘er

gath•er•ing

GATT *Business.* (General Agreement on Tariffs and Trade)

gauche

gauche∘ly

gauche•ness

gau•che•rie

gau•cho n., pl. gau•chos.

gaud∘i∘ly

gaud∘i•ness

gaud∘y adj., gaud•i∘er, gaud•i∘est.

gauge v., gauged, gaug•ing. (measure: cf. GAGE; GOUGE)

Gau•guin

Gaul (ancient France: cf. GALL)

gaunt adj., gaunt∘er, gaunt•est.

gaunt•let

gaunt•ness

gauze

gauz∘y adj., gauz•i∘er, gauz•i∘est.

gave

gav∘el v., gav•eled or gav•elled, gav•el•ing or gav•el•ling.

ga•votte

G.A.W. *Business.* (guaranteed annual wage)

gawk v., gawked, gawk•ing.

gawk∘i∘ly

gawk∘i•ness

gawk∘y adj., gawk•i∘er, gawk•i∘est.

gay adj., gay∘er, gay•est.

gay•e∘ty

gay∘ly

gaze *v.*, gazed, gaz•
ing.

ga•ze◦bo *n., pl.* ga•
ze•bos or ga•ze•
boes.

ga•zelle *n., pl.* ga•
zelles or ga•zelle.

ga•zette

gaz•et•teer

GB *Computers.* (giga-
byte)

Gb *Computers.* (gigabit)

gear *v.*, geared, gear•
ing.

gear•shift

gear•wheel or gear
wheel

gee

geese

gee•zer

ge•fil◦te fish

Gei•ger count◦er

gei•sha *n., pl.* gei•sha
or gei•shas.

gel¹ (colloid: cf. JELL)

gel² *v.*, gelled, gel•
ling.

gel◦a•tin

ge•lat◦i•nous

geld *v.*, geld◦ed,
geld•ing.

gel◦id

gem

gem◦i•nate *v.*,
gem◦i•nat◦ed,
gem◦i•nat•ing.

gem◦i•na•tion

Gem◦i•oni *n., pl.*
Gem◦i•no•rum.

gem◦o◦log◦i•cal

gem•ol◦o◦gist

gem•ol◦o◦gy or
gem•mol◦o◦gy

gem•stone

gen•darme *n., pl.*
gen•darmes.

gen•der

gen•der bend◦er

gene

gene splic◦ing

ge◦ne◦a•log◦i•cal or
ge◦ne◦a•log◦ic

ge◦ne◦al◦o◦gist

ge◦ne◦al◦o◦gy *n., pl.*
ge◦ne◦al◦o•gies.

gen•er◦a

gen•er◦al

general part•ner *Busi-
ness.*

general part•ner•ship
Business.

general prac•ti◦
tion◦er

general store

gen•er•al•is◦si•mo
n., pl. gen•er•al•is•
si•mos.

gen•er•al◦i•ty *n., pl.*
gen•er•al◦i•ties.

gen•er•al◦i•za•tion

gen•er•al•ize *v.*,
gen•er•al•ized,
gen•er•al•iz◦ing.

gen•er•al•ship

gen•er◦ate *v.*, gen•
er•at◦ed, gen•er•
at◦ing.

gen•er◦a•tion

Gen•er◦a•tion X

gen•er◦a•tion◦al

gen•er◦a•tive

gen•er◦a•tor

ge•ner◦ic

generic prod•uct *Busi-
ness.*

gen•er•ous

gen•er•ous◦ly

gen◦e•osis *n., pl.*
gen◦e•oses.

ge•net◦ic

genetic code

genetic en◦gi•neer•
ing

gen•et•ic fin•ger•
print•ing

ge•net◦o◦i•cal◦ly

ge•net◦o◦i•cist

ge•net•ics

Ge•ne◦va

Gen•ghis Khan

gen◦ial

ge•ni•al◦i◦ty

gen•ial◦ly

ge•nie

gen◦i•tal (of genitalia:
cf. GENTEEL; GENTILE;
GENTLE)

gen◦i•ta•li◦a or
gen◦i•tals

gen◦i•tive

gen◦i•to•u◦ri◦nar◦y

gen•ius *n., pl.* gen•
ius◦es, gen◦i•i.
(guardian spirits; ex-
ceptional intellects: cf.
GENUS)

gen•lock *Computers.*

Gen◦o◦a

gen◦o•cide

ge•nome

ge•no◦mic DNA

gen◦o•type

gen◦re *n., pl.* gen◦res.

gent

gen•teel (polite: cf.
GENITAL; GENTLE)

gen•tian

gen•tile (not Jewish:
cf. GENITAL; GENTLE)

gen•til◦i◦ty

gen•tle¹ *v.*, gen•tled,
gen•tling.

gen•tle² *adj.*, gen•
tler, gen•tlest.
(kindly)

gen◦tle•folk or
gen◦tle•folks *n., pl.*

gen◦tle•man *n., pl.*
gen◦tle•men.

gen◦tle•man◦ly

gen•tle•ness

gen•tle•wom•an *n.*, *pl.* gen•tle•wom•en.

gen•tly

gen•tri•fi•ca•tion

gen•tri•fy *v.*, gen•tri•fied, gen•tri•fy•ing.

gen•try

gen∘u•flect *v.*, gen∘u•flect∘ed, gen∘u•flect•ing.

gen∘u•flec•tion

gen•u•ine

gen•u•ine•ly

gen•u•ine•ness

ge•nus *n.*, *pl.* gen∘e∘ra or ge•nus∘es. (subdivision: cf. GENIUS)

ge∘o•cen•tric

ge•ode

ge∘o•des∘ic

ge∘o•od∘e∘sy

ge∘o•det∘ic

ge•og•ra•pher

ge∘o•graph∘i•cal

ge∘o•graph∘i•cal∘ly

ge•og•ra•phy

ge∘o•log∘i•cal

ge•ol∘o∘gist

ge•ol∘o∘gy

ge∘o•mag•ne•tism

ge∘o•met•ric

ge∘o•met•ri•cal

ge∘o•met•ri•cal∘ly

ge•om∘e•try

ge∘o•phys∘i•cal

ge∘o•phys∘i•cist

ge∘o•phys•ics

ge∘o•po•lit∘i•cal

ge∘o•pol∘i•tics

George

Geor•gia (GA)

Geor•gian

ge∘o•sta•tion•ar∘y

ge∘o•syn•cline

ge∘o•ther•mal or ge∘o•ther•mic

ge•ra•ni•um

ger•bil

ger•er•os∘i∘ty

ger∘i•at•ric

ger∘i•at•rics

germ

Ger•man (the language)

ger•mane (relevant)

Ger•man∘ic

ger•ma•ni•um

Ger•ma•ny

ger•mi•cid∘al

ger•mi•cide

ger•mi•nal

ger•mi•nate *v.*, ger•mi•nat∘ed, ger•mi•nat•ing.

ger•mi•na•tion

ge•ron•to•log∘i•cal

ger•on•tol∘o•gist

ger•on•tol∘o•gy

ger•ry•man•der *v.*, ger•ry•man•dered, ger•ry•man•der•ing.

Gersh•win

ger•und

Ge•sta∘po

ges•tate *v.*, ges•tat∘ed, ges•tat•ing.

ges•ta•tion

ges•ta•tion•al

ges•tat•tion∘al car•ri∘er

ges•tic∘u•late *v.*, ges•tic∘u•lat∘ed, ges•tic∘u•lat•ing.

ges•tic∘u•la•tion

ges•tur∘al

ges•ture *v.*, ges•tured, ges•tur•ing. (movement: cf. JESTER)

ge•sund•heit

get *v.*, got, got or got•ten, get•ting.

get-to∘geth∘er

get∘a∘way

Get•tys•burg

get∘up or get-up

gew•gaw

gey•ser

Gha∘na

Gha•na•ian or Gha•ni∘an

ghast∘ly *adj.*, ghast•li∘er, ghast•li∘est. (horrible)

gher•kin

ghet∘to *n.*, *pl.* ghet•tos or ghet•toes.

ghet•to•ize, *v.*, ghet•to•ized, ghet•to•iz•ing.

ghost

ghost∘ly (spectral)

ghost•writ∘er or ghost writ∘er

ghost•writ•ten

ghoul (demon: cf. GOAL)

ghoul•ish

Gia•co•met•ti

gi•ant

gi•ant∘ess

gib•ber *v.*, gib•bered, gib•ber•ing.

gib•ber•ish

gib•bet *n.*, *v.*, gib•bet∘ed, gib•bet•ing.

gib•bon

gibe *v.*, gibed, gib•ing. (to taunt: cf. JIBE; JIVE)

gib•let

Gi•bral•tar

gid•di•ness

gid○dy *adj.,* gid•
di•er, gid•di•est.
Gide
gift
gift○ed
gig (job: cf. JIG)
gig○a•bit (Gb) *Computers.*
gig○a•byte (GB) *Computers.*
gi•gan•tic
gig•gle *v.,* gig•gled,
gig•gling.
gig•gly
GIGO *Computers.* (garbage in, garbage out)
gig○o○lo *n., pl.*
gig○o○los.
Gi○la mon•ster
gild *v.,* gild○ed, gild•
ing. (to coat with
gold: cf. GUILD)
gill
gilt (gold: cf. GUILT)
gilt-edged or gilt-edge
Business.
gim•bals
gim•crack
gim•crack•er○y
gim•let
gim○me cap
gim•mick *v.,* gim•
micked, gim•mick•
ing.
gim•mick○ry
gim•mick○y
gimp
gimp○y *adj.,* gimp•
i○er, gimp•i•est.
gin *v.,* ginned, gin•
ning.
gin•ger
ginger ale
gin○ger•bread
gin•ger○ly
gin○ger•snap

gin•ger○y
ging•ham
gin•gi•vi•tis
gink○go or ging○ko,
n., pl. gink•goes or
ging•koes.
Gin•nie Mae *Business.*
(Government National
Mortgage Association)
gin•seng
Gip○sy *n., pl.* Gip•
sies.
gi•raffe
gird *v.,* gird○ed or
girt, gird•ing.
gird○er
gir•dle *v.,* gir•dled,
gir•dling.
girl
girl Fri•day *n., pl.* girl
Fri•days.
girl scout
girl•friend
girl•hood
girl•ish
girt
girth
gis○mo or giz○mo, *n.,*
pl. gis•mos.
gist (essence: cf. JEST)
give *v.,* gave, giv○en,
giv•ing.
give-and-take
give•a○way
give•back *Business.*
giv○en
giv○er
giz○mo *n., pl.* giz•
mos.
giz•zard
gla•cial
gla•cial○ly
gla•cier (ice mass: cf.
GLAZIER)
glad *adj.,* glad•der,
glad•dest.

glad hand *n., pl.*
glad-hand *v.,* glad-
hand○ed, glad-
hand○ing.
glad•den *v.,* glad-
dened, glad•den•
ing.
glade
glad•i•a•tor
glad•i•a•to•ri•al
glad•i•o•lus *n., pl.*
glad•i•o•lus, glad•
i•o○li, glad•i•o•
lus○es.
glad○ly
glad•ness
glad•some
glam•or•ize or glam•
our•ize *v.,* glam•or•
ized, glam•or•iz•
ing.
glam•or•ous
glam•our or glam○or
glamour stock *Business.*
glance *v.,* glanced,
glanc•ing.
gland
glan•du•lar
glans *n., pl.* glan•des.
glare *v.,* glared, glar•
ing.
glar•ing○ly
Glas•gow
glas•nost
glass *v.,* glassed,
glass•ing.
glass ceil•ing
glass○es
glass•ware
glass○y *adj.,* glass•
i○er, glass•i•est.
glau•co○ma
glaze *v.,* glazed, glaz•
ing.
gla•zier (glass installer:
cf. GLACIER)

gleam v., gleamed, gleam•ing.

glean v., gleaned, glean•ing.

glee

glee•ful

glen

Glen•dale

glib

glib∘ly

glib•ness

glide v., glid∘ed, glid•ing.

glid∘er

glim•mer v., glim•mered, glim•mer•ing.

glimpse v., glimpsed, glimps•ing.

glint v., glint∘ed, glint•ing.

glis•san∘do n., pl. glis•san∘di or glis•san•dos.

glis•ten v., glis•tened, glis•ten•ing.

glitch

glit•ter v., glit•tered, glit•ter•ing.

glit•ter∘y

glitz∘y adj., glitz•i∘er, glitz•i•est.

gloam•ing

gloat v., gloat∘ed, gloat•ing.

glob

glob∘al

glo•bal warm•ing

glob•al•ism

glob•al•ist

glob•al∘ly

globe

globe•trot•ter

glob∘u•lar

glob•ule

glob∘u•lin

glock•en•spiel

gloom

gloom∘y adj., gloom•i∘er, gloom•i•est.

glop

glop∘py adj., glop•pi∘er, glop•pi•est.

glor∘i∘fi•ca•tion

glo•ri∘fy v., glo•ri•fied, glo•ri•fy•ing.

glo•ri∘ous

glo•ri•ous∘ly

glo∘ry n., pl. glo•ries; v., glo•ried, glo•ry•ing.

gloss v., glossed, gloss•ing.

glos•sa∘ry n., pl. glos•sa•ries.

glos∘so•la•li∘a

gloss∘y adj., gloss•i∘er, gloss•i•est.

glot•tal

glot•tis n., pl. glot•tis∘es, glot•ti•des.

glove

gloved

glow v., glowed, glow•ing.

glow∘er v., glow•ered, glow•er•ing.

glow•ing

glow•worm

glu•cose

glue v., glued, glu•ing.

glue∘y adj., glue•i∘er, glue•i•est.

glum adj., glum•mer, glum•mest.

glum∘ly

glum•ness

glut v., glut•ted, glut•ting.

glu•ten

glu•ten•ous (like gluten)

glu•ti•nous (sticky)

glut•ton•ous (greedy)

glut•ton•ous∘ly

glut•ton∘y

glyc•er∘in or glyc•er•ine

glyc•er∘ol

gly•co∘gen

gnarled

gnash v., gnashed, gnash•ing.

gnat

gnaw v., gnawed, gnaw•ing.

gneiss

gnome

gnom•ish

GNP or **G.N.P.** Business (gross national product).

gnu n., pl. gnus, gnu. (antelope: cf. KNEW; NEW)

go v., went, gone, go•ing, goes.

go-a∘head

go-be∘tween

go-get∘er

go-get∘ting

go-go

go/•no-go Business.

go pub•lic Business.

goad v., goad∘ed, goad•ing.

goal (aim: cf. GHOUL)

goal∘ie

goal•keep∘er

goal•keep•ing

goat

goat∘ee

goat•herd

goat•skin

gob

gob•ble v., gob•bled, gob•bling.

gob•ble•dy•gook or
   gob•ble•de•gook
gob•bler
Go○bi
gob•let
gob•lin
God
god•child *n., pl.* god•
   chil•dren.
god•daugh•ter
god•dess
god•fa•ther
God•head
god•hood
Go•di•va
god•less
god•like
god•li•ness
god○ly *adj.,* god•
   li○er, god•li•est.
god•moth○er
god•par•ent
god•send
god•son
God•win Aus•ten
Goe•the
go•fer or go-fer
gog•gle *v.,* gog•gled,
   gog•gling.
go○ings-on
goi•ter
gold dig•ger
gold re•serve *Busi-
   ness.*
gold stand•ard *Busi-
   ness.*
gold•brick
gold○en
golden hand•cuffs
   Business.
golden hand•shake
   Business.
golden par○a•chute
   Business.
gold•en•rod
gold•finch

gold•fish *n., pl.* gold•
   fish or gold•fish○es.
gold•smith
golf *v.,* golfed, golf•
   ing.
golf○er
Go•li•ath
gol○ly
go•nad
gon•do•la *n., pl.*
   gon•do•las.
gon•do•lier
gone
gon○er
gong
gon•or•rhe•a
goo
goo•ber
good *adj.,* bet•ter,
   best.
good-by or good○by,
   n., pl. good-bys or
   good-byes.
good de•liv•er○y
   Business.
good-for-noth•ing
Good Fri•day
good-heart○ed or
   good•heart○ed
good-heart○ed•ness
good-look○ing
good-na○tured
good-na○tured○ly
good-hu○mored
good•ies
good○ly
good•ness
good•will or good
   will
good○y-good○y *n. pl.*
   good○y-good○ies.
goo○ey *adj.,* goo•
   i○er, goo•i•est.
goof *v.,* goofed,
   goof•ing.
goof-off *n.*

goof•ball
goof○y *adj.,* goof•
   i○er, goof•i•est.
gook
goon
goose *n., pl.* geese,
   goos○es; *v.,* goosed,
   goos○ing. (birds or
   pokes. prods)
goose flesh or goose•
   flesh
goose•ber○ry *n., pl.*
   goose•ber•ries.
GOP or G.O.P. ("Grand
   Old Party," Republican
   party).
go•pher
Gor•ba•chev
gore *v.,* gored, gor•
   ing.
gorge *v.,* gorged,
   gorg•ing.
gor•geous
gor•geous○ly
go•ril○la *n., pl.* go•
   ril•las. (large ape: cf.
   GUERRILLA or GUERILLA)
gor○i•ness
Gor○ki
gor•man•dize, *v.,*
   gor•man•dized,
   gor•man•diz•ing.
gorse
gor○y *adj.,* gor•i○er,
   gor•i•est.
gosh
gos•hawk
gos•ling
gos•pel
gos•sa•mer
gos•sip *v.,* gos•siped
   or gos•sipped, gos•
   sip•ing or gos•sip•
   ping.
gos•sip○y
got
Goth

goth∘ic

go∘to n., pl. go•tos.
Computers.

got•ten

Gou∘da

gouge v., gouged,
goug•ing. (to scoop
out: cf. GAGE; GAUGE)

goug∘er

gou•lash

gourd

gour•mand (big eater)

gour•met (epicure)

gout

gout∘y

gov•ern v., gov•
erned, gov•ern•ing.

gov•ern•a∘ble

gov•ern•ance

gov•ern•ess

gov•ern•ment

government bond
Business.

gov•ern•men•tal

gov•er•nor

gov•er•nor•ship

gown

Go∘ya

gppm Computers.
(graphics pages per
minute)

grab v., grabbed,
grab•bing.

grab•ber

grace v., graced, grac•
ing.

grace•ful

grace•ful∘ly

grace•less

grace•less∘ly

grace•less•ness

gra•cious

gra•cious∘ly

gra•cious•ness

grack∘le

grad

gra•da•tion

grade v., grad∘ed,
grad•ing.

grade in•fla•tion

grade•fla•tion

gra•di•ent

grad•u∘al

grad•u•al•ism

grad•u•al•ly

grad•u•ate v., grad•
u•at∘ed, grad•u•
at•ing.

grad•u•a•tion

graf•fi∘ti n., sing.
graf•fi∘to.

graft v., graft∘ed,
graft•ing.

graft∘er

gra•ham

grail

grain

grain∘i•ness

grain∘y adj., grain•
i∘er, grain•i•est.

gram•mar

gram•mar•i∘an

gram•mat∘i•cal

gram•mat∘i•cal∘ly

gra•na∘ry n., pl. gra•
na•ries.

grand n., pl. grands,
grand; adj.,
grand∘er, grand•est.
(pianos or money)

grand mal

grand•child n., pl.
grand•chil•dren.

grand•daugh•ter

grande dame n., pl.
grandes dames.

gran•dee

gran•deur

grand•fa•ther

gran•dil•o∘quence

gran•dil•o∘quent

gran•di•ose

grand∘ly

grand∘ma n., pl.
grand•mas.

grand•moth∘er

grand•ness

grand∘pa

grand•son

grand•stand

grange

gran•ite

gran∘ny or gran•nie
n., pl. gran•nies.

gra•no•la

grant v., grant∘ed,
grant•ing.

gran•tee

gran•tor

grants•man•ship

gran•u•lar

gran•u•lar•i∘ty

gran•u•late v.,
gran•u•lat∘ed,
gran•u•lat•ing.

gran•u•la•tion

gran•ule

grape

grape•fruit

grape•shot

grape•vine

graph v., graphed,
graph•ing.

graph∘ic

graphic nov∘el

graph∘i•cal us∘er in•
ter•face (GUI) Com-
puters.

graph∘i•cal∘ly

graph•ics Computers.

graph∘ics-based Com-
puters.

graphics tab•let Com-
puters.

graph•ite

graph•ol∘o•gist

graph•ol∘o•gy

grap•nel

grap•ple *v.*, grap•pled, grap•pling.

grasp *v.*, grasped, grasp•ing.

grass

grass•hop•per

grass◦y *adj.*, grass•i◦er, grass•i◦est.

grate[1] (metal frame: cf. GREAT)

grate[2] *v.*, grat◦ed, grat•ing.

grate•ful

grate•ful◦ly

grate•ful•ness

grat◦er

grat◦i•fi•ca•tion

grat◦i•fy *v.*, grat•i◦fied, grat•i•fy◦ing.

grat•ing

grat◦is

grat◦i•tude

gra•tu◦i•tous

gra•tu◦i◦ty *n.*, *pl.* gra•tu◦i•ties.

gra•va•men *n.*, *pl.* gra•vam◦i◦na.

grave *adj.*, grav◦er, grav•est.

grav◦el

grav•el◦ly

grav◦el◦ly

grave•stone

grave•yard

grav◦id

gra•vim◦e•ter

grav◦i•tate *v.*, grav◦i•tat◦ed, grav◦i•tat•ing.

grav◦i•ta•tion

grav◦i•ta•tion◦al

grav◦i◦ty

gra•vure

gra◦vy *n.*, *pl.* gra• vies.

gray or grey *v.*,

grayed or greyed, gray•ing or grey• ing; *adj.*, gray◦er or grey◦er, gray•est or grey•est.

gray mar•ket *Business.*

gray scal•ing *Computers.*

gray•beard

gray•ish

gray•mail *Business.*

gray•mail◦er *Business.*

gray•ness

graze *v.*, grazed, graz•ing.

graz•ing

grease *v.*, greased, greas•ing. (soft fat: cf. GREECE)

grease•paint or grease paint

greas◦i•ness

greas◦y *adj.*, greas• i◦er, greas•i•est.

great *v.*, great◦er, great•est. (large; important: cf. GRATE)

Great At•trac•tor

great•coat

great•heart◦ed

great◦ly

great•ness

grebe

Gre•cian

Greece (the country: cf. GREASE)

greed

greed◦i◦ly

greed◦i•ness

greed◦y *adj.*, greed• i◦er, greed•i•est.

Greek

Greek Or•tho•dox Church

greek•ing *Computers.*

green *v.*, greened,

green•ing; *adj.*, green◦er, green•est.

green-eyed

green•back

green•belt

green◦er◦y

green•gro◦cer

green•horn

green•house *n.*, *pl.* green•hous◦es.

greenhouse ef•fect

greenhouse gas

green•ish

Green•land

Green•land◦er

green•mail *Business.*

green•mail◦er *Business.*

green•ness

green•room

Greens•bo◦ro

green•sward

Green•wich

greet *v.*, greet◦ed, greet•ing.

gre•gar•i◦ous

Gre•go•ri◦an cal•en• dar

grem•lin

Gre•na◦da

gre•nade

Gre•na•di◦an

gren◦a•dier

gren◦a•dine

grew

grey *v.*, greyed, grey• ing; *adj.*, grey◦er, grey•est.

grey•hound or gray• hound

grid

grid◦dle

grid◦dle•cake

grid•i◦ron

grid•lock

grief

griev•ance *Business.*
grievance com•mit•tee
grieve *v.,* grieved, griev•ing.
griev•ous
griev•ous•ly
grif•fin or grif•fon
grill *v.,* grilled, grill•ing. (to broil)
grille (grating)
grim *adj.,* grim•mer, grim•mest.
grim•ace *v.,* grim•aced, grim•ac•ing.
grime
grim•ly
Grimm
grim•ness
grim•y *adj.,* grim•i•er, grim•i•est.
grin *v.,* grinned, grin•ning.
grind *v.,* ground, grind•ing.
grind•er
grind•stone
grip *v.,* gripped, grip•ping. (to grasp)
gripe *v.,* griped, grip•ing. (to complain)
grippe (influenza)
gris•ly (gruesome: cf. GRISTLY; GRIZZLY)
grist
gris•tle
gris•tly *adj.,* gris•tli•er, gris•tli•est. (cartilaginous: cf. GRISLY; GRIZZLY)
grit *v.,* grit•ted, grit•ting.
grits
grit•ty *adj.,* grit•ti•er, grit•ti•est.
griz•zled
griz•zly *n., pl.* griz•zlies. (bear: cf. GRISLY; GRISTLY)

groan *v.,* groaned, groan•ing. (moan: cf. GROWN)
groats
gro•cer
gro•cer•y *n., pl.* gro•cer•ies.
grog
grog•gi•ly
grog•gi•ness
grog•gy *adj.,* grog•gi•er, grog•gi•est.
groin
grom•met or grum•met
groom *v.,* groomed, groom•ing.
groove[1] (indentation: cf. GROVE)
groove[2] *v.,* grooved, groov•ing.
groov•i•est
groov•y *adj.,* groov•i•er, groov•i•est.
grope *v.,* groped, grop•ing.
gros•beak
gros•grain
gross *n., pl.* gross or gross•es; *v.,* grossed, gross•ing; *adj.,* gross•er, gross•est.
gross mar•gin *Business.*
gross na•tion•al prod•uct (GNP) *Business.*
gross prof•it *Business.*
gross sales *Business.*
gross•ly
gross•ness
gro•tesque
gro•tesque•ly
grot•to *n., pl.* grot•toes or grot•tos.

grouch *v.,* grouched, grouch•ing.
grouch•y *adj.,* grouch•i•er, grouch•i•est.
ground *v.,* ground•ed, ground•ing.
ground•hog or ground hog
ground•less
ground•swell
group *v.,* grouped, group•ing.
group dis•count *Business.*
group in•sur•ance *Business.*
group ther•a•py
group•er *n., pl.* group•er or group•ers.
group•ie
group•ware *Computers.*
grouse *n., pl.* grouse or grous•es; *v.,* groused, grous•ing.
grout *v.,* grout•ed, grout•ing.
grove (orchard: cf. GROOVE)
grov•el *v.,* grov•eled or grov•elled, grov•el•ing or grov•el•ling.
grow *v.,* grew, grown, grow•ing.
grow•er
growl *v.,* growled, growl•ing.
grown (matured: cf. GROAN)
grown•up
growth
growth fund *Business.*
growth stock *Business.*

grub v., grubbed,
grub•bing.
grub•bi•ness
grub•by adj., grub•
bi∘er, grub•bi•est.
grub•stake
grudge v., grudged,
grudg•ing.
grudg•ing∘ly
gru•el
gru•el•ing
grue•some
grue•some∘ly
grue•some•ness
gruff adj., gruff∘er,
gruff•est.
gruff∘ly
gruff•ness
grum•ble v., grum•
bled, grum•bling.
grum•bler
grump∘i•ness
grump∘y adj., grump•
i∘er, grump•i•est.
grun∘gy adj., grun•
gi∘er, grun•gi•est.
grun•ion
grunt v., grunt∘ed,
grunt•ing.
Gru•yère
gua•ca•mo•le
Gua•da•la•ja∘ra
Guam
Guang•zhou or
Kwang•chow
gua•nine
gua∘no
gua•ra∘ni n., pl. gua•
ra∘ni or gua•ra•nis.
guar•an•tee v., guar•
an•teed, guar•an•
tee•ing.
guaranteed an•nu∘al
wage (G.A.W.) Busi-
ness.
guar•an•tor Business.
guar•an∘ty n., pl.

guar•an•ties; v.,
guar•an•tied, guar•
an•ty•ing. Business.
guard v., guard∘ed,
guard∘ing.
guard•ed∘ly
guard•house n., pl.
guard•hous∘es.
guard•i∘an
guard•i•an•ship
Gua•te•ma∘la
Gua•te•ma•lan
gua∘va n., pl. gua•
vas.
gu•ber•na•to•ri∘al
Guern•sey n., pl.
Guern•seys.
guer•ril∘la or gue•
ril∘la n., pl. guer•ril•
las. (irregular soldier:
cf. GORILLA)
guess v., guessed,
guess∘ing. (did
guess)
guest (visitor)
guf•faw v., guf•
fawed, guf•faw•ing.
GUI Computers. (graphi-
cal user interface)
guid•ance
guide v., guid∘ed,
guid•ing.
guide•book
guid∘ed mis•sile
guide•line
guild (organization: cf.
GILD)
guil•der
guile
guile•ful
guile•less
guil•lo•tine v., guil•
lo•tined, guil•lo•
tin•ing.
guilt (blame: cf. GILT)
guilt∘i∘ly
guilt•less

guilt∘y adj., guilt•
i∘er, guilt•i•est.
guin∘ea n., pl. guin•
eas.
Guin∘ea-Bis∘sau
guin∘ea pig
Guin•e∘an
guise
gui•tar
gui•tar•ist
gulch
gul•den n., pl. gul•
dens or gul•den.
gulf
Gulf War
gull v., gulled, gull•
ing.
gul•let
gul•li•bil•i∘ty
gul•li∘ble
gul∘ly n., pl. gul•lies.
gulp v., gulped, gulp•
ing.
gum v., gummed,
gum•ming.
gum ar∘a•bic
gum•bo n., pl. gum•
bos.
gum•drop
gum∘my adj., gum•
mi∘er, gum•mi•est.
gump•tion
Gum∘ri
gum•shoe
gun v., gunned, gun•
ning.
gun-shy
gun•boat
gun•cot•ton
gun•fight
gun•fire
gung-ho
gunk
gun•lock
gun•man n., pl. gun•
men.

gun•ner
gun•ner•y
gun•ny•sack
gun•point
gun•pow•der
gun•shot
gun•smith
gun•wale or gun•nel
gup•py n., pl. gup•
  pies.
gur•gle v., gur•gled,
  gur•gling.
gur•ney n., pl. gur•
  neys.
gu•ru n., pl. gu•rus.
gush v., gushed,
  gush•ing.
gush•er
gush•y adj., gush•
  i•er, gush•i•est.
gus•set
gus•sy v., gus•sied,
  gus•sy•ing.

gust v., gust•ed,
  gust•ing.
gus•ta•to•ry
gus•to
gust•y adj., gust•i•er,
  gust•i•est. (windy)
gut v., gut•ted, gut•
  ting.
gut•less
guts•y adj., guts•i•er,
  guts•i•est. (coura-
  geous)
gut•ter
gut•ter•snipe
gut•tur•al
guy v., guyed, guy•
  ing.
Guy•a•na
Guy•a•nese
guz•zle v., guz•zled,
  guz•zling.
guz•zler
gym

gym•na•si•um n., pl.
  gym•na•si•ums or
  gym•na•si•a.
gym•nast
gym•nas•tic
gym•nas•tics
gym•no•sperm
gy•ne•co•log•i•cal
gy•ne•col•o•gist
gy•ne•col•o•gy
gyp v., gypped, gyp•
  ping.
gyp•sum
Gyp•sy n., pl. Gyp•
  sies.
gyp•sy moth
gy•rate v., gy•rat•ed,
  gy•rat•ing.
gy•ra•tion
gyr•fal•con
gy•ro
gy•ro•com•pass
gy•ro•scope

H

H-•bomb (hydrogen
  bomb)
ha or hah
ha-ha
ha•be•as cor•pus
hab•er•dash•er
hab•er•dash•er•y n.,
  pl. hab•er•dash•er•
  ies.
ha•bil•i•ments
hab•it
hab•it-form•ing
hab•it•a•bil•i•ty
hab•it•a•ble
hab•it•ant
hab•i•tat
hab•i•ta•tion
ha•bit•u•al
ha•bit•u•al•ly

ha•bit•u•ate v., ha•
  bit•u•at•ed, ha•
  bit•u•at•ing.
ha•bit•u•a•tion
ha•bit•u•é
ha•ci•en•da n., pl.
  ha•ci•en•das.
hack v., hacked, hack•
  ing.
hack•er Computers.
hack•ie
hack•les
hack•ney n., pl. hack•
  neys.
hack•neyed
hack•saw or hack saw
had
had•dock n., pl. had•
  dock or had•docks.
Ha•des

had•n't
hadst
haf•ni•um
hag
hag•gard
hag•gard•ness
hag•gis
hag•gle v., hag•gled,
  hag•gling.
hag•i•og•ra•pher
hag•i•og•ra•phy
Hague, The
hai•ku n., pl. hai•ku.
hail (to greet; ice: cf.
  HALE)
hail•stone
hail•storm
hair (tresses: cf. HARE)
hair-rais•ing

hair trig•ger n.

hair-trig∘ger adj.

hair•ball

hair•breadth or hairs•
breadth

hair•brush

hair•cloth

hair•cut

hair•do n., pl. hair•
dos.

hair•dress∘er

hair•dress•ing

hair∘i•ness

hair•less

hair•like

hair•line

hair•piece

hair•pin

hairs•breadth

hair•split•ting

hair•spring

hair•style or hair style

hair•styl•ist

hair∘y adj., hair•i∘er,
hair•i•est.

Hai∘ti

Hai•tian

hajj or hadj n., pl.
hajj∘es or hadj∘es.

haj∘ji or hadj∘i, n., pl
haj•jis or hadj∘is.

hake n., pl. hake or
hakes.

hal•berd

hal•cy∘on

hale[1] v., haled, hal•
ing.

hale[2] (healthy: cf. HAIL)

half n., pl. halves.

half-and-half

half-baked

half-breed

half-caste

half-cocked

half-du∘plex mode
Computers.

half-height drive *Com-
puters.*

half-life or half life n.,
pl. half-lives or half-
lives.

half-mast

half-slip

half-track or half•
track

half-truth n., pl. half-
truths.

half-wit

half-wit∘ted

half•back

half•heart∘ed

half•heart•ed•ly

half•heart•ed•ness

half•pen•ny n., pl.
half-pen∘nies or
half•pence.

half•time or half-time

half•tone

half•way

halfway house

hal∘i•but n., pl.
hal∘i•but or hal∘i•
buts.

Hal∘i•fax

hal∘i•to•sis

hall (room: cf. HAUL)

hal•le•lu•jah or hal•
le•lu•iah

hall•mark

hal•low v., hal•
lowed, hal•low•ing.
(to make holy: cf.
HALO; HOLLOW)

Hal•low•een or Hal•
low•e'en

hal•lu•ci•nate v.,
hal•lu•ci•nat∘ed,
hal•lu•ci•nat•ing.

hal•lu•ci•na•tion

hal•lu•ci•na•to∘ry

hal•lu•ci•no•gen

hal•lu•ci•no•gen∘ic

hall•way

ha∘lo n., pl. ha•los or
ha•loes; v., ha•loed,
ha∘lo•ing. (ring of
light: cf. HALLOW; HOL-
LOW)

hal∘o•gen

halt v., halt∘ed, halt•
ing.

hal•ter

halt•ing∘ly

hal•vah

halve v., halved, halv•
ing. (to divide in two:
cf. HAVE)

halves

hal•yard

ham v., hammed,
ham•ming.

Ham•burg

ham•burg∘er

Ham•il•ton

ham•let

ham•mer v., ham•
mered, ham•mer•
ing.

ham∘mer•head

ham∘mer•lock or
ham•mer lock

Ham•mer•stein

ham∘mer•toe

ham•mock

ham∘my

ham•per v., ham•
pered, ham•per•ing.

ham•ster

ham•string v., ham•
strung, ham•string•
ing.

Han•cock

hand v., hand∘ed,
hand•ing.

hand-me-down

hand-to-hand

hand-to-mouth *Busi-
ness.*

hand-to-mouth buy•
ing

hand•bag
hand•ball
hand•bar•row
hand•bill
hand•book
hand•car
hand•cart
hand•clasp
hand•craft v., hand•craft∘ed, hand•craft•ing.
hand•cuff v., hand•cuffed, hand•cuff•ing.
Han•del
hand•ful n., pl. hand•fuls.
hand•gun
hand∘i•cap v., hand∘i•capped, hand∘i•cap•ping.
hand∘i•cap•per
hand∘i•craft
hand∘i•ly
hand∘i•ness
hand∘i•work
hand•ker•chief
han•dle v., han•dled, han•dling.
han∘dle•bar
han•dler
hand•made (made by hand)
hand•maid or hand•maid∘en (servant)
hand•out
hand•pick v., hand•picked, hand•pick•ing.
hand•rail
hands-off
hands-on
hand•saw
hand•set
hand•shake
hand•some adj.,

hand•som∘er, hand•som∘est. (attractive: cf. HANSOM)
hand•some•ly
hand•some•ness
hand•spring
hand•stand
hand•work
hand•writ•ing
hand•writ•ten
hand∘y adj., hand∘i∘er, hand•i•est.
hand∘y•man n., pl. hand∘y•men.
hang v., hung, hanged, hang•ing.
hang glid•ing
hang-up or hang∘up
hang∘ar (airplane shed: cf. HANGER)
hang•dog
hang∘er (garment holder: cf. HANGAR)
hang∘er-on n., pl. hang∘ers-on.
hang•ing
hang•man n., pl. hang•men.
hang•nail
hang•out
hang∘o∘ver
hank
han•ker v., han•kered, han•ker•ing.
han∘ky or han•kie, n., pl. han•kies.
han∘ky-pan∘ky
Han•ni•bal
Ha•noi
han•som (cab: cf. HANDSOME)
Ha•nuk•kah or Cha•nu•kah
hap•haz•ard
hap•haz•ard∘ly
hap•less

hap•loid
hap∘ly
hap•pen v., hap•pened, hap•pen•ing.
hap∘pen•stance
hap•pi∘ly
hap•pi•ness
hap∘py adj., hap•pi∘er, hap•pi•est.
hap∘py-go-luck∘y
ha∘ra-ki∘ri
ha•rangue v., ha•rangued, ha•rangu•ing.
Ha•ra∘re
ha•rass v., ha•rassed, ha•rass•ing.
ha•rass•ment
Har•bin
har•bin•ger
har•bor v., har•bored, har•bor•ing.
hard adj., hard∘er, hard•est.
hard-and-fast
hard-bit∘ten
hard-boiled
hard card Computers.
hard-cod∘ed Computers.
hard cop∘y n., pl. hard copies. Computers.
hard-cop∘y adj. Computers.
hard-core
hard cur•ren∘cy Business.
hard disk Computers.
hard fonts Computers.
hard goods Business.
hard hat or hard•hat n., pl.
hard-hat adj.
hard-line or hard•line
hard-lin∘er

hard-nosed
hard re•turn *Comput-ers.*
hard-shell or hard-shelled
hard-wired *Computers.*
hard•back
hard•ball
hard•bound
hard•cov•er
hard•en *v.,* hard•ened, hard•en•ing.
hard•en•er
hard•head○ed or hard-head○ed
hard•head•ed•ness
hard•heart○ed
hard•heart•ed•ness
har•di•hood
har•di•ly (robustly: cf. HARDLY)
har•di•ness
Har•ding
hard○ly (scarcely: cf. HARDLY)
hard•ness
hard•pan
hard•scrab•ble
hard•ship
hard•stand
hard•tack
hard•top
hard•ware
hard•ware in•ter•rupt *Computers.*
hard•ware plat•form *Computers.*
hard•wood
har○dy *adj.,* har•di○er, har•di•est.
hare *n., pl.* hares or hare. (rabbit: cf. HAIR)
Ha○re Krish○na
hare•brained or hair•brained
hare•lip

har○em
hark *v.,* harked, hark•ing.
hark○en *v.,* hark•ened, hark•en•ing. (hearken)
Har•lem
Har•lem•ite
har•le•quin
har•lot
har•lot○ry
harm *v.,* harmed, harm•ing.
harm•ful
harm•ful○ly
harm•less
harm•less○ly
har•mon○ic
har•mon•i•ca *n., pl.* har•mon•i•cas.
har•mon•i•cal○ly
har•mon•ics
har•mo•ni•ous
har•mo•ni•ous○ly
har•mo•ni○um
har•mo•ni•za•tion
har•mo•nize *v.,* har•mo•nized, har•mo•niz•ing.
har•mo○ny *n., pl.* har•mo•nies.
har•ness *v.,* har•nessed, har•ness•ing.
harp *v.,* harped, harp•ing.
harp○er (one who harps)
Har•pers Fer○ry (site of John Brown's raid)
harp•ist
har•poon *v.,* har•pooned, har•poon•ing.
harp•si•chord
harp•si•chord•ist

har○py *n., pl.* har•pies.
har•ri•dan
har•ri○er
Har•ris•burg
Har•ri•son
har•row
har•row•ing
har○ry *v.,* har•ried, har•ry•ing.
harsh
harsh○ly
harsh•ness
hart *n., pl.* harts or hart. (deer: cf. HEART)
Hart•ford
har○um-scar○um
har•vest *v.,* har•vest○ed, har•vest•ing.
har•vest○er
has
has-been
hash *v.,* hashed, hash•ing.
hash•ish
Ha•sid *n., pl.* Ha•sid○im.
Ha•sid○ic
has○n't
hasp
has•sle *v.,* has•sled, has•sling.
has•sock
hast
has○ta la vis○ta
haste
has•ten *v.,* has•tened, has•ten•ing.
hast•i○ly
hast○y *adj.,* hast•i○er, hast•i•est.
hat
hatch *v.,* hatched, hatch•ing.
hatch•back

hatch•er•y *n., pl.*
  hatch•er•ies.
hatch◦et *v.*, hatch•
  et◦ed, hatch•et•ing.
hatch•way
hate *v.*, hat◦ed, hat•
  ing.
hate•ful
hate•ful◦ly
hate•ful•ness
hat◦er
hath
hat•less
ha•tred
hat•ted
hat•ter
hau•berk
haugh•ti◦ly
haugh•ti•ness
haugh◦ty *adj.*,
  haugh•ti◦er,
  haugh•ti•est.
haul *v.*, hauled, haul•
  ing. (to drag: cf. HALL)
haul•age *Business.*
haunch (hip: cf. HUNCH)
haunt *v.*, haunt◦ed,
  haunt•ing.
haunt•ing◦ly
haute cou•ture
haute cui•sine
hau•teur
Ha•van◦a
have¹ *n., pl.* haves.
have² *v.*, had, hav•
  ing. (to possess: cf.
  HALVE)
have-not
ha•ven (refuge: cf.
  HEAVEN)
have◦n't
hav•er•sack
hav◦oc
Ha•wai◦i (HI)
Ha•wai•ian

hawk *v.*, hawked,
  hawk•ing.
hawk-eyed
hawk◦er
Haw•kins
hawk•ish
haw•ser
haw•thorn
Haw•thorne ef•fect
  Business.
hay (dried grass: cf.
  HEY)
hay fe•ver
hay◦cock
Hay◦dn
Hayes
hay•fork
hay•loft
hay•mak◦er
hay•mow
hay•seed
hay•stack
Hay•ward
hay•wire
haz•ard *v.*, haz•
  ard◦ed, haz•ard•
  ing.
haz•ard•ous
haz•ard•ous◦ly
haze *v.*, hazed, haz•
  ing.
ha•zel
ha◦zel•nut
ha•zi◦ly
ha•zi•ness
ha◦zy *adj.*, ha•zi◦er,
  ha•zi•est.
HDTV (high-definition
  television)
he, *n., pl.* they, hes;
  him, *pl.* them; his, *pl.*
  their; his, *pl.* theirs.
he-man *n., pl.* he-men.
head *v.*, head◦ed,
  head•ing.
head crash *Computers.*

head-on
head•ache
head•band
head•bang◦er
head•board
head•dress
head•first
head•gear
head•hunt◦er
head•hunt•ing
head•ing
head•land
head•less
head•light
head•line *v.*, head•
  lined, head•lin•ing.
head•lock
head•long
head•man *n., pl.*
  head•men.
head•mas•ter
head•mis•tress
head•phone
head•piece
head•quar•ters *n., pl.*
  head•quar•ters.
head•rest
head•room
head•set
heads•man or head•
  man *n., pl.* heads•
  men or head•men
head•stall
head•stone
head•strong
head•wait◦er
head•wa•ters
head•way
head•wind
head•word
head◦y *adj.*, head•
  i◦er, head•i•est.
heal *v.*, healed, heal•
  ing. (to get well: cf.
  HEEL; HE'LL)
heal◦er

health
health•ful
health•i∘ly
health∘y *adj.*, health•
i∘er, health•i•est.
heap *v.*, heaped,
heap•ing.
hear *v.*, heard, hear•
ing. (to listen: cf.
HERE)
heard (did listen: cf.
HERD)
hear∘er
hear•ing
hear•ing-ear dog
hark∘en or hark∘en
v., heark•ened,
heark•en•ing.
hear•say
hearse
heart (the organ: cf.
HART)
heart at•tack
heart-to-heart
heart•ache
heart•beat
heart•break
heart•break•ing
heart•bro•ken
heart•burn
heart∘en *v.*, heart•
ened, heart•en•ing.
heart•en•ing∘ly
heart•felt
hearth
hearth•stone
heart•i∘ly
heart•i•ness
heart•less
heart•less∘ly
heart•less•ness
heart•rend•ing
heart•rend•ing∘ly
heart•sick
heart•strings
heart•throb

heart•warm•ing
heart∘y *n.*, *pl.* heart•
ies; *adj.*, heart•i∘er,
heart•i•est.
heat *v.*, heat∘ed,
heat•ing.
heat•ed∘ly
heat∘er
heath
hea•then *n.*, *pl.* hea•
thens or hea•then.
heath∘er
heat•stroke
heave *v.*, heaved or
hove, heav•ing.
heave-ho *n.*, *pl.*
heave-hos.
heav∘en (abode of
God: cf. HAVEN)
heav•en∘ly
heav•en•ward
heav•i∘ly
heav•i•ness
heav∘y *n.*, *pl.* heav•
ies; *adj.*, heav•i∘er,
heav•i•est.
heav∘y-du∘ty
heav∘y-hand∘ed
heav∘y-hand∘ed∘ly
heav∘y-hand∘ed•ness
heav∘y-heart∘ed
heav∘y∘set
heav∘y∘weight
He•bra∘ic
He•brew
Heb•ri•des, the
heck
heck∘le *v.*, heck•led,
heck•ling.
heck•ler
hec•tare
hec•tic
hec∘to•gram
hec∘to•li∘ter
hec∘to•me∘ter

hec•tor *v.*, hec•tored,
hec•tor•ing.
he'd
hedge *v.*, hedged,
hedg•ing.
hedge fund *Business.*
hedge•hog
hedge•row
he•don•ism
he•don•ist
he•don•is•tic
hee•bie-jee•bies
heed *v.*, heed∘ed,
heed•ing.
heed•ful
heed•less
hee•haw
heel[1] (back of foot: cf.
HEAL; HE'LL)
heel[2] *v.*, heeled, heel•
ing.
heel•less
heft *v.*, heft∘ed, heft•
ing.
heft•i•ness
heft∘y *adj.*, heft•i∘er,
heft•i•est.
he•gem∘o•ny *n.*, *pl.*
he•gem∘o•nies.
he•gi∘ra or he•ji∘ra
n., *pl.* he•gi•ras or
he•ji•ras.
Hei•del•berg
heif∘er
height
height∘en *v.*, height•
ened, height•en•
ing.
height•ism
Heim•lich ma•neu•
ver
hei•nous
heir (inheritor: cf. AIR;
E'ER; ERE; ERR)
heir ap•par•ent *n.*, *pl.*
heirs ap•par•ent.
heir pre•sump•tive

n., pl. **heirs pre•**
sump•tive.
heir•ess
heir•loom
heist v., heist○ed,
heist•ing.
held
Hel○en
Hel•e○na
hel○i•cal
hel○i•cal-scan car•
tridge *Computers.*
hel○i•cop•ter
he○li○o•cen•tric
he○li○o•graph
he○li○o•trope
hel○i•port
he•li○um
he•lix n., pl. hel○i•ces
or he•lix○es.
he'll (he will: cf. HEAL;
HEEL)
hell
hell•bent
hell•cat
hel•le•bore
Hel•len○ic
Hel•len•ism
Hel•len•is•tic
hell•gram•mite
hell•hole
hel•lion
hell•ish
hell•ish○ly
hel○lo n., pl. hel•los.
helm
hel•met
hel•met○ed
helms•man n., pl.
helms•men.
hel○ot
help v., helped, help•
ing.
help○er
help•ful
help•ful○ly

help•ful•ness
help○ing
help•less
help•less○ly
help•less•ness
help•mate or help•
meet
Hel•sin○ki
hel○ter-skel○ter
Hel•ve○tia
hem v., hemmed,
hem•ming.
he○ma•tite
he○ma•tol○o•gist
he○ma•tol○o•gy
he○ma•to•ma n., pl.
he○ma•to•mas or
he○ma•to•ma○ta.
Hem•ing•way
hem○i•sphere
hem○i•spher•ic
hem•line
hem•lock
he○mo•glo•bin
he○mo•phil○i•a
he○mo•phil○i•ac
hem•or•rhage v.,
hem•or•rhaged,
hem•or•rhag•ing.
hem•or•rhag○ic
hem•or•rhoid
he○mo•stat
hemp
hem•stitch, v., hem•
stitch○ed, hem•
stitch•ing, n.
hen
hence (from now: cf.
THENCE; WHENCE)
hence•forth
hench•man n., pl.
hench•men.
he○na n., pl. hen•
nas; v., hen•naed,
hen•na•ing.
hen•peck

hen•pecked
hen○ry n., pl. hen•ries
or hen•rys.
hep
hep○a•rin
he•pat○ic
hep○a•ti•tis
hep•tath•lon
her
He○ra
her•ald v., her•
ald○ed, her•ald•ing.
he•ral•dic
her•ald○ry
herb
her•ba•ceous
her•bage
herb○al
herb•al○ist
her•bi•cid○al
herb○i•cide
her•bi•vore
her•biv○o○rous
her•cu•le○an
Her•cu•les
herd[1] (group of ani-
mals: cf. HEARD)
herd[2] v., herd○ed,
herd•ing.
here (in this place: cf.
HEAR)
here•a○bout or here•
a○bouts
here•af○ter
here•by
he•red○i•tar○y
he•red•i○ty
here○in
here•in•af○ter or
here•in•be○low
here○of
her•e○sy n., pl. her•
e•sies.
her○e•tic
he•ret○i•cal

here•to or here•
un•to
here•to•fore
here•up•on
here•with
her•it•a•ble
her•it•age
her•maph•ro•dite
her•maph•ro•dit•ic
Her•mes
her•met•i•cal•ly
her•mit
her•mit•age
her•ni•a n., pl. her•
ni•as or her•ni•ae.
her•ni•ate, v., her•
ni•at•ed, her•ni•
at•ing.
he•ro n., pl. he•ros,
he•roes. (brave peo-
ple; sandwiches)
He•rod•o•tus
he•ro•ic
he•ro•i•cal•ly
her•o•in (drug)
her•o•ine (admired
woman)
her•o•ism
her•on
her•pes
herpes sim•plex
herpes zos•ter
her•pe•tol•o•gy
Herr n., pl. Her•ren.
her•ring n., pl. her•
ring or her•rings.
her•ring•bone
hers
her•self
her•sto•ry, n., pl.
her•sto•ries.
hertz n., pl. hertz or
hertz•es.
he's
hes•i•tan•cy
hes•i•tant

hes•i•tant•ly
hes•i•tate v., hes•i•
tat•ed, hes•i•tat•
ing.
hes•i•tat•ing•ly
hes•i•ta•tion
Hes•se
het•er•o•dox
het•er•o•dox•y
het•er•o•ge•ne•i•ty
het•er•o•ge•ne•ous
heterogeneous net•
work Computers.
het•er•o•sex•u•al
het•er•o•sex•u•al•
i•ty
heu•ris•tic
hew v., hewed,
hewed or hewn,
hew•ing. (to chop: cf.
HUE; HUGH)
hex v., hexed, hex•
ing.
hex•a•gon
hex•ag•o•nal
hex•am•e•ter
hey (the exclamation:
cf. HAY)
hey•day
hi
HI (Hawaii)
hi-fi n., pl. hi-fis.
hi-res Computers.
Hi•a•le•ah
hi•a•tus n., pl. hi•a•
tus•es or hi•a•t us.
hi•ba•chi n., pl. hi•
ba•chis.
hi•ber•nate v., hi•
ber•nat•ed, hi•ber•
nat•ing.
hi•ber•na•tion
hi•bis•cus n., pl. hi•
bis•cus•es.
hic•cup or hic•cough
v., hic•cuped or hic•
cupped or hic•

coughed, hic•cup•
ing or hic•cup•ping
or hic•cough•ing.
hick
hick•ey, n., pl. hick•
eys.
hick•o•ry n., pl. hick•
o•ries.
hid•den
hid•den agen•da
hidden file Computers.
hidden re•serves Busi-
ness.
hidden tax Business.
hide[1] v., hid, hid•den,
hid•ing. (to conceal)
hide[2] v., hid•ed, hid•
ing. (to thrash)
hide-and-seek
hide•a•way
hide•bound
hid•e•ous
hid•e•ous•ly
hid•e•ous•ness
hide•out or hide-out
hie v., hied, hie•ing.
hi•er•ar•chic or
hi•er•ar•chi•cal
hierarchical file sys•
tem Computers.
hi•er•ar•chi•cal•ly
hi•er•ar•chy n., pl.
hi•er•ar•chies.
hi•er•o•glyph•ic
hig•gle•dy-
pig•gle•dy
high n., pl. highs; adj.,
high•er, high•est.
high con•cept
high-den•si•ty Com-
puters.
high fi•del•i•ty n.
high-fi•del•i•ty adj.
high-five v., high-
fived, high-fiv•ing.
high-flown
high fre•quen•cy n.

high-fre○quen○cy *adj.*
high-hand○ed
high-hand○ed○ly
high-hand○ed○ness
high-hat *v.,* high-hat○ted, high-hat○ting.
high jinks (frolics: cf. JINX)
high-lev○el
high-level lan○guage *Computers.*
high mem○o○ry *Computers.*
high-mind○ed
high-mind○ed○ness
high-oc○cu○pan○cy ve○hi○cle (HOV)
high-pres○sure *v.,* high-pres○sured, high-pres○sur○ing.
high-res○o○lu○tion *Computers.*
high-rise or high○rise
high-sound○ing
high-spir○ited
high-strung
high-tech
high-ten○sion
high-test
high-toned
high top
high•ball *v.,* high•balled, high•ball•ing.
high•born
high•boy
high•brow
high•chair
high○er (taller: cf. HIRE)
high○er-up
high•fa•lu•tin or high•fa•lu•ting
high•land
high•light

high○ly
high•ness
high•road
high•tail
high•way
high•way•man *n., pl.* high•way•men.
hi•jack *v.,* hi•jacked, hi•jack•ing.
hi•jack○er
hike *v.,* hiked, hik•ing.
hik○er
hi•lar•i•ous
hi•lar•i•ous○ly
hi•lar•i○ty
hill
hill•bil○ly *n., pl.* hill•bil•lies.
hill•ock
hill•side
hill•top
hill○y *adj.,* hill•i○er, hill•i•est.
hilt
him (objective case of "he": cf. HYMN)
Him○a•la•yan
Him○a•la•yas
him•self
hind *n., pl.* hinds or hind.
hin•der[1] *v.,* hin•dered, hin•der•ing. (to prevent)
hind○er[2] (in the rear)
Hin○di
hind•most
hind•quar•ter
hin•drance
hind•sight
Hin○du *n., pl.* Hin•dus.
Hin•du•ism
Hin•du•stan
Hin•du•sta•ni

hinge *v.,* hinged, hing•ing.
hint *v.,* hint○ed, hint•ing.
hin○ter•land
hip *adj.,* hip•per, hip•pest.
hip-hop
hip•bone
hip•hug•ger
hip•ness
hip•pie *n., pl.* hip•pies.
hip○po
Hip•po•crat○ic oath
hip•po•drome
hip•po•pot○a•mus *n., pl.* hip•po•pot○a•mus○es or hip•po•pot○a○mi.
hip•ster
hire *v.,* hired, hir•ing. (to employ: cf. HIGHER)
hire•ling
hir•ing hall *Business.*
Hi•ro•shi•ma
hir•sute
hir•sute•ness
his
His•pan○ic
His•pan•io○la
hiss *v.,* hissed, hiss•ing.
his•ta•mine
his•to•gram
his•tol○o•gist
his•tol○o○gy
his•to•ri○an
his•tor○ic
his•tor○i•cal
historical cost *Business.*
his•tor○i•cal○ly
his•to•ric○i○ty
his•to•ri•og•ra•phy,

n., pl. his•to•ri•og•
ra•phies.
his•to•ry *n., pl.* his•
to•ries.
his•tri•on•ic
his•tri•on•i•cal•ly
his•tri•on•ics
hit *v.,* hit, hit•ting.
hit-and-run
hit-or-miss
hitch *v.,* hitched,
hitch•ing.
hitch•hike *v.,* hitch•
hiked, hitch•hik•ing.
hitch•hik•er
hith•er
hith•er•to
Hit•ler
hit•ter
HIV (human immunode-
ficiency virus)
hive
hives
HMO (health mainte-
nance organization)
Ho Chi Minh
hoa•gy or hoa•gie,
n., pl. hoa•gies.
hoard *v.,* hoard•ed,
hoard•ing. (to amass:
cf. HORDE)
hoard•er
hoar•frost
hoar•i•ness
hoarse *adj.,* hoars•er,
hoars•est. (husky in
tone: cf. HORSE)
hoarse•ly
hoarse•ness
hoar•y *adj.,* hoar•
i•er, hoar•i•est.
hoax *v.,* hoaxed,
hoax•ing.
hoax•er
hob•ble *v.,* hob•bled,
hob•bling.

hob•by *n., pl.* hob•
bies.
hob•by•horse
hob•by•ist
hob•gob•lin
hob•nail
hob•nailed
hob•nob *v.,* hob•
nobbed, hob•nob•
bing.
ho•bo *n., pl.* ho•bos
or ho•boes.
hock *v.,* hocked,
hock•ing.
hock•ey
hock•shop
ho•cus-po•cus
hodge•podge
Hodg•kin's disease
hoe *v.,* hoed, hoe•ing.
hoe•cake
hoe•down
hog *v.,* hogged, hog•
ging.
hog-wild
ho•gan
hog•gish
hogs•head
hog•tie *v.,* hog•tied,
hog•ty•ing.
hog•wash
hoi pol•loi
hoist *v.,* hoist•ed,
hoist•ing.
hok•ey *adj.,* hok•i•er,
hok•i•est.
ho•kum
hold *v.,* held, hold•
ing.
hold•er
holder in due course
Business.
hold•ing
holding com•pa•ny
Business.
hold•o•ver

hold•up
hole[1] (opening: cf.
WHOLE)
hole[2] *v.,* holed, hol•
ing.
hol•ey (full of holes:
cf. HOLY; WHOLLY)
hol•i•day (day of com-
memoration: cf. HOLY
DAY)
ho•li•er-than-thou
ho•li•ness
ho•lis•tic
Hol•land
hol•lan•daise sauce
Hol•land•er
hol•ler *v.,* hol•lered,
hol•ler•ing.
Hol•ler•ith code *Com-
puters.*
hol•low[1] *v.,* hol•
lowed, hol•low•ing.
hol•low[2] *adj.,* hol•
low•er, hol•low•
est. (empty: cf. HAL-
LOW; HALO)
hol•low•ness
hol•ly *n., pl.* hol•lies.
hol•ly•hock
Hol•ly•wood
Holmes
hol•mi•um
hol•o•caust
Hol•o•cene
hol•o•gram
hol•o•graph
hol•o•graph•ic
ho•log•ra•phy
Hol•stein
hol•ster *v.,* hol•
stered, hol•ster•ing.
ho•ly *adj.,* ho•li•er,
ho•li•est. (sacred: cf.
HOLEY; WHOLLY)
holy day (religious
feast day: cf. HOLIDAY)
Ho•ly Ghost

hom•age

hom•burg

home v., homed, hom•ing.

home-mak•ing

home of•fice *Business.*

home shop•ping *Business.*

home•bod•y n., pl. home•bod•ies.

home•boy

home•com•ing

home•grown

home•land

home•less

home•like

home•li•ness

home•ly adj., home•li•er, home•li•est. (unattractive: cf. HOMEY or HOMY)

home•made

home•mak•er

ho•me•o•box gene

ho•me•o•path•ic

ho•me•op•a•thy

ho•me•o•sta•sis

ho•me•o•stat•ic

hom•er

Ho•mer

Ho•mer•ic

home•room or home room

home•school•ing

home•sick

home•sick•ness

home•spun

home•stead

home•stretch

home•ward

home•work

hom•ey or hom•y, adj., hom•i•er, hom•i•est. (cozy: cf. HOMELY)

hom•i•cid•al

hom•i•cide

hom•i•let•ics

hom•i•ly n., pl. hom•i•lies. (sermon: cf. HOMINY)

hom•ing pi•geon

hom•i•nid

hom•i•ny (hulled corn: cf. HOMILY)

Ho•mo sa•pi•ens

ho•mo•ge•ne•i•ty

ho•mo•ge•ne•ous (alike: cf. HOMOGENOUS)

ho•mog•e•ni•za•tion

ho•mog•e•nized

ho•mog•e•nous (of common origin: cf. HOMOGENEOUS)

hom•o•graph

ho•mol•o•gous

hom•o•nym

ho•mo•phile

ho•mo•pho•bi•a

hom•o•phone

ho•mo•sex•u•al

ho•mo•sex•u•al•i•ty

hom•y adj., hom•i•er, hom•i•est.

hon

hon•cho n., pl. hon•chos.

Hon•du•ran

Hon•du•ras

hone v., honed, hon•ing.

hon•est

hon•est•ly

hon•es•ty

hon•ey n., pl. hon•eys.

hon•ey•bee or hon•ey bee

hon•ey•comb

hon•ey•dew

hon•eyed or hon•ied

hon•ey•moon v., hon•ey•mooned, hon•ey•moon•ing.

hon•ey•moon•er

hon•ey•suck•le

Hong Kong

Ho•ni

honk v., honked, honk•ing.

honk•y-tonk

Hon•o•lu•lu

hon•or v., hon•ored, hon•or•ing.

hon•or•a•ble

hon•or•a•bly

hon•o•rar•i•um n., pl. hon•o•rar•i•ums or hon•o•rar•i•a.

hon•or•ar•y

hon•or•if•ic

Hon•shu

hooch or hootch

hood

hood•ed

hood•lum

hoo•doo n., pl. hoo•doos; v., hoo•dooed, hoo•doo•ing.

hood•wink v., hood•winked, hood•wink•ing.

hoo•ey

hoof n., pl. hoofs or hooves or hoof.

hook v., hooked, hook•ing.

hook•ah n., pl. hook•ahs.

hook•er

hook•up

hook•worm

hook•y or hook•ey

hoo•li•gan

hoo•li•gan•ism

hoop (circular band: cf. WHOOP)

hoop•la

hoo•ray

hoose•gow

Hoo•sier

hoot v., hoot○ed, hoot•ing.

hoot•en•an•ony n., pl. hoot•en•an•nies.

Hoo•ver

hop v., hopped, hop•ping.

hope v., hoped, hop•ing.

hope•ful

hope•ful○ly

hope•less

hope•less○ly

hope•less•ness

hop•head

Ho○pi n., pl. Ho•pis or Ho○pi.

hop•per

hop•sack•ing

hop•scotch

Hor•ace

horde (crowd: cf. HOARD)

hore•hound

ho•ri•zon

hor○i•zon•tal

horizontal in•te•gra•tion Business.

hor○i•zon•tal merg○er Business.

horizontal scroll•ing Computers.

hor○i•zon•tal○ly Business.

hor•mo•nal

hor•mone

horn

horned

hor•net

horn•less

horn•pipe

horn○y adj., horn•i○er, horn•i•est.

hor○o•log○ic

ho•rol○o○gist

ho•rol•o○gy

hor○o•scope

hor•ren•dous

hor•ri•ble

hor•ri•bly

hor•rid

hor•rif○ic

hor•ri•fy v., hor•ri•fied, hor•ri•fy•ing.

hor•ri•fy•ing○ly

hor•ror

hors de com•bat

hors d'oeuvre n., pl. hors d'oeuvre or hors d'oeuvres.

horse n., pl. hors○es or horse; v., horsed, hors•ing. (the animal: cf. HOARSE)

horse fly or horse•fly

horse•back

horse•flesh

horse•hair

horse•hide

horse•laugh

horse•less

horse•man n., pl. horse•men.

horse•man•ship

horse•play

horse•pow○er

horse•rad•ish

horse•shoe

horse•tail

horse•whip v., horse•whipped, horse•whip•ping.

horse•wom○an n., pl. horse•wom○en.

hors○y adj., hors•i○er, hors•i•est.

hor•ta•to○ry

hor•ti•cul•tur○al

hor•ti•cul•ture

ho•san○na n., pl. ho•san•nas.

hose n., pl. hose, hos○es; v., hosed, hos•ing. (stockings or tubes)

ho•sier○y

hos•pice

hos•pi•ta○ble (receptive)

hos•pi•tal (medical institution)

hos•pi•tal•i○ty n., pl. hos•pi•tal•i•ties.

hos•pi•tal•i○za•tion

hos•pi•tal•ize v., hos•pi•tal•ized, hos•pi•tal•iz•ing.

host v., host○ed, host•ing.

host com•put○er Computers.

hos•tage

hos•tel (lodging place: cf. HOSTILE)

host•ess v., host•essed, host•ess•ing.

hos•tile (antagonistic: cf. HOSTEL)

hostile take○o○ver Business.

hos•til•i•ties

hos•til•i○ty

hot adj., hot•ter, hot•test.

hot-blood○ed

hot-but•ton

hot cake or hot•cake

hot dog n.

hot-dog or hot•dog v., hot-dogged, hot-dog○ging or hot-dog•ging.

hot key Computers.

hot link Computers.

hot rod[1] n.

hot-rod[2] v., hot-

rod○ded, hot-
rod○ding.
hot rod•der
hot spot or hot•spot
hot•bed
hot•box or hot box
ho•tel
ho•te•lier
hot•foot *n., pl.* hot•
foots.
hot•head
hot•head○ed
hot•head•ed•ness
hot•house
hot○ly
hot•shot
hound *v.,* hound○ed,
hound•ing.
hound's-tooth
hour (60 minutes: cf.
OUR)
hour•glass
hou○ri *n., pl.* hou•ris.
hour○ly
house *n., pl.* hous○es;
v., housed, hous•
ing.
house mu○sic
house sit•ter or
house-sit○ter
house•boat
house•boy
house•break *v.,*
house•broke,
house•bro○ken,
house•break○ing.
house•break○er
house•coat
house•fa○ther
house•fly, *n., pl.*
house•flies.
house•ful *n., pl.*
house•fuls.
house•hold
house•hold○er
house•hus•band

house•keep○er
house•keep○ing
house•maid
house•man *n., pl.*
house•men.
house•moth○er
house•par•ent
house•plant
house•sit or house-sit,
v., house•sat,
house•sit•ting or
house•sit○ting.
house•top
house•wares
house•warm○ing
house•wife *n., pl.*
house•wives.
house•wife○ly
house•work
hous○ing
Hous•ton
HOV (high-occupancy
vehicle)
hove
hov○el
hov○er *v.,* hov•ered,
hov•er•ing.
hov○er•craft *n., pl.*
hov○er•craft.
how
how-do-you-do or
how-de-do, *n., pl.*
how-do-you-dos.
how-to
How•ard
how•be○it
how•dah
how•ev○er
how•itz○er
howl *v.,* howled,
howl○ing.
howl○er
how•so•ev○er
hoy•den
hoy•den○ish
Hoyle

hua•ra•che *n., pl.*
hua•ra•ches.
hub
hub-and-spoke
hub•bub
hub•cap
hu•bris
huck○le•ber○ry *n., pl.*
huck○le•ber○ries.
huck•ster
HUD (Department of
Housing and Urban
Development)
hud•dle *v.,* hud•dled,
hud•dling.
Hud•son
hue (color: cf. HEW;
HUGH)
huff *v.,* huffed, huff•
ing.
huff○y *adj.,* huff•i○er,
huff•i•est.
hug *v.,* hugged, hug•
ging.
huge *adj.,* hug○er,
hug•est.
huge○ly
huge•ness
hug○ger-mug○ger
Hugh (the name: cf.
HEW; HUE)
Hu○go
Hu•gue•not
huh
hu○la *n., pl.* hu•las.
hulk
hulk•ing
hull
hul•la•ba•loo *n., pl.*
hul•la•ba•loos.
hum *v.,* hummed,
hum•ming.
hu•man (of people)
Hu○man Ge•nome
Proj•ect
hu•man re•sourc○es
Business.

human rights
hu•mane (compassion-
ate)
hu•mane•ly
hu•mane•ness
hu○man•ism
hu○man•ist
hu○man•is•tic
hu○man•i•tar•i•an
hu○man•i•tar•i•an•
ism
hu○man•i•ties
hu○man•i○ty
hu○man•ize v.,
hu○man•ized,
hu○man•iz•ing.
hu○man•kind
hu○man•ly
hu○man•oid
hum•ble v., hum•
bled, hum•bling;
adj., hum•bler,
hum•blest.
hum•bly
hum•bug v., hum•
bugged, hum•bug•
ging.
hum•ding○er
hum•drum
hu•mer○al
hu•mer•ous n., pl. hu•
mer•i. (arm bone: cf.
HUMOROUS)
hu•mid
hu•mid○i•fi•ca•tion
hu•mid○i•fi○er
hu•mid•i•fy v., hu•
mid•i•fied, hu•mid•
i•fy•ing.
hu•mid•i○ty
hu•mi•dor
hu•mil•i○ate v., hu•
mil○i•at○ed, hu•
mil○i•at•ing.
hu•mil○i•at•ing○ly
hu•mil○i•a•tion
hu•mil•i•ty

hum•mer
hum•ming•bird
hum•mock
hu•mon•gous
hu•mor v., hu•mored,
hu•mor•ing.
hu•mor•ist
hu•mor•less
hu•mor•ous (funny:
cf. HUMERUS)
hu•mor•ous○ly
hump v., humped,
hump•ing.
hump•back
hump•backed
humph
hu•mus
Hum•vee
Hun
Hu○nan
hunch[1] n. (suspicion:
cf. HAUNCH)
hunch[2] v., hunched,
hunch•ing.
hunch•back
hunch•backed
hun•dred n., pl. hun•
dreds or hun•dred.
hun•dred•fold
hun•dredth
hun•dred•weight n.,
pl. hun•dred•
weights or hun•
dred•weight.
hung
Hun•gar•i○an
Hun•ga○ry
hun•ger v., hun•
gered, hun•ger•ing.
hun•gri○ly
hun•gry adj., hun•
gri○er, hun•gri•est.
hunk
hun•ker v., hun•
kered, hun•ker•ing.
hunk○y-do○ry

hunt v., hunt○ed,
hunt•ing.
hunt○er
hunt•ress
hunts•man n., pl.
hunts•men.
Hunts•ville
hur•dle[1] n. (barrier: cf.
HURTLE)
hur•dle[2] v., hur•dled,
hur•dling.
hur•dler
hur○dy-gur○dy n., pl.
hur○dy-gur○dies.
hurl v., hurled, hurl•
ing.
hurl○er
hurl○y-burl○y
Hu•ron n., pl. Hu•
rons or Hu•ron.
hur•rah or hur•ray v.,
hur•rahed or hur•
rayed, hur•rah•ing
or hur•ray•ing.
hur•ri•cane
hur•ried○ly
hur○ry n., pl. hur•ries;
v., hur•ried, hur•ry•
ing.
hurt v., hurt, hurt•
ing.
hurt•ful
hur•tle v., hur•tled,
hur•tling. (to rush:
cf. HURDLE)
hus•band v., hus•
band○ed, hus•
band•ing.
hus•band○ry
hush v., hushed,
hush•ing.
hush-hush
husk v., husked,
husk•ing.
husk•i○ly
husk○i•ness
husk○y n., pl. husk•

ies; *adj.*, husk•i∘er,
husk•i•est.
hus•sar
hus∘sy *n.*, *pl.* hus•
sies.
hus•tings
hus•tle *v.*, hus•tled,
hus•tling.
hus•tler
hut
hutch
hutz∘pa or hutz•pah
Hux•ley
huz∘zah *n.*, *pl.* huz•
zahs; *v.*, huz•zahed,
huz•zah•ing.
hy•a•cinth
hy•brid
hy•dra *n.*, *pl.* hy•dras
or hy•drae.
hy•dran•gea *n.*, *pl.*
hy•dran•geas.
hy•drant
hy•drau•lic
hy•drau•lics
hy•dro *n.*, *pl.* hy•
dros.
hy∘dro•car•bon
hy∘dro•ceph∘a•lus or
hy•dro•ceph•a∘ly
hy∘dro•chlo•ric ac∘id
hy∘dro•cor•ti•sone
hy•dro•dy•nam•ics
hy∘dro•e•lec•tric
hy∘dro•e•lec•tric•
i∘ty
hy∘dro•foil
hy∘dro•gen
hydrogen bomb
hy•dro•gen per•ox•
ide
hy•drog∘e∘nate, *v.*,
hy•drog∘e∘nat•ed,
hy•drog∘e∘nat•ing.
hy∘dro•gen•a∘tion
hy•drol∘o∘gy

hy•drom•e∘ter
hy•drom•e∘try
hy∘dro•pho•bi∘a
hy∘dro•phone
hy∘dro•plane
hy∘dro•pon∘ic
hy∘dro•pon•ics
hy•dro•sphere
hy•dro•stat∘ic
hy•dro•stat•ics
hy•dro•ther∘a∘py
hy•drous
hy•drox∘ide
hy•e∘ona *n.*, *pl.* hy•e•
nas.
hy•giene
hy•gi∘en∘ic
hy•gi∘en∘i•cal∘ly
hy•gien•ist
hy•grom•e∘ter
hy•grom•e∘try
hy•men
hy•me•ne∘al
hymn (song: cf. HIM)
hym•nal
hype
hy•per
hy∘per•ac•tive
hy∘per•ac•tiv•i∘ty
hy∘per•bar∘ic
hy∘per•bo•la *n.*, *pl.*
hy∘per•bo•las.
(curve)
hy∘per•bo•le (exag-
geration)
hy∘per•bol∘ic or
hy∘per•bol∘i•cal
hy∘per•crit∘i•cal
hy∘per•crit∘i•cal∘ly
hy∘per•gly•ce•mi∘a
hy∘per•gly•ce•mic
hy∘per•in•fla•tion
Business.
hy∘per•me•di∘a *Com-
puters.*
hy∘per•sen•si•tive

hy∘per•sen•si•tive•
ness or hy∘per•sen•
si•tiv•i∘ty
hy∘per•son∘ic
hy∘per•ten•sion
hy∘per•ten•sive
hy∘per•text *Comput-
ers.*
hy∘per•thy•roid
hy∘per•thy•roid•ism
hy∘per•troph∘ic
hy∘per•tro•phy
hy∘per•ven•ti•late
v., hy∘per•ven•ti•
lat∘ed, hy∘per•ven•
ti•lat•ing.
hy∘per•ven•ti•la•
tion
hy•phen
hy•phen•ate *v.*, hy•
phen•at∘ed, hy•
phen•at•ing.
hy•phen•a•tion
hyp•no•sis *n.*, *pl.*
hyp•no•ses.
hyp•not∘ic
hyp•not∘i•cal∘ly
hyp•no•tism
hyp•no•tist
hyp•no•tiz∘a∘ble
hyp•no•tize *v.*, hyp•
no•tized, hyp•no•
tiz•ing.
hy∘po, *n.*, *pl.* hy•pos.
v., hy∘poed, hy∘po•
ing.
hy∘po•al•ler•gen∘ic
hy∘po•chon•dri∘a
hy∘po•chon•dri∘ac
hy•poc∘ri•sy *n.*, *pl.*
hy•poc∘ri•sies.
hyp∘o•crite
hyp∘o•crit∘i•cal
hyp∘o•crit∘i•cal∘ly
hy∘po•der•mic
hy∘po•gly•ce•mi∘a
hy∘po•gly•ce•mic

hy•pot•e•nuse

hy•po•thal•a•mus, n., pl. hy•po•thal•a•mi.

hy•poth•e•ca•tion Business.

hy•po•ther•mi•a

hy•poth•e•sis n., pl. hy•poth•e•ses.

hy•poth•e•size v., hy•poth•e•sized, hy•poth•e•siz•ing.

hy•po•thet•i•cal

hy•po•thet•i•cal•ly

hy•po•thy•roid

hy•po•thy•roid•ism

hys•sop

hys•ter•ec•to•my n., pl. hys•ter•ec•to•mies.

hys•te•ri•a

hys•ter•i•cal

hys•ter•ics

I

I n., pl. we, I's; me, pl. us; my, pl. our; mine, pl. ours. (me: cf. AYE: EYE)

I-•beam point•er Computers.

IA (Iowa)

i•amb

i•am•bic

I•be•ri•a

I•be•ri•an

i•bex n., pl. i•bex•es or i•bi•ces or i•bex. (mountain goat)

i•bi•dem

i•bis n., pl. i•bis•es or i•bis. (wading bird)

Ib•sen

i•bu•pro•fen

ICC Business. (Interstate Commerce Commission)

ice v., iced, ic•ing.

ice cream

ice skate¹ n.

ice-skate² v., ice-skat•ed, ice-skat•ing.

ice•berg

ice•bound

ice•box

ice•break•er

ice•cap

iced

Ice•land

Ice•lan•dic

ice•man n., pl. ice•men.

ich•thy•ol•o•gy

i•ci•cle

i•ci•ly

i•ci•ness

ic•ing

ick•y adj., ick•i•er, ick•i•est.

i•con

i•con•ic

i•co•nic•i•ty

i•con•o•clasm

i•con•o•clast

i•con•o•clas•tic

ic•tus n., pl. ic•tus•es or ic•tus.

ICU (intensive care unit)

i•cy adj., i•ci•er, i•ci•est.

ID¹ (Idaho)

ID² n., pl. IDs or ID's. (identification)

I'd (I would)

id

I•da•ho (ID)

I•da•ho•an

i•de•a

i•de•al (perfect: cf. IDLE; IDOL; IDYLL)

i•de•al•ism

i•de•al•ist

i•de•al•is•tic

i•de•al•i•za•tion

i•de•al•ize v., i•de•al•ized, i•de•al•iz•ing.

i•de•al•ly

i•dée fixe n., pl. i•dée fixes.

i•dem

i•den•ti•cal

i•den•ti•cal•ly

i•den•ti•fi•a•ble

i•den•ti•fi•ca•tion

i•den•ti•fied goods Business.

i•den•ti•fy v., i•den•ti•fied, i•den•ti•fy•ing.

i•den•ti•ty n., pl. i•den•ti•ties.

id•e•o•gram

i•de•o•log•i•cal

i•de•ol•o•gy n., pl. i•de•ol•o•gies.

ides

id•i•o•cy n., pl. id•i•o•cies.

id•i•om

id•i•o•mat•ic

id•i•o•mat•i•cal•ly

id•i•o•path•ic

id•i•o•syn•cra•sy n., pl. id•i•o•syn•cra•sies.

id•i•o•syn•crat•ic

id•i•ot

id•i•ot•ic
id•i•ot•i•cal•ly
i•odle *adj.,* i•odler, i•odlest; *v.,* i•odled, i•odling. (inactive; to be idle: cf. IDEAL; IDOL; IDYLL)
i•odle•ness
i•odler
i•odly
i•odol (object of worship: cf. IDEAL; IDLE; IDYLL)
i•odol•a•ter
i•odol•a•trous
i•odol•a•try
i•odol•ize *v.,* i•odol•ized, i•odol•iz•ing.
i•odyll (pastoral poem: cf. IDEAL; IDLE; IDOL)
i•odyl•lic
i.e. (that is: cf. E.G.)
IEEE *Computers.* (Institute of Electrical and Electronics Engineers)
if
if•o•fy *adj.,* if•fi•er, if•fi•est.
ig•loo *n., pl.* ig•loos.
ig•ne•ous
ig•nite *v.,* ig•nit•ed, ig•nit•ing.
ig•ni•tion
ig•no•bil•i•ty
ig•no•ble
ig•no•bly
ig•no•min•i•ous
ig•no•min•i•ous•ly
ig•no•min•y
ig•no•ra•mus *n., pl.* ig•no•ra•mus•es.
ig•no•rance
ig•no•rant
ig•no•rant•ly
ig•nore *v.,* ig•nored, ig•nor•ing.

i•gua•ona *n., pl.* i•gua•nas.
IL (Illinois)
il•o•e•oi•tis
il•e•oum *n., pl.* il•e•ums. (intestine)
Il•o•i•ad
il•o•i•oum *n., pl.* il•o•i•oa. (hip bone)
ilk
I'll (I will: cf. AISLE; ISLE)
ill *adj.* (sick)
ill-ad•vised
ill-ad•vis•ed•ly
ill-bred
ill-fat•ed
ill-got•ten
ill-hu•mor
ill-hu•mored
ill-man•nered
ill-na•tured
ill-na•tured•ly
ill-na•tured•ness
ill-starred
ill-treat *v.,* ill-treat•ed, ill-treat•ing.
ill-treat•ment
ill-use *v.,* ill-used, ill-us•ing.
ill will *n*
ill-willed *adj.*
il•le•gal
il•le•gal•i•oty
il•le•gal•ly
il•leg•i•bil•i•oty
il•leg•i•ble (hard to read: cf. ELIGIBLE)
il•leg•i•bly
il•le•git•o•i•ma•cy
il•le•git•o•i•mate
il•le•git•o•i•mate•ly
il•lib•er•al
il•lic•oit (illegal: cf. ELICIT)
il•lic•it•ly
il•lic•it•ness

il•lim•it•a•oble
il•lim•it•a•bly
ill•in'
Il•li•nois (IL)
il•lit•er•a•ocy
il•lit•er•ate
ill•ness
il•log•oi•cal
il•log•oi•cal•ly
il•lu•mi•nate *v.,* il•lu•mi•nat•ed, il•lu•mi•nat•ing.
il•lu•mi•nat•ing•ly
il•lu•mi•na•tion
il•lu•mine *v.,* il•lu•mined, il•lu•min•ing.
il•lu•sion (false idea: cf. ALLUSION)
il•lu•sive (deceptive: cf. ALLUSIVE; ELUSIVE)
il•lu•so•ory
il•lus•trate *v.,* il•lus•trat•ed, il•lus•trat•ing.
il•lus•tra•tion
il•lus•tra•tive
il•lus•tra•tive•ly
il•lus•tra•tor
il•lus•tri•ous
il•lus•tri•ous•ly
il•lus•tri•ous•ness
I'm (I am)
im•age *v.,* im•aged, im•ag•ing.
im•age•ory
i•omag•oi•na•ble
im•ag•oi•nar•y
im•ag•oi•na•tion
im•ag•oi•na•tive
im•ag•oi•na•tive•ly
im•ag•ine *v.,* im•ag•ined, im•ag•in•ing, im•ag•ines. (forms a mental image)
i•oma•ogo *n., pl.* i•oma•

goes or i•ma•gi•
nes. (adult insects)
i•mam
im•bal•ance
im•be•cile
im•be•cil•ic
im•bed v., im•bed•
ded, im•bed•ding.
im•bibe v., im•bibed,
im•bib•ing.
im•bri•ca•tion
im•bro•glio n., pl.
im•bro•glios.
im•bue v., im•bued,
im•bu•ing.
IMF or I.M.F. Business.
(International Mone-
tary Fund).
im•i•tate v., im•i•
tat•ed, im•i•tat•
ing.
im•i•ta•tion
im•i•ta•tive
im•i•ta•tor
im•mac•u•late
im•mac•u•late•ly
im•ma•nence
im•ma•nent (inherent:
cf. EMINENT; IMMINENT)
im•ma•te•ri•al
im•ma•ture
im•ma•ture•ly
im•ma•tur•i•ty
im•meas•ur•a•ble
im•meas•ur•a•bly
im•me•di•a•cy
im•me•di•ate
im•me•di•ate•ly
im•me•mo•ri•al
im•mense
im•mense•ly
im•men•si•ty
im•merse v., im•
mersed, im•mers•
ing.
im•mers•i•ble

im•mer•sion
im•mi•grant
im•mi•grate v., im•
mi•grat•ed, im•mi•
grat•ing. (to come to
a new country: cf. EMI-
GRATE)
im•mi•nence
im•mi•nent (impend-
ing: cf. EMINENT; IMMA-
NENT)
im•mi•nent•ly
im•mo•bile
im•mo•bil•i•ty
im•mo•bi•li•za•tion
im•mo•bi•lize v., im•
mo•bi•lized, im•
mo•bi•liz•ing.
im•mod•er•ate
im•mod•er•ate•ly
im•mod•est
im•mod•est•ly
im•mod•es•ty
im•mo•late v., im•
mo•lat•ed, im•mo•
lat•ing.
im•mo•la•tion
im•mor•al (licentious:
cf. AMORAL; IMMORTAL)
im•mo•ral•i•ty n., pl.
im•mo•ral•i•ties.
im•mor•al•ly
im•mor•tal (everlast-
ing)
im•mor•tal•i•ty
im•mor•tal•ize v.,
im•mor•tal•ized,
im•mor•tal•iz•ing.
im•mor•tal•ly
im•mov•a•bil•i•ty
im•mov•a•ble or im•
move•a•ble
im•mune
im•mu•ni•ty
im•mu•ni•za•tion
im•mu•nize v., im•

mu•nized, im•mu•
niz•ing.
im•mu•no•log•i•cal
im•mu•nol•o•gy
im•mu•no•sup•pres•
sive
im•mure v., im•
mured, im•mur•ing.
im•mu•ta•bil•i•ty
im•mu•ta•ble
im•mu•ta•bly
imp
im•pact v., im•
pact•ed, im•pact•
ing.
impact print•er Com-
puters.
im•pair v., im•paired,
im•pair•ing.
im•pair•ment
im•pa•la n., pl. im•
pal•as or im•pal•a.
im•pale v., im•paled,
im•pal•ing.
im•pale•ment
im•pal•pa•ble
im•pal•pa•bly
im•pan•el v., im•
pan•eled or im•
pan•elled, im•pan•
el•ing or im•pan•
el•ling.
im•part v., im•
part•ed, im•part•
ing.
im•par•tial
im•par•ti•al•i•ty
im•par•tial•ly
im•pass•a•ble (not
passable: cf. IMPASSI-
BLE; IMPOSSIBLE)
im•passe
im•pas•si•ble (incapa-
ble of suffering)
im•pas•sioned
im•pas•sioned•ly
im•pas•sive

im•pas•sive•ly
im•pas•siv•i•ty
im•pas•to
im•pa•tience (lack of patience)
im•pa•tiens n., pl. im•pa•tiens. (the plant)
im•pa•tient
im•pa•tient•ly
im•peach v., im•peached, im•peach•ing.
im•peach•a•ble
im•peach•ment
im•pec•cabil•i•ty
im•pec•ca•ble
im•pec•ca•bly
im•pe•cu•ni•ous
im•pe•cu•ni•ous•ness
im•ped•ance
im•pede v., im•ped•ed, im•ped•ing.
im•ped•i•ment
im•ped•i•men•ta n., pl.
im•pel v., im•pelled, im•pel•ling.
im•pend v., im•pend•ed, im•pend•ing.
im•pen•e•tra•bil•i•ty
im•pen•e•tra•ble
im•pen•e•tra•bly
im•pen•i•tence
im•pen•i•tent
im•per•a•tive
im•per•a•tive•ly
im•per•cep•ti•ble
im•per•cep•ti•bly
im•per•cep•tive
im•pre•cate
im•per•fect

im•per•fec•tion
im•per•fect•ly
im•per•fect•ness
im•per•fo•rate
im•pe•ri•al
im•pe•ri•al•ism
im•pe•ri•al•ist
im•pe•ri•al•is•tic
im•per•il v., im•per•iled or im•per•illed, im•per•il•ing or im•per•il•ling.
im•per•il•ment
im•pe•ri•ous
im•pe•ri•ous•ly
im•pe•ri•ous•ness
im•per•ish•a•ble
im•per•ma•nence
im•per•ma•nent
im•per•ma•nent•ly
im•per•me•a•bil•i•ty
im•per•me•a•ble
im•per•son•al
im•per•son•al•ly
im•per•son•ate v., im•per•son•at•ed, im•per•son•at•ing.
im•per•son•a•tion
im•per•son•a•tor
im•per•ti•nence
im•per•ti•nent
im•per•ti•nent•ly
im•per•turb•a•bil•i•ty
im•per•turb•a•ble
im•per•turb•a•bly
im•per•vi•ous
im•per•vi•ous•ly
im•pe•ti•go
im•pet•u•os•i•ty
im•pet•u•ous
im•pet•u•ous•ly
im•pe•tus
im•pi•e•ty
im•pinge v., im•

pinged, im•ping•ing.
im•pinge•ment
im•pi•ous
im•pi•ous•ly
imp•ish
imp•ish•ly
imp•ish•ness
im•plac•a•bil•i•ty
im•plac•a•ble
im•plac•a•bly
im•plant v., im•plant•ed, im•plant•ing.
im•plau•si•bil•i•ty
im•plau•si•ble
im•plau•si•bly
im•ple•ment v., im•ple•ment•ed, im•ple•ment•ing.
im•ple•men•ta•tion
im•pli•cate v., im•pli•cat•ed, im•pli•cat•ing.
im•pli•ca•tion
im•plic•it
implicit cost *Business.*
im•plic•it•ly
im•plied war•ran•ty *Business.*
im•plode v., im•plod•ed, im•plod•ing.
im•plore v., im•plored, im•plor•ing.
im•plor•ing•ly
im•plo•sion
im•ply v., im•plied, im•ply•ing.
im•po•lite
im•po•lite•ly
im•pol•i•tic
im•pon•der•a•ble
im•port v., im•port•ed, im•port•ing.

import quo○ta *Business.*
im•por•tance
im•por•tant
im•por•tant○ly
im•por•ta•tion *Business.*
im•port○er *Business.*
im•por•tu•nate
im•por•tu•nate○ly
im•por•tune *v.,* im•
  por•tuned, im•por•
  tun•ing.
im•por•tun•i○ty
im•pose *v.,* im•posed,
  im•pos•ing.
im•pos•ing○ly
im•po○si•tion
im•pos•si•bil•i○ty
im•pos•si•ble (not
  possible: cf. IMPASSA-
  BLE; IMPOSSIBLE)
im•pos•si•bly
im•post
im•pos•tor or im•
  post○er (pretender)
im•pos•ture (fraud)
im•po•tence
im•po•tent
im•po•tent○ly
im•pound *v.,* im•
  pound○ed, im•
  pound•ing.
im•pov•er•ish *v.,* im•
  pov•er•ished, im•
  pov•er•ish•ing.
im•pov•er•ish•ment
im•prac•ti•ca•ble
  (not feasible)
im•prac•ti•cal (not
  useful)
im•prac•ti•cal•i○ty
im•pre•ca•tion
im•pre•cise
im•pre•ci•sion or im•
  pre•cise•ness
im•preg•na•bil•i○ty

im•preg•na•ble
im•preg•nate *v.,* im•
  preg•nat○ed, im•
  preg•nat•ing.
im•preg•na•tion
im•pre•sa•ri○o *n., pl.*
  im•pre•sa•ri○os.
im•press *v.,* im•
  pressed, im•press•
  ing.
im•pres•si•bil•i○ty
im•pres•si•ble
im•pres•sion
im•pres•sion•a•ble
im•pres•sion•ism
im•pres•sion•ist
im•pres•sive
im•pres•sive○ly
im•pres•sive•ness
im•press•ment
im•prest fund
im•pri•ma•tur
im•print *v.,* im•
  print○ed, im•print•
  ing.
im•pris○on *v.,* im•
  pris○oned, im•pris•
  on•ing.
im•pris•on•ment
im•prob•a•bil•i○ty
im•prob•a•ble
im•prob•a•bly
im•promp○tu *n., pl.*
  im•promp•tus.
im•prop○er
im•prop•er○ly
im•pro•pri•e○ty *n.,*
  pl. im•pro•pri•e•
  ties.
im•prove *v.,* im•
  proved, im•prov•
  ing.
im•prove•ment
im•prov○i•dence
im•prov○i•dent
im•prov○i•dent○ly
im•prov○i•sa•tion

im•prov○i•sa•tion•al
im•pro•vise *v.,* im•
  pro•vised, im•pro•
  vis•ing.
im•pru•dence
im•pru•dent
im•pu•dence
im•pu•dent
im•pu•dent○ly
im•pugn *v.,* im•
  pugned, im•pugn•
  ing.
im•pulse
impulse i○tem *Busi-*
  ness.
im•pul•sion
im•pul•sive
im•pul•sive○ly
im•pul•sive•ness
im•pu•ni○ty
im•pure
im•pure○ly
im•pure•ness
im•pur•i○ty
im•put•a•ble
im•pu•ta•tion
im•pute *v.,* im•
  put○ed, im•put•ing.
im•put○ed in•ter•est
  Business.
in (within: cf. INN)
IN (Indiana)
in ab•sen•tia
in-depth
in ex•tre•mis
in-flight or in•flight
in-house *Business.*
in-law
in-line skate
in me•mo•ri○am
in re (in the matter of)
in-res○i•dence
in si○tu
in to○to
in vi•tro
in•a•bil•i○ty

in•ac•ces•si•ble
in•ac•tion
in•ac•ti•vate v., in•ac•ti•vat•ed, in•ac•ti•vat•ing.
in•ad•e•qua•cy
in•ad•e•quate
in•ad•e•quate•ly
in•ad•mis•si•ble
in•ad•vert•ence
in•ad•vert•ent
in•ad•vert•ent•ly
in•ad•vis•a•ble
in•al•ien•a•ble
in•am•o•ra•ta n., pl. in•am•o•ra•tas.
in•ane (lacking sense: cf. INSANE)
in•ane•ly
in•an•i•mate
in•an•i•ty
in•apt (not fitting: cf. INEPT)
in•ar•tic•u•late
in•ar•tic•u•late•ly
in•ar•tic•u•late•ness
in•as•much as
in•at•ten•tion
in•at•ten•tive
in•au•gu•ral
in•au•gu•rate v., in•au•gu•rat•ed, in•au•gu•rat•ing.
in•au•gu•ra•tion
in•board
in•born
in•bound
in•bred
in•breed
Inc. Business. (incorporated)
In•ca
in•cal•cu•la•ble
in•cal•cu•la•bly
In•can
in•can•des•cence

in•can•des•cent
in•can•ta•tion
in•ca•pa•bil•i•ty
in•ca•pa•ble
in•ca•pa•bly
in•ca•pac•i•tate v., in•ca•pac•i•tat•ed, in•ca•pac•i•tat•ing.
in•ca•pac•i•ty
in•car•cer•ate v., in•car•cer•at•ed, in•car•cer•at•ing.
in•car•cer•a•tion
in•car•na•dine
in•car•nate
in•car•na•tion
in•cen•di•ar•y n., pl. in•cen•di•ar•ies.
in•cense
in•censed
in•cen•tive
in•cep•tion
in•cer•ti•tude
in•ces•sant
in•ces•sant•ly
in•cest
in•ces•tu•ous
inch v., inched, inch•ing.
in•cho•ate
inch•worm
in•ci•dence
in•ci•dent
in•ci•den•tal
in•ci•den•tal•ly
in•cin•er•ate v., in•cin•er•at•ed, in•cin•er•at•ing.
in•cin•er•a•tion
in•cin•er•a•tor
in•cip•i•ent
in•cip•i•ent•ly
in•cise v., in•cised, in•cis•ing.
in•ci•sion
in•ci•sive

in•ci•sive•ly
in•ci•sor
in•cite v., in•cit•ed, in•cit•ing. (to stir up: cf. INSIGHT)
in•cite•ment
in•ci•vil•i•ty
in•clem•ent
in•cli•na•tion
in•cline v., in•clined, in•clin•ing.
in•clude v., in•clud•ed, in•clud•ing.
in•clu•sion
in•clu•sive
in•clu•sive•ly
in•clu•sive•ness
in•cog•ni•to
in•co•her•ence
in•co•her•ent
in•co•her•ent•ly
in•com•bus•ti•ble
in•come
income fund Business.
income state•ment Business.
income tax Business.
in•com•men•su•rate
in•com•mu•ni•ca•do
in•com•pa•ra•ble
in•com•pat•i•bil•i•ty
in•com•pat•i•ble
in•com•pat•i•bly
in•com•pe•tence
in•com•pe•tent
in•com•pe•tent•ly
in•com•plete
in•com•plete•ly
in•com•plete•ness
in•com•pre•hen•si•ble
in•con•ceiv•a•ble
in•con•clu•sive
in•con•gru•i•ty

in•con•gru•ous
in•con•gru•ous•ly
in•con•se•quen•tial
in•con•se•quen•
  tial•ly
in•con•sid•er•a•ble
in•con•sid•er•ate
in•con•sid•er•ate•ly
in•con•sid•er•ate•
  ness
in•con•sist•en•cy, n.,
  pl. in•con•sist•en•
  cies.
in•con•sist•ent
in•con•sol•a•ble
in•con•spic•u•ous
in•con•spic•u•ous•ly
in•con•spic•u•ous•
  ness
in•con•stan•cy
in•con•stant
in•con•stant•ly
in•con•test•a•ble
in•con•test•a•bly
in•con•ti•nence
in•con•ti•nent
in•con•tro•vert•i•ble
in•con•ven•ience v.,
  in•con•ven•ienced,
  in•con•ven•ienc•
  ing.
in•con•ven•ient
in•con•ven•ient•ly
in•cor•po•rate v., in•
  cor•po•rat•ed, in•
  cor•po•rat•ing.
  Business.
in•cor•po•ra•tion
  Business.
in•cor•po•re•al
in•cor•rect
in•cor•rect•ly
in•cor•ri•gi•ble
in•cor•ri•gi•bly
in•cor•rupt•i•ble
in•crease v., in•

creased, in•creas•
  ing.
in•creas•ing•ly
in•cred•i•ble (unbe-
  lievable)
in•cred•i•bly
in•cre•du•li•ty
in•cred•u•lous (skep-
  tical)
in•cre•ment
in•cre•men•tal
  back•up Computers.
incremental cost Busi-
  ness.
incremental rev•e•
  nue Business.
in•crim•i•nate v., in•
  crim•i•nat•ed, in•
  crim•i•nat•ing.
in•crim•i•na•tion
in•crim•i•na•to•ry
in•crust or en•crust,
  v., in•crust•ed, in•
  crust•ing.
in•crus•ta•tion
in•cu•bate v., in•cu•
  bat•ed, in•cu•bat•
  ing.
in•cu•ba•tion
in•cu•ba•tor
in•cu•bus n., pl. in•
  cu•bi or in•cu•
  bus•es.
in•cul•cate v., in•cul•
  cat•ed, in•cul•cat•
  ing.
in•cul•ca•tion
in•cul•pa•ble
in•cul•pate v., in•
  cul•pat•ed, in•cul•
  pat•ing.
in•cum•ben•cy
in•cum•bent
in•cu•nab•u•la
in•cur v., in•curred,
  in•cur•ring.
in•cur•a•ble

in•cur•a•bly
in•cu•ri•ous
in•cur•sion
in•debt•ed
in•de•cen•cy
in•de•cent
in•de•cent•ly
in•de•ci•pher•a•ble
in•de•ci•sion
in•de•ci•sive
in•de•ci•sive•ly
in•de•ci•sive•ness
in•dec•o•rous
in•deed
in•de•fat•i•ga•ble
in•de•fat•i•ga•bly
in•de•fea•si•ble
in•de•fen•si•ble
in•de•fen•si•bly
in•de•fin•a•ble
in•def•i•nite
in•def•i•nite•ly
in•del•i•ble
in•del•i•bly
in•del•i•ca•cy
in•del•i•cate
in•del•i•cate•ly
in•dem•ni•fi•ca•tion
in•dem•ni•fy v., in•
  dem•ni•fied, in•
  dem•ni•fy•ing.
in•dem•ni•ty n., pl.
  in•dem•ni•ties.
in•dent v., in•
  dent•ed, in•dent•
  ing.
in•den•ta•tion
in•den•ture v., in•
  den•tured, in•den•
  tur•ing.
in•de•pend•ence
in•de•pend•ent
independent au•di•
  tor Business.
independent con•
  trac•tor Business.

in•de•pend•ent•ly
in•de•scrib•a•ble
in•de•scrib•a•bly
in•de•struct•i•bil•i•ty
in•de•struct•i•ble
in•de•ter•mi•na•cy
in•de•ter•mi•nate
in•dex n., pl. in•dex•es or in•di•ces.
index ar•bi•trage Business.
in•dex•a•tion Business.
in•dex•er
In•di•a
In•di•an
In•di•an•a (IN)
In•di•an•an or In•di•an•i•an
In•di•an•ap•o•lis
in•di•cate v., in•di•cat•ed, in•di•cat•ing.
in•dic•a•tive
in•di•ca•tor
in•dict v., in•dict•ed, in•dict•ing. (to accuse: cf. INDITE)
in•dict•a•ble
in•dict•ment
in•dif•fer•ence
in•dif•fer•ent
in•dif•fer•ent•ly
in•dig•e•nous (native to)
in•di•gent (poor)
in•di•gest•i•ble
in•di•ges•tion
in•dig•nant
in•dig•nant•ly
in•dig•na•tion
in•dig•ni•ty n., pl. in•dig•ni•ties.
in•di•go
in•di•rect

indirect tax Business.
in•di•rect•ly
in•di•rect•ness
in•dis•creet
in•dis•creet•ly
in•dis•cre•tion
in•dis•crim•i•nate
in•dis•pen•sa•bil•i•ty
in•dis•pen•sa•ble
in•dis•posed
in•dis•po•si•tion
in•dis•put•a•ble
in•dis•put•a•bly
in•dis•sol•u•ble
in•dis•tinct
in•dis•tinct•ly
in•dite v., in•dit•ed, in•dit•ing. (to compose: cf. INDICT)
in•di•um
in•di•vid•u•al
individual re•tire•ment ac•count (IRA) Business.
in•di•vid•u•al•ism
in•di•vid•u•al•ist
in•di•vid•u•al•i•ty
in•di•vid•u•al•ize, v., in•di•vid•u•al•ized, in•di•vid•u•al•iz•ing.
in•di•vid•u•al•ly
in•di•vid•u•ate, v., in•di•vid•u•at•ed, in•di•vid•u•at•ing.
in•di•vid•u•a•tion
in•di•vis•i•bil•i•ty
in•di•vis•i•ble
in•di•vis•i•bly
In•do-Eu•ro•pe•an
In•do•chi•na
In•do•chi•nese n., pl. In•do•chi•nese.
in•doc•tri•nate v.,

in•doc•tri•nat•ed,
in•doc•tri•nat•ing.
in•doc•tri•na•tion
in•do•lence
in•do•lent
in•dom•i•ta•ble
in•dom•i•ta•bly
In•do•ne•sia
In•do•ne•sian
in•door
in•doors
in•du•bi•ta•ble
in•du•bi•ta•bly
in•duce v., in•duced, in•duc•ing.
in•duce•ment
in•duct v., in•duct•ed, in•duct•ing.
in•duct•ance
in•duc•tee
in•duc•tion
in•duc•tive
in•dulge v., in•dulged, in•dulg•ing.
in•dul•gence v., in•dul•genced, in•dul•genc•ing.
in•dul•gent
in•dus•tri•al Business. (of industry: cf. INDUS-TRIOUS)
industrial es•pi•o•nage Business.
industrial goods Business.
in•dus•tri•al-strength
in•dus•tri•al•ism Business.
in•dus•tri•al•ist Business.
in•dus•tri•al•i•za•tion Business.
in•dus•tri•al•ize v., in•dus•tri•al•ized, in•dus•tri•al•iz•ing. Business.

in•dus•tri•ous (diligent: cf. INDUSTRIAL)
in•dus•tri•ous•ly
in•dus•tri•ous•ness
in•dus•try n., pl. in•dus•tries.
in•dwell
in•e•bri•at•ed
in•e•bri•a•tion
in•ed•i•bil•i•ty
in•ed•i•ble
in•ed•u•ca•ble
in•ef•fa•ble
in•ef•fa•bly
in•ef•fec•tive
in•ef•fec•tu•al
in•ef•fi•ca•cy (lack of power)
in•ef•fi•cien•cy (wastefulness)
in•ef•fi•cient
in•ef•fi•cient•ly
in•e•o•las•tic de•mand *Business.*
inelastic sup•ply *Business.*
in•el•e•gant
in•el•oi•gi•bil•i•ty
in•el•oi•gi•ble
in•e•luc•ta•ble
in•ept (incompetent: cf. INAPT)
in•ept•i•tude
in•ept•ly
in•ept•ness
in•e•qual•i•ty n., pl. in•e•qual•i•ties.
in•eq•ui•ta•ble
in•eq•ui•ty n., pl. in•eq•ui•ties.
in•er•rant
in•ert
in•er•tia
in•er•tial
in•ert•ly
in•es•cap•a•ble

in•es•cap•a•bly
in•es•ti•ma•ble
in•es•ti•ma•bly
in•ev•oi•ta•bil•i•ty
in•ev•oi•ta•ble
in•ev•oi•ta•bly
in•ex•act
in•ex•act•ly
in•ex•cus•a•ble
in•ex•cus•a•bly
in•ex•haust•i•ble
in•ex•haust•i•bly
in•ex•oo•ra•ble
in•ex•oo•ra•bly
in•ex•pen•sive
in•ex•pe•ri•enced
in•ex•pert
in•ex•pi•a•ble
in•ex•pli•ca•ble
in•ex•pli•ca•bly
in•ex•press•i•ble
in•ex•tin•guish•a•ble
in•ex•tri•ca•ble
in•fal•li•bil•i•ty
in•fal•li•ble
in•fal•li•bly
in•fa•mous
in•fa•my n., pl. in•fa•mies.
in•fan•cy n., pl. in•fan•cies.
in•fant
in•fant in•dus•try *Business.*
in•fan•ti•cide
in•fan•tile
in•fan•try
in•fan•try•man n., pl. in•fan•try•men.
in•fat•u•ate v., in•fat•u•at•ed, in•fat•u•at•ing.
in•fat•u•a•tion
in•fect v., in•fect•ed, in•fect•ing.

in•fec•tion
in•fec•tious
in•fec•tious•ly
in•fec•tious•ness
in•fe•lic•oi•tous
in•fe•lic•oi•ty
in•fer v., in•ferred, in•fer•ring.
in•fer•ence
in•fer•en•tial
in•fe•ri•or
in•fe•ri•or•i•ty
in•fer•nal
in•fer•no n., pl. in•fer•nos.
in•fer•tile
in•fer•til•i•ty
in•fest v., in•fest•ed, in•fest•ing.
in•fes•ta•tion
in•fi•del
in•fi•del•i•ty n., pl. in•fi•del•i•ties.
in•field
in•field•er
in•fight•ing
in•fil•trate v., in•fil•trat•ed, in•fil•trat•ing.
in•fil•tra•tion
in•fil•tra•tor
in•fi•nite
in•fi•nite•ly
in•fin•oi•tes•oi•mal
in•fin•oi•tes•oi•mal•ly
in•fin•oi•tive (verb form)
in•fin•oi•ty (boundlessness)
in•firm
in•fir•ma•ory n., pl. in•fir•ma•ries.
in•fir•mi•ty n., pl. in•fir•mi•ties.
in•flame v., in•flamed, in•flam•ing.

in•flam•ma•bil•i•ty
in•flam•ma•ble
in•flam•ma•tion
in•flam•ma•to•ry
in•flat•a•ble
in•flate v., in•flat•ed, in•flat•ing.
in•fla•tion
in•fla•tion•ar•y *Business.*
inflationary spi•ral *Business.*
in•flect v., in•flect•ed, in•flect•ing.
in•flec•tion (voice tone)
in•flex•i•bil•i•ty
in•flex•i•ble
in•flex•i•bly
in•flict v., in•flict•ed, in•flict•ing.
in•flic•tion (something imposed)
in•flo•res•cence
in•flow
in•flu•ence v., in•flu•enced, in•flu•enc•ing.
in•flu•en•tial
in•flu•en•za
in•flux
in•fo
in•fold v., in•fold•ed, in•fold•ing.
in•fo•mer•cial
in•form v., in•formed, in•form•ing.
in•for•mal
in•for•mal•i•ty
in•for•mal•ly
in•form•ant
in•for•ma•tion
information su•per•high•way
in•form•a•tive

in•form•er
in•fo•tain•ment
in•fra
in•frac•tion
in•fra•red or in•fra-red
in•fra•son•ic
in•fra•struc•ture
in•fre•quen•cy
in•fre•quent
in•fre•quent•ly
in•fringe v., in•fringed, in•fring•ing.
in•fringe•ment
in•fu•ri•ate v., in•fu•ri•at•ed, in•fu•ri•at•ing.
in•fu•ri•at•ing•ly
in•fuse v., in•fused, in•fus•ing.
in•fu•sion
in•gen•ious (inventive)
in•gen•ious•ly
in•gé•nue or in•ge•nue
in•ge•nu•i•ty
in•gen•u•ous (artless)
in•gen•u•ous•ly
in•gen•u•ous•ness
in•gest v., in•gest•ed, in•gest•ing.
in•ges•tion
in•glo•ri•ous
in•glo•ri•ous•ly
in•got
in•grained
in•grate
in•gra•ti•ate v., in•gra•ti•at•ed, in•gra•ti•at•ing.
in•gra•ti•a•tion
in•grat•i•tude
in•gre•di•ent

in•gress
in•grown
in•gui•nal
in•hab•it v., in•hab•it•ed, in•hab•it•ing.
in•hab•it•a•ble
in•hab•it•ant
in•hal•ant
in•ha•la•tor
in•hale v., in•haled, in•hal•ing.
in•hal•er
in•here v., in•hered, in•her•ing.
in•her•ent
in•her•ent•ly
in•her•it v., in•her•it•ed, in•her•it•ing.
in•her•it•ance
inheritance tax *Business.*
in•hib•it v., in•hib•it•ed, in•hib•it•ing.
in•hi•bi•tion
in•hib•i•tor
in•hu•man
in•hu•mane
in•hu•mane•ly
in•hu•man•i•ty
in•im•i•cal
in•im•i•ta•ble
in•iq•ui•tous
in•iq•ui•ty n., pl. in•iq•ui•ties.
in•i•tial v., in•i•tialed or in•i•tialled, in•i•tial•ing or in•i•tial•ling.
initial mark•up *Business.*
in•i•tial•ly
in•i•ti•ate v., in•i•ti•at•ed, in•i•ti•at•ing.
in•i•ti•a•tion
in•i•ti•a•tive

in•ject v., in•ject○ed,
   in•ject•ing.
in•jec•tion
in•jec•tor
in•junc•tion
in•jure v., in•jured,
   in•jur•ing.
in•ju•ri•ous
in•ju•ry n., pl. in•ju•
   ries.
in•jus•tice
ink v., inked, ink•ing.
ink-jet print○er Com-
   puters.
ink•blot
ink○i•ness
ink•ling
ink•well
ink○y adj., ink•i○er,
   ink•i•est.
in•laid
in•land
in•lay v., in•laid, in•
   lay•ing.
in•let
in•mate
in•most
inn (hotel: cf. IN)
in•nards
in•nate
in•nate○ly
in•nate•ness
in•ner
in○ner-di○rect○ed
in•ner•most
in•ner•sole
in•ner•spring
in•ner•vate v., in•
   ner•vat○ed, in•ner•
   vat•ing. (to invigor-
   ate: cf. ENERVATE)
in•ner•va•tion
in•ning
inn•keep○er
in•no•cent
in•no•cent○ly

in•noc•u•ous
in•noc•u•ous○ly
in•no•vate v., in•no•
   vat○ed, in•no•vat•
   ing.
in•no•va•tion
in•nu•en•do n., pl.
   in•nu•en•dos or in•
   nu•en•does.
in•nu•mer•a•ble
in•nu•mer•ate
in•oc•u•late v., in•
   oc•u•lat○ed, in•
   oc•u•lat•ing.
in•oc•u•la•tion
in•of•fen•sive
in•of•fen•sive○ly
in•op•er•a○ble
in•op•er•a○tive
in•op•por•tune
in•or•di•nate
in•or•di•nate○ly
in•or•gan○ic
in•pa○tient
in•put v., in•put○ted
   or in•put, in•put•
   ting.
input de•vice Comput-
   ers.
in○put/•out○put Com-
   puters.
in•quest
in•qui•e•tude
in•quire or en•quire
   v., in•quired, in•
   quir•ing.
in•quir○er
in•quir•ing○ly
in•quiry○ or en•qui•
   ry n., pl. in•quir•ies.
in•qui•si•tion
in•quis•i•tive
in•quis•i•tive•ness
in•quis•i•tor
in•road
in•sane (mad: cf. IN-
   ANE)

in•sane○ly
in•san•i•ty
in•sa•tia•bil•i•ty
in•sa•tia•ble
in•sa•tia•bly
in•scribe v., in•
   scribed, in•scrib•ing.
in•scrip•tion
in•scru•ta•bil•i•ty
in•scru•ta○ble
in•seam
in•sect
in•sec•ti•cide
in•sec•ti•vore
in•sec•tiv○o•rous
in•se•cure
in•se•cure○ly
in•se•cu•ri•ty n., pl.
   in•se•cu•ri•ties.
in•sem•i•nate v., in•
   sem•i•nat○ed, in•
   sem•i•nat•ing.
in•sem•i•na•tion
in•sen•sate
in•sen•si•bil•i•ty
in•sen•si○ble
in•sen•si•bly
in•sen•si•tive
in•sen•si•tive○ly
in•sen•si•tiv•i•ty
in•sen•ti•ence
in•sen•ti•ent
in•sep•a•ra○ble
in•sert v., in•sert○ed,
   in•sert•ing. (to put
   in)
in•sert mode Comput-
   ers.
in•ser•tion
in•set[1] (something set
   in)
in•set[2] v., in•set, in•
   set•ting.
in•shore
in•side
in•sid○er

insider trad•ing *Business.*

in•sid◦i•ous

in•sight (understanding: cf. INCITE)

in•sig•ni◦a *n.*, *pl.* in•sig•ni◦a or in•sig•ni◦as.

in•sin•cere

in•sin•cere◦ly

in•sin•cer•i◦ty

in•sin◦u•ate *v.*, in•sin◦u•at◦ed, in•sin◦u•at•ing.

in•sin◦u•a•tion

in•sip◦id

in•sist *v.*, in•sist◦ed, in•sist•ing.

in•sist•ence

in•sist•ent

in•so•far

in•sole

in•so•lence

in•so•lent

in•so•lent◦ly

in•sol◦u•bil◦i◦ty

in•sol◦u•ble

in•sol•ven◦cy

in•sol•vent

in•som•ni◦a

in•som•ni◦ac

in•so•much as

in•sou•ci◦ance

in•sou•ci◦ant

in•spect *v.*, in•spect◦ed, in•spect•ing.

in•spec◦tion

in•spec◦tor

in•spi•ra◦tion

in•spi•ra◦tion◦al

in•spire *v.*, in•spired, in•spir•ing.

in•spir◦it, *v.*, in•spir•it◦ed, in•spir•it•ing.

in•sta•bil◦i◦ty

in•stall *v.*, in•stalled, in•stall•ing.

in•stal•la◦tion

in•stall•ment

installment plan *Business.*

installment pur•chase *Business.*

installment sale *Business.*

in•stance

in•stant

in•stan•ta•ne•ous

in•stan•ta•ne•ous◦ly

in•stan•ter

in•stant◦ly

in•state *v.*, in•stat◦ed, in•stat•ing.

in•stead

in•step

in•sti•gate *v.*, in•sti•gat◦ed, in•sti•gat•ing.

in•sti•ga◦tion

in•sti•ga•tor

in•still *v.*, in•stilled, in•still•ing.

in•stinct

in•stinc•tive *v.*,

in•sti•tute *v.*, in•sti•tut◦ed, in•sti•tut•ing.

in•sti•tu◦tion

in•sti•tu◦tion◦al

in•sti•tu◦tion•al◦i•za◦tion

in•sti•tu◦tion•al•ize *v.*, in•sti•tu◦tion•al◦ized, in•sti•tu◦tion•al•iz•ing.

in•struct *v.* in•struct◦ed, in•struct•ing.

in•struc◦tion

in•struc◦tion◦al

in•struc◦tive

in•struc◦tor

in•stru•ment

in•stru•men•tal

in•stru•men•tal•ist

in•stru•men•tal◦i•ty, *n.*, *pl.* in•stru•men•tal•i◦ties.

in•stru•men•ta◦tion

in•sub•or•di•nate

in•sub•or•di•na◦tion

in•sub•stan•tial

in•suf•fer•a◦ble

in•suf•fer•a◦bly

in•suf•fi•cient

in•suf•fi•cient◦ly

in•su•lar

in•su•lar•i◦ty

in•su•late *v.*, in•su•lat◦ed, in•su•lat•ing.

in•su•la◦tion

in•su•la•tor

in•su•lin

in•sult *v.*, in•sult◦ed, in•sult•ing.

in•su•per•a◦ble

in•sup•port•a◦ble

in•sur•a◦ble

insurable risk *Business.*

in•sur•ance *Business.* (protection: cf. ASSURANCE)

in•sure *v.*, in•sured, in•sur•ing.

in•sur◦er *Business.*

in•sur•gence

in•sur•gent

in•sur•mount•a◦ble

in•sur•rec◦tion

in•sur•rec◦tion•ist

in•tact

in•tagl◦io *n.*, *pl.* in•tagl•ios or in•ta•gli•i.

in•take

in•tan•gi◦ble

intangible as•set *Business.*

in•te•ger
in•te•gral
in•te•grate v., in•te•grat∘ed, in•te•grat•ing.
integrated ar•chi•tec•ture Computers.
integrated cir•cuit Computers.
integrated soft•ware Computers.
in•te•gra•tion
in•teg•ri•ty
in•teg•u•ment
in•tel•lect
in•tel•lec•tu•al
intellectual prop•er∘ty
in•tel•lec•tu•al•ize v., in•tel•lec•tu•al•ized, in•tel•lec•tu•al•iz•ing.
in•tel•lec•tu•al∘ly
in•tel•li•gence
in•tel•li•gent
in•tel•li•gent ter•mi∘nal Computers.
in•tel•li•gent∘ly
in•tel•li•gent•si∘a
in•tel•li•gi•bil•i∘ty
in•tel•li•gi•ble
in•tel•li•gi•bly
in•tem•per•ance
in•tem•per•ate
in•tend v., in•tend∘ed, in•tend•ing.
in•tend∘ed
in•tense (extreme: cf. INTENTS)
in•tense∘ly
in•ten•si•fi•ca•tion
in•ten•si•fi∘er
in•ten•si•fy v., in•ten•si•fied, in•ten•si•fy•ing.

in•ten•si∘ty n., pl. in•ten•si•ties.
in•ten•sive
in•tent n., pl. in•tents. (purposes: cf. INTENSE)
in•ten•tion
in•ten•tion∘al
in•ten•tion•al∘ly
in•tent∘ly
in•tent•ness
in•ter v., in•terred, in•ter•ring.
in•ter- (between; among; cf. INTRA-)
in∘ter•act v., in∘ter•act∘ed, in∘ter•act•ing.
in∘ter•ac•tion
in∘ter•ac•tive
interactive pro•gram Computers.
in∘ter•breed v., in∘ter•bred, in∘ter•breed•ing.
in∘ter•cede v., in∘ter•ced∘ed, in∘ter•ced∘ing.
in∘ter•cept v., in∘ter•cept∘ed, in∘ter•cept•ing.
in∘ter•cep•tion
in∘ter•cep•tor
in∘ter•ces•sion
in∘ter•change v., in∘ter•changed, in∘ter•chang•ing.
in∘ter•change•a∘ble
in∘ter•col•le•giate
in∘ter•com
in∘ter•com•mu•ni•cate, v., in∘ter•com•mu•ni•cat∘ed, in∘ter•com•mu•ni•cat•ing.
in∘ter•con•nect v., in∘ter•con•nect∘ed,

in∘ter•con•nect•ing.
in∘ter•con•ti•nen•tal
in∘ter•cos•tal
in∘ter•course
in∘ter•cul•tur•al
in∘ter∘de•nom•i•na•tion∘al
in∘ter∘de•part•men•tal
in∘ter∘de•pend•ence
in∘ter∘de•pend•ent
in∘ter•dict v., in∘ter•dict∘ed, in∘ter•dict•ing.
in∘ter•dic•tion
in∘ter•dis•ci•pli•nar∘y
in•ter•est
in•ter•est∘ed
in•ter•est•ing
in∘ter•face v., in∘ter•faced, in∘ter•fac•ing. Computers.
in∘ter•faith
in∘ter•fere v., in∘ter•fered, in∘ter•fer•ing.
in∘ter•fer•ence
in∘ter•fer∘on
in•ter∘im
in•te•ri∘or
in∘ter•ject v., in∘ter•ject∘ed, in∘ter•ject•ing.
in∘ter•jec•tion
in∘ter•lace v., in∘ter•laced, in∘ter•lac•ing.
in∘ter•lard v., in∘ter•lard∘ed, in∘ter•lard•ing.
in∘ter•leave fac•tor Computers.
in∘ter•leu•kin
in∘ter•lock v., in∘ter•

locked, in○ter•lock•
ing.
in○ter•loc○u•to○ry
in○ter•lope v.,
    in○ter•loped,
    in○ter•lop•ing.
in○ter•lop○er
in○ter•lude
in○ter•mar•riage
in○ter•mar○ry v.,
    in○ter•mar•ried,
    in○ter•mar•ry•ing.
in○ter•com•mu•ni•
cate
in○ter•me○di•ar○y n.,
    pl. in○ter•me○di•ar•
ies.
in○ter•me○di•ate
in•ter•ment (burial:
    cf. INTERNMENT)
in○ter•mez○zo n., pl.
    in○ter•mez○zos or
    in○ter•mez○zi.
in•ter•mi•na•ble
in•ter•mi•na•bly
in○ter•min•gle v.,
    in○ter•min•gled,
    in○ter•min•gling.
in○ter•mis•sion
in•ter•mit•tent
in•ter•mix v., in○ter•
    mixed, in○ter•mix•
ing.
in•tern v., in•terned,
    in•tern•ing.
in•ter•nal
internal au•dit Busi-
ness.
internal au•di•tor
Business.
internal-com○bus○
tion en•gine
internal com•mand
Computers.
internal fonts Comput-
ers.

internal mo•dem
Computers.
internal rev○e•nue
Business.
in•ter•nal•ize v., in•
    ter•nal•ized, in•ter•
    nal•iz•ing.
in•ter•nal○ly
in•ter•na•tion○al
in○ter•na•tion•al○ly
in•ter•ne○cine
in○ter•net
in•tern•ist
in•tern•ment (confine-
    ment: cf. INTERMENT)
in•tern•ship
in○ter•of•fice
in○ter•pel•la•tion
    (questioning: cf. INTER-
    POLATION)
in○ter•per•son○al
in○ter•plan○e•tar○y
in○ter•play
in•ter•po•late v., in•
    ter•po•lat○ed, in•
    ter•po•lat•ing.
in○ter•po•la•tion (in-
    sertion: cf. INTERPELLA-
    TION)
in○ter•pose v.,
    in○ter•posed,
    in○ter•pos•ing.
in○ter•po•si•tion
in•ter•pret
in•ter•pre•ta•tion
in•ter•pret○er
in•ter•pre•tive
in○ter•ra○cial
in○ter•re•lat○ed
in•ter•ro•gate v., in•
    ter•ro•gat○ed, in•
    ter•ro•gat•ing.
in•ter•ro•ga•tion
in○ter•rog○a•tive
in•ter•rog○a•tor
in•ter•rog○a•to○ry

n., pl. in•ter•rog○a•
to○ries.
in•ter•rupt¹ n., Com-
puters.
in•ter•rupt² v., in•
    ter•rupt○ed, in•ter•
    rupt•ing.
in•ter•rup•tion
in○ter•scho○las•tic
in○ter•sect v., in•ter•
    sect○ed, in•ter•
    sect•ing.
in○ter•sec•tion
in○ter•ses•sion
in○ter•sperse v., in•
    ter•spersed, in•ter•
    spers•ing.
in○ter•state (between
    states: cf. INTESTATE; IN-
    TRASTATE)
in○ter•stel•lar
in○ter•stice n., pl. in•
    ter•stic○es.
in○ter•twine v., in•
    ter•twined, in•ter•
    twin•ing.
in○ter•ur•ban
in•ter•val
in○ter•vene v., in•
    ter•vened, in•ter•
    ven•ing.
in○ter•view v., in•
    ter•viewed, in•ter•
    view•ing.
in○ter•view○er
in○ter•vo•cal○ic
in○ter•weave v., in•
    ter•wove or in•ter•
    weaved, in•ter•
    weaved or in•ter•
    wo○ven, in•ter•
    weav•ing.
in•tes•ta○cy
in•tes•tate (without a
    will: cf. INTERSTATE; IN-
    TRASTATE)
in•tes•ti•nal

in•tes•tine
in•ti•fa○da
in•ti•mate v., in•ti•mat○ed, in•ti•mat•ing.
in•ti•mate○ly
in•ti•ma•tion
in•tim○i•date v., in•tim○i•dat○ed, in•tim○i•dat•ing.
in•tim○i•da•tion
in○to
in•tol•er•a○ble
in•tol•er•a•bly
in•tol•er•ance
in•tol•er•ant
in•to•na•tion
in•tone v., in•toned, in○ton•ing.
in•tox○i•cant
in•tox○i•cate v., in•tox○i•cat○ed, in•tox○i•cat•ing.
in•tox○i•ca•tion
in○tra- (within: cf. IN-TER-)
in•trac•ta•bil•i○ty
in•trac•ta○ble
in○tra•mu○ral
in•tran•si•gence
in•tran•si•gent or in•tran•si•geant
in•tran•si•tive
in•tran•si•tive○ly
in○tra•pre•neur Business.
in○tra•state (within a state: cf. INTERSTATE; IN-TESTATE)
in○tra•u○ter○o•ine
in○tra•ve○nous
in○tra•ve○nous○ly
in•trep○oid
in•trep•id○ly
in•tri•ca○cy n., pl. in•tri•ca•cies.

in•tri•cate
in•trigue v., in•trigued, in•tri•guing.
in•tri•guer
in•tri•guing○ly
in•trin•sic
in•trin•si•cal○ly
in○tro•duce v., in○tro•duced, in○tro•duc•ing.
in○tro•duc•tion
in○tro•duc•to○ry
in•tro○it
in○tro•spec•tion
in○tro•spec•tive
in○tro•ver•sion
in○tro•vert v., in○tro•vert○ed, in○tro•vert•ing.
in•trude v., in•trud○ed, in•trud•ing.
in•trud○er
in•tru•sion
in•tru•sive
in•tu○it v., in•tu•it○ed, in•tu•it•ing.
in•tu•i•tion
in•tu•i•tive
In•u○it or In•nu○it n., pl. In•u•its or In•u○it.
in•un•date v., in•un•dat○ed, in•un•dat•ing.
in•un•da•tion
in•ure v., in•ured, in•ur•ing.
in•vade v., in•vad○ed, in•vad•ing.
in•vad○er
in•val○id[1] (not valid)
in•va•lid[2] v., in•va•lid○ed, in•va•lid•ing. (sick person)
in•val○i•date v., in•

val○i•dat○ed, in•val○i•dat•ing.
in•val○i•da•tion
in•val•u•a○ble
in•var•i•a○ble
in•var•i•a•bly
in•va•sion
in•vec•tive
in•veigh v., in•veighed, in•veigh•ing.
in•vei•gle v., in•vei•gled, in•vei•gling.
in•vent v., in•vent○ed, in•vent•ing.
in•ven•tion
in•ven•tive
in•ven•tive•ness
in•ven•tor
in•ven•to○ry n., pl. in•ven•to•ries; v., in•ven•to•ried, in•ven•to•ry•ing. Business.
In•ver•ness
in•verse
in•verse○ly
in•ver•sion
in•vert v., in•vert○ed, in•vert•ing.
in•ver•te•brate
in•vert○ed tree Computers.
in•vest v., in•vest○ed, in•vest•ing.
in•ves•ti•gate v., in•ves•ti•gat○ed, in•ves•ti•gat•ing.
in•ves•ti•ga•tion
in•ves•ti•ga•tor
in•ves•ti•ture
in•vest•ment Business.
investment bank Business.

investment com•
pa•ny *Business.*
in•ves•tor *Business.*
in•vet•er•ate
in•vid•i•ous
in•vid•i•ous•ly
in•vig•or•ate *v.,* in•
vig•or•at•ed, in•
vig•or•at•ing.
in•vin•ci•bil•i•ty
in•vin•ci•ble
in•vi•o•la•bil•i•ty
in•vi•o•la•ble
in•vi•o•late
in•vis•i•bil•i•ty
in•vis•i•ble
invisible hand *Busi-
ness.*
in•vis•i•bly
in•vi•ta•tion
in•vi•ta•tion•al
in•vite *v.,* in•vit•ed,
in•vit•ing.
in•vi•tee
in•vit•ing
in•vo•ca•tion
in•voice *v.,* in•voiced,
in•voic•ing. *Business.*
in•voke *v.,* in•voked,
in•vok•ing.
in•vol•un•tar•i•ly
in•vol•un•tar•y
in•vo•lu•tion
in•volve *v.,* in•
volved, in•volv•ing.
in•volve•ment
in•vul•ner•a•bil•i•ty
in•vul•ner•a•ble
in•ward or in•wards
in•ward•ly
I/O *Computers.* (input/
output)
i•o•dide
i•o•dine
i•o•dize *v.,* i•o•
dized, i•o•diz•ing.

i•on
I•on•ic (of classical
Greek architecture)
i•on•ic (of ions)
i•on•i•za•tion
i•on•ize *v.,* i•on•
ized, i•on•iz•ing.
i•on•iz•er
i•on•o•sphere
i•on•o•spher•ic
i•o•ta *n., pl.* i•o•tas.
IOU or I.O.U. *n., pl.*
IOUs or IOU's or I.O.
U.'s.
I•o•wa (IA)
I•o•wan
ip•e•cac
ip•so fac•to
IRA or I.R.A. *Business.*
(individual retirement
account).
I•ran
I•ra•ni•an
I•raq
I•ra•qi
i•ras•ci•bil•i•ty
i•ras•ci•ble (easily an-
gered; cf. ERASABLE)
i•rate
i•rate•ly
ire
Ire•land
i•ren•ic
ir•i•des•cence
ir•i•des•cent
i•rid•i•um
i•ris *n., pl.* i•ris•es
(for 1)or i•ris or
i•ri•des (for 2). **1.**
(parts of eye) **2.**
(plants)
I•rish
I•rish•man *n., pl.*
I•rish•men.
I•rish•wom•an *n., pl.*
I•rish•wom•en.

irk *v.,* irked, irk•ing.
irk•some
i•ron *v.,* i•roned,
i•ron•ing.
i•ron•clad
i•ron•ic
i•ron•i•cal•ly
i•ron•ing
i•ron•ware
i•ron•work
i•ro•ny *n., pl.* i•ro•
nies.
Ir•o•quoi•an
Ir•o•quois *n., pl.*
Ir•o•quois.
ir•ra•di•ate *v.,* ir•ra•
di•at•ed, ir•ra•di•
at•ing.
ir•ra•di•a•tion
ir•ra•tion•al
ir•ra•tion•al•ly
ir•re•cov•er•a•ble
ir•re•deem•a•ble
ir•ref•u•ta•ble
ir•reg•u•lar
ir•reg•u•lar•i•ty
ir•rel•e•vance
ir•rel•e•vant (not per-
tinent; cf. IRREVERENT)
ir•re•li•gious
ir•re•me•di•a•ble
ir•re•me•di•a•bly
ir•rep•a•ra•ble
ir•re•place•a•ble
ir•re•press•i•ble
ir•re•proach•a•ble
ir•re•sist•i•ble
ir•re•sist•i•bly
ir•res•o•lute
ir•res•o•lu•tion
ir•re•spec•tive
ir•re•spon•si•bil•
i•ty
ir•re•spon•si•ble
ir•re•spon•si•bly
ir•re•triev•a•ble

ir•rev•er•ence
ir•rev•er•ent (lacking respect: cf. IRRELEVANT)
ir•re•vers•i•ble
ir•rev•o•ca•ble
ir•rev•o•ca•bly
ir•ri•ga•ble
ir•ri•gate v., ir•ri•gat•ed, ir•ri•gat•ing.
ir•ri•ga•tion
ir•ri•ta•bil•i•ty
ir•ri•ta•ble
ir•ri•ta•bly
ir•ri•tant
ir•ri•tate v., ir•ri•tat•ed, ir•ri•tat•ing.
ir•ri•ta•tion
ir•rupt v., ir•rupt•ed, ir•rupt•ing.
IRS Business. (Internal Revenue Service)
is
I•saac
I•sa•iah
ISDN Computers. (integrated services digital network)
i•sin•glass
I•sis
Is•lam
Is•lam•a•bad
Is•lam•ic
is•land
is•land•er

isle (island: cf. AISLE; I'LL)
is•let (small island: cf. EYELET)
isn't (is not)
i•so•bar
i•so•late v., i•so•lat•ed, i•so•lat•ing.
i•so•la•tion
i•so•la•tion•ism
i•so•la•tion•ist
i•so•mer
i•so•met•ric
i•sos•ce•les
i•so•tope
Is•ra•el
Is•rae•li n., pl. Is•rae•lis or Is•rae•li.
Is•ra•el•ite
is•su•ance
is•sue v., is•sued, is•su•ing.
Is•tan•bul
isth•mi•an
isth•mus n., pl. isth•mus•es or isth•mi.
it n., pl. they; it, pl. them; its, pl. their; its, pl. theirs.
I•tal•ian
i•tal•ic
i•tal•i•ci•za•tion
i•tal•i•cize v., i•tal•i•cized, i•tal•i•ciz•ing.

i•tal•ics
It•a•ly
itch v., itched, itch•ing.
itch•y adj., itch•i•er, itch•i•est.
-ite
i•tem
i•tem•i•za•tion
i•tem•ize v., i•tem•ized, i•tem•iz•ing.
itemized de•duc•tions Business.
itemized state•ment Business.
it•er•ate v., it•er•at•ed, it•er•at•ing.
it•er•a•tion
i•tin•er•ant
i•tin•er•ar•y n., pl. i•tin•er•ar•ies.
it'll (it will)
its (belonging to it)
it's (it is)
it•self
it•ty-bit•ty or it•sy-bit•sy
IUD (intrauterine device)
I've
i•vo•ry n., pl. i•vo•ries.
i•vy
I•wo Ji•ma

J

jab v., jabbed, jab•bing.
jab•ber v., jab•bered, jab•ber•ing.
ja•bot
jack v., jacked, jack•ing.
jack-in-the-box or

jack-in-a-box n., pl. jack-in-the-box•es.
jack-in-the-pul•pit n., pl. jack-in-the-pul•pits.
jack-o'-lan•tern
jack-of-all-trades n., pl. jacks-of-all-trades.

jack rab•bit
jack•al
jack•a•napes
jack•ass
jack•boot
jack•daw
jack•et v., jack•et•ed, jack•et•ing.

jack•ham•mer
jack•knife *n.*, *pl.* jack•knives; *v.*, jack•knifed, jack•knif•ing.
jack•pot
jack•screw
Jack•son
Jack•son•ville
jack•straw
Ja•cob
Jac•quard loom
Ja•cuz°zi *Trademark.*
jade
jad°ed
jade•ite
jag *v.*, jagged, jag•ging. (jerked, jogged)
jag°ged (raggedly notched)
jag•ged°ly
jag•gies, *n.*, *pl.* Computers.
jag•uar
jai a°lai
jail *v.*, jailed, jail•ing.
jail•bird
jail•break
jail°er
Ja•kar°ta or Dja•kar°ta
ja•la•pe°ño or ja•la•pe°no *n.*, *pl.* ja•la•pe•ños or ja•la•pe•nos.
ja•lop°y *n.*, *pl.* ja•lop•ies.
jal•ou•sie (louvered shutter: cf. JEALOUSY)
jam *v.*, jammed, jam•ming. (to squeeze; fruit preserve: cf. JAMB)
jam-packed
jam ses•sion
Ja•mai°ca
Ja•mai•can

jamb (vertical side-piece: cf. JAM)
jam•bo•ree (merry gathering: cf. JUBILEE)
James•town
jam•mies
Jane Doe
Jan•et[1] (woman's name)
Ja•net[2] (French psychologist)
jan•gle *v.*, jan•gled, jan•gling.
jan•i•tor
jan•i•to•ri•al
Jan•u•ar°y
ja•pan *v.*, ja•panned, ja•pan•ning.
Ja•pan
Jap°a•nese *n.*, *pl.* Jap°a•nese.
jar *v.*, jarred, jar•ring.
jar•di•niere
jar•gon
jar•ring°ly
jas•mine or jes•sa•mine
jas•per
ja°to or JATO *n.*, *pl.* ja•tos or JATOs. (jet-assisted takeoff)
jaun•dice
jaun•diced
jaunt
jaun•ti°ly
jaun•ti•ness
jaun°ty *adj.*, jaun•ti°er, jaun•ti•est.
Ja°va
Jav°a•nese
jave•lin
jaw *v.*, jawed, jaw•ing.
jaw•bone *v.*, jaw•boned, jaw•bon•ing.
jaw•break°er

jawed
jaw•less
jay
Jay•cee
jay•walk *v.*, jay•walked, jay•walk•ing.
jay•walk°er
jazz *v.*, jazzed, jazz•ing.
jazz•er•cise
jazz°y *adj.*, jazz•i°er, jazz•i•est.
JCS or J.C.S. (Joint Chiefs of Staff).
jeal•ous (envious: cf. ZEALOUS)
jeal•ous°ly
jeal•ous°y *n.*, *pl.* jeal•ous•ies. (envy: cf. JALOUSIE)
jeans
Jeep *Trademark.*
jeer *v.*, jeered, jeer•ing.
jeer•ing°ly
Jef•fer•son
Jef•fer•so•ni•an
Je•ho•vah
Je•ho•vah's Wit•ness°es
je•june (insipid)
je•ju•num (part of intestine)
jell *v.*, jelled, jell•ing. (to congeal: cf. GEL)
Jell-°O *Trademark.*
jel°ly *n.*, *pl.* jel•lies.
jel°ly roll
jel°ly•bean
jel°ly•fish *n.*, *pl.* jel°ly•fish or jel°ly•fish°es.
jel°ly•like
jen°ny *n.*, *pl.* jen•nies.
jeop•ard•ize *v.*, jeop•

ard•ized, jeop•ard•
iz•ing.
jeop•ard•y
jer•e•mi•ad
Jer•e•mi•ah
Jer•i•cho
jerk v., jerked, jerk•
ing.
jer•kin
jerk•wa•ter
jerk•y¹ adj., jerk•i•er,
jerk•i•est. (spas-
modic)
jer•ky² (jerked meat)
jer•ry-built
jer•sey n., pl. jer•
seys.
Je•ru•sa•lem
jest v., jest∘ed, jest•
ing. (joke; to jest: cf.
GIST)
jest∘er (clown: cf. GES-
TURE)
jest•ing•ly
Jes•u∘it
Jes•u•it∘i•cal
Je•sus
jet v., jet•ted, jet•
ting.
jet lag or jet•lag
jet-pro∘pelled
jet set
jet-set∘er
jet stream
jet•lin∘er
jet•sam (cargo thrown
overboard: cf. JETTISON)
jet•ti∘son v., jet•ti•
soned, jet•ti•son•
ing. (to discard: cf.
JETSAM)
jet∘ty n., pl. jet•ties.
Jew
jew∘el
jewel box
jew•eled or jew•elled

jew•el∘er
jew•el•like
jew•el•ry
Jew•ish
Jew•ish•ness
Jew•ry (Jewish people:
cf. JURY)
Jez∘e•bel
jib
jibe v., jibed, jib•ing.
(to agree: cf. GIBE; JIVE)
jif∘fy or jiff n., pl. jif•
fies or jiffs.
jig v., jigged, jig•ging.
(dance: cf. GIG)
jig•ger v., jig•gered,
jig•ger•ing.
jig•gle v., jig•gled,
jig•gling. (move jerk-
ily: cf. JINGLE)
jig•gly adj., jig•gli∘er,
jig•gli•est.
jig•saw
ji•had
jilt v., jilt∘ed, jilt•ing.
Jim Crow n.
Jim-Crow adj.
jim-dan∘dy
jim∘my n., pl. jim•
mies; v., jim•mied,
jim•my•ing.
jim∘son•weed
jin∘gle¹ (ringing sound:
cf. JIGGLE)
jin•gle² v., jin•gled,
jin•gling.
jin•gly adj., jin•gli∘er,
jin•gli•est.
jin∘go
jin•go•ism
jin•go•ist
jin•go•is∘tic
jinn or jin∘ni n., pl.
jinns or jinn; jin•nis
or jin∘ni.
jin•rik∘i•sha or jin•
rik•sha n., pl. jin•

rik∘i•shas or jin•rik•
shas.
jinx (bad luck: cf. HIGH
JINKS)
j.i.t. Business. (just-in-
time manufacturing)
jit•ney n., pl. jit•neys.
jit•ter v., jit•tered,
jit•ter•ing.
jit•ter•bug
jit•ters
jit•ter∘y
jive v., jived, jiv•ing.
(the music: cf. GIBE;
JIBE)
job v., jobbed, job•
bing.
job ac•tion
job a∘nal•o•y•sis Busi-
ness.
job bid•ding Business.
job lot Business.
job shop
job•ber Business.
job•hold∘er
job•less
job•less•ness
jock
jock∘ey n., pl. jock•
eys; v., jock•eyed,
jock•ey•ing.
jock•strap
jo•cose (playful: cf
JOCUND)
joc∘u•lar
joc∘u•lar•i∘ty
joc•und (cheerful: cf.
JOCOSE)
jodh•pur
jog v., jogged, jog•
ging.
jog•ger
jog•gle v., jog•gled,
jog•gling.
Jo•han•nes•burg
john
John Doe

John•son
joie de vi•vre
join v., joined, join•
ing.
join•er
join field Computers.
joint
joint con•tract Busi•
ness.
joint-stock com•
pa•ny Business.
joint ten•an•cy Busi•
ness.
joint ten•ant Business.
joint ven•ture Busi•
ness.
joint•ly
joist
joke v., joked, jok•
ing.
jok•er
jok•ing•ly
jol•li•ty
jol•ly n., pl. jol•lies;
v., jol•lied, jol•ly•
ing; adj., jol•li•er,
jol•li•est.
jolt v., jolt•ed, jolt•
ing.
Jo•nah
Jones
jon•quil
Jon•son
Jor•dan
Jor•da•ni•an
Jo•seph
josh v., joshed, josh•
ing. (to tease: cf. JOSS
STICK)
josh•ing•ly
Josh•u•a
joss stick (incense: cf.
JOSH)
jos•tle v., jos•tled,
jos•tling.
jot v., jot•ted, jot•
ting.

joule
jounce v., jounced,
jounc•ing.
jour•nal
journal vouch•er
jour•nal•ese
jour•nal•ism
jour•nal•ist
jour•nal•is•tic
jour•ney n., pl. jour•
neys; v., jour•neyed,
jour•ney•ing.
jour•ney•man n., pl.
jour•ney•men.
joust¹ (medieval com•
bat: cf. JUST)
joust² v., joust•ed,
joust•ing.
jo•vi•al
jo•vi•al•i•ty
jo•vi•al•ly
jowl
jowled
jowl•y adj., jowl•i•er,
jowl•i•est.
joy
Joyce
Joyc•e•an
joy•ful
joy•ful•ly
joy•ful•ness
joy•less
joy•ous
joy•ous•ly
joy•ous•ness
joy•ride v., joy•rode,
joy•rid•den, joy•
rid•ing.
joy•rid•er
joy•stick Computers.
JP or J.P. (justice of the
peace)
Jr. (junior)
ju•bi•lant
ju•bi•lant•ly
ju•bi•la•tion

ju•bi•lee (anniversary
celebration: cf. JAMBO•
REE)
Ju•da•ic
Ju•da•ism
Ju•das
Ju•de•o-Chris•tian or
Ju•dae•o-Chris•tian
judge v., judged,
judg•ing.
judge•ship
judg•ment
judg•men•tal
ju•di•ca•to•ry, n., pl.
ju•di•ca•to•ries,
adj.
ju•di•ca•ture
ju•di•cial (of courts:
cf. JUDICIOUS)
ju•di•cial•ly
ju•di•ci•ar•y n., pl.
ju•di•ci•ar•ies.
ju•di•cious (prudent:
cf. JUDICIAL)
ju•di•cious•ly
ju•di•cious•ness
ju•do
jug
Jug•ger•naut
jug•gle v., jug•gled,
jug•gling.
jug•gler (tosser and
catcher of balls)
jug•u•lar (vein in
neck)
juice v., juiced, juic•
ing.
juice•less
juic•er
juic•i•ly
juic•i•ness
juic•y adj., juic•i•er,
juic•i•est.
ju•jit•su
ju•jube
juke•box
ju•lep

ju•li•enne
Ju•ly
jum•ble v., jum•bled, jum•bling.
jum•bo n., pl. jum•bos.
jumbo cer•tif•i•cate *Business.*
jump v., jumped, jump•ing.
jump-start v., jump-start•ed, jump-start•ing.
jump•er
jump•i•ness
jump•ing-off place
jump•suit
jump•y adj., jump•i•er, jump•i•est.
jun•co n.,pl. jun•cos.
junc•tion (meeting point)
junc•ture (critical point of time)
June
Ju•neau
jun•gle
jun•ior (Jr.)
ju•ni•per

junk v., junked, junk•ing.
junk bond *Business.*
junk mail
Jun•ker (Prussian aristocrat)
jun•ket v., jun•ket•ed, jun•ket•ing.
jun•ke•teer or jun•ket•er
junk•ie n , pl. junk•ies.
junk•y adj., junk•i•er, junk•i•est.
Ju•no
jun•ta n., pl. jun•tas.
Ju•pi•ter
Ju•ras•sic
ju•rid•i•cal
ju•ris•dic•tion *Business.*
ju•ris•dic•tion•al strike
ju•ris•pru•dence
ju•rist
ju•ror
ju•ry n., pl. ju•ries. (verdict-rendering group: cf. JEWRY)

ju•ry-rigged
just (equitable: cf. JOUST)
just-in-time man•u•fac•tur•ing (j.i.t) *Business.*
jus•tice
justice of the peace (JP)
jus•ti•fi•a•ble
jus•ti•fi•a•bly
jus•ti•fi•ca•tion
jus•ti•fy v., jus•ti•fied, jus•ti•fy•ing.
just•ly
just•ness
jut v., jut•ted, jut•ting.
jute
ju•ve•nile
ju•venile delin•quency
ju•venile delin•quent
jux•ta•pose v., jux•ta•posed, jux•ta•pos•ing.
jux•ta•po•si•tion
JV or J.V. (joint venture)

K

ka•bob
ka•bu•ki
Ka•bul
kad•dish n., pl. kad•di•shim.
kaf•fee•klatsch or kaf•fee klatsch
Kaf•ka
kai•ser
kale
ka•lei•do•scope
ka•lei•do•scop•ic
ka•mi•ka•ze n., pl. ka•mi•ka•zes.

Kam•pa•la
Kam•pu•che•a
Kam•pu•che•an
kan•ban *Business.*
Kan•din•sky
kan•ga•roo n., pl. kan•ga•roos or kan•ga•roo.
Kan•san
Kan•sas (KS)
Kant
Kant•i•an
ka•o•lin
ka•pok

kap•pa n., pl. kap•pas.
ka•put
Ka•ra•chi
Kar•a•kul or car•a•cul
ka•ra•o•ke
kar•at (gold weight: cf. CARAT; CARET; CARROT)
ka•ra•te
Kar•en (woman's name)
kar•ma

kar•mic (of fate: cf. COMIC)
kart•ing
ka•sha
Kat•man∘du or Kath•man∘du
ka∘ty•did
kay∘ak v., kay•aked, kay•ak•ing.
kay∘o n., pl. kay∘os; v., kay•oed, kay∘o•ing.
ka•zoo n., pl. ka•zoos.
KB Computers. (kilobyte)
Kb Computers. (kilobit)
Keats
ke•bab or ka•bob
keel v., keeled, keel•ing.
keen v., keened, keen•ing; adj., keen•er, keen•est.
keen∘ly
keen•ness
keep v., kept, keep•ing.
keep∘er
keep•ing
keep•sake
keg
kelp
Kelt (Celt)
Kelt∘ic
kel•vin
ken v., kenned or kent, ken•ning.
ken•nel v., ken•neled or ken•nelled, ken•nel•ing or ken•nel•ling.
Ken•tuck∘i∘an
Ken•tuck∘y (KY)
Ken∘ya
Ken•yan

Ke•ogh ac•count Business.
Keogh plan Business.
kept
ker∘a•tin
ker∘chief
Ker•mit Computers.
ker•nel (seed: cf. COLONEL)
ker∘o•sene or ker∘o•sine
kes•trel
ketch
ketch∘up or cat•sup
ket•tle
ket∘tle•drum
key n., pl. keys; v., keyed, key•ing. (lock opener: cf. CAY; QUAY)
key-man in•sur•ance Business.
key•board v., key•board∘ed, key•board•ing.
key•hole
Keynes•i∘an Business.
key•note
key•not∘er
key•pad Computers.
key•punch v., key•punched, key•punch•ing.
key•punch∘er
key•stone
KGB or **K.G.B.** (Soviet secret police)
khak∘i n., pl. khak∘is.
khan
Khar•kov
Khar•toum
kib•butz n., pl. kib•but•zim. (Israeli community settlement)
kib•itz v., kib•itzed, kib•itz∘ing. (to meddle)
kib•itz∘er

ki•bosh
kick v., kicked, kick•ing.
kick•back Business.
kick∘er
kick•off or kick-off
kick•stand
kick∘y adj., kick•i∘er, kick•i∘est.
kid v., kid•ded, kid•ding.
kid•der
kid•die or kid∘dy, n., pl. kid•dies.
kid•nap v., kid•napped or kid•naped, kid•nap•ping or kid•nap•ing.
kid•nap•per or kid•nap∘er
kid•ney n., pl. kid•neys.
kiel•ba∘sa n., pl. kiel•ba∘sas or kiel•ba∘sy.
Ki∘ev
Ki∘ga∘li
kill v., killed, kill•ing. (to slay: cf. KILN; KIN)
kill-joy or kill•joy
kill∘er
kill•ing
kiln (oven: cf. KILL; KIN)
ki∘lo n., pl. ki•los.
kil∘o•bit (Kb) Computers.
kil∘o•byte (KB) Computers.
kil∘o•flop Computers.
kil∘o•gram
kil∘o•hertz n., pl. kil∘o•hertz or kil∘o•hertz∘es.
kil∘o•me•ter
kil∘o•ton
kil∘o•watt
kilt

kilt○ed
kil•ter
ki•mo○no *n.*, *pl.* ki•
mo○nos.
kin (relatives: cf. KILL;
KILN)
kind *adj.*, kind○er,
kind•est.
kin○der•gar•ten
kind•heart○ed
kind•heart•ed○ly
kind•heart•ed•ness
kin•dle *v.*, kin•dled,
kin•dling. (to begin
burning)
kin•dling (material for
starting fire)
kind○ly *adj.*, kind•
li○er, kind•li○est.
(benevolent)
kind•ness
kin•dred
kin○e•scope
kin•es○the•sia
kin•es○thet○ic
ki•net○ic
kin•folk or kin•folks
n., *pl.*
king
king-size or king-sized
king•dom
king•fish○er
king○ly
king•pin
king•ship
Kings•ton
Kings•town
kink *v.*, kinked, kink•
ing.
kin•ka•jou *n.*, *pl.* kin•
ka•jous.
kink○y *adj.*, kink•i○er,
kink•i○est.
Kin•sha○sa
kin•ship

kins•man *n.*, *pl.* kins•
men.
kins•wom○an *n.*, *pl.*
kins•wom○en.
ki•osk
Kip•ling
kip•per
Ki•ri•ba○ti
kis•met
kiss
kiss-and-tell
kiss•a○ble
kiss○er
kit
kitch○en
kitch○en•ette
kite *v.*, kit○ed, kit•
ing.
kith
kitsch
kitsch○y
kit•ten
kit•ten•ish
kit○ty *n.*, *pl.* kit•ties.
kit○ty-cor○nered or
kit○ty-cor○ner
ki○wi *n.*, *pl.* ki○wis.
KKK or K.K.K. (Ku Klux
Klan)
klep○to•ma•ni○a
klep○to•ma•ni○ac
klieg light
kludge *v.*, kludged,
kludg•ing. *Comput-
ers.*
klutz
klutz○i•ness
klutz○y *adj.*, klutz•
i○er, klutz•i○est.
knack (aptitude: cf.
KNOCK)
knack•wurst or
knock•wurst
knap•sack
knave (rogue: cf. NAVE)
knav•er○y

knav•ish
knead *v.*, knead○ed,
knead•ing. (to work
dough: cf. NEED)
knee *v.*, kneed, knee•
ing.
knee-deep
knee•cap *v.*, knee•
capped, knee•cap•
ping.
kneel *v.*, knelt or
kneeled, kneel•ing.
knee•sock
knew (did know: cf.
GNU; NEW)
knick•ers
knick•knack
knife *n.*, *pl.* knives; *v.*,
knifed, knif•ing.
knight *v.*, knight○ed,
knight•ing. (noble; to
confer knighthood
upon: cf. NIGHT)
knight-er○rant *n.*, *pl.*
knights-er○rant.
knight•hood
knight•li•ness
knight○ly
knish
knit *v.*, knit•ted or
knit, knit•ting. (to
join: cf. NIT)
knit•ter
knit•wear
knob
knock *v.*, knocked,
knock•ing. (to strike:
cf. KNACK)
knock-knee
knock-kneed
knock○down
knock○er
knock•out
knock•wurst
knoll
knot *v.*, knot•ted,

knot•ting. (tied cluster: cf. NOT)

knot•hole

knot•ty adj., knot•ti•er, knot•ti•est.

know v., knew, known, know•ing. (to understand: cf. NO)

know-how

know-it-all

know•a•ble

know•ing

know•ing•ly

knowl•edge

knowl•edge•a•ble or knowl•edg•a•ble

knows (understands: cf. NOES; NOSE)

Knox•ville

knuck•le v., knuck•led, knuck•ling.

knuck•le•head

knuck•le•head•ed•y

knurl v., knurled, knurl•ing.

KO n., pl. KOs or KO's; v., KO'd, KO'•ing. (knockout)

ko•a•o•la n., pl. ko•a•las.

kohl (black powder: cf. COAL)

kohl•ra•o•bi n., pl. kohl•ra•bies.

ko•o•la n., pl. ko•las. (nut: cf. COLA; COLA)

kook

kook•y adj., kook•i•er, kook•i•est. (eccentric: cf. COOKIE)

ko•peck or ko•pek

Ko•ran (Islamic text)

Ko•re•a

Ko•re•an (language of Korea)

ko•sher v., ko•shered, ko•sher•ing.

kow•tow v., kow•towed, kow•tow•ing.

Krem•lin

Krem•lin•ol•o•gy

Krish•na

kro•na n., pl. kro•nor. (Swedish coin)

kró•ona n., pl. kro•nur. (Icelandic coin)

kro•ne[1] n., pl. kro•nen. (former Austrian coin)

kro•one[2] n., pl. kro•ner. (Danish or Norwegian coin)

kryp•ton

KS (Kansas)

Ku Klux Klan (KKK)

Ku Klux•er

Kua•la Lum•pur

ku•dos

kud•zu n., pl. kud•zus.

kum•quat

kung fu

Kurd (member of Asian people: cf. CURD)

Ku•wait

Ku•wai•ti

kvetch v., kvetched, kvetch•ing.

kwa•cha n., pl. kwa•chas.

Kwang•chow

KY (Kentucky)

kye

Kyo•to

Kyu•shu

L

L-•do•o•pa

LA (Louisiana)

la-di-da or la-de-da

La Paz

lab

la•bel v., la•beled or la•belled, la•bel•ing or la•bel•ling.

la•bi•al

la•bile

la•bi•um n., pl. la•bi•a.

la•bor v., la•bored, la•bor•ing.

la•bor-in•ten•sive Business.

labor re•la•tions Business.

lab•o•o•ra•to•ry n., pl. lab•o•o•ra•to•ries. (scientific workshop: cf. LAVATORY)

la•bored

la•bo•ri•ous

la•bo•ri•ous•ly

la•bor-sav•ing or la•bor-sav•ing Business.

Lab•ra•dor

la•bur•num, n., pl. la•bur•nums.

lab•y•rinth

lab•y•rin•thine

lac (resin: cf. LACK)

lace v., laced, lac•ing. (netlike fabric: cf. LAZE)

lac•er•ate v., lac•er•at•ed, lac•er•at•ing.

lac•er•a•tion

lach•ry•mal (of tears)

lach•ry•mose (mournful)

lack v., lacked, lack•ing. (deficiency: cf. LAC)

lack○a•dai•si•cal

lack○ey n., pl. lack•eys.

lack•lus•ter

la•con○ic

la•con○i•cal○ly

lac•quer v., lac•quered, lac•quer•ing.

lac•ri•mal

la•crosse

lac•tate v., lac•tat○ed, lac•tat•ing.

lac•ta•tion

lac•tic

lactic ac○id

lac•tose

la•cu○na n., pl. la•cu•nae or la•cu•nas.

lad

lad•der

lad•die

lad○en

lad•ing

la•dle v., la•dled, la•dling.

la○dy n., pl. la•dies.

la○dy-in-wait○ing n., pl. la○dies-in-wait○ing.

la○dy•bug

la○dy•fin•ger

la○dy•like

la○dy•love

la○dy's-slip○per or la○dy-slip○per

la○dy•ship

La•fa•yette

lag v., lagged, lag•ging.

la•ger

lag•gard

lag•gard○ly

lag•ging in•di•ca•tor *Business.*

la•gniappe

la•goon

La•gos

La•hore

laid

laid-back

lain (past participle of "lie": cf. LANE)

lair (den: cf. LAYER)

lais•sez faire or lais•ser faire *Business.*

la•i○ty

lake

lal○ly•gag or lol○ly•gag v., lal○ly•gagged, lal○ly•gag•ging.

lam v., lammed, lam•ming. (to thrash: cf. LAMB)

la○ma n., pl. la•mas. (monk: cf. LLAMA)

La•ma○ism

la•ma•ser○y n., pl. la•ma•ser○ies.

La•maze meth○od

lamb (young sheep: cf. LAM)

lam•ba○da

lam•baste or lam•bast v., lam•bast○ed, lam•bast•ing.

lamb○da n., pl. lamb•das.

lam•bent

lam•bent○ly

lamb•kin

lame adj. lam○er, lam•est. (disabled)

la○mé (the fabric)

lame•brain

lame•brained

lame○ly

lame•ness

la•ment v., la•ment○ed, la•ment•ing.

la•ment•a○ble

lam•en•ta•tion

lam•i○na n., pl. lam•i○nae or lam•i•nas.

lam○i•nar

lam○i•nate v., lam○i•nat○ed, lam○i•nat•ing.

lam○i•na•tion

lamp

lamp•black

lam•poon v., lam•pooned, lam•poon•ing.

lamp•post

lam•prey n., pl. lam•preys.

LAN *Computers.* (local area network)

lance v., lanced, lanc•ing.

Lan•ce•lot

lanc○er

lan•cet

land v., land○ed, land•ing.

land-of○fice busi•ness

land•fall

land•fill

land•hold○er

land•ing

land•lad○y, n.,pl. land•la•dies.

land•locked

land•lord *Business.*

land•lub•ber

land•mark v., land•marked, land•mark•ing.

land•mass

land of○fice

land•scape v., land•

scaped, land•scap•ing.

landscape o•ri•en•ta•tion *Computers.*

land•scap•er

land•slide

lane (path: cf. LAIN)

lan•guage

lan•guid

lan•guish *v.*, lan•guished, lan•guish•ing.

lan•guor

lan•guor•ous

lank *adj.*, lank•er, lank•est.

lank•i•ness

lank•y *adj.*, lank•i•er, lank•i•est.

lan•o•lin

Lan•sing

lan•tern

lan•tern-jawed

lan•tha•num

lan•yard

La•os

La•o•tian

lap *v.*, lapped, lap•ping.

lap belt

lap dog

la•pel

lap•i•dar•y *n.*, *pl.* lap•i•dar•ies.

lap•in

lap•is laz•u•li

Lap•land

Lapp

lap•pet

lapse *v.*, lapsed, laps•ing. (to subside; error: cf. ELAPSE)

lap•top *Computers.*

laptop com•put•er *Computers.*

lap•wing

lar•board

lar•ce•nous

lar•ce•ny *n.*, *pl.* lar•ce•nies.

larch

lard *v.*, lard∘ed, lard•ing.

lar•der¹ (pantry)

lard∘er² (one that lards)

lar•es and pe•na•tes *n.*, *pl.*

large *adj.*, larg∘er, larg•est.

large-foot∘print com•put∘er *Computers.*

large•ly

large•ness

lar•gess or lar•gesse

lar∘go *n.*, *pl.* lar•gos.

lar•i•at

lark

lark•spur

lar∘va *n.*, *pl.* lar•vae. (young insect: cf. LAVA)

lar•val

la•ryn•ge•al

lar•yn•gi•tis

lar•ynx *n.*, *pl.* la•ryn•ges or lar•ynx∘es.

la•sa•gna

las•civ•i•ous

la•ser

laser disc *Computers.*

laser print∘er *Computers.*

lash *v.*, lashed, lash•ing.

lass

las•sie

las•si•tude

las∘so *n.*, *pl.* las•sos or las•soes; *v.*, las•soed, las∘so•ing.

last *v.*, last∘ed, last•ing.

last-in first-out (LIFO) *Business.*

last•ing•ly

last∘ly

latch *v.*, latched, latch•ing.

latch•key *n.*, *pl.* latch•keys.

late *adj.*, lat∘er, lat•est. (afterward: cf. LATTER)

late•com∘er

late•ly

la•ten•cy

late•ness

la•tent

lat•er•al

lat•er•al∘ly

la•tex

lath *n.*, *pl.* laths. (strip of wood)

lathe (machine)

lath∘er *v.*, lath•ered, lath•er•ing.

lath•er∘y

Lat∘in

Lat∘in A•mer•i•ca

Lat∘in A•mer•i•can *n.*

Lat∘in-A•mer•i•can *adj.*

La•ti•na *n.*, *pl.* La•ti•nas.

La•ti•no *n.*, *pl.* La•ti•nos.

lat∘i•tude

lat∘i•tu•di•nar•i•an

la•trine

la•tte

lat•ter (second of two: cf. LATER)

Lat•ter-day Saint

lat•tice

lat•ticed

lat•tice•work

Lat•vi•a

Lat•vi•an

laud v., laud•ed,
laud•ing. (to praise:
{f. CUM LAUDE and
LORD)

laud•a•ble

laud•a•bly

lau•da•num

laud○a•to○ry

laugh v., laughed,
laugh•ing.

laugh•a•ble

laugh•a•bly

laugh•ing•ly

laugh•ing•stock

laugh•ter

launch v., launched,
launch•ing.

launch○er

laun•der v., laun•
dered, laun•der•ing.

laun•der•ette or
laun•drette

laun•dress

Laun•dro•mat Trade-
mark.

laun•dry n., pl. laun•
dries.

laun○dry•man n., pl.
laun○dry•men.

laun○dry•wom○an n.,
pl. laun○dry•
wom○en.

lau•re•ate

lau•rel

la•va (molten rock: cf.
LARVA)

lav•a•liere or lav•a•
lier

lav○a•to○ry n., pl.
lav○a•to○ries. (wash-
room: cf. LABORATORY)

lav•en•der

lav•ish v., lav•ished,
lav•ish•ing.

lav•ish•ly

law

law-a○bid○ing

law•break•er

law•break•ing

law•ful

law•ful•ly

law•giv•er

law•less

law•less•ness

law•mak•er

law•man n., pl. law•
men.

lawn

law•ren•ci•um

law•suit

law•yer

lax adj., lax○er, lax•
est.

lax○a•tive

lax•i○ty

lax○ly

lax•ness

lay v., laid, lay•ing.
(to set down; secular:
cf. LEI; LIE; LYE)

lay-a○way plan Busi-
ness.

lay○er v., lay•ered,
lay•er•ing. (stratum:
cf. LAIR)

lay•ette

lay•man n., pl. lay•
men.

lay•off Business.

lay•out

lay○o○ver

Laz○a•rus

laze v., lazed, laz•ing.
(to loaf: cf. LACE)

la•zi○ly

la•zi•ness

la○zy adj., la•zi○er,
la•zi•est.

la○zy Su•san or la○zy
su•san

la○zy•bones

lb. n., pl. lbs, lb.

LBO Business. (lever-
aged buyout)

LCD n., pl. **LCDs** or
LCD's. Computers. (liquid crystal display)

lea (meadow: cf. LEE)

leach v., leached,
leach•ing. (to filter:
cf. LEECH)

lead[1] (soft metal: cf.
LED)

lead[2] v., led, lead•ing.
(to guide)

lead○ed (made with
lead)

lead○en (heavy)

lead○er (guide: cf.
LIEDER)

lead•er•less

lead•er•ship

lead•ing

leading in•di•ca•tor
Business.

leaf n., pl. leaves,
leafs; v., leafed,
leaf•ing. (unit of foli-
age; to turn pages: cf.
LIEF)

leaf•hop•per

leaf•less

leaf•let v., leaf•
let○ed or leaf•let•
ted, leaf•let•ing or
leaf•let•ting.

leaf•stalk

leaf○y adj., leaf•i○er,
leaf•i•est.

league v., leagued,
lea•guing.

leak v., leaked, leak•
ing. (where liquid es-
capes; to leak: cf.
LEEK)

leak•age

leak○y adj., leak•i○er,
leak•i•est.

lean v., leaned, lean•

ing; adj., lean∘er, lean•est. (to incline; thin: cf. LIEN)

lean-to n., pl. lean-tos.

lean•ness

leap v., leaped or leapt, leap•ing.

leap•frog v., leap•frogged, leap•frog•ging.

learn v., learned or learnt, learn•ing. (ascertained)

learn mode Computers.

learn∘ed (erudite)

learn∘er

learn•ing

learn∘ing-dis∘a∘bled

lease v., leased, leas•ing.

lease•back Business.

lease•hold

lease•hold∘er

leash v., leashed, leash•ing.

least (smallest: cf. LEST)

least•wise

leath∘er

leath•er•neck

leath•er∘y

leave v., left, leav•ing.

leave-tak∘ing

leav∘en v., leav•ened, leav•en•ing.

leav•en•ing

leav•ings

Leb∘a∘nese n., pl. Leb∘a∘nese.

Leb∘a∘non

lech∘er (lewd person: cf. LECTURE)

lech•er•ous

lech•er•ous•ly

lech•er∘y

lec∘i∘thin

lec•tern

lec•ture v., lec•tured, lec•tur•ing. (discourse: cf. LECHER)

lec•tur∘er

led (guided: cf. LEAD)

LED n., pl. LEDs or LED's. Computers. (light-emitting diode)

ledge

ledg∘er Business.

lee (shelter: cf. LEA)

leech v., leeched, leech•ing. (bloodsucking insect; to cling to; drain: cf. LEACH)

leek (the vegetable: cf. LEAK)

leer v., leered, leer•ing.

leer∘y adj., leer•i∘er, leer•i•est.

lees

lee•ward

lee•way

left

left-hand

left-hand∘ed

left wing n.

left-wing adj.

left-wing∘er

left•ism

left•ist

left∘o∘ver

left∘y n., pl. left•ies.

leg v., legged, leg•ging.

leg•a∘cy n., pl. leg•a∘cies.

le•gal

le•gal in•stru•ment Business.

legal ten∘der Business.

le•gal•ese

le•gal•ism

le•gal•is•tic

le•gal•i∘ty

le•gal∘i•za∘tion

le•gal•ize v., le•gal•ized, le•gal•iz•ing.

le•gal∘ly

leg•ate

leg∘a•tee

le•ga•tion

le•ga∘to

leg•end

leg•end•ar∘y

leg∘er•de•main

leg•ged

leg•gings

leg∘gy adj., leg•gi∘er, leg•gi•est.

Leg•horn

leg•i•bil•i∘ty

leg•i∘ble

leg•i•bly

le•gion (multitude: cf. LESION)

le•gion•ar∘y n., pl. le•gion•ar•ies.

le•gion•naire

le•gion•naires' dis•ease

leg•is•late v., leg•is•lat∘ed, leg•is•lat•ing.

leg•is•la•tion

leg•is•la•tive

leg•is•la•tor

leg•is•la•ture

le•git

le•git∘i•ma∘cy

le•git∘i•mate∘ly

le•git∘i•mize v., le•git∘i•mized, le•git∘i•miz•ing.

leg•less

leg•man n., pl. leg•men.

leg•room

leg•ume

le•gu•mi•nous

leg•work

lei *n., pl.* leis. (wreath: cf. LAY; LIE; LYE)

Leip•zig

lei•sure

lei•sure•ly

leit•mo•tif

lem•ming

lem○on

lemon law *Business.*

lem○on•ade

lem○on○y

le•mur

lend *v.,* lent, lend•ing.

lend-lease

lend○er

lends (gives temporary use of: cf. LENS)

length

length○en *v.,* length• ened, length•en• ing.

length•wise or length•wa ys

length○y *adj.,* length• i○er, length•i•est.

le•ni•en○cy

le•ni•ent

le•ni•ent○ly

Le•nin

Le•nin•grad

Le•nin•ism

Le•nin•ist

len○i•tive

lens *n., pl.* lens○es. (eyepiece: cf. LENDS)

Lent (religious fast)

lent (did lend)

Lent○en

len•til (the legume: cf. LINTEL)

Le○o

le•one (monetary unit of Sierra Leone)

le○o•nine

leop•ard

le•o•tard

lep○er

lep•re•chaun

lep•ro○sy

lep•rous

lep○ton

les•bi○an

les•bi•an•ism

lese ma•jes○ty or lèse majesty

le•sion (wound: cf. LE- GION)

Le•so•tho

less

les•see

less○en *v.,* less•ened, less•en•ing. (to de- crease: cf. LESSON)

less○er (smaller: cf. LES- SOR)

les•son (instruction: cf. LESSEN)

les•sor (one who gives a lease: cf. LESSER)

lest (unless: cf. LEAST)

let *v.,* let, let•ting.

let•down

le•thal

le•thal○ly

le•thar•gic

le•thar•gi•cal○ly

leth○ar•gy

let's (let us)

lets (permits)

let•ter *v.,* let•tered, let•ter•ing.

letter bomb

letter car•rier

letter of cred○it *Busi- ness.*

let○ter-per○fect

let○ter-qual○i○ty *Com- puters.*

let○ter•head

let○ter•ing

let○ter•press

let•tuce

let○up

leu•ke•mi○a

leu•ke•mic

leu•ko•cyte or leu• co•cyte

lev○ee (embankment: cf. LEVY)

lev○el *v.,* lev•eled or lev•elled, lev•el•ing or lev•el•ling.

lev○el○er

lev○el•head○ed

lev○el•head•ed•ness

lev○el○ly

lev○el•ness

lev○er *v.,* lev•ered, lev•er•ing.

lev•er•age *v.,* lev•er• aged, lev•er•ag○ ing.

leveraged buy•out (LBO) *Business.*

le•vi•a•than

Le•vi's *Trademark.*

lev○i•tate *v.,* lev○i• tat○ed, lev○i•tat○ ing. (to rise)

lev○i•ta•tion

lev•i○ty (gaiety)

lev○y *n., pl.* lev•ies; *v.,* lev•ied, lev○y• ing. (tax: cf. LEVEE)

lewd *adj.,* lewd○er, lewd•est.

lewd○ly

lewd•ness

lex○i•cal

lex○i•cog•ra•pher

lex○i•co•graph○ic

lex○i•cog•ra•phy

lex○i•con

LF *Computers.* (line feed)

li•a•bil•i○ty *n., pl.* li• a•bil•i•ties.

liability in•sur•ance *Business.*

li•a•ble (responsible: cf. LIBEL)

li•ai•son

li•ar (one who tells un-truths: cf. LYRE)

lib

li•ba•tion

li•bel *v.,* li•beled or li•belled, li•bel•ing or li•bel•ling. (defa-mation: cf. LIABLE)

li•bel•ous

lib•er•al

lib•er•al•ism

lib•er•al•i•ty

lib•er•al•i•za•tion

lib•er•al•ize *v.,* lib•er•al•ized, lib•er•al•iz•ing.

lib•er•al•ly

lib•er•ate *v.,* lib•er•at•ed, lib•er•at•ing.

lib•er•a•tion

lib•er•a•tor

Li•be•ri•a

Li•be•ri•an

lib•er•tar•i•an

lib•er•tine

lib•er•ty *n., pl.* lib•er•ties.

li•bid•i•nous

li•bi•do *n., pl.* li•bi•dos.

Li•bra *n., pl.* Li•bras.

li•brar•i•an

li•brar•y *n., pl.* Li•brar•ies.

li•bret•tist

li•bret•to *n., pl.* li•bret•tos or li•bret•ti.

Li•bre•ville

Lib•y•a

Lib•y•an

lice

li•cense *v.,* li•censed, li•cens•ing.

li•cen•see *Business.*

li•cen•ti•ate

li•cen•tious

li•cen•tious•ly

li•cen•tious•ness

li•chee

li•chen (fungus: cf. LIKEN)

lic•it

lick *v.,* licked, lick•ing.

lick•e•ty-split

lick•ing

lic•o•rice

lid

lie¹ *v.,* lay, lain, ly•ing. (to recline)

lie² *v.,* lied, ly•ing. (to speak falsely: cf. LAY; LEI; LYE)

lie de•tec•tor

Liech•ten•stein

lied *n., pl.* lied•er. (art songs: cf. LEADER)

lief (gladly: cf. LEAF)

liege

Li•ège

lien *Business.* (claim: cf. LEAN)

lieu (stead: cf. LOO)

lieu•ten•ant

lieutenant colo•nel

life *n., pl.* lives.

life•-care

life in•sur•ance *Busi-ness.*

life-size or life-sized

life style or life-style

life•blood

life•boat

life•guard

life•less

life•like

life•line

life•long

lif•er

life•sav•er

life•sav•ing

life•time

life•work

LIFO *Business.* (last in, first out)

lift *v.,* lift•ed, lift•ing.

lift•off or lift-off

lig•a•ment

lig•a•ture *v.,* lig•a•tured, lig•a•tur•ing.

light *v.,* light•ed or lit, light•ing; *adj.,* light•er, light•est.

light bar *Computers.*

light-e•mit•ting di•ode (LED) *Computers.*

light-fin•gered

light-foot•ed

light-mind•ed

light-year

light•en *v.,* light•ened, light•en•ing. (making lighter: cf. LIGHTNING)

light•en•er

light•er

light•face

light•head•ed

light•heart•ed

light•heart•ed•ly

light•heart•ed•ness

light•house *n., pl.* light•hous•es.

light•ing

light•ly

light•ness

light•ning (electrical discharge in sky: cf. LIGHTNING)

light pen *Computers.*

light•weight

lig•ne•ous

lik•a•bil•i•ty

lik•a•ble or like•
a•ble

like v., liked, lik•ing.

like-mind•ed

like-mind•ed•ness

like•li•hood

like•ly adj., like•li•er,
like•li•est.

lik•en v., lik•ened,
lik•en•ing. (to com-
pare: cf. LICHEN)

like•ness

like•wise

lik•ing

li•lac

Lil•li•pu•tian

Li•long•we

lilt v., lilt•ed, lilt•ing.

lil•y n., pl. lil•ies.

lil•y-liv•ered

li•ma bean

limb (appendage: cf.
LIMN)

lim•ber v., lim•bered,
lim•ber•ing.

lim•ber•ness

limb•less

lim•bo n., pl. lim•bos.

Lim•burg•er

lime

lime•ade

lime•light

lim•er•ick

lime•stone

lim•it v., lim•it•ed,
lim•it•ing.

lim•i•ta•tion

lim•it•ed

limited li•a•bil•i•ty
com•pa•ny Business.

limited part•ner

limited part•ner•ship
Business.

limited war•ran•ty
Business.

lim•it•er

lim•it•less

limn v., limned, limn•
ing. (to draw: cf. LIMB)

lim•o n., pl. lim•os.

lim•ou•sine

limp v., limped, limp•
ing; adj., limp•er,
limp•est.

lim•pet (marine ani-
mal)

lim•pid (clear)

lim•pid•i•ty

limp•ly

limp•ness

lin•age (number of
lines: cf. LINEAGE)

linch•pin

Lin•coln

lin•den

line v., lined, lin•ing.

line ed•i•tor Comput-
ers.

line feed (LF) Comput-
ers.

line of cred•it Busi-
ness.

line print•er Comput-
ers.

line printer ter•mi•
nal Computers.

lin•e•age (ancestry: cf.
LINAGE)

lin•e•al (of direct de-
scent: cf. LINEAR)

lin•e•a•ment (feature:
cf. LINIMENT)

lin•e•ar (of lines: cf.
LINEAL)

lin•e•ar•i•ty

line•back•er

line•man n., pl. line•
men. (football player;
telephone repairman:
cf. LINESMAN)

lin•en

lin•er

lines•man n., pl.

lines•men. (sports of-
ficial: cf. LINEMAN)

line•up

lin•ger v., lin•gered,
lin•ger•ing.

lin•ge•rie

lin•ger•ing

lin•ger•ing•ly

lin•go n., pl. lin•goes.

lin•gua fran•ca n., pl.
lin•gua fran•cas.

lin•gual

lin•gui•ne or lin•
gui•ni

lin•guist

lin•guis•tic

lin•guis•tics

lin•i•ment (salve: cf.
LINEAMENT)

lin•ing

link v., linked, link•
ing.

link-ed•it v., link-
ed•it•ed, link-ed•it•
ing. Computers.

link ed•i•tor Comput-
ers.

link•age

link•er Computers.

links (golf course: cf.
LYNX)

link•up

lin•net

li•no•le•um

Lin•o•type Trademark.

lin•seed oil

lint

lin•tel (beam: cf. LEN-
TIL)

lint•y adj., lint•i•er,
lint•i•est.

li•on

li•on•heart•ed

li•on•ize v., li•on•
ized, li•on•iz•ing.

lip v., lipped, lip•ping.

lip-sync or lip-synch *v.*, lip-synced or lip-synched, lip-sync○ing or lip-synch○ing.

lip○o○id

lip○o○fill•ing

lip○o○suc•tion

lip•read *v.*, lip•read, lip•read•ing.

lip•read○er

lip•read•ing

lip•stick

liq•ue•fac•tion

liq•ue•fi•a○ble

liq•ue•fi○er

liq•ue○fy *v.*, liq•ue•fied, liq•ue•fy•ing.

li•queur (alcoholic beverage that is a cordial: cf. LIQUOR)

liq•uid

liq•uid crys•tal dis•play (LCD) *Computers.*

liq•ui•date *v.*, liq•ui•dat○ed, liq•ui•dat•ing.

liq•ui•da•tion

liquidation val○ue *Business.*

liq•ui•da○tor *Business.*

li•quid•i○ty *Business.*

liq•uid•ize, *v.*, liq•uid•ize, liq•uid•iz•ing.

liq•uor (any alcoholic beverage: cf. LIQUEUR)

li○ra *n.*, *pl.* li•ras or li○re.

Lis•bon

lisle

lisp *v.*, lisped, lisp•ing.

lis•some or lis•som

list *v.*, list○ed, list•ing.

list price *Business.*

list bro•ker *Business.*

listed stock *Business.*

lis•ten *v.*, lis•tened, lis•ten•ing.

lis•ten○er

list•ing

list•less

list•less○ly

list•less•ness

Liszt

lit•a○ny *n.*, *pl.* lit•a•nies.

li•tchi or li•chee *n.*, *pl.* li•tchis or li•chees.

li•ter (liquid measure: cf. LITTER)

lit•er•a○cy

lit•er○al (exact: cf. LIT-TORAL)

lit•er•al○ly

lit•er•al•ness

lit•er•ar○y

lit•er•ate (educated)

lit○e•ra○ti (well-educated people)

lit•er○a•ture (written works: cf. LITTÉRATEUR or LITTERATEUR)

lithe *adj.*, lith○er, lith○est.

lithe•some

lith•i○um

lith○o•graph *v.*, lith○o•graphed, lith○o•graph•ing.

li•thog•ra•pher

lith○o•graph○ic

li•thog•ra•phy

lith○o•sphere

Lith○u•a•ni○a

Lith○u•a•ni○an

lit○i•gant

lit○i•gate *v.*, lit○i•gat○ed, lit○i•gat•ing.

lit○i•ga•tion

lit○i•ga•tor

li•ti•gious

li•ti•gious•ness

lit•mus

lit•ter *v.*, lit•tered, lit•ter•ing. (strewn objects: cf. LITER)

lit•té•ra•teur or lit•te•ra•teur (writer: cf. LITERATURE)

lit○ter•bug

lit•ter○er

little[1] *adj.*, less or less○er, least.

lit•tle[2] *adj.*, lit•tler, lit•tlest.

lit○tle•neck

lit•to•ral (of a shore: cf. LITERAL)

li•tur•gi•cal

lit•ur•gist

lit•ur○gy *n.*, *pl.* lit•ur•gies.

liv•a•bil•i○ty

liv•a○ble or live•a○ble

live *v.*, lived, liv•ing.

lived (did live: cf. LIVID)

live•li•hood

live•li•ness

live•long

live○ly *adj.*, live•li○er, live•li•est.

liv○en *v.*, liv•ened, liv•en•ing.

liv○er

liv•er•ied

liv•er•ish

Liv•er•pool

Liv•er•pud•li○an

liv○er•wort

liv○er•wurst

liv•er○y *n.*, *pl.* liv•er•er•ies.

lives

live•stock

liv•id (enraged;

flushed; ashen: cf.
LIVED)
liv•id•ly
liv•ing
living will
liz•ard
lla•ma n., pl. lla•mas.
(the animal: cf. LAMA)
lla•nos. n., pl. lla•nos.
LISP Computers. (pro-
gramming language)
lo (behold!: cf. LOW)
lo-res Computers. (low-
resolution)
load v., load°ed,
load•ing. (burden: cf.
LODE)
load fund Business.
load°er Computers.
loaf n., pl. loaves; v.,
loafed, loaf•ing.
loaf°er
Loaf°er Trademark.
loam
loan v., loaned, loan•
ing. (to lend: cf. LONE)
loan shark
loan°er
loan•shark•ing
loan•word
loath (reluctant)
loathe v., loathed,
loath•ing. (to hate)
loath•some
loath•some•ness
loaves
lob v., lobbed, lob•
bing.
lo•bar
lob°by n., pl. lob•
bies; v., lob•bied,
lob•by•ing.
lob°by•ist
lobe
lo•bot•o°my n., pl.
lo•bot•o•mies.

lob•ster n., pl. lob•
ster or lob•sters.
lo•cal (confined)
lo•cal-ar•e•a net•
work (LAN) Comput-
ers.
lo•cale (place)
lo•cal•i•ty n., pl. lo•
cal•i•ties.
lo•cal•i•za•tion
lo•cal•ize v., lo•cal•
ized, lo•cal•iz•ing.
lo•cal•ly
lo•cat•a•ble
lo•cate v., lo•cat°ed,
lo•cat•ing.
lo•cat°er
lo•ca•tion
loch (lake)
lock v., locked, lock•
ing. (fastener; to fas-
ten)
lock°er
lock°et
lock•jaw
lock•out Business.
locks (fasteners: cf. LOX)
lock•smith
lock•step
lock°up
lo•co
lo•co•mo•tion
lo•co•mo•tive
lo•co•mo•tor
lo°co•weed
lo•cus n., pl. lo•ci. (lo-
cality)
lo•cust (the insect)
lo•cu•tion
lode (mineral deposit:
cf. LOAD)
lo•den
lode•star
lode•stone
lodge v., lodged,

lodg•ing. (cabin; to
stick: cf. LOGE)
lodg°er
lo•ess (loamy deposit:
cf. LOOSE; LOSE; LOSS)
loft v., loft°ed, loft•
ing.
loft•i•ly
loft°i•ness
loft°y adj., loft•i°er,
loft•i•est.
log v., logged, log•
ging.
log in or log on Com-
puters.
log off or log out
Computers.
lo•gan•ber°ry n., pl.
lo•gan•ber•ries.
log•a•rithm
log•a•rith•mic
loge (theater section:
cf. LODGE)
log•ger
log°ger•head
log°ic
log°i•cal
logical da°ta struc•
ture Computers.
log°i•cal°ly
lo•gi•cian
lo•gi•ness
lo•gis•tics
log•jam
lo°go n., pl. lo°gos.
LOGO Computers. (pro-
gramming language)
log°o•type
log•roll•ing
lo°gy adj., lo•gi°er,
lo•gi•est.
loin
loin•cloth n., pl. loin•
cloths.
loi•ter v., loi•tered,
loi•ter•ing.
loi•ter°er

loll v., lolled, loll•ing.
lol•li•pop
Lo•o•mé
Lon•don
lone (solitary: cf. LOAN)
lone•li•ness
lone•ly adj., lone•li•er, lone•li•est.
lon•er
lone•some
lone•some•ness
long v., longed, long•ing; v., long•er, long•est.
long dis•tance n.
long-dis•tance adj.
long-drawn-out
long-lived
long-play•ing
long-range
long-suf•fer•ing
long-term as•set Business.
long-wind•ed
long•boat
lon•gev•i•ty
long•hair
long•hand
long•ing
long•ing•ly
lon•gi•tude
lon•gi•tu•di•nal
long•shore•man n., pl. long•shore•men.
long•stand•ing
long-term
long•time
long•word Computers.
loo n., (toilet: cf. LIEU)
look v., looked, look•ing.
look-and-feel Computers.
look-see
look•er

look•er-on n., pl. look•ers-on.
look•ing glass
look•out
loom v., loomed, loom•ing.
loon
loon•y n., pl. loon•ies.
loony tunes
loop v., looped, loop•ing. (closed circuit; to make a closed circuit: cf. LOUPE)
loop•hole
loop•y adj., loop•i•er, loop•i•est.
loose v., loosed, loos•ing; adj., loos•er, loos•est. (to release; unattached: cf. LOESS; LOSE; LOSS)
loose can•non
loose-leaf
loose•ly
loos•en v., loos•ened, loos•en•ing.
loose•ness
loot v., loot•ed, loot•ing. (booty; to pillage: cf. LUTE)
loot•er
lop v., lopped, lop•ping. (to cut off)
lope v., loped, lop•ing. (to run slowly)
lop•sid•ed
lop•sid•ed•ly
lop•sid•ed•ness
lo•qua•cious
lo•qua•cious•ness
lo•quac•i•ty
lo•ran
lord v., lord•ed, lord•ing. (noble: cf. LAUD; CUM LAUDE)

lord•ly adj., lord•li•er, lord•li•est.
lord•ship
lore
lor•gnette
lorn
lor•ry n., pl. lor•ries.
Los An•ge•les
lose v., lost, los•ing. (to misplace: cf. LOESS; LOOSE; LOSS)
los•er
loss (something lost: cf. LOESS; LOOSE; LOSE)
loss lead•er Business.
loss ra•tio Business.
lost
lot
Lo•thar•i•o n., pl. Lo•thar•i•os.
lo•tion
lot•ter•y n., pl. lot•ter•ies.
lot•to
lo•tus n., pl. lo•tus•es.
loud adj., loud•er, loud•est.
loud•ly
loud•mouth n., pl. loud•mouths.
loud•mouthed
loud•ness
loud•speak•er
Lou•is
Lou•i•si•an•a (LA)
Lou•is•ville
lounge v., lounged, loung•ing.
loupe (small magnifier: cf. LOOP)
louse n., pl. lice (for 1) or lous•es (for 2), v., loused, lous•ing. 1. (insects), 2. (lowlifes); 3. (to delouse)
lous•i•ly

lous•i•ness
lous•y adj., lous•i•er, lous•i•est.
lout
lou•ver or lou•vre
lou•vered
lov•a•ble or love•a•ble
lo•va•stat•in
love v., loved, lov•ing.
love han•dles.
love•bird
love•less
love•li•ness
love•lorn
love•ly n., pl. love•lies; adj., love•li•er, love•li•est.
love•mak•ing
lov•er
love•sick
lov•ing
lov•ing•ly
low v., lowed, low•ing; adj., low•er, low•est. (to moo; not high: cf. LO)
low-cal (low-calorie)
low-key or low-keyed
low-lev•el for•mat Computers.
low-level lan•guage Computers.
low-mind•ed
low-rent
low-res•o•lu•tion Computers.
low-rise
low-spir•it•ed
low•brow
low•down
low•er v., low•ered, low•er•ing.
low•er class n.
low•er-class adj.

low•er•case
low•land
low•life n., pl. low•lifes.
low•li•ness
low•ly adj., low•li•er, low•li•est.
low•ness
lox (cured salmon: cf. LOCKS)
loy•al
loy•al•ist
loy•al•ly
loy•al•ty
loz•enge
LSD (hallucinogenic drug, lysergic acid diethylamide)
LSI Computers. (large-scale integration)
Ltd. or ltd. Business. (limited).
Lu•an•da
lu•au n., pl. lu•aus.
Lub•bock
lube v., lubed, lub•ing.
lu•bri•cant
lu•bri•cate v., lu•bri•cat•ed, lu•bri•cat•ing.
lu•bri•ca•tion
lu•bri•ca•tor
lu•bri•cious
lu•bric•i•ty
lu•cid
lu•cid•i•ty
lu•cid•ly
Lu•ci•fer
Lu•cite Trademark.
luck v., lucked, luck•ing.
luck•i•ly
luck•less
luck•y adj., luck•i•er, luck•i•est.

lu•cra•tive
lu•cra•tive•ly
lu•cra•tive•ness
lu•cre
lu•cu•brate v., lu•cu•brat•ed, lu•cu•brat•ing.
lu•cu•bra•tion
Lud•dite
lu•di•crous
lu•di•crous•ly
lu•di•crous•ness
luff v., luffed, luff•ing.
lug v., lugged, lug•ging.
lug•ga•ble com•put•er Computers.
lug•gage
lu•gu•bri•ous
lu•gu•bri•ous•ly
lu•gu•bri•ous•ness
Luke
luke•warm
luke•warm•ly
luke•warm•ness
lull v., lulled, lull•ing.
lull•a•by n., pl. lull•a•bies.
lum•ba•go
lum•bar (of the loins)
lum•ber v., lum•bered, lum•ber•ing. (cut timber; to cut timber)
lum•ber•jack
lum•ber•man
lum•ber•yard
lu•mi•nar•y n., pl. lu•mi•nar•ies.
lu•mi•nes•cence
lu•mi•nes•cent
lu•mi•nos•i•ty
lu•mi•nous
lu•mi•nous•ly
lum•mox

lump *v.*, lumped, lump•ing.
lump○i○ness
lump•y *adj.*, lump•i○er, lump•i•est.
lu•na○cy
lu•nar
lu•na•tic
lunch *v.*, lunched, lunch•ing.
lunch•box com•put○er *Computers.*
lunch•eon
lunch•eon•ette
lunch•room
lung
lunge *v.*, lunged, lung○ing.
lunk•head
lu•pine
lu•pus
lurch *v.*, lurched, lurch○ing.
lure *v.*, lured, lur•ing.
lu•rid
lu•rid○ly
lu•rid○ness
lurk *v.*, lurked, lurk•ing.
Lu•sa○ka
lus•cious
lus•cious•ness

lush *adj.*, lush○er, lush•est.
lush•ness
lust *v.*, lust○ed, lust○ing.
lus•ter
lus•ter•less
lust•ful
lust•i○ly
lust○i•ness
lus•trous
lust○y *adj.*, lust•i○er, lust•i•est.
lute (stringed instrument: cf. LOOT)
lu•te•ti○um
Lu•ther
Lu•ther○an
Lu•ther•an•ism
Lux•em•bourg
lux○u•ri•ance
lux○u•ri•ant (abundant: cf. LUXURIOUS)
lux○u•ri•ant○ly
lux○u•ri•ate *v.*, lux○u•ri•at○ed, lux○u•ri•at○ing.
lux○u•ri•ous (sumptuous: cf. LUXURIANT)
lux○u•ri•ous○ly
lux○u•ri•ous•ness

lux•u○ry *n.*, *pl.* lux•u•ries.
ly•ce○um
lye (alkaline solutio⟩ cf. LAY; LEI; LIE)
ly○ing
ly○ing-in *n.*, *pl.* ly○ings-in, ly○ing-ins.
Lyme dis•ease
lymph
lymph node
lym•phat○ic
lym•phoid
lym•pho•ma *n.*, *pl.* lym•pho•mas, lym•pho•ma○ta.
lynch *v.*, lynched, lynch•ing.
lynch○er
lynx *n.*, *pl.* lynx○es or lynx. (the animal: cf. LINKS)
Ly•ons
lyre (small harp: cf. LIAR)
lyr○ic
lyr○i•cal○ly
lyr○i•cism
lyr○i•cist
ly•ser○gic ac○id di•eth○yl•am○ide (LSD)

M

MA (Massachusetts)
M.A. (Master of Arts)
ma *n.*, *pl.* mas.
ma'am
ma•ca•bre
mac•ad○am
mac•ad•am•ize *v.*, mac•ad•am•iz○ed, mac•ad•am•iz○ing.
Ma•cao
ma•caque

mac•a•ro•ni
mac•a•roon
ma•caw
mace (clublike weapon; spice)
Mace *v.*, Maced, Macing. *Trademark.* (chemical spray)
Mac○e○do•ni○a
Mac○e○do•ni○an
mac•er•ate *v.*, mac•

er•at○ed, mac•er•at•ing.
mac•er•a•tion
mach or Mach
ma•chet○e *n.*, *pl.* ma•chet○es.
Mach○i•a•vel•li○an
mach○i•na•tion
ma•chine *v.*, ma•chined, ma•chin○ing.

ma•chine-
  de•pend•ent
  Computers.
ma•chine gun
ma•chine-
  in•de•pend•ent
  Computers.
machine lan•guage
  Computers.
ma•chine-read•a•ble
  Computers.
ma•chin•er•y
ma•chin•ist
ma•chis•mo
ma•cho *n., pl.* ma•
  chos.
Mac•in•tosh *Trade-
  mark.*
mack•er•el *n., pl.*
  mack•er•el or
  mack•er•els.
mack•i•naw
mack•in•tosh (rain-
  coat: cf. MCINTOSH;
  MACINTOSH)
mac•ra•mé
mac•ro *n., pl.* mac•
  ros. *Computers.*
mac•ro•bi•ot•ic
mac•ro•bi•ot•ics
mac•ro•cosm
mac•ro•ec•o•nom•
  ics *Business.*
ma•cron
mac•ro•scop•ic
mad *adj.,* mad•der,
  mad•dest.
Mad•a•gas•car
mad•am *n., pl.* ma•
  dams.
mad•ame (Mme.) *n.,*
  pl. mes•dames.
mad•cap
mad•den *v.,* mad•
  dened, mad•den•
  ing.
mad•der

mad•ding
made *v.,* made, mak•
  ing. (produced: 'f.
  MAID)
made-to-or•der
made-up
Ma•dei•ra
mad•e•moi•selle
  (Mlle.) *n., pl.*
  mad•e•moi•selles or
  mes•de•moi•selles.
mad•house *n., pl.*
  mad•hous•es.
Mad•i•son (city)
mad•ly
mad•man *n., pl.* mad•
  men.
mad•ness
Ma•don•na
Ma•dras
mad•ras (fabric)
Ma•drid
mad•ri•gal
mad•wom•an *n., pl.*
  mad•wom•en.
mael•strom
mae•nad
maes•tro *n., pl.*
  maes•tros.
Ma•fi•a
ma•fi•o•so *n., pl.*
  ma•fi•o•si or ma•
  fi•o•sos.
mag•a•zine
Ma•gel•lan
ma•gen•ta
mag•got
Ma•gi *n.* (pl. of Ma-
  gus)
mag•ic
mag•i•cal
mag•i•cal•ly
ma•gi•cian
mag•is•te•ri•al
mag•is•trate
mag•ma

mag•na
Mag•na Car•ta or
  Char•ta
mag•na•nim•i•ty
mag•nan•i•mous
  (great)
mag•nan•i•mous•ly
mag•nate (influential
  person)
mag•ne•sia
mag•ne•si•um (min-
  eral mixture)
mag•net (metal that
  attracts iron)
mag•net•ic
magnetic bub•ble
  Computers.
magnetic disk *Comput-
  ers.*
magnetic drum *Com-
  puters.*
magnetic res•o•nance
  im•ag•ing (MRI)
mag•net•i•cal•ly
mag•net•ism
mag•ne•tite
mag•net•ize *v.,* mag•
  net•ized, mag•net•
  iz•ing.
mag•ne•to *n., pl.*
  mag•ne•tos.
mag•ne•tom•e•ter
mag•ni•fi•ca•tion
mag•nif•i•cence
mag•nif•i•cent
mag•nif•i•cent•ly
mag•ni•fi•er
mag•ni•fy *v.,* mag•
  ni•fied, mag•ni•fy•
  ing.
mag•nil•o•quence
mag•nil•o•quent
mag•ni•tude
mag•no•lia *n., pl.*
  mag•no•lias.
mag•num
magnum o•pus

mag•pie
Ma•gus n., pl. Ma•gi.
Mag•yar
mah-jongg or mah•jong
ma•ha•ra•jah n., pl. ma•ha•ra•jahs.
ma•ha•ra•nee n., pl. ma•ha•ra•nees.
ma•ha•ri•shi n., pl. ma•ha•ri•shis.
ma•hat•ma n., pl. ma•hat•mas.
Ma•hi•can n., pl. Ma•hi•cans or Ma•hi•can.
Mah•ler
ma•hog•a•ny
ma•hout
maid (servant: cf. MADE)
maid•en
maid•en•hair
maid•en•head
maid•en•hood
maid•en•ly
maid•serv•ant
mail v., mailed, mail•ing. (letters; to mail: cf. MALE)
mail merge Computers.
mail or•der Business.
mail-or•der Business.
mail•box
mail•er
mail•lot
mail•man n., pl. mail•men.
maim v., maimed, maim•ing.
main
main mem•o•ry Computers.
Maine (ME)
Main•er
main•frame Computers.

main•land
main line n., pl.
main•line v., main•lined, main•lin•ing.
main•ly
main•mast
main•sail
main•spring
main•stay
main•stream
main•tain v., main•tained, main•tain•ing.
main•tain•a•ble
main•te•nance
maî•tre d' or mai•tre d' n., pl. maî•tre d's or mai•tre d's.
maî•tre d'ho•tel n., pl. maî•tres d'ho•tel.
maize (corn: cf. MAZE)
ma•jes•tic
ma•jes•ti•cal•ly
maj•es•ty n., pl. maj•es•ties.
ma•jol•i•ca
ma•jor v., ma•jored, ma•jor•ing.
ma•jor-do•mo n., pl. ma•jor-•do•mos.
major med•i•cal Business.
ma•jor•ette
ma•jor•i•ty n., pl. ma•jor•i•ties.
make v.
make-be•lieve
make-do n., pl. make-•dos.
make-work
mak•er
make•shift
make•up or make-up
mak•ing
mal•a•chite

mal•ad•just•ed
mal•ad•just•ment
mal•a•droit
mal•a•dy n., pl. mal•a•dies.
Mal•a•gas•y Re•pub•lic
ma•laise
mal•a•mute or mal•e•mute
mal•a•prop•ism
ma•lar•i•a
ma•lar•i•al
ma•lar•key
mal•a•thi•on
Ma•la•wi n., pl. Ma•la•wis or Ma•la•wi.
Ma•la•wi•an
Ma•lay
Mal•a•ya•lam
Ma•lay•sia
Ma•lay•sian
mal•con•tent
Mal•dives
male (masculine: cf. MAIL)
mal•e•dic•tion
mal•e•fac•tion
mal•e•fac•tor
ma•lef•ic
ma•lef•i•cence
ma•lef•i•cent
male•ness
ma•lev•o•lence
ma•lev•o•lent
ma•lev•o•lent•ly
mal•fea•sance
mal•for•ma•tion
mal•formed
mal•func•tion v., mal•func•tioned, mal•func•tion•ing.
Ma•li
mal•ice
ma•li•cious
ma•li•cious•ly

ma•lign *v.*, ma•
ligned, ma•lign•ing.
ma•lig•nan•cy
ma•lig•nant
ma•lin•ger *v.*, ma•
lin•gered, ma•lin•
ger•ing.
ma•lin•ger•er
mall (shopping center:
cf. MAUL)
mall rat
mal•lard *n.*, *pl.* mal•
lards or mal•lard.
mal•le•a•bil•i•ty
mal•le•a•ble
mal•let
mal•le•ous *n.*, *pl.* mal•
le•i.
mall•ing
mal•low
mal•nour•ished
mal•nu•tri•tion
mal•oc•clu•sion
mal•o•dor•ous
mal•prac•tice
malt
Mal•ta
malt•ed milk
Mal•thu•sian
malt•ose
mal•treat *v.*, mal•
treat•ed, mal•treat•
ing.
mal•treat•ment
ma•ma or mam•ma,
n., *pl.* ma•mas.
mam•ba
mam•bo *n.*, *pl.* mam•
bos; *v.*, mam•boed,
mam•bo•ing.
mam•mal
mam•ma•li•an
mam•ma•ry
mam•mo•gram
mam•mog•ra•phy
mam•mon

mam•mon•ism
mam•moth
man *n.*, *pl.* men; *v.*,
manned, man•ning.
man-eat•er
man-eat•ing
man Fri•day *n.*, *pl.*
men Fri•day or Fri•
days.
man-hour
man-made
man-of-war *n.*, *pl.*
men-•of-•war.
man-sized or man-size
man•a•cle *v.*,
man•a•cled,
man•a•cling. (ma•
chine tool)
man•age *v.*, man•
aged, man•ag•ing.
man•age•a•ble
man•age•ment *Busi•
ness.*
management con•
sult•ant *Business.*
management in•for•
ma•tion sys•tem
Computers.
man•ag•er *Business.*
man•a•ge•ri•al *Busi•
ness.*
ma•ña•na *n.*, *pl.* ma•
ña•nas.
man•a•tee *n.*, *pl.*
man•a•tees.
Man•ches•ter
Man•chu *n.*, *pl.* Man•
chus or Man•chu.
Man•chu•ri•a
Man•chu•ri•an
man•da•mus, *n.*, *pl.*
man•da•mus•es.
man•da•rin
man•date *v.*, man•
dat•ed, man•dat•
ing.
man•da•to•ry

man•di•ble
man•dib•u•lar
man•do•lin
man•drake
man•drel or man•dril
man•drill (monkey)
mane
ma•nège or ma•nege
(horsemanship: cf. MÉ•
NAGE)
ma•neu•ver
ma•neu•ver•a•ble
man•ful
man•ful•ly
man•ga•nese
mange
man•ger
man•gi•ness
man•gle *v.*, man•
gled, man•gling.
man•go *n.*, *pl.* man•
goes or man•gos.
man•grove
man•gy *adj.*, man•
gi•er, man•gi•est.
man•han•dle *v.*,
man•han•dled,
man•han•dling.
Man•hat•tan
man•hole
man•hood
man•hunt
ma•ni•a *n.*, *pl.* ma•
ni•as.
ma•ni•ac
ma•ni•a•cal
man•ic
man•ic-de•pres•sive
man•i•cure *v.*,
man•i•cured,
man•i•cur•ing.
man•i•cur•ist
man•i•fest *v.*, man•i•
fest•ed, man•i•
fest•ing.
man•i•fes•ta•tion

man•i•fest•ly
man•i•fes•to n., pl.
man•i•fes•tos or
man•i•fes•toes.
man•i•fold
man•i•kin or man•
ni•kin
Ma•nil•a
man•i•oc
ma•nip•u•la•ble
ma•nip•u•late v.,
ma•nip•u•lat•ed,
ma•nip•u•lat•ing.
ma•nip•u•la•tion
ma•nip•u•la•tive
ma•nip•u•la•tor
Man•i•to•ba
man•kind
man•li•ness
man•ly adj., man•
li•er, man•li•est.
Mann
man•na
manned
man•ne•quin or
man•i•kin
man•ner (way: cf.
MANOR)
man•nered
man•ner•ism
man•ner•ly
man•nish
ma•noeu•vre v., ma•
noeu•vred, ma•
noeu•vring.
man•or (estate: cf.
MANNER)
ma•no•ri•al
man•pow•er
man•qué
man•sard roof
manse
man•serv•ant n., pl.
men•serv•ants.
man•sion
man•slaugh•ter

man•sue•tude
man•ta n., pl. man•
tas.
man•tel (fireplace
frame)
man•til•la n., pl.
man•til•las.
man•tis n., pl. man•
tis•es or man•tes.
man•tis•sa
man•tle (cloak)
man•tra n., pl. man•
tras.
man•u•al
man•u•al•ly
man•u•fac•ture v.,
man•u•fac•tured,
man•u•fac•tur•ing.
Business.
man•u•fac•tur•er
Business.
man•u•fac•tur•ing
Business.
manufacturing cost
Business.
manufacturing o•ver•
head *Business.*
man•u•mis•sion
man•u•mit v.,
man•u•mit•ted,
man•u•mit•ting.
ma•nure v., ma•
nured, ma•nur•ing.
man•u•script
Manx
man•y adj., more,
most.
Mao Ze•dong or Mao
Tse-tung
Mao•ism
Mao•ist
Ma•o•ri n., pl. Ma•o•
ris or Ma•o•ri.
map v., mapped,
map•ping.
map file *Computers.*
ma•ple

mar v., marred, mar•
ring.
mar•a•bou n., pl.
mar•a•bous.
ma•rac•a n., pl. ma•
rac•as.
mar•a•schi•no
mar•a•thon
mar•a•thon•er
ma•raud
ma•raud•er
mar•ble v., mar•bled,
mar•bling.
mar•ble•ize v., mar•
ble•ized, mar•ble•
iz•ing.
mar•cel v., mar•
celled, mar•cel•ling.
march v., marched,
march•ing.
march•er
mar•chion•ess
Mar•di Gras
mare (female horse: cf.
MAYOR)
ma•re n., pl. ma•ri•a.
(dark lunar plain)
mare's-nest
mar•ga•rine
mar•gin v., mar•
gined, mar•gin•ing.
margin call *Business.*
margin rate *Business.*
mar•gin•al
mar•gi•na•li•a
mar•gue•rite
ma•ri•a•chi n., pl.
ma•ri•a•chis.
Ma•rie An•toi•nette
mar•i•gold
ma•ri•jua•na
ma•rim•ba n., pl.
ma•rim•bas.
ma•ri•na n., pl. ma•
ri•nas.
mar•i•nade (seasoned
liquid)

mar•i•nate v., mar•i•nat•ed, mar•i•nat•ing. (to steep in marinade)

ma•rine

mar•i•ner

mar•i•on•ette

mar•i•tal (of marriage: cf. MARSHAL; MARTIAL)

mar•i•tal•ly

mar•i•time

mar•jo•ram

mark v., marked, mark•ing. (visible impression; to mark: cf. MARQUE)

mark price Business.

mark•down Business.

marked

mark•ed•ly

mark•er

mar•ket v., mar•ket•ed, mar•ket•ing.

mar•ket e•con•o•my Business.

mar•ket price Business.

market re•search Business.

market share Business.

market val•ue Business.

mar•ket•a•ble Business.

mar•ket•er Business.

mar•ket•ing Business.

mar•ket•place Business.

mark•ka n., pl. mark•kaa.

Mar•kov chain Business.

marks•man n., pl. marks•men

marks•man•ship

mark•up Business.

mar•lin n., pl. mar•lin or mar•lins.

mar•line•spike

mar•ma•lade

mar•mo•set

mar•mot

ma•roon

marque (product model: cf. MARK)

mar•quee (theater sign)

mar•quess (British nobleman)

mar•que•try n., pl. mar•que•tries.

mar•quis n., pl. mar•quis•es or mar•quis. (European nobleman)

mar•quise n., pl. mar•quis•es. (European noblewoman)

mar•qui•sette

mar•riage (wedding: cf. MIRAGE)

mar•riage•a•ble

mar•row

mar•ry v., mar•ried, mar•ry•ing.

Mars

Mar•seilles

marsh

mar•shal[1] n.

mar•shal[2] v., mar•shaled or mar•shalled, mar•shal•ing or mar•shal•ling. (police officer: cf. MARITAL; MARTIAL)

marsh•mal•low

marsh•y adj., marsh•i•er, marsh•i•est.

mar•su•pi•al

mart

mar•ten n., pl. mar•tens or mar•ten. (animal: cf. MARTIN)

mar•tial (warlike: cf. MARITAL; MARSHAL)

Mar•tian

mar•tin (the bird: cf. MARTEN)

mar•ti•net

mar•tin•gale

mar•ti•ni n., pl. mar•ti•nis.

mar•tyr v., mar•tyred, mar•tyr•ing.

mar•tyr•dom

mar•vel v., mar•veled or mar•velled, mar•vel•ing or mar•vel•ling.

mar•vel•ous

mar•vel•ous•ly

Marx•i•an

Marx•ism

Marx•ist

Mar•y

Mar•y•land (MD)

mar•zi•pan

mas•car•a v., mas•car•aed, mas•car•a•ing.

mas•cot

mas•cu•line

mas•cu•lin•i•ty

ma•ser

mash v., mashed, mash•ing.

mask v., masked, mask•ing. (face covering: cf. MASQUE)

mas•och•ism

mas•och•ist

mas•och•is•tic

mas•och•is•ti•cal•ly

ma•son

Ma•son•ic

ma•son•ry

masque (elaborate play: cf. MASK)

mas•quer•ade v.,

mas•quer•ad•ed,
mas•quer•ad•ing.
mas•quer•ad•er
mass
mass mar•ket•ing
Business.
mass me•di•a
mass-pro•duce v.,
mass-•pro•duced,
mass-•pro•duc•ing.
Business.
mass pro•duc•tion
Business.
mass stor•age Computers.
Mas•sa•chu•setts
(MA)
mas•sa•cre v., mas•
sa•cred, mas•sa•
cring.
mas•sage v., mas•
saged, mas•sag•ing.
massed (assembled: cf.
MAST)
mas•seur
mas•seuse
mas•sive
mas•sive•ly
mas•sive•ness
mast (upright pole: cf.
MASSED)
mas•tec•to•my n., pl.
mas•tec•to•mies.
mas•ter v., mas•
tered, mas•ter•ing.
mas○ter•ful
mas○ter•ful○ly
mas○ter○ly
mas○ter•mind v.,
mas○ter•mind○ed,
mas○ter•mind○ing.
mas○ter•piece
mas○ter•stroke
mas○ter•work
mas•ter○y
mast•head
mas•ti•cate v., mas•

ti•cat○ed, mas•ti•
cat•ing.
mas•ti•ca•tion
mas•tiff
mas•to•don
mas•toid
mas•tur•bate v.,
mas•tur•bat○ed,
mas•tur•bat•ing.
mas•tur•ba•tion
mat (pad: cf. MATTE)
mat•a•dor
match v., matched,
match•ing.
match•book
match•less
match•mak○er
mate v., mat○ed,
mat•ing, n. (to
marry; spouse)
ma○té or ma○te n., pl.
ma•tés or ma•tes.
(beverage)
ma•te•ri•al (substance: cf. MATÉRIEL)
ma•te•ri•al•ism
ma•te•ri•a•list
ma•te•ri•al•is•tic
ma•te•ri•al•i•za•
tion
ma•te•ri•al•ize v.,
ma•te•ri•al•ized,
ma•te•ri•al•iz•ing.
ma•te•ri•al○ly
ma•te•ri•als han•
dling Business.
ma•té•ri•el (equipment: cf. MATERIAL)
ma•ter•nal
ma•ter•nal○ly
ma•ter•ni○ty
math
math co•proc•es•sor
Computers.
math○e•mat•i•cal
math○e•mat•i•cal○ly
math○e•ma•ti•cian

math○e•mat•ics
mat•i•née or mat•i•
nee
ma○tri•arch
ma○tri•ar•chal
ma○tri•ar•chy
mat•ri•cid○al
mat•ri•cide
ma•tric•u•late v.,
ma•tric•u•lat○ed,
ma•tric•u•lat•ing.
ma•tric•u•la•tion
mat○ri•mo•ni○al
mat○ri•mo•ny n., pl.
mat○ri•mo•nies.
ma•trix n., pl. ma•tri•
ces or ma•trix○es.
ma•tron
ma•tron○ly
matte (dull: cf. MAT)
mat•ted[1] (having a
dull surface)
mat•ted or matt○ed[2]
(padded)
mat•ter v., mat•
tered, mat•ter•ing.
mat○ter-of-fact
mat○ter-of-fact○ly
Mat•thew
mat•ting[1] (pad; material for pads)
mat•ting or matt•ing[2]
(dull surface; finishing
with a dull surface)
mat•tress
mat○u•ra•tion
ma•ture v., ma•tured,
ma•tur•ing.
ma•ture○ly
ma•tu•ri○ty
maturity yield Business.
mat○zo or mat•zoh,
n., pl. mat•zos or
mat•zot, mat•zohs
or mat•zoth.
maud•lin

maul v., mauled, maul•ing. (to handle roughly: cf. MALL)

Mau•pas•sant

Mau•ri•ta•ni•a

Mau•ri•ta•ni•an

Mau•ri•tian

Mau•ri•tius

mau•so•le•um n., pl. mauve

ma•ven or ma•vin

mav•er•ick

maw

mawk•ish

mawk•ish•ly

max◦i n., pl. max◦is.

max•il•la n., pl. max•il•lae.

max•il•lar•y

max◦im

max◦i•mal

max◦i•mal•ly

max◦i•mize v., max◦i•mized, max◦i•miz•ing.

max◦i•mum n., pl. max◦i•mums or max◦i•ma.

may v., might.

Ma•ya n., pl. Ma•yas or Ma•ya.

May◦an

may•be n., pl. may•bes.

may•flow◦er

may•fly n., pl. may•flies.

may•hem

may◦o

may•on•naise

may◦or (city official: cf. MARE; MARE)

may•or•al

may•or•al◦ty

May•pole

maze (labyrinth: cf. MAIZE)

ma•zur◦ka n., pl. ma•zur•kas.

Mb *Computers.* (megabit)

MB *Computers.* (megabyte)

MBA or **M.B.A.** *Business.* (Master of Business Administration).

Mc◦Coy

Mc•In•tosh (the apple: cf. MACKINTOSH; MACINTOSH)

Mc•Kin•ley

MD (doctor of medicine)

MD (Maryland)

mdse. (merchandise)

ME (Maine)

me

mead

mead◦ow

mead◦ow•lark

mea•ger

mea•ger◦ly

meal

meal•time

meal◦y adj., meal•i◦er, meal•i•est.

meal◦y-mouthed or meal◦y•mouthed

mean[1] (midway point: cf. MEDIAN)

mean[2] v., meant, mean•ing; adj., mean◦er, mean•est. (to intend; unkind: cf. MIEN)

me•an•der v., me•an•dered, me•an•der•ing.

mean•ing

mean•ing•ful

mean•ing•less

mean◦ly

mean•ness

meant

mean•time

mea•sles

mea•sly adj., mea•sli◦er, mea•sli•est.

meas•ur•a◦ble

meas•ur•a•bly

meas•ure v., meas•ured, meas•ur•ing.

meas•ure•less

meas•ure•ment

meat (flesh food: cf. MEET; METE)

meat•ball

meat◦y adj., meat•i◦er, meat•i•est.

Mec◦ca

me•chan◦ic

me•chan◦i•cal

mechanical mouse *Computers.*

me•chan◦i•cal◦ly

me•chan◦ics

mech•an•ism

mech◦a•nis•tic

mech◦a•ni•za•tion

mech◦a•nize v., mech◦a•nized, mech◦a•niz•ing.

med◦al (metal disk: cf. MEDDLE; METAL; METTLE)

med•al•ist

me•dal•lion

med•dle v., med•dled, med•dling. (to interfere)

med•dler

med◦dle•some

me•di•a n., pl. me•di◦a or me•di•ums.

me•di◦al

me•di◦an (middle number: cf. MEAN)

me•di•ate v., me•di•at◦ed, me•di•at•ing.

me·di·a·tion
me·di·a·tor
med○ic
med○i·ca○ble
Med○i·caid
med○i·cal
med○i·cal○ly
me·dic○a·ment
Med○i·care
med○i·cate v.,
  med○i·cat○ed,
  med○i·cat·ing.
med○i·ca·tion
me·dic○i·nal
me·di·e○val or me·
  di·ae·val
me·di·e○val·ist
me·di·o·cre
me·di·oc·ri·ty
med○i·tate v.,
  med○i·tat○ed,
  med○i·tat·ing.
med○i·ta·tion
med○i·ta·tive
Med○i·ter·ra·ne○an
me·di·um n., pl.
me·di·um-
  res○o○lu○tion
  Computers.
med·ley n., pl. med·
  leys.
me·dul○la ob○
  long○a○ta n., pl. me-
  dulla ob·long○a·
  tas.
meek adj., meek○er,
  meek·est.
meek○ly
meek·ness
meer·schaum
meet v., met, meet·
  ing. (to encounter: cf.
  MEAT; METE)
meg○a·bit (Mb) Com-
  puters.
meg○a·byte (MB)
  Computers.

meg○a·cy·cle
meg○a·flop (MFLOP)
  Computers.
meg○a·hertz n., pl.
  meg○a·hertz or
  meg○a·hertz○es.
meg○a·hit
meg○a·lo·ma·ni○a
meg○a·lo·ma·ni○ac
meg○a·lop·o·lis
meg○a·phone
meg○a·ton
mei·o·sis
mel○a·mine
mel·an·cho·li○a
mel·an·chol·y
Mel○a·ne·sia
Mel○a·ne·sian
mé·lange n., pl. mé·
  langes.
mel○a·nin
mel○a·nism
mel○a·no·ma n., pl.
  mel○a·no·mas or
  mel○a·no·ma·ta.
Mel○ba toast
Mel·bourne
meld v., meld○ed,
  meld·ing.
me·lee or mê·lée
mel○·io·rate v., mel·
  io·rat○ed, mel·io·
  rat·ing.
mel·io·ra·tion
mel·lif·lu·ous
mel·lif·lu·ous○ly
mel·low v., mel·
  lowed, mel·low·ing;
  adj., mel·low○er,
  mel·low·est.
me·lod○ic
me·lod○i·cal○ly
me·lo·di·ous
me·lo·di·ous○ly
me·lo·di·ous·ness

mel○o·dra·ma n., pl.
  mel○o·dra·mas.
mel○o·dra·mat○ic
mel○o·dy n., pl. mel·
  o·dies.
mel○on
melt v., melt○ed,
  melt·ing.
melt·down
Mel·ville
mem·ber
mem·ber·ship
mem·brane
mem·bra·nous
me·men·to n., pl.
  me·men·tos or me·
  men·toes.
mem○o n., pl.
  mem○os.
mem·oir
mem○o·ra·bil·i○a
mem○o·ra○ble
mem○o·ra·bly
mem○o·ran·dum n.,
  pl. mem○o·ran·
  dums or mem○o·
  ran○da.
me·mo·ri○al
mem○o·ri·za·tion
mem○o·rize v.,
  mem○o·rized,
  mem○o·riz·ing.
mem○o·ry n., pl.
  mem○o·ries.
memory dump Com-
  puters.
mem○o·ry-res○i·dent
  Computers.
Mem·phis
men
men·ace v., men·
  aced, men·ac·ing.
men·ac·ing○ly
mé·nage or me·nage
  (household: cf. MA-
  NÈGE)
me·nag·er·ie

mend v., mend∘ed,
mend•ing.
men•da•cious
men•da•cious•ly
men•dac•i∘ty
Men•del
men•de•le•vi∘um
Men•dels•sohn
men•di•cant
men•folk or men•
folks
men•ha•den
me•ni∘al
me•nin•ges n.pl.,
sing. me•ninx
men•in•gi•tis
me•nis•cus n., pl.
me•nis∘ci or me•
nis•cus∘es.
Men•non•ite
men∘o∘pau∘sal
men∘o∘pause
me•nor∘ah
men•ses
men•stru∘al
men•stru•ate v.,
men•stru•at∘ed,
men•stru•at•ing.
men•stru•a•tion
men•sur•a∘ble
men•su•ra•tion
mens•wear
men•tal
men•tal•ist
men•tal•i∘ty
men•tal∘ly
men•thol
men•tho•lat∘ed
men•tion v., men•
ti∘ned, men•tion•
ing.
men•tor
men∘u n., pl. men∘us.
menu bar Computers.
men∘u-driv∘en Com-
puters.

me∘ow
mer•can•tile Business.
mer•ce•nar∘y n., pl.
mer•ce•nar•ies.
mer•cer
mer•cer∘i•za•tion
mer•cer•ize v., mer•
cer•ized, mer•cer•
iz∘ing.
mer•chan•dise v.,
mer•chan•dised,
mer•chan•dis•ing.
Business.
merchandise mart
Business.
mer•chan•dis∘er Busi-
ness.
mer•chan•dis•ing
Business.
mer•chant Business.
merchant bank Busi-
ness.
mer•chant•man n., pl.
mer•chant•men.
mer•ci•ful
mer•ci•ful∘ly
mer•ci•less
mer•ci•less∘ly
mer•cu•ri∘al
mer•cu•ric
mer•cu•rous
mer•cu∘ry
mer•cy n., pl. mer•
cies.
mere adj., mer•est.
mere∘ly
mer∘e∘tri•cious (taw-
dry: cf. MERITORIOUS)
mer•gan•ser n., pl.
mer•gan•sers or
mer•gan•ser.
merge v., merged,
merg•ing.
merg∘ee Business.
merg∘er Business.
me•rid•i∘an
me•ringue

me•ri∘no, n., pl. me•
ri∘nos.
mer•it v., mer•it∘ed,
mer•it•ing.
merit rat•ing Business.
mer∘i•to•ri•ous
(praiseworthy: cf. MER-
ETRICIOUS)
Mer•lin
mer•maid
mer•man n., pl. mer•
men.
mer•ri∘ly
mer•ri•ment
mer∘ry adj., mer•
ri∘er, mer•ri•est.
mer∘ry-go-round
mer∘ry•mak∘er
mer∘ry•mak•ing
me∘sa n., pl. me•sas.
mé•sal•li•ance n., pl.
mé•sal•li•anc∘es.
mes•cal
mes•ca•line
mes•dames (Mmes.)
mes•de•moi•selles
(Mlles.)
mesh v., meshed,
mesh•ing.
mes•mer•ism
mes•mer•ize v., mes•
mer•ized, mes•mer•
iz•ing.
Mes∘o•lith∘ic
Mes∘o•po•ta•mi∘a
Mes∘o•po•ta•mi∘an
mes∘o•sphere
Mes∘o•zo∘ic
mes•quite
mess v., messed,
mess•ing.
mes•sage
mes•sei•gneurs
mes•sen•ger
Mes•si∘ah
Mes•si•an∘ic

mes•sieurs (MM.)

mess•i•ly

messoi•ness (to allot:
cf. MEAT; MEET)

Messrs. (pl. of Mr.)

messoy adj., mess•
i•er, mess•i•est.

mes•ti◦zo n., pl. mes•
ti◦zos or mes•ti•
zoes.

met

met◦a•bol◦ic

me•tab◦o◦lism

me•tab◦o•lite

me•tab◦o•lize v.,
me•tab◦o•lized,
me•tab◦o•liz•ing.

met◦a•car•pal

met◦a•car•pus n., pl.
met◦a•car◦pi.

met◦al (element: cf.
MEDAL; MEDDLE; METTLE)

met◦al•head

me•tal•lic

me•tal•li•cal◦ly

met◦al•lur•gist

met◦al•lur◦gy

met◦a•mor•phic

met◦a•mor•phism

met◦a•mor•phose v.,
met◦a•mor•phosed,
met◦a•mor•phos•
ing; n., pl. met◦a•
mor•phos◦es.

met◦a•mor•pho◦sis
n., pl. met◦a•mor•
pho•ses.

met◦a•phor

met◦a•phor◦i•cal

met◦a•phor◦i•cal◦ly

met◦a•phys◦i•cal

met◦a•phys◦ics

me•tas•ta•sis n., pl.
me•tas•ta•ses.
(spread of malignant
cells: cf. METATHESIS)

me•tas•ta•size v.,

me•tas•ta•sized,
me•tas•ta•siz•ing.

met◦a•stat◦ic

met◦a•tar•sal

met◦a•tar•sus n., pl.
met◦a•tar◦si.

me•tath◦e•sis n., pl.
me•tath◦e•ses.
(transposition: cf. ME-
TASTASIS)

mete v., met◦ed,
met•ing. (to allot: cf.
MEAT; MEET)

me•tem•psy•cho•sis,
n., pl. me•tem•psy•
cho•ses.

me•te◦or

me•te◦or◦ic

me•te◦or•ite

me•te◦or•oid

me•te◦or◦o•log◦i•
cal

me•te◦or◦ol◦o•gist

me•te◦or◦ol◦o•gy

me•ter v., me•tered,
me•ter•ing.

me•ter-kil◦o◦o–gram-
sec◦ond

meth◦a•done

meth•ane

meth◦a•nol

me•thinks v., me•
thought.

meth◦od

me•thod◦i•cal

me•thod◦i•cal◦ly

Meth•od•ist

meth•od◦o◦log◦i•cal

Me•thu•se•lah

meth◦yl

me•tic◦u•lous

me•tic◦u•lous◦ly

me•tic◦u•lous•ness

mé•tier or me•tier

me•tre

met◦ric

metric sys•tem

met•ri•ca•tion

met•ri•cize v., met•
ri•cized, met•ri•ciz•
ing.

met•rics

met◦ro n., pl. met•
ros.

met◦ro•nome

Met•ro•plex

me•trop◦o•lis n., pl.
me•trop◦o•lis◦es.

met◦ro•pol◦i•tan

met•tle (fortitude: cf.
MEDAL; MEDDLE; METAL)

met•tle•some

mew v., mewed,
mew•ing.

mewl v., mewled,
mewl•ing.

Mex◦i•can

Mex◦i◦co

mez•za•nine

mez◦zo-so◦pran◦o
n., pl. mez◦zo-•
so◦pran◦o.

mfg. (manufacturing)

MFLOP Computers.
(mega floating-point
operations per second)

MFM Computers. (modi-
fied frequency modula-
tion)

mfr. n., pl. mfrs. (man-
ufacturer)

mgr. or Mgr. (man-
ager).

MHz (megahertz)

MI (Michigan)

MIA (missing in action)

Mi•am◦i

mi•as◦ma n., pl. mi•
as•mas.

mi◦ca

mice

Mi•chel•an•ge•lo

Mich◦i•gan (MI)

Mich•i•gan•der or
Mich•i•gan•ite
mi•cro n., pl. mi•cros.
Computers.
mi•crobe
mi•cro•bi•ol•o•gist
mi•cro•bi•ol•o•gy
mi•cro•chip *Comput-
ers.*
mi•cro•com•put•er
Computers.
mi•cro•cosm
mi•cro•ec•o•nom•ics
Business.
mi•cro•fiche
mi•cro•film
mi•cro•flop•py n., pl.
mi•cro•flop•pies.
Computers.
mi•cro•groove
mi•cro•jus•ti•fi•ca•
tion *Computers.*
mi•cro•man•age, v.,
mi•cro•man•aged,
mi•cro•man•ag•ing.
mi•crom•e•ter
mi•cron n., pl. mi•
crons.
Mi•cro•ne•sia
Mi•cro•ne•sian
mi•cro•or•gan•ism
mi•cro•phone
mi•cro•proc•es•sor
Computers.
mi•cro•scope
mi•cro•scop•ic
mi•cro•scop•i•cal•ly
mi•cros•co•py
mi•cro•spac•ing *Com-
puters.*
mi•cro•sur•ger•y
mi•cro•wav•a•ble
mi•cro•wave v.,
mi•cro•waved,
mi•cro•wav•ing.
mid
mid•air

Mi•das
mid•day
mid•den
mid•dle
mid•dle-aged
Mid•dle A•mer•i•
can n.
Mid•dle-A•mer•i•can
adj.
middle class n.
mid•dle-class adj.
Mid•dle East
middle man•age•
ment *Business.*
middle man•ag•er
Business.
mid•dle-of-the-road
Mid•dle West
mid•dle•brow
mid•dle•man n., pl.
mid•dle•men.
mid•dle•weight
mid•dling
mid•dy n., pl. mid•
dies. (blouse: cf. MIDI;
MIDI)
Mid•east
Mid•east•ern
midge
midg•et
mid•i n., pl. mid•is.
(skirt: cf. MIDDY)
MIDI *Computers.* (musi-
cal instrument digital
interface)
mid•land
mid•night
mid•point
mid•riff
mid•ship•man n., pl.
mid•ship•men.
midst
mid•stream
mid•sum•mer
mid•term
mid•town

mid•way
mid•week
Mid•west
Mid•west•ern
Mid•west•ern•er
mid•wife n., pl. mid•
wives.
mid•wife•ry
mid•win•ter
mid•year
mien (demeanor: cf.
MEAN)
miff
miffed
might (power: cf. MITE)
might•i•ly
might•i•ness
might•y adj., might•
i•er, might•i•est.
mi•gnon•ette
mi•graine
mi•grant
mi•grate v., mi•
grat•ed, mi•grat•
ing.
mi•gra•tion
mi•gra•to•ry
mi•ka•do n., pl. mi•
ka•dos.
mike v., miked, mik•
ing.
mil (unit of length: cf.
MILL)
mi•la•dy n., pl. mi•
la•dies.
Mi•lan
mild adj., mild•er,
mild•est.
mil•dew v., mil•
dewed, mil•dew•
ing.
mild•ly
mild•ness
mile
mile•age or mil•age
mile•post

mil•er

mile•stone

mi•lieu n., pl. mi•
lieus or mi•lieux.

mil•i•tan•cy

mil•i•tant

mil•i•tant•ly

mil•i•ta•rism

mil•i•ta•rist

mil•i•ta•ris•tic

mil•i•ta•rize, n., pl.
mil•i•ta•rized,
mil•i•ta•riz•ing.

mil•i•tar•y

mil•i•tate v., mil•i•
tat•ed, mil•i•tat•
ing. (to have an effect:
cf. MITIGATE)

mi•li•tia

mi•li•tia•man n., pl.
mi•li•tia•men.

milk v., milked, milk•
ing.

milk•i•ness

milk•maid

milk•man n., pl. milk•
men.

milk shake or milk•
shake

milk•sop

milk•weed

milk•y adj., milk•i•er,
milk•i•est.

mill v., milled, mill•
ing. (factory; to grind:
cf. MIL)

mill•age

mil•le•nar•y (a thou-
sand: cf. MILLINERY)

mil•len•ni•al

mil•len•ni•um n., pl.
mil•len•ni•ums or
mil•len•ni•a.

mill•er (one who mills)

Mil•ler (last name)

mil•let

mil•li•gram

mil•li•li•ter

mil•li•me•ter

mil•li•ner

mil•li•ner•y (women's
hats: cf. MILLENARY)

mil•lion n., pl. mil•
lions or mil•lion.

mil•lion•aire

mil•lionth

mil•li•pede

mill•race

mill•stone

mill•stream

mill•wright

milque•toast

milt

Mil•ton

Mil•wau•kee

mime v., mimed,
mim•ing.

mim•e•o•graph v.,
mim•e•o•graphed,
mim•e•o•graph•
ing.

mi•me•sis

mi•met•ic

mim•ic v., mim•icked,
mim•ick•ing.

mim•ic•ry n., pl.
mim•ic•ries.

mi•mo•sa n., pl. mi•
mo•sas.

min•a•ret

min•a•to•ry

mince v., minced,
minc•ing. (to chop
fine: cf. MINTS)

mince•meat

mind v., mind•ed,
mind•ing.

mind-blow•ing

mind•ful

mind•less

mine v., mined, min•
ing.

min•er (mine worker:
cf. MINOR)

min•er•al

min•er•al•o•gist

min•er•al•o•gy

Mi•ner•va

min•e•stro•ne

mine•sweep•er

min•gle v., min•gled,
min•gling.

min•i n., pl. min•is.

min•i•a•ture

min•i•a•tur•ist

min•i•a•tur•i•za•
tion

min•i•a•tur•ize v.,
min•i•a•tur•ized,
min•i•a•tur•iz•ing.

min•i•bike

min•i•bus

min•i•com•put•er
Computers.

min•im

min•i•mal

minimal re•cal•cu•
la•tion Computers.

min•i•mal•ism

min•i•mal•ist

min•i•mal•ly

min•i•max Business.

min•i•mi•za•tion

min•i•mize v., min•i•
mized, min•i•miz•
ing.

min•i•mum n., pl.
min•i•mums or
min•i•ma.

minimum wage Busi-
ness.

min•ion

min•i•se•ries n., pl.
min•i•se•ries.

min•i•skirt

min•is•ter v., min•is•
tered, min•is•ter•
ing.

min•is•te•ri•al

min•is•trant

min•is•tra•tion

min•is•try *n., pl.*
min•is•tries.

min•i•van

mink *n., pl.* **minks** or
mink.

Min•ne•ap•o•lis

min•ne•sing•er

Min•ne•so•ta (MN)

Min•ne•so•tan

min•now *n., pl.* min•
nows or min•now.

Mi•no•an

mi•nor (lesser: cf.
MINER)

mi•nor•i•ty *n., pl.*
mi•nor•i•ties.

minority in•ter•est
Business.

min•ox•i•dil

min•strel

min•strel show

min•strel•sy

mint *v.,* mint○ed,
mint•ing.

mint ju•lep

mints (candies: cf.
MINCE)

mint○y *adj.,* mint•
i○er, mint•i•est.

min○u•end

min•u○et

mi•nus

mi•nus sign

mi•nus•cule

min•ute¹ *v.,* min•
ut○ed, min•ut•ing.
(to note down; 60
seconds)

mi•nute² *adj.,* mi•
nut•est. (very small)

min•ute steak

mi•nute○ly

Min•ute•man *n., pl.*
Min•ute•men.

mi•nute•ness

mi•nu•ti•a *n., pl.* mi•
nu•ti○ti○ae.

minx

Mi○o•cene

MIPS *Computers.* (mil-
lion instructions per
second)

mir○a•cle

mi•rac•u•lous

mi•rac•u•lous○ly

mi•rage (illusion: cf.
MARRIAGE)

Mi○•ran•dize, *v.,* Mi○
ran•dized, Mi•ran•
diz○ing.

mire

mir•ror *v.,* mir•rored,
mir•ror•ing.

mirth

mirth•ful

MIS *Computers.* (management information
system)

mis•ad•ven•ture

mis•al•li•ance

mis•an•thrope

mis•an•throp○ic

mis•an•thro○py

mis•ap•pre•hend *v.,*
mis•ap•pre•
hend○ed, mis•ap•
pre•hend•ing.

mis•ap•pre•hen•sion

mis•ap•pro•pri•ate
v., mis•ap•pro•pri•
at○ed, mis•ap•pro•
pri•at•ing.

mis•ap•pro•pri•a•
tion

mis•be•got•ten

mis•be•have *v.,* mis•
be•haved, mis•be•
hav○ing.

mis•be•hav•ior

misc. (miscellaneous)

mis•call *v.,* mis•
called, mis•call•ing.

mis•car•riage

mis•car○ry *v.,* mis•

car•ried, mis•car•
ry○ing.

mis•cast *v.,* mis•cast,
mis•cast•ing.

mis•ceg○e•na•tion

mis•cel•la•ne•ous

mis•cel•la•ny *n., pl.*
mis•cel•la•nies.

mis•chance

mis•chief

mis•chie•vous

mis•chie•vous○ly

mis•con•ceive *v.,*
mis•con•ceived,
mis•con•ceiv•ing.

mis•con•cep•tion

mis•con•duct *v.,* mis•
con•duct○ed, mis•
con•duct•ing.

mis•con•strue *v.,*
mis•con•strued,
mis•con•stru•ing.

mis•count *v.,* mis•
count○ed, mis•
count•ing.

mis•cre•ant

mis•cue

mis•deed

mis•de•mean○or

mis•di•rect *v.,* mis•
di•rect○ed, mis•di•
rect•ing.

mise-en-scène *n., pl.*
mise-•en-•scènes.

mi•ser

mis•er•a•ble

mis•er•a•bly

mi•ser•li•ness

mi•ser○ly

mis•er○y *n., pl.* mis•
er•ies.

mis•fea•sance

mis•fire *v.,* mis•fired,
mis•fir•ing.

mis•fit

mis•for•tune

mis•giv•ing

mis•guide v., mis•guid•ed, mis•guid•ing.

mis•han•dle v., mis•han•dled, mis•han•dling.

mis•hap

mish•mash

mis•in•form v., mis•in•formed, mis•in•form•ing.

mis•in•for•ma•tion

mis•in•ter•pret v., mis•in•ter•pret•ed, mis•in•ter•pret•ing.

mis•in•ter•pre•ta•tion

mis•judge v., mis•judged, mis•judg•ing.

mis•judg•ment

mis•lay v., mis•laid, mis•lay•ing.

mis•lead v., mis•led, mis•lead•ing.

mis•man•age v., mis•man•aged, mis•man•ag•ing.

mis•man•age•ment

mis•match v., mis•matched, mis•match•ing.

mis•no•mer

mi•sog•a•mist

mi•sog•a•my (hostility to marriage)

mi•sog•y•nist

mi•sog•y•ny (hostility to women)

mis•place v., mis•placed, mis•plac•ing.

mis•play v., mis•played, mis•play•ing.

mis•print v., mis•print•ed, mis•print•ing.

mis•pri•sion

mis•pro•nounce v., mis•pro•nounced, mis•pro•nounc•ing.

mis•pro•nun•ci•a•tion

mis•quote v., mis•quot•ed, mis•quot•ing.

mis•read v., mis•read, mis•read•ing.

mis•rep•re•sent v., mis•rep•re•sent•ed, mis•rep•re•sent•ing.

mis•rep•re•sen•ta•tion

mis•rule

miss n., pl. miss•es;. v., missed, miss•ing.

mis•sal (prayer book: cf. MISSILE; MISSIVE)

missed (failed: cf. MIST)

mis•shap•en

mis•sile

mis•sile•ry

miss•ing

mis•sion

mis•sion•ar•y n., pl. mis•sion•ar•ies.

Mis•sis•sip•pi (MS)

Mis•sis•sip•pi•an

mis•sive (letter: cf. MIS•SAL; MISSILE)

Mis•sour•i (MO)

Mis•sour•i•an

mis•spell v., mis•spelled, mis•spell•ing.

mis•spell•ing

mis•spend v., mis•spent, mis•spend•ing.

mis•state v., mis•stat•ed, mis•stat•ing.

mis•state•ment

mis•step

mist v., mist•ed, mist•ing. (haze; to become misty: cf. MISSED)

mis•take v., mis•took, mis•tak•en, mis•tak•ing.

mis•tak•en•ly

mis•ter

mist•i•ness

mis•tle•toe

mis•treat v., mis•treat•ed, mis•treat•ing.

mis•treat•ment

mis•tress

mis•tri•al

mis•trust v., mis•trust•ed, mis•trust•ing.

mis•trust•ful

mist•y adj., mist•i•er, mist•i•est.

mis•un•der•stand v., mis•un•der•stood, mis•un•der•stand•ing.

mis•un•der•stand•ing

mis•use v., mis•used, mis•us•ing.

mite (small thing: cf. MIGHT)

mit•i•gate v., mit•i•gat•ed, mit•i•gat•ing. (to make less severe: cf. MILITATE)

mit•i•ga•tion

mi•to•sis

mitt

mit•ten

mix v., mixed, mix•ing.

mix-up
mixed cost *Business.*
mixed e○con○o○my
  Business.
mixed-up
mix○er
mix•ture
Miz○o○ram
miz•zen
miz•zen•mast
Mlle. *n., pl.* Mlles.
  (mademoiselle)
MM. (messieurs)
Mme. *n., pl.* Mmes.
  (madame)
MN (Minnesota)
mne•mon○ic (aiding
  the memory: cf. PNEU-
  MONIC)
MO (Missouri)
moan *v.,* moaned,
  moan•ing.
moat (trench: cf. MOTE)
mob *v.,* mobbed,
  mob•bing.
mo•bile
mo•bil•i○ty
mo•bi•li○za•tion
mo•bi•lize *v.,* mo•bi•
  lized, mo•bi•liz•ing.
mob•ster
moc•ca•sin
mo•cha
mock *v.,* mocked,
  mock•ing.
mock-up or mock○up
mock•er○y
mock•ing•bird
mock•ing○ly
mod
mod○al (of a mode: cf.
  MODEL)
mo•dal•i○ty
mode (manner: cf.
  MOWED)
mod•el *v.,* mod•eled

or mod•elled, mod•
  el•ing or mod•el•
  ling. (example: cf.
  MODAL)
mo•dem *Computers.*
  (modulator-
  demodulator)
mod•er•ate *v.,* mod•
  er•at○ed, mod•er•
  at•ing.
mod•er•ate○ly
mod•er•a•tion
mod•er○a•tor
mod•ern
mod•ern•ism
mod•ern•ist
mod•ern•is•tic
mo•der•ni○ty
mod•ern•i•za•tion
mod•ern•ize *v.,* mod•
  ern•ized, mod•ern•
  iz•ing.
mod•ern•ness
mod•est
mod•est○ly
mod•es○ty
mod○i•cum
mod○i•fi•ca•tion
mod○i•fi○er
mod○i•fy *v.,* mod•i•
  fied, mod•i•fy•ing.
mod•ish
mod•ish○ly
mod•ish•ness
mo•diste
mod○u•lar
modular ar•chi•tec•
  ture *Computers.*
mod○u•late *v.,*
  mod○u•lat○ed,
  mod○u•lat•ing.
mod○u•la•tion
mod○u•la•tor
mod○u•la○tor-
  de○mod○u•la○tor
  Computers. (modem)
mod•ule

mo•dus op○e•ran○di
mo•gul
mo•hair
Mo•ham•med
Mo•ham•med○an
Mo•ham•med•an•
  ism
Mo•hawk *n., pl.* Mo•
  hawks or Mohawk.
Mo•he•gan *n., pl.*
  Mo•he•gans or Mo•
  hegan.
Mo•hi•can *n., pl.*
  Mo•hi•cans or Mo•
  hi•can.
moi•e○ty *n., pl.* moi•
  e•ties.
moi○ré *n., pl.* moi•rés.
moist *adj.,* moist○er,
  moist•est.
mois•ten *v.,* mois•
  tened, mois•ten•
  ing.
moist•en○er
moist○ly
moist•ness
mois•ture
mois•tur•ize *v.,*
  mois•tur•ized,
  mois•tur•iz•ing.
mois•tur•iz○er
mo•lar
mo•las•ses
mold *v.,* mold○ed,
  mold•ing.
mold○er *v.,* mold•
  ered, mold•er•ing.
mold•ing
mold○y *adj.,* mold•
  i○er, mold•i•est.
mole
mo•lec○u•lar
mol○e•cule
mole•hill
mole•skin
mo•lest *v.,* mo•

lest•ed, mo•lest•
ing.
mo•les•ta•tion
mo•lest•er
Mo•liè̀e
moll
mol•li•fi•ca•tion
mol•li•fi◦er
mol•li◦fy v., mol•li•
fied, mol•li•fy•ing.
mol•lusk or mol•lusc
mol◦ly•cod•dle v.,
mol◦ly•cod•dled,
mol◦ly•cod•dling.
molt v., molt◦ed,
molt•ing.
mol•ten
mo•lyb•de•num
mom
mom-and-pop store
Business.
mo•ment
mo•men•tar•i◦ly
mo•men•tar◦y
mo•men•tous
mo•men•tous•ness
mo•men•tum n., pl.
mo•men◦ta or mo•
men•tums.
mom◦my or mom•
mie, n., pl. mom•
mies.
mommy track
Mon•a◦co
mon•arch
mo•nar•chi•cal or
mo•nar•chic
mon•ar•chism
mon•ar•chist
mon•ar•chist◦ic
mon•ar•chy n., pl.
mon•ar•chies.
mon•as•ter◦y n., pl.
mon•as•ter•ies.
mo•nas•tic
mo•nas•ti•cism

mon•au•ral
Mon•day
Mon•dri◦an
mon◦e•tar•i◦ly
mon◦e•ta•rism Busi-
ness.
mon◦e•ta•rist Busi-
ness.
mon◦e•tar◦y
mon◦ey
mon◦ey-chang◦er
Business.
money mar•ket Busi-
ness.
money of ac•count
Business.
money or•der Busi-
ness.
mon◦ey•bags
mon◦ey•eyed
mon◦ey•lend◦er Busi-
ness.
mon◦ey•mak◦er
mon◦ey•mak◦ing
mon•eys or mon•ies
mon•ger
Mon•gol
Mon•go•li◦a
Mon•go•li◦an
mon•gol•ism
Mon•gol•oid
mon•goose n., pl.
mon•goos◦es.
mon•grel
mon•ied
mon◦i•ker or mon•
ick◦er
mon•ism
mon•ist
mo•nis•tic
mon◦i•tor v., mon◦i•
tored, mon◦i•tor•
ing.
mon◦i•to◦ry
monk
mon•key n., pl. mon•

keys; v., mon•keyed,
mon•key•ing.
mon•key wrench
mon◦key•shines
mon◦o
mon◦o•chro•mat◦ic
mon◦o•chro•mat◦i•
cal◦ly
mon◦o•chrome
monochrome mon◦i•
tor Computers.
mon◦o•cle
mon◦o•cled
mon◦o•clo•nal
mon◦o•cot◦y•le•
don◦ous
mo•noc◦u•lar
mo•nog◦a•mous
mo•nog◦a•mous•ly
mo•nog◦a◦my
mon◦o•gram v.,
mon◦o•grammed,
mon◦o•gram•ming.
mon◦o•graph
mon◦o•lin•gual
mon◦o•lith
mon◦o•lith◦ic
mon◦o•log◦ist or
mon◦o•logu•ist
mon◦o•logue or
mon◦o•log
mon◦o•ma•ni◦a n.,
pl. mon◦o•ma•
ni◦as.
mon◦o•ma•ni◦ac
mon◦o•mer
mon◦o•nu•cle◦o•sis
mon◦o•phon◦ic
mo•nop◦o•list Busi-
ness.
mo•nop◦o•lis•tic
Business.
mo•nop◦o•lize v.,
mo•nop◦o•lized,
mo•nop◦o•liz•ing.
mo•nop◦o•ly n., pl.

mo•nop•o•lies.
Business.
mo•nop•so•ny *n., pl.*
mo•nop•so•nies.
Business.
mon•o•rail
mon•o•so•di•um
glu•ta•mate (MSG)
mon•o•spac•ing *Computers.*
mon•o•syl•lab•ic
mon•o•syl•la•ble
mon•o•the•ism
mon•o•the•ist
mon•o•the•is•tic
mon•o•tone
mo•not•o•nous
mo•not•o•nous•ly
mo•not•o•nous•ness
mo•not•o•ny
mon•ox•ide
Mon•roe
mon•sei•gneur *n., pl.*
mes•sei•gneurs.
mon•sieur *n., pl.*
mes•sieurs.
mon•si•gnor *n., pl.*
mon•si•gnors or
mon•si•gno•ri.
mon•soon
mon•ster
mon•stros•i•ty
mon•strous
mon•tage *n., pl.*
mon•tag•es.
Mon•tan•a (MT)
Mon•tan•an
Mon•te Car•lo
Mon•tes•so•ri
meth•od
Mon•te•vi•de•o
Mont•gom•er•y
month
month•ly *n., pl.*
month•lies.
Mont•pel•ier

Mont•re•al
mon•u•ment
mon•u•men•tal
mon•u•men•tal•ly
moo *n., pl.* moos; *v.,*
mooed, moo•ing.
mooch *v.,* mooched,
mooch•ing.
mooch•er
mood
mood•i•ly
mood•i•ness
mood•y *adj.,* mood•
i•er, mood•i•est.
moon
moon•beam
moon•light
moon•lit
moon•scape
moon•shine
moon•shot or moon
shot
moon•stone
moon•struck
moon•walk
moor *v.,* moored,
moor•ing.
Moor•ish
moose *n., pl.* moose.
(the animal: cf. MOUSE;
MOUSSE)
moot (debatable: cf.
MUTE)
mop *v.,* mopped,
mop•ping.
mope *v.,* moped,
mop•ing. (brooded)
mo•ped (motorized bi-
cycle with pedals)
mop•pet
mo•raine
mor•al (ethical)
mo•rale (mood)
mor•al•ist
mor•al•is•tic
mor•al•is•ti•cal•ly

mo•ral•i•ty *n., pl.*
mo•ral•i•ties.
mor•al•ize *v.,* mor•
al•ized, mor•al•iz•
ing.
mor•al•ly
mo•rass
mor•a•to•ri•um *n.,*
pl. mor•a•to•ri•a or
mor•a•to•ri•ums.
mo•ray *n., pl.* mo•
rays.
mor•bid
mor•bid•i•ty
mor•bid•ly
mor•dan•cy
mor•dant
more *adj.,* more, most.
mo•rel
more•o•ver
mo•res
morgue
mor•i•bund
Mor•mon
Mor•mon•ism
morn (morning: cf.
MOURN)
morn•ing (early part of
day: cf. MOURNING)
morn•ing glo•ry or
morn•ing-glo•ry
Mo•roc•can
Mo•roc•co
mo•ron
mo•ron•ic
mo•ron•i•cal•ly
mo•rose
mo•rose•ly
mo•rose•ness
mor•pheme
mor•phe•mic
mor•phine
mor•pho•log•i•cal
mor•phol•o•gy
mor•row
Morse code

mor•sel

mor•tal

mor•tal•i•ty *n.*, *pl.*
mor•tal•i•ties.

mor•tal•ly

mor•tar *v.*, mor•
tared, mor•tar•ing.

mor•tar•board

mort•gage *v.*, mort•
gaged, mort•gag•
ing. *Business.*

mortgage bond *Busi-
ness.*

mort•ga•gee *Business.*

mort•ga•gor or
mort•gag•er *Busi-
ness.*

mor•ti•cian

mor•ti•fi•ca•tion

mor•ti•fy *v.*, mor•ti•
fied, mor•ti•fy•ing.

mor•tise

mor•tu•ar•y *n.*, *pl.*
mor•tu•ar•ar•ies.

mo•sa•ic (inlaid stone)

Mo•sa•ic (of Moses)

Mos•cow

Mo•ses

mo•sey *v.*, mo•seyed,
mo•sey•ing.

mosh

mosh pit

Mos•lem *n.*, *pl.* Mos•
lems, Mos•lem.

mosque

mos•qui•to *n.*, *pl.*
mos•qui•toes or
mos•qui•tos.

moss

moss•back

moss•y *adj.*, moss•
i•er, moss•i•est.

most

most•ly

mote (speck: cf. MOAT)

mo•tel

mo•tet

moth *n.*, *pl.* moths.

moth•ball *v.*, moth•
balled, moth•ball•
ing.

moth•er *v.*, moth•
ered, moth•er•ing.

moth•er-in-law *n.*, *pl.*
moth•ers-•in-•law.

moth•er-of-pearl

moth•er•board *Com-
puters.*

moth•er•hood

moth•er•land

moth•er•less

moth•er•li•ness

moth•er•ly

mo•tif (theme: cf. MO-
TIVE)

mo•tile

mo•til•i•ty

mo•tion *v.*, mo•
tioned, mo•tion•ing.

motion pic•ture

mo•tion•less

mo•ti•vate *v.*, mo•ti•
vat•ed, mo•ti•vat•
ing.

mo•ti•va•tion

mo•ti•va•tion•al

mo•tive (purpose: cf.
MOTIF)

mot•ley

mo•to•cross

mo•tor *v.*, mo•tored,
mo•tor•ing.

mo•tor•bike

mo•tor•boat

mo•tor•cade

mo•tor•car

mo•tor•cy•cle *v.*,
mo•tor•cy•cled,
mo•tor•cy•cling.

mo•tor•cy•clist

mo•tor•ist

mo•tor•man *n.*, *pl.*
mo•tor•men.

mot•tle *v.*, mot•tled,
mot•tling.

mo•to *n.*, *pl.* mot•
toes or mot•tos.

moue *n.*, *pl.* moues.

mound

mount

moun•tain

Moun•tain stand•ard
time (MST)

moun•tain•eer

moun•tain•ous

moun•tain•top

moun•te•bank

Moun•tie *n.*, *pl.*
Moun•ties.

mount•ing

mourn *v.*, mourned,
mourn•ing. (to
grieve: cf. MORN)

mourn•er

mourn•ful

mourn•ful•ly

mourn•ing (grieving:
cf. MORNING)

mouse *n.*, *pl.* mice.
(the rodent: cf. MOOSE;
MOUSSE)

mouse point•er *Com-
puters.*

mouse•pad *Computers.*

mous•er

mouse•trap

mous•i•ness

mousse (whipped des-
sert: cf. MOOSE; MOUSE)

mous•tache

mous•y *adj.*, mous•
i•er, mous•i•est.

mouth *n.*, *pl.* mouths;
v., mouthed, mouth•
ing.

mouth-wa•ter•ing

mouth•ful *n.*, *pl.*
mouth•fuls.

mouth•part

mouth•piece

mouth•wash
mou•ton (sheepskin fur: cf. MUTTON)
mov•a•ble or move•a•ble
movable rul•er *Computers.*
move *v.,* moved, mov•ing.
move•ment
mov•er
mov•ie
mov•ing
mov•ing-bar men•u *Computers.*
mow *v.,* mowed, mowed or mown, mow•ing. (cut down: cf. MODE)
Mo•zam•bique
Mo•zart
Mo•zar•te•an
moz•za•rel•la
mpg or m.p.g. (miles per gallon).
mph or m.p.h. (miles per hour).
Mr. *n.,* pl. Messrs.
MRI (magnetic resonance imaging)
Mrs. *n.,* pl. Mmes.
MS (Mississippi)
Ms. *n.,* pl. Mses.
MSG (monosodium glutamate)
MSI *Business.* (Marketing Science Institute)
MST or M.S.T. (Mountain standard time).
MT (Montana)
MTBF *Computers.* (mean time between failures)
mtg. (mortgage)
mu
much *adj.*
mu•ci•lage

mu•ci•lag•i•nous
muck
muck•rak•er
mu•cous (of mucus)
mu•cus
mud
mud•di•ness
mud•dle *v.,* mud•dled, mud•dling.
mud•dle•head•ed
mud•dy *v.,* mud•died, mud•dy•ing; *adj.,* mud•di•er, mud•di•est.
mud•sling•ing
muen•ster
mu•ez•zin
muff *v.,* muffed, muff•ing.
muf•fin
muf•fle
muf•fler
muf•ti *n.,* pl. muf•tis.
mug *v.,* mugged, mug•ging.
mug•ger
mug•gi•ness
mug•gy *adj.,* mug•gi•er, mug•gi•est.
mug•wump
Mu•ham•mad
Mu•ham•mad•an
Mu•ham•mad•an•ism
muk•luk
mu•lat•to *n.,* pl. mu•lat•toes.
mul•ber•ry *n.,* pl. mul•ber•ries.
mulch
mulct
mule
mu•le•teer
mul•ish
mull *v.,* mulled, mull•ing.

mul•lah *n.,* pl. mul•lahs.
mul•lein
mul•let *n.,* pl. mul•let or mul•lets.
mul•li•gan stew
mul•li•ga•taw•ny
mul•lion
mul•ti•dis•ci•pli•nar•y
mul•ti•far•i•ous
mul•ti•far•i•ous•ly
mul•ti•far•i•ous•ness
mul•ti•form
mul•ti•fre•quen•cy mon•i•tor *Computers.*
mul•ti•func•tion pe•riph•er•al *Computers.*
mul•ti•me•di•a
mul•ti•na•tion•al
mul•ti•ple
mul•ti•ple-choice
mul•ti•ple scle•ro•sis
mul•ti•plex *v.,* mul•ti•plexed, mul•ti•plex•ing.
mul•ti•pli•cand
mul•ti•pli•ca•tion
mul•ti•plic•i•ty *n.,* pl. mul•ti•plic•i•ties.
mul•ti•pli•er
multiplier ef•fect *Business.*
mul•ti•ply *v.,* mul•ti•plied, mul•ti•ply•ing.
mul•ti•proc•ess•ing *Computers.*
mul•ti•scan•ning mon•i•tor *Computers.*
mul•ti•stage
mul•ti•task•ing *Computers.*
mul•ti•tude

mul•ti•tu•di•nous

mul•ti•us•er *Comput-
ers.*

mul•ti•vi•ta•min

mum

mum•ble *v.,* mum•
bled, mum•bling.

mum•bler

mum•ble•ty•peg

mum•bo jum•bo

mum•mer

mum•mi•fi•ca•tion

mum•mi•fy *v.,* mum•
mi•fied, mum•mi•
fy•ing.

mum•my *n., pl.*
mum•mies; *v.,*
mum•mied, mum•
my•ing.

mumps

munch *v.,* munched,
munch•ing.

mun•dane

Mu•nich

mu•nic•i•pal

municipal bond *Busi-
ness.*

mu•nic•i•pal•i•ty *n.,
pl.* mu•nic•i•pal•i•
ties.

mu•nif•i•cence

mu•nif•i•cent

mu•nif•i•cent•ly

mu•ni•tions

mu•ral

mu•ral•ist

mur•der *v.,* mur•
dered, mur•der•ing.

mur•der•er

mur•der•ess

mur•der•ous

mur•der•ous•ly

mu•ri•at•ic ac•id

murk

murk•i•ly

murk•i•ness

murk•y *adj.,* murk•
i•er, murk•i•est.

mur•mur *v.,* mur•
mured, mur•mur•
ing.

mur•rain

mus•ca•tel

mus•cle *v.,* muscled,
muscling. (body tis-
sue: cf. MUSSEL)

mus•cle•bound

mus•cu•lar

mus•cu•lar dys•tro•
phy

mus•cu•lar•i•ty

mus•cu•la•ture

muse *v.,* mused, mus•
ing.

mu•sette

mu•se•um

mush *v.,* mushed,
mush•ing.

mush•i•ness

mush•room *v.,* mush•
roomed, mush•
room•ing.

mush•y *adj.,* mush•
i•er, mush•i•est.

mu•sic

mu•si•cal (of music)

mu•si•cale (musical
gathering)

mu•si•cal•i•ty

mu•si•cal•ly

mu•si•cian

mu•si•cian•ship

mu•si•col•o•gist

mu•si•col•o•gy

musk

mus•keg

mus•kel•lunge *n., pl.*
mus•kel•lung•es or
mus•kel•lunge.

mus•ket

mus•ket•eer

mus•ket•ry

musk•i•ness

musk•mel•on

musk•ox or musk ox,
n., pl. musk•ox•en.

musk•rat *n., pl.*
musk•rats or musk•
rat.

Mus•lim *n., pl.* Mus•
lims or Mus•lim. (ad-
herent of the religion)

mus•lin (cotton fabric)

muss *v.,* mussed,
muss•ing.

mus•sel

Mus•so•li•ni

muss•y *adj.,* muss•
i•er, muss•i•est.

must

mus•tache or mous•
tache

mus•tached

mus•tang

mus•tard

mus•ter *v.,* mus•
tered, mus•ter•ing.
(gathered)

mus•ti•ness

must•n't

mus•ty *adj.,* must•
i•er, must•i•est.

mu•ta•bil•i•ty

mu•ta•ble

mu•tant

mu•tate *v.,* mu•
tat•ed, mu•tat•ing.

mu•ta•tion

mute *adj.,* mut•er,
mut•est; *v.,* mut•ed,
mut•ing. (silent: cf.
MOOT)

mute•ly

mute•ness

mu•ti•late *v.,* mu•ti•
lat•ed, mu•ti•lat•
ing.

mu•ti•la•tion

mu•ti•neer

mu•ti•nous

mu•ti•ny n., pl. mu•ti•nies; v., mu•ti•nied, mu•ti•ny•ing.

mutt

mut•ter v., mut•tered, mut•ter•ing.

mut•ton

mut•ton•chops

mu•tu•al

mutual fund Business.

mu•tu•al•ly

muu•muu n., pl. muu•muus.

muz•zle v., muz•zled, muz•zling.

my

My•an•mar

my•as•the•ni•a

my•as•then•ic

my•col•o•gist

my•col•o•gy

my•e•li•tis

My•lar Trademark.

my•na or my•nah n., pl. my•nas or my•nahs.

my•o•pi•a

my•op•ic

myr•i•ad

myrrh

myr•tle

my•self

mys•te•ri•ous

mys•te•ri•ous•ly

mys•ter•y n., pl. mys•ter•ies.

mys•tic

mys•ti•cal

mys•ti•cal•ly

mys•ti•cism

mys•ti•fi•ca•tion

mys•ti•fy v., mys•ti•fied, mys•ti•fy•ing.

mys•tique

myth

myth•i•cal

myth•o•log•i•cal

my•thol•o•gist

my•thol•o•gy n., pl. my•thol•o•gies.

N

N-•bomb (neutron bomb)

NA or N.A. (not applicable).

nab v., nabbed, nab•bing.

na•bob

na•cre•ous

na•dir

nag v., nagged, nag•ging.

Na•hua•tl

nai•ad n., pl. nai•ads or nai•a•des.

nail v., nailed, nail•ing.

Nai•ro•bi

na•ive or na•ïve

na•ive•ly

na•ive•té or na•ïve•té

na•ked

na•ked•ly

na•ked•ness

nam•by-pam•by n.,

pl. nam•by-pam•bies.

name v., named, nam•ing.

name brand Business.

name•a•ble

name•less

name•ly

name•plate

name•sake

Na•mib•i•a

Na•mib•i•an

nan•keen

Nan•king

nan•ny n., pl. nan•nies.

nan•o•sec•ond

nap v., napped, nap•ping.

na•palm v., na•palmed, na•palm•ing.

nape

naph•tha

naph•tha•lene or naph•tha•line

nap•kin

Na•ples

na•po•le•on

Na•po•le•on•ic

narc or nark

nar•cis•sism

nar•cis•sist (self-centered person)

nar•cis•sis•tic

nar•cis•sus n., pl. nar•cis•sus or nar•cis•sus•es or nar•cis•si. (the flower)

nar•co•sis

nar•co•ter•ror•ism

nar•cot•ic

nar•co•tize v., nar•co•tized, nar•co•tiz•ing.

nar•oes n., pl. nar•ois.

nar•rate v., nar•rat•ed, nar•rat•ing.

nar•ra•tion

nar•ra•tive

nar•ra•tor

nar•row v., nar•

rowed, nar•row•
ing; *adj.*, nar•
row•er, nar•row•
est.
nar•row-mind∘ed
nar•row-
mind∘ed∘ness
nar•row∘ly
nar•whal
nar∘y
NASA (National Aero-
nautics and Space Ad-
ministration)
na•sal
na•sal•i∘ty
na•sal•i∘za•tion
na•sal•ize *v.*, na•sal•
ized, na•sal•iz•ing.
na•sal∘ly
nas•cence
nas•cent
NASDAQ *Business.* (Na-
tional Association of
Securities Dealers Au-
tomated Quotations)
Nash•ville
nas•ti∘ly
nas•ti•ness
nas•tur•tium *n.*, *pl.*
nas•tur•tiums.
nas∘ty *n.*, *pl.* nas•ties;
adj., nas•ti∘er, nas•
ti∘est.
na•tal
na•tes *n.pl.*
na•tion
na•tion∘al
national bank *Busi-
ness.*
national brand *Busi-
ness.*
national debt *Business.*
na•tion•al•ism
na•tion•al•ist
na•tion•al•is•tic
na•tion•al•i∘ty *n.*, *pl.*
na•tion•al•i•ties.

na•tion•al∘i∘za•tion
na•tion•al•ize *v.*, na•
tion•al•ized, na•
tion•al•iz•ing.
na•tion•al∘ly
na•tion•hood
na•tion•wide
na•tive
Na•tive A∘mer∘i•can
na•tiv•ism
na•tiv•i∘ty *n.*, *pl.* na•
tiv•i•ties.
nat∘ty *adj.*, nat•ti∘er,
nat•ti∘est.
nat∘u∘ral
natural se•lec•tion
nat∘u∘ral•ism
nat∘u∘ral•ist
nat∘u∘ral•is•tic
nat∘u∘ral•i∘za•tion
nat∘u∘ral•ize *v.*,
nat∘u∘ral•ized,
nat∘u∘ral•iz•ing.
nat∘u∘ral∘ly
na•ture
Nau•ga•hyde *Trade-
mark.*
naught or nought (cf.
NOUGHAT)
naugh•ti∘ly
naugh•ti•ness
naugh∘ty *adj.*,
naugh•ti∘er,
naugh•ti∘est.
nau•se∘a
nau•se•ate *v.*, nau•
se•at∘ed, nau•se•
at•ing.
nau•se•at•ing∘ly
nau•seous
nau•ti•cal
nau•ti•cal∘ly
nau•ti•lus *n.*, *pl.* nau•
ti•lus∘es or nau•
ti∘li.
Nav•a∘jo or Nav•
a∘ho *n.*, *pl.* Nav•a•

jos or Nav•a•joes or
Nav•a∘jo; Nav•a•
hos or Nav•a•hoes
or Nav•a•ho.
na•val (of a ship)
nave (church area: cf.
KNAVE)
na•vel (umbilicus)
navel or•ange
nav∘i•ga•bil•i∘ty
nav∘i•ga∘ble
nav∘i•gate *v.*, nav∘i•
gat∘ed, nav∘i•gat•
ing.
nav∘i•ga•tion
nav∘i•ga•tor
na•vy *n.*, *pl.* na•vies.
nay (no: cf. NEIGH; NEE)
nay•say∘er
Naz∘a∘reth
Na∘zi *n.*, *pl.* Na•zis.
Na•zism
NBS or **N.B.S.** (National
Bureau of Standards).
NC (North Carolina)
n/c or NC (no charge)
NC-17 (motion-picture
rating)
ND (North Dakota)
NE (Nebraska)
ne plus ul•tra
Ne•an•der•thal
neap
Ne•a•pol∘i•tan
near *v.*, neared, near•
ing; *adj.*, near∘er,
near•est.
near-let∘ter qual•i∘ty
Computers.
near mon∘ey *Business.*
near∘by
near∘ly
near•ness
near•sight∘ed
near•sight•ed•ness

neat *adj.*, neat∘er, neat•est.

neath or 'neath

neat∘ly

neat•ness

Ne•bras∘ka (NE)

Ne•bras•kan

neb•u∘la *n., pl.* neb•u•lae or neb•u•las.

neb∘u•lar

neb∘u•lous

nec•es•sar•i∘ly

nec•es•sar∘y

ne•ces•si•tate *v.*, ne•ces•si•tat∘ed, ne•ces•si•tat•ing.

ne•ces•si∘ty *n., pl.* ne•ces•si•ties.

neck *v.*, necked, neck•ing.

neck•er•chief

neck•lace

neck•line

neck•tie

ne•crol•o∘gy *n., pl.* ne•crol•o•gies.

nec∘ro•man•cer

nec∘ro•man∘cy

ne•crop∘o•lis *n., pl.* ne•crop∘o•lis∘es.

ne•cro∘sis

ne•crot∘ic

nec•tar

nec•tar•ine

nee or née (born: cf. NAY; NEIGH)

need *v.*, need∘ed, need•ing, needs or need. (to require: cf. KNEAD)

need•ful

need∘i•ness

nee•dle *v.*, nee•dled, nee•dling.

needle trades *Business.*

nee∘dle•point

need•less

need•less∘ly

need•less•ness

nee∘dle•work

need∘n't

needs

need∘y *adj.*, need•i∘er, need•i•est.

ne'er

ne'er-do-well

ne•far∘i•ous

ne•gate *v.*, ne•gat∘ed, ne•gat•ing.

ne•ga•tion

neg∘a•tive

negative float *Business.*

negative in•come *Business.*

negative income tax *Business.*

negative op•tion *Business.*

neg∘a•tive∘ly

neg∘a•tive•ness

neg∘a•tiv•ism

neg∘a•tiv•i∘ty

ne•glect *v.*, ne•glect∘ed, ne•glect•ing.

ne•glect•ful

ne•glect•ful∘ly

neg•li•gee or neg•li•gée *n., pl.* neg•li•gees or neg•li•gées.

neg•li•gence

neg•li•gent (careless)

neg•li•gent∘ly

neg•li•gi∘ble (unimportant)

ne•go•ti•a•bil•i∘ty

ne•go•ti•a∘ble

negotiable bond *Business.*

negotiable in•stru•ment *Business.*

ne•go•ti•ate *v.*, ne•go•ti•at∘ed, ne•go•ti•at•ing.

ne•go•ti•a•tion

ne•go•ti•a•tor

Neg•ri∘tude

Ne•gro *n., pl.* Ne•groes.

Ne•groid

Neh∘ru

neigh (whinny: cf. NAY; NEE)

neigh•bor

neigh•bor•hood

neigh•bor•ing

neigh•bor•li•ness

neigh•bor∘ly

nei•ther (not either: cf. NETHER)

nel•son

nem∘a•tode

nem∘e•sis *n., pl.* nem∘e•ses.

ne∘o•clas•si•cal

ne∘o•clas•si•cism

ne∘o•co•lo•ni•al

ne∘o•co•lo•ni•al•ism

ne∘o•dym•i∘um

Ne∘o•lith∘ic

ne•ol∘o∘gism

ne∘on

ne∘o•na•tal

ne∘o•nate

ne∘o•phyte

ne∘o•plasm

ne∘o•plas•tic

ne∘o•prene

Ne•pal

Nep∘a•lese

ne•pen•the

neph∘ew

neph•rite

ne•phrit∘ic

ne•phri•tis

nep∘o•tism

nep•o•tist
Nep•tune
nep•tu•ni•um
nerd
nerd•y *adj.*, nerd•i•er, nerd•i•est.
Ne•ro
nerve *v.*, nerved, nerv•ing.
nerve cell
nerve•less
nerv•ous
nerv•ous•ly
nerv•ous•ness
nerv•y *adj.*, nerv•i•er, nerv•i•est.
nest *v.*, nest•ed, nest•ing.
nest•er
nes•tle *v.*, nes•tled, nes•tling. (pressing affectionately)
nest•ling (young bird)
net *v.*, net•ted, net•ting.
net earn•ings *Business.*
net in•come *Business.*
net prof•it *Business.*
net sales *Business.*
net worth *Business.*
neth•er (lower: cf. NEI-THER)
neth•erworld or neth•er•world
Neth•er•lands
neth•er•most
net•ting
net•tle
net•tle•some
net•work *v.*, net•worked, net•work•ing.
network com•put•er
network in•ter•face card *Computers.*

network serv•er *Computers.*
net•work•er
net•work•ing
neu•ral
neu•ral net•work *Computers.*
neu•ral•gia
neu•ral•gic
neur•as•the•ni•a
neur•as•then•ic
neu•ri•tis
neu•ro•im•mu•nol•o•gy
neu•ro•log•i•cal
neu•rol•o•gist
neu•rol•o•gy
neu•ron
neu•ron•al
neu•ro•sis *n.*, *pl.* neu•ro•ses.
neu•ro•sur•geon
neu•ro•sur•ger•y
neu•rot•ic
neu•rot•ic•al•ly
neu•rot•i•cism
neu•ro•trans•mit•ter
neu•ter *v.*, neu•tered, neu•ter•ing. (asexual)
neu•tral (not taking sides)
neu•tral•ism
neu•tral•ist
neu•tral•i•ty
neu•tral•i•za•tion
neu•tral•ize *v.*, neu•tral•ized, neu•tral•iz•ing.
neu•tral•ly
neu•tri•no *n.*, *pl.* neu•tri•nos.
neu•tron
Ne•vad•a (NV)
Ne•vad•an
nev•er

nev•er-nev•er land
nev•er•more
nev•er•the•less
ne•vus *n.*, *pl.* ne•vi.
new *adj.*, new•er, new•est. (recent: cf. GNU; KNEW)
New Bed•ford
New Bruns•wick
new-col•lar
New Eng•land
New Eng•land•er
new-fash•ioned
New Hamp•shire (NH)
New Hamp•shir•ite
New Jer•sey (NJ)
New Jer•sey•ite
New Mex•ico (NM)
New Or•le•ans
New Tes•ta•ment
New York (NY)
New York Stock Ex•change (NYSE) *Business.*
New York•er
New Zea•land
New Zea•land•er
New•ark
new•born *n.*, *pl.* new•born or new•borns.
new•com•er
new•el
new•fan•gled
New•found•land
new•ly
new•ly•wed
new•ness
New•port News
news
news•boy
news•cast
news•cast•er
news•deal•er
news•let•ter

news•man *n., pl.*
  news•men.
news•pa•per
news•pa•per•man *n.,*
  pl. newspaper•men.
news•pa•per•
  wom•an *n., pl.*
  newspaper•
  wom•en.
new•speak
news•print
news•reel
news•stand
news•wor•thi•ness
news•wor•thy
news•y *adj.,* news•
  i•er, news•i•est.
newt
new•ton
New•to•ni•an
next
next-door
nex•us *n., pl.* nex•us.
Nez Percé *n., pl.* Nez
  Per•cés *or* Nez Percé.
NF (no funds)
NH (New Hampshire)
ni•a•cin
Ni•ag•a•ra Falls
nib
nib•ble *v.,* nib•bled,
  nib•bling.
nibs
Nic•a•ra•gua
Nic•a•ra•guan
nice *adj.,* nic•er, nic•
  est.
nice•ly
nice•ness
ni•ce•ty *n., pl.* ni•
  ce•ties.
niche (recess)
nick (dent; to dent)
nick•el *v.,* nick•eled
  or nick•elled, nick•

el•ing *or* nick•el•
  ling.
nick•el•o•de•on
nick•er *v.,* nick•ered,
  nick•er•ing.
nick•name *v.,* nick•
  named, nick•nam•
  ing.
nic•o•tine
nic•o•tin•ic ac•id
niece
Nie•tzsche
nif•ty *adj.,* nif•ti•er,
  nif•ti•est.
Ni•ger
Ni•ge•ri•a
Ni•ge•ri•an
nig•gard•ly
nig•gling
nigh
night (darkness: cf.
  KNIGHT)
night•cap
night•clothes
night•club *v.,* night•
  clubbed, night•club•
  bing.
night•fall
night•gown
night•hawk
night•ie *n., pl.* night•
  ies.
night•in•gale
night•ly
night•mare
night•mar•ish
night•shade
night•shirt
night•spot
night•time
night•walk•er
ni•hil•ism
ni•hil•ist
ni•hil•is•tic
nil
Nile

nim•ble
nim•ble•ness
nim•bly
nim•bus *n., pl.* nim•bi
  or nim•bus•es.
Nim•rod
nin•com•poop
nine
nine•pins
nine•teen
nine•teenth
nine•ti•eth
nine•ty *n., pl.* nine•
  ties.
nin•ny *n., pl.* nin•
  nies.
Nin•ten•do *Trade-*
  mark.
ninth
ni•o•bi•um
nip *v.,* nipped, nip•
  ping.
nip•per
nip•ple
Nip•pon
Nip•pon•ese
nip•py *adj.,* nip•
  pi•er, nip•pi•est.
nir•va•na
Ni•sei *n., pl.* Ni•sei.
ni•si
nit (insect egg: cf. KNIT)
ni•ter
nit•pick *or* nit-pick, *v.,*
  nit•picked, nit•pick•
  ing *or* nit•pick•ing.
nit•pick•er
ni•trate
ni•tric ac•id
ni•tri•fy, *v.,* ni•tri•
  fied, ni•tri•fy•ing.
ni•trite
ni•tro•cel•lu•lose
ni•tro•gen
ni•trog•e•nous
ni•tro•glyc•er•in

ni•trous ox•ide
nit∘ty-grit∘ty
nit•wit
nix *v.*, nixed, nix•ing.
Nix∘on
NJ (New Jersey)
NLRB *Business.* (National Labor Relations Board)
NM (New Mexico)
No
no[1] (negative: cf. KNOW)
no[2] *n.*, *pl.* noes or nos.
no-brain∘er
no-fault in•sur•ance *Business.*
no-frills serv•ice *Business.*
no-good
no-load fund *Business.*
no-name
no-no *n.*, *pl.* no-nos or no-no's.
no-non∘sense
no one
no-show
no-trump
no-win
No∘ah
No•bel prize
No•bel•ist
no•bel•i∘um
no•bil•i∘ty
no•ble *adj.*, no•bler, no•blest.
no∘ble•man *n.*, *pl.* no∘ble•men.
no∘ble•ness
no•blesse o∘blige
no∘ble•wom∘an *n.*, *pl.* no∘ble•wom∘en.
no•bly
no•bod∘y *n.*, *pl.* no•bod•ies.
noc•tur•nal
noc•turne

nod *v.*, nod•ded, nod•ding.
nod∘al
node
nod∘u•lar
nod•ule
No∘el
no-fault *Business.*
nog•gin
noise *v.*, noised, nois•ing.
noise•less
noise•less∘ly
noise•mak∘er
nois•i∘ly
nois•i•ness
noi•some (obnoxious)
nois∘y *adj.*, nois•i∘er, nois•i•est. (loud)
nol∘le pros∘e∘qui
no∘lo con•ten•de∘re
nom de plume *n.*, *pl.* noms de plume.
no•mad
no•mad∘ic
no•men•cla•ture
no•men•kla•tu∘ra
nom∘i•nal
nominal cap∘i•tal *Business.*
nominal val∘ue *Business.*
nominal wag∘es *Business.*
nom∘i•nal∘ly
nom∘i•nate *v.*, nom∘i•nat∘ed, nom∘i•nat•ing.
nom∘i•na•tion
nom∘i•na•tive
nom∘i•nee
non com•pos men•tis
non se•qui•tur
non trop∘po
non-∘U (not upperclass)

non•age
non∘a•ge•nar•i∘an
non•a∘ligned
non•a∘lign•ment
non•ap•pear•ance
nonce
non•cha•lance
non•cha•lant
non•cha•lant∘ly
non•com
non•com•bat•ant
non•com•mis•sioned of•ficer
non•com•mit•tal
non•com•mit•tal∘ly
non•con•duc•tor
non•con•form•ist
non•con•form•i∘ty
non•con•trib∘u•to∘ry *Business.*
non•co∘op∘er•a∘tion or non∘co-op∘er∘a∘tion
non•cu•mu•la•tive *Business.*
non•cur•rent *Business.*
non•dair∘y *Business.*
non•de•duc•ti•ble
non•de•script
none (not one: cf. NUN)
non•en•ti∘ty *n.*, *pl.* non•en•ti•ties.
none•such
none•the•less
non•e∘vent
non•fat
non•fic•tion
non•im•pact print∘er *Computers.*
non•in∘ter•ac•tive pro•gram *Computers.*
non•in∘ter•laced mon∘i•tor *Computers.*
non•in∘ter•ven•tion

non•met∘al
non•ob∘jec•tive
non•op•er∘a•tive *Business.*
non•pa∘reil
non•par•ti•san
non•per•son
non•plus *v.,* non•plussed or non•plused, non•plus•sing or non•plus•ing.
non•prof∘it *Business.*
non•pro•lif•er•a•tion
non•re•cur•ring charge *Business.*
non•res∘i•dent
non•re•stric•tive
non•sched•uled
non•sec•tar•i∘an
non•sense
non•sen•si•cal
non•sen•si•cal∘ly
non•sex•ist
non•skid
non•stand•ard
non•stick
non•stop
non•sup•port
non•tax•a∘ble *Business.*
non•un•ion
non•vi∘o•lence
non•vi∘o•lent
non•vol∘a•tile mem∘o∘ry *Computers.*
noo•dle
nook
noon
noon•light•ing
noose
nope
nor
Nor•dic

norm
nor•mal
nor•mal•ize *v.,* nor•mal•ized, nor•mal•iz•ing.
nor•mal∘ly
Nor•man
Nor•man∘dy
nor•ma•tive
norm•ing
Nor•plant *Trademark.*
Norse
Norse•man *n., pl.* Norse•men.
north
North A∘mer∘i∘ca
North Car∘o∘li∘na (NC)
North Car∘o∘lin•i∘an
North Da•ko∘ta (ND)
North Da•ko•tan
north•east
north•east∘er
north•east•ern
north•er∘ly
north•ern
north•ern∘er
north•ern•most
north•ward
north•west
north•west•er∘ly
north•west•ern
Nor•way
Nor•we•gian
nos. or Nos. (numbers).
nose *n., v.,* nosed, nos•ing. (organ of smell: cf. KNOWS; NOES)
nose•bleed
nose-dive *v.,* nose-dived, nose-div•ing.
nose•gay
nosh
nos•i∘ly
nos∘i•ness
nos•tal•gia

nos•tal•gic
nos•tal•gi•cal∘ly
nos•tril
nos•trum
nos∘y or nos∘ey, *adj.,* nos•i∘er, nos•i•est.
not (no: cf. KNOT)
no∘ta be∘ne
no•ta•ble
no•ta•bly
no•ta•ri•za•tion
no•ta•rize *v.,* no•ta•rized, no•ta•riz•ing.
no•ta∘ry *n., pl.* no•ta•ries.
no•ta•tion
notch
notch ba∘by
note *v.,* not∘ed, not•ing.
note•book
notebook com•put∘er *Computers.*
not∘ed
note-pa•per
notes re•ceiv•a∘ble *Business.*
note•wor•thy
noth•ing
noth•ing•ness
no•tice *v.,* no•ticed, no•tic•ing.
no•tice•a∘ble
no•tice•a•bly
no•ti•fi•ca•tion
no•ti•fy *v.,* no•ti•fied, no•ti•fy•ing.
no•tion
no•tion•al
no•to•ri•e∘ty
no•to•ri•ous
no•to•ri•ous∘ly
not•with•stand•ing
nou•gat (the candy)
nought (nothing)
noun

nour•ish v., nour•
ished, nour•ish•ing.
nour•ish•ment
nou•veau riche n., pl.
nou•veaux riches.
nou•velle cui•sine
no•va n., pl. no•vas
or no•vae.
No•va Sco•tia
No•va Sco•tian
no•va•tion
nov•el
nov•el•ette
nov•el•ist
nov•el•oi•za•tion
nov•el•ize v., novel•
ized, novel•iz•ing.
no•vel•la n., pl. no•
vel•las.
nov•el•ty n., pl. nov•
el•ties.
No•vem•ber
no•ve•na
nov•ice
no•vi•ti•ate
No•vo•caine Trade-
mark.
now
NOW ac•count Busi-
ness. (negotiable order
of withdrawal ac-
count)
now•a•days
no•where
no•wise
nox•ious
noz•zle (spout: cf. NUZ-
ZLE)
NSF Business. (not suffi-
cient funds)
NSFnet Computers. (Na-
tional Science Founda-
tion network)
nt. wt. (net weight)
nth
nu•ance
nub•bin

nub•by adj., nub•
bi•er, nub•bi•est.
nu•bile
nu•cle•ar
nuclear re•ac•tor
nu•cle•ate v., nu•
cle•at•ed, nu•cle•
at•ing.
nu•cle•a•tion
nu•cle•ic ac•id
nu•cle•o•lar
nu•cle•o•lus n., pl.
nu•cle•o•li.
nu•cle•on
nu•cle•ous n., pl. nu•
cle•i or nu•cle•
us•es.
nude adj., nud•er,
nud•est.
nudge v., nudged,
nudg•ing.
nud•ism
nud•ist
nu•di•ty
nu•ga•to•ry
nug•get
nui•sance
nuisance tax
nuke v., nuked, nuk•
ing.
null
null char•ac•ter Com-
puters.
null-mo•dem ca•ble
Computers.
nul•li•fi•ca•tion
nul•li•fy v., nul•li•
fied, nul•li•fy•ing.
nul•li•ty
numb v., numbed,
numb•ing.
numb•er¹ adj., numb•
est. (more incapable
of sensation)
num•ber² (figure; to
count)

number crunch•ing
Computers.
num•bered ac•count
Business.
num•ber•less
numb•ly
numb•ness
nu•mer•o•a•cy
nu•mer•al
nu•mer•a•tor
nu•mer•ic key•pad
Computers.
numeric mode Com-
puters.
nu•mer•i•cal or nu•
mer•ic
nu•mer•i•cal•ly
nu•mer•ol•o•gist
nu•mer•ol•o•gy
nu•mer•ous
nu•mis•mat•ics
nu•mis•ma•tist
num•skull or numb•
skull
nun (woman in reli-
gious order: cf. NONE)
nun•ci•o n., pl. nun•
ci•os.
nun•ner•y n., pl.
nun•ner•ies.
nup•tial
nurse v., nursed,
nurs•ing.
nurse•maid
nurs•er•y n., pl.
nurs•er•ies.
nurs•er•y•man n., pl.
nurs•er•y•men.
nurs•ling or nurse•
ling
nur•ture v., nur•
tured, nur•tur•ing.
nut
nut•crack•er
nut•hatch
nut•meat
nut•meg

nut•pick
nu•tri•a
nu•tri•ent
nu•tri•ment
nu•tri•tion
nu•tri•tion•al
nu•tri•tion•al•ly
nu•tri•tion•ist
nu•tri•tious
nu•tri•tious•ly
nu•tri•tious•ness

nu•tri•tive
nuts
nut•shell
nut•ti•ly
nut•ti•ness
nut•ty adj., nut•ti•er,
  nut•ti•est.
nuz•zle v., nuz•zled,
  nuz•zling. (to snug-
  gle: cf. NOZZLE)
NV (Nevada)

NY (New York)
nyb•ble Computers.
NYC or N.Y.C. (New
  York City).
ny•lon
nymph
nym•pho•ma•ni•a
nym•pho•ma•ni•ac
NYSE Business. (New
  York Stock Exchange)

O

oaf
oaf•ish
oak
oak•en
oa•kum
oar (long paddle: cf.
  O'ER; OR; ORE)
oar•lock
oars•man n., pl. oars•
  men.
OAS (Organization of
  American States)
OASI Business. (Old
  Age and Survivors In-
  surance)
o•a•sis n., pl.
  o•a•ses.
oat
oath n., pl. oaths.
oat•meal
ob•bli•ga•to n., pl.
  ob•bli•ga•tos or
  ob•bli•ga•ti.
ob•du•ra•cy
ob•du•rate
ob•du•rate•ness
o•be•di•ence
o•be•di•ent
o•bei•sance
o•bei•sant
ob•e•lisk
o•bese

o•be•si•ty
o•bey v., o•beyed,
  o•bey•ing.
ob•fus•cate v., ob•
  fus•cat•ed, ob•fus•
  cat•ing.
ob•fus•ca•tion
ob•fus•ca•to•ry
o•bi n., pl. o•bis,
  o•bi.
o•bit
ob•i•ter dic•tum n.,
  pl. ob•i•ter dic•ta.
o•bit•u•ar•y n., pl.
  o•bit•u•ar•ies.
ob•ject v., ob•
  ject•ed, ob•ject•ing.
object code Computers.
ob•ject-o•ri•en•ted
  Computers.
ob•jec•tion
ob•jec•tion•a•ble
ob•jec•tive
ob•jec•tiv•i•ty
ob•jec•tor
ob•jet d'art n., pl.
  ob•jets d'art.
ob•late
ob•li•gate v., ob•li•
  gat•ed, ob•li•gat•
  ing.
ob•li•ga•tion

ob•blig•a•to•ry
o•blige v., o•bliged,
  o•blig•ing.
ob•li•gee Business.
ob•li•gor Business.
o•blique
o•blique•ness
o•bliq•ui•ty
ob•lit•er•ate v., ob•
  lit•er•at•ed, ob•lit•
  er•at•ing.
ob•lit•er•a•tion
ob•liv•i•on
ob•liv•i•ous
ob•liv•i•ous•ness
ob•long
ob•lo•quy n., pl. ob•
  lo•quies.
ob•nox•ious
o•boe
o•bo•ist
ob•scene
ob•scen•i•ty
ob•scu•rant•ism
ob•scu•rant•ist
ob•scure v., ob•
  scured, ob•scur•ing.
ob•scure•ly
ob•scur•i•ty
ob•se•qui•ous
ob•serv•ance
ob•serv•ant

ob•ser•va•tion

ob•serv•a•to•ry n., pl. ob•serv•a•to•ries.

ob•serve v., ob•served, ob•serv•ing.

ob•serv•er

ob•sess v., ob•sessed, ob•sess•ing.

ob•ses•sion

ob•sess•ive

ob•sess•ive•ly

ob•sid•i•an

ob•so•les•cence

ob•so•les•cent

ob•so•lete

ob•sta•cle

ob•stet•ri•cal or ob•stet•ric

ob•ste•tri•cian

ob•stet•rics

ob•sti•na•cy

ob•sti•nate

ob•strep•er•ous

ob•struct v., ob•struct•ed, ob•struct•ing.

ob•struc•tion

ob•struc•tion•ism

ob•struc•tion•ist

ob•struc•tive

ob•struc•tive•ness

ob•tain v., ob•tained, ob•tain•ing.

ob•tain•a•ble

ob•trude v., ob•trud•ed, ob•trud•ing.

ob•tru•sion

ob•tru•sive

ob•tru•sive•ness

ob•tuse

ob•verse

ob•vi•ate v., ob•vi•at•ed, ob•vi•at•ing.

ob•vi•a•tion

ob•vi•ous

oc•a•ri•na n., pl. oc•a•ri•nas.

oc•ca•sion v., oc•ca•sioned, oc•ca•sion•ing.

oc•ca•sion•al

Oc•ci•dent

oc•ci•den•tal

oc•clude v., oc•clud•ed, oc•clud•ing.

oc•clu•sion

oc•clu•sive

oc•cult

oc•cult•ism

oc•cu•pan•cy

oc•cu•pant

oc•cu•pa•tion

oc•cu•pa•tion•al

oc•cu•py v., oc•cu•pied, oc•cu•py•ing.

oc•cur v., oc•curred, oc•cur•ring.

oc•cur•rence

o•cean

o•cea•naut

o•cean•go•ing or o•cean-go•ing

o•ce•an•ic

o•cea•nog•ra•pher

o•cea•no•graph•ic

o•cea•nog•ra•phy

oc•e•lot

o•cher or o•chre

o'•clock

OCR Computers. (optical character recognition)

oc•ta•gon

oc•tag•o•nal

oc•tane

oc•tave

oc•ta•vo n., pl. oc•ta•vos.

oc•tet

Oc•to•ber

oc•to•ge•nar•i•an

oc•to•pus n., pl. oc•to•pus•es or oc•to•pi.

oc•to•roon

oc•u•lar

oc•u•list

OD (overdose)

o•da•lisque

odd adj., odd•er, odd•est.

odd-e•ven pric•ing Business.

odd foot•er Computers.

odd•ball

odd•i•ty n., pl. odd•i•ties.

odd•ment

odds

odds-on

ode (poem: cf. OWED)

O•din

o•di•ous

o•di•um

o•dom•e•ter

o•dor

o•dor•if•er•ous

o•dor•ous

O•dys•se•us

Od•ys•sey n., pl. Od•ys•seys.

oed•i•pal

Oed•i•pus

OEM Computers. (original equipment manufacturer)

oe•nol•o•gist

oe•nol•o•gy or e•nol•o•gy

oe•no•phile

o'er (over: cf. OAR; OR; ORE)

oeu•vre n., pl. oeu•vres.

of (belonging to)

off (away from)
off-col○or
off-hour
off-key
off-lim○its
off-line or off•line *Computers.*
off-load or off•load
off-put○ting
off-sea○son
off-the-cuff
off-the-rec○ord
off-the-shelf
off-the-wall
off-white
of•fal (garbage: cf. AW-FUL)
off•beat
of•fend *v.,* of•fend○ed, of•fend•ing.
of•fense or of•fence
of•fen•sive
of•fer *v.,* of•fered, of•fer•ing.
of•fer•ing
of•fer•to○ry *n., pl.* of•fer•to○ries.
off•hand
off•hand•ed○ly
off•hand•ed•ness
of•fice
office au○to•ma○tion *Computers.*
office park *Business.*
of•fice•hold○er
of•fi•cer
of•fi•cial (authorized: cf. OFFICIOUS)
of•fi•cial•dom
of•fi•cial•ly
of•fi•ci•ant
of•fi•ci•ate *v.,* of•fi•ci•at○ed, of•fi•ci•at•ing.

of•fi•cious (meddle-some: cf. OFFICIAL)
off•ing
off•ish
off•print
off•set *v.,* off•set, off•set•ting.
off•shoot
off•shore
off•side
off•spring *n., pl.* off•spring.
off•stage
off•track
oft
of•ten
o○gle *v.,* o○gled, o○gling.
o○gre
OH (Ohio)
oh *n., pl.* oh's or ohs; ohed, oh•ing. (excla-mation of surprise: cf. OWE)
O○hi○o (OH)
ohm
o○ho
oil *v.,* oiled, oil•ing.
oil•cloth
oili○ness
oil•skin
oil○y *adj.,* oil•i○er, oil•i•est.
oink *v.,* oinked, oink•ing.
oint•ment
O○jib○wa or O○jib•way *n., pl.* O○jib•was or O○jib○wa; O○jib•ways or O○jib•way.
OK[1] (Oklahoma)
OK or O.K.[2] *n., pl.* OKs or OK's or O.K.'s; *v.,* OK'd or O.K.'ed, OK'○ing or O.K.'○ing.

o○kay *n., pl.* o○kays;. *v.,* o○kayed, o○kay•ing.
o○key-doke or o○key-do○key
O○ki•na○wa
O○ki•na○wan
O○kla•ho○ma (OK)
O○kla•ho○man
o○kra *n., pl.* o○kras.
old *adj.,* old○er or eld○er, old•est or eld•est.
old-fash○ioned
Old Tes○ta•ment
old-time
old-tim○er
Old World *n.*
old-world *adj.*
old○en
old○ie
old-line
Ol•du•vai Gorge
o○lé *n., pl.* o○lés.
o○le•ag○i•nous
o○le•an•der
o○le•o○mar•ga•rine
ol•fac•to○ry
ol○i•garch
ol○i•gar•chic
ol○i•gar•chy *n., pl.* ol○i•gar•chies.
Ol○i•go•cene
ol○i•gop○o○ly *n., pl.* ol○i•gop○o○lies. *Business.*
ol•ive
O○lym•pi○a
O○lym•pic
O○lym•pus
Om
O○man
O○ma○ni
OMB or O.M.B. *Business.* (Office of Man-agement and Budget).

om•buds•man n., pl.
om•buds•men.
o•ome•ga n., pl.
o•ome•gas.
o•ome•ga-o3 fat•ty
ac•id
om•e•let or om•e•
lette
o•men
om•i•nous
o•mis•sion
o•mit v., o•mit•ted,
o•mit•ting.
om•ni•bus n., pl. om•
ni•bus•es.
om•nip•o•tence
om•nip•o•tent
om•ni•pres•ence
om•ni•pres•ent
om•nis•cience
om•nis•cient
om•ni•um-gath•
er•um n., pl.
om•ni•um-
gath•er•ums.
om•ni•vore
om•niv•o•rous
on
on-board mem•o•ry
Computers.
on-board mo•dem
Computers.
on spec Business.
on-the-job train•ing
Business.
o•nan•ism
once
once-o•ver
on•co•gene
on•co•log•i•cal
on•col•o•gist
on•col•o•gy
on•com•ing
on•co•vi•rus
one (single: cf. WON)
one-di•men•sion•al

one-on-one
one-shot
one-sid•ed
one-sid•ed•ness
one-track
one-up•man•ship
one-way
O•nei•da n., pl.
O•nei•das or
O•nei•da.
O'•Neill
one-lin•er
one•ness
on•er•ous
one•self or one's self
one-time or one•time
on•go•ing
on•ion
on•ion•skin
on-line or on•line
Computers.
on-line serv•ice Com-
puters.
on•look•er
on•look•ing
on•ly
on•o•mat•o•poe•ia
on•o•mat•o•poe•ic
or on•o•mat•o•po•
et•ic
On•on•da•ga n., pl.
On•on•da•gas or
On•on•da•ga.
on•rush
on•rush•ing
on•set
on•slaught
On•tar•i•o
on•to
on•to•ge•net•ic or
on•to•gen•ic
on•tog•e•ony or on•
to•gen•e•sis
on•to•log•i•cal or
on•to•log•ic
on•tol•o•gy

o•nus n., pl. o•
nus•es.
on•ward or on•wards
on•yx
oo•dles
OOP Computers. (ob-
ject-oriented program-
ming)
OOPL Computers. (ob-
ject-oriented program-
ming language)
ooze v., oozed, ooz•
ing.
o•pac•i•ty
o•pal
o•pal•es•cence
o•pal•es•cent
o•paque
OPEC (Organization of
Petroleum Exporting
Countries)
Op-Ed (newspaper
page)
o•pen
o•pen-and-shut
o•pen-date la•bel•
ing Business.
open dis•play Busi-
ness.
o•pen-end Business.
o•pen-end•ed Busi-
ness.
o•pen-faced
o•pen-heart sur•
ger•y
o•pen-heart•ed
o•pen-hearth
o•pen mar•ket Busi-
ness.
o•pen-mind•ed
o•pen•er
o•pen-hand•ed
o•pen•ing
o•pen•work
op•er•a¹ n., pl. op•
er•as. (music drama)

o•per•a² (plural of opus)

op•er•a•ble

op•er•ate v., op•er•at•ed, op•er•at•ing.

op•er•at•ic

op•er•at•ing en•vi•ron•ment Computers.

operating ex•pens•es Business.

operating in•come Business.

operating sys•tem Computers.

op•er•a•tion

op•er•a•tion•al

op•er•a•tive

op•er•a•tor

op•er•et•ta n., pl. op•er•et•tas.

oph•thal•mol•o•gist

oph•thal•mol•o•gy

o•pi•ate

o•pine v., o•pined, o•pin•ing.

o•pin•ion

o•pin•ion•at•ed

o•pi•um

o•pos•sum n., pl. o•pos•sums or o•pos•sum.

op•po•nent

op•por•tune

op•por•tun•ism

op•por•tun•ist

op•por•tun•is•tic

op•por•tu•ni•ty n., pl. op•por•tu•ni•ties.

op•pose v., op•posed, op•pos•ing.

op•po•site (facing: cf. APPOSITE)

op•po•si•tion (resistance: cf. APPOSITION)

op•press v., op•pressed, op•press•ing.

op•pres•sion

op•pres•sive

op•pres•sor

op•pro•bri•ous

op•pro•bri•um

opt v., opt•ed, opt•ing.

op•tic

op•ti•cal

optical disc Computers.

op•ti•cal mouse Computers.

optical scan•ner Computers.

optical scan•ning Computers.

op•ti•cal•ly

op•ti•cian

op•tics

op•ti•mal

op•ti•mism

op•ti•mist

op•ti•mis•tic

op•ti•mum n., pl. op•ti•ma or op•ti•mums.

op•tion

op•tion•al

op•to•me•chan•i•cal mouse Computers.

op•tom•e•trist

op•tom•e•try

op•u•lence

op•u•lent

o•pus n., pl. o•pus•es or o•pe•ra.

or (otherwise: cf. OAR; O'ER; ORE)

OR (Oregon)

or °bi

or•a•cle (shrine: cf. AURICLE)

o•rac•u•lar

o•ral (spoken: cf. AU-RAL)

or•ange

or•ange•ade

o•rang•u•tan or o•rang•u•tang or o•orang•ou•tang

o•rate v., o•rat•ed, o•rat•ing.

o•ra•tion

or•a•tor

or•a•tor•i•cal

or•a•to•ri•o n., pl. or•a•to•ri•os.

or•a•to•ry

orb

or•bit v., or•bit•ed, or•bit•ing.

or•bit•al

or•chard

or•ches•tra n., pl. or•ches•tras.

or•ches•tral

or•ches•trate v., or•ches•trat•ed, or•ches•trat•ing.

or•ches•tra•tion

or•ches•tra•tor

or•chid

or•dain v., or•dained, or•dain•ing.

or•dain•ment

or•deal

or•der v., or•dered, or•der•ing.

order cy•cle Business.

or•der•li•ness

or•der•ly n., pl. or•der•lies.

or•di•nal

or•di•nance (law: cf. ORDNANCE)

or•di•nar•i•ly

or•di•nar•i•ness

or•di•nar•y

ordinary in•come Business.

or•di•nate
or•di•na•tion
ord•nance (military weapons: cf. ORDINANCE)
Or•do•vi•cian
or•dure
ore (mineral: cf. O'ER; OR)
o•reg•a•no
Or•e•gon (OR)
O•res•tes
or•gan
or•gan•dy or or•gan•die n., pl. or•gan•dies.
or•gan•elle
or•gan•ic
or•gan•i•cal•ly
or•gan•ism
or•gan•ist
or•gan•i•za•tion
or•gan•i•za•tion•al
or•gan•ize v., or•gan•ized, or•gan•iz•ing.
or•gan•ized
or•gan•iz•er
or•gan•za
or•gasm v., or•gasmed, or•gasm•ing.
or•gas•mic
or•gas•tic
or•gi•as•tic
or•gy n., pl. or•gies.
o•ri•el
o•ri•ent v., o•ri•ent•ed, o•ri•ent•ing.
o•ri•en•tal
o•ri•en•ta•tion
or•i•fice
o•ri•fi•cial
o•ri•ga•mi
or•i•gin

o•rig•i•nal
o•rig•i•nal•i•ty
o•rig•i•nal•ly
o•rig•i•nate v., o•rig•i•nat•ed, o•rig•i•nat•ing.
o•rig•i•na•tion
o•rig•i•na•tor
o•ri•ole
O•ri•on
Or•lon Trademark.
or•mo•lu
or•na•ment v., or•na•ment•ed, or•na•ment•ing.
or•na•men•tal
or•na•men•ta•tion
or•nate
or•nate•ly
or•nate•ness
or•ner•i•ness
or•ner•y
or•ni•thol•o•gy
o•ro•tund
o•ro•tun•di•ty
or•phan v., or•phaned, or•phan•ing.
or•phan•age
Or•phe•us
or•ris
or•tho•don•tal
or•tho•don•tic
or•tho•don•tics
or•tho•don•tist
or•tho•dox
or•tho•dox•y
or•tho•graph•ic
or•thog•ra•phy
or•tho•pe•dic
or•tho•pe•dics
or•tho•pe•dist
Or•well
Or•well•i•an
or•zo

os¹ n., pl. os•sa. (bone)
os² n., pl. o•ra. (mouth)
O•sage n., pl. O•sag•es or O•sage.
O•sa•ka
os•cil•late v., os•cil•lat•ed, os•cil•lat•ing. (to go back and forth)
os•cu•late v., os•cu•lat•ed, os•cu•lat•ing. (to kiss)
OSHA Business. (Occupational Safety and Health Administration)
o•sier
Os•lo
os•mi•um
os•mo•sis
os•mot•ic
os•prey n., pl. os•preys.
os•se•ous
os•si•fi•ca•tion
os•si•fy v., os•si•fied, os•si•fy•ing.
os•ten•si•ble
ostensible part•ner Business.
os•ten•ta•tion
os•ten•ta•tious
os•te•o•path
os•te•op•a•thy
os•te•o•po•ro•sis
os•tra•cism
os•tra•cize v., os•tra•cized, os•tra•ciz•ing.
os•trich
OTC Business. (over-the-counter)
oth•er
oth•er•wise
oth•er•world•ly
o•ti•ose

o•to•lar•yn•gol•o•gist

o•to•lar•yn•gol•o•gy

Ot•ta•wa *n.*, *pl.* Ot•ta•was or Ot•ta•wa.

ot•ter *n.*, *pl.* ot•ters or ot•ter.

ot•to•man *n.*, *pl.* ot•to•mans.

Oua•ga•dou•gou

ou•bli•ette

ouch

ought (should: cf. AUGHT)

Oui•ja *Trademark.*

ounce

our (belonging to us: cf. HOUR)

ours

our•selves

oust *v.*, oust•ed, oust•ing.

oust•er

out

out-and-out

out-of-bod•y

out-of-date

out-of-doors

out-of-the-way

out•age

out•back

out•bal•ance *v.*, out•bal•anced, out•bal•anc•ing.

out•board

out•bound

out•break

out•build•ing

out•burst

out•cast

out•class *v.*, out•classed, out•class•ing.

out•come

out•crop *v.*, out•cropped, out•crop•ping.

out•cry *n.*, *pl.* out•cries.

out•dat•ed

out•dis•tance *v.*, out•dis•tanced, out•dis•tanc•ing.

out•do *v.*, out•did, out•done, out•do•ing.

out•door

out•doors

out•er

out•er•most

out•er•wear

out•field

out•field•er

out•fit *v.*, out•fit•ted, out•fit•ting.

out•fit•ter

out•flank *v.*, out•flanked, out•flank•ing.

out•flow

out•fox *v.*, out•foxed, out•fox•ing.

out•go *n.*, *pl.* out•goes; *v.*, out•went, out•gone, out•go•ing.

out•grow *v.*, out•grew, out•grown, out•grow•ing.

out•growth

out•house *n.*, *pl.* out•hous•es.

out•ing

out•land•ish

out•last *v.*, out•last•ed, out•last•ing.

out•law *v.*, out•lawed, out•law•ing.

out•lay

out•let

out•line *v.*, out•lined, out•lin•ing.

outline font *Computers.*

out•live *v.*, out•lived, out•liv•ing.

out•look

out•ly•ing

out•ma•neu•ver *v.*, out•ma•neu•vered, out•ma•neu•ver•ing.

out•mod•ed

out•num•ber

out•pa•tient or out-pa•tient

out•place•ment *Business.*

out•post

out•pour•ing

out•put *v.*, out•put•ted or out•put, out•put•ting.

output de•vice *Computers.*

out•rage *v.*, out•raged, out•rag•ing.

out•ra•geous

out•rank *v.*, out•ranked, out•rank•ing.

out•reach *v.*, out•reached, out•reach•ing.

out•rig•ger

out•right

out•run *v.*, out•ran, out•run, out•run•ning.

out•sell *v.*, out•sold, out•sell•ing.

out•set

out•shine *v.*, out•shone, out•shin•ing.

out•side

out•sid•er

out•size
out•skirt
out•smart v., out•smart∘ed, out•smart•ing.
out•source v., out•sourced, out•sourc•ing. *Business.*
out•spo•ken
out•spread v., out•spread, out•spread•ing.
out•stand•ing
out•stretch v., out•stretched, out•stretch•ing.
out•strip v., out•stripped, out•strip•ping.
out•take
out•vote v., out•vot∘ed, out•vot•ing.
out•ward
out•weigh v., out•weighed, out•weigh•ing.
out•wit v., out•wit∘ted, out•wit•ting.
out•work v., out•worked, out•work•ing.
ou∘zo
o∘va
o∘val
O∘val Of•fice
o∘va∘ry n., pl. o∘va∘ries.
o∘vate
o∘va•tion
ov∘en
o∘ver
o∘ver-the-count∘er (OTC) *Business.*
o∘ver•a∘chieve v., o∘vera∘chieved, o∘vera∘chiev•ing.

o∘ver•a∘chiev∘er
o∘ver•act v., o∘ver•act∘ed, o∘ver•act•ing.
o∘ver•age
o∘ver•all
o∘ver•arm
o∘ver•awe v., o∘ver•awed, o∘ver•aw•ing.
o∘ver•bal•ance v., o∘ver•bal•anced, o∘ver•bal•anc•ing.
o∘ver•bear•ing
o∘ver•bite
o∘ver•blown
o∘ver•board
o∘ver•bought *Business.*
o∘ver•cast
o∘ver•charge v., o∘ver•charged, o∘ver•charg•ing.
o∘ver•coat
o∘ver•come v., o∘ver•came, o∘ver•come, o∘ver•com•ing.
o∘ver∘do v., o∘ver•did, o∘ver•done, o∘ver•do•ing. (to overindulge: cf. OVERDUE)
o∘ver•dose (OD)
o∘ver•draft *Business.*
o∘ver•draw v., o∘ver•drew, o∘ver•drawn, o∘ver•draw•ing.
o∘ver•drive
o∘ver•due (late: cf. OVERDO)
o∘ver•flight
o∘ver•flow v., o∘ver•flowed, o∘ver•flow•ing.

overflow er•ror *Computers.*
o∘ver•fly v., o∘ver•flew, o∘ver•flown, o∘ver•fly•ing.
o∘ver•grow v., o∘ver•grew, o∘ver•grown, o∘ver•grow•ing.
o∘ver•grown
o∘ver•growth
o∘ver•hand
o∘ver•hang v., o∘ver•hung, o∘ver•hang•ing.
o∘ver•haul v., o∘ver•hauled, o∘ver•haul•ing.
o∘ver•head
overhead scan•ner *Computers.*
o∘ver•hear v., o∘ver•heard, o∘ver•hear•ing.
o∘ver•joyed
o∘ver•kill
o∘ver•laid win•dows *Computers.*
o∘ver•land
o∘ver•lap v., o∘ver•lapped, o∘ver•lap•ping.
o∘ver•lay
o∘ver•look v., o∘ver•looked, o∘ver•look•ing.
o∘ver•lord v., o∘ver•lord∘ed, o∘ver•lord•ing.
o∘ver∘ly
o∘ver•much
o∘ver•night
o∘ver•pass
o∘ver•play v., o∘ver•played, o∘ver•play•ing.
o∘ver•pow∘er v.,

o•ver•pow•ered,
o•ver•pow•er•ing.
o•ver•qual•i•fied
o•ver•reach *v.*,
o•ver•reached,
o•ver•reach•ing.
o•ver•ride *v.*, o•ver•
rode, o•ver•rid•
den, o•ver•rid•ing.
o•ver•rule *v.*, o•ver•
ruled, o•ver•rul•
ing.
o•ver•run *v.*, o•ver•
ran, o•ver•run,
o•ver•run•ning.
o•ver•seas or o•ver•
sea
o•ver•see *v.*, o•ver•
saw, o•ver•seen,
o•ver•see•ing.
o•ver•se•er
o•ver•sexed
o•ver•shad•ow *v.*,
o•ver•shad•owed,
o•ver•shad•ow•ing.
o•ver•shoe
o•ver•shoot *v.*,
o•ver•shot, o•ver•
shoot•ing.
o•ver•sight
o•ver•size or o•ver•
sized
o•ver•sleep *v.*,
o•ver•slept, o•ver•
sleep•ing.
o•ver•state *v.*,
o•ver•stat•ed,
o•ver•stat•ing.
o•ver•stay *v.*, o•ver•
stayed, o•ver•stay•
ing.

o•ver•step *v.*, o•ver•
stepped, o•ver•
step•ping.
o•ver•strike mode
Computers.
o•ver•stuffed
o•ver•sub•scribe *v.*,
o•ver•sub•scribed,
o•ver•sub•scrib•
ing.
o•vert
o•ver•take *v.*, o•ver•
took, o•ver•tak•en,
o•ver•tak•ing.
o•ver•throw *v.*,
o•ver•threw,
o•ver•thrown,
o•ver•throw•ing.
o•ver•time *Business.*
o•vert•ly
o•ver•tone
o•ver•ture
o•ver•turn *v.*, o•ver•
turned, o•ver•turn•
ing.
o•ver•view
o•ver•ween•ing
o•ver•whelm *v.*,
o•ver•whelmed,
o•ver•whelm•ing.
o•ver•write *v.*,
o•ver•wrote,
o•ver•writ•ten,
o•ver•writ•ing.
o•ver•wrought
Ov•id
o•vi•duct
o•vip•a•rous
o•void
ov•u•lar
ov•u•late *v.*, ov•u•

lat•ed, ov•u•lat•
ing.
ov•u•la•tion
ov•ule
o•vum *n.*, *pl.* o•va.
ow (expression of pain)
owe *v.*, owed, ow•
ing. (to be indebted:
cf. OH)
owed (did owe: cf.
ODE)
owl
owl•ish
own *v.*, owned, own•
ing.
own•er
own•er•ship
ox *n.*, *pl.* ox•en or
ox•es.
ox•blood
ox•bow
ox•ford
ox•i•dant
ox•i•da•tion
ox•ide
ox•i•dize *v.*, ox•i•
dized, ox•i•diz•ing.
ox•i•diz•er
ox•y•a•cet•y•lene
ox•y•gen
ox•y•gen•ate *v.*,
ox•y•gen•at•ed,
ox•y•gen•at•ing.
ox•y•gen•a•tion
ox•y•mo•ron
oys•ter
o•zone
ozone hole
ozone lay•er

P&L *Business.* (profit and loss)

PA (Pennsylvania)

pa

pab•u•lum

PAC *n., pl.* **PACs** or **PAC's.** (political action committee)

Pac-Man de•fense *Business.*

pace¹ *v.,* **paced, pac•ing.** (step; to step)

pa•ce² (with due re-spect)

pace•mak•er

pac•er

pace•set•ter

pach•y•derm

pach•y•san•dra *n., pl.* **pach•y•san•dras.**

pa•cif•ic

Pa•cif•ic O•cean

Pacific time (PT)

pac•i•fi•ca•tion

pac•i•fi•er

pac•i•fism

pac•i•fist

pac•i•fy *v.,* **pac•i•fied, pac•i•fy•ing.**

pack *v.,* **packed, pack•ing.**

pack•age *v.,* **pack•aged, pack•ag•ing.**

packed (bundled: cf. PACT)

packed file *Computers.*

pack•er

pack•et

pack•et-switched *Computers.*

pack•horse

pack•ing

pack•sad•dle

pact (agreement: cf. PACKED)

pad *v.,* **pad•ded, pad•ding.**

pad char•ac•ter *Computers.*

pad•dle *v.,* **pad•dled, pad•dling.**

pad•dock

pad•dy *n., pl.* **pad•dies.** (rice field: cf. PATTY)

pad•lock *v.,* **pad•locked, pad•lock•ing.**

pa•dre *n., pl.* **pa•dres.**

pae•an

pa•gan

pa•gan•ism

page *v.,* **paged, pag•ing.**

page de•scrip•tion lan•guage *Computers.*

page-mode mem•o•ry *Computers.*

page print•er *Computers.*

page-white dis•play

pag•eant

pag•eant•ry

paged vir•tu•al mem•o•ry *Computers.*

pag•i•na•tion

pa•go•da *n., pl.* **pa•go•das.**

paid (pd.)

paid-in cap•i•tal *Business.*

paid-in sur•plus *Business.*

pail (bucket: cf. PALE)

pail•ful *n., pl.* **pail•fuls.**

pain *v.,* **pained, pain•ing.** (suffering: cf. PANE)

Paine

pain•ful

pain•ful•ly

pain•kill•er

pain•kill•ing

pain•less

pain•less•ly

pains•tak•ing

pains•tak•ing•ly

paint *v.,* **paint•ed, paint•ing.**

paint pro•gram *Computers.*

paint•brush

paint•er

paint•ing

pair *n., pl.* **pairs** or **pair.** (two: cf. PARE; PEAR)

pais•ley *n., pl.* **pais•leys.**

pa•ja•mas

Pa•ki•stan

Pa•ki•sta•ni

pal *v.,* **palled, pal•ling.**

pal•ace

pal•a•din

pal•an•quin

pal•at•a•ble

pal•a•tal

pal•ate (roof of mouth: cf. PALLET; PALETTE)

pa•la•tial

Pa•lat•i•nate

pal•a•tine

pa•lav•er

pale *v.,* **paled, pal•ing;. *adj.,* **pal•er,**

pal•est. (lacking color: cf. PAIL)
pale•face
pale•ness
Pa•le•o•cene
pa•le•on•tol•o•gist
pa•le•on•tol•o•gy
Pa•le•o•zo•ic
Pal•es•tine
Pal•es•tin•i•an
pal•ette (paint tablet: cf. PALATE; PALLET)
pal•frey n., pl. pal•freys.
pal•i•mo•ny
pal•imp•sest
pal•in•drome
pal•ing
pal•i•sade
pall v., palled, pall•ing. (gloomy effect: cf. PAUL)
pal•la•di•um n., pl. pal•la•di•a.
pall•bear•er
pal•let (bed: cf. PALATE; PALETTE)
pal•li•ate v., pal•li•at•ed, pal•li•at•ing.
pal•li•a•tion
pal•li•a•tive
pal•lid
pal•ling¹ (associating as pals)
pall•ing² (becoming tiresome)
pal•lor
palm v., palmed, palm•ing. (part of hand; the tree: cf. PSALM)
pal•mate or pal•mat•ed
Pal•mer (last name)
palm•er (pilgrim)
pal•met•to n., pl.

pal•met•tos or pal•met•toes.
palm•ist
palm•is•try
palm•top Computers.
palmtop com•put•er Computers.
palm•y adj., palm•i•er, palm•i•est.
pal•o•mi•no n., pl. pal•o•mi•nos.
pal•pa•ble
pal•pa•bly
pal•pate v., pal•pat•ed, pal•pat•ing. (to examine by touch)
pal•pa•tion
pal•pi•tate v., pal•pi•tat•ed, pal•pi•tat•ing. (to throb)
pal•pi•ta•tion
pal•sied
pal•sy n., pl. pal•sies.
pal•tri•ness
pal•try (trifling: cf. POULTRY)
pam•pas
pam•per v., pam•pered, pam•per•ing.
pam•phlet
pam•phlet•eer
Pam•yat
pan v., panned, pan•ning.
Pan-A•mer•i•can
pan•a•ce•a n., pl. pan•a•ce•as.
pa•nache
Pan•a•ma n., pl. Pan•a•mas.
Pan•a•ma Ca•nal
Pan•a•ma•ni•an
pan•cake
pan•chro•mat•ic
pan•cre•as
pan•cre•at•ic

pan•da n., pl. pan•das.
pan•dem•ic
pan•de•mo•ni•um n., pl. pan•de•mo•ni•ums.
pan•der v., pan•dered, pan•der•ing.
Pan•do•ra
pane (window section: cf. PAIN)
pan•e•gyr•ic
pan•el v., pan•eled or pan•elled, pan•el•ing or pan•el•ling.
pan•el•ist
pang
pan•han•dle v., pan•han•dled, pan•han•dling.
pan•han•dler
pan•ic v., pan•icked, pan•ick•ing.
pan•ick•y
pan•nier or pan•ier
pan•o•ply n., pl. pan•o•plies.
pan•o•ram•a n., pl. pan•o•ram•as.
pan•o•ram•ic
pan•sy n., pl. pan•sies.
pant v., pant•ed, pant•ing.
pan•ta•loon
pan•the•ism
pan•the•ist
pan•the•is•tic
pan•the•is•ti•cal
pan•the•on
pan•ther n., pl. pan•thers or pan•ther.
pant•ies
pan•to•mime v., pan•to•mimed, pan•to•mim•ing.
pan•to•mim•ic

pan•to•mim•ist
pan•to•then•ic ac○id
pan•try n., pl. pan•tries.
pants
pant•suit or pants suit
pant○y•hose
pant○y•waist
pap
Pap test
pa○pa n., pl. pa•pas.
pa•pa○cy n., pl. pa•pa•cies.
pa•pal
pa•pa○ya n., pl. pa•pa•yas.
pa•per v., pa•pered, pa•per•ing.
paper clip
paper prof○it Business.
paper trail
pa○per-white dis•play Computers.
pa○per•back
pa○per•board
pa○per•boy
pa○per•hang○er
pa○per•hang•ing
pa○per•weight
pa○per•work
pa○pier-mâ○ché
pa•poose
pap•ri○ka
Pap○ua New Guin○ea
pa•py•rus n., pl. pa•py○ri or pa•py•rus○es.
par v., parred, par•ring.
par ex•cel•lence
par val○ue Business.
par○a•ble
pa•rab•o○la n., pl. pa•rab•o•las.
par○a•chute v.,

par○a•chut○ed, par○a•chut•ing.
par○a•chut•ist
pa•rade v., pa•rad○ed, pa•rad•ing.
pa•rad○er
par○a•digm
par○a•dise
par○a•di•si•a•cal
par○a•di•si•a•cal○ly[1]
par○a•di•si•a•cal○ly[2]
par○a•dox
par○a•dox○i•cal
par○a•dox○i•cal•ly
par•af•fin
par○a•gon
par○a•graph v., par○a•graphed, par○a•graph•ing.
Par○a•guay
Par○a•guay○an
par○a•keet
par○a•le•gal
par•al•lax
par•al•lel v., par•al•leled, par•al•lel•ing.
parallel in○ter•face Computers.
parallel port Computers.
parallel print○er Computers.
parallel proc•ess•ing Computers.
par•al•lel○o•gram
pa•ral○y•sis n., pl. pa•ral○y•ses.
par○a•lyze v., par○a•lyzed, par○a•lyz•ing.
par○a•lyz•ing○ly
Par○a•mar•i○bo
par○a•me•ci○um n., pl. par○a•me•ci○a.
par○a•med○i•cal
pa•ram○e•ter (math

variable; limit: cf. PE•RIMETER)
par○a•met•ric or par○a•met•ri•cal
par○a•mil○i•tar○y
par○a•mount
par○a•mour
par○a•noi○a
par○a•pet
par○a•pher•na○lia
par○a•phrase v., par○a•phrased, par○a•phras•ing.
par○a•ple•gi○a
par○a•ple•gic
par○a•pro•fes•sion○al
par○a•psy•chol○o○gist
par○a•psy•chol○o○gy
par○a•site
par○a•sol
par○a•sym•pa•thet○ic
par○a•thi○on
par○a•thy○roid
par○a•troop
par•bake v., par•baked, par•bak•ing.
par•boil v., par•boiled, par•boil•ing.
par•cel v., par•celed or par•celled, par•cel•ing or par•cel•ling.
parcel post
parch v., parched, parch•ing.
parch•ment
par•don v., par•doned, par•don•ing.
par•don•a○ble
par•don•a○bly
pare v., pared, par•ing. (to trim: cf. PAIR; PEAR)
par•e○gor○ic

par•ent *v.*, par•
ent•ed, par•ent•
ing.
parent di•rec•to•ry
Computers.
par•ent•age
pa•ren•tal
parental leave
pa•ren•the•sis *n., pl.*
pa•ren•the•ses.
par•ent•hood
par•ent•ing
pa•re•sis
pa•ret•oic
pa•re•ove or par•ove
par•fait
par•oi-mu•tu•el or
par•oi•mu•tu•el
pa•ri•oah
pa•ri•e•tal
Par•is
par•ish (church dis-
trict: cf. PERISH)
pa•rish•ion•er
par•i•o•ty *n., pl.* par•i•
ties.
parity check *Comput-
ers.*
parity check•ing *Com-
puters.*
park *v.*, parked, park•
ing.
par•ka *n., pl.* par•kas.
park•ing me•ter
Par•kin•son's disease
park•way
par•lance
par•lay (to bet)
par•ley *n., pl.* par•
leys; *v.*, par•leyed,
par•ley•ing. (confer-
ence)
par•lia•ment
par•lia•men•tar•i•an
par•lor
Par•me•san

par•mi•gia•na
pa•ro•chi•al
par•o•o•dy *n., pl.* par•
o•dies; *v.*, par•o•
died, par•o•dy•ing.
pa•role *v.*, pa•roled,
pa•rol•ing.
par•ox•ysm
par•quet *v.*, par•
queted, par•quet•
ing.
par•que•try
par•ri•cid•al
par•ri•cide
par•rot *v.*, par•
rot•ed, par•rot•ing.
par•ory *n., pl.* par•ries;
v., par•ried, par•ry•
ing.
parse *v.*, parsed, pars•
ing.
par•si•mo•ny
pars•ley
pars•nip
par•son
par•son•age
part *v.*, part•ed, part•
ing.
part-song
part-time
part-tim•er
par•take *v.*, par•took,
par•tak•en, par•
tak•ing.
par•terre
par•the•no•gen•e•
sis
par•the•no•
ge•net•ic
Par•the•non
par•ti-col•ored or
par•ty-col•ored
par•tial
par•tial•ly
par•tic•i•pate *v.*,
par•tic•i•pat•ed,
par•tic•i•pat•ing.

par•tic•i•pa•tive
par•tic•i•pa•to•ry
par•ti•ci•ple
par•ti•cle
par•tic•u•lar
par•tic•u•lar•i•za•
tion
par•tic•u•lar•ize *v.*,
par•tic•u•lar•ized,
par•tic•u•lar•iz•
ing.
par•tic•u•late
part•ing
par•ti•san
par•ti•san•ship
par•ti•tion *v.*, par•ti•
tioned, par•ti•tion•
ing.
part•ly
part•ner *v.*, part•
nered, part•ner•ing.
par•tridge *n., pl.* par•
tridg•es or par•
tridge.
par•tu•ri•tion
part•way
par•o•ty *n., pl.* par•
ties; *v.*, par•tied,
par•ty•ing.
par•ve•onu *n., pl.* par•
ve•nus.
Pas•a•de•na
pas•cal
Pas•cal (programming
language)
pas•chal
pa•sha *n., pl.* pa•
shas.
pass *v.*, passed, pass•
ing.
pass-through *Business.*
pass•a•ble (accepta-
ble: cf. PASSIBLE)
pass•a•bly
pas•sage *v.*, pas•
saged, pas•sag•ing.
pas•sage•way

pass•book
pas○sé
passed (did pass: cf.
  PAST)
pas•sel
pas•sen•ger
pass○er○by or pass○
  er-by n., pl. pass•
  ers○by or pass○
  ers-by.
pass•i•ble (capable of
  emotion: cf. PASSABLE)
pas•sim
pass•ing
pas•sion
pas•sion•ate
pas•sion•ate○ly
pas•sive
passive in•come Busi-
  ness.
pas•sive smok•ing
pas•sive○ly
pass•key n., pl. pass•
  keys.
Pass○o○ver
pass•port
pass•word
past (former time: cf.
  PASSED)
pas○ta n., pl. pas•tas.
paste v., past○ed,
  past○ing.
paste•board
pas•tel
pas•tern
Pas•teur
pas•teur○i•za○tion
pas•teur•ize v., pas•
  teur○ized, pas•teur•
  iz○ing.
pas•teur•iz○er
pas•tiche
pas•time
past○i•ness
pas•tor
pas•to•ral (rustic)

pas•to•rale (musical
  composition)
pas•tra○mi
pas•try n., pl. pas•
  tries.
pas•tur•age
pas•ture v., pas•
  tured, pas•tur•ing.
past○y n., pl. past○ies.
pat v., pat•ted, pat•
  ting.
patch v., patched,
  patch•ing.
patch•a○ble
patch○er
patch○i•ness
patch•work
patch○y adj., patch•
  i○er, patch•i•est.
pate (top of head)
pâte (pottery paste)
pâ○té n., pl. pâ•tés.
  (meat paste)
pa•tel○la n., pl. pa•
  tel•las or pa•tel•lae.
pa•tel•lar
pat•ent v., pat•
  ent○ed, pat•ent•
  ing. Business.
pat•ent○ly
pa○ter•fa•mil•i•o○as
pa•ter•nal
pa•ter•nal•ism
pa•ter•nal•is•tic
pa•ter•nal○ly
pa•ter•ni○ty
pa○ter•nos•ter
Pat•er•son
path n., pl. paths.
pa•thet○ic
pa•thet○i•cal○ly
path•find○er
path○name Computers.
pa•tho○o•gen
pa•thol○o•gist

pa•thol○o•gy n., pl.
  pa•thol○o•gies.
pa•thos (tender qual-
  ity: cf. BATHOS)
path•way
pa•tience (forbear-
  ance)
pa•tient n., pl. pa•
  tients. (doctor's cli-
  ents)
pa•tient○ly
pat•i○na n., pl. pat•
  ti•nas.
pat○i○o n., pl. pat•
  i○os.
pat•ness
pat•ois n., pl. pat•ois.
pa•tri•arch
pa•tri•ar•chal
pa•tri•cian
pat•ri•cide
pat•ri•mo○ny n., pl.
  pat•ri•mo•nies.
pa•tri○ot
pa•tris•tic or pa•
  tris•ti•cal
pa•tris•ti•cal○ly
pa•trol v., pa•trolled,
  pa•trol•ling.
pa•trol•man n., pl.
  pa•trol•men.
pa•tron
pa•tron•age
pa•tron•ize v., pa•
  tron○ized, pa•tron•
  iz○ing.
pat•ro•nym○ic
pat○sy n., pl. pat•sies.
pat•ter v., pat•tered,
  pat•ter•ing.
pat•tern v., pat•
  terned, pat•tern•
  ing.
pat•terned
pat○ty n., pl. pat•ties.
  (flat mass: cf. PADDY)
pau•ci○ty

Paul (the name: cf. PALL)
Paul Bun•yan
Pau•line¹ (first name)
Paul•ine² (of the apostle Paul)
paunch
pau•per
pause v., paused, paus•ing. (delay: cf. PAWS)
pave v., paved, pav•ing.
pave•ment
pa•vil•ion
pav•ing
Pav•lov
Pav•lov•i•an
paw v., pawed, paw•ing.
pawn v., pawned, pawn•ing.
pawn•bro•ker
pawn•bro•king
pawn•shop
paw•paw
paws (animal feet: cf. PAUSE)
pay v., paid, pay•ing.
pay•back Business.
pay◦ee Business.
pay◦er Business.
pay•load
pay•mas•ter
pay•ment (pmt.)
pay•off
pay•o◦la
pay•out Business.
pay•roll Business.
payroll tax Business.
PBS (Public Broadcasting System)
PBX (telephone)
PC¹ n., pl. PCs or PC's. Computers. (personal computer)

PC² (politically correct)
pd. (paid)
p/e Business. (price-earnings ratio)
pea n., pl. peas.
peace (freedom from war: cf. PIECE)
peace•mak◦er
peace•mak•ing
peace•time
peach
pea•cock n., pl. pea•cocks or pea•cock.
peak (pointed top: cf. PEEK; PIQUE)
peaked¹ (pointed: cf. PEEKED; PIQUED)
peak◦ed² (pale and thin)
peak•ed•ness
peal v., pealed, peal•ing. (to resound: cf. PEEL)
pea•nut
pear (the fruit: cf. PAIR; PARE)
pearl (the gem: cf. PURL)
Pearl Har•bor
peas•ant
peat
peat◦y adj., peat•i◦er, peat•i•est.
peb•ble
peb•bled
pe•can
pec•ca•dil◦lo n., pl. pec•ca•dil•loes or pec•ca•dil•los.
pec•ca•ry n., pl. pec•ca•ries or pec•ca•ry.
peck v., pecked, peck•ing.
pec•tin
pec•tin•ous
pec•to•ral
pec•u•late v., pec•u•

lat◦ed, pec•u•lat•ing.
pec•u•la•tion
pe•cu•liar
pe•cu•liar◦ly
pe•cu•ni•ar◦y
ped◦a•gogue
ped◦a•go◦gy
ped◦al v., ped•aled or ped•alled, ped•al•ing or ped•al•ling. (foot lever; to propel with a pedal: cf. PEDDLE)
ped•ant
pe•dan•tic
ped•dle v., ped•dled, ped•dling. (to sell)
ped•er•as◦ty
ped•es•tal
pe•des•tri◦an
pe•di•at◦ric
pe•di•a•tri•cian
pe•di•at•rics
ped◦i•cab
ped◦i•cure
ped◦i•cur•ist
ped◦i•gree
ped◦i•ment
pe•dom◦e•ter
peek v., peeked, peek•ing. (to look: cf. PEAK; PIQUE)
peel v., peeled, peel•ing. (to strip: cf. PEAL)
peep v., peeped, peep•ing.
peep•hole
peer v., peered, peer•ing. (equal; to look: cf. PIER)
peer-to-peer Computers.
peer•less
peeve
peeved
pee•vish

pee•vish•ly
pee•vish•ness
pee•wee
peg v., pegged, peg•
  ging.
Peg○a•sus
peg•legged
peign•oir
pe•jo○ra•tive
Pe•king
Pe•king•ese or Pe•
  kin•ese n., pl. Pe•
  king•ese or Pe•kin•
  ese.
pe•koe
pel○i•can
pell-mell or pell•mell
pel•la•gra
pel•let
pel•lu•cid
pel•lu•cid○ly
pelt v., pelt○ed, pelt•
  ing.
pel•vic
pel•vis n., pl. pel•
  vis○es.
pem•mi•can
pen v., penned, pen•
  ning.
pen name
pe•nal
pe•nal○i•za•tion
pe•nal•ize v., pe•
  nal○ized, pe•nal•iz•
  ing.
pen•al○ty n., pl. pen•
  al•ties.
pen•ance (punishment:
  cf. PENNANTS)
pence
pen•chant
pen•cil v., pen•ciled
  or pen•cilled, pen•
  cil•ing or pen•cil•
  ling.
pend•ant
pend•ent

pend•ing
pen•du•lous
pen•du•lum
pen○e•trate v.,
  pen○e•trat○ed,
  pen○e•trat•ing.
pen○e•trat•ing
pen○e•trat•ing○ly
pen○e•tra•tion
penetration pric•ing
  Business.
pen•guin
pen○i•cil•lin
pe•nile
pen•in•su○la n., pl.
  pen•in•su○las.
pen•in•su•lar
pe•nis n., pl. pe•
  nis○es or pe•nes.
pen○i•tent
pen○i•ten•tia○ry n.,
  pl. pen○i•ten•tia•
  ries.
pen○i•tent○ly
pen•knife n., pl. pen•
  knives.
pen•light
pen•man n., pl. pen•
  men.
pen•man•ship
Penn
pen•nant n., pl. pen•
  nants. (flags: cf. PEN-
  ANCE)
pen•ni•less
Penn•syl•va•nia (PA)
pen○ny, n., pl. pen•
  nies (U.S.), pence
  (Britain).
pen○ny-pinch○ing
pen•sion Business.
pension plan Business.
pen•sive
pen•sive○ly
pent
pent-up

pen○ta•cle
pen○ta•gon
pen•tag○o○nal
pen•tam○e•ter
Pen○ta•teuch
pen•tath•lon
Pen○te•cost
pent•house n., pl.
  pent•hous○es.
pe•nu•che
pe•nul•ti•mate
pe•num•bra n., pl.
  pe•num•brae or pe•
  num•bras.
pe•nu○ri•ous
pe•nu○ri•ous•ness
pen•u○ry
pe○on
pe○o○ny n., pl. pe•○•
  nies.
peo•ple n., pl. peo•
  ples; v., peo•pled,
  peo•pling.
people me○ter
pep v., pepped, pep•
  ping.
pep•per v., pep•
  pered, pep•per•ing.
pep○per•corn
pep○per○i•ness
pep○per•mint
pep○per•○o○ni n., pl.
  pep○per•○o○nis.
pep○per•y
pep•sin
pep•tic
per an•num
per cap•i○ta
per di○em
per se
per-share Business.
per•ad•ven•ture
per•am•bu•la•tor
per•cale
per•ceiv•a○ble

per•ceive v., per•
   ceived, per•ceiv•ing.
per•cent or per cent
per•cent•age
per•cen•tile
per•cep•ti•ble
per•cep•ti•bly
per•cep•tion
per•cep•tive
per•cep•tive•ly
per•cep•tive•ness
per•cep•tiv•i•ty
per•cep•tu•al
per•cep•tu•al•ly
perch n., pl. perch or
   perch•es; v.,
   perched, perch•ing.
per•chance
per•cip•i•ent
per•co•late v., per•
   co•lat•ed, per•co•
   lat•ing.
per•co•la•tor
per•cus•sion
per•cus•sion•ist
per•di•tion
per•e•gri•na•tion
per•emp•to•ri•ly
per•emp•to•ri•ness
per•emp•to•ry
per•en•ni•al
per•en•ni•al•ly
pe•re•stroi•ka
per•fect¹ adj. (faultless:
   cf. PREFECT²)
per•fect² v., per•
   fect•ed, per•fect•
   ing.
per•fect•i•bil•i•ty
per•fect•i•ble
per•fec•tion
per•fec•tion•ism
per•fec•tion•ist
per•fect•ness
per•fi•dy n., pl. per•
   fi•dies.

per•fo•rate v., per•
   fo•rat•ed, per•fo•
   rat•ing.
per•force
per•form v., per•
   formed, per•form•
   ing.
per•for•mance
performance rat•ing
   Business.
per•form•er
per•fume v., per•
   fumed, per•fum•
   ing.
per•fum•er•y n., pl.
   per•fum•er•ies.
per•func•to•ri•ly
per•func•to•ri•ness
per•func•to•ry
per•haps
per•i•car•di•um n.,
   pl. per•i•car•di•a.
Per•i•cles
per•i•gee
per•i•he•li•on n., pl.
   per•i•he•li•a.
per•il v., per•iled or
   per•illed, per•il•ing
   or per•il•ling.
pe•rim•e•ter (bound-
   ary: cf. PARAMETER)
per•i•ne•al
per•i•ne•um n., pl.
   per•i•ne•a.
pe•ri•od
pe•ri•od•ic (recurring
   at intervals)
periodic acid (chemi-
   cal)
periodic ex•pense
   Business.
periodic in•ven•to•ry
   Business.
pe•ri•od•i•cal
pe•ri•od•i•cal•ly
per•i•o•don•tal
per•i•pa•tet•ic

pe•riph•er•al
peripheral de•vice
   Computers.
pe•riph•er•al•ly
pe•riph•er•y n., pl.
   pe•riph•er•ies.
per•i•scope
per•ish v., per•ished,
   per•ish•ing. (to die:
   cf. PARISH)
per•ish•a•bil•i•ty
per•ish•a•ble
per•i•stal•sis n., pl.
   per•i•stal•ses.
per•i•stal•tic
per•i•to•ne•al
per•i•to•ne•um n.,
   pl. per•i•to•ne•ums
   or per•i•to•ne•a.
per•i•to•ni•tis
per•i•wig
per•jure v., per•jured,
   per•jur•ing.
per•jur•er
per•ju•ry n., pl. per•
   ju•ries.
perk¹ n. Business. (per-
   quisite)
perk² v., perked,
   perk•ing. (to become
   cheerful; to percolate)
per•ma•frost
per•ma•nent
per•ma•nent•ly
per•me•a•ble
per•me•ate v., per•
   me•at•ed, per•me•
   at•ing.
Per•mi•an
per•mis•si•ble
per•mis•sion
per•mis•sive
per•mis•sive•ly
per•mis•sive•ness
per•mit v., per•mit•
   ted, per•mit•ting.
per•mu•ta•tion

per•ni•cious
per•ni•cious•ly
per•ni•cious•ness
per•o•ra•tion
per•ox•ide v., per•
ox•id•ed, per•ox•
id•ing.
per•pen•dic•u•lar
per•pen•dic•u•lar•
i•ty
per•pen•dic•u•lar•ly
per•pe•trate v., per•
pe•trat•ed, per•pe•
trat•ing.
per•pe•tra•tion
per•pe•tra•tor
per•pet•u•al
perpetual in•ven•
to•ry Business.
per•pet•u•al•ly
per•pet•u•ate v.,
per•pet•u•at•ed,
per•pet•u•at•ing.
per•pet•u•a•tion
per•pe•tu•i•ty
per•plex v., per•
plexed, per•plex•
ing.
per•qui•site Business.
(benefit: cf. PREREQUI-
SITE)
per•se•cute v., per•
se•cut•ed, per•se•
cut•ing. (to harass:
Cf. PROSECUTE)
per•se•cu•tor
per•se•vere v., per•
se•vered, per•se•
ver•ing.
Per•sia
Per•sian
Persian Gulf
per•si•flage
per•sim•mon
per•sist v., per•
sist•ed, per•sist•
ing.

per•snick•et•y
per•son
per•so•na non gra•ta
per•son•a•ble
per•son•age
per•son•al (private: cf.
PERSONNEL)
personal com•put•er
(PC) Computers.
personal prop•er•ty
Business.
per•son•al•i•ty n., pl.
per•son•al•i•ties.
per•son•al•ize v.,
per•son•al•ized,
per•son•al•iz•ing.
per•son•i•fy v., per•
son•i•fied, per•
son•i•fy•ing.
per•son•nel (employ-
ees: cf. PERSONAL)
per•spec•tive (view:
cf. PROSPECTIVE)
per•spi•ca•cious
per•spi•ca•cious•ly
per•spi•cac•i•ty
per•spic•u•ous
per•spic•u•ous•ly
per•spic•u•ous•ness
per•spi•ra•tion
per•spire v., per•
spired, per•spir•ing.
per•suade v., per•
suad•ed, per•suad•
ing.
per•sua•sion
pert (jaunty)
PERT chart (program
evaluation and review
technique chart)
per•tain v., per•
tained, per•tain•ing.
per•ti•na•cious
per•ti•na•cious•ly
per•ti•nac•i•ty
per•ti•nence
per•ti•nent

per•ti•nent•ly
pert•ly
pert•ness
per•turb v., per•
turbed, per•turb•
ing.
per•turb•a•ble
Pe•ru
pe•ruse v., pe•rused,
pe•rus•ing.
per•vade v., per•
vad•ed, per•vad•
ing.
per•va•sive
per•verse
per•verse•ly
per•ver•sion
per•ver•si•ty n., pl.
per•ver•si•ties.
per•vert v., per•
vert•ed, per•vert•
ing.
per•vert•i•ble
pe•se•ta n., pl. pe•
se•tas.
pesk•i•ly
pesk•i•ness
pes•ky adj., pes•
ki•er, pes•ki•est.
pe•so n., pl. pe•sos.
pes•si•mism
pes•si•mist
pes•si•mis•tic
pes•si•mis•ti•cal•ly
pest
pes•ter v., pes•tered,
pes•ter•ing.
pes•ti•cid•al
pes•ti•cide
pes•tif•er•ous
pes•ti•lence
pes•ti•lent
pes•tle
pet v., pet•ted, pet•
ting.

PET (positron emission tomography)
pet•al
pet•aled or pet•alled
pe•tard
pe•ter v., pe•tered, pe•ter•ing.
pet•i•ole
pe•tit (lesser: cf. PETTY)
petit bour•geois (member of lower middle class)
petit four n., pl. pet•its fours. (small tea cake)
pe•tite (diminutive)
pe•ti•tion v., pe•ti•tioned, pe•ti•tion•ing.
pe•ti•tion•er
pet•rel (the bird: cf. PETROL)
pet•ri•fy v., pet•ri•fied, pet•ri•fy•ing.
pet•ro•chem•i•cal
pet•ro•dol•lars Business.
pet•rol (gasoline: cf. PETREL)
pet•ro•la•tum
pe•tro•le•um
pet•ro•log•ic or pet ro•log•i•cal
pet•ro•log•i•cal•ly
pe•trol•o•gist
pe•trol•o•gy
pet•ti•coat
pet•ti•fog•ger
pet•ti•fog•ging
pet•ti•ly
pet•ti•ness
pet•ty adj., pet•ti•er, pet•ti•est. (insignificant: cf. PETIT; PETITE)
petty cash Business.
pet•ou•lance
pet•ou•lant

pet•ou•lant•ly
pe•tu•nia n., pl. pe•tu•nias.
pew
pe•wee
pew•ter
pe•yo•ote
PG (motion-picture rating)
PG-13 (motion-picture rating)
phag•o•cyte
phag•o•cyt•ic
pha•lan•ger
pha•lanx n., pl. pha•lanx•es or pha•lan•ges.
phal•lus n., pl. phal•li or phal•lus•es.
phan•tasm
phan•tas•ma•go•ri•a n., pl. phan•tas•ma•go•ri•as.
phan•tas•mal
phan•tas•mic
phan•tas•mi•cal
phan•ta•sy n., pl. phan•ta•sies;. v., phan•ta•sied, phan•ta•sy•ing. (fantasy)
phan•tom
phantom stock Business.
phan•tom•like
Phar•aoh
Phar•i•see
phar•ma•ceu•ti•cal
phar•ma•cist
phar•ma•co•log•i•cal or phar•ma•co•log•ic
phar•ma•col•o•gist
phar•ma•col•o•gy
phar•ma•co•poe•ia or phar•ma•co•pe•ia n., pl. phar•

ma•co•poe•ias or phar•ma•co•pe•ias.
phar•ma•cy n., pl. phar•ma•cies.
phar•yn•gi•tis
phar•ynx n., pl. pha•ryn•ges or phar•ynx•es.
phase v., phased, phas•ing. (aspect; to phase: cf. FAZE)
phase•out or phase-out
Ph.D. (Doctor of Philosophy)
pheas•ant
phe•no•bar•bi•tal
phe•nol
phe•no•lic
phe•nom•e•non n., pl. phe•nom•e•na or phe•nom•e•nons.
phe•no•type
phe•no•typ•ic or phe•no•typ•i•cal
pher•o•mo•nal
pher•o•mone
phi
phi•al
Phil•a•del•phi•a
phi•lan•der v., phi•lan•dered, phi•lan•der•ing.
phi•lan•der•er
phi•lan•thro•py n., pl. phi•lan•thro•pies.
phil•a•tel•ic
phil•a•tel•i•cal•ly
phi•lat•e•list
phi•lat•e•ly
phil•har•mon•ic
phi•lip•pic
Phil•ip•pines
phil•is•tine
phil•o•den•dron n.,

pl. phil•o•den•
drons *or* phil•o•
den•dra.

phi•lol•o•gy

phi•los•o•pher

phil•o•soph•i•cal

phi•los•o•phize *v.,*
phi•los•o•phized,
phi•los•o•phiz•ing.

phi•los•o•phy *n., pl.*
phi•los•o•phies.

phil•ter (potion: cf. FIL-
TER)

phle•bi•tis

phle•bot•o•my *n., pl.*
phle•bot•o•mies.

phlegm

phleg•mat•ic

phleg•mat•i•cal•ly

phlox *n., pl.* phlox *or*
phlox•es. (the flower:
cf. FLOCKS)

Phnom Penh

pho•bi•a *n., pl.* pho•
bi•as.

pho•bic

phoe•be *n., pl.* phoe•
bes.

Phoe•ni•cia

phoe•nix

phone *v.,* phoned,
phon•ing.

phone phreak

pho•neme

pho•net•ics

phon•ics

pho•ni•ness

pho•no•graph

pho•no•log•i•cal *or*
pho•no•log•ic

pho•nol•o•gist

pho•nol•o•gy *n., pl.*
pho•nol•o•gies.

pho•ny *n., pl.* pho•
nies; *v.,* pho•nied,
pho•ny•ing; *adj.,*

pho•ni •er, pho•ni•
est.

phoo•ey

phos•phate

phos•phor

phos•pho•res•cence

phos•pho•res•cent

phos•phor•ic ac•id

phos•pho•rus

pho•to•cell

pho•to•cop•y *n., pl.*
pho•to•cop•ies;
pho•to•cop•ied,
pho•to•cop•y•ing.

pho•to•e•lec•tric

pho•to•en•grav•er

pho•to•gen•ic

pho•to•graph *v.,*
pho•to•graphed,
pho•to•graph•ing.

pho•to•graph•a•ble

pho•tog•ra•phy

pho•to•jour•nal•ism

pho•to•jour•nal•ist

pho•to•me•chan•i•
cal

pho•tom•e•ter

pho•to•mi•cro•
graph

pho•to•mi•crog•ra•
phy

pho•to•mur•al

pho•to•mu•ral•ist

pho•ton

pho•ton•ic

pho•to•sen•si•tive

pho•to•sen•si•ti•za•
tion

pho•to•sen•si•tize
v., pho•to•sen•si•
tized, pho•to•sen•
si•tiz•ing.

pho•to•syn•the•sis

pho•to•syn•thet•ic

pho•to•syn•thet•i•
cal•ly

phrase *v.,* phrased,
phras•ing.

phra•se•ol•o•gy

phreak

phre•nol•o•gy

phy•lac•ter•y *n., pl.*
phy•lac•ter•ies.

phy•log•e•nist

phy•log•e•ny

phy•lum *n., pl.*
phy•la.

phys•ic (medicine: cf.
PHYSIQUE; PSYCHIC)

phys•i•cal (of the
body: cf. FISCAL)

physical data struc-
ture *Computers.*

physical in•ven•to•ry
Business.

physical mem•o•ry
Computers.

phys•i•cal•ly

phy•si•cian

phys•i•cist

phys•ics

phys•i•og•no•my *n.,
pl.* phys•i•og•no•
mies.

phys•i•ol•o•gy

phys•i•o•ther•a•pist

phys•i•o•ther•a•py

phy•sique (body struc-
ture: cf. PHYSIC; PSY-
CHIC)

pi (Greek letter: cf. PIE)

pi•a•nis•si•mo *n., pl.*
pi•a•nis•si•mos.

pi•an•ist

pi•an•o¹ *n., pl.* pi•
an•os. (musical in-
strument)

pi•a•no² *adj.* (soft;
softly)

pi•an•o•forte

pi•as•ter *or* pi•as•tre

pi•az•za *n., pl.* pi•
az•zas *or* piaz•ze.

pic *n.*, *pl.* pix or pics.

pi○ca *n.*, *pl.* pi•cas.

pic○a•resque (roguish: cf. PICTURESQUE)

Pi•cas○so

pic○a•yune

pic•co○lo *n.*, *pl.* pic•co○los.

pick *v.*, picked, pick•ing.

pick○ax or pick•axe *n.*, *pl.* pick•ax•es.

pick•er○el *n.*, *pl.* pick○el or pick•els.

pick○et *v.*, pick•et○ed, pick•et•ing.

pick•et○er

pick○le *v.*, pick•led, pick•ling.

pick•pock○et

pick○up

pick○y *adj.*, pick•i○er, pick•i•est.

pic•nic *v.*, pic•nicked, pic•nick•ing.

pic•nick○er

pi○co•sec•ond

pic•to•ri○al

pic•ture *v.*, pic•tured, pic•tur•ing. (image: cf. PITCHER)

pic•tur•esque (quaint: cf. PICARESQUE)

pic•tur•esque○ly

pic•tur•esque•ness

pid•dling

pidg○in (jargon: cf. PI•GEON)

pie (pastry: cf. PI)

pie-eyed

pie•bald

piece *v.*, pieced, piec•ing. (portion: cf. PEACE)

pièce de ré•sis•tance *n.*, *pl.* pièces de ré•sis•tance.

piece•meal

piece•work *Business.*

piece•work○er *Business.*

pied

pied-à-terre *n.*, *pl.* pieds-à-terre.

pier (dock: cf. PEER)

pierce *v.*, pierced, pierc•ing.

Pierre

pi•e○ty *n.*, *pl.* pi•e•ties.

pif•fle

pig *v.*, pigged, pig•ging.

pi•geon (the bird: cf. PIDGIN)

pi○geon-toed

pi•geon•hole *v.*, pi•geon•holed, pi•geon•hol•ing.

pig•gish

pig•gish•ness

pig○gy or pig•gie, *n.*, *pl.* pig•gies; *adj.*, pig•gi○er, pig•gi•est.

pig○gy•back[1] *adv.*

pig○gy•back[2] *v.*, *adj.* pig○gy•backed, pig○gy•back•ing.

pig•head○ed

pig•head•ed•ness

pig•ment *v.*, pig•ment○ed, pig•ment•ing.

pig•men•ta•tion

pig•ment○ed

pig•pen

pig•skin

pig•tail

pike *n.*, *pl.* pike or pikes.

pik○er

pi•laf

pi•las•ter

pi•las•tered

Pi•late

pil•chard

pile *v.*, piled, pil•ing.

piles

pile○up

pil•fer *v.*, pil•fered, pil•fer•ing.

pil•fer•age

pil•grim

pil•grim•age

pill

pil•lage *v.*, pil•laged, pil•lag•ing.

pil•lar

pil•lared

pill•box

pil•lion

pil•lo○ry *n.*, *pl.* pil•lo•ries; *v.*, pil•lo•ried, pil•lo•ry•ing.

pil•low *v.*, pil•lowed, pil•low•ing.

pil○low•case

pi•lot *v.*, pi•lot○ed, pi•lot•ing.

pi○lot•house *n.*, *pl.* pi○lot•hous•es.

PIM *Computers.* (personal information manager)

pi•men○to *n.*, *pl.* pi•men•tos.

pimp *v.*, pimped, pimp•ing.

pim•per•nel

pim•ple

PIN *Computers.* (personal identification number)

pin *v.*, pinned, pin•ning.

pin feed *Computers.*

pin○a•fore

pi•ña○ta *n.*, *pl.* pi•ña•tas.

pin•ball machine

pince-nez *n., pl.* pince-nez.

pin•cers

pinch *v.,* pinched, pinch•ing.

pinch-hit *v,* pinch-hit, pinch-hit○ting.

pin•cush•ion

pine *v.,* pined, pin•ing.

pin•e○al gland

pine-ap○ple

ping

Ping-Pong *Trademark.*

pin•head

pin•hole

pin•ion (gear; wing: cf. PIÑON; PINYIN)

pink *adj.,* pink○er, pink•est.

pink•eye

pink○ie or pink○y, *n., pl.* pink•ies.

pink•ing shears

pin•na•cle

pi•noch○le

pi•ñon *n., pl.* pi•ñons or pi•ño•nes. (pine nut: cf. PINION; PINYIN)

pin•point *v.,* pin•point○ed, pin•point•ing.

pin•prick

pin•set•ter

pin•striped

pint

pin○to *n., pl.* pin•tos.

pin○up

pin•wheel

pin•yin (Chinese transliteration system: cf. PINION; PIÑON)

pi•o•neer *v.,* pi•o•neered, pi•o•neer•ing.

pi•ous

pi•ous○ly

pi•ous•ness

pip

pipe *v.,* piped, pip•ing.

pipe•line

pip•pin

pip•squeak

pi•quan○cy

pi•quant

pique *v.,* piqued, piqu○ing. (to irritate: cf. PEAK; PEEK)

pi•qué (the fabric)

piqued (aroused: cf. PEAKED; PEEKED)

pi•ra○cy *n., pl.* pi•ra•cies.

pi•ra•nha *n., pl.* pi•ra•nhas or pi•ra•nha.

pi•rate *v.,* pi•rat○ed, pi•rat•ing.

pi•rat○i•cal

pir•ou•ette *v.,* pir•ou•et○ted, pir•ou•et•ting.

pis•ca•to○ry or pis•ca•to•ri•al

Pis•ces

pis•mire

pis•tach○i○o *n., pl.* pis•ta•chi○os.

pis•til (flower part)

pis•tol (handgun)

pis○tol-whip *v.,* pis○tol-whipped, pis○tol-whip○ping.

pis•ton

pit *v.,* pit○ted, pit•ting.

pi○ta *n., pl.* pi•tas.

pit-a-pat

pitch *v.,* pitched, pitch•ing.

pitch-black

pitch-dark

pitch•blende

pitch○er (container; baseball player: cf. PICTURE)

pitch•fork

pitch•man *n., pl.* pitch•men.

pit○e○ous

pit○e○ous○ly

pit○e○ous•ness

pit•fall

pith

pith○y *adj.,* pith•i○er, pith•i•est.

pit○i•a○ble

pit○i•ful

pit○i•ful○ly

pit○i•less

pit○i•less○ly

pit○i•less•ness

pi•ton

pit•tance

pit○ter-pat○ter *v.,* pit○ter-pat○tered, pit○ter-pat○ter○ing.

Pitts•burgh

pi•tu•i•tar○y *n., pl.* pi•tu•i•tar•ies.

pit○y *n., pl.* pit•ies; pit•ied, pit○y•ing.

pit○y•ing○ly

piv○ot *v.,* piv•ot○ed, piv•ot•ing.

pix *n., pl.* of pic.

pix○el *Computers.*

pix○ie or pix○y, *n., pl.* pix•ies.

pi•zazz or piz•zazz

piz○za *n., pl.* piz•zas.

piz•ze•ri○a *n., pl.* piz•ze•ri•as.

piz•zi•ca○to *n., pl.* piz•zi•ca•ti.

pl. (plural)

P/L or P&L *Business.* (profit and loss).

PL/1 *Computers.* (programming language)

plac•ard
pla•cate v., pla•
 cat○ed, pla•cat•ing.
place v., placed, plac•
 ing.
pla•ce○bo n., pl. pla•
 ce○bos or pla•
 ce○boes.
place•ment
pla•cen○ta n., pl. pla•
 cen•tas or pla•cen•
 tae.
pla•cen•tal
plac○id
pla•cid•i○ty or plac•
 id•ness
plac•id○ly
plack○et
pla•gia•rize v., pla•
 gia○rized, pla•gia•
 riz•ing.
plague v., plagued,
 pla○guing. (epidemic
 disease; to torment: cf.
 PLAQUE)
plaid
plain adj., plain○er,
 plain•est. (clear: cf.
 PLANE)
plain va•nil○la
plain•clothes•man or
 plain•clothes man
 n., pl. plain•clothes•
 men or plain•clothes
 men.
plain○ly
plain•ness
plains•man n., pl.
 plains•men.
plain•song
plaint
plain•tiff (one who
 sues)
plain•tive (mournful)
plain•tive○ly
plait v., plait○ed,
 plait•ing. (braid; to

braid: cf. PLAT; PLATE;
 PLEAT)
plan v., planned,
 plan•ning.
pla•nar
plane v., planed,
 plan•ing. (airplane;
 tool; to use a plane:
 cf. PLAIN)
plan○et
plan○e○tar•i○um n.,
 pl. plan○e○tar○i•ums
 or plan○e○tar○i○a.
plan○e○tes○i•mal
plank
plank•ton
plan•ner
plant v., plant○ed,
 plant•ing.
plant•a○ble
plan•tain
plan•tar (of the sole of
 the foot)
plan•ta•tion
plant○er (one who
 plants:
plaque (inscribed tab-
 let: cf. PLAGUE)
plas○ma
plasma dis•play Com-
 puters.
plas•ter v., plas•
 tered, plas•ter•ing.
plas○ter•board
plas•ter○er
plas•tic
plastic sur•ger○y
plat v., plat•ted, plat•
 ting. (map: cf. PLAIT;
 PLEAT)
plate v., plat○ed,
 plat•ing. (dish)
plate-tec○ton○ic
pla•teau n., pl. pla•
 teaus or pla•teaux;
 v., pla•teaued, pla•
 teau•ing.

plat•form
plat○i•num
plat○i•tude
Pla○to
Pla•ton○ic
pla•toon
plat•ter
plat○y n., pl. plat○y or
 plat○ys or plat•ies.
plat○y•pus n., pl.
 plat○y•pus○es or
 plat○y○pi.
plau•dit
plau•si•bil•i○ty
plau•si○ble
plau•si•bly
play v., played, play•
 ing.
play-off
play•act v., play•
 act○ed, play•act•
 ing.
play•back
play•bill
play•boy
play○er
play•ful
play•ful○ly
play•ful•ness
play•go○er
play•ground
play•house n., pl.
 play•hous○es.
play•mate
play•pen
play•thing
play•wright
pla○za n., pl. pla○zas.
plea n., pl. pleas.
plead v., plead○ed or
 pled, plead•ing.
plead•a○ble
plead○er
pleas•ant
pleas•ant○ly
pleas•ant•ness

pleas•ant∘ry n., pl.
  pleas•ant•ries.
please v., pleased,
  pleas•ing.
pleas•ing∘ly
pleas•ur•a∘ble
pleas•ur•a•bly
pleas•ure
pleat v., pleat∘ed,
  pleat•ing. (crease: cf.
  PLAIT; PLAT; PLATE)
ple•be∘ian
pleb∘i•scite
plec•trum n., pl. plec•
  tra, plec•trums.
pled
pledge v., pledged,
  pledg•ing.
Pleis•to•cene
ple•na∘ry
plen∘i•po•ten•ti•
  ar∘y n., pl. plen∘i•
  po•ten•ti•ar•ies.
plen∘i•tude
plen•te∘ous
plen•te•ous•ness
plen•ti•ful
plen•ti•ful∘ly
plen∘ty
pleu•ri∘sy
Plex∘i•glas Trademark.
plex∘us n., pl. plex•
  us∘es or plex∘us.
pli•a•bil∘i•ty
pli•a∘ble
pli•an∘cy
pli•ant
pli•ers
plight v., plight∘ed,
  plight•ing.
plod v., plod•ded,
  plod•ding.
plod•der
plod•ding∘ly
plop v., plopped,
  plop•ping.

plot v., plot•ted,
  plot•ting.
plov∘er
plow v., plowed,
  plow•ing.
plow•a∘ble
plow∘er
plow•share
ploy
pluck v., plucked,
  pluck•ing.
pluck•i∘ly
pluck∘i•ness
pluck∘y adj., pluck•
  i∘er, pluck•i•est.
plug v., plugged,
  plug•ging.
plug-com∘pat∘i•ble
  Computers.
plum (the fruit)
plum•age
plum•aged
plumb[1] (perpendicular)
plumb[2] v., plumbed,
  plumb•ing. (to meas-
  ure, as depth)
plumb∘er
plumb•ing
plume
plum•met v., plum•
  met∘ed, plum•met•
  ing.
plump v., plumped,
  plump•ing; adj.,
  plump∘er, plump•
  est.
plump•ness
plun•der v., plun•
  dered, plun•der•ing.
plun•der•a∘ble
plun•der∘er
plunge v., plunged,
  plung•ing.
plung∘er
plunk v., plunked,
  plunk•ing.
plunk∘er

plu•per•fect
plu•ral
plu•ral•ism
plu•ral•ist
plu•ral•is•tic
plu•ral•is•ti•cal∘ly
plu•ral•i∘ty n., pl.
  plu•ral•i•ties.
plu•ral∘i•za•tion
plu•ral•ize v., plu•
  ral∘ized, plu•ral•iz•
  ing.
plus
plush adj., plush∘er,
  plush•est.
plush∘ly
Plu•tarch
Plu•to
plu•toc•ra∘cy n., pl.
  plu•toc•ra•cies.
plu•ton
plu•to•ni∘um
ply n., pl. plies; v.,
  plied, ply•ing.
Plym•outh
ply•wood
PMS (premenstrual syndrome)
pmt. (payment)
pneu•mat∘ic
pneu•mo•ni∘a
pneu•mon∘ic (of the
  lungs: cf. MNEMONIC)
poach v., poached,
  poach•ing.
pock∘et v., pock•
  et∘ed, pock•et•ing.
pock∘et•book
pock∘et•knife n., pl.
  pock∘et•knives.
pock•marked
pod
po•di•a•try
po•di∘um n., pl. po•
  di•ums or po•di∘a.
Poe

po•em
po•e•sy *n., pl.* po•e•sies.
po•et
poet lau•re•ate *n., pl.* po•ets lau•re•ate.
po•et•ic
po•et•ry
po•grom
poi
poign•an•cy
poign•ant
poign•ant•ly
poin•ci•an•a *n., pl.* poin•ci•an•as.
poin•set•ti•a *n., pl.* poin•set•ti•as.
point
point-and-click *Computers.*
point of pur•chase *n. Business.*
point-of-purchase *adj. Business.*
point-blank
point•er
poin•til•lism
poin•til•list
point•less
point•less•ly
point•less•ness
poise *v.,* poised, pois•ing.
poised
poi•son *v.,* poi•soned, poi•son•ing.
poison pill *Business.*
poi•son•er
poke *v.,* poked, pok•ing.
pok•er (card game: cf. POLKA)
pok•i•ly
pok•i•ness
pok•y *adj.,* pok•i•er, pok•i•est.

pol
Po•land
po•lar
Po•lar•ois
po•lar•i•ty *n., pl.* po•lar•i•ties.
po•lar•i•za•tion
po•lar•ize *v.,* po•lar•ized, po•lar•iz•ing.
Po•lar•oid *Trademark.*
pole *v.,* poled, pol•ing. (long rod; to use a pole: cf. POLL)
pole vault *n.*
pole-vault•er
pole•cat *n., pl.* pole•cats or pole•cat.
po•lem•ic
po•lem•ics
pole•star
pole-vault *v.,* pole-vault•ed, pole-vault•ing.
po•lice *v.,* po•liced, po•lic•ing.
po•lice•man *n., pl.* po•lice•men.
pol•i•cy *n., pl.* pol•i•cies.
pol•i•cy•hold•er *Business.*
po•li•o•my•e•li•tis
Po•lish (of Poland)
pol•ish *v.,* pol•ished, pol•ish•ing. (to make glossy)
Po•lit•bu•ro
po•lite *adj.,* po•lit•er, po•lit•est.
po•lite•ly
po•lite•ness
pol•i•tesse
pol•i•tic
po•lit•i•cal
po•lit•i•cal•ly
politically cor•rect
pol•i•ti•cian

po•lit•i•cize *v.,* po•lit•i•cized, po•lit•i•ciz•ing.
po•lit•i•co *n., pl.* po•lit•i•cos.
pol•i•tics
Polk
pol•ka *n., pl.* pol•kas; *v.,* pol•kaed, pol•ka•ing. (lively dance: cf. POKER)
poll *v.,* polled, poll•ing. (survey: cf. POLE)
pol•len
pol•li•nate *v.,* pol•li•nat•ed, pol•li•nat•ing.
pol•li•na•tion
pol•li•wog or pol•ly•wog
poll•ster
pol•lute *v.,* pol•lut•ed, pol•lut•ing.
pol•lut•er
po•lo
pol•o•naise
po•lo•ni•um
pol•ter•geist
pol•y•clin•ic
pol•y•es•ter
pol•y•eth•yl•ene
po•lyg•a•mist
po•lyg•a•my
pol•y•glot
pol•y•glot•ism
pol•y•gon
po•lyg•o•nal
pol•y•graph *v.,* pol•y•graphed, pol•y•graph•ing.
pol•y•he•dral
pol•y•he•dron *n., pl.* pol•y•he•drons, pol•y•he•dra.
pol•y•math
pol•y•mer

portcullis

pol•y•mer•ase chain re•ac•tion
Pol•y•ne•sia
pol•y•no•mi•al
pol•yp
po•lyph•o•o•ny
pol•y•sty•rene
pol•y•syl•lab•ic
pol•y•syl•la•ble
pol•y•tech•nic
pol•y•the•ism
pol•y•the•ist
pol•y•the•is•tic
pol•y•the•is•ti•cal
pol•y•un•sat•u•rat•ed
pol•y•vi•nyl
po•made
pome•gran•ate
pom•mel v., pom•meled or pom•melled, pom•mel•ing or pom•mel•ling. (knob: cf. PUM•MEL)
pomp
pom•pa•dour
pom•pa•no n., pl. pom•pa•no, pom•pa•nos.
pom•pom or pom-pom
pomp•ous
pomp•ous•ly
pon•cho n., pl. pon•chos.
pond
pon•der v., pon•dered, pon•der•ing.
pon•der•o•sa pine
pon•der•ous
pon•der•ous•ly
pone
pon•gee
pon•iard
pon•tiff

pon•tif•i•cate v., pon•tif•i•cat•ed, pon•tif•i•cat•ing.
pon•toon
poo•ny n., pl. poo•nies; v., poo•nied, poo•ny•ing.
poo•ny•tail
Pon•zi scheme Business.
pooch
poo•dle
pooh
pooh-pooh v., pooh-poohed, pooh-pooh•ing.
pool v., pooled, pool•ing.
poop v., pooped, poop•ing.
poor adj., poor•er, poor•est. (impoverished: cf. PORE; POUR)
poor•house n., pl. poor•hous•es.
pop v., popped, pop•ping.
pop-up u•til•i•ty Computers.
pop-up win•dow Computers.
pop•corn
pope
pop•gun
pop•in•jay
pop•lar (the tree: cf. POPULAR)
pop•lin
pop•o•ver
pop•py n., pl. pop•pies.
pop•py•cock
pop•u•lace (common people: cf. POPULOUS)
pop•u•lar (well-liked: cf. POPLAR)
pop•u•lar•i•za•tion

pop•u•lar•ize v., pop•u•lar•ized, pop•u•lar•iz•ing.
pop•u•lar•ly
pop•u•late v., pop•u•lat•ed, pop•u•lat•ing.
pop•u•la•tion
pop•u•lism
pop•u•list
pop•u•lous (thickly populated: cf. POPU•LACE)
por•ce•lain
porch
por•cine
por•cu•pine
pore v., pored, por•ing. (tiny opening; to read: cf. POOR; POUR)
por•gy n., pl. por•gy or por•gies.
pork
porn or por•no
por•no•graph•ic
por•nog•ra•phy
po•rous
po•rous•ness
por•phy•rit•ic
por•phy•ry
por•poise n., pl. por•poise or por•pois•es.
por•ridge
por•rin•ger
port v., port•ed, port•ing.
Port-au-Prince
Port More•sby
Port-of-Spain
port•a•ble
portable com•put•er Computers.
por•tage v., por•taged, por•tag•ing.
por•tal
port•cul•lis

por•tend v., por•
tend•ed, por•tend•
ing.
por•tent
por•ten•tous
por•ten•tous•ly
por•ter
por•ter•house
port•fo•li•o n., pl.
port•fo•li•os.
port•hole
por•ti•co n., pl. por•
ti•coes or por•ti•
cos.
por•ti•coed
por•tiere or por•tiére
por•tiered
por•tion v., por•
tioned, por•tion•
ing.
Port•land
port•li•ness
port•ly adj., port•
li•er, port•li•est.
port•man•teau n., pl.
port•man•teaus or
port•man•teaux.
Por•to No•vo
por•trait
por•trait o•ri•en•ta•
tion Computers.
por•trait•ist
por•trai•ture
por•tray v., por•
trayed, por•tray•
ing.
Por•tu•gal
Por•tu•guese n., pl.
Por•tu•guese.
pose v., posed, pos•
ing.
Po•sei•don
pos•er (puzzling prob-
lem)
po•seur (affected per-
son)
posh

pos•it v., pos•it•ed,
pos•it•ing.
po•si•tion v., po•si•
tioned, po•si•tion•
ing.
po•si•tion•al
pos•i•tive
pos•i•tive•ness
pos•i•tron
pos•se
pos•sess v., pos•
sessed, pos•sess•
ing.
pos•ses•sion
pos•ses•sive
pos•ses•sive•ly
pos•ses•sive•ness
pos•ses•sor
pos•si•ble
pos•sum n., pl. pos•
sums or pos•sum.
post v., post•ed,
post•ing.
post of•fice n.
post-of•fice adj.
post•age
post•al
post•card or post card
post•date v., post•
dat•ed, post•dat•
ing.
post•er
pos•te•ri•or
pos•te•ri•or•i•ty
pos•te•ri•or•ly
pos•ter•i•ty
pos•tern
post•fem•i•nism
post•fem•i•nist
post•grad•u•ate
post•haste
post•hu•mous
post•hu•mous•ly
post•hyp•not•ic
pos•til•ion
pos•til•ioned

post•in•dus•tri•al
post•lude
post•man n., pl. post•
men.
post•mark v., post•
marked, post•mark•
ing.
post•mas•ter
post•mod•ern
post•mod•ern•ism
post•mod•ern•ist
post•mor•tem
post•na•sal
post•op•er•a•tive
post•op•er•a•tive•ly
post•paid
post•par•tum
post•pone v., post•
poned, post•pon•
ing.
post•pone•ment
post•pran•di•al
post•proc•es•sor
Computers.
post•script
post•struc•tur•al•ism
pos•tu•late v., pos•
tu•lat•ed, pos•tu•
lat•ing.
pos•tu•la•tion
pos•tur•al
pos•ture v., pos•
tured, pos•tur•ing.
post•war
po•sy n., pl. po•sies.
pot v., pot•ted, pot•
ting.
po•ta•bil•i•ty
po•ta•ble
pot•ash
po•tas•si•um
po•ta•to n., pl. po•
ta•toes.
pot•bel•lied
pot•bel•ly n., pl. pot•
bel•lies.

precision

pot•boil∘er
po•tent
po•ten•tate
po•ten•tial
po•ten•tial∘ly
pot•herb
pot•hold∘er
pot•hole
pot•hook
po•tion
pot•latch
pot•luck
Po•to•mac
pot•pie
pot•pour∘ri n., pl.
  pot•pour•ris.
pot•sherd
pot•shot
pot•tage
pot•ted
pot•ter
pot•ter∘y
pouch
poul•tice
poul•try (fowl: cf. PAL-
  TRY)
pounce v., pounced,
  pounc•ing.
pound n., pl. pounds
  or pound; v.,
  pound∘ed, pound•
  ing.
pour v., poured,
  pour•ing. (to send
  flowing: cf. PORE; POOR)
pout v., pout∘ed,
  pout•ing.
pov•er∘ty
pov∘er∘ty-strick∘en
pow•der v., pow•
  dered, pow•der•ing.
power v., pow•ered,
  pow•er•ing.
pow∘er us∘er Comput-
  ers.

pow∘er•bro•ker or
  pow∘er bro•ker
pow•er•ful
pow•er•ful∘ly
pow∘er•house n., pl.
  pow∘er•hous∘es.
pow•er•less
pow•wow
pox
pp. (pages)
PR (Puerto Rico)
prac•ti•ca∘ble (feasi-
  ble)
prac•ti•cal (useful)
prac•ti•cal•i∘ty
prac•ti•cal∘ly
prac•tice v., prac•
  ticed, prac•tic•ing.
prac•ti•tion∘er
Prae•to•ri∘an Guard
prag•mat∘ic
prag•mat∘i•cal∘ly
prag•ma•tism
prag•ma•tist
Prague
Prai∘a
prai•rie
praise v., praised,
  prais•ing.
praise•wor•thi∘ly
praise•wor•thi•ness
praise•wor•thy
pra•line
prance v., pranced,
  pranc•ing.
prank
pra•se∘o•dym•i∘um
prate v., prat∘ed,
  prat•ing.
prat•fall
prat•tle v., prat•tled,
  prat•tling.
prawn
pray v., prayed, pray•
  ing. (to entreat: cf.
  PREY)

prayer¹ (worshipful pe-
  tition)
pray∘er² (one who
  prays)
preach v., preached,
  preach•ing.
pre•am•ble
pre•ar•range v., pre•
  ar•ranged, pre•ar•
  rang•ing.
pre•ar•range•ment
Pre•cam•bri•an or
  Pre-Cam∘bri•an
pre•can•cer•ous
pre•car∘i•ous
pre•car∘i•ous∘ly
pre•cau•tion
pre•cau•tion•ar∘y
pre•cede v., pre•
  ced∘ed, pre•ced•
  ing. (to go before: cf.
  PROCEED)
prec∘e•dence (prior-
  ity)
prec∘e•dent n., pl.
  prec∘e•dents. (exam-
  ples)
pre•ced•ing
pre•cept
pre•cep•tor
pre•cinct
pre•ci•os•i∘ty
pre•cious
pre•cious•ness
prec∘i•pice
pre•cip∘i•tant
pre•cip∘i•tate v.,
  pre•cip∘i•tat∘ed,
  pre•cip∘i•tat•ing.
pre•cip∘i•tate∘ly
pre•cip∘i•ta•tion
pre•cip∘i•tous
pré•cis n., pl. preé•
  cis. (summary)
pre•cise (exact)
pre•cise∘ly
pre•ci•sion

pre•clude *v.*, pre•
clud∘ed, pre•clud•
ing.

pre•co•cious

pre•coc•i∘ty

pre•cog•ni•tion

pre•cog•ni•tive

pre-Co∘lum∘bi∘an

pre•con•ceived

pre•con•cep•tion

pre•con•di•tion *v.*,
pre•con•di•tioned,
pre•con•di•tion•
ing.

pre•cur•sor

pre•cur•so∘ry

pre•date *v.*, pre•
dat∘ed, pre•dat•
ing.

pre•da•tion

pred∘a•tor

pred∘a•to∘ry

pre•de•cease *v.*, pre•
de•ceased, pre•de•
ceas∘ing.

pred∘e•ces•sor

pre•des•ti•na•tion

pre•des•tine *v.*, pre•
des•tined, pre•des•
tin∘ing.

pre•de•ter•mi•na•
tion

pre•de•ter•mine *v.*,
pre•de•ter•mined,
pre•de•ter•min•ing.

pre•dic∘a•ment

pred∘i•cate

pre•dict *v.*, pre•
dict∘ed, pre•dict•
ing.

pre•dict•a∘ble

pre•dic•tion (proph-
ecy)

pre•di•gest *v.*, pre•
di•gest∘ed, pre•di•
gest∘ing.

pre•di•lec•tion (pref-
erence)

pre•dis•pose *v.*, pre•
dis•posed, pre•dis•
pos∘ing.

pre•dis•po•si•tion

pre•dom∘i•nance

pre•dom∘i•nant

pre•dom∘i•nant∘ly

pre•dom∘i•nate *v.*,
pre•dom∘i•nat∘ed,
pre•dom∘i•nat•ing.

pre•em∘i•nence

pre•em∘i•nent or
pre-em∘i∘nent

pre•em∘i•nent∘ly

pre•empt or pre-empt
v., pre•empt∘ed,
pre•empt•ing or
pre-empt∘ing.

pre•emp•tion

pre•emp•tive

preemptive right *Busi-
ness.*

preen *v.*, preened,
preen•ing.

pre•fab

pre•fab•ri•cat∘ed

pre•fab•ri•ca•tion

pref•ace *v.*, pref•
aced, pref•ac∘ing.

pref∘a•to∘ry

pre•fect (magistrate:
cf. PERFECT)

pre•fec•ture

pre•fer *v.*, pre•ferred,
pre•fer•ring.

pref•er•a∘ble

pref•er•a∘bly

pref•er•ence

pref•er•en•tial

pref•er•ment

preferred stock *Busi-
ness.*

pre•fig•ure *v.*, pre•
fig•ured, pre•fig•
ur∘ing.

pre•fix

preg•nan∘cy

preg•nant

pre•hen•sile

pre•his•tor∘ic

pre•judge *v.*, pre•
judged, pre•judg•
ing.

pre•judg•ment

prej∘u•dice *v.*,
prej∘u•diced,
prej∘u•dic∘ing.

prej∘u•di•cial

prel•a∘cy

prel•ate

pre•lim∘i•nar∘y *n.*,
pl. pre•lim∘i•nar•
ies.

pre•lit•er•ate

prel•ude

pre•mar∘i•tal

pre•ma•ture

pre•ma•ture∘ly

pre•med∘i•tate *v.*,
pre•med∘i•tat∘ed,
pre•med∘i•tat•ing.

pre•med∘i•ta•tion

pre•mier (leading;
prime minister)

pre•miere *v.*, pre•
miered, pre•mier•
ing. (first perfor-
mance; to give a pre-
miere)

prem•ise

pre•mi∘um *Business.*

pre•mo•ni•tion

pre•mon∘i•to∘ry

pre•na•tal

pre•na•tal∘ly

pre•oc•cu•pa•tion

pre•oc•cu•py *v.*, pre•
oc•cu•pied, pre•
oc•cu•py∘ing.

pre•op•er∘a•tive

pre•or•dain *v.*, pre•

or•dained, pre•or•dain•ing.

prep *v.*, prepped, prep•ping.

prep school

pre•pack•age *v.*, pre•pack•aged, pre•pack•ag•ing.

pre•paid *Business.*

prepaid ex•pense *Business.*

prep○a•ra•tion

pre•par○a•to○ry

pre•pare *v.*, pre•pared, pre•par•ing.

pre•par○ed•ness

pre•pay *v.*, pre•paid, pre•pay•ing.

pre•pay•ment

pre•pon•der•ance

pre•pon•der•ant

prep○o•si•tion (grammatical form: cf. PROP-OSITION)

prep○o•si•tion○al

pre•pos•sess *v.*, pre•pos•sessed, pre•pos•sess•ing.

pre•pos•sess•ing

pre•pos•ter○ous

prep○py or prep•pie *n., pl.* prep•pies.

pre•puce

pre•quel

pre•re○cord *v.*, pre•re○cord○ed, pre•re○cord•ing.

pre•req•ui•site (precondition: cf. PERQUI-SITE)

pre•re○tail•ing *Business.*

pre•rog○a•tive

pres•age *v.*, pres•aged, pres•ag•ing.

pres•by•o•pi○a

pres•by•te•ri○an

pre•school

pre•school○er

pre•science

pre•scient

pre•scribe *v.*, pre•scribed, pre•scrib•ing. (to order: cf. PRO-SCRIBE)

pre•scrip•tion

pre•scrip•tive

pres•ence (being at a place)

pres•ent¹ (gift; here)

pre•sent² *v.*, pre•sent○ed, pre•sent•ing. (to give)

pre•sent•a○ble

pres•en•ta•tion

presentation graph•ics *Computers.*

pres○ent-day

pre•sen•ti•ment

pres•ent○ly

pres•er•va•tion

pres•er•va•tion•ist

pre•serv○a•tive

pre•serve *v.*, pre•served, pre•serv•ing.

pre•serv○er

pre•set *v.*, pre•set, pre•set•ting.

pre•side *v.*, pre•sid○ed, pre•sid•ing.

pres○i•den○cy

pres○i•dent

pres○i•den•tial

pre•sid•i•um *n., pl.* pre•sid○i•ums or pre•sid•i○a.

press *v.*, pressed, press•ing.

press○er

press•ing

press•man *n., pl.* press•men.

pres•sure *v.*, pres•sured, pres•sur•ing.

pres•sur•ize *v.*, pres•sur•ized, pres•sur•iz•ing.

pres○ti•dig○i•ta•tion

pres•tige

pres•tig•ious

pres○to *n., pl.* pres•tos.

pre•sum•a○ble

pre•sum•a○bly

pre•sume *v.*, pre•sumed, pre•sum•ing.

pre•sump•tion

pre•sump•tive

pre•sump•tu○ous

pre•sup•pose *v.*, pre•sup•posed, pre•sup•pos•ing.

pre•sup•po•si•tion

pre•teen

pre•tend *v.*, pre•tend○ed, pre•tend•ing.

pre•tend○er

pre•tense

pre•ten•sion

pre•ten•tious

pre•ten•tious○ly

pre•ten•tious•ness

pret•er○it or pret•er•ite

pre•ter•nat○u•ral

pre•test

pre•text

Pre•to•ri○a

pret•ti○fy *v.*, pret•ti•fied, pret•ti•fy•ing.

pret•ti○ly

pret•ti•ness

pret○ty *n., pl.* pret•ties; *v.*, pret•tied, pret•ty•ing; *adj.*, pret•ti○er, pret•ti•est.

pret•zel

pre•vail v., pre•vailed, pre•vail•ing.

prev○a•lence

prev○a•lent

pre•var○i•cate v., pre•var○i•cat○ed, pre•var○i•cat•ing.

pre•var○i•ca•tion

pre•var○i•ca•tor

pre•vent v., pre•vent○ed, pre•vent•ing.

pre•vent•a•ble or pre•vent○i•ble

pre•ven•tion

pre•ven•tive or pre•vent○a•tive

preventive main•te•nance Business.

pre•view v., pre•viewed, pre•view•ing.

pre•vi•ous

pre•vi•ous○ly

pre•war

prex○y n., pl. prex•ies.

prey v., preyed, prey•ing. (victim; to victimize: cf. PRAY)

pri•ap○ic

price v., priced, pric•ing. Business.

price con•trol Business.

price-earn○ings ra•ti○o (p/e) Business.

price e○las•tic•i○ty Business.

price in•dex Business.

price lead○er Business.

price war Business.

price•less

prick v., pricked, prick•ing.

prick○le v., prick•led, prick•ling.

prick○ly adj., prick•li○er, prick•li•est.

pride v., prid○ed, prid•ing.

prie-dieu n., pl. prie-dieus or prie-dieux.

priest

priest•ess

priest•hood

priest○ly adj., priest•li○er, priest•li•est.

prig

prig•gish

prim adj., prim•mer, prim•mest.

pri○ma don○na n., pl. pri○ma don•nas.

pri○ma fa•ci○e

pri•ma○cy

pri•mal

pri•ma•ri○ly

pri•ma○ry n., pl. pri•ma•ries.

primary li•a•bil•i○ty Business.

primary of•fer•ing Business.

pri•mate

prime v., primed, prim•ing.

prime rate Business.

prim○er

pri•me•val or pri•mae•val

prim○i•tive

prim○ly

prim•ness

pri○mo•gen○i•tor

pri○mo•gen○i•ture

pri•mor•di○al

primp v., primped, primp•ing.

prim•rose

prince

prince○ly adj., prince•li○er, prince•li•est.

prin•cess

prin•ci•pal (foremost)

prin•ci•pal•i○ty n., pl. prin•ci•pal•i•ties.

prin•ci•pal○ly

prin•ci•ple (fundamental law)

prin•ci•pled

print v., print○ed, print•ing.

print qual○i○ty mode Computers.

print serv○er Computers.

print spool○er Computers.

print spool•ing Computers.

print•a○ble

print○ed cir•cuit

printed circuit board

print○er

print○ing

print•out Computers.

print•wheel Computers.

pri○or

pri•or•ess

pri•or○i•tize v., pri•or○i•tized, pri•or○i•tiz•ing.

pri•or○i○ty n., pl. pri•or•i•ties.

pri•o○ry n., pl. pri•o•ries.

prism

pris•mat○ic

pris○on

pris•on○er

pris•si○ly

pris•si•ness

pris○sy adj., pris•si○er, pris•si•est.

pris•tine

prith○ee

pri•va•cy *n., pl.* pri•
va•cies.

pri•vate

private en•ter•prise
Business.

private la•bel *Busi-
ness.*

private sec•tor *Busi-
ness.*

pri•va•teer

pri•vate•ly

pri•va•tion

priv•et

priv•i•lege

priv•i•leged

priv•y *n., pl.* priv•ies.

prize *v.,* prized, priz•
ing.

prize•fight or prize
fight

prize•fight•er

pro *n., pl.* pros.

pro for•ma

pro forma in•voice
Business.

pro-life

pro-lif•er

pro tem•po•re

prob•a•bil•i•ty *n., pl.*
prob•a•bil•i•ties.

prob•a•ble

prob•a•bly

pro•bate *v.,* pro•
bat•ed, pro•bat•
ing.

pro•ba•tion

pro•ba•tion•ar•y

pro•ba•tion•er

probe *v.,* probed,
prob•ing.

pro•bi•ty

prob•lem

prob•lem•at•ic or
prob•lem•at•i•cal

pro•bos•cis *n., pl.*
pro•bos•cis•es or
pro•bos•ci•des.

pro•caine

pro•ce•dur•al

pro•ce•dure

pro•ceed *v.,* pro•
ceed•ed, pro•ceed•
ing. (to continue: cf.
PRECEDE)

proc•ess *n., pl.* proc•
ess•es; *v.,* proc•
essed, proc•ess•ing.

process cost•ing *Busi-
ness.*

proc•ess num•ber
Computers.

pro•ces•sion

pro•ces•sion•al

proc•es•sor

pro-choice or pro•
choice

pro-choic•er

pro•claim *v.,* pro•
claimed, pro•claim•
ing.

proc•la•ma•tion

pro•cliv•i•ty *n., pl.*
pro•cliv•i•ties.

pro•cras•ti•nate *v.,*
pro•cras•ti•nat•ed,
pro•cras•ti•nat•ing.

pro•cras•ti•na•tion

pro•cras•ti•na•tor

pro•cre•ate *v.,* pro•
cre•at•ed, pro•cre•
at•ing.

pro•cre•a•tion

pro•cre•a•tive

Pro•crus•te•an

Pro•crus•tes

proc•tol•o•gist

proc•tol•o•gy

proc•tor *v.,* proc•
tored, proc•tor•ing.

pro•cur•a•ble

proc•u•ra•tor

pro•cure *v.,* pro•
cured, pro•cur•ing.

pro•cure•ment

pro•cur•er

prod *v.,* prod•ded,
prod•ding.

prod•i•gal

prod•i•gal•i•ty

pro•di•gious

pro•di•gious•ly

prod•i•gy *n., pl.*
prod•i•gies. (genius:
cf. PROTÉGÉ)

prod•uce¹ (vegetables)

pro•duce² *v.,* pro•
duced, pro•duc•ing.
(to make)

pro•duc•er

producer goods *Busi-
ness.*

prod•uct

product cost *Business.*

product di•ver•si•fi•
ca•tion *Business.*

product li•a•bil•i•ty

product mix

prod•uct-o•ri•ent•ed

pro•duc•tion *Business.*

production budg•et
Business.

production con•trol
Business.

pro•duc•tive

pro•duc•tive•ly

pro•duc•tive•ness

pro•duc•tiv•i•ty *Busi-
ness.*

prof

Prof. (professor)

prof•a•na•tion

pro•fane *v.,* pro•
faned, pro•fan•ing.

pro•fane•ly

pro•fan•i•ty *n., pl.*
pro•fan•i•ties.

pro•fess *v.,* pro•
fessed, pro•fess•ing.

pro•fes•sion

pro•fes•sion•al

pro•fes•sion•al•ism
pro•fes•sion•al•ly
pro•fes•sor
pro•fes•so•ri•al
prof•fer v., prof•
fered, prof•fer•ing.
pro•fi•cien•cy
pro•fi•cient
pro•fi•cient•ly
pro•file v., pro•filed,
pro•fil•ing.
prof•it v., prof•it•ed,
prof•it•ing. Business.
(gain: cf. PROPHET)
prof•it-and-loss (P/L)
Business.
profit cen•ter Busi-
ness.
profit shar•ing Busi-
ness.
prof•it•a•bil•i•ty
Business.
prof•it•a•ble Busi-
ness.
prof•it•a•bly Busi-
ness.
prof•it•eer v.,
prof•it•eered,
prof•it•eer•ing.
prof•it•less
prof•li•ga•cy
prof•li•gate
pro•found
pro•found•ly
pro•fun•di•ty
pro•fuse
pro•fuse•ly
pro•fu•sion
pro•gen•i•tor
prog•e•ny n., pl.
prog•e•ny or prog•
e•nies.
pro•ges•ter•one
prog•na•thous or
prog•nath•ic
prog•no•sis n., pl.
prog•no•ses.

prog•nos•ti•cate v.,
prog•nos•ti•cat•ed,
prog•nos•ti•cat•
ing.
prog•nos•ti•ca•tion
prog•nos•ti•ca•tor
pro•gram v., pro•
grammed or pro•
gramed, pro•gram•
ming or pro•gram•
ing.
program trad•ing
Business.
pro•gram•ma•ble
Computers.
pro•gram•mat•ic
pro•grammed in•
struc•tion Computers.
pro•gram•mer Com-
puters.
pro•gram•ming lan•
guage Computers.
prog•ress¹ (develop-
ment)
pro•gress² v., pro•
gressed, pro•gress•
ing. (to develop)
pro•gres•sion
pro•gres•sive
pro•gres•sive•ly
pro•hib•it v., pro•
hib•it•ed, pro•hib•
it•ing.
pro•hi•bi•tion
pro•hi•bi•tion•ist
pro•hib•i•tive
pro•hib•i•to•ry
proj•ect¹ (something
planned)
pro•ject² v., pro•
ject•ed, pro•ject•
ing. (to protrude)
pro•jec•tile
pro•jec•tion
pro•jec•tion•ist
pro•jec•tor
pro•le•gom•e•non

n., pl. pro•le•
gom•e•na.
pro•le•tar•i•an
pro•le•tar•i•at
pro•lif•er•ate v.,
pro•lif•er•at•ed,
pro•lif•er•at•ing.
pro•lif•er•a•tion
pro•lif•ic
pro•lif•i•cal•ly
pro•lix
pro•lix•i•ty
PROLOG Computers.
(programming lan-
guage)
pro•logue or pro•log
pro•long v., pro•
longed, pro•long•
ing.
pro•lon•ga•tion
prom
PROM Computers. (pro-
grammable read-only
memory)
prom•e•nade v.,
prom•e•nad•ed,
prom•e•nad•ing.
Pro•me•the•us
prom•i•nence
prom•i•nent
prom•i•nent•ly
prom•is•cu•i•ty
prom•is•cu•ous
prom•is•cu•ous•ly
prom•ise v., prom•
ised, prom•is•ing.
prom•is•so•ry note
Business.
prom•on•to•ry n., pl.
prom•on•to•ries.
pro•mote v., pro•
mot•ed, pro•mot•
ing.
pro•mot•er
pro•mo•tion
pro•mo•tion•al
prompt v.,

prompt•ed, prompt•
ing; *adj.*, prompt•er,
prompt•est.
prompt•er
prompt•ly
prompt•ness
prom•ul•gate *v.*,
prom•ul•gat•ed,
prom•ul•gat•ing.
prom•ul•ga•tion
prone
prong
pronged
prong•horn *n.*, *pl.*
prong•horns or
prong•horn.
pro•nom•i•nal
pro•noun
pro•nounce *v.*, pro•
nounced, pro•
nounc•ing.
pro•nounce•a•ble
pro•nounced
pro•nounce•ment
pron•to
pro•nun•ci•a•tion
proof *v.*, proofed,
proof•ing.
proof•read *v.*, proof•
read, proof•read•
ing.
proof•read•er
prop *v.*, propped,
prop•ping.
prop•a•gan•da
prop•a•gan•dist
prop•a•gan•dize *v.*,
prop•a•gan•dized,
prop•a•gan•diz•
ing.
prop•a•gate *v.*,
prop•a•gat•ed,
prop•a•gat•ing.
prop•a•ga•tion
pro•pane
pro•pel *v.*, pro•
pelled, pro•pel•ling.

pro•pel•lant
pro•pel•ler
pro•pen•si•ty *n.*, *pl.*
pro•pen•si•ties.
prop•er
prop•er•ly
prop•er•tied
prop•er•ty *n.*, *pl.*
prop•er•ties. *Busi-
ness.*
proph•e•cy *n.*, *pl.*
proph•e•cies. (pre-
diction)
proph•e•sy *v.*,
proph•e•sied,
proph•e•sy•ing. (to
foretell)
proph•et (person who
speaks for God; one
who foretells: cf.
PROFIT)
pro•phet•ic
pro•phy•lac•tic
pro•phy•lax•is *n.*, *pl.*
pro•phy•lax•es.
pro•pin•qui•ty
pro•pi•ti•ate *v.*, pro•
pi•ti•at•ed, pro•pi•
ti•at•ing.
pro•pi•ti•a•tion
pro•pi•ti•a•to•ry
pro•pi•tious
pro•po•nent
pro•por•tion
pro•por•tion•al
proportional pitch
Computers.
pro•por•tion•ate
pro•pos•al
pro•pose *v.*, pro•
posed, pro•pos•ing.
prop•o•si•tion (offer:
cf. PREPOSITION)
pro•pound *v.*, pro•
pound•ed, pro•
pound•ing.
pro•pri•e•tar•y

pro•pri•e•tor *Busi-
ness.*
pro•pri•e•tor•ship
Business.
pro•pri•e•ty *n.*, *pl.*
pro•pri•e•ties.
pro•pul•sion
pro•rate *v.*, pro•
rat•ed, pro•rat•ing.
pro•sa•ic
pro•sce•ni•um *n.*, *pl.*
pro•sce•ni•ums or
pro•sce•ni•a.
pro•sciut•to
pro•scribe *v.*, pro•
scribed, pro•scrib•
ing. (to prohibit: cf.
PRESCRIBE)
pro•scrip•tion
prose
pros•e•cute *v.*,
pros•e•cut•ed,
pros•e•cut•ing. (to
begin legal
proceedings: cf. PERSE-
CUTE)
pros•e•cu•tion
pros•e•cu•tor
pros•e•lyt•ism
pros•e•lyt•ize *v.*,
pros•e•lyt•ized,
pros•e•lyt•iz•ing.
pros•e•lyt•iz•er
pros•o•dy
pros•pect *v.*, pros•
pect•ed, pros•pect•
ing.
pro•spec•tive (poten-
tial: cf. PERSPECTIVE)
pros•pec•tor
pro•spec•tus *n.*, *pl.*
pro•spec•tus•es.
Business.
pros•per *v.*, pros•
pered, pros•per•ing.
pros•per•i•ty
pros•per•ous

pros•tate (male gland:
cf. PROSTRATE)

pros•the•sis *n., pl.*
pros•the•ses.

pros•thet•ic

pros•ti•tute *v.,* pros•
ti•tut•ed, pros•ti•
tut•ing.

pros•ti•tu•tion

pros•trate (lying flat:
cf. PROSTATE)

pros•tra•tion

pros•y *adj.,* pros•i•er,
pros•i•est.

prot•ac•tin•i•um

pro•tag•o•nist

pro•te•an (changea-
ble: cf. PROTEIN)

pro•tect *v.,* pro•
tect•ed, pro•tect•
ing.

pro•tec•tion

pro•tec•tion•ism
Business.

pro•tec•tion•ist *Busi-
ness.*

pro•tec•tive

pro•tec•tive•ly

pro•tec•tive•ness

pro•tec•tor

pro•tec•tor•ate

pro•té•gé *n., pl.* pro•
té•gés. (one guided
by another: cf. PROD-
IGY)

pro•té•gée *n., pl.*
pro•té•gées. (a
woman or girl guided
by another)

pro•tein (food source:
cf. PROTEAN)

pro•test *v.,* pro•
test•ed, pro•test•
ing.

Prot•es•tant

Prot•es•tant•ism

prot•es•ta•tion

pro•to•col

pro•ton

pro•to•plasm

pro•to•type *v.,*
pro•to•typed,
pro•to•typ•ing.

pro•to•zo•an *n., pl.*
pro•to•zo•ans or
pro•to•zo•a.

pro•tract *v.,* pro•
tract•ed, pro•tract•
ing.

pro•trac•tion

pro•trac•tor

pro•trude *v.,* pro•
trud•ed, pro•trud•
ing.

pro•tru•sion

pro•tu•ber•ance

pro•tu•ber•ant

proud *adj.,* proud•er,
proud•est.

proud•ly

prov•a•bil•i•ty

prov•a•ble

prove *v.,* proved,
prov•en, prov•ing.

prov•e•nance

Pro•ven•çal

prov•en•der

prov•erb

pro•ver•bi•al

pro•vide *v.,* pro•
vid•ed, pro•vid•ing.

prov•i•dence

prov•i•dent

prov•i•den•tial

prov•i•den•tial•ly

prov•i•dent•ly

pro•vid•er

prov•ince

pro•vin•cial

pro•vin•cial•ism

pro•vi•sion¹

pro•vi•sion² *v.,* pro•

vi•sioned, pro•vi•
sion•ing.

pro•vi•sion•al

pro•vi•sion•al•ly

pro•vi•so *n., pl.* pro•
vi•sos or pro•vi•
soes.

prov•o•ca•tion

pro•voc•a•tive

pro•voc•a•tive•ly

pro•voke *v.,* pro•
voked, pro•vok•ing.

pro•vo•lo•ne

pro•vost

prow

prow•ess

prowl *v.,* prowled,
prowl•ing.

prowl•er

prox•im•i•ty

prox•y *n., pl.* prox•
ies.

proxy fight *Business.*

Pro•zac *Trademark.*

prude

pru•dence

pru•dent

pru•den•tial

pru•dent•ly

prud•er•y

prud•ish

prune *v.,* pruned,
prun•ing.

pru•ri•ence

pru•ri•ent

Prus•sia

Prus•sian

pry *v.,* pried, pry•ing.

psalm (hymn: cf. PALM)

psalm•ist

pseu•do *n., pl.* pseu•
dos.

pseu•do•code *Com-
puters.*

pseu•do•nym

pshaw

psi

psit•ta•co•sis

pso•ri•a•sis

psst or pst

psych *v.,* psyched, psych•ing.

psy•che

psych•e•del•ic

psy•chi•at•ric

psy•chi•a•trist

psy•chi•a•try

psy•chic (mental: cf. PHYSIC; PHYSIQUE)

psy•cho *n., pl.* psy•chos.

psy•cho•a•nal•y•sis

psy•cho•an•a•lyst

psy•cho•an•a•lyze *v.,* psy•cho•an•a•lyzed, psy•cho•an•a•lyz•ing.

psy•cho•dra•ma

psy•cho•gen•ic

psy•cho•log•i•cal

psy•chol•o•gist

psy•chol•o•gy

psy•cho•neu•ro•sis *n., pl.* psy•cho•neu•ro•ses.

psy•cho•path

psy•cho•path•ic

psy•cho•sex•u•al

psy•cho•sis *n., pl.* psy•cho•ses.

psy•cho•so•mat•ic

psy•cho•ther•a•pist

psy•cho•ther•a•py *n., pl.* psy•cho•ther•a•pies.

psy•chot•ic

psy•cho•tron•ic

PT or P.T. (Pacific time)

ptar•mi•gan *n., pl.* ptar•mi•gans or ptar•mi•gan.

pter•o•dac•tyl

Ptol•e•my

pto•maine

pub

pu•ber•ty

pu•bes•cence

pu•bes•cent

pu•bic (of the lower abdomen)

pub•lic (of the community)

public cor•po•ra•tion *Business.*

public do•main soft•ware *Computers.*

public sale *Business.*

public sec•tor *Business.*

pub•lic-serv•ice

pub•lic-spir•it•ed

public u•til•i•ty *Business.*

pub•li•ca•tion

pub•li•cist

pub•lic•i•ty

pub•li•cize *v.,* pub•li•cized, pub•li•ciz•ing.

pub•lic•ly

pub•lish *v.,* pub•lished, pub•lish•ing.

pub•lish•er

Puc•ci•ni

puce

puck

puck•er *v.,* puck•ered, puck•er•ing.

pud•ding

pud•dle *v.,* pud•dled, pud•dling.

pudg•y *adj.,* pudg•i•er, pudg•i•est.

pueb•lo *n., pl.* pueb•los.

pu•er•ile

pu•er•il•i•ty

pu•er•per•al

Puer•to Ri•can

Puerto Ri•co (PR)

puff *v.,* puffed, puff•ing.

puff•ball

puf•fin

puff•i•ness

puff•y *adj.,* puff•i•er, puff•i•est.

pug

pug-nosed

pu•gi•lism

pu•gi•list

pu•gi•lis•tic

pug•na•cious

pug•na•cious•ly

pug•nac•i•ty

pu•is•sance

puke *v.,* puked, puk•ing.

puk•ka

pul•chri•tude

pul•ing (whimpering)

pull *v.,* pulled, pull•ing. (drawing toward oneself)

pull-down men•u *Computers.*

pull-up or pull•up

pull•back

pul•let

pul•ley *n., pl.* pul•leys.

Pull•man *n., pl.* Pull•mans. *Trademark.*

pull•out

pull•o•ver

pul•mo•nar•y

pulp *v.,* pulped, pulp•ing.

pul•pit

pulp•y *adj.,* pulp•i•er, pulp•i•est.

pul•sar

pul•sate *v.,* pul•sat•ed, pul•sat•ing.

pul•sa•tion
pulse v., pulsed, puls•ing.
pul•ver•i•za•tion
pul•ver•ize v., pul•ver•ized, pul•ver•iz•ing.
pu•ma n., pl. pu•mas.
pum•ice
pum•mel v., pum•meled or pum•melled, pum•mel•ing or pum•mel•ling. (to beat: cf. POM•MEL)
pump v., pumped, pump•ing.
pump prim•ing *Business.*
pump•er
pum•per•nick•el
pump•kin
pun v., punned, pun•ning.
punch v., punched, punch•ing.
punch card *Computers.*
punch-drunk
punch•y adj., punch•i•er, punch•i•est.
punc•til•i•ous
punc•til•i•ous•ly
punc•til•i•ous•ness
punc•tu•al
punc•tu•al•i•ty
punc•tu•al•ly
punc•tu•ate v., punc•tu•at•ed, punc•tu•at•ing.
punc•tu•a•tion
punc•ture v., punc•tured, punc•tur•ing.
pun•dit
pun•di•to•ry
pun•gen•cy
pun•gent
pun•gent•ly

pu•ni•ness
pun•ish v., pun•ished, pun•ish•ing.
pun•ish•a•ble
pun•ish•ment
pu•ni•tive
punk
punk rock
punk rock•er
pun•ster
punt v., punt•ed, punt•ing.
punt•er
pu•ny adj., pu•ni•er, pu•ni•est.
pup
pu•pa n., pl. pu•pae or pu•pas.
pu•pal (of a pupa)
pu•pil (student)
pup•pet
pup•pet•eer
pup•pet•ry
pup•py n., pl. pup•pies.
pur•blind
pur•chas•a•ble
pur•chase v., pur•chased, pur•chas•ing.
purchase or•der *Business.*
pur•chas•er
pur•chas•ing a•gent *Business.*
pure adj., pur•er, pur•est.
pure•bred
pu•rée or pu•ree v., pu•réed or pu•reed, pu•rée•ing or pu•ree•ing.
pure•ly
pur•ga•tive
pur•ga•to•ry
purge v., purged, purg•ing.

pu•ri•fi•ca•tion
pu•ri•fi•er
pu•ri•fy v., pu•ri•fied, pu•ri•fy•ing.
Pu•rim
pu•rine
pur•ism
pur•ist
pu•ri•tan
pu•ri•tan•i•cal
pu•ri•tan•ism
pu•ri•ty
purl v., purled, purl•ing. (knitting stitch; to purl: cf. PEARL)
pur•lieu n., pl. pur•lieus.
pur•loin v., pur•loined, pur•loin•ing.
pur•ple v., pur•pled, pur•pling; adj., pur•pler, pur•plest.
pur•plish
pur•port v., pur•port•ed, pur•port•ing.
pur•port•ed
pur•port•ed•ly
pur•pose
pur•pose•ful
pur•pose•less
purr v., purred, purr•ing.
purse v., pursed, purs•ing.
purs•er
pur•su•a•ble
pur•su•ance
pur•su•ant
pur•sue v., pur•sued, pur•su•ing.
pur•su•er
pur•suit
pu•ru•lence
pu•ru•lent

pur•vey v., pur•
veyed, pur•vey•ing.
pur•vey•or
pur•view
pus (body fluid in
sores: cf. PUSS)
push v., pushed,
push•ing.
push but•ton n.
push-but•ton adj.
push mon•ey Busi-
ness.
push-up
push•er
push•i•ness
push•o•ver
push•y adj., push•
i•er, push•i•est.
pu•sil•la•nim•i•ty
pu•sil•lan•i•mous
pus•like
puss (cat: cf. PUS)
puss•like
puss•y¹ v., puss•ies.
(cat)
pus•sy² adj., pus•
si•er, pus•si•est.
(puslike)
puss•y•foot v.,
puss•y•foot•ed,
puss•y•foot•ing.
pus•tule

put v., put, put•ting.
(to place: cf. PUTT)
put-call ra•tio Busi-
ness.
put-down or put•
down
put-on
put op•tion Business.
pu•ta•tive
pu•tre•fac•tion
pu•tre•fy v., pu•tre•
fied, pu•tre•fy•ing.
pu•tres•cence
pu•tres•cent
pu•trid
putsch
putt v., putt•ed,
putt•ing. (golf stroke:
cf. PUT)
put•ter¹ (one who
puts)
putt•er² (club for hit-
ting golf stroke)
put•ter³ (to occupy
oneself casually)
put•ter•er
put•ting¹ (placing)
putt•ing² (hitting the
golf stroke)
put•tre•fac•tion
put•ty v., put•tied,
put•ty•ing.

puz•zle v., puz•zled,
puz•zling.
puz•zle•ment
puz•zler
pyg•my n., pl. pyg•
mies.
py•jam•as
py•lon
py•lor•ic
py•lo•rus n., pl. py•
lo•ri.
Pyong•yang
py•or•rhe•a or py•
or•rhoe•a
py•ra•can•tha
pyr•a•mid v., pyr•a•
mid•ed, pyr•a•mid•
ing.
pyramid sell•ing Busi-
ness.
py•ram•i•dal
pyre
Pyr•e•nees
py•re•thrin
Py•rex Trademark.
py•rim•i•dine
py•rite or py•rites
py•ro•ma•ni•ac
py•ro•tech•nics
Pyr•rhic vic•to•ry
Py•thag•o•ras
Py•thag•o•re•an
py•thon

Q

Qa•tar
Qa•tar•i
Q.E.D. (which was to
be demonstrated)
QIC Computers. (quar-
ter-inch cartridge)
qt., n., pl. qt., qts.
(quart)
qua
quack, v., quacked,
quack•ing.

quack•er•y
quad
quad den•si•ty Com-
puters.
quad•ran•gle
quad•ran•gu•lar
quad•rant
quad•ra•phon•ic or
quad•ri•phon•ic
quad•rat•ic
quad•ren•ni•al

quad•ren•ni•um, n.,
pl. quad•ren•ni•
ums, quad•ren•
ni•a.
quad•ri•ceps, n., pl.
quad•ri•ceps•es,
quad•ri•ceps.
quad•ri•lat•er•al
quad•ri•lat•er•al•ly
quad•rille
quad•ril•lion, n., pl.

quad•ril•lions or
quad•ril•lion.
quad•ri•ple•gi•a
quad•ri•ple•gic
quad•ru•ped
quad•ru•pe•dal
quad•ru•ple, v.,
quad•ru•pled,
quad•ru•pling.
quad•ru•plet
quad•ru•pli•cate
quaff, v., quaffed,
quaff•ing. (to drink:
cf. COIF)
quag•mire
qua•hog or qua-haug
quail¹ v., quailed,
quail•ing. (to shrink
with fear)
quail² n., pl. quails or
quail. (the bird)
quaint, adj.,
quaint•er, quaint•
est.
quaint•ly
quaint•ness
quake, v., quaked,
quak•ing.
Quak•er
Quak•er•ism
quak•y, adj., quak•
i•er, quak•i•est.
qual•i•fi•ca•tion
qual•i•fied
qual•i•fy, v., qual•i•
fied, qual•i•fy•ing.
qual•i•ta•tive
qual•i•ta•tive•ly
qual•i•ty, n., pl.
qual•i•ties.
quality as•sur•ance
Business.
quality cir•cle Busi-
ness.
quality time
qualm

quan•da•ry, n., pl.
quan•da•ries.
quant Business.
quan•ti•fy, v., quan•
ti•fied, quan•ti•fy•
ing.
quan•ti•ta•tive
quan•ti•ty, n., pl.
quan•ti•ties.
quan•tum, n., pl.
quan•ta.
quar•an•tine, v.,
quar•an•tined,
quar•an•tin•ing.
quark
quar•rel, v., quar•
reled or quar•relled,
quar•rel•ing or
quar•rel•ling.
quar•rel•some
quarry, n., pl. quar•
ries; v., quar•ried,
quar•ry•ing.
quart
quar•ter, v., quar•
tered, quar•ter•ing.
quar•ter-inch car•
tridge (QIC) Comput-
ers.
quar•ter•back
quar•ter•ly, n., pl.
quar•ter•lies.
quar•ter•mas•ter
quar•tet
quar•to, n., pl. quar•
tos.
quarts (32-ounce units)
quartz (mineral)
qua•sar
quash, v., quashed,
quash•ing. (to sub-
due: cf. SQUASH)
qua•si
qua•si•crys•tal
Quat•er•nar•y
quat•rain

qua•ver, v., qua•
vered, qua•ver•ing.
qua•ver•er
qua•ver•ing•ly
quay (wharf: cf. CAY;
KEY)
Quayle
quea•si•ness
quea•sy, adj., quea-
si•er, queasi•est.
Que•bec
queen
queen-size or queen-
sized
queen•ly, adj.,
queen•li•er, queen•
li•est.
Queens
queer, adj., queer•er,
queer•est.
quell, v., quelled,
quell•ing.
quench, v., quenched,
quench•ing.
quench•er
quench•less
quer•u•lous
quer•u•lous•ly
que•ry, n., pl. que•
ries; v., que•ried,
que•ry•ing.
query by ex•am•ple
Computers.
query lan•guage Com-
puters.
quest, v., quest•ed,
quest•ing.
ques•tion, v., ques•
tioned, ques•tion•
ing.
question mark
ques•tion•a•ble
ques•tion•naire
queue, v., queued,
queu•ing. (line; se-
quence: cf. CUE)

quib•ble, *v.*, quib•bled, quib•bling.
quib•bler
quiche
quick, *adj.*, quick∘er, quick•est.
quick-and-dirt∘y
quick-freeze, *v.*, quick-froze, quick-fro∘zen, quick-freez∘ing.
quick-tem∘pered
quick-wit∘ted
quick∘en, *v.*, quick•ened, quick•en•ing.
quick∘ie
quick∘lime
quick•ness
quick•sand
quick•sil•ver
quid pro quo, *n.*, *pl.* quid pro quos or quids pro quo.
qui•es•cence
qui•es•cent
qui∘et, *v.*, qui•et∘ed, qui•et∘ing;. *adj.*, qui•et∘er, qui•et•est. (still: cf. QUITE; QUIT)
qui∘et∘ly
qui•e•tude
qui•e•tus, *n.*, *pl.* qui•e•tus∘es.

quill
quilt, *v.*, quilt∘ed, quilt•ing.
quilt∘ed
quilt∘er
quince
qui∘nine
quint
quin•tes•sence
quin•tes•sen•tial
quin•tet
quin•til•lion, *n.*, *pl.* quin•til•lions or quin•til•lion.
quin•tu•ple, *v.*, quin•tu•pled, quin•tu•pling.
quin•tu•plet
quip, *v.*, quipped, quip•ping.
quip•ster
quire (24 sheets: cf. CHOIR)
quirk
quirk∘i•ness
quirk∘y, *adj.*, quirk•i∘er, quirk•i•est.
quirt
quis•ling
quit, *v.*, quit or quit•ted, quit•ting. (to leave: cf. QUIET; QUITE)
quit•claim *Business.*

quite (very)
Qui∘to
quits
quit•tance
quit•ter
quiv∘er, *v.*, quiv•ered, quiv•er•ing.
quiv•er∘y
quix•ot∘ic
quiz, *n.*, *pl.* quiz•zes; *v.*, quizzed, quiz•zing.
quiz•zi•cal
quiz•zi•cal∘ly
quoit
quon•dam
Quon•set hut *Trademark.*
quo•rum
quo∘ta (allotment)
quo•ta•tion
quotation mark
quote, *v.*, quot∘ed, quot•ing. (saying; to repeat another's words)
quoth
quo•tid•i∘an
quo•tient
q.v. (which see)
QWERTY (standard typewriter or computer keyboard)

R

R&D *Business.* (research; development)
Ra or Re
Ra•bat
rab•bet (a notch in timber: cf. RABBIT)
rab∘bi *n.*, *pl.* rab•bis. (clergy: cf. RABIES)
rab•bin•ate
rab•bin∘i•cal

rab•bit *n.*, *pl.* rab•bits or rab•bit. *(the animal: cf. RABBET)*
rab•ble
rab∘ble-rous∘er
rab∘ble-rous∘ing
Rab∘e•lais
Rab∘e•lai•si∘an
rab∘id

ra•bies (disease: cf. RABBIS)
rac•coon *n.*, *pl.* rac•coons or rac•coon.
race *v.*, raced, rac•ing.
race•horse
ra•ceme
rac∘er
race•track
race•way

ra•chit•ic
ra•chi•tis
ra•cial
ra•cial•ism
ra•cial•ist
ra•cial•ly
raci•ly
raci•ness
rac•ism
rac•ist
rack v., racked, rack•ing.
rack job•ber Business.
rack•et
rack•et•eer v., rack•et•eered, rack•et•eer•ing.
rack•ing•ly
rac•on•teur
rac•quet•ball
racy adj., raci•er, raci•est.
rad
ra•dar
ra•dar•scope
ra•di•al
ra•di•ance
ra•di•ant
ra•di•ant•ly
ra•di•ate v., ra•di•at•ed, ra•di•at•ing.
ra•di•a•tion
ra•di•a•tor
rad•i•cal
rad•i•cal•ism
rad•i•cal•i•za•tion
rad•i•cal•ize v., rad•i•cal•ized, rad•i•cal•iz•ing.
rad•i•cal•ly
ra•dic•chi•o
ra•di•i
ra•di•o n., pl. ra•di•os; v., ra•di•oed, ra•di•o•ing.
ra•di•o tel•e•scope

ra•di•o•ac•tive
ra•di•o•ac•tive•ly
ra•di•o•ac•tiv•i•ty
ra•di•o•gram
ra•di•o•i•so•tope
ra•di•o•i•so•top•ic
ra•di•ol•o•gist
ra•di•ol•o•gy
ra•di•om•e•ter
ra•di•o•met•ric
ra•di•om•e•try
ra•di•o•scop•ic or ra•di•o•scop•i•cal
ra•di•os•co•py
ra•di•o•tel•e•graph v., ra•di•o•tel•e•graphed, ra•di•o•tel•e•graph•ing.
ra•di•o•tel•e•graph•ic
ra•di•o•te•leg•ra•phy
ra•di•o•tel•e•phone v., ra•di•o•tel•e•phoned, ra•di•o•tel•e•phon•ing.
ra•di•o•ther•a•pist
ra•di•o•ther•a•py
rad•ish
ra•di•um
ra•di•us n., pl. ra•di•i or ra•di•us•es.
ra•don
RAF or **R.A.F.** (Royal Air Force)
raf•fi•a
raff•ish
raff•ish•ly
raff•ish•ness
raf•fle v., raf•fled, raf•fling.
raft
raf•ter
rag v., ragged, rag•ging. (did tease: cf. RAGGED)
ra•ga n., pl. ra•gas.

rag•a•muf•fin
rag•bag
rage v., raged, rag•ing.
rag•ged (tattered: cf. RAGGED)
rag•ged•ness
rag•ged•y
rag•ing•ly
rag•lan sleeve
ra•gout
rag•tag and bob•tail
rag•time
rag•weed
rah
raid v., raid•ed, raid•ing.
raid•er
rail v., railed, rail•ing.
rail•ler•y
rail•road v., rail•road•ed, rail•road•ing.
rail•way
rai•ment
rain v., rained, rain•ing. (shower; to rain: cf. REIGN; REIN)
rain check or rain•check
rain for•est
rain•bow
rain•coat
rain•drop
rain•fall
rain•i•er (more rainy)
Rai•nier (the mountain)
rain•mak•er
rain•storm
rain•wa•ter
rain•y adj., rain•i•er, rain•i•est.
raise v., raised, rais•ing. (to lift: cf. RAYS; RAZE)

rai•sin

rai•son d'ê•tre n., pl. rai•sons d'ê•tre.

ra•jah n., pl. ra•jahs.

rake v., raked, rak• ing.

rake-off

rak•ish

rak•ish•ly

rak•ish•ness

Ra•leigh

ral•ly n., pl. ral•lies; v., ral•lied, ral•ly• ing.

RAM Computers. (ran-dom-access memory)

ram v., rammed, ram• ming.

RAM cache Computers.

RAM disk Computers.

RAM-res•i•dent Com-puters.

ram•ble v., ram•bled, ram•bling.

ram•bler

ram•bunc•tious

ram•bunc•tious•ness

ram•e•kin

ram•i•fi•ca•tion

ram•i•fy v., ram•i• fied, ram•i•fy•ing.

ram•jet

ramp

ram•page v., ram• paged, ram•pag• ing.

ramp•ant

ramp•ant•ly

ram•part

ram•rod

ram•shack•le

ran

ranch v., ranched, ranch•ing.

ranch house

ranch•er n., pl. ranch• ers.

ranch•man n., pl. ranch•men.

ran•cid

ran•cor

ran•cor•ous

rand n., pl. rand.

ran•dom

ran•dom-ac•cess mem•o•ry (RAM) Computers.

ran•dom•i•za•tion

ran•dom•ize v., ran• dom•ized, ran• dom•iz•ing.

ran•dom•iz•er

ran•dom•ly

rand•y adj., rand• i•er, rand•i•est.

rang

range v., ranged, rang•ing.

rang•er

Ran•goon

rang•y adj., rang• i•er, rang•i•est.

rank v., ranked, rank• ing; adj., rank•er, rank•est.

rank and file

ran•kle v., ran•kled, ran•kling.

ran•sack v., ran• sacked, ran•sack• ing.

ran•som v., ran• somed, ran•som• ing.

rant v., rant•ed, rant• ing.

rap v., rapped, rap• ping. (to strike: cf. WRAP)

ra•pa•cious

ra•pac•i•ty

rape v., raped, rap• ing.

Raph•a•el

rap•id

ra•pid•i•ty

rap•id•ly

rap•ids

ra•pi•er

rap•ine

rap•ist

rapped (struck: cf. RAPT; WRAPPED)

rap•per

rap•port

rap•proche•ment

rap•scal•lion

rapt (engrossed: cf. RAPPED; WRAPPED)

rapt•ly

rapt•ness

rap•ture

rap•tur•ous

ra•ra a•vis n., pl. ra• rae a•ves.

rare adj., rar•er, rar• est.

rare•bit

rar•e•fac•tion

rar•e•fy v., rar•e•fied, rar•e•fy•ing.

rare•ly

rar•ing

rar•i•ty

ras•cal

ras•cal•ly

rash adj., rash•er, rash•est.

rash•ly

rash•ness

rasp v., rasped, rasp• ing.

rasp•ber•ry n., pl. rasp•ber•ries.

rasp•y adj., rasp•i•er, rasp•i•est.

ras•ter graph•ics *Computers.*

rat *v.,* rat•ted, rat•ting.

ratch•et *v.,* ratch•et•ed, ratch•et•ing.

rate *v.,* rat•ed, rat•ing.

rate cut•ting *Business.*

rath○er

raths•kel•ler

rat○i•fi•ca•tion

rat○i•fy *v.,* rat•i•fied, rat•i•fy•ing.

rat•ing

ra•tio *n., pl.* ra•tios.

ra•ti•oc○i•nate *v.,* ra•ti•oc○i•nat○ed, ra•ti•oc○i•nat•ing.

ra•ti•oc○i•na•tion

ra•tion *v.,* ra•tioned, ra•tion•ing.

ra•tion•al (reasonable)

ra•tion•ale (logical basis)

ra•tion•al•ism

ra•tion•al•ist

ra•tion•al•is•tic

ra•tion•al•i•ty

ra•tion•al•i•za•tion

ra•tion•al•ize *v.,* ra•tion•al•ized, ra•tion•al•iz•ing.

ra•tion•al•ly

rat•like

rat•tan

rat•tle *v.,* rat•tled, rat•tling.

rat•tle•brained

rat•tler

rat○tle•snake

rat○tle•trap

rat•tling

rat•trap

rat○ty *adj.,* rat•ti○er, rat•ti•est.

rau•cous

rau•cous•ly

rau•cous•ness

raun•chi•ness

raun•chy *adj.,* raun•chi○er, raun•chi•est.

rav•age *v.,* rav•aged, rav•ag•ing.

rave *v.,* raved, rav•ing.

Ra•vel (composer)

rav○el *v.,* rav•eled or rav•elled, rav•el•ing or rav•el•ling. (to disentangle; to entangle)

ra•ven[1] (the bird)

rav○en[2] *v.,* rav•ened, rav•en•ing. (to prowl for food)

rav•en•ous

rav•en•ous•ly

ra•vine

rav•ing

ra•vi•○○li

rav•ish *v.,* rav•ished, rav•ish•ing.

rav•ish○er

rav•ish•ing

rav•ish•ment

raw *adj.,* raw○er, raw•est.

raw•boned

raw•hide

raw•ness

ray

ray○on

rays (light beams: cf. RAISE; RAZE)

raze or rase *v.,* razed or rased, raz•ing or ras•ing. (to tear down)

ra•zor

razz *v.,* razzed, razz•ing.

raz○zle-daz○zle

rcpt. (receipt)

re (with reference to)

re-tread *v.,* re-trod, re-trod○den or re-trod, re-tread○ing. *(to walk again)*

re-up *v.,* re-upped, re-up○ping.

reach *v.,* reached, reach•ing.

re•act *v.,* re•act○ed, re•act•ing.

re•ac•tance

re•ac•tant

re•ac•tion

read *v.,* read, read•ing. (did read: cf. RED)

read-me file *Computers.*

read-on•ly *Computers.*

read-only mem○o•ry (ROM) *Computers.*

read•a•bil•i•ty

read•a•ble

read○er

read•er•ship

read•ing

read•out or read-out

read/•write head *Computers.*

read○y *v.,* read•ied, read○y•ing; *adj.,* read•i○er, read•i•est.

read○y•made or read○y-made

Rea•gan

re•a•gent

re○al (true: cf. REEL)

real ac•count *Business.*

real es•tate *Business.*

real in•come *Business.*

real prop•er○ty *Business.*

re•al-time clock *Computers.*

real-time sys•tem *Computers.*

re•al•ism

re•al•i•ty *n., pl.* re•al•i•ties. (real thing: cf. REALTY)

re•al•iz•a•ble

realizable val•ue *Business.*

re•al•ize *v.,* re•al•ized, re•al•iz•ing. (to understand: cf. RE-LIES)

re•al•ly

realm

re•al•po•li•tik

Re•al•tor *Business.*

re•al•ty *Business.* (property: cf. REALITY)

ream *v.,* reamed, ream•ing.

ream•er

reap *v.,* reaped, reap•ing.

reap•er

rear *v.,* reared, rear•ing.

rear•most

rear•ward

rea•son *v.,* rea•soned, rea•son•ing.

rea•son•a•ble

rea•son•a•ble•ness

rea•son•a•bly

re•as•sur•ance

re•as•sure *v.,* re•as•sured, re•as•sur•ing.

re•as•sur•ing•ly

re•bate *v.,* re•bat•ed, re•bat•ing. *Business.*

re•bat•er

reb•el¹ (one who revolts)

re•bel² *v.,* re•belled, re•bel•ling. (to revolt)

re•bel•lion

re•bel•lious

re•bel•lious•ly

re•bel•lious•ness

re•birth

re•boot *v.,* re•boot•ed, re•boot•ing. *Computers.*

re•bound *v.,* re•bound•ed, re•bound•ing. (to spring back: cf. REDOUND)

re•buff *v.,* re•buffed, re•buff•ing.

re•buke *v.,* re•buked, re•buk•ing.

re•buk•ing•ly

re•bus *n., pl.* re•bus•es.

re•but *v.,* re•but•ted, re•but•ting.

re•but•tal

rec. (receipt; record)

re•cal•ci•trance

re•cal•ci•trant

re•call *v.,* re•called, re•call•ing.

re•cant *v.,* re•cant•ed, re•cant•ing.

re•can•ta•tion

re•cap *v.,* re•capped, re•cap•ping.

re•ca•pit•u•late *v.,* re•ca•pit•u•lated, re•ca•pit•u•lat•ing.

re•ca•pit•u•la•tion

re•cap•ture *v.,* re•cap•tured, re•cap•tur•ing.

recd. or rec'd. (received)

re•cede *v.,* re•ced•ed, re•ced•ing.

re•ceipt

re•ceiv•a•ble

re•ceive *v.,* re•ceived, re•ceiv•ing.

re•ceiv•er

re•ceiv•er•ship *Business.*

re•ceiv•ing a•pron *Business.*

re•cent

re•cent•ly

re•cep•ta•cle

re•cep•tion

re•cep•tion•ist

re•cep•tive

re•cep•tor

re•cess *v.,* re•cessed, re•cess•ing.

re•ces•sion *Business.*

re•ces•sive

re•cher•che

re•cid•i•vism

re•cid•i•vist

re•ci•pe *n., pl.* re•ci•pes.

re•cip•i•ent

re•cip•ro•cal

re•cip•ro•cate *v.,* re•cip•ro•cat•ed, re•cip•ro•cat•ing.

re•cip•ro•ca•tion

rec•i•proc•i•ty

re•cit•al

rec•i•ta•tion

rec•i•ta•tive

re•cite *v.,* re•cit•ed, re•cit•ing.

reck•less

reck•less•ly

reck•less•ness

reck•on *v.,* reck•oned, reck•on•ing.

re•claim *v.,* re•claimed, re•claim•ing.

rec•la•ma•tion

re•cline *v.,* re•clined, re•clin•ing.

re•clin•er
rec•luse
re•clu•sive
rec•og•ni•tion
rec•og•niz•a•ble
re•cog•ni•zance
rec•og•nize v., rec•
og•nized, rec•og•
niz•ing.
re•coil v., re•coiled,
re•coil•ing.
rec•ol•lect v., rec•ol•
lect•ed, rec•ol•lect•
ing.
rec•ol•lec•tion
re•com•bi•nant
rec•om•mend v., rec•
om•mend•ed, rec•
om•mend•ing.
rec•om•men•da•tion
rec•om•pense v., rec•
om•pensed, rec•
om•pens•ing.
rec•on•cil•a•ble
rec•on•cile v., rec•
on•ciled, rec•on•
cil•ing.
rec•on•cil•i•a•tion
rec•on•dite
re•con•nais•sance
re•con•noi•ter v., re•
con•noi•tered, re•
con•noi•ter•ing.
re•con•sid•er v., re•
con•sid•ered, re•
con•sid•er•ing.
re•con•sid•er•a•tion
re•con•sti•tute v.,
re•con•sti•tut•ed,
re•con•sti•tut•ing.
re•con•struct v., re•
con•struct•ed, re•
con•struct•ing.
re•con•struc•tion
rec•ord[1] n.
re•cord[2] v., re•

cord•ed, re•cord•
ing.
re•cord•a•ble
re•cord•er
re•cord•ing
re-count v., re-
count•ed, re-
count•ing. (to count
again)
re•count v., re•
count•ed, re•count•
ing. (to narrate)
re•coup v., re•
couped, re•coup•
ing.
re•course
re-cov•er v., re-cov•
ered, re-cov•er•ing.
(to cover again)
re•cov•er v., re•cov•
ered, re•cov•er•ing.
(to regain)
re•cov•er•a•ble
re•cov•er•y
re-cre•ate v., re-cre•
at•ed, re-cre•at•ing.
(to create anew)
rec•re•ate v., rec•re•
at•ed, rec•re•at•
ing. (to amuse one-
self)
rec•re•a•tion
rec•re•a•tion•al
re•crim•i•nate v., re•
crim•i•nat•ed, re•
crim•i•nat•ing.
re•crim•i•na•tion
re•cru•des•cence
re•cruit v., re•
cruit•ed, re•cruit•
ing.
re•cruit•er
re•cruit•ment
rec•tal
rec•tal•ly
rec•tan•gle
rec•ti•fi•a•ble

rec•ti•fi•ca•tion
rec•ti•fi•er
rec•ti•fy v., rec•ti•
fied, rec•ti•fy•ing.
rec•ti•lin•e•ar
rec•ti•tude
rec•to n., pl. rec•tos.
rec•tor
rec•to•ry n., pl. rec•
to•ries.
rec•tum n., pl. rec•
tums or rec•ta.
re•cum•ben•cy
re•cum•bent
re•cu•per•ate v., re•
cu•per•at•ed, re•
cu•per•at•ing.
re•cu•per•a•tion
re•cu•per•a•tive
re•cur v., re•curred,
re•cur•ring.
re•cur•rence
re•cur•rent
re•cur•rent•ly
re•cy•cla•ble
re•cy•cle v., re•cy•
cled, re•cy•cling.
red adj., red•der, red•
dest. (the color: cf.
READ)
red-blood•ed
red carpet n.
red-carpet adj.
red-hand•ed
red-hot
red-let•ter
red-light dis•trict
red•cap
red•coat
red•den v., red•
dened, red•den•ing.
red•dish
re•deem v., re•
deemed, re•deem•
ing.
re•deem•a•ble

re•deem∘er
re•demp•tion
redemption price *Business.*
re•demp•tive
red•head
red•head∘ed
re•dis•count *v.,* re•dis•count∘ed, re•dis•count•ing. *Business.*
re•dis•trict *v.,* re•dis•trict∘ed, re•dis•trict•ing.
red•line *v.,* red•lined, red•lin•ing.
red•lined text *Computers.*
red•neck or red-neck
red•ness
red∘o•lence
red∘o•lent
re•doubt
re•doubt•a∘ble
re•dound *v.,* re•dound∘ed, re•dound•ing. (to result: cf. RE-BOUND)
re•dress *v.,* re•dressed, re•dress•ing.
red•skin
re•duce *v.,* re•duced, re•duc•ing.
re•duc•tion
re•duc•tive
re•dun•dan∘cy
re•dun•dant
re•dux
red•wood
reed
reed∘i•ness
reed∘y *adj.,* reed•i∘er, reed•i•est.
reef
reef∘er
reek *v.,* reeked, reek•ing. (to smell strongly: cf. WREAK; WRECK)
reel *v.,* reeled, reel•ing. (spool; to sway: cf. REAL)
re•en•try *n., pl.* re•en•tries.
re•face *v.,* re•faced, re•fac•ing.
re•fec•to•ry *n., pl.* re•fec•to•ries.
re•fer *v.,* re•ferred, re•fer•ring.
ref•er•oee *v.,* ref•er•eed, ref•er•ee•ing. (arbitrator: cf. REVERIE)
ref•er•ence
ref•er•en•dum *n., pl.* ref•er•en•dums or ref•er•en∘da.
ref•er•ent
re•fer•ral
re•fill *v.,* re•filled, re•fill•ing.
re•fill•a∘ble
re•fine *v.,* re•fined, re•fin•ing.
re•fine•ment
re•fin•er∘y *n., pl.* re•fin•er•ies.
re•flag *v.,* re•flagged, re•flag•ging.
re•fla•tion *Business.*
re•flect *v.,* re•flect∘ed, re•flect•ing.
re•flec•tion
re•flec•tive
re•flec•tive∘ly
re•flec•tor
re•flex
re•flex•ive
re•flex•ive∘ly
re•for•est *v.,* re•for•est∘ed, re•for•est•ing.
re•for•est•a•tion

re-form *v.,* re-formed, re-form∘ing. (to form again)
re•form *v.,* re•formed, re•form•ing. (to end wrong conduct)
ref•or•ma•tion
re•form∘a•to∘ry *n., pl.* re•form∘a•to•ries.
re•form∘er
re•fract *v.,* re•fract∘ed, re•fract•ing.
re•frac•tion
re•frac•tive
re•frac•to∘ry
re•frain *v.,* re•frained, re•frain•ing.
re•fresh *v.,* re•freshed, re•fresh•ing.
refresh rate *Computers.*
re•fresh∘er
re•fresh•ing
re•fresh•ment
re•frig•er•ant
re•frig•er•ate *v.,* re•frig•er•at∘ed, re•frig•er•at•ing.
re•frig•er•a•tion
re•frig•er∘a•tor
ref•uge *v.,* ref•uged, ref•ug•ing.
ref∘u•gee
re•ful•gence
re•ful•gent
re•fund *v.,* re•fund∘ed, re•fund•ing.
re•fund•a∘ble
re•fur•bish *v.,* re•fur•bished, re•fur•bish•ing.
re•fur•bish•ment

re•fus•al
refusal to deal *Business*.
ref•use¹ (garbage)
re•fuse² *v.*, re•fused, re•fus•ing. (say no)
re•fut•a•ble
ref•u•ta•tion
re•fute *v.*, re•fut•ed, re•fut•ing.
re•gal (royal)
re•gale *v.*, re•galed, re•gal•ing. (to entertain)
re•ga•li•a
re•gal•ly
re•gard *v.*, re•gard•ed, re•gard•ing.
re•gard•ing
re•gard•less
re•gat•ta *n.*, *pl.* re•gat•tas.
re•gen•cy *n.*, *pl.* re•gen•cies.
re•gen•er•a•cy
re•gen•er•ate *v.*, re•gen•er•at•ed, re•gen•er•at•ing.
re•gen•er•a•tion
re•gen•er•a•tive
re•gent
reg•gae
reg•i•cide
re•gime or ré•gime
reg•i•men
reg•i•ment *v.*, reg•i•ment•ed, reg•i•ment•ing.
reg•i•men•tal
reg•i•men•ta•tion
Re•gi•na
re•gion
re•gion•al
re•gion•al•ism
re•gion•al•ly

reg•is•ter *v.*, reg•is•tered, reg•is•ter•ing. (to enroll)
reg•is•trant
reg•is•trar (record keeper)
reg•is•tra•tion
reg•is•try *n.*, *pl.* reg•is•tries.
reg•nant
re•gress *v.*, re•gressed, re•gress•ing.
re•gres•sion
re•gres•sive
re•gret *v.*, re•gret•ted, re•gret•ting.
re•gret•ful
re•gret•ta•ble
re•group *v.*, re•grouped, re•group•ing.
reg•u•lar
reg•u•lar•i•ty
reg•u•lar•ize *v.*, reg•u•lar•ized, reg•u•lar•iz•ing.
reg•u•lar•ly
reg•u•late *v.*, reg•u•lat•ed, reg•u•lat•ing.
reg•u•la•tion
reg•u•la•tive
reg•u•la•tor
reg•u•la•to•ry
re•gur•gi•tate *v.*, re•gur•gi•tat•ed, re•gur•gi•tat•ing.
re•gur•gi•ta•tion
re•hab *v.*, re•habbed, re•hab•bing.
re•ha•bil•i•tate *v.*, re•ha•bil•i•tat•ed, re•ha•bil•i•tat•ing.
re•ha•bil•i•ta•tion
re•ha•bil•i•ta•tive
re•hash *v.*, re•

hashed, re•hash•ing.
re•hears•al
re•hearse *v.*, re•hearsed, re•hears•ing.
Reich
reign *v.*, reigned, reign•ing. (sovereignty; to rule: cf. RAIN; REIN)
re•im•burse *v.*, re•im•bursed, re•im•burs•ing.
re•im•burse•ment
rein *v.*, reined, rein•ing. (strap of harness; to use a rein)
re•in•car•nate
re•in•car•na•tion
rein•deer *n.*, *pl.* rein•deer or rein•deers.
re•in•force or re•en•force *v.*, re•in•forced or re•en•forced, re•in•forc•ing or re•en•forc•ing.
re•in•force•ment
re•in•state *v.*, re•in•stat•ed, re•in•stat•ing.
re•in•state•ment
re•in•sure *v.*, re•in•sured, re•in•sur•ing. *Business*.
re•in•vest•ment *Business*.
reinvestment rate *Business*.
REIT *Business*. (real-estate investment trust)
re•it•er•ate *v.*, re•it•er•at•ed, re•it•er•at•ing.
re•it•er•a•tion

re•ject v., re•ject•ed, re•ject•ing.
re•jec•tion
re•joice v., re•joiced, re•joic•ing.
re•join v., re•joined, re•join•ing.
re•join•der
re•ju•ve•nate v., re•ju•ve•nat•ed, re•ju•ve•nat•ing.
re•ju•ve•na•tion
re•lapse v., re•lapsed, re•laps•ing.
re•late v., re•lat•ed, re•lat•ing.
re•la•tion
re•la•tion•al da•ta•base *Computers.*
re•la•tion•ship
rel○a•tive
rel○a•tive•ly
rel○a•tiv•i•ty
re•lax v., re•laxed, re•lax•ing.
re•lax•ant
re•lax•a•tion
re•lay v., re•layed, re•lay•ing.
re•lease v., re•leased, re•leas•ing.
rel○e•gate v., rel○e•gat•ed, rel○e•gat•ing.
rel○e•ga•tion
re•lent v., re•lent•ed, re•lent•ing.
re•lent•less
re•lent•less•ly
re•lent•less•ness
rel○e•vance
rel○e•vant
re•li•a•bil•i•ty
re•li•a○ble
re•li•a•bly
re•li•ance
re•li•ant

rel○ic
re•lief
re•lies (depends on: cf. REALIZE)
re•lieve v., re•lieved, re•liev•ing.
re•li•gion
re•li•gious n., pl. re•li•gious.
re•li•gious•ly
re•lin•quish v., re•lin•quished, re•lin•quish•ing.
re•lin•quish•ment
rel○i•quar○y n., pl. rel○i•quar•ies.
re•lish v., re•lished, rel•ish•ing.
re•live v., re•lived, re•liv•ing.
re•lo•cate v., re•lo•cat•ed, re•lo•cat•ing.
re•lo•ca•tion
re•luc•tance
re•luc•tant
re•luc•tant•ly
re○ly v., re•lied, re•ly•ing.
rem (radiation measure)
REM (rapid eye movement)
re•main v., re•mained, re•main•ing.
re•main•der v., re•main•dered, re•main•der•ing.
re•mand v., re•mand○ed, re•mand•ing.
re•mark v., re•marked, re•mark•ing.
re•mark•a○ble
re•mark•a•bly
Rem•brandt

re•me•di•al
remedial main•te•nance *Business.*
re•me•di•al•ly
rem○e•dy n., pl. rem○e•dies; v., rem○e•died, rem○e•dy•ing.
re•mem•ber v., re•mem•bered, re•mem•ber•ing.
re•mem•brance
re•mind v., re•mind○ed, re•mind•ing.
re•mind○er
rem○i•nisce v., rem○i•nisced, rem○i•nisc•ing.
rem○i•nis•cence
rem○i•nis•cent
re•miss
re•mis•sion
re•miss•ness
re•mit v., re•mit•ted, re•mit•ting.
re•mit•tance
rem•nant
re•mod○el v., re•mod•eled or re•mod•elled, re•mod•el•ing or re•mod•el•ling.
re•mon•strance
re•mon•strate v., re•mon•strat○ed, re•mon•strat•ing.
re•morse
re•morse•ful
re•morse•less
re•mote adj., re•mot○er, re•mot•est.
remote con•trol n.
remote-con○trol adj.
re•mote•ly
re•mote•ness
re•mov•a○ble

removable car•tridge *Computers.*

re•mov•al

re•move *v.*, re•moved, re•mov•ing.

re•mu•ner•ate *v.*, re•mu•ner•at•ed, re•mu•ner•at•ing.

re•mu•ner•a•tion

re•mu•ner•a•tive

Ren•ais•sance

re•nal

rend *v.*, rent, rend•ing.

ren•der[1] *v.*, ren•dered, ren•der•ing. (to provide; to represent)

rend•er[2] (one who tears)

ren•dez•vous *n.*, *pl.* ren•dez•vous; *v.*, ren•dez•voused, ren•dez•vous•ing.

ren•di•tion

ren•e•gade

re•nege *v.*, re•neged, re•neg•ing.

re•new *v.*, re•newed, re•new•ing.

re•new•a•ble

re•new•al

ren•net

ren•nin

Re•no

Re•noir

re•nounce *v.*, re•nounced, re•nounc•ing.

re•nounce•ment

ren•o•vate *v.*, ren•o•vat•ed, ren•o•vat•ing.

ren•o•va•tion

ren•o•va•tor

re•nown

rent *v.*, rent•ed, rent•ing.

rent•al *Business.*

rent•er

re•nun•ci•a•tion

re•or•der point *Business.*

rep

re•pair[1]

re•pair[2] *v.*, re•paired, re•pair•ing.

re•pair•man *n.*, *pl.* re•pair•men.

rep•a•ra•ble or re•pair•a•ble

rep•a•ra•tion

rep•ar•tee

re•past

re•pa•tri•ate *v.*, re•pa•tri•at•ed, re•pa•tri•at•ing.

re•pa•tri•a•tion

re•pay *v.*, re•paid, re•pay•ing.

re•pay•ment

re•peal *v.*, re•pealed, re•peal•ing.

re•peat *v.*, re•peat•ed, re•peat•ing.

re•peat•ed•ly

re•peat•er

re•pel *v.*, re•pelled, re•pel•ling.

re•pel•lent or re•pel•lant

re•pent *v.*, re•pent•ed, re•pent•ing.

re•pent•ance

re•pent•ant

re•per•cus•sion

rep•er•toire

rep•er•to•ry *n.*, *pl.* rep•er•to•ries.

rep•e•ti•tion

rep•e•ti•tious

re•pet•i•tive

re•pine *v.*, re•pined, re•pin•ing.

re•place *v.*, re•placed, re•plac•ing.

re•place•a•ble

re•place•ment

replacement cost *Business.*

re•play *v.*, re•played, re•play•ing.

re•plen•ish *v.*, re•plen•ished, re•plen•ish•ing.

re•plen•ish•ment

re•plete

re•ple•tion

rep•li•ca *n.*, *pl.* rep•li•cas.

rep•li•cate *v.*, rep•li•cat•ed, rep•li•cat•ing.

rep•li•ca•tion

re•ply *n.*, *pl.* re•plied, re•ply•ing, re•plies.

re•po *Business.*

re•port *v.*, re•port•ed, re•port•ing.

report writ•er *Computers.*

re•port•age

re•port•ed•ly

re•port•er

re•pose *v.*, re•posed, re•pos•ing.

re•pose•ful

re•pos•i•to•ry *n.*, *pl.* re•pos•i•tor•ies.

re•pos•sess *v.*, re•pos•sessed, re•pos•sess•ing.

re•pos•ses•sion *Business.*

rep•re•hen•si•ble

rep•re•hen•si•bly

rep•re•sent *v.*, rep•

re•sent•ed, rep•re•
sent•ing.
rep•re•sen•ta•tion
rep•re•sen•ta•
tion∘al
rep•re•sent∘a•tive
re•press v., re•
pressed, re•press•
ing.
re•pres•sion
re•pres•sive
re•prieve v., re•
prieved, re•priev•
ing.
rep•ri•mand v., rep•
ri•mand∘ed, rep•ri•
mand•ing.
re•pris∘al
re•prise v., re•prised,
re•pris•ing.
re•proach v., re•
proached, re•
proach•ing.
re•proach•ful
re•proach•ful∘ly
rep•ro•bate
re•pro•duce v., re•
pro•duced, re•pro•
duc•ing.
re•pro•duc•i∘ble
re•pro•duc•tion
reproduction cost
Business.
re•pro•duc•tive
re•proof
re•prove v., re•
proved, re•prov•ing.
re•prov•ing∘ly
rep•tile
rep•til∘i∘an
re•pub•lic
re•pub•li•can
Re•pub•li•can Par∘ty
re•pub•li•can•ism
re•pu•di•ate v., re•
pu•di•at∘ed, re•
pu•di•at•ing.

re•pu•di•a•tion
re•pug•nance
re•pug•nant
re•pulse v., re•
pulsed, re•puls•ing.
re•pul•sion
re•pul•sive
re•pul•sive∘ly
re•pul•sive•ness
re•pur•chase a∘gree•
ment Business.
rep∘u•ta•bil•i∘ty
rep∘u•ta∘ble
rep∘u•ta•tion
re•pute
re•put∘ed
re•put•ed∘ly
re•quest v., re•
quest∘ed, re•quest•
ing.
req•ui∘em
re•quire v., re•quired,
re•quir•ing.
re•quire•ment
req•ui•site
req•ui•si•tion v.,
req•ui•si•tioned,
req•ui•si•tion•ing.
Business.
re•quit∘al
re•quite v., re•
quit∘ed, re•quit•
ing.
re•run v., re•ran, re•
run, re•running.
re•sale
re•scind v., re•
scind∘ed, re•scind•
ing.
re•scis•sion Business.
res•cue v., res•cued,
res•cu•ing.
res•cu∘er
re•search v., re•
searched, re•search•
ing.
re•search∘er

re•sec•tion
re•sem•blance
re•sem•ble v., re•
sem•bled, re•sem•
bling.
re•sent v., re•
sent∘ed, re•sent•
ing.
re•sent•ful
re•sent•ful∘ly
re•sent•ment
res•er•pine
res•er•va•tion
re•serve v., re•
served, re•serv•ing.
reserve bank Business.
reserve re•quire•
ment Business.
reserved word Com-
puters.
re•serv•ist
res•er•voir
re•set but•ton Com-
puters.
re•side v., re•sid∘ed,
re•sid•ing.
res∘i•dence (home: cf.
RESIDENTS)
res∘i•den∘cy n., pl.
res∘i•den•cies.
res∘i•dent
resident buy∘er Busi-
ness.
resident fonts Comput-
ers.
res∘i•den•tial
re•sid∘u∘al
residual in•come Busi-
ness.
residual val∘ue Busi-
ness.
res∘i•due
re•sign v., re•signed,
re•sign•ing.
res•ig•na•tion
re•signed
re•sign•ed∘ly

re•sil•ience
re•sil•ient
res◦in
re•sist v., re•sist◦ed, re•sist•ing.
re•sist•ance
re•sist•ant
re•sist◦er (one who resists)
re•sis•tor (electrical device)
re•size v., re•sized, re•siz•ing. *Computers.*
re•sole v., re•soled, re•sol•ing.
res◦o•lute
res◦o•lute◦ly
res◦o•lu•tion
re•solv•a•ble
re•solve v., re•solved, re•solv•ing.
res◦o•nance
res◦o•nant
res◦o•nate v., res◦o•nat◦ed, res◦o•nat•ing.
res◦o•na•tor
re•sort v., re•sort◦ed, re•sort•ing.
re•sound v., re•sound◦ed, re•sound•ing.
re•sound•ing◦ly
re•source
re•source•ful
re•source•ful•ness
re•spect v., re•spect◦ed, re•spect•ing.
re•spect•a•bil•i•ty
re•spect•a◦ble
re•spect•a•bly
re•spect•ful
re•spect•ful◦ly (with deference)
re•spect•ing

re•spec•tive
re•spec•tive◦ly (sequentially)
res•pi•ra•tion
res•pi•ra•tor
res•pi•ra•to◦ry
re•spire v., re•spired, re•spir•ing.
res•pite
re•splend•ent
re•splend•ent◦ly
re•spond v., re•spond◦ed, re•spond•ing.
re•spond•ent
re•sponse
re•spon•si•bil•i•ty n., pl. re•spon•si•bil•i•ties.
re•spon•si◦ble
re•spon•si•bly
re•spon•sive
re•spon•sive◦ly
re•spon•sive•ness
rest v., rest◦ed, rest•ing. (repose: cf. WREST)
res•tau•rant
res•tau•ra•teur n., pl. res•tau•ra•teurs.
rest•ful
rest•ful◦ly
res•ti•tu•tion
res•tive
res•tive◦ly
rest•less
rest•less◦ly
rest•less•ness
res•to•ra•tion
re•stor◦a•tive
re•store v., re•stored, re•stor•ing.
re•strain v., re•strained, re•strain•ing.
re•straint

restraint of trade *Business.*
re•strict v., re•strict◦ed, re•strict•ing.
re•strict◦ed stock *Business.*
re•stric•tion
re•stric•tive
re•sult v., re•sult◦ed, re•sult•ing.
re•sult•ant
ré•su◦mé or re•su◦me (summary of past jobs)
re•sume v., re•sumed, re•sum•ing. (to continue)
re•sump•tion
re•sur•gence
re•sur•gent
res•ur•rect v., res•ur•rect◦ed, res•ur•rect•ing.
res•ur•rec•tion
re•sus•ci•tate v., re•sus•ci•tat◦ed, re•sus•ci•tat•ing.
re•sus•ci•ta•tion
re•sus•ci•ta•tor
re•tail v., re•tailed, re•tail•ing. *Business.*
re•tail sales *Business.*
re•tail◦er *Business.*
re•tail•ing *Business.*
re•tain v., re•tained, re•tain•ing.
re•tained earn•ings *Business.*
re•tain◦er
re•take v., re•took, re•tak◦en, re•tak•ing.
re•tal◦i•ate v., re•tal◦i•at◦ed, re•tal◦i•at•ing.
re•tal◦i•a•tion

re•tal•i•a•tive or re•tal•i•a•to•ry

re•tard v., re•tard•ed, re•tard•ing.

re•tard•ant

re•tar•da•tion

re•tard•ed

retch v., retched, retch•ing. (to vomit: cf. WRETCH)

re•ten•tion

re•ten•tive

re•ten•tive•ness

ret•i•cence

ret•i•cent

Ret•in-A

ret•i•na n., pl. ret•i•nas or ret•i•nae.

ret•i•nue

re•tire v., re•tired, re•tir•ing.

re•tire•ment

re•tir•ing

re•tool v., re•tooled, re•tool•ing.

re•tort v., re•tort•ed, re•tort•ing.

re•touch v., re•touched, re•touch•ing.

re•trace v., re•traced, re•trac•ing.

re•tract v., re•tract•ed, re•tract•ing.

re•tract•a•ble or re•tract•i•ble

re•trac•tion

re•tread

re-tread v., re-trod, re-trod•den or re-trod, re-trod•ding. (to walk again)

re•treat v., re•treat•ed, re•treat•ing.

re•trench v., re•trenched, re•trench•ing.

re•trench•ment

ret•ri•bu•tion

re•trib•u•tive

re•triev•al

re•trieve v., re•trieved, re•triev•ing.

re•triev•er

ret•ro

ret•ro•ac•tive

retroactive pay Business.

ret•ro•ac•tive•ly

ret•ro•fit v., ret•ro•fit•ted, ret•ro•fit, ret•ro•fit•ting.

ret•ro•grade

ret•ro•gress v., ret•ro•gressed, ret•ro•gress•ing.

ret•ro•gres•sion

ret•ro•gres•sive

ret•ro•rock•et

ret•ro•spect

ret•ro•spec•tive

ret•ro•spec•tive•ly

re•turn v., re•turned, re•turn•ing.

return key Computers.

re•turn•a•ble

re•turn•ee

Reu•ben sand•wich

re•un•ion

Ré•u•nion

rev v., revved, rev•ving.

re•vamp v., re•vamped, re•vamp•ing.

re•veal v., re•vealed, re•veal•ing.

rev•eil•le (bugle call)

rev•el v., rev•eled or rev•elled, rev•el•ing or rev•el•ling.

rev•e•la•tion

rev•el•er or rev•el•ler

rev•el•ry (merrymaking)

re•venge v., re•venged, re•veng•ing.

re•venge•ful

rev•e•nue Business.

revenue bond Business.

re•ver•ber•ate v., re•ver•ber•at•ed, re•ver•ber•at•ing.

re•ver•ber•a•tion

re•vere v., re•vered, re•ver•ing.

rev•er•ence

rev•er•end (minister)

rev•er•ent (respectful)

rev•er•en•tial

rev•er•ent•ly

rev•er•ie (musing: cf. REFEREE)

re•ver•sal

re•verse v., re•versed, re•vers•ing.

reverse split Business.

reverse vid•e•o Computers.

re•vers•i•ble

re•ver•sion

re•vert v., re•vert•ed, re•vert•ing.

re•vet•ment

re•view v., re•viewed, re•view•ing. (critique: cf. RE-VUE)

re•view•er

re•vile v., re•viled, re•vil•ing.

re•vile•ment

re•vise v., re•vised, re•vis•ing.

re•vi•sion

re•vi•sion•ism
re•vi•sion•ist
re•vi•tal•i•za•tion
re•vi•tal•ize v., re•vi•tal•ized, re•vi•tal•iz•ing.
re•viv•al
re•viv•al•ist
re•vive v., re•vived, re•viv•ing.
re•vivi•i•fi•ca•tion
re•vivi•i•fy v., re•vivi•i•fied, re•vivi•i•fy•ing.
rev•o•ca•ble or re•vok•a•ble
rev•o•ca•tion
re•voke v., re•voked, re•vok•ing.
re•volt v., re•volt•ed, re•volt•ing.
rev•o•lu•tion
rev•o•lu•tion•ar•y n., pl. rev•o•lu•tion•ar•ies.
rev•o•lu•tion•ize v., rev•o•lu•tion•ized, rev•o•lu•tion•iz•ing.
re•volve v., re•volved, re•volv•ing.
re•volv•er
re•volv•ing cred•it Business.
revolving fund Business.
revolving loan Business.
re•vue (theatrical entertainment: cf. RE-VIEW)
re•vul•sion
re•ward v., re•ward•ed, re•ward•ing. (recompense)
re•word v., re•word•ed, re•word•

ing. (to change wording)
re•write v., re•wrote, re•writ•ten, re•writ•ing.
Rey•kja•vik
RFD or R.F.D. (rural free delivery)
RGB mon•i•tor Computers. (red, green, blue monitor)
Rh factor (antigens in blood)
rhap•sod•ic or rhap•sod•i•cal
rhap•so•dize v., rhap•so•dized, rhap•so•diz•ing.
rhap•so•dy n., pl. rhap•so•dies.
rhe•a n., pl. rhe•as.
rhe•o•stat
rhe•sus mon•key
rhet•o•ric
rhe•tor•i•cal
rhe•tor•i•cal•ly
rheu•mat•ic
rheu•ma•tism
rheu•ma•toid
rheum•y adj., rheum•i•er, rheum•i•est. (ill with a cold: cf. ROOMY)
Rhine
rhine•stone
rhi•ni•tis
rhi•no n., pl. rhi•nos or rhi•no.
rhi•noc•er•os n., pl. rhi•noc•er•os•es or rhi•noc•er•os.
rhi•zome
rho (Greek letter: cf. ROE; ROW)
Rhode Is•land (RI)
Rho•de•sia
Rho•de•sian

rho•do•den•dron
rhom•boid
rhom•bus n., pl. rhom•bus•es.
Rhone or Rhône
rhu•barb
rhyme v., rhymed, rhym•ing. (verse)
rhym•er
rhythm (beat)
rhyth•mic or rhyth•mi•cal
rhyth•mi•cal•ly
RI (Rhode Island)
ri•al
rib v., ribbed, rib•bing.
rib•ald
rib•ald•ry
rib•bon v., rib•boned, rib•bon•ing.
ri•bo•fla•vin
ri•bo•nu•cle•ic ac•id
rice
rich adj., rich•er, rich•est.
Rich•ards
rich•es n.pl.
rich•ly
Rich•mond
rich•ness
Rich•ter scale
rick•ets
rick•et•y adj., rick•et•i•er, rick•et•i•est.
rick•rack or ric•rac
rick•shaw
ric•o•chet v., ric•o•cheted or ric•o•chet•ted, ric•o•chet•ing or ric•o•chet •ting.
ri•cot•ta
rid v., rid, rid•ding.
rid•dance

rid•den
rid•dle *v.*, rid•dled, rid•dling.
ride *v.*, rode, rid•den, rid•ing.
rid•er
rid•er•less
rid•er•ship
ridge
ridged
ridge•pole
ridg∘y *adj.*, ridg•i∘er, ridg•i•est.
rid∘i•cule *v.*, rid∘i•culed, rid∘i•cul•ing.
ri•dic•u•lous
ri•dic∘u•lous∘ly
ri•dic∘u•lous•ness
riel
rife
riff
rif•fle *v.*, rif•fled, rif•fling. (to shuffle: cf. RIFLE)
riff•raff
ri•fle *v.*, ri•fled, ri•fling. (firearm: cf. RIFFLE)
ri•fle•man *n.*, *pl.* ri•fle•men.
rif•lip
rift
rig *v.*, rigged, rig•ging.
rig∘a•ma•role (rigmarole)
rig•ging
right *adj.*, right∘er, right•est; *v.*, right∘ed, right•ing. (correct; to make right: cf. RITE; WRIGHT; WRITE)
right hand *n.*
right-hand *adj.*
right-hand∘ed
right-hand∘ed∘ness
right-mind∘ed

right of way or right-of-way, *n.*, *pl.* rights of way or right of ways or rights-of-way, right-of-ways.
right-to-life
right-to-lif∘er
right-to-work *Business.*
right wing *n.*
right-wing *adj.*
right-wing∘er
right•eous
right•eous∘ly
right•eous•ness
right•ful
right•ful∘ly
right•ist
right∘ly
right•ness
rights on *Business.*
rig•id
ri•gid•i∘ty or rig•id•ness
rig•id∘ly
rig•ma•role or rig∘a•ma•role
rig∘or
rig∘or mor•tis
rig•or•ous
rig•or•ous∘ly
rile *v.*, riled, ril•ing.
rill
rim *v.*, rimmed, rim•ming.
rime
rind
ring¹ *v.*, rang, rung, ring•ing. (to sound, as a bell: cf. WRING)
ring² *v.*, ringed, ring•ing. (to encircle: cf. WRING)
ring to•pol∘o∘gy *Computers.*
ring∘er
ring•lead∘er

ring•let
ring•mas•ter
ring•side
ring•worm
rink
rink∘y-dink
rinse *v.*, rinsed, rins•ing.
Ri∘o de Ja•nei∘ro
Rio Gran∘de
ri∘ot *v.*, ri•ot∘ed, ri•ot•ing.
ri•ot∘er
ri•ot•ous
RIP (rest in peace)
rip *v.*, ripped, rip•ping.
ripe *adj.*, rip∘er, rip•est.
rip∘en *v.*, rip•ened, rip•en•ing.
ripe•ness
rip-off or rip-off
ri•poste *v.*, ri•post∘ed, ri•post•ing.
rip•per
rip•ple *v.*, rip•pled, rip•pling.
ripple ef•fect *Computers.*
rip∘ple-through ef•fect *Computers.*
rip-roar∘ing
rip•saw
rip•tide
RISC *Computers.* (reduced instruction set computer)
rise *v.*, rose, ris∘en, ris•ing.
ris∘er
ris•i•bil•i•ty
ris•i•ble
ris•ing
risk *v.*, risked, risk•ing.

risk ar•bi•trage *Business.*
risk cap•i•tal *Business.*
risk man•age•ment *Business.*
risk•y *adj.*, risk•i•er, risk•i•est. (hazardous)
ris•qué (not quite proper)
rite (ceremony: cf. RIGHT; WRIGHT; WRITE)
rit•u•al
rit•u•al•ism
rit•u•al•is•tic
rit•u•al•ly
ritz•y *adj.*, ritz•i•er, ritz•i•est.
ri•val *v.*, ri•valed or ri•valled, ri•val•ing or ri•val•ling.
ri•val•ry
riv•en
riv•er
riv•er•side
riv•et *v.*, riv•et•ed or riv•et•ted, riv•et•ing or riv•et•ting.
riv•et•er
Rivoi•ier•a
riv•u•let
Ri•yadh
ri•yal or ri•al

RLL *Computers.* (run length limited)
RNA (transmitter of genetic information)
roach *n., pl.* roach•es or roach.
road (street: cf. RODE; ROWED)
road show or road•show
road•bed
road•block
road•run•ner
road•side

road•ster
road•way
road•work
roam *v.*, roamed, roam•ing.
roan
roar *v.*, roared, roar•ing.
roast *v.*, roast•ed, roast•ing.
roast•er
rob *v.*, robbed, rob•bing.
rob•ber
rob•ber•y *n., pl.* rob•ber•ies.
robe *v.*, robed, rob•ing.
rob•in
ro•bot
ro•bot•ic
ro•bot•ics
ro•bust
ro•bust•ly
ro•bust•ness
Roch•es•ter
rock *v.*, rocked, rock•ing.
rock and roll
rock jock
rock-ribbed
rock•er
rock•et *v.*, rock•et•ed, rock•et•ing.
rocket sci•en•tist
rock•et•ry
rock•y *adj.*, rock•i•er, rock•i•est.
ro•co•co
rod
rode (did ride: cf. ROAD; ROWED)
ro•dent
ro•de•o *n., pl.* ro•de•os.
Rodg•ers

Ro•din
roe (fish eggs: cf. RHO; ROW)
Roent•gen or Rönt•gen
rogue (scoundrel: cf. ROUGE)
ro•guer•y
ro•guish
Ro•hyp•nol
roil *v.*, roiled, roil•ing. (to induce turbulence: cf. ROYAL)
roist•er *v.*, roist•ered, roist•er•ing.
roist•er•er
role or rôle (actor's part).
role-play•ing
roll *v.*, rolled, roll•ing. (bread; to turn over)
roll•back
roll•er
roll•er skate *n.*
roll•er-skate *v.*, roll•er-skat•ed, roll•er-skat•ing.
rol•lick•ing
roll•o•ver *Business.*
rollover mort•gage *Business.*
ro•ly-po•ly
ROM *Computers.* (read-only memory)
ro•maine
Ro•man
ro•man à clef *n., pl.* ro•mans à clef.
Roman Cath•o•lic
ro•mance *v.*, ro•manced, ro•manc•ing.
Ro•man•esque
Ro•ma•ni•a or Ru•ma•ni•a
Ro•ma•ni•an
ro•man•tic

ro•man•ti•cal•ly
ro•man•ti•cism
ro•man•ti•cize v.,
　ro•man•ti•cized,
　ro•man•ti•ciz•ing.
Rom○a○ny
Rome
Ro•me○o n., pl. Ro•
　me○os.
romp v., romped,
　romp•ing.
romp○er
Rom○u•lus
ron•deau (poem)
ron○do (musical form)
roof n., pl. roofs; v.,
　roofed, roof•ing.
roof○er
roof•less
roof•top
rook v., rooked, rook•
　ing.
rook•er○y n., pl.
　rook•er•ies.
rook○ie
room v., roomed,
　room•ing.
room○er (lodger: cf.
　RUMOR)
room•ette
room•ful
room○i•ness
room•mate
room○y adj., room•
　i○er, room•i•est.
　(spacious: cf. RHEUMY)
Roo•se•velt
roost v., roost○ed,
　roost•ing.
roost○er
root v., root○ed,
　root•ing. (plant part:
　cf. ROUT; ROUTE)
root di•rec•to•ry
　Computers.
root○er
root•less

root•stock
rope v., roped, rop•
　ing.
Roque•fort *Trade-
　mark.*
Ror•schach test
ro•sa○ry n., pl. ro•sa•
　ries.
rose (the flower; did
　rise: cf. ROWS)
ro○sé (pink wine)
ro•se○ate
Ro•seau
rose•bud
rose•bush
rose-col○ored
rose•mar○y n., pl.
　rose•mar•ies.
ro•sette
rose•wood
Rosh Ha•sha•nah
ros○in
ros○i•ness
ros•ter
ros•trum n., pl. ros•
　trums or ros•tra.
ros○y adj., ros•i○er,
　ros•i•est.
rot v., rot•ted, rot•
　ting.
ro•ta○ry n., pl. ro•ta•
　ries.
ro•tate v., ro•tat○ed,
　ro•tat•ing.
ro•ta•tion
ro•ta•vi•rus
rote (repetition: cf.
　WROTE)
rot•gut
ro•tis•ser○ie
ro•tor
ro○to•till○er
rot•ten adj., rot•
　ten○er, rot•ten•est.
rot•ten•ness
Rot•ter•dam

ro•tund
ro•tun○da n., pl. ro•
　tun•das.
ro•tun•di○ty
rou•é n., pl. rou•és.
rouge v., rouged,
　roug•ing. (red cos-
　metic: cf. ROGUE)
rough adj., rough○er,
　rough•est;. v.,
　roughed, rough•ing.
　(coarse; to make
　rough: cf. RUFF)
rough-and-read○y
rough-and-tum○ble
rough•age
rough○en
rough-hewn
rough•house, v.,
　rough•housed,
　rough•hous•ing.
rough○ly
rough•neck
rough•ness
rough•shod
rou•lette
Rou•ma•ni○a (Roma-
　nia)
Rou•ma•ni○an
round v., round○ed,
　round•ing; adj.,
　round○er, round•
　est.
round lot *Business.*
round-shoul○dered
round table n.
round-table adj.
round-the-clock
round trip n.
round-trip adj.
round•a○bout
round○ly
round•ness
round○up
round•worm
rouse v., roused,

rous•ing. (to awaken: cf. ROWS)

Rous•seau

roust•a∘bout

rout v., rout∘ed, rout•ing. (to defeat: cf. ROOT)

route v., rout∘ed, rout•ing. (course of travel)

route sheet Business.

rou•tine

rou•tine∘ly

rove v., roved, rov•ing.

rov∘er

row v., rowed, row•ing. (to propel with oars: cf. RHO; ROE)

row•boat

row•di•ness

row∘dy n., pl. row•dies; adj., row•di∘er, row•di∘est.

row•dy•ism

rowed (did row: cf. ROAD; RODE)

row∘el v., row•eled, row•el•ing, row•elled, row•el•ling.

row∘er

rows[1] (lines: cf. ROSE)

rows[2] (quarrels: cf. ROUSE)

roy∘al (of a sovereign: cf. ROIL)

roy•al•ist

roy•al∘ly

roy•al∘ty n., pl. roy•al•ties.

RSVP (please respond to this invitation; from French répondez s'il vous plaît)

rub v., rubbed, rub•bing.

ru•ba∘to n., pl. ru•ba•tos or ru•ba•ti.

rub•ber

rubber stamp n.

rub∘ber-stamp v.

rub•ber•ize v., rub•ber•ized, rub•ber•iz•ing.

rub∘ber•neck v., rub•ber•necked, rub•ber•neck•ing.

rub•ber∘y

rub•bish

rub•ble (broken stone)

rub•down

rube

ru•bel∘la

Ru∘bens

Ru∘bik's Cube

ru•ble or rou•ble (monetary unit)

ru•bric

ru∘by n., pl. ru•bies.

ruck•sack

ruck∘us

rud•der

rud•der•less

rud•di•ness

rud∘dy adj., rud•di∘er, rud•di•est.

rude adj., rud∘er, rud•est.

rude∘ly

rude•ness

ru•di•ment

ru•di•men•ta∘ry

rue v., rued, ru•ing.

rue•ful

rue•ful∘ly

ruff (collar: cf. ROUGH)

ruf•fi∘an

ruf•fle v., ruf•fled, ruf•fling.

rug

Rug∘by

rug•ged

rug•ged∘ly

rug•ged•ness

Ruhr

ru•in v., ru•ined, ru•in•ing. (destruction: cf. RUNE)

ru•in•a•tion

ru•in•ous

rule v., ruled, rul•ing.

rul∘er

ruler line Computers.

rul•ing

rum

Ru•ma•ni∘a (Romania)

rum•ba n., pl. rum•bas; v., rum•baed, rum∘ba•ing.

rum•ble v., rum•bled, rum•bling.

ru•mi•nant

ru•mi•nate v., ru•mi•nat∘ed, ru•mi•nat•ing.

ru•mi•na•tion

ru•mi•na•tive

rum•mage v., rum•maged, rum•mag•ing.

rum∘my

ru•mor v., ru•mored, ru•mor•ing. (hearsay: cf. ROOMER)

rump

rum•ple v., rum•pled, rum•pling.

rum•pus

run v., ran, run, run•ning.

run-in

run-of-the-mill

run-on

run-through

run•a∘bout

run•a∘round

run•a∘way

run•down

rune (alphabetic character: cf. RUIN)
rung (did ring; cross-piece: cf. WRUNG)
run○ic
run•ner
run○ner-up *n., pl.* run○ners-up.
run○ny *adj.,* run•ni○er, run•ni○est.
run•off
runt
run•time *Computers.*
runtime er•ror *Computers.*
runtime ver•sion *Computers.*
runtish

runt○y *adj.,* runt•i○er, runt•i○est.
run○way
ru•pee
ru•pi○ah *n., pl.* ru•pi○ah *or* ru•pi•ahs.
rup•ture *v.,* rup•tured, rup•tur•ing.
ru•ral
ruse
rush
rusk
rus•set
Rus•sia
Rus•sian
rust *v.,* rust○ed, rust•ing.
rus•tic
rus•ti•ca•tion

rust○i•ness
rus•tle *v.,* rus•tled, rus•tling.
rustler
rust○y *adj.,* rust•i○er, rust•i○est.
rut *v.,* rut○ted, rut•ting.
ru•ta•ba○ga *n., pl.* ru•ta•ba•gas..
Ruth
ruth•less
ruth•less○ly
ruth•less•ness
Rwan○da
Rwan•dan
Rx (prescription)
ry○a rug
rye (the grain: cf. WRY)
Ryu•kyu Is•lands

S

S&L (savings-and-loan)
Sab•bath
sab•bat○i•cal
sa•ber
sa•ber•like
sa•ber•met•rics
Sa•bin vac•cine
sa•ble *n., pl.* sa•bles *or* sa•ble.
sab○o•tage *v.,* sab○o•taged, sab○o•tag•ing.
sab○o•teur
sa•bra *n., pl.* sa•bras.
SAC (Strategic Air Command)
sac (pouch, as of animal: cf. SACK)
sac•cha•rin (sugar substitute)
sac•cha•rine (excessively sweet)
sac•er•do•tal

sa•chet (small scented bag: cf. SASHAY)
sack (bag: cf. SAC)
sack•cloth
sack•ful *n., pl.* sack•fuls.
sac○ra•ment
sac○ra•men•tal
Sac○ra•men○to
sa•cred
sacred mon•ster
sa•cred•ness
sac○ri•fice *v.,* sac○ri•ficed, sac○ri•fic•ing.
sac○ri•fi•cial
sac○ri•lege
sac○ri•le•gious
sac○ri•le•gious○ly
sac○ris•tan
sac○ris○ty *n., pl.* sac○ris•ties.
sac○ro•il○i○ac
sac○ro•sanct
sac○ro•sanct•ness

sac•rum *n., pl.* sac○ra.
sad *adj.,* sad•der, sad•dest.
sad•den *v.,* sad•dened, sad•den•ing.
sad•dle *v.,* sad•dled, sad•dling.
sad○dle•bag
Sad•du•cee
sa•dism
sa•dist
sa•dis•tic
sa•dis•ti•cal○ly
sad○ly
sad•ness
sa○do•mas○o•chism
sa○do•mas○o•chist
sa○do•mas○o•chis•tic
sa•fa○ri *n., pl.* sa•fa•ris.
safe *adj.,* saf○er, saf•est.
safe-con○duct

safe-de•pos•it
safe•guard v., safe•
  guard•ed, safe•
  guard•ing.
safe•keep•ing
safe•ly
safe•ness
safe•ty n., pl. safe•
  ties.
safety stock Business.
saf•flow•er
saf•fron
sag v., sagged, sag•
  ging.
sa•ga n., pl. sa•gas.
sa•ga•cious
sa•gac•i•ty
sage adj., sag•er,
  sag•est.
sage•brush
sag•gy adj., sag•
  gi•er, sag•gi•est.
Sag•it•tar•i•us
Sa•har•a
sa•hib
said
Sai•gon
sail v., sailed, sail•ing.
  (to travel by boat: cf.
  SALE)
sail•boat
sail•cloth
sail•fish n., pl. sail•
  fish or sail•fish•es.
sail•or
saint
saint•ed
saint•hood
saint•li•ness
saint•ly
sake[1] (benefit; purpose)
sa•ke or sa•ké[2] (Japa-
  nese fermented rice
  beverage)
sa•laam v., sa•
  laamed, sa•laam•

ing. (bow; to bow: cf.
  SALAMI)
sal•a•ble or sale•
  a•ble
sa•la•cious
sa•la•cious•ly
sa•la•cious•ness
sal•ad
sal•a•man•der
sa•la•mi n., pl. sa•la•
  mis. (sausage: cf. SA-
  LAAM)
sal•a•ried Business.
sal•a•ry n., pl. sal•a•
  ries. Business.
sale (act of selling: cf.
  SAIL)
sale and lease•back
  Business.
sale•a•ble Business.
Sa•lem
sales a•gent Business.
sales check Business.
sales com•mis•sion
  Business.
sales pro•mo•tion
  Business.
sales quo•ta Business.
sales rep•re•sent•
  a•tive Business.
sales slip Business.
sales tax Business.
sales•clerk Business.
sales•man n., pl.
  sales•men. Business.
sales•man•ship Busi-
  ness.
sales•per•son Busi-
  ness.
sales•room Business.
sales•wom•an n., pl.
  sales•wom•en. Busi-
  ness.
sal•i•cyl•ic ac•id
sa•li•ence
sa•li•ent
sa•li•ent•ly

sa•line
sa•lin•i•ty
Salis•bur•y steak
sa•li•va
sal•i•var•y
sal•i•vate v., sal•i•
  vat•ed, sal•i•vat•
  ing.
sal•i•va•tion
Salk vaccine
sal•low adj., sal•
  low•er, sal•low•est.
sal•low•ness
sal•ly n., pl. sal•lies;
  v., sal•lied, sal•ly•
  ing.
salm•on n., pl. salm•
  ons or salm•on.
sal•mo•nel•la
sa•lon (reception
  room)
sa•loon (barroom)
sal•sa
salt v., salt•ed, salt•
  ing.
salt•cel•lar
salt•ed
sal•tine
salt•i•ness
salt•pe•ter or salt•
  pe•tre
salt•shak•er
salt•wa•ter
salt•y adj., salt•i•er,
  salt•i•est.
sa•lu•bri•ous
sal•u•tar•y
sal•u•ta•tion
sa•lute v., sa•lut•ed,
  sa•lut•ing.
Sal•va•dor
Sal•va•do•ran or
  Sal•va•do•ri•an
sal•vage v., sal•
  vaged, sal•vag•ing.
  (to save: cf. SELVAGE)
sal•vage•a•ble

sal•va•tion
salve¹ (hail!)
salve² v., salved, salv•ing. (ointment; to soothe, to salvage)
sal•ver¹ (tray)
salv•er² (one who soothes or salvages)
sal•vo n., pl. sal•vos or sal•voes.
sa•mar•i•um
sam•ba n., pl. sam•bas; v., sam•baed, sam•ba•ing.
same
same•ness
sam•iz•dat
Sa•mo•a
Sa•mo•an
sam•o•var
sam•pan
sam•ple v., sam•pled, sam•pling.
sam•pler
Sam•son
Sam•u•el
sam•u•rai n., pl. sam•u•rai.
San An•to•ni•o
San Di•e•go
San Fran•cis•can
San Fran•cis•co
San Sal•va•dor
Sa•n'a or Sa•naa
san•a•to•ri•um n., pl. san•a•to•ri•ums or san•a•to•ri•a.
sanc•ti•fi•ca•tion
sanc•ti•fy v., sanc•ti•fied, sanc•ti•fy•ing.
sanc•ti•mo•ni•ous
sanc•ti•mo•ni•ous•ly
sanc•tion v., sanc•tioned, sanc•tion•ing.
sanc•ti•ty

sanc•tu•ar•y n., pl. sanc•tu•ar•ies.
sanc•tum n., pl. sanc•tums or sanc•ta.
sand v., sand•ed, sand•ing.
san•dal
san•daled
san•dal•wood
sand•bag v., sand•bagged, sand•bag•ging.
sand•bank
sand•blast v., sand•blast•ed, sand•blast•ing.
sand•box
sand•er n., pl. sand•ers. (those who sand)
San•ders (last name)
sand•hog
sand•i•ness
sand•lot
sand•man n., pl. sand•men.
sand•pa•per v., sand•pa•pered, sand•pa•per•ing.
sand•pi•per
sand•stone
sand•storm
sandwich v., sand•wiched, sand•wich•ing.
sand•wich gen•er•a•tion
sand•y adj., sand•i•er, sand•i•est.
sane adj., san•er, san•est.
sane•ly
sang
sang-froid
san•gri•a or san•gri•a
san•gui•nar•y
san•guine

san•i•tar•i•um n., pl. san•i•tar•i•ums or san•i•tar•i•a.
san•i•tar•y
san•i•ta•tion
san•i•tize v., san•i•tized, san•i•tiz•ing.
san•i•tized
san•i•ty
sank
sans
sans ser•if
San•skrit
San•ta Claus
Santa Fe
San•te•rí•a or San•te•ri•a
San•ti•a•go
San•to Do•min•go
Sao Pau•lo
São To•mé and Prín•ci•pe or Sao To•me and Prin•ci•pe
sap v., sapped, sap•ping.
sa•pi•ence
sa•pi•ent
sap•less
sap•ling
sap•phire
sap•pi•ness
sap•py adj., sap•pi•er, sap•pi•est.
sap•ro•phyte
sap•ro•phyt•ic
sap•suck•er
Sar•a•cen
Sar•ah
sa•ran
sar•casm
sar•cas•tic
sar•cas•ti•cal•ly
sar•co•ma n., pl. sar•co•mas or sar•co•ma•ta.
sar•coph•a•gus n., pl.

sar•coph•a•gi or
sar•coph•a•gus•es.
sar•dine n., pl. sar•
dine or sar•dines.
Sar•din•i•a
sar•don•ic
sar•don•i•cal•ly
sa•ori n., pl. sa•ris.
sa•rong
sar•sa•pa•ril•la
sar•to•ri•al
sar•to•ri•al•ly
SASE (self-addressed
stamped envelope)
sash
sa•shay v., sa•
shayed, sa•shay•
ing. (to walk: cf. SA-
CHET)
Sas•katch•e•wan
sass v., sassed, sass•
ing.
sas•sa•fras
sas•sy adj., sas•si•er,
sas•si•est.
SAT Trademark
sat
Sa•tan
sa•tan•ic
satch•el
sate v., sat•ed, sat•
ing.
sa•teen
sat•el•lite
sa•ti•ate v., sa•ti•
at•ed, sa•ti•at•ing.
sa•ti•a•tion
sa•ti•e•ty
sat•in
sat•in•wood
sat•ire (irony: cf. SA-
TYR)
sa•tir•i•cal
sat•i•rist (humorous
writer: cf. SITARIST)

sat•i•rize v., sat•i•
rized, sat•i•riz•ing.
sat•is•fac•tion
sat•is•fac•to•ri•ly
sat•is•fac•to•ry
sat•is•fy v., sat•is•
fied, sat•is•fy•ing.
sa•to•ri
sa•trap
sat•u•ra•ble
sat•u•rate v., sat•u•
rat•ed, sat•u•rat•
ing.
sat•u•ra•tion
Sat•ur•day
Sat•ur•day-night
spe•cial
Sat•urn
sat•ur•nine
sa•tyr (woodland deity:
cf. SATIRE)
sa•ty•ri•a•sis
sa•tyr•ic
sauce v., sauced,
sauc•ing.
sauce•pan
sau•cer
sau•ci•ly
sau•ci•ness
sau•cy adj., sau•ci•er,
sau•ci•est.
Sau•di A•ra•bi•a
sau•er•kraut
Saul
sau•na n., pl. sau•
nas.
saun•ter v., saun•
tered, saun•ter•ing.
sau•ri•an
sau•sage
sau•té v., sau•téed,
sau•té•ing.
Sau•ternes
sav•a•ble or save•
a •ble

sav•age v., sav•aged,
sav•ag•ing.
sav•age•ly
sav•age•ry
sa•van•na or sa•
van•nah n., pl. sa•
van•nas or sa•van•
nahs.
Sa•van•nah
sa•vant n., pl. sa•
vants.
save v., saved, sav•
ing.
sav•er (one who saves:
cf. SAVOR)
sav•ings ac•count
Business.
sav•ings-and-loan
(S&L) Business.
savings bank Business.
savings bond Business.
sav•ior or sav•iour
sa•voir-faire
sa•vor v., sa•vored,
sa•vor•ing. (to taste
with relish: cf. SAVER)
sa•vor•y
sav•vy adj., sav•
vi•er, sav•vi•est.
saw v., sawed, saw•
ing.
saw-toothed
saw•bones n., pl.
saw•bones.
saw•buck
saw•dust
saw•horse
saw•mill
saw•yer
sax
Sax•on
sax•o•phone
sax•o•phon•ist
say v., said, say•ing.
say-so n., pl. say-sos.
SBA Business. (Small

Business Administration)
SC (South Carolina)
scab
scab•bard
scab•by adj., scab•bi•er, scab•bi•est.
sca•bies
scab•rous
scads
scaf•fold
scal•a•ble font Computers.
scal•a•wag
scald v., scald○ed, scald•ing.
scale v., scaled, scal•ing.
scal•lion
scal•lop v., scal•loped, scal•lop•ing.
scalp v., scalped, scalp•ing.
scal•pel
scalp○er
scal•y adj., scal•i○er, scal•i•est.
scam v., scammed, scam•ming.
scamp v., scamped, scamp•ing.
scamp○er v., scamp•ered, scamp•er•ing.
scam○pi n., pl. scam○pi.
scan v., scanned, scan•ning.
scan•dal
scan•dal•ize v., scan•dal•ized, scan•dal•iz•ing.
scan○dal•mon•ger
scan•dal•ous
scan•dal•ous○ly
Scan•di•na•vi○a
Scan•di•na•vi○an

Scan•lon plan Business.
scan•ner
scan•sion
scant
scant•ies
scant•i○ly
scant○i•ness
scant○ly
scant•ness
scant○y adj., scant•i○er, scant•i•est.
scape•goat
scape•grace
scap○u•la n., pl. scap○u•las or scap○u•lae.
scap○u•lar
scar v., scarred, scar•ring.
scar○ab
scarce adj., scarc○er, scarc•est.
scarce○ly
scar•ci○ty
scare v., scared, scar•ing.
scare•crow
scarf n., pl. scarfs or scarves.
scar○i•fi•ca•tion
scar○i•fy v., scar○i•fied, scar○i•fy•ing.
scar○i•ness
scar•let
scar○y adj., scar•i○er, scar•i•est.
scat v., scat•ted, scat•ting.
scath•ing
scath•ing○ly
scat○o•log○i•cal
sca•tol○o○gy
scat○ter v., scat•tered, scat•ter•ing.
scat○ter•brain

scat○ter•brained
scav•enge v., scav•enged, scav•eng•ing.
scav•en•ger
sce•nar○i○o n., pl. sce•nar○i•os.
sce•nar•ist
scene (place of action: cf. SEEN)
scen•er○y
sce•nic
sce•ni•cal○ly
scent (odor: cf. CENT; SENT)
scent○ed
scents (odors: cf. CENTS; SENSE)
scep•ter
scep•tered
scep•tic
sched•ule v., sched•uled, sched•ul•ing.
sche•mat○ic
scheme v., schemed, schem•ing.
schem○er
scher○zo n., pl. scher•zos or scher○zi.
Schick test
schil•ling
schism
schis•mat○ic
schist
schiz•oid
schiz○o○phre•ni○a
schiz○o○phren○ic
schle•miel
schlep v., schlepped, schlep•ping.
schlock
schmaltz or schmalz
schmaltz○y adj., schmaltz•i○er, schmaltz•i•est.
Schmidt

schnapps
schnau•zer
schnook
schol○ar
schol•ar•ly
schol•ar•ship
scho•las•tic
scho•las•ti•cal○ly
school v., schooled,
　school•ing.
school•boy
school•girl
school•house n., pl.
　school•hous○es.
school•marm
school•mas•ter
school•mate
school•room
school•teach○er
school•teach•ing
school•work
school•yard
schoon○er
Schu•bert
schuss v., schussed,
　schuss•ing.
schwa n., pl. schwas.
sci•at○ic
sci•at○i○ca
sci•ence
science fic•tion
sci•en•tif○ic
sci•en•tif○i○cal○ly
sci•en•tist
sci-fi (science fiction)
scim○i•tar
scin•til○la n., pl. scin•
　til•las.
scin•til•late v., scin•
　til•lat○ed, scin•til•
　lat○ing.
scin•til•la•tion
sci○on
scis•sor v., scis•sored,
　scis•sor•ing.
scis•sors

scle•ro•sis n., pl.
　scle•ro•ses.
scle•rot○ic
scoff v., scoffed,
　scoff•ing.
scoff•law
scold v., scold○ed,
　scold•ing.
sco•li○o•sis
sconce
scone
scoop v., scooped,
　scoop•ing.
scoot v., scoot○ed,
　scoot•ing.
scoot○er
scope v., scoped,
　scop•ing.
scor•bu○tic
scorch v., scorched,
　scorch•ing.
score n., pl. scores or
　score; scored, scor•
　ing.
score•board
score•less
scor○er
scorn v., scorned,
　scorn•ing.
scorn•ful
scorn•ful○ly
Scor•pi○o n., pl. Scor•
　pi○os.
scor•pi○on
scot-free
scotch v., scotched,
　scotch•ing. (to put an
　end to)
Scotch tape Trade-
　mark.
Scotch•man n., pl.
　Scotch•men.
Scot•land
Scots
Scots•man n., pl.
　Scots•men.

Scots•wom○an n., pl.
　Scots•wom○en.
Scot•tie
Scot•tish (of Scotland)
scoun•drel
scour v., scoured,
　scour•ing.
scourge v., scourged,
　scourg•ing.
scout v., scout○ed,
　scout•ing.
scout•mas•ter
scow
scowl v., scowled,
　scowl•ing.
scrab•ble v., scrab•
　bled, scrab•bling.
Scrab•ble Trademark.
scrab•bler
scrag•gly adj., scrag•
　gli○er, scrag•gli○est.
scram v., scrammed,
　scram•ming.
scram•ble v., scram•
　bled, scram•bling.
scram•bler
scrap v., scrapped,
　scrap•ping.
scrap heap or scrap•
　heap
scrap•book
scrape v., scraped,
　scrap•ing.
scrap○er
scrap•per
scrap•ple
scrap•py adj., scrap•
　pi○er, scrap•pi○est.
scratch v., scratched,
　scratch•ing.
scratch○i•ness
scratch○y adj.,
　scratch•i○er,
　scratch•i○est.
scrawl v., scrawled,
　scrawl•ing.

scrawloy *adj.*, scrawl•i•er, scrawl•i•est.

scrawnoi•ness

scream *v.*, screamed, scream•ing.

screamoer

screech

screechoy *adj.*, screech•i•er, screech•i•est.

screen

screen an•oi•ma•tor *Computers.*

screen blank•er *Computers.*

screen cap•ture *Computers.*

screen dump *Computers.*

screen flick•er *Computers.*

screen sav•er *Computers.*

screen•play

screen•writ•er

screw *v.*, screwed, screw•ing.

screw•ball

screw•driv•er

screwoy *adj.*, screw•i•er, screw•i•est.

scrib•ble *v.*, scrib•bled, scrib•bling.

scrib•bler

scribe

scrim

scrim•mage *v.*, scrim•maged, scrim•mag•ing.

scrimp *v.*, scrimped, scrimp•ing.

scrim•shaw

scrip (currency; certificate)

script (handwriting)

script lan•guage *Computers.*

scrip•tur•al

scrip•ture

script•writ•er

scrive•ner

scrod

scrofou•la

scrofou•lous

scroll *v.*, scrolled, scroll•ing.

Scrooge

scro•tal

scro•tum *n.*, *pl.* scro•ta or scro•tums.

scrounge *v.*, scrounged, scroung•ing.

scroungoer

scroungoy *adj.*, scroung•i•er, scroung•i•est.

scrub[1]

scrub[2] *v.*, scrubbed, scrub•bing.

scrub•ber

scruboby *adj.*, scrub•bi•er, scrub•bi•est.

scruff

scruffoy *adj.*, scruff•i•er, scruff•i•est.

scrump•tious

scrunch *v.*, scrunched, scrunch•ing.

scru•ple *v.*, scru•pled, scru•pling.

scru•pu•los•i•ty

scru•pu•lous

scru•pu•lous•ly

scru•ti•nize *v.*, scru•ti•nized, scru•ti•niz•ing.

scru•tiony *n.*, *pl.* scru•ti•nies.

SCSI port *Computers.* (small computer systems interface port)

scu•ba *n.*, *pl.* scu•bas;

v., scu•baed, scu•ba•ing.

scud *v.*, scud•ded, scud•ding.

scuff *v.*, scuffed, scuff•ing.

scuf•fle *v.*, scuf•fled, scuf•fling.

scull (oar: cf. SKULL)

scul•leroy *n.*, *pl.* scul•ler•ies.

scul•lion

sculpt *v.*, sculpt•ed, sculpt•ing.

sculp•tor (artist)

sculp•tur•al

sculp•ture (three-dimensional art)

scum

scumomy *adj.*, scum•mi•er, scum•mi•est.

scup•per

scur•ril•oi•ty

scur•ril•ous

scur•ril•ous•ly

scuroy *adj.*, scur•ried, scur•ry•ing.

scurovy

scutch•eon

scut•tle *v.*, scut•tled, scut•tling.

scut•tle•butt

scuzzoy *adj.*, scuzz•i•er, scuzz•i•est.

scythe *v.*, scythed, scyth•ing.

SD (South Dakota)

SDR *Business.* (special drawing rights)

sea (ocean: cf. SEE)

sea horse or sea•horse

sea•bed

sea•board

sea•coast

sea•faroer

sea•far•ing

sea•food
sea•go•ing
seal n., pl. seals or seal; v., sealed, seal•ing.
seal•ant
seal•er
seal•ing (closing tightly: cf. CEILING)
seal•skin
seam (stitched juncture: cf. SEEM)
sea•man n., pl. sea•men. (sailor: cf. SE-MEN)
sea•man•ship
seamed
seam•less
seam•stress
seam•y adj., seam•i•er, seam•i•est.
sé•ance
sea•plane
sea•port
sear v., seared, sear•ing. (to burn: cf. SEER; SERE)
search v., searched, search•ing.
search-and-re•place Computers.
search•light
sea•scape
sea•shell or sea shell
sea•shore
sea•sick
sea•sick•ness
sea•side
sea•son v., sea•soned, sea•son•ing. (time of year; to give flavor to)
sea•son•a•ble (timely)
sea•son•al (of the season)

seasonal un•em•ploy•ment Business.
sea•son•al•ly
sea•son•ing
seat v., seat•ed, seat•ing.
seat belt
Se•at•tle
sea•ward
sea•wa•ter
sea•way
sea•weed
sea•wor•thy
se•ba•ceous
seb•or•rhe•a
SEC or S.E.C. Business. (Securities and Exchange Commission).
se•cant
se•cede v., se•ced•ed, se•ced•ing.
se•ces•sion
se•ces•sion•ist
se•clud•ed
se•clu•sion
sec•ond v., sec•ond•ed, sec•ond•ing.
second class n.
sec•ond-class adj.
sec•ond-guess v., sec•ond-guessed, sec•ond-guess•ing.
sec•ond hand n.
sec•ond-rate
sec•ond-sto•ry man
sec•ond-string•er
sec•ond•ar•i•ly
sec•ond•ar•y n., pl. sec•ond•ar•ies.
secondary mar•ket Business.
secondary of•fer•ing Business.
secondary stor•age Computers.

sec•ond•hand adj.
secondhand smoke
sec•ond•ly
se•cre•cy
se•cret
sec•re•tar•i•al
sec•re•tar•i•at
sec•re•tar•y n., pl. sec•re•tar•ies.
se•crete v., se•cret•ed, se•cret•ing.
se•cre•tion
se•cre•tive
se•cret•ly
sect
sec•tar•i•an
sec•tion v., sec•tioned, sec•tion•ing.
sec•tion•al
sec•tion•al•ism
sec•tor
sec•u•lar
sec•u•lar•ism
sec•u•lar•ist
sec•u•lar•i•za•tion
sec•u•lar•ize v., sec•u•lar•ized, sec•u•lar•iz•ing.
se•cure v., se•cured, se•cur•ing.
se•cured loan
se•cure•ly
se•cu•ri•ty n., pl. se•cu•ri•ties.
security an•a•lyst
secy or sec'y (secretary)
se•dan
se•date v., se•dat•ed, se•dat•ing.
se•date•ly
se•da•tion
sed•a•tive
sed•en•tar•y
Se•der n., pl. Se•ders or Se•da•rim.

sedge
sed○i•ment
sed○i•men•ta•ry
sed○i•men•ta•tion
se•di•tion
se•di•tious
se•duce v., se•duced, se•duc•ing.
se•duc•er
se•duc•tive
sed○u•lous
see v., saw, seen, see•ing. (to perceive: cf. SEA)
see-through
seed[1] n., pl. seeds or seed. (plant ovule: cf. CEDE)
seed[2] v., seed○ed, seed•ing.
seed mon○ey Business.
seed○i•ness
seed•less
seed•ling
seed○y adj., seed•i○er, seed•i•est.
see•ing
seek v., sought, seek•ing.
seek time Computers.
seek○er
seem v., seemed, seem•ing. (to appear: cf. SEAM)
seem•ing○ly
seem•li•ness
seem○ly adj., seem•li○er, seem•li•est.
seen (viewed: cf. SCENE)
seep v., seeped, seep•ing.
seep•age
se○er[1] (one who sees)
seer[2] (prophet: cf. SEAR; SERE)

seer•suck○er
see•saw v., see•sawed, see•saw•ing.
seethe v., seethed, seeth•ing.
seg•ment v., seg•ment○ed, seg•ment•ing.
seg•men•ta•tion
seg•ment○ed vir•tu○al mem•o○ry Computers.
seg•re•gate v., seg•re•gat○ed, seg•re•gat•ing.
seg•re•ga•tion
seg•re•ga•tion•ist
se•gue v., se•gued, se•gue•ing.
sei•gnior
seine
seis•mic
seis•mo•graph
seis•mog•ra•pher
seis•mo•graph○ic
seis•mog•ra•phy
seis•mo•log○ic
seis•mo•log○i•cal
seis•mol•ogy
seize v., seized, seiz•ing.
sei•zure
sel•dom
se•lect v., se•lect○ed, se•lect•ing.
se•lec•tion
se•lec•tive
se•lect•man n., pl. se•lect•men.
se•lec•tor
sel○e•nite
se•le•ni○um
sel○e•nog•ra•pher
sel○e•nog•ra•phy
self n., pl. selves.

self-ad○dressed
self-as○sur○ance
self-cen○tered
self-con○fi○dence
self-con○fi○dent
self-con○scious
self-con○scious○ly
self-con○scious○ness
self-con○tained
self-con○trol
self-con○trolled
self-de○fense
self-de○ni○al
self-de○struct v., self-de○struct○ed, self-de○struct•ing.
self-de○struc•tion
self-de○struc•tive
self-de○ter○mi○na○tion
self-es○teem
self-ev○i○dent
self-ex○plan○a○to○ry
self-ex○pres○sion
self-ful○fill○ing
self-gov○ern○ing
self-gov○ern○ment
self-im○age
self-im○por○tance
self-im○por○tant
self-in○sur○ance Business.
self-in○sure v., self-in○sured, self-in○sur○ing. Business.
self-in○ter○est
self-liq○ui○dat○ing Business.
self-made
self-pos○ses○sion
self-pro○pelled or self-pro○pel○ling
self-reg○u○lat○ing
self-re○li○ance
self-re○li○ant
self-re○spect

self-re○straint
self-right○eous
self-right○eous○ly
self-right○eous○ness
self-sac○ri○fice
self-sac○ri○fic○ing
self-seek○ing
self-serv○ice
self-serv○ing
self-start○er
self-start○ing
self-styled
self-suf○fi○cien○cy
self-suf○fi○cient
self-taught
self-wind○ing
self•ish
self•ish○ly
self•ish•ness
self•less
self•less○ly
self•less•ness
self•same
sell v., sold, sell•ing.
  Business. (to offer for
  money: cf. CELL)
sell-off *Business.*
sell-through *Business.*
sell○er *Business.* (one
  who sells: cf. CELLAR)
sell•ers' mar•ket *Busi-
  ness.*
sell•ing point *Busi-
  ness.*
sell•out
selt•zer
sel•vage (fabric edge:
  cf. SALVAGE)
selves
se•man•tic
semantic er•ror
se•man•ti•cist
se•man•tics
sem○a•phore v.,
  sem○a•phored,
  sem○a•phor•ing.

sem•blance
se•men (male repro-
  ductive fluid: cf. SEA-
  MAN)
se•mes•ter
sem○i n., pl. sem○is.
sem○i•am○a•teur
sem○i•an○nu○al
sem○i•au○to•mat○ic
sem○i•cir○cle
sem○i•cir○cu○lar
sem○i•co•lon
sem○i•con○duc•tor
sem○i•fi•nal
sem○i•fi•nal•ist
sem○i•month○ly n.,
  pl. sem○i•month•
  lies.
sem○i•nal
sem○i•nar
sem○i•nar•i○an
sem○i•nar○y n., pl.
  sem○i•nar•ies.
Sem○i•nole n., pl.
  Sem○i•noles or
  Sem○i•nole.
se•mi•ot○ics
sem○i•per•me•a○ble
sem○i•pre•cious
sem○i•pri○vate
sem○i•pro•fes•
  sion○al
sem○i•skilled
Sem•ite
Se•mit○ic
sem○i•tone
sem○i•trail○er
sem○i•trop○i○cal
sem○i•var•i•a○ble
  cost *Business.*
sem○i•vow○el
sem○i•week○ly n., pl.
  sem○i•week•lies.
sen•ate
sen○a•tor
sen○a•to○ri○al

send v., sent, send•
  ing.
send-off
send○er
Sen○e○ca n., pl.
  Sen○e•cas or
  Sen○e○ca.
Sen○e•gal
Sen○e•ga•lese n., pl.
  Sen○e•ga•lese.
se•nes•cence
se•nes•cent
se•nile
se•nil•i○ty
sen•ior
sen•ior•i○ty n., pl.
  sen•ior•i•ties.
sen○na
se•ñor n., pl. se•ñors
  or se•ño•res.
se•ño•ra n., pl. se•
  ño•ras.
se•ño•ri○ta n., pl. se•
  ño•ri•tas.
sen•sa•tion
sen•sa•tion○al
sen•sa•tion•al•ism
sen•sa•tion•al•is•tic
sense[1] n. (faculty: cf.
  CENTS; SCENTS)
sense[2] v., sensed,
  sens•ing. (to feel)
sense•less
sens○es (faculties: cf.
  CENSUS)
sen•si•bil•i○ty n., pl.
  sen•si•bil•i•ties.
sen•si•ble
sen•si•bly
sen•si•tive
sen•si•tiv•i○ty
sen•si•ti•za•tion
sen•si•tize v., sen•si•
  tized, sen•si•tiz○
  ing.
sen•sor
sen•so○ry

sen•su•al
sen•su•al•i•ty
sen•su•al•ly
sen•su•ous
sen•su•ous•ly
sen•su•ous•ness
sent (did send: cf. CENT; SCENT)
sen•te•men•tal•ist
sen•tence v., sen•tenced, sen•tenc•ing.
sen•ten•tious
sen•tient
sen•ti•ment
sen•ti•men•tal
sen•ti•men•tal•i•ty
sen•ti•men•tal•ize v., sen•ti•men•tal•ized, sen•ti•men•tal•iz•ing.
sen•ti•men•tal•ly
sen•ti•nel
sen•try n., pl. sen•tries.
Seoul
se•pal
sep•a•ra•ble
sep•a•rate v., sep•a•rat•ed, sep•a•rat•ing.
sep•a•rate•ly
sep•a•ra•tion
sep•a•ra•tism
sep•a•ra•tist
sep•a•ra•tor
se•pi•a
sep•sis
Sep•tem•ber
sep•tet
sep•tic
sep•ti•ce•mi•a
sep•tu•a•ge•nar•i•an
Sep•tu•a•gint

sep•tum n., pl. sep•ta.
sep•ul•cher
se•pul•chral
se•quel
se•quence v., se•quenced, se•quenc•ing.
se•quenc•ing
se•quen•tial
sequential ac•cess Computers.
se•ques•ter v., se•ques•tered, se•ques•ter•ing.
se•ques•tra•tion
se•quin
se•quined
se•quoi•a n., pl. se•quoi•as.
se•ra
se•ra•glio n., pl. se•ra•glios.
se•ra•pe n., pl. se•ra•pes.
ser•aph n., pl. ser•aphs or ser•a•phim.
se•raph•ic
Serb
Ser•bi•a
Ser•bi•an
Ser•bo-Cro•a•tian
sere (withered: cf. SEAR; SEER)
ser•e•nade v., ser•e•nad•ed, ser•e•nad•ing.
ser•en•dip•i•tous
ser•en•dip•i•ty
se•rene
se•rene•ly
se•ren•i•ty
serf (peasant: cf. SURF)
serf•dom
serge (cloth: cf. SURGE)
ser•geant

se•ri•al (story in installments; of a sequence: cf. CEREAL)
serial bond Business.
serial in•ter•face Computers.
serial mouse Computers.
serial print•er Computers.
se•ri•al•i•za•tion
se•ri•al•ize v., se•ri•al•ized, se•ri•al•iz•ing.
se•ries n., pl. se•ries. (related group)
ser•if
se•ri•ous (important)
se•ri•ous•ly
se•ri•ous•ness
ser•mon
ser•mon•ize v., ser•mon•ized, ser•mon•iz•ing.
se•rol•o•gist
se•rol•o•gy
se•rous
ser•pent
ser•pen•tine
ser•rat•ed
ser•ra•tion
ser•ried
se•rum n., pl. se•rums or se•ra.
serv•ant
serve v., served, serv•ing.
serv•er
serv•er-based Computers.
serv•ice n., v., serv•iced, serv•ic•ing. (help; to repair)
Ser•vice (the poet)
service book
service busi•ness Business.

service cen•ter *Business.*
service charge *Business.*
serv•ice•a•ble
serv•ice•man *n.*, *pl.* serv•ice•men.
ser•vi•ette
ser•vile
ser•vil•i•ty
serv•ing
ser•vi•tor
ser•vi•tude
ser•vo *n.*, *pl.* ser•vos.
ser•vo•mech•an•ism
ser•vo•mo•tor
ses•a•me
ses•qui•cen•ten•ni•al
ses•sion (meeting: cf. CESSION)
set *v.*, set, set•ting.
set-to *n.*, *pl.* set-tos.
set•back
set•tee
set•ter
set•ting
set•tle *v.*, set•tled, set•tling.
set•tle•ment
set•tler
set•up
sev•en
sev•en•teen
sev•en•teen•year lo•cust
sev•en•teenth
sev•enth
sev•en•ti•eth
sev•en•ty *n.*, *pl.* sev•en•ties.
sev•er *v.*, sev•ered, sev•er•ing.
sev•er•al
sev•er•al•ly
sev•er•ance

severance pay *Business.*
severance tax *Business.*
se•vere
se•vere•ly
se•vere•ness
se•ver•i•ty
Se•ville
sew *v.*, sewed, sewn or sewed, sew•ing. (to stitch: cf. so; sow)
sew•age or sew•er•age
sew•er
sex
sex•a•ge•nar•i•an
sex•i•ly
sex•i•ness
sex•ism
sex•ist
sex•less
sex•pot
sex•tant
sex•tet or sex•tette
sex•ton
sex•tu•ple *v.*, sex•tu•pled, sex•tu•pling.
sex•u•al
sex•u•al•i•ty
sex•u•al•ly
sex•y *adj.*, sex•i•er, sex•i•est.
Sey•chelles
SF or s-of (science fiction).
sh or shh
shab•bi•ly
shab•bi•ness
shab•by *adj.*, shab•bi•er, shab•bi•est.
shack *v.*, shacked, shack•ing.
shack•le *v.*, shack•led, shack•ling.

shad *n.*, *pl.* shad or shads.
shade *v.*, shad•ed, shad•ing.
shad•i•ness
shad•ow *v.*, shad•owed, shad•ow•ing.
shadow price *Business.*
shadow•box *v.*, shad•ow•boxed, shad•ow•box•ing.
shad•ow•y *adj.*, shad•ow•i•er, shad•ow•i•est.
shad•y *adj.*, shad•i•er, shad•i•est.
shaft
shag *v.*, shagged, shag•ging.
shag•gi•ness
shag•gy *adj.*, shag•gi•er, shag•gi•est.
shah
shake *v.*, shook, shak•en, shak•ing.
shake-up
shake•down
shak•er
Shake•speare
Shake•spear•e•an or Shake•spear•i•an
shak•y *adj.*, shak•i•er, shak•i•est.
shale
shall
shal•lot
shal•low *adj.*, shal•low•er, shal•low•est.
sha•lom
shalt
sham *v.*, shammed, sham•ming.
sha•man
sham•ble *v.*, sham•bled, sham•bling.
sham•bles

shame v., shamed,
  sham•ing.
shame•faced
shame•ful
shame•ful•ly
shame•less
sham•poo v., sham•
  pooed, sham•poo•
  ing.
sham•rock
shang•hai v., shang•
  haied, shang•hai•
  ing.
Shan○gri-la
shan't (shall not)
Shan•tung
shan•ty n., pl. shan•
  ties. (hut: cf. CHANTEY)
shape v., shaped,
  shap•ing.
shape•less
shape•less•ness
shape○ly adj., shape•
  li•er, shape•li•est.
shard or sherd
share v., shared, shar•
  ing.
share•crop•per
share•hold○er Business.
share•ware Computers.
shark
shark•skin
sharp adj., sharp○er,
  sharp•est.
sharp-eyed
sharp-tongued
sharp○en v., sharp•
  ened, sharp•en•ing.
sharp•en○er
sharp○ly
sharp•ness
sharp•shoot○er
sharp•shoot•ing
shat•ter v., shat•
  tered, shat•ter•ing.

shat○ter•proof
shave v., shaved,
  shaved or shav○en,
  shav•ing.
shav○er
Shaw
shawl
Shaw•nee n., pl.
  Shaw•nees or
  Shaw•nee.
s/he
she n., pl. they, shes.
sheaf n., pl. sheaves.
shear v., sheared,
  sheared or shorn,
  shear•ing. (to clip: cf.
  SHEER)
sheath (a case)
sheathe v., sheathed,
  sheath•ing. (to en-
  case)
she-bang
she'd
shed v., shed, shed•
  ding.
sheen
sheep n., pl. sheep.
sheep•dog or sheep
  dog
sheep•fold
sheep•ish
sheep•ish○ly
sheep•ish•ness
sheep•skin
sheer adj., sheer○er,
  sheer•est. (transpar-
  ent: cf. SHEAR)
sheer•ness
sheet
sheet-fed scan•ner
  Computers.
sheet feed○er Comput-
  ers.
sheet•ing
sheik or sheikh (Arab
  chief: cf. CHIC; CHICK)

sheik•dom or sheikh•
  dom
shek○el
shelf n., pl. shelves.
she'll (she will)
shell v., shelled, shell•
  ing.
shell-shocked
shel•lac or shel•lack
  v., shel•lacked, shel•
  lack•ing.
Shel•ley
shell•fish n., pl. shell•
  fish or shell•fish○es.
shel•ter v., shel•
  tered, shel•ter•ing.
shelve v., shelved,
  shelv•ing.
she•nan○i•gans
shep•herd v., shep•
  herd○ed, shep•
  herd•ing.
sher•bet
sher•iff
Sher○pa n., pl. Sher•
  pas.
sher○ry n., pl. sher•
  ries.
she's (she is)
shib•bo•leth
shied
shield v., shield○ed,
  shield•ing.
shift v., shift○ed,
  shift•ing.
shift click•ing Comput-
  ers.
shift-click Computers.
shift•i○ly
shift○i•ness
shift•less
shift•less•ness
shift○y adj., shift•
  i○er, shift•i•est.
shill v., shilled, shill•
  ing. (posing as a cus-
  tomer)

shil•le•lagh

shil•ling (old British coin)

shil•ly-shal•ly v., shil•ly-shal•lied, shil•ly-shal•ly•ing.

shim•mer v., shim•mered, shim•mer•ing.

shim•mer•y

shin v., shinned, shin•ning.

shin•bone

shin•dig

shine v., shone or shined, shin•ing.

shin•er

shin•gle v., shin•gled, shin•gling.

shin•gles

shin•i•ness

shin•ny v., shin•nied, shin•ny•ing.

Shin•to

Shin•to•ist

shin•y adj., shin•i•er, shin•i•est.

ship v., shipped, ship•ping.

ship•board

ship•build•er

ship•build•ing

ship•mate

ship•ment

ship•per

ship•ping

ship•shape

ship•wreck v., ship•wrecked, ship•wreck•ing.

ship•yard

shire

shirk v., shirked, shirk•ing.

shirk•er

shirred eggs

shirt•ing

shirt•tail

shirt•waist

shish ke•bab

shiv

Shi•va or Si•va

shiv•er v., shiv•ered, shiv•er•ing.

shiv•er•y

shlep or shlepp v., shlepped, shlep•ping.

shoal

shoat

shock v., shocked, shock•ing.

shock jock

shock•er

shock•ing

shock•proof

shod

shod•di•ly

shod•di•ness

shod•dy adj., shod•di•er, shod•di•est.

shoe n., pl. shoes; v., shod or shoed, shoe•ing. (foot covering: cf. SHOO)

shoe•horn

shoe•lace

shoe•less

shoe•mak•er

shoe•shine

shoe•string

shoe•tree

sho•gun

sho•gun•ate

shone (did shine: cf. SHOWN)

shoo (to send away: cf. SHOE)

shoo-in

shook

shoot v., shot, shoot•ing. (to fire a gun: cf. CHUTE)

shoot•er

shoot•out

shop v., shopped, shop•ping.

shop•keep•er

shop•lift v., shop•lift•ed, shop•lift•ing.

shop•lift•er

shoppe

shop•per

shop•ping cen•ter

shop•talk

shop•worn

shore v., shored, shor•ing.

shore•bird

shore•line

shorn

short adj., short•er, short•est.

short cir•cuit n.

short-cir•cuit v., short-cir•cuit•ed, short-cir•cuit•ing.

short-hand•ed

short-lived

short or•der n.

short-or•der adj.

short-range

short sale Business.

short sell•ing Business.

short shrift

short-tem•pered

short term n.

short-term adj.

short-term debt Business.

short ton

short-waist•ed

short-wind•ed

short•age

short•bread

short•cake

short•change v.,

short•changed,
short•chang•ing.
short•com•ing
short•cut
short•en v., short•
ened, short•en•ing.
short•hand
Short•horn
short•ly
short•ness
short•sight○ed
short•sight•ed•ly
short•sight•ed•ness
short•stop
short•wave
short•word *Computers.*
Sho•sho○ne or Sho•
sho○ni n., pl. Sho•
sho•nes or Sho•
sho•nis, Sho•
sho○ne or Sho•
sho○ni.
shot n., pl. shots or
shot.
shot clock
shot-put○ter
shot•gun v., shot•
gunned, shot•gun•
ning.
should
shoul•der v., shoul•
dered, shoul•der•
ing.
should○n't
shout v., shout○ed,
shout•ing.
shove v., shoved,
shov•ing.
shov○el v., shov•eled
or shov•elled, shov•
el•ing or shov•el•
ling.
shov•el•ful n., pl.
shov•el•fuls.
show v., showed,
shown, show•ing.
show•boat

show•case v., show•
cased, show•cas•
ing.
show•down
show○er v., show•
ered, show•er•ing.
show•i○ly
show○i•ness
show•ing
show•man n., pl.
show•men.
show•man•ship
shown (did show: cf.
SHONE)
show-off
show•piece
show•place
show•room
show○y adj., show•
i○er, show•i•est.
shpt. (shipment)
shrank
shrap•nel
shred v., shred•ded,
shred, shred•ding.
shred•der
Shreve•port
shrew
shrewd adj.,
shrewd○er, shrewd•
est.
shrewd○ly
shrewd•ness
shrew•ish
shriek v., shrieked,
shriek•ing.
shrike
shrill adj., shrill○er,
shrill•est.
shrill•ness
shril○ly
shrimp n., pl. shrimps
or shrimp.
shrine
shrink v., shrank or
shrunk, shrunk or

shrunk○en, shrink•
ing.
shrink-wrap v., shrink-
wrapped, shrink-
wrap○ping.
shrink•a○ble
shrink•age *Business.*
shrive v., shrove or
shrived, shriv○en or
shrived, shriv•ing.
shriv○el v., shriv•eled
or shriv•elled, shriv•
el•ing or shriv•el•
ling.
shroud v., shroud○ed,
shroud•ing.
shrove
shrub
shrub•ber○y
shrub○by adj., shrub•
bi○er, shrub•bi•est.
shrug v., shrugged,
shrug•ging.
shrunk
shrunk○en
shtg. (shortage)
shuck v., shucked,
shuck•ing.
shud•der v., shud•
dered, shud•der•
ing. (to tremble: cf.
SHUTTER)
shuf•fle v., shuf•fled,
shuf•fling.
shuf○fle•board
shun v., shunned,
shun•ning.
shunt v., shunt○ed,
shunt•ing.
shush v., shushed,
shush•ing.
shut v., shut, shut•
ting.
shut-in
shut•down
shut•eye
shut•out

shut•ter v., shut•
tered, shut•ter•ing.
(window cover: cf.
SHUDDER)

shut•ter•bug

shut•tle v., shut•tled,
shut•tling.

shut○tle•cock

shy n., pl. shies; v.,
shied, shy•ing; adj.,
shy•er or shi•er,
shy•est or shi•est.

Shy•lock

shy○ly

shy•ness

shy•ster

Si•am

Si•a•mese n., pl. Si•
a•mese.

Si•be•ri•a

Si•be•ri•an

sib○i•lance

sib○i•lant

sib•ling

sib○yl

sic (SO)

Si•cil•ian

Sic○i○ly

sick adj., sick○er, sick•
est. (ill)

sick•bed

sick○en v., sick•ened,
sick•en•ing.

sick○le

sick○ly adj., sick•li○er,
sick•li•est.

sick•ness

sick•out

sick•room

side v., sid○ed, sid•
ing. (edge: cf. SIGHED)

side arm n.

side•arm adj.

side•bar

side•board

side•burns

side•car

side•kick

side•light

side•line v., side•
lined, side•lin•ing.

side•long

side•man n. pl. side•
men.

si•de•re•al

side•sad•dle

side•show

side•split•ting

side•step v., side•
stepped, side•step•
ping.

side•stream smoke

side•stroke v., side•
stroked, side•strok•
ing.

side•swipe v., side•
swiped, side•swip•
ing.

side•track v., side•
tracked, side•track•
ing.

side•walk

side•wall

side•ways

sid○ing

si•dle v., si•dled, si•
dling.

siege

si•en•na

si•er○ra n., pl. si•er•
ras.

Si•er○ra Le•o○ne

si•es○ta n., pl. si•es•
tas.

sieve

sift v., sift○ed, sift•
ing.

SIG Computers. (special
interest group)

sigh v., sighed, sigh•
ing.

sighed (did sigh: cf.
SIDE)

sighs (audible exhala-
tions: cf. SIZE)

sight (vision: cf. CITE;
SITE)

sight draft Business.

sight-read v., sight-
read, sight-read○ing.

sight○ed

sight•less

sight•see•ing

sight•se○er

sig○ma n., pl. sig•
mas.

sign[1] n. (indication: cf.
SINE)

sign[2] v., signed, sign•
ing. (to use sign lan-
guage)

sig•nal v., sig•naled
or sig•nalled, sig•
nal•ing or sig•nal•
ling.

sig•nal○ly

sig•na•to○ry n., pl.
sig•na•to•ries.

sig•na•ture

signature loan Busi-
ness.

sign•board

sign○er

sig•net (small seal: cf.
CYGNET)

sig•nif○i•cance

sig•nif○i•cant

sig•nif○i•cant○ly

sig•ni•fi•ca○tion

sig•ni○fy v., sig•ni•
fied, sig•ni•fy•ing.

si•gnor n., pl. si•
gnors.

si•gno○ra n., pl. si•
gno•ras.

si•gno•ri○na n., pl.
si•gno•ri•nas.

sign•post

Sikh

si•lage

si•lence *v.*, si•lenced, si•lenc•ing.

si•lenc•er

si•lent

silent part•ner *Business.*

si•lent•ly

sil•hou•ette *v.*, sil•hou•et•ted, sil•hou•et•ting.

sil∘i∘ca

sil∘i∘cate

sil∘i∘con (chemical element in sand; computer chips)

Sil∘i∘con Val•ley

sil∘i∘cone (fluid polymer)

sil∘i∘co•sis

silk

silk∘en

silk•screen *v.*, silk•screened, silk•screen•ing.

silk•worm

silk∘y *adj.*, silk•i∘er, silk•i•est.

sill

sil•li•ness

sil∘ly *n.*, *pl.* sil•lies; *adj.*, sil•li∘er, sil•li•est.

si∘lo *n.*, *pl.* si∘los.

silt *v.*, silt∘ed, silt•ing.

silt∘y

Si•lu∘ri∘an

sil•ver *v.*, sil•vered, sil•ver•ing.

sil∘ver-tongued

sil∘ver•fish *n.*, *pl.* sil∘ver•fish or sil∘ver•fish ∘es.

sil∘ver•smith

sil∘ver•ware

sil•ver∘y

sim∘i∘an

sim∘i•lar

sim∘i•lar•i∘ty

sim∘i•lar•ly

sim∘i•le

si•mil∘i•tude

SIMM *Computers.* (single in-line memory module)

sim•mer *v.*, sim•mered, sim•mer•ing.

si∘mon-pure

si•mo∘ny

sim•pa•ti•co

sim•per *v.*, sim•pered, sim•per•ing.

sim•ple *adj.*, sim•pler, sim•plest. (plain: cf. SIMPLISTIC)

simple in•ter•est *Business.*

sim∘ple•mind∘ed or sim∘ple-mind∘ed

sim•ple•ness

sim∘ple•ton

sim•plic•i∘ty

sim•pli•fi•ca•tion

sim•pli•fy *v.*, sim•pli•fied, sim•pli•fy•ing.

sim•plis•tic (oversimplified: cf. SIMPLE)

sim•ply

sim∘u•late *v.*, sim∘u•lat∘ed, sim∘u•lat•ing.

sim∘u•la•tion

sim∘u•la•tor

si•mul•cast *v.*, si•mul•cast, si•mul•cast∘ed, si•mul•cast•ing.

si•mul•ta•ne∘ous

si•mul•ta•ne∘ous•ly

sin *v.*, sinned, sin•ning.

sin tax *Business.*

Si•nai

since

sin•cere

sin•cere∘ly

sin•cer•i∘ty

sine (angle ratio: cf. SIGN)

si∘ne di∘e

si∘ne qua non

si•ne∘cure

sin∘ew

sin•ew∘y

sin•ful

sing *v.*, sang, sung, sing•ing. (vocalizing: cf. SINGEING)

sing-a∘long

sing•a∘ble

Sin•ga•pore

singe *v.*, singed, singe•ing. (scorching: cf. SINGING)

sing∘er

sin•gle *v.*, sin•gled, sin•gling.

sin•gle-breast∘ed

sin•gle-den∘si∘ty *Computers.*

sin•gle-en∘try *Business.*

sin•gle-hand∘ed

sin•gle-hand∘ed∘ly

sin•gle-lens re•flex cam•er∘a

sin•gle-mind∘ed

sin•gle-mind∘ed∘ly

sin•gle-pre∘ci∘sion *Computers.*

sin•gle-sid∘ed *Computers.*

sin•gle-track

sin•gle•ton

sin•gly

sing•song

sin•gu•lar

sin•gu•lar•i∘ty

sin•gu•lar•ly

Sin•ha•lese *n., pl.*
Sin•ha•lese.
sin•is•ter
sink *v.,* sank or sunk,
sunk or sunk•en,
sink•ing.
sink•a•ble
sink•er
sink•hole
sink•ing fund *Busi-
ness.*
sin•ner
sin•u•ous
si•nus *n., pl.* si•
nus•es.
si•nus•i•tis
Sioux *n., pl.* Sioux.
sip *v.,* sipped, sip•
ping.
si•phon
sir
sire *v.,* sired, sir•ing.
si•ren
sir•loin
si•roc•co *n., pl.* si•
roc•cos.
sis
si•sal
sis•si•fied
sis•sy *n., pl.* sis•sies.
sis•ter
sis•ter-in-law *n., pl.*
sis•ters-in-law.
sis•ter•hood
sis•ter•ly
Sis•y•phus
sit *v.,* sat, sit•ting.
sit-down
sit-in
sit-up
si•tar
si•tar•ist (musician: cf.
SATIRIST)
sit•com
site *v.,* sit•ed, sit•ing.

(location: cf. CITE;
SIGHT)
sit•ter
sit•ting
sit•u•at•ed
sit•u•a•tion
six
six-pack
six-shoot•er
six•pence *n., pl.* six•
pence or six•
penc•es.
six•teen
six•teenth
sixth
six•ti•eth
six•ty *n., pl.* six•ties.
siz•a•ble or size•
a•ble
size (dimensions: cf.
SIGHS)
siz•zle *v.,* siz•zled,
siz•zling.
skate[1] *n., pl.* skates or
skate. (the fish)
skate[2] *v.,* skat•ed,
skat•ing. (ice skate or
roller skate; to skate)
skate•board
skat•er
ske•dad•dle
skeet
skein
skel•e•tal
skel•e•ton
skep•tic or scep•tic
skep•ti•cal or scep•
ti•cal
skep•ti•cal•ly
skep•ti•cism or scep•
ti•cism
sketch *v.,* sketched,
sketch•ing.
sketch•y *adj.,* sketch•
i•er, sketch•i•est.
skew *v.,* skewed,
skew•ing.

skew•er *v.,* skew•
ered, skew•er•ing.
ski *n., pl.* skis or ski;
v., skied, ski•ing.
skid *v.,* skid•ded,
skid•ding.
ski•er
skiff
skilled
skil•let
skill•ful
skill•ful•ly
skim *v.,* skim,
skimmed, skim•
ming.
skimp *v.,* skimped,
skimp•ing.
skimp•i•ness
skimp•y *adj.,* skimp•
i•er, skimp•i•est.
skin *v.,* skinned, skin•
ning.
skin-deep
skin div•er
skin div•ing
skin flick
skin•flint
skin•ni•ness
skin•ny *adj.,* skin•
ni•er, skin•ni•est.
skin•ny-dip *v.,*
skin•ny-dipped,
skin•ny-dip•ping.
skin•tight
skip *v.,* skipped, skip•
ping.
skip loss *Business.*
skip•per
skir•mish *v.,* skir•
mished, skir•mish•
ing.
skirt *v.,* skirt•ed,
skirt•ing.
skit
skit•ter *v.,* skit•tered,
skit•ter•ing.
skit•tish

skoal

skosh

skul•dug•ger○y or skull•dug•gery *n.*, *pl.* skul•dug•ger•ies.

skulk *v.*, skulked, skulk•ing.

skull (skeleton of head: cf. SCULL)

skull•cap

skunk *n.*, *pl.* skunks or skunk.

sky *n.*, *pl.* skies; *v.*, skied or skyed, sky•ing.

sky-high

sky mar•shal

sky•cap

sky•div•ing or sky div•ing

sky•jack *v.*, sky•jacked, sky•jack•ing.

sky•jack○er

sky•lark *v.*, sky•larked, sky•lark•ing.

sky•light

sky•line or sky line

sky•rock•et *v.*, sky•rock•et○ed, sky•rock•et•ing.

sky•scrap○er

sky•ward

sky•writ○er

sky•writ•ing

slab

slack *v.*, slacked, slack•ing; *adj.*, slack○er, slack•est.

slack○en *v.*, slack•ened, slack•en•ing.

slack○er

slack•ness

slacks

slag

slain

slake *v.*, slaked, slak•ing.

sla•lom

slam *v.*, slammed, slam•ming.

slam-bang

slam dance

slam•mer

slan•der *v.*, slan•dered, slan•der•ing.

slan•der○er

slan•der•ous

slang

slang○y *adj.*, slang•i○er, slang•i•est.

slant *v.*, slant○ed, slant•ing.

slant•wise

slap *v.*, slapped, slap•ping.

slap•dash

slap•hap○py

slap•stick

slash *v.*, slashed, slash•ing.

slash-and-burn

slash○er

slat

slate *v.*, slat○ed, slat•ing.

slate PC *Computers.*

slath○er *v.*, slath•ered, slath•er•ing.

slat•ted

slat•tern○ly

slaugh•ter *v.*, slaugh•tered, slaugh•ter•ing.

slaugh•ter•house *n.*, *pl.* slaugh•ter•hous○es.

Slav

slave *v.*, slaved, slav•ing.

slav○er *v.*, slav•ered, slav•er•ing.

slav•er○y

Slav○ic

slav•ish

slav•ish○ly

slaw

slay *v.*, slew, slain, slay•ing. (to kill: cf. SLEIGH)

slay○er

sleaze

slea•zi•ness

slea○zy *adj.*, slea•zi○er, slea•zi•est.

sled

sledge *v.*, sledged, sledg•ing.

sledge•ham•mer

sleek *adj.*, sleek○er, sleek•est.

sleek•ness

sleep *v.*, slept, sleep•ing.

sleep○er

sleep•i○ly

sleep•i•ness

sleep•less

sleep•less•ness

sleep•walk *v.*, sleep•walked, sleep•walk•ing.

sleep•walk○er

sleep•wear

sleep○y *adj.*, sleep•i○er, sleep•i•est.

sleet

sleet○y *adj.*, sleet•i○er, sleet•i•est.

sleeve

sleeve•less

sleigh (sled: cf. SLAY)

sleight of hand

slen•der *adj.*, slen•der○er, slen•der•est.

slen•der•ize *v.*, slen•der•ized, slen•der•iz•ing.

slen•der•ness

slept

sleuth

slew (large quantity; killed: cf. SLUE)

slice v., sliced, slic•ing.

slic∘er

slick adj., slick∘er, slick•est.

slick∘ly

slick•ness

slide v., slid, slid•ing.

slid∘er

slight adj., slight∘er, slight•est.

slight∘ly

slight•ness

slim v., slimmed, slim•ming; adj., slim•mer, slim•mest.

slim dis•ease

slime

slim∘i•ness

slim•ness

slim∘y adj., slim•i∘er, slim•i•est.

sling v., slung, sling•ing.

sling•shot

slink v., slunk, slink•ing.

slink∘y adj., slink•i∘er, slink•i•est.

slip v., slipped, slip•ping.

slip-up

slip•case

slip•cov∘er

slip•knot or slip knot

slip•page

slip•per

slip•per∘y

slip•shod

slit v., slit, slit•ting.

slith∘er v., slith•ered, slith•er•ing.

sliv∘er

slob

slob•ber v., slob•bered, slob•ber•ing.

sloe (a fruit: cf. SLOW)

sloe-eyed

slog v., slogged, slog•ging.

slo•gan

sloop

slop v., slopped, slop•ping.

slope v., sloped, slop•ing.

slop•pi•ness

slop∘py adj., slop•pi∘er, slop•pi•est.

slosh v., sloshed, slosh•ing.

slot

sloth

sloth•ful

slot∘ted

slouch v., slouched, slouch•ing.

slough v., sloughed, slough•ing.

Slo•vak

slov∘en∘ly

slow v., slowed, slow•ing; adj., slow∘er, slow•est. (not fast; to slow: cf. SLOE)

slow mo•tion n.

slow-mo•tion adj.

slow-wit∘ted

slow-wit∘ted∘ly

slow•down

slow∘ly

slow•ness

slow•poke

sludge

slue v., slued, slu•ing. (to turn: cf. SLEW)

slug v., slugged, slug•ging.

slug•gard

slug•ger

slug•gish

slug•gish•ness

sluice v., sluiced, sluic•ing.

slum v., slummed, slum•ming.

slum•ber v., slum•bered, slum•ber•ing.

slum•lord

slump v., slumped, slump•ing.

slung

slunk

slur v., slurred, slur•ring.

slurp v., slurped, slurp•ing.

slush v., slushed, slush•ing.

slush∘y adj., slush•i∘er, slush•i•est.

slut

sly adj., sly∘er or sli∘er, sly•est or sli•est.

sly∘ly

sly•ness

smack v., smacked, smack•ing.

smack∘ers

small adj., small∘er, small•est.

small busi•ness Business.

small-foot∘print com•put∘er Computers.

small-mind∘ed

small-scale

small-time

small•ish

small•ness

small•pox

smart adj., smart∘er, smart•est.

smart al•eck or
smart al•ec *n.*

smart-al•eck *adj.*

smart-al•eck•y

smart ter•mi•nal
Computers.

smart∘en *v.*, smart•
ened, smart•en•ing.

smart∘ly

smart•ness

smash *v.*, smashed,
smash•ing.

smash-up

smash•ing

smat•ter•ing

smear *v.*, smeared,
smear•ing.

smell *v.*, smelled or
smelt, smell•ing.

smell∘y *adj.*, smell•
i∘er, smell•i•est.

smelt *n.*, *pl.* smelt or
smelts; *v.*, smelt∘ed,
smelt•ing.

smelt∘er

smid•gen or smid•gin

smile *v.*, smiled, smil•
ing.

smil•ing∘ly

smirk *v.*, smirked,
smirk•ing.

smite *v.*, smote, smit•
ten, smit•ing.

smith

smith•er•eens

smith∘y *n.*, *pl.* smith•
ies.

smock

smog

smog∘gy *adj.*, smog•
gi∘er, smog•gi•est.

smoke *v.*, smoked,
smok•ing.

smoke and mir•rors

smoke•less

smok∘er

smoke•stack

smok∘i•ness

smok∘y *adj.*, smok•
i∘er, smok•i•est.

smol•der or smoul•
der *v.*, smol•dered,
smol•der•ing.

smooch *v.*, smooched,
smooch•ing.

smooth *adj.*,
smooth∘er, smooth•
est; *v.*, smoothed,
smooth•ing.

smooth∘ly

smooth•ness

smor•gas•bord or
smör•gas•bord

smote

smoth∘er *v.*, smoth•
ered, smoth•er•ing.

smudge *v.*, smudged,
smudg•ing.

smudg∘y *adj.*, smudg•
i∘er, smudg•i•est.

smug *adj.*, smug∘ger,
smug•gest.

smug•gle *v.*, smug•
gled, smug•gling.

smug•gler

smug∘ly

smug•ness

smut

smut•ti•ness

smut∘ty *adj.*, smut•
ti∘er, smut•ti•est.

snack *v.*, snacked,
snack•ing.

snag *v.*, snagged,
snag•ging.

snail

snake *v.*, snaked,
snak•ing.

snake•like

snak∘y *adj.*, snak•
i∘er, snak•i•est.

snap *v.*, snapped,
snap•ping.

snap•drag∘on

snap•per

snap•pish

snap∘py *adj.*, snap•
pi∘er, snap•pi•est.

snap•shot

snare *v.*, snared, snar•
ing.

snarl *v.*, snarled,
snarl•ing.

snarl•ing∘ly

snatch *v.*, snatched,
snatch•ing.

sneak *v.*, sneaked or
snuck, sneak•ing.

sneak∘er

sneak∘y *adj.*, sneak•
i∘er, sneak•i•est.

sneer *v.*, sneered,
sneer•ing.

sneeze *v.*, sneezed,
sneez•ing.

sneeze•guard

snick∘er *v.*, snick•
ered, snick•er•ing.

snide

sniff *v.*, sniffed, sniff•
ing.

sniff∘er *ad Business.*

snif•fle *v.*, snif•fled,
snif•fling.

snif•ter

snig•ger *v.*, snig•
gered, snig•ger•ing.

snig•let

snip *v.*, snipped, snip•
ping.

snipe *n.*, *pl.* snipes or
snipe; *v.*, sniped,
snip•ing.

snip∘er

snip•pet

snip∘py *adj.*, snip•
pi∘er, snip•pi•est.

snit

snitch *v.*, snitched,
snitch•ing.

sniv•el *v.*, sniv•eled

or sniv•elled, sniv•
el•ing or sniv•el•
ling.

snob

snob•ber•y

snob•bish

snob•bish•ness

snood

snoop v., snooped,
snoop•ing.

snoop•y adj., snoop•
i•er, snoop•i•est.

snoot•i•ness

snoot•y adj., snoot•
i•er, snoot•i•est.

snooze v., snoozed,
snooz•ing.

snore v., snored,
snor•ing.

snor•kel v., snor•
keled, snor•kel•ing.

snor•kel•er

snort v., snort•ed,
snort•ing.

snot

snot•ty adj., snot•
ti•er, snot•ti•est.

snout

snow v., snowed,
snow•ing.

snow•ball v., snow•
balled, snow•ball•
ing.

Snow•belt or Snow
Belt

snow•bound

snow•drift

snow•drop

snow•fall

snow•flake

snow•man n., pl.
snow•men.

snow•mo•bile v.,
snow•mo•biled,
snow•mo•bil•ing.

snow•plow v., snow•

plowed, snow•
plow•ing.

snow•shoe

snow•storm

snow•suit

snow•y adj., snow•
i•er, snow•i•est.

snub v., snubbed,
snub•bing.

snub-nosed

snuck

snuff v., snuffed,
snuff•ing.

snuff•box

snuf•fle v., snuf•fled,
snuf•fling.

snug adj., snug•ger,
snug•gest.

snug•gle v., snug•
gled, snug•gling.

snug•ly

so (thus; cf. SEW; SOW)

so-and-so n., pl. so-
and-sos.

so-called

so long

so-so or so so

soak v., soaked, soak•
ing.

soap v., soaped,
soap•ing.

soap op•er•a

soap•box or soap box

soap•i•ness

soap•stone

soap•suds

soap•y adj., soap•
i•er, soap•i•est.

soar v., soared, soar•
ing. (to fly upward: cf.
SORE)

soared (did soar: cf.
SWARD; SWORD)

sob v., sobbed, sob•
bing.

sob•bing•ly

so•ber v., so•bered,

so•ber•ing; adj., so•
ber•er, so•ber•est.

so•ber•ly

so•bri•e•ty

so•bri•quet

soc•cer

so•cia•bil•i•ty

so•cia•ble

so•cia•bly

so•cial

social se•cu•ri•ty
Business.

so•cial•ism

so•cial•ist

so•cial•is•tic

so•cial•ite

so•cial•i•za•tion

so•cial•ize v., so•
cial•ized, so•cial•iz•
ing.

so•cial•ly

so•ci•e•tal

so•ci•e•ty n., pl. so•
ci•e•ties.

so•ci•o•ec•o•nom•ic

so•ci•o•log•i•cal

so•ci•ol•o•gist

so•ci•ol•o•gy

so•ci•o•path

sock n., pl. socks; v.,
socked, sock•ing.

sock•et

Soc•ra•tes

So•crat•ic

sod

so•da n., pl. so•das.

sod•den

so•di•um

sodium pen•to•thal

sod•om•y

so•fa n., pl. so•fas.

sofa bed or so•fa•
bed

So•fi•a

soft adj., soft•er,
soft•est.

soft-boiled

soft cop○y *Computers.*

soft-core

soft-cov•er

soft cur•ren○cy *Business.*

soft fonts *Computers.*

soft goods *Business.*

soft-heart○ed

soft ped○al *n.*

soft-ped•al *v.,* soft-ped○aled or soft-ped○alled, soft-ped○al○ing, soft-ped○al•ling.

soft re•turn *Computers.*

soft-sec○tored *Computers.*

soft soap *n.*

soft-soap *v.,* soft-soaped, soft-soap○ing.

soft•ball

soft○en *v.,* soft•ened, soft•en•ing.

soft•en○er

soft○ly

soft•ness

soft•ware *Computers.*

software in•ter•rupt *Computers.*

software pi•ra○cy *Computers.*

software plat•form *Computers.*

soft•wood

soft○y or soft○ie, *n. pl.* soft•ties.

sog•gi•ness

sog○gy *adj.,* sog•gi○er, sog•gi•est.

soi•gné or soi•gnée

soil *v.,* soiled, soil•ing.

soi•ree or soi•ree

so•journ *v.,* so•

journed, so•journ•ing.

sol•ace *v.,* sol•aced, sol•ac•ing.

so•lar

so•lar○i•um *n., pl.* so•lar○i•ums or so•lar○i○a.

sold

sol•der *v.,* sol•dered, sol•der•ing. (fusible alloy)

sol•der○er

sol•dier *v.,* sol•diered, sol•dier•ing. (military person; to be a soldier)

sol•dier○ly

sole *n., pl.* sole or so•les. *Business.* (only; the fish: cf. SOUL)

sole pro•pri•e•tor•ship

sol○e○cism

sole○ly

sol•emn

so•lem•ni•ty

sol•em•nize *v.,* sol•em•nized, sol•em•niz•ing.

sol•emn○ly

so•le○noid

so•lic○it *v.,* so•lic•it○ed, so•lic•it•ing.

so•lic○i•ta•tion

so•lic○i•tor

so•lic○i•tous

so•lic○i•tude

sol○id

sol○id-state

sol○i•dar•i○ty *n., pl.* sol○i•dar•i•ties.

so•lid○i•fi•ca•tion

so•lid○i○fy *v.,* so•lid○i•fied, so•lid○i•fy•ing.

so•lid○i•ty

sol•id○ly

so•lil○o•quize *v.,* so•lil○o•quized, so•lil○o•quiz•ing.

so•lil○o•quy *n., pl.* so•lil○o•quies.

sol•ip•sism

sol○i•taire

sol○i•tar○y *n., pl.* sol○i•tar•ies.

sol○i•tude

so•lo *n., pl.* so•los or so•li; *v.,* so•loed, so•lo•ing.

so•lo•ist

Sol○o•mon

sol•stice

sol•u•bil•i•ty

sol•u○ble

sol•ute

so•lu•tion

solve *v.,* solved, solv•ing.

sol•ven○cy

sol•vent

solv○er

So•ma•li○a

So•ma•li○an

so•mat○ic

som•ber

som•ber○ly

som•bre○ro *n., pl.* som•bre○ros.

some (certain: cf. SUM)

some•bod○y *n., pl.* some•bod•ies.

some•day

some•how

some•one

some•place

som•er•sault *v.,* som•er•sault○ed, som•er•sault•ing.

some•thing

some•time

some•times

some•what
some•where
som•nam•bu•lism
som•nam•bu•list
som•no•lence
som•no•lent
son (male child: cf. SUN)
son-in-law n., pl. sons-in-law.
so•nar
so•na◦ta n., pl. so•na•tas.
song
song•bird
song•fest
song•ster
son◦ic
son•net
son◦ny
so•nor•i◦ty
so•no•rous
soon adj., soon◦er, soon•est.
soot
sooth (truth)
soothe v., soothed, sooth•ing. (to calm)
sooth•ing
sooth•ing◦ly
sooth•say◦er
sooth•say•ing
soot◦y adj., soot•i◦er, soot•i•est.
sop v., sopped, sop•ping.
SOP (standard operating procedure)
soph•ism
soph•ist
so•phis•ti•cate
so•phis•ti•cat◦ed
so•phis•ti•ca•tion
soph•ist◦ry n., pl. soph•ist•ries.
Soph◦o•cle◦an

Soph◦o•cles
soph◦o•more
soph◦o•mor◦ic
sop◦o•rif◦ic
sop•ping
sop◦py adj., sop•pi◦er, sop•pi•est.
so•pran◦o n., pl. so•pran◦os.
sor•bet
sor•cer◦er
sor•cer•ess
sor•cer◦y
sor•did
sor•did•ness
sore adj., sor◦er, sor•est. (painful: cf. SOAR)
sore•head
sore◦ly
sore•ness
sor•ghum
so•ror•i◦ty n., pl. so•ror•i•ties.
sor•rel
sor•ri◦ly
sor•row sor•rowed, sor•row•ing.
sor•row•ful
sor•row•ful◦ly
sor◦ry adj., sor•ri◦er, sor•ri•est.
sort v., sort◦ed, sort•ing.
sort◦er
sor•tie v., sor•tied, sor•tie•ing.
SOS n., pl. SOSs or SOS's. (signal for help)
sot◦to vo◦ce
sou•brette
souf•flé
sought
sou•kous
soul (spirit: cf. SOLE)
soul•ful

soul•ful◦ly
soul•ful•ness
soul•less
sound v., sound◦ed, sound•ing; adj., sound◦er, sound•est.
sound•less
sound◦ly
sound•ness
sound•proof v., sound•proofed, sound•proof•ing.
sound•track or sound track
soup v., souped, soup•ing.
soup•çon
soup◦y adj., soup•i◦er, soup•i•est.
sour v., soured, sour•ing;. adj., sour◦er, sour•est.
source v., sourced, sourc◦ing.
source code Computers.
source di•rec•to◦ry Computers.
sour•dough
sour◦ly
sour•ness
sour•puss
souse
soused
south
South Car◦o•li◦na (SC)
South Da•ko◦ta (SD)
south•east
South•east A◦sia
south•east•ern
south•east•ward
south•ern
south•ern◦er
south•paw
south•ward

south•west
south•west•er•ly
south•west•ern
sou•ve•nir
sov•er•eign
sov•er•eign•ty *n., pl.*
  sov•er•eign•ties.
So•vi•et
sow *v.,* sowed, sown
  or sowed, sow•ing.
  (to plant: cf. SEW; SO)
So•we•to
sox
soy
soy•bean
spa *n., pl.* spas.
space *v.,* spaced,
  spac•ing.
space buy•er *Business.*
space shut•tle
space sta•tion
space•craft *n., pl.*
  space•crafts or
  space•craft.
spaced-out
space•flight
space•man *n., pl.*
  space•men.
space•port
space•ship
space•suit
space•walk
spac•ey or spac•y
  adj., spac•i•er, spac•
  i•est.
spa•cious
spa•cious•ly
spa•cious•ness
spack•le *v.,* spack•
  led, spack•ling.
spade *v.,* spad•ed,
  spad•ing.
spade•ful *n., pl.*
  spade•fuls.
spade•work
spa•ghet•ti

Spain
spake
span *v.,* spanned,
  span•ning.
span•dex
span•gle
span•gled
Span•iard
span•iel
Span•ish
Span•ish A•mer•i•
  can *n.*
Span•ish-A•mer•i•
  can *adj.*
spank *v.,* spanked,
  spank•ing.
span•ner
spar *v.,* sparred, spar•
  ring.
spare *v.,* spared, spar•
  ing.
spare•ribs
spar•ing
spar•ing•ly
spark *v.,* sparked,
  spark•ing.
spar•kle *v.,* spar•kled,
  spar•kling.
spar•kler
spar•row
sparse
sparse•ly
sparse•ness or spar•
  si•ty
Spar•ta
Spar•tan
spasm
spas•mod•ic
spas•mod•i•cal•ly
spas•tic
spat
spate
spa•tial
spat•ter *v.,* spat•
  tered, spat•ter•ing.

spat•u•la *n., pl.*
  spat•u•las.
spav•ined
spawn *v.,* spawned,
  spawn•ing.
spay *v.,* spayed, spay•
  ing.
speak *v.,* spoke, spo•
  ken, speak•ing.
speak•eas•y *n., pl.*
  speak•eas•ies.
speak•er
speak•er-
  de•pend•ent *Com•
  puters.*
spear *v.,* speared,
  spear•ing. (the
  weapon; to spear: cf.
  SPHERE)
spear•head *v.,* spear•
  head•ed, spear•
  head•ing.
spear•mint
spec *v.,* spec'd or
  specked or specced,
  spec'•ing or speck•
  ing or spec•cing.
spe•cial
special char•ac•ter
  Computers.
special draw•ing
  rights (SDR) *Business.*
special jour•nal *Busi•
  ness.*
spe•cial•ist
spe•cial•i•za•tion
spe•cial•ize *v.,* spe•
  cial•ized, spe•cial•
  iz•ing.
spe•cial•ly
spe•cial•ty *n., pl.*
  spe•cial•ties.
spe•cie (coined money:
  cf. SPECIES)
spe•cies *n., pl.* spe•
  cies.
spe•cif•ic

spe•cif•ic lien *Business.*

spe•cif•i•cal•ly

spec•i•fi•ca•tion

spec•i•fic•i•ty

spec•i•fy *v.,* spec•i•fied, spec•i•fy•ing.

spec•i•men

spe•cious

spe•cious•ly

speck *v.,* specked, speck•ing.

speck•le *v.,* speck•led, speck•ling.

specs

spec•ta•cle

spec•tac•u•lar

spec•tac•u•lar•ly

spec•ta•tor

spec•ter

spec•tral

spec•tro•scope

spec•tro•scop•ic

spec•tros•co•py

spec•trum *n., pl.* spec•tra *or* spec•trums.

spec•u•late *v.,* spec•u•lat•ed, spec•u•lat•ing.

spec•u•la•tion

spec•u•la•tive

spec•u•la•tor

speech

speech•less

speed *v.,* sped *or* speed•ed, speed•ing.

speed•boat

speed•er

speed•i•ly

speed•om•e•ter

speed•ster

speed•up

speed•way

speed•y *adj.,* speed•i•er, speed•i•est.

spe•le•ol•o•gist

spe•le•ol•o•gy

spell *v.,* spelled, spell•ing.

spell check•er *Computers.*

spell•bind•er

spell•bind•ing

spell•bound

spell•er

spell•ing

spe•lunk•er

spend *v.,* spent, spend•ing.

spend•a•ble

spend•er

spend•thrift

spent

sperm *n., pl.* sperm *or* sperms.

sper•mat•o•zo•on *n., pl.* sper•mat•o•zo•a.

sper•mi•cide

spew *v.,* spewed, spew•ing.

sphere (ball: cf. SPEAR)

spher•i•cal

sphe•roid

sphinc•ter

sphinx *n., pl.* sphinx•es *or* sphin•ges.

spice *v.,* spiced, spic•ing.

spic•i•ness

spick-and-span

spic•y *adj.,* spic•i•er, spic•i•est.

spi•der

spiel

spiff•y *adj.,* spiff•i•er, spiff•i•est.

spig•ot

spike *v.,* spiked, spik•ing.

spik•y *adj.,* spik•i•er, spik•i•est.

spill *v.,* spilled *or* spilt, spill•ing.

spill•age

spill•way

spin *v.,* spun, spin•ning.

spin con•trol

spin doc•tor

spi•na bif•i•da

spin•ach

spi•nal

spin•dle

spin•dly *adj.,* spin•dli•er, spin•dli•est.

spine

spine•less

spin•et

spin•na•ker

spin•ner

spin-off *or* spin•off

spin•ster

spin•ster•hood

spin•y *adj.,* spin•i•er, spin•i•est.

spi•ra•cle

spi•ral *v.,* spi•raled *or* spi•ralled, spi•ral•ing *or* spi•ral•ling.

spire

spir•it *v.,* spir•it•ed, spir•it•ing.

spir•it•less

spir•it•u•al

spir•it•u•al•ism

spir•it•u•al•ist

spir•it•u•al•is•tic

spir•it•u•al•i•ty

spir•it•u•al•ly

spir•it•u•ous

spi•ro•chete

spit[1] *v.,* spit *or* spat,

spit•ting. (eject saliva)

spit² v., **spit•ted, spit•ting.** (impale on a spit)

spit•ball

spite

spite•ful

spit•fire

spit•tle

spit•toon

splash v., **splashed, splash•ing.**

splash•down

splash•y adj., **splash•i•er, splash•i•est.**

splat

splat•ter v., **splat•tered, splat•ter•ing.**

splay v., **splayed, splay•ing.**

splay•foot•ed

spleen

splen•did

splen•did•ly

splen•dor

sple•net•ic

splice v., **spliced, splic•ing.**

splint v., **splint•ed, splint•ing.**

splint•er¹ (one who splints)

splin•ter² v., **splin•tered, splin•ter•ing** (sharp piece of wood; to break into pieces)

splin•ter•y

split v., **split, split•ting.**

split-lev•el

splotch v., **splotched, splotch•ing.**

splotch•y adj., **splotch•i•er, splotch•i•est.**

splurge v., **splurged, splurg•ing.**

splut•ter v., **splut•tered, splut•ter•ing.**

spoil v., **spoiled** or **spoilt, spoil•ing.**

spoil•age

spoil•er

spoil•sport

Spo•kane

spoke

spo•ken

spokes•man n., pl. **spokes•men.**

spokes•wom•an n., pl. **spokes•wom•en.**

spo•li•a•tion

sponge v., **sponged, spong•ing.**

spong•er

spong•y adj., **spong•i•er, spong•i•est.**

spon•sor v., **spon•sored, spon•sor•ing.**

spon•sor•ship

spon•ta•ne•i•ty

spon•ta•ne•ous

spon•ta•ne•ous•ly

spoof v., **spoofed, spoof•ing.**

spook v., **spooked, spook•ing.**

spook•y adj., **spook•i•er, spook•i•est.**

spool v., **spooled, spool•ing.**

spool•er Computers.

spool•ing Computers.

spoon v., **spooned, spoon•ing.**

spoon-feed v., **spoon-fed, spoon-feed•ing.**

spoon•bill

spoon•er•ism

spoon•ful n., pl. **spoon•fuls.**

spoor (animal trail)

spo•rad•ic

spo•rad•i•cal•ly

spore (seed)

sport

sport•ing

spor•tive

sports•cast

sports•cast•er

sports•cast•ing

sports•man n., pl. **sports•men.**

sports•man•like

sports•man•ship

sport•y adj., **sport•i•er, sport•i•est.**

spot v., **spot•ted, spot•ting.**

spot check n.

spot-check v., **spot-checked, spot-check•ing.**

spot mar•ket

spot trad•ing Business.

spot•less

spot•light v., **spot•light•ed** or **spot•lit, spot•light•ing.**

spot•ted

spot•ter

spot•ti•ness

spot•ty adj., **spot•ti•er, spot•ti•est.**

spous•al

spouse

spout v., **spout•ed, spout•ing.**

sprain v., **sprained, sprain•ing.**

sprang

sprat n., pl. **sprats** or **sprat.**

sprawl v., **sprawled, sprawl•ing.**

spray v., **sprayed, spray•ing.**

spread *v.*, spread, spread•ing.

spread-ea•gle *v.*, spread-ea•gled, spread-ea•gling.

spread•sheet *Computers.*

spree

sprig

spright•li•ness

spright•ly *adj.*, spright•li•er, spright•li•est.

spring *v.*, sprang or sprung, sprung, spring•ing.

spring•board

Spring•field

spring•time

spring•y *adj.*, spring•i•er, spring•i•est.

sprin•kle *v.*, sprin•kled, sprin•kling.

sprin•kler

sprin•kling

sprint *v.*, sprint•ed, sprint•ing.

sprint•er

sprite

spritz *v.*, spritzed, spritz•ing.

sprock•et

sprout *v.*, sprout•ed, sprout•ing.

spruce *v.*, spruced, spruc•ing.

sprung

spry *adj.*, spry•er or spri•er, spry•est or spri•est.

spud

spume

spu•mo•ni or spu•mo•ne

spun

spunk

spunk•y *adj.*, spunk•i•er, spunk•i•est.

spur *v.*, spurred, spur•ring.

spurge

spu•ri•ous

spu•ri•ous•ly

spu•ri•ous•ness

spurn *v.*, spurned, spurn•ing.

spurt *v.*, spurt•ed, spurt•ing.

sput•nik

sput•ter *v.*, sput•tered, sput•ter•ing.

spu•tum *n.*, *pl.* spu•ta.

spy *n.*, *pl.* spies; *v.*, spied, spy•ing.

spy•glass

squab *n.*, *pl.* squabs or squab.

squab•ble *v.*, squab•bled, squab•bling.

squad

squad•ron

squal•id

squall *v.*, squalled, squall•ing.

squal•or

squa•mous or squa•mose

squan•der *v.*, squan•dered, squan•der•ing.

square *v.*, squared, squar•ing; *adj.*, squar•er, squar•est.

square dance *n.*

square-dance *v.*, square-danced, square-danc•ing.

square-rigged

square•ly

square•ness

squash *n.*, *pl.* squash•es or squash;

v., squashed, squash•ing. (to crush; the vegetable: cf. QUASH)

squash•y *adj.*, squash•i•er, squash•i•est.

squat *v.*, squat•ted, squat•ting.

squat•ter

squaw

squawk *v.*, squawked, squawk•ing.

squeak *v.*, squeaked, squeak•ing.

squeak•y *adj.*, squeak•i•er, squeak•i•est.

squeal *v.*, squealed, squeal•ing.

squeal•er

squeam•ish

squeam•ish•ness

squee•gee *v.*, squee•geed, squee•gee•ing.

squeez•a•ble

squeeze *v.*, squeezed, squeez•ing.

squelch *v.*, squelched, squelch•ing.

squib

squid *n.*, *pl.* squid or squids.

squig•gle

squint *v.*, squint•ed, squint•ing.

squire *v.*, squired, squir•ing.

squirm *v.*, squirmed, squirm•ing.

squir•rel *n.*, *pl.* squir•rels or squir•rel; *v.*, squir•reled or squir•relled, squir•rel•ing or squir•rel•ling.

squirt *v.*, squirt∘ed,
squirt•ing.

squish *v.*, squished,
squish•ing.

SRAM *Computers.*
(static random access
memory)

Sri Lan∘ka

Sri Lan•kan

SSI *Business.* (Supple-
mental Security In-
come)

SST (supersonic trans-
port)

St. (street)

St. Pe•ters•burg

**St. Vin•cent and the
Gren∘a•dines**

stab *v.*, stabbed,
stab•bing.

sta•bil•i∘ty

sta•bi•li•za•tion

sta•bi•lize *v.*, sta•bi•
lized, sta•bi•liz•ing.

sta•bi•liz∘er

sta•ble *v.*, sta•bled,
sta•bling;. *adj.*, sta•
bler, sta•blest.

stac•ca∘to *n.*, *pl.*
stac•ca•tos or stac•
ca∘ti.

stack *v.*, stacked,
stack•ing.

sta•di∘um *n.*, *pl.* sta•
di•ums or sta•di∘a.

staff[1] *n.*, *pl.* staffs or
staves. (stick)

staff[2] *n.*, *pl.* staffs; *v.*,
staffed, staff•ing.
(group of employees;
to employ: cf. STAPH)

staff∘er

staff•ing *Business.*

stag

stage *v.*, staged, stag•
ing.

stage•coach

stage•craft

stage•hand

stage•struck or stage-
struck

stag•fla•tion *Business.*

stag•ger *v.*, stag•
gered, stag•ger•ing.

stag•nant

stag•nate *v.*, stag•
nat∘ed, stag•nat•
ing.

stag•na•tion

staid (sedate: cf.
STAYED)

staid∘ly

stain *v.*, stained,
stain•ing.

stain•less

stair (step: cf. STARE)

stair•case

stair•way

stair•well or stair well

stake *v.*, staked, stak•
ing. (post; to wager:
cf. STEAK)

stake•out

sta•lac•tite (deposit
hanging from cave
ceiling)

sta•lag•mite (deposit
on cave floor)

stale *adj.*, stal∘er,
stal∘est.

stale•mate *v.*, stale•
mat∘ed, stale•mat•
ing.

stale•ness

Sta•lin

stalk *v.*, stalked,
stalk•ing. (plant
stem; to pursue: cf.
STORK)

stall *v.*, stalled, stall•
ing.

stal•lion

stal•wart

sta•men *n.*, *pl.* sta•
mens or stam∘i∘na.

stam∘i∘na

stam•mer *v.*, stam•
mered, stam•mer•
ing.

stam•mer∘er

stam•mer•ing∘ly

stamp *v.*, stamped,
stamp•ing.

stam•pede *v.*, stam•
pede, •ped∘ed, •
ped∘ing.

stance

stanch or staunch *v.*,
stanched or
staunched, stanch•
ing or staunch•ing.
(to stop a flow: cf.
STAUNCH)

stan•chion

stand *v.*, stood,
stand•ing.

stand•ard

stand∘ard-bear∘er

stand•ard cost sys•
tem *Business.*

stand•ard of liv•ing
Business.

stand•ard∘i•za•tion

stand•ard•ize *v.*,
stand•ard•ized,
stand•ard•iz•ing.

stand∘by *n.*, *pl.*
stand•bys.

standby costs *Business.*

stand∘ee

stand-in

stand•ing

stand•off or stand-off

stand•off•ish or
stand-off∘ish

stand•out or stand-
out

stand•pipe

stand•point

stand•still

stand-up or stand∘up

stank

stan∘za n., pl. stan•
zas.

staph (staphylococcus:
cf. STAFF)

staph∘y∘lo∘coc•cus
n., pl. staph∘y∘lo•
coc∘ci.

sta•ple v., sta•pled,
sta•pling.

sta•pler

star v., starred, star•
ring.

star to•pol∘o∘gy
Computers.

star•board

starch v., starched,
starch•ing.

starch∘y adj., starch•
i∘er, starch•i•est.

star•dom

stare v., stared, star•
ing. (to gaze: cf. STAIR)

star•fish n., pl. star•
fish or star•fish∘es.

star•gaz∘er

star•gaz∘ing

stark adj., stark∘er,
stark∘est.

stark•ness

star•less

star•let

star•light

star•ling

star•lit

star∘ry adj., star•
ri∘er, star•ri•est.

star∘ry-eyed

start v., start∘ed,
start•ing.

start bit Computers.

start-up time Business.

start∘er

star•tle v., star•tled,
star•tling.

start-up

star•va•tion

starve v., starved,
starv•ing.

starve•ling

stash v., stashed,
stash•ing.

state v., stat∘ed, stat•
ing.

state bank Business.

state of the art n.

state-of-the-art adj.

state•craft

state•hood

state•house n., pl.
state•hous∘es.

state•less

state•less•ness

state•li•ness

state∘ly adj., state•
li∘er, state•li•est.

state•ment

Stat∘en Is•land

state•room

state•side

states•man n., pl.
states•men.

states•man•like

states•man•ship

stat∘ic

static RAM (SRAM)
Computers.

static var•i•a∘ble
Computers.

sta•tion v., sta•
tioned, sta•tion•ing.

sta•tion•ar∘y (fixed in
place)

sta•tion•er∘y (writing
materials)

sta•tis•tic

sta•tis•ti•cal

stat∘is•sti•cian

sta•tis•tics

stat∘u•ar∘y

stat∘ue (sculpture: cf.
STATURE; STATUTE)

stat∘u•esque

stat∘u•ette

stat•ure (height: cf.
STATUE; STATUTE)

sta•tus

status quo

stat•ute (law: cf.
STATUTE; STATURE)

stat∘tuspbrk;to∘ry

statutory tax rate
Business.

staunch or stanch adj.,
staunch∘er,
staunch•est. (stead-
fast: cf. STANCH)

staunch∘ly

stave v., staved or
stove, stav•ing.

stay

stayed (remained: cf.
STAID)

stead

stead•fast

stead•fast∘ly

stead•i∘ly

stead∘y n., pl. stead•
ies; v., stead•ied,
stead∘y•ing; adj.,
stead•i∘er, stead•i•
est.

steak (cut of meat: cf.
STAKE)

steal v., stole, sto•len.
(to rob: cf. STEEL)

stealth

stealth•i∘ly

stealth∘y adj.,
stealth•i∘er,
stealth•i•est.

steam v., steamed,
steam•ing.

steam•boat

steam∘er

steam•fit•ter or
steam fit•ter

steam•roll•er v.,

steam•roll•ered, steam•roll•er•ing.

steam•ship

steam○y *adj.*, steam•i○er, steam•i•est.

steed

steel (refined iron: cf. STEAL)

steel○y *adj.*, steel•i○er, steel•i•est.

steep *v.*, steeped, steep•ing; *adj.*, steep○er, steep•est.

stee•ple

stee○ple•chase

stee○ple•jack

steep○ly

steep•ness

steer[1] *n.*, *pl.* steers or steer. *(the animal)*

steer[2] *v.*, steered, steer•ing. (to guide)

steer•age

steg○o○•saur

stein

stel•lar

stem *v.*, stemmed, stem•ming.

stem•ware

stench

sten•cil *v.*, sten•ciled or sten•cilled, sten•cil•ing or sten•cil•ling.

sten○o○ *n.*, *pl.* sten○os.

ste•nog•ra•pher

sten○o•graph○ic

ste•nog•ra•phy

sten○to•ri○an

step *v.*, stepped, step•ping. (a gait; to step: cf. STEPPE)

step-down

step-up

step•broth○er

step•child *n.*, *pl.* step•child•ren.

step•daugh•ter

step•fa•ther

step•lad•der

step•moth○er

step•par•ent

steppe (a plain: cf. STEP)

stepped cost *Business.*

step•ping•stone or step•ping stone

step•sis•ter

step•son

ster○e○o○ *n.*, *pl.* ster○e○os.

ster○e○o○•phon○ic

ster○e○o○•scope

ster○e○o○•type *v.*, ster○e○o○•typed, ster○e○o○•typ•ing.

ster○e○o○•typ○ic

ster•ile

ste•ril•i○ty

ster○i•li•za•tion

ster○i•lize *v.*, ster○i•lized, ster○i•liz•ing.

ster○i•liz○er

ster•ling

stern *adj.*, stern○er, stern•est.

stern○ly

stern•ness

ster•num *n.*, *pl.* ster○na or ster•nums.

ste•roid

ster•to•rous

stet *v.*, stet•ted, stet•ting.

steth○o•scope

ste•ve•dore

stew *v.*, stewed, stew•ing.

stew•ard

stew•ard•ess

stew•ard•ship

stick *v.*, stuck, stick•ing.

stick-in-the-mud

stick○er

sticker price *Business.*

sticker shock *Business.*

stick○i•ness

stick○le•back

stick•ler

stick•pin

stick○up

stick○y *adj.*, stick•i○er, stick•i•est.

stiff *v.*, stiffed, stiff•ing; *adj.*, stiff○er, stiff•est.

stiff-arm *v.*, stiff-armed, stiff-arm○ing.

stiff-necked

stiff○en *v.*, stiff•ened, stiff•en•ing.

stiff•en○er

stiff○ly

stiff•ness

sti•fle *v.*, sti•fled, sti•fling.

stig○ma *n.*, *pl.* stig•ma○ta or stig•mas.

stig•ma•tize *v.*, stig•ma•tized, stig•ma•tiz•ing.

stile (set of steps: cf. STYLE)

sti•let○to *n.*, *pl.* sti•let•tos or sti•let•toes.

still *v.*, stilled, still•ing; *adj.*, still○er, still•est.

still life *n.*, still lifes.

still-life *adj.*

still•birth

still•born

still•ness

stilt

stilt○ed

Stil•ton

stim•u•lant

stim•u•late v., stim•u•lat•ed, stim•u•lat•ing.

stim•u•la•tion

stim•u•lus n., pl. stim•u•li.

sting v., stung, sting• ing.

sting∘er

stin•gi∘ly

stin•gi•ness

sting•ray

stin•gy adj., stin• gi∘er, stin•gi•est.

stink v., stank or stunk, stunk, stink• ing.

stink∘er

stint (period of time)

sti•pend

stip•ple v., stip•pled, stip•pling.

stip∘u•late v., stip∘u• lat∘ed, stip∘u•lat• ing.

stip∘u•la•tion

stir v., stirred, stir• ring.

stir-cra∘zy

stir-fry v., stir-fried, stir-fry∘ing.

stir•rer

stir•ring

stir•rup

stitch v., stitched, stitch•ing.

stoat

stock v., stocked, stock•ing.

stock cer•tif∘i•cate Business.

stock com•pa∘ny Business.

stock div∘i•dend Business.

stock ex•change Business.

stock mar•ket Business.

stock op•tion Business.

stock quo•ta•tion Business.

stock reg•is•tra•tion Business.

stock split Business.

stock-still

stock ta•ble

stock•ade

stock•brok∘er Busi- ness.

stock•hold∘er Busi- ness.

Stock•holm

stock∘i•ness

stock∘i•nette

stock•ing

stock•job•ber Busi- ness.

stock•keep∘er

stock•pile v., stock• piled, stock•pil•ing.

stock∘y adj., stock• i∘er, stock•i•est.

stock•yard

stodg∘i•ness

stodg∘y adj., stodg• i∘er, stodg•i•est.

sto∘gy or sto•gie n., pl. sto•gies.

sto∘ic

sto•i•cal

sto•i•cal∘ly

sto•i•cism

stoke v., stoked, stok• ing.

stok∘er

stole

sto•len (robbed)

stol∘id

stol•id∘ly

stol•len (sweet bread)

stom•ach

stom∘ach•ache

stom•ach∘er

stomp v., stomped, stomp•ing.

stone n., pl. stones or stone; v., stoned, ston•ing.

stone•wall v., stone• walled, stone•wall• ing.

ston∘i•ness

ston∘y adj., ston•i∘er, ston•i•est.

stood

stooge

stool

stoop v., stooped, stoop•ing. (to bend: cf. STOUP)

stop v., stopped, stop•ping.

stop bit Computers.

stop or•der Business.

stop pay•ment Busi- ness.

stop•cock

stop•gap

stop•light

stop•o∘ver

stop•page

stop•per

stop•watch

stor•age

storage de•vice Com- puters.

store v., stored, stor• ing.

store•front

store•house n., pl. store•hous∘es.

store•keep∘er

store•room

sto•ried

stork n., pl. storks or

stork. (the bird: cf. STALK)

storm *v.*, stormed, storm•ing.

storm•i∘ly

storm∘y *adj.*, storm• i∘er, storm•i•est.

sto∘ry *n.*, *pl.* sto•ries.

sto∘ry•board

sto∘ry•book

sto∘ry•tell∘er

sto∘ry•tell•ing

stoup (basin: cf. STOOP)

stout *adj.*, stout∘er, stout•est.

stout-heart∘ed

stout∘ly

stout•ness

stove

stove•pipe

stow *v.*, stowed, stow•ing.

stow•age

stow•a∘way

stra•bis•mus

strad•dle *v.*, strad• dled, strad•dling.

strafe *v.*, strafed, straf•ing.

strag•gle *v.*, strag• gled, strag•gling.

strag•gler

strag•gly *adj.*, strag• gli∘er, strag•gli•est.

straight *adj.*, straight∘er, straight•est. (direct: cf. STRAIT)

straight-arm *v.*, straight-armed, straight-arm∘ing.

straight-edge

straight-faced

straight•a∘way

straight•edge

straight∘en *v.*,

straight•ened, straight•en•ing.

straight•en•ing.

straight•for•ward

straight•ness

strain *v.*, strained, strain•ing.

strain∘er

strait (narrow water- way: cf. STRAIGHT)

strait-laced

strait•jack∘et

strand *v.*, strand∘ed, strand•ing.

strange *v.*, strang∘er, strang•est. (odder)

strange∘ly

strange•ness

stran•ger (newcomer)

stran•gle *v.*, stran• gled, stran•gling.

stran•gle•hold

stran•gler

stran•gu•la•tion

strap *v.*, strapped, strap•ping.

strap•less

stra∘ta

strat∘a•gem

stra•te•gic

stra•te•gi•cal∘ly

strat∘e•gist

strat∘e•gy *n.*, *pl.* strat∘e•gies.

strat∘i•fi•ca•tion

strat∘i•fy *v.*, strat∘i• fied, strat∘i•fy•ing.

strat∘o•sphere

stra•tum *n.*, *pl.* stra∘ta or stra•tums.

Strauss

Stra•vin•sky

straw

straw•ber∘ry *n.*, *pl.* straw•ber•ries.

stray *v.*, strayed, stray•ing.

streak *v.*, streaked, streak•ing.

streak∘er

streak∘y *adj.*, streak• i∘er, streak•i•est.

stream *v.*, streamed, stream•ing.

stream∘er

stream•line *v.*, stream•lined, stream•lin•ing.

street

street name *Business.*

street-smart

street•car

street•walk∘er

street•wise

strength

strength∘en

stren•u•ous

stren•u•ous∘ly

stren•u•ous•ness

strep

strep∘to•coc•cus *n.*, *pl.* strep∘to•coc•ci.

strep∘to•my•cin

stress *v.*, stressed, stress•ing.

stressed-out

stress•ful

stretch *v.*, stretched, stretch•ing.

stretch•a∘ble

stretch∘er

stretch∘y *adj.*, stretch•i∘er, stretch•i•est.

strew *v.*, strewed, strewn or strewed, strew•ing.

stri•at∘ed

strick∘en

strict *adj.*, strict∘er, strict•est.

strict∘ly

strict•ness

stric•ture

stride *v.*, strode, strid•den, strid•ing.

stri•dent

stri•dent•ly

strife

strike *v.*, struck, struck; strick•en, strik•ing. (hit) or (afflicted)

strike fund *Business.*

strike•out

strik•er

strik•ing price *Business.*

string *v.*, strung, string•ing.

strin•gen•cy

strin•gent

strin•gent•ly

string•er

string•y *adj.*, string•i•er, string•i•est.

strip *v.*, stripped, strip•ping.

strip-min•ing

strip-search *v.*, strip-searched, strip-search•ing.

stripe

striped

strip•ling

strip•per

strip•tease

strip•teas•er

strive *v.*, strove or strived, striv•en or strived, striv•ing.

strobe

stro•bo•scope

strode

stroke *v.*, stroked, strok•ing.

stroll *v.*, strolled, stroll•ing.

stroll•er

strong *adj.*, strong•er, strong•est.

strong-arm *v.*, strong-armed, strong-arm•ing.

strong-mind•ed

strong•box

strong•hold

strong•ly

strong•man *n.*, pl. strong•men.

stron•ti•um

strop *v.*, stropped, strop•ping.

strove

struck

struc•tur•al

structure *v.*, struc•tured, struc•tur•ing.

structured pro•gram•ming *Computers.*

stru•del

strug•gle *v.*, strug•gled, strug•gling.

strum *v.*, strummed, strum•ming.

strum•pet

strung

strut *v.*, strut•ted, strut•ting.

strych•nine

stub *v.*, stubbed, stub•bing.

stub•ble

stub•born

stub•born•ness

stub•by *adj.*, stub•bi•er, stub•bi•est.

stuc•co *n.*, pl. stuc•coes or stuc•cos;. *v.*, stuc•coed, stuc•co•ing.

stuck

stuck-up

stud *v.*, stud•ded, stud•ding.

stud•book

stu•dent

stud•ied

stu•di•o *n.*, pl. stu•di•os.

stu•di•ous

stud•y *n.*, pl. stud•ies; *v.*, stud•ied, stud•y•ing.

stuff *v.*, stuffed, stuff•ing.

stuff•i•ness

stuff•ing

stuff•y *adj.*, stuff•i•er, stuff•i•est.

stul•ti•fi•ca•tion

stul•ti•fy *v.*, stul•ti•fied, stul•ti•fy•ing.

stum•ble *v.*, stum•bled, stum•bling.

stump *v.*, stumped, stump•ing.

stun *v.*, stunned, stun•ning.

stung

stunk

stun•ning

stun•ning•ly

stunt *v.*, stunt•ed, stunt•ing.

stu•pe•fac•tion

stu•pe•fy *v.*, stu•pe•fied, stu•pe•fy•ing.

stu•pen•dous

stu•pid *adj.*, stu•pid•er, stu•pid•est.

stu•pid•i•ty

stu•por

stur•di•ly

stur•di•ness

stur•dy *adj.*, stur•di•er, stur•di•est.

stur•geon *n.*, pl. stur•geon or stur•geons.

stut•ter *v.*, stut•tered, stut•ter•ing.

stut•ter•er

sty *n.*, pl. sties.

Styg•i•an
style v., styled, styl•ing. (mode; fashion: cf. STILE)
styl•ish
styl•ist
sty•lis•tic
sty•lis•ti•cal•ly
styl•ize adj., styl•ized, styl•iz•ing.
sty•lus n., pl. sty•li or sty•lus•es.
sty•mie n., pl. sty•mies; v., sty•mied, sty•mie•ing.
styp•tic
sty•rene
Sty•ro•foam Trademark.
Styx
sua•sion
suave
suave•ly
sub v., subbed, sub•bing.
sub ro•sa
sub•a•tom•ic
sub•com•mit•tee
sub•com•pact
sub•con•scious
sub•con•scious•ly
sub•con•ti•nent
sub•con•tract v., sub•con•tract•ed, sub•con•tract•ing.
sub•con•trac•tor
sub•cul•ture
sub•cu•ta•ne•ous
sub•deb
sub•di•rec•to•ry n. pl. sub•di•rec•to•ries. Computers.
sub•di•vide v., sub•di•vid•ed, sub•di•vid•ing.
sub•di•vi•sion

sub•due v., sub•dued, sub•du•ing.
sub•head
sub•ject v., sub•ject•ed, sub•ject•ing.
sub•jec•tion
sub•jec•tive
sub•jec•tiv•i•ty
sub•ju•gate v., sub•ju•gat•ed, sub•ju•gat•ing.
sub•ju•ga•tion
sub•junc•tive
sub•lease v., sub•leased, sub•leas•ing.
sub•let v., sub•let, sub•let•ting.
sub•li•cense v., sub•li•censed, sub•li•cens•ing. Business.
sub•li•cen•see Business.
sub•li•cen•sor Business.
sub•li•mate v., sub•li•mat•ed, sub•li•mat•ing.
sub•li•ma•tion
sub•lime v., sub•limed, sub•lim•ing.
sub•lim•i•nal
sub•lim•i•ty
sub•ma•chine gun
sub•mar•gin•al
sub•ma•rine
sub•merge v., sub•merg•ing.
sub•mer•gence
sub•merse v., sub•mersed, sub•mers•ing.
sub•mers•i•ble
sub•mer•sion
sub•mi•cro•scop•ic

sub•mis•sion
sub•mis•sive
sub•mit v., sub•mit•ted, sub•mit•ting.
sub•nor•mal
sub•or•bit•al
sub•or•di•nate v., sub•or•di•nat•ed, sub•or•di•nat•ing.
sub•or•di•na•tion
sub•orn v., sub•orned, sub•orn•ing.
sub•or•na•tion
sub•plot
sub•poe•na or sub•pe•na n., pl. sub•poe•nas; v., sub•poe•naed, sub•poe•na•ing.
sub•rou•tine Computers.
sub•scribe v., sub•scribed, sub•scrib•ing.
sub•scrib•er
sub•script
sub•scrip•tion
sub•se•quent
sub•se•quent•ly
sub•ser•vi•ence
sub•ser•vi•ent
sub•set
sub•side v., sub•sid•ed, sub•sid•ing.
sub•sid•ence
sub•sid•i•ar•y n., pl. sub•sid•i•ar•ies.
subsidiary ac•count Business.
sub•si•dize v., sub•si•dized, sub•si•diz•ing.
sub•si•dy n., pl. sub•si•dies.
sub•sist v., sub•sist•ed, sub•sist•ing.

sub•sist•ence
sub•soil
sub•son•ic
sub•stance
sub•stand•ard
sub•stan•tial
sub•stan•tial•ly
sub•stan•ti•ate v., sub•stan•ti•at•ed, sub•stan•ti•at•ing.
sub•stan•ti•a•tion
sub•stan•tive
sub•sta•tion
sub•sti•tute v., sub•sti•tut•ed, sub•sti•tut•ing.
sub•sti•tu•tion
sub•stra•tum n., pl. sub•stra•ta or sub•stra•tums.
sub•struc•ture
sub•sume v., sub•sumed, sub•sum•ing.
sub•teen
sub•ter•fuge
sub•ter•ra•ne•an
sub•ti•tle v., sub•ti•tled, sub•ti•tling.
sub•tle adj., sub•tler, sub•tlest.
sub•tle•ty
sub•to•tal v., sub•to•taled or sub•to•talled, sub•to•tal•ing or sub•to•tal•ling.
sub•tract v., sub•tract•ed, sub•tract•ing.
sub•trac•tion
sub•tra•hend
sub•trop•i•cal
sub•urb
sub•ur•ban
sub•ur•ban•ite
sub•ur•bi•a

sub•ven•tion
sub•ver•sion
sub•ver•sive
sub•vert v., sub•vert•ed, sub•vert•ing.
sub•way
suc•ceed v., suc•ceed•ed, suc•ceed•ing.
suc•cess
suc•cess•ful
suc•cess•ful•ly
suc•ces•sion
suc•ces•sive
suc•ces•sive•ly
suc•ces•sor
suc•cinct
suc•cinct•ly
suc•cinct•ness
suc•cor v., suc•cored, suc•cor•ing. (to help: cf. SUCKER)
suc•co•tash
suc•cu•lence
suc•cu•len•cy
suc•cu•lent
suc•cumb v., suc•cumbed, suc•cumb•ing.
such
such and such
such•like
suck v., sucked, suck•ing.
suck•er v., suck•ered, suck•er•ing. (gullible person; to make a sucker of: cf. SUCCOR)
suck•le v., suck•led, suck•ling.
su•crose
suc•tion v., suc•tioned, suc•tion•ing.
Su•dan
Su•da•nese
sud•den

sud•den•ly
sud•den•ness
suds
suds•y adj., suds•i•er, suds•i•est.
sue v., sued, su•ing.
suede or suède
su•et
Su•ez Ca•nal
suf•fer v., suf•fered, suf•fer•ing.
suf•fer•ance
suf•fer•er
suf•fer•ing
suf•fice v., suf•ficed, suf•fic•ing.
suf•fi•cien•cy
suf•fi•cient
suf•fi•cient•ly
suf•fix
suf•fo•cate v., suf•fo•cat•ed, suf•fo•cat•ing.
suf•fo•ca•tion
suf•frage
suf•fra•gette
suf•fra•gist
suf•fuse v., suf•fused, suf•fus•ing.
suf•fu•sion
sug•ar v., sug•ared, sug•ar•ing.
sug•ar•cane or sug•ar cane
sug•ar•coat v., sug•ar•coat•ed, sug•ar•coat•ing.
sug•ar•less
sug•ar•plum
sug•ar•y
sug•gest v., sug•gest•ed, sug•gest•ing.
sug•gest•i•bil•i•ty
sug•gest•i•ble
sug•ges•tion

sug•ges•tive

sug•ges•tive•ly

su◦i ge•ne•ris

su◦i•cid◦al

su◦i•cide

suit v., suit•ed, suit• ing. (set of clothes; to adapt: cf. SUITE; SWEET)

suit•a•bil•i•ty

suit•a◦ble

suit•a•bly

suit•case

suite (series of rooms: cf. SUIT; SWEET)

suit•ing

suit◦or

su•ki•ya◦ki

Suk•koth or Suk•kot

sul◦fa (the drug)

sul•fate

sul•fide

sul•fur (the chemical element)

sul•fu•ric

sulk v., sulked, sulk• ing.

sulk•i◦ly

sulk◦i•ness

sulk◦y n., pl. sulk•ies; adj., sulk•i◦er, sulk• i•est.

sul•len

sul•len◦ly

sul•len•ness

sul◦ly v., sul•lied, sul•ly•ing.

sul•phur

sul•tan

sul•tan•ate

sul•try adj., sul• tri◦er, sul•tri•est.

sum¹ (total: cf. SOME)

sum² v., summed, sum•ming.

su•mac

Su•ma•tra

sum•mar•i◦ly

sum•ma•rize v., sum• ma•rized, sum•ma• riz•ing.

sum•ma◦ry n., pl. sum•ma•ries. (synopsis)

sum•ma•tion

sum•mer v., sum• mered, sum•mer• ing.

sum◦mer•house n., pl. sum◦mer• hous◦es.

sum◦mer•time

sum◦mer◦y (like summer)

sum•mit

sum•mon v., sum• moned, sum•mon• ing.

sum•mons n., pl. sum•mons◦es.

su◦mo

sump•tu◦ous

sun (star: cf. SON)

Sun Yat-sen

sun•bath n., pl. sun• baths.

sun•bathe v., sun• bathed, sun•bath• ing.

sun•bath◦er

sun•beam

Sun•belt or Sun Belt

sun•bon•net

sun•burn v., sun• burned or sun• burnt, sun•burn• ing.

sun•burst

sun•dae (ice cream with toppings)

Sun•day (day of the week)

sun•der v., sun• dered, sun•der•ing.

sun•di◦al

sun•down

sun•dries

sun•dry

sun•flow◦er

sung

sun•glass◦es

sunk

sunk cost Business.

sunk◦en

sun•lamp

sun•light

sun•lit

sun◦ny adj., sun• ni◦er, sun•ni•est.

sun•rise

sunrise in•dus•try Business.

sun•roof n., pl. sun• roofs.

sun•screen or sun screen

sun•set

sunset in•dus•try Business.

sun•shine

sun•spot

sun•stroke

sun•tan v., sun• tanned, sun•tan• ning.

sun◦up

sup v., supped, sup• ping.

su•per

su◦per•a◦bun•dance

su◦per•a◦bun•dant

su◦per•an•nu•at◦ed

su•perb

su•perb◦ly

su◦per•car•go n., pl. su◦per•car•goes or su◦per•car•gos.

su◦per•charge v., su◦per•charged, su◦per•charg•ing.

su•per•charg•er
su•per•cil•i•ous
su•per•com•put•er
Computers.
su•per•con•duc•tiv•
i•ty
su•per•con•duc•tor
su•per•del•e•gate
su•per•e•go *n., pl.*
su•per•e•gos.
su•per•er•o•ga•tion
su•per•e•rog•a•
to•ry
su•per•fi•cial
su•per•fi•ci•al•i•ty
su•per•fi•cial•ly
su•per•flu•i•ty
su•per•flu•ous
su•per•he•ro *n., pl.*
su•per•he•roes.
su•per•high•way
su•per•hu•man
su•per•im•pose *v.,*
su•per•im•posed,
su•per•im•pos•ing.
su•per•in•tend *v.,*
su•per•in•tend•ed,
su•per•in•tend•ing.
su•per•in•ten•dence
su•per•in•ten•
den•cy
su•per•in•tend•ent
su•pe•ri•or
su•pe•ri•or•i•ty
su•per•la•tive
su•per•la•tive•ly
su•per•man *n., pl.*
su•per•men.
su•per•mar•ket
su•per•nal
su•per•nat•u•ral
su•per•no•va *n., pl.*
su•per•no•vas or
su•per•no•vae.
su•per•nu•mer•ar•y
n., pl. su•per•nu•
mer•ar•ies.

su•per•pow•er
su•per•saur
su•per•script
su•per•scrip•tion
su•per•sede *v.,*
su•per•sed•ed,
su•per•sed•ing.
su•per•son•ic
su•per•star
su•per•sti•tion
su•per•sti•tious
su•per•string theo•ry
su•per•struc•ture
su•per•sym•me•try
su•per•tank•er
su•per•vene *v.,*
su•per•vened,
su•per•ven•ing.
su•per•ven•tion
su•per•vise *v.,*
su•per•vised,
su•per•vis•ing.
su•per•vi•sion
su•per•vi•sor
su•per•vi•so•ry
su•pine
sup•per
sup•plant *v.,* sup•
plant•ed, sup•
plant•ing.
sup•ple *adj.,* sup•pler,
sup•plest.
sup•ple•ment *v.,*
sup•ple•ment•ed,
sup•ple•ment•ing.
sup•ple•men•ta•ry
sup•pli•ant
sup•pli•cant
sup•pli•cate *v.,* sup•
pli•cat•ed, sup•pli•
cat•ing.
sup•pli•ca•tion
sup•pli•er
sup•ply¹ *n., pl.* sup•
plies; *v.,* sup•plied,
sup•ply•ing. (quan-

tity on hand; to fur-
nish)
sup•ply² (in a supple
way)
sup•ply-side *Business.*
sup•port *v.,* sup•
port•ed, sup•port•
ing.
support group
sup•port•er
sup•port•ive
sup•pose *v.,* sup•
posed, sup•pos•ing.
sup•pos•ed•ly
sup•po•si•tion
sup•pos•i•to•ry *n.,*
pl. sup•pos•i•to•
ries.
sup•press *v.,* sup•
pressed, sup•press•
ing.
sup•pres•sant
sup•pres•sion
sup•pu•ra•tion
su•pra•na•tion•al
su•prem•a•cist
su•prem•a•cy
su•preme
Supreme Be•ing
Supreme Court
su•preme•ly
sur•cease
sur•charge *v.,* sur•
charged, sur•charg•
ing.
sure *adj.,* sur•er, sur•
est.
sure•fire
sure•foot•ed
sure•ly
sure•ness
sur•e•ty *n., pl.*
sur•e•ties. *Business.*
surety bond *Business.*
surf *v.,* surfed, surf•
ing. (waves; to ride a
surfboard: cf. SERF)

sur•face v., sur•faced, sur•fac•ing.
surf•board
sur•feit
sur•feit∘ed
surf∘er
surf•ing
surge v., surged, surg•ing.
sur•geon
sur•ger∘y
sur•gi•cal
sur•gi•cal∘ly
Su•ri•na∘me or Su•ri•nam
Su•ri•na•mese
sur•li•ness
sur∘ly adj., sur•li∘er, sur•li•est.
sur•mise v., sur•mised, sur•mis•ing.
sur•mount v., sur•mount∘ed, sur•mount•ing.
sur•name
sur•named
sur•pass v., sur•passed, sur•pass•ing.
sur•plice (vestment)
sur•plus (excess)
surplus val∘ue Business.
sur•prise v., sur•prised, sur•pris•ing.
sur•pris•ing∘ly
sur•re∘al
sur•re•al•ism
sur•re•al•ist
sur•re•al•is•tic
sur•ren•der v., sur•ren•dered, sur•ren•der•ing.
sur•rep•ti•tious
sur•ro•gate
sur•round v., sur•

round∘ed, sur•round•ing.
sur•tax v., sur•taxed, sur•tax•ing.
sur•veil•lance
sur•vey n., pl. sur•veys; v., sur•veyed, sur•vey•ing.
sur•vey∘or
sur•viv∘al
sur•viv•al•ist
sur•vive v., sur•vived, sur•viv•ing.
sur•vi•vor
sus•cep•ti•bil•i∘ty
sus•cep•ti•ble
sus•pect v., sus•pect∘ed, sus•pect•ing.
sus•pend v., sus•pend∘ed, sus•pend•ing.
sus•pend∘ers
sus•pense
suspense ac•count Business.
sus•pense•ful
sus•pen•sion
sus•pi•cion
sus•pi•cious
sus•pi•cious∘ly
sus•tain v., sus•tained, sus•tain•ing.
sus•te•nance
su•ture v., su•tured, su•tur•ing.
Su∘va
svelte
swab or swob v., swabbed or swobbed, swab•bing or swob•bing.
swad•dle v., swad•dled, swad•dling.
swag
swag•ger v., swag•

gered, swag•ger•ing.
Swa•hi•li
swain
swal•low v., swal•lowed, swal•low•ing.
swal∘low•tail
swam
swa∘mi n., pl. swa•mis.
swamp v., swamped, swamp•ing.
swamp∘y adj., swamp•i∘er, swamp•i•est.
swan
swank v., swanked, swank•ing; adj., swank∘er, swank•est.
swank∘y adj., swank•i∘er, swank•i•est.
swans•down
swap v., swapped, swap•ping.
swapping in Computers.
swapping out Computers.
sward (turf: cf. SOARED; SWORD)
swarm v., swarmed, swarm•ing.
swarth∘y adj., swarth•i∘er, swarth•i•est.
swash•buck•ler
swas•ti∘ka n., pl. swas•ti•kas.
swat v. swat∘ted, swat•ting.
swatch
swath (strip)
swathe v., swathed, swath•ing. (to wrap)
swat•ter

sway *v.*, swayed, sway•ing.

sway•back or sway•backed

Swa∘zi•land

swear *v.*, swore, sworn, swear•ing.

swear•word

sweat *v.*, sweat or sweat∘ed, sweat•ing.

sweat eq•ui∘ty *Business.*

sweat∘er

sweat•pants or sweat pants

sweat•shirt

sweat•shop *Business.*

sweat∘y *adj.*, sweat•i∘er, sweat•i∘est.

Swede

Swe•den

Swed•ish

sweep *v.*, swept, sweep•ing.

sweep∘er

sweep•ing∘ly

sweeps

sweep•stakes

sweet *adj.*, sweet∘er, sweet•est. (sugary: cf. SUIT; SUITE)

sweet-talk *v.*, sweet-talked, sweet-talk∘ing.

sweet•bread

sweet•bri∘er or sweet•bri∘ar

sweet∘en *v.*, sweet•ened, sweet•en∘ing.

sweet•en∘er

sweet•heart

sweetheart con•tract *Business.*

sweet∘ish

sweet∘ly

sweet•meat

sweet•ness

swell *v.*, swelled, swol•len or swelled, swell•ing.

swell•head∘ed

swel•ter *v.*, swel•tered, swel•ter•ing.

swept

swept•back

swerve *v.*, swerved, swerv•ing.

swift *adj.*, swift∘er, swift•est.

swift∘ly

swift•ness

swig *v.*, swigged, swig•ging.

swill *v.*, swilled, swill•ing.

swim *v.*, swam, swum, swim•ming.

swim•mer

swim•suit

swin•dle *v.*, swin•dled, swin•dling.

swin•dler

swine *n.*, *pl.* swine.

swing *v.*, swung, swing•ing.

swing loan *Business.*

swing∘er

swipe *v.*, swiped, swip•ing.

swirl *v.*, swirled, swirl•ing.

swish *v.*, swished, swish•ing.

Swiss *n.*, *pl.* Swiss.

switch *v.*, switched, switch•ing.

switch-hit *v.*, switch-hit, switch-hit∘ting.

switch-hit∘ter

switch•blade

switch•board

switch∘er

Switz∘er•land

swiv•el *v.*, swiv•eled or swiv•elled, swiv•el•ing or swiv•el•ling.

swiz∘zle stick

swob *v.*, swobbed, swob•bing.

swol•len

swoon *v.*, swooned, swoon•ing.

swoop *v.*, swooped, swoop•ing.

sword (weapon with blade: cf. SOARED; SWARD)

sword•fish *n.*, *pl.* sword•fish∘es or sword•fish.

sword•play

swords•man *n.*, *pl.* swords•men.

swore

sworn

swum

swung

Syb∘a•rite

Syb∘a•rit∘ic

syc∘a•more

syc∘o•phan∘cy

syc∘o•phant

syc∘o•phan•tic

Syd•ney

syl•lab∘ic

syl•lab∘i•ca•tion or syl•lab∘i•fi•ca•tion

syl•lab∘i•fy *v.*, syl•lab∘i•fied, syl•lab∘i•fy•ing.

syl•la•ble

syl•la•bus *n.*, *pl.* syl•la•bus∘es or syl•la•bi.

syl•lo•gism

syl•lo•gis•tic

sylph

syl•van

sym•bi•o•sis *n.*, *pl.* sym•bi•o•ses.

sym•bi•ot•ic

sym•bol (sign: cf. CYM-BAL)

sym•bol•ic

sym•bol•i•cal•ly

sym•bol•ism

sym•bol•ize *v.*, sym•bol•ized, sym•bol•iz•ing.

sym•met•ri•cal

sym•met•ri•cal•ly

sym•me•try *n.*, *pl.* sym•me•tries.

sym•pa•thet•ic

sym•pa•thet•i•cal•ly

sym•pa•thize *v.*, sym•pa•thized, sym•pa•thiz•ing.

sym•pa•thiz•er

sym•pa•thy *n.*, *pl.* sym•pa•thies.

sym•phon•ic

sym•pho•ny *n.*, *pl.* sym•pho•nies.

sym•po•si•um *n.*, *pl.* sym•po•si•ums or sym•po•si•a.

symp•tom

symp•to•mat•ic

syn•a•gogue

syn•apse

sync or synch *v.*, synced or synched,

sync•ing or synch•ing.

syn•chro•ni•za•tion

syn•chro•nize *v.*, syn•chro•nized, syn•chro•niz•ing.

syn•chro•nous

syn•co•pate *v.*, syn•co•pat•ed, syn•co•pat•ing.

syn•co•pa•tion

syn•co•pe

syn•di•cate *v.*, syn•di•cat•ed, syn•di•cat•ing.

syn•di•ca•tion *Business.*

syn•di•ca•tor *Business.*

syn•drome

syn•er•gism

syn•er•gis•tic

syn•fu•el

syn•od

syn•o•nym

syn•on•y•mous

syn•op•sis *n.*, *pl.* syn•op•ses.

syn•tac•tic or syn•tac•ti•cal

syn•tax

syntax er•ror *Computers.*

syn•the•sis *n.*, *pl.* syn•the•ses.

syn•the•size *v.*, syn•the•sized, syn•the•siz•ing.

syn•the•siz•er

syn•thet•ic

synthetic fu•el

syn•thet•i•cal•ly

synth•pop

syph•i•lis

syph•i•lit•ic

Syr•a•cuse

Syr•i•a

Syr•i•an

sy•ringe

syr•up

syr•up•y

sys•op *Computers.*

sys•tem

system call *Computers.*

sys•tem•at•ic

sys•tem•at•i•cal•ly

sys•tem•a•tize *v.*, sys•tem•a•tized, sys•tem•a•tiz•ing.

sys•tem•ic

sys•tem•i•cal•ly

sys•tems a•nal•y•sis *Computers.*

systems an•a•lyst *Computers.*

systems soft•ware *Computers.*

sys•to•le

sys•tol•ic

T

T-•ac•count *Business.* (the bookkeeping account)

T-•bill *Business.* (treasury bill)

T-•bond *Business.* (treasury bond)

T-•bone steak

T cell (thymus-derived cell)

T-•note *Business.* (treasury note)

T-•shirt or tee shirt

T square

tab *v.*, tabbed, tab•bing.

tab char•ac•ter *Computers.*

tab•by *n.*, *pl.* tab•bies.

tab•er•nac•le

ta•ble *v.*, ta•bled, ta•bling.

ta•ble d'hôte *n., pl.*
ta•bles d'hôte.
ta∘ble-hop *v.,* ta∘ble-
hopped, ta∘ble-
hop∘ping.
ta∘ble-hop∘per
tab•leau *n., pl.* tab•
leaux *or* tab•leaus.
*(picturesque grouping:
cf.* TABLOID*)*
ta∘ble•cloth *n., pl.*
ta∘ble•cloths.
ta∘ble•land
ta∘ble•spoon
ta∘ble•spoon•ful *n.,
pl.* ta∘ble•spoon•
fuls.
tab•let
ta∘ble•ware
tab•loid (newspaper:
cf. TABLEAU)
ta•boo *n., pl.* ta•
boos.
tab∘u•lar
tab∘u•late *v.,* tab∘u•
lat∘ed, tab∘u•lat•
ing.
tab∘u•la•tion
tab∘u•la•tor
ta•cet (musical direc-
tion: cf. TACIT)
ta•chom∘e•ter
tach∘y•car•di∘a
tac∘it (implied)
tac∘it•ly
tac∘it•ness
tac∘i•turn
tac∘i•tur•ni•ty
tack *v.,* tacked, tack•
ing.
tacked (nailed: cf. TACT)
tack∘i•ness
tack∘le *v.,* tack•led,
tack•ling.
tack•ler
tacks (nails: cf. TAX)

tack∘y *adj.,* tack•i∘er,
tack•i•est.
ta•co *n., pl.* ta•cos.
Ta•co∘ma
tact (diplomacy: cf.
TACKED)
tact•ful
tact•ful∘ly
tac•ti•cal
tac•ti•cal∘ly
tac•ti•cian
tac•tics
tac•tile
tact•less
tact•less∘ly
tad
tad•pole
taf•fe∘ta *n., pl.* taf•
fe∘tas.
taf∘fy *n., pl.* taf•fies.
Taft
tag *v.,* tagged, tag•
ging.
Ta•ga•log *n., pl.* Ta•
ga•logs *or* Ta•ga•
log.
Ta•hi∘ti
Ta•hi•tian
t'ai chi ch'uan *or* tai
chi chuan
tail *v.,* tailed, tail•ing.
(rear part; to follow:
cf. TALE)
tail coat *or* tail•coat
tail•gate *v.,* tail•
gat∘ed, tail•gat•ing.
tail•gat∘er
tail•less
tail•light
tai•lor *v.,* tai•lored,
tai•lor•ing.
tail•pipe
tail•spin
taint *v.,* taint∘ed,
taint•ing.
Tai•pei

Tai•wan
Tai•wan•ese *n., pl.*
Tai•wan•ese.
take *v.,* took, tak•en,
tak•ing.
take•a∘ble
take•off
take•out
take•o∘ver
tak∘er
tak∘ing
talc
tal•cum pow•der
tale (story: cf. TAIL)
tale•bear∘er
tal•ent
tal•ent∘ed
tal•is•man *n., pl.* tal•
is•mans.
talk *v.,* talked, talk•
ing.
talk ra∘di∘o
talk∘a•tive
talk∘a•tive•ness
talk∘er
talk∘ing-to *n., pl.*
talk∘ing-tos.
tall *adj.,* tall∘er, tall•
est.
Tal•la•has•see
tal•low
tal∘ly *n., pl.* tal•lies;
v., tal•lied, tal•ly•
ing.
tal•ly∘ho *n., pl.* tal•
ly•hos.
Tal•mud
Tal•mud∘ic
tal∘on
tam
tam-o'-shan∘ter
tam•a∘ble *or* tame•
a∘ble
ta•ma∘le *n., pl.* ta•
ma∘les.
tam∘a•rind

tam•bou•rine

tame v., tamed, tam•
ing; adj., tam•er,
tam•est.

tame•a•ble

tame•ly

tame•ness

tam•er

Tam•il

tamp v., tamped,
tamp•ing.

Tam•pa

tam•per v., tam•
pered, tam•per•ing.

tam•pon

tan v., tanned, tan•
ning; adj., tan•ner,
tan•nest.

tan•a•ger

tan•dem

T'ang or Tang

tan•ge•lo n., pl. tan•
ge•los.

tan•gent

tan•gen•tial

tan•ge•rine

tan•gi•bil•i•ty

tan•gi•ble

tangible as•set Busi-
ness.

tan•gi•bly

tan•gle v., tan•gled,
tan•gling.

tan•go n., pl. tan•
gos; v., tan•goed,
tan•go•ing.

tank

tan•kard

tank•er

tank•ful n., pl. tank•
fuls.

tan•ner•y n., pl. tan•
ner•ies.

tan•nin

tan•sy n., pl. tan•sies.

tan•ta•lize v., tan•

ta•lized, tan•ta•liz•
ing.

tan•ta•liz•er

tan•ta•liz•ing•ly

tan•ta•lum

tan•ta•mount

tan•trum

Tan•za•ni•a

Tan•za•ni•an

Tao•ism

Tao•ist

tap v., tapped, tap•
ping.

tap dance

tap-danc•er

tape v., taped, tap•
ing.

tap•er¹ (one who
tapes)

ta•per² v., ta•pered,
ta•per•ing. (candle;
to become thinner at
one end)

tap•es•try n., pl. tap•
es•tries.

tape•worm

tap•i•o•ca

ta•pir n., pl. ta•pirs or
ta•pir. (the animal)

tap•per

tap•root

taps

tar v., tarred, tar•ring.

tar•an•tel•la n., pl.
tar•an•tel•las. (the
dance)

ta•ran•tu•la n., pl.
ta•ran•tu•las. (the
spider)

tar•di•ly

tar•di•ness

tar•dy adj., tar•di•er,
tar•di•est.

tare (weight: cf. TEAR)

tar•get v., tar•
get•ed, tar•get•ing.

tar•iff Business.

tar•nish v., tar•
nished, tar•nish•ing.

ta•ro n., pl. ta•ros.
(edible tuber)

ta•rot cards (cards for
fortune telling)

tar•pau•lin

tar•pon n., pl. tar•
pons or tar•pon.

tar•ra•gon

tar•ry v., tar•ried,
tar•ry•ing.

tar•sal

tar•sus n., pl. tar•si.

tart v., tart•ed, tart•
ing; adj., tart•er,
tart•est.

tar•tan

tar•tar

tar•tar•ic ac•id

tart•ly

tart•ness

task

task switch•ing Com-
puters.

task•mas•ter

Tas•ma•ni•a

Tas•ma•ni•an

tas•sel

tas•seled or tas•
selled

taste v., tast•ed, tast•
ing.

taste•ful

taste•ful•ly

taste•less

taste•less•ly

tast•er

tast•i•ness

tast•y adj., tast•i•er,
tast•i•est.

tat v., tat•ted, tat•
ting.

ta•ta•mi n., pl. ta•
ta•mi or ta•ta•mis.

tat•ter

tat•ter•de•mal•ion

tat•tered

tat•ter•sall

tat•ting

tat•tle v., tat•tled,
tat•tling.

tat•tler

tat•tle•tale

tat•too n., pl. tat•
toos; v., tat•tooed,
tat•too•ing.

tat•too•ist

tau

taught (did teach: cf.
TAUT)

taunt v., taunt•ed,
taunt•ing. (to mock)

taunt•ing•ly

taupe

Tau•rus

taut adj., taut•er,
taut•est. (tense: cf.
TAUGHT; TAUNT)

taut•ly

taut•ness

tau•to•log•ic or tau•
tol•o•gous

tau•tol•o•gy n., pl.
tau•tol•o•gies.

tav•ern

taw•dri•ness

taw•dry adj., taw•
dri•er, taw•dri•est.

taw•ni•ness

taw•ny adj., taw•
ni•er, taw•ni•est.

tax v., taxed, tax•ing.
(money paid to gov-
ernment; to impose a
tax: cf. TACKS)

tax-de•ferred Busi-
ness.

tax-ex•empt Business.

tax ex•emp•tion Busi-
ness.

tax-free Business.

tax lien Business.

tax rate Business.

tax re•turn Business.

tax shel•ter Business.

tax-shel•tered Busi-
ness.

tax shield Business.

tax•a•ble Business.

tax•er

tax•i n., pl. tax•is; v.,
tax•ied, tax•i•ing.

tax•i•cab

tax•i•der•mist

tax•i•der•my

tax•o•nom•ic

tax•on•o•my

tax•pay•er

tax•pay•ing

Tay•lor

tbs. or tbsp. (table-
spoon).

Tchai•kov•sky

tea (beverage: cf. TEE)

teach v., taught,
teach•ing.

teach•er

tea•cup

teak

tea•ket•tle

teal n., pl. teals or
teal.

team v., teamed,
team•ing. (group; to
join together: cf. TEEM)

team•mate

team•ster

team•work

tea•pot

tear¹ v., tore, torn,
tear•ing. (rip; to rip:
cf. TARE)

tear² v., teared, tear•
ing. (drop of fluid
from eye; to weep: cf.
TIER)

tear gas n.

tear-gas v., tear-

gassed, tear-
gas∘sing.

tear-off men•u Com-
puters.

tear•drop

tear•jerk∘er

teas (beverages)

tease v., teased, teas•
ing. (to provoke)

tea•sel

teas•ing•ly

tea•spoon

tea•spoon•ful n., pl.
tea•spoon•fuls.

teat

tech∘ie

tech•ne•ti•um

tech•ni•cal

tech•ni•cal•i•ty n.,
pl. tech•ni•cal•i•
ties.

tech•ni•cal•ly

tech•ni•cian

Tech•ni•col∘or Trade-
mark.

tech•nics (study of a
mechanical art)

tech•nique n., pl.
tech•niques. (skilled
methods)

tech•no-thrill∘er

tech•noc•ra∘cy n., pl.
tech•noc•ra•cies.

tech•no•log∘i•cal

tech•no•log∘i•cal•ly

tech•nol∘o∘gist

tech•nol∘o∘gy n., pl.
tech•nol∘o∘gies.

tech•no•pop

tec•ton•ics

ted∘dy bear

te•di•ous

te•di•ous•ly

te•di•um

tee v., teed, tee•ing.
(golf peg; to strike a

golf ball from a tee: cf. TEA)

tee shirt (T-shirt)

teem *v.*, teemed, teem•ing. (to swarm: cf. TEAM)

teen

teen•age or teen• aged

teen•ag•er

tee•ny *adj.*, tee• ni•er, tee•ni•est.

teen•y•bop•per

tee•pee (tepee)

tee•ter *v.*, tee•tered, tee•ter•ing.

teeth (plural of tooth)

teethe *v.*, teethed, teeth•ing. (to grow teeth)

tee•to•tal•er

Tef•lon *Trademark.*

Te•gu•ci•gal•pa

Te•he•ran or The•ran

tek•tite

Tel A•viv

tel•e•cast *v.*, tel•e• cast or tel•e• cast•ed, tel•e•cast• ing.

tel•e•cast•er

tel•e•com•mu•ni• ca•tions

tel•e•com•mut•ing

tel•e•con•fer•ence *v.*, tel•e•con•fer• enced, tel•e•con• fer•enc•ing.

tel•e•cop•y *v.*, tel•e• cop•ied, tel•e• cop•y•ing.

tel•e•gen•ic

tel•e•gram

tel•e•graph *v.*, tel•e• graphed, tel•e• graph•ing.

te•leg•ra•pher or te• leg•ra•phist

te•leg•ra•phy

tel•e•ki•ne•sis

tel•e•mar•ket•er *Business.*

tel•e•mar•ket•ing *Business.*

te•lem•e•ter *v.*, te• lem•e•tered, te• lem•e•ter•ing.

tel•e•met•ric

te•lem•e•try

tel•e•o•log•i•cal ar• gu•ment

tel•e•ol•o•gy

tel•e•path•ic

tel•e•path•i•cal•ly

te•lep•a•thy

tel•e•phone *v.*, tel•e•phoned, tel•e•phon•ing.

tel•e•phone tag

tel•e•phon•ic

te•leph•o•ny

tel•e•pho•to

tel•e•play

tel•e•por•ta•tion

tel•e•scope *v.*, tel•e• scoped, tel•e•scop• ing.

tel•e•scop•ic

tel•e•thon

Tel•e•type *Trademark.*

tel•e•van•ge•lism

tel•e•van•ge•list

tel•e•vise *v.*, tel•e• vised, tel•e•vis•ing.

tel•e•vi•sion (TV)

tel•ex *v.*, tel•exed, tel•ex•ing. *Business.*

tell *v.*, told, tell•ing.

tell•er

Tel•ler

tell•ing•ly

tell•tale

tel•lu•ri•um

tel•ly *n.*, *pl.* tel•lies.

Tel•star *Trademark.*

te•mer•i•ty

temp *Business.*

tem•per *v.*, tem• pered, tem•per•ing.

tem•pe•ra (painting technique: cf. TEMPURA)

tem•per•a•ment

tem•per•a•men•tal

tem•per•ance

tem•per•ate

tem•per•ate•ly

tem•per•ate•ness

tem•per•a•ture

tem•pest

tem•pes•tu•ous

tem•pes•tu•ous•ly

tem•pes•tu•ous•ness

tem•plate

tem•ple

tem•po *n.*, *pl.* tem• pos or tem•pi.

tem•po•ral

tem•po•rar•i•ly

tem•po•rar•y *n.*, *pl.* tem•po•rar•ies.

tem•po•rize *v.*, tem• po•rized, tem•po• riz•ing.

tempt *v.*, tempt•ed, tempt•ing.

temp•ta•tion

tempt•ing•ly

tem•pu•ra (Japanese food: cf. TEMPERA)

ten

ten•a•ble

te•na•cious

te•na•cious•ly

ten•an•cy *n.*, *pl.* ten• an•cies.

ten•ant *v.*, ten• ant•ed, ten•ant•

ing. (occupant; to dwell: cf. TENET)

tend *v.*, tend∘ed, tend•ing.

ten•den∘cy *n.*, *pl.* ten•den∘cies.

ten•den•tious

tend∘er[1] (one who tends; auxiliary ship)

ten•der[2] *v.*, ten•dered, ten•der∘ing; *adj.*, ten•der∘er, ten•der•est. (to bid; soft)

ten∘der-heart∘ed

ten∘der of•fer *Business.*

ten∘der∘er

ten∘der•foot *n.*, *pl.* ten∘der•foots or ten∘der•feet.

ten∘der•ize *v.*, ten∘der•ized, ten∘der•iz∘ing.

ten∘der•iz∘er

ten∘der•loin

ten•der•ly

ten•der•ness

ten•di∘ni•tis

ten•don (cord connecting muscle; bone: cf. TENON)

ten•dril

ten∘e•brous

ten∘e•ment

ten∘et (belief: cf. TEN-ANT)

ten•fold

Ten•nes•se∘an

Ten•nes•see (TN)

ten•nis

Ten•ny•son

ten∘on (projection inserted into mortise: cf. TENDON)

ten∘or (male singer; purport: cf. TENURE)

ten•pins

tense *v.*, tensed, tens•ing; *adj.*, tens∘er, tens•est.

tense∘ly

tense•ness

ten•sile

ten•sion *v.*, ten•sioned, ten•sion•ing.

tent

ten•ta•cle

ten•ta•cled

ten•tac∘u•lar

ten•ta•tive

ten•ta•tive∘ly

ten•ta•tive•ness

ten∘ter•hook

tenth

ten∘u•ous

ten∘u•ous∘ly

ten∘u•ous•ness

ten•ure (term: cf. TENOR)

te•pee or tee•pee

tep∘id

te•qui•la

ter∘a•bit (Tb) *Computers.*

ter∘a•byte (TB) *Computers.*

ter•bi∘um

ter•cen•ten•ar∘y *n.*, *pl.* ter•cen•ten•ar•ies.

ter∘i•ya∘ki

term *v.*, termed, term•ing.

term bond *Business.*

term in•sur•ance *Business.*

ter•ma•gant

ter•mi•na∘ble

ter•mi•nal

terminal em∘u•la•tion *Computers.*

ter•mi•nal∘ly

ter•mi•nate *v.*, ter•mi•nat∘ed, ter•mi•nat•ing.

ter•mi•na•tor

ter•mi•no•log∘i•cal

ter•mi•nol∘o∘gy *n.*, *pl.* ter•mi•nol∘o∘gies.

ter•mi•nus *n.*, *pl.* ter•mi∘ni or ter•mi•nus∘es.

ter•mite

tern (the bird: cf. TURN)

ter•na∘ry

terp•si•cho•re∘an

ter∘ra cot∘ta *n.*, *pl.* ter∘ra cot•tas.

terra fir∘ma

terra in•cog•ni∘ta

ter•race *v.*, ter•raced, ter•rac•ing.

ter•rain

ter•ra•pin

ter•rar∘i∘um *n.*, *pl.* ter•rar∘i•ums or ter•rar∘i•a.

ter•raz∘zo

ter•res•tri∘al

ter•res•tri•al∘ly

ter•ri∘ble

ter•ri∘bly

ter•ri∘er

ter•rif∘ic

ter•rif∘i•cal∘ly

ter•ri•fy *v.*, ter•ri•fied, ter•ri•fy•ing.

ter•ri•fy•ing∘ly

ter•ri•to•ri∘al

ter•ri•to•ry *n.*, *pl.* ter•ri•to•ries.

ter•ror

ter•ror•ism

ter•ror•ist

ter•ror•ize *v.*, ter•ror•ized, ter•ror•iz•ing.

ter∘ory *n., pl.* ter∘ries.
terse
terse∘ly
terse•ness
ter∙ti•ar∘y
test *v.,* test∘ed, test•ing.
tes•ta•ment
tes•tate
tes•ta•tor
tes•tes
tes•ti•cle
tes•tic•u•lar
tes•ti•fy *v.,* tes•ti•fied, tes•ti•fy•ing.
tes•ti•mo•ni•al
tes•ti•mo•ny
tes•tis *n., pl.* tes•tes.
tes•tos•ter•one
tes∘ty *adj.,* tes•ti•er, tes•ti•est.
tet∘a•nal
tet∘a•nus
tête-à-tête *n., pl.* tête-à-têtes.
teth∘er *v.,* teth•ered, teth•er•ing.
tet∘ra *n., pl.* tet•ras.
tet∘ra•cy•cline
tet∘ra•gram
tet∘ra•he•dral
tet∘ra•he•dron *n., pl.* tet∘ra•he•drons or tet∘ra•he•dra.
te•tram∘e•ter
Teu•ton
Teu•ton∘ic
tev∘a•tron
Tex∘an
Tex∘as (TX)
text
text ed∘i•tor
text file *Computers.*
text•book
tex•tile
tex•tu∘al

tex•tur∘al
tex•ture *v.,* tex•tured, tex•tur•ing.
Thai *n., pl.* Thais.
Thai•land
thal∘a•mus *n., pl.* thal∘a•mi.
tha∘lid∘o∘mide
thal•li•um
Thames
than (compared to: cf. THEN)
than∘a•tol∘o∘gy
thane
thank *v.,* thanked, thank•ing.
thank•ful
thank•ful•ly
thank•ful•ness
thank•less
thank•less•ly
thanks•giv•ing
that *n., pl.* those.
thatch *v.,* thatched, thatch•ing.
Thatch∘er
that's (that is)
thaw *v.,* thawed, thaw•ing.
the
the∘a•ter or thea•tre
the•at•ri•cal
the•at•ri•cal•i∘ty
the•at•ri•cal•ly
thee
thee•ing and thou•ing
theft
their (belonging to them: cf. THERE; THEY'RE)
theirs
the•ism
the•ist
the•is•tic
them

the•mat∘ic
the•mat∘i•cal∘ly
theme
them•selves
then (at that time: cf. THAN)
thence (from that place: cf. HENCE; WHENCE)
thence•forth
the•oc•ra∘cy *n., pl.* the•oc•ra•cies.
the•o•crat∘ic
the•o•lo•gian
the•o•log∘i•cal
the•ol∘o∘gy *n., pl.* the•ol∘o∘gies.
the•o•rem
the•o•ret∘i•cal
the•o•ret∘i•cal∘ly
the•o•re•ti•cian
the•o•rist
the•o•rize *v.,* the•o•rized, the•o•riz•ing.
the•o∘ry *n., pl.* the•o∘ries.
The•o∘ry of Eve•ry•thing
the•os∘o∘phy
ther∘a•peu•tic *adj.*
ther∘a•peu•tics *n.*
ther∘a•pist
ther∘a•py *n., pl.* ther∘a•pies.
there (at that place: cf. THEIR; THEY'RE)
there•a∘bout or there•a∘bouts
there•af∘ter
there∘at
there∘by
there•for (in exchange)
there•fore (consequently)
there∘in

there○of
there○on
there•to or there•un○to
there•to•fore
there•up○on
there•with
ther•mal
thermal print○er *Computers.*
ther○mo•dy•nam•ics
ther•mom○e•ter
ther○mo•nu○cle•ar
ther○mo•plas•tic
ther•mos
ther○mo•stat
the•sau•rus *n., pl.* the•sau•rus•es or the•sau○ri.
these
The•se○us
the•sis *n., pl.* the•ses.
Thes•pi○an
the○ta
they, them, their, theirs.
they're (they are: cf. THEIR; THERE)
thi•a•mine or thi•a•min
thick *adj.,* thick○er, thick•est.
thick-skinned
thick○en *v.,* thick○ened, thick•en○ing.
thick•en○er
thick○et
thick•head○ed
thick○ly
thick•ness
thick•set
thief *n., pl.* thieves.
thiev•er○y
thiev•ing
thigh
thigh•bone

thim•ble
thim•ble•ful *n., pl.* thim•ble•fuls.
Thim•phu or Thim○bu
thin *v.,* thinned, thin•ning; *adj.,* thin•ner, thin•nest.
thine
thing
thing○a•ma•bob
think *v.,* thought, think•ing.
think tank
think○er
thin○ly
thin•ner
thin•ness
thin-skinned
third
third-class
third de•gree *n.*
third-de•gree *adj.*
third mar•ket *Business.*
third-rate
Third World
thirst *v.,* thirst○ed, thirst•ing.
thirst•i○ly
thirst○y *adj.,* thirst•i○er, thirst•i•est.
thir•teen
thir•teenth
thir•ti•eth
thir○ty *n., pl.* thir•ties.
this *n., pl.* these.
this•tle
this○tle•down
thith○er
thong (leather strip: cf. TONG; TONGUE)
Thor
tho•rac○ic
tho•rax *n., pl.* tho•rax○es or tho•ra•ces.
Tho•reau
tho•ri○um
thorn
thorn○y *adj.,* thorn•i○er, thorn•i•est.
thor•ough (complete: cf. THREW; THROUGH)
thor•ough•bred
thor•ough•fare
thor•ough•go•ing
thor•ough○ly
thor•ough•ness
those
thou, thee, thy, thine.
though
thought
thought•ful
thought•ful○ly
thought•ful•ness
thought•less
thought•less○ly
thought•less•ness
thou•ing
thou•sand *n., pl.* thou•sands or thou•sand.
thou•sandth
thrall
thrash *v.,* thrashed, thrash•ing. (to strike: cf. THRESH)
thread *v.,* thread○ed, thread•ing.
thread•bare
threat
threat○en *v.,* threat•ened, threat•en•ing.
three
three-di•men○sion○al
three•fold
three•score
three•some
thren○o•dy *n., pl.* thren○o•dies.

thresh v., threshed, thresh•ing. (to beat out grain: cf. THRASH)

thresh•er

thresh•old

threw (did throw: cf. THOROUGH; THROUGH)

thrice

thrift

thrift•i•ly

thrift•less

thrifts Business.

thrift•shop

thrift∘y adj., thrift•i∘er, thrift•i•est.

thrill v., thrilled, thrill•ing.

thrill∘er

thrive v., thrived, thriv•ing.

throat

throat•i•ly

throat∘y adj., throat•i∘er, throat•i•est.

throb v., throbbed, throb•bing.

throes (pangs: cf. THROWS)

throm•bo•sis

throm•bus n., pl. throm∘bi.

throne (royal chair: cf. THROWN)

throng v., thronged, throng•ing.

throt•tle v., throt•tled, throt•tling.

through (by means of: cf. THOROUGH; THREW)

through•out

through•put Computers.

through•way (thru-way)

throw v., threw, thrown, throw•ing. (hurled: cf. THRONE)

throw•a∘way

throw•back

throw∘er

throws (does hurl: cf. THROES)

thru (through)

thrum v., thrummed, thrum•ming.

thrush

thrust v., thrust, thrust•ing.

thru•way or through•way

thud v., thud•ded, thud•ding.

thug

thu•li∘um

thumb v., thumbed, thumb•ing.

thumb•nail

thumb•screw

thumb•tack v., thumb•tacked, thumb•tack•ing.

thump v., thumped, thump•ing.

thun•der v., thun•dered, thun•der•ing.

thun∘der•bolt

thun∘der•clap

thun∘der•cloud

thun∘der•head

thun∘der•ous

thun∘der•show∘er

thun∘der•storm

thun∘der•struck

Thurs•day

thus

thwack v., thwacked, thwack•ing.

thwart v., thwart∘ed, thwart•ing.

thy

thyme (the herb: cf. TIME)

thy•mus n., pl. thy•mus•es or thy•mi.

thy•roid

thy•roid•ec•to•my

thy•rox∘in

thy•self

ti•ar∘a n., pl. ti•ar∘as.

Ti•ber

Ti•bet

Ti•bet∘an

tib∘i∘a n., pl. tib∘i∘ae or tib•i∘as.

tic (muscle spasm)

tick[1] (the arachnid)

tick[2] v., ticked, tick•ing. (click; did click)

tick-tack-toe or tic-tac-toe

tick∘er tape

tick∘et v., tick•et∘ed, tick•et•ing.

tick•ing

tick∘le v., tick•led, tick•ling.

tick•ler

tickler file Business.

tick•lish

tick•lish•ness

tid∘al

tid•bit

tid∘dly•winks

tide v., tid∘ed, tid•ing. (rise and fall of ocean; to carry: cf. TIED)

tide•land

tide•wa•ter

ti•di•ly

ti•di•ness

ti•dings

ti∘dy v., ti•died, ti•dy•ing; adj., ti•di∘er, ti•di•est.

tie, v., tied, ty•ing. (fastened: cf. TIDE)

tie-dye v., tie-dyed, tie-dye○ing.

tie-in

tie rod

tie-up

tier (row: cf. TEAR)

tiered

tiff

TIFF (tagged image file format) *Computers.*

Tif•fa○ny glass

ti•ger n., pl. ti•gers or ti•ger.

tight adj., tight○er, tight•est.

tight-fist○ed or tight• fist○ed

tight-lipped

tight○en v., tight• ened, tight•en○ing.

tight○ly

tight•ness

tight•rope

tights

tight•wad

ti•gress (female tiger)

Ti•gris (river)

tike (tyke)

til○de n., pl. til•des.

tile v., tiled, til•ing.

tiled win•dows *Computers.*

till[1] (until)

till[2] v., tilled, till•ing. (to plow)

till•age

till○er[1] (one who tills)

til•ler[2] (rudder part)

tilt v., tilt○ed, tilt•ing.

tim•bale n., pl. tim• bales.

tim•ber (wood)

tim•bered

tim•ber•line

tim•bre (sound quality)

time v., timed, tim• ing. (duration; to measure time: cf. THYME)

time-and-mo○tion *Business.*

time de•pos○it *Business.*

time draft *Business.*

time-hon○ored

time loan *Business.*

time-out or time•out, n., pl. time-outs.

time-shar○ing *Computers.*

time•card

time•keep○er

time•less

time○ly adj., time• li○er, time•li○est.

time•piece

tim○er

time•ta○ble

time•worn

tim○id

ti•mid•i○ty

tim○id○ly

tim○ing

tim•or•ous

tim•or•ous•ness

Tim○o•thy

tim•pa○ni or tym• pa○ni

tim•pa•nist

tin v., tinned, tin• ning.

tin par○a•chute *Business.*

tin plate or tin•plate

tinc•ture

tin•der

tin○der•box

tine

tin•foil

tinge v., tinged, tinge••ing or ting• ing.

tin•gle v., tin•gled, tin•gling.

tin•gly adj., tin• gli○er, tin•gli○est.

ti•ni•ness

tin•ker v., tin•kered, tin•ker•ing.

tin•ker○er

tin•kle v., tin•kled, tin•kling.

tin•ni○ly

tin•ni•ness

tin•ni•tus

tin○ny adj., tin•ni○er, tin•ni○est.

tin•sel

tint v., tint○ed, tint• ing.

tin•tin•nab○u•la• tion

tin•type

ti○ny adj., ti•ni○er, ti•ni○est.

tip v., tipped, tip• ping.

tip•off

tip•per

tip•ple v., tip•pled, tip•pling.

tip•pler

tip•si○ly

tip•si•ness

tip•ster

tip○sy adj., tip•si○er, tip•si•est.

tip•toe v., tip•toed, tip•toe•ing.

tip•top

ti•rade

Ti•ra•në or Ti•ra•na

tire v., tired, tir•ing.

tire•less

tire•less○ly

tire•some

tire•some∘ly
tis (it is)
tis•sue
tit
ti•tan
ti•tan∘ic
ti•ta•ni∘um
tithe v., tithed, tith•ing.
Ti•tian
tit•il•late v., tit•il•lat∘ed, tit•il•lat•ing.
tit•il•la•tion
ti•tle v., ti•tled, ti•tling.
title bar Computers.
title search Business.
tit•mouse n., pl. tit•mice.
tit•ter v., tit•tered, tit•ter•ing.
tit•tle
tit∘u•lar
tiz∘zy n., pl. tiz•zies.
TM (trademark)
TN (Tennessee)
TNT (the explosive)
to (toward: cf. too; two)
to-do n., pl. to-dos.
toad
toad•stool
toad∘y n., pl. toad•ies, toad•ied, toad∘y•ing.
toast v., toast∘ed, toast•ing.
toast∘er
toast•mas•ter
toast∘y adj., toast•i∘er, toast•i∘est.
to•bac•co n., pl. to•bac•cos or to•bac•coes.
to•bac•co•less

to•bac•co•nist
to•bog•gan v., to•bog•ganed, to•bog•gan•ing.
toc•sin (alarm bell: cf. toxin)
to•day
tod•dle v., tod•dled, tod•dling.
tod•dler
tod∘dy n., pl. tod•dies.
toe v., toed, toe•ing. (foot digit; to touch with the toes: cf. tow)
toe•hold or toe-hold
toe•nail
tof•fee
to∘fu
to∘ga n., pl. to•gas.
to•gaed
to•geth∘er
to•geth•er•ness
tog•gle key Computers.
To∘go
To∘go•lese
togs
toil v., toiled, toil•ing. (labor; to toil)
toile (transparent fabric)
toil∘er
toi•let (bathroom fixture)
toi•let∘ry n., pl. toi•let•ries.
toi•lette (grooming)
toil•some
toke v., toked, tok•ing.
to•ken v., to•kened, to•ken•ing.
to∘ken-ring net•work Computers.
to•ken•ism
To•ky∘o

To•ky∘o•ite
told
tole (metalware: cf. toll)
To•le∘do
tol•er•a∘ble
tol•er•a∘bly
tol•er•ance
tol•er•ant
tol•er•ant∘ly
tol•er•ate v., tol•er•at∘ed, tol•er•at•ing.
tol•er•a•tion
toll v., tolled, toll•ing. (fee; to sound: cf. tole)
toll•booth n., pl. toll•booths.
toll•gate
Tol•stoy or Tol•stoi
tol∘u•ene
tom
Tom Col•lins
tom-tom
tom∘a•hawk
to•ma∘to n., pl. to•ma•toes.
tomb (grave: cf. tome)
tom•boy
tom•boy•ish
tomb•stone
tom•cat v., tom•cat∘ted, tom•cat•ting.
tome (book: cf. tomb)
tom•fool•er∘y
Tom∘my gun
to•mog•ra•phy
to•mor•row
ton
ton∘al
to•nal•i∘ty n., pl. to•nal•i•ties.
tone v., toned, ton•ing.
tone arm or tone•arm

tone-deaf
tone•less
ton○er
tong (tongs, a two-armed implement: cf. THONG; TONGUE)
Ton○ga
tongs
tongue v., tongued, tongu•ing. (organ in mouth; to play tones)
tongue-lash○ing
tongue-tied
ton○ic
to•night
ton•nage
ton•sil
ton•sil•lec•to○my n., pl. ton•sil•lec•to•mies.
ton•sil•li•tis
ton•so○ri○al
ton•sure
ton•sured
ton○y adj., ton•i○er, ton•i•est.
To○ny n., pl. To•nys.
too (also; excessive: cf. TO; TWO)
took
tool v., tooled, tool•ing. (implement; to shape with a tool: cf. TULLE)
toon
toot v., toot○ed, toot•ing.
tooth n., pl. teeth.
tooth•ache
tooth•brush
toothed
tooth•less
tooth•paste
tooth•pick
tooth•some

tooth○y adj., tooth•i○er, tooth•i•est.
top-down pro•gram•ming Computers.
top flight n.
top-flight adj.
top-heav○y
top-lev○el
top man•age•ment Business.
top-se○cret
to•paz
top•coat
To•pe○ka
to•pi○ar○y
top○ic
top○i•cal
top•knot
top•less
top•mast
top•most
top•notch or top-notch
top○o○graph○ic or top○o○graph○i•cal
to•pog•ra•phy n., pl. to•pog•ra•phies. (surface features: cf. TYPOGRAPHY)
top○o○log○ic
to•pol○o○gy
top•ping
top•ple v., top•pled, top•pling.
TOPS Computers. (transparent operating system)
top•sail
top•side
top•soil
top○sy-tur○vy
toque
To•rah n., pl. To•rahs.
torch v., torched, torch•ing.
torch•bear○er

torch•light
tore
tor○e○a•dor
tor•ment v., tor•ment○ed, tor•ment•ing.
tor•men•tor
torn
tor•na○do n., pl. tor•na•does or tor•na•dos.
To•ron○to
To•ron•to•ni○an
tor•pe○do n., pl. tor•pe•does; v., tor•pe•doed, tor•pe○do•ing.
tor•pid
tor•por
torque
tor•rent
tor•ren•tial
tor•rid
tor•rid•i•ty
tor•sion
tor○so n., pl. tor•sos or tor○si.
tort (wrongful act)
torte n., pl. tortes. (rich cake)
tor•tel•li○ni
tor•til○la n., pl. tor•til•las.
tor•toise
tor•toise•shell or tor-toise shell
tor•tu•ous (twisting: cf. TORTUROUS)
tor•tu•ous○ly
tor•ture v., tor•tured, tor•tur•ing.
tor•tur○er
tor•tur•ous (painful: cf. TORTUOUS)
To○ry n., pl. To•ries.
toss v., tossed, toss•ing.

toss○up

tot v., tot•ted, tot•ting.

to•tal v., to•taled or to•talled, to•tal•ing or to•tal•ling.

to•tal○i•tar○i•an

to•tal○i•tar○i•an•ism

to•tal•i○ty

to•tal•i○za•tor

to•tal○ly

tote v., tot○ed, tot•ing.

to•tem

tot•ter v., tot•tered, tot•ter•ing.

tou•can

touch v., touched, touch•ing.

touch and go n.

touch-and-go adj.

touch tab•let Computers.

touch•a○ble

touch•down

tou•ché

touched

touch○i○ly

touch○i•ness

touch•ing

touch•ing○ly

touch•screen Computers.

touch•stone

touch○y adj., touch•i○er, touch•i•est.

touch○y-feel○y

tough v., toughed, tough•ing; adj., tough○er, tough•est.

tough-mind○ed

tough○en v., tough•ened, tough•en•ing.

tough○ly

tough•ness

tou•pee

tour v., toured, tour•ing.

tour de force n., pl. tours de force.

Tou•rette's syn○drome

tour•ism

tour•ist

tour•is○ta

tour•ma•line

tour•na•ment

tour•ni•quet

tou•sle v., tou•sled, tou•sling.

tout v., tout○ed, tout•ing.

tow v., towed, tow•ing. (to pull: cf. TOE)

tow-head○ed

tow•age

to•ward or to•wards

tow○el v., tow•eled or tow•elled, tow•el•ing or tow•el•ling.

tow○er v., tow•ered, tow•er•ing.

tower con•fig•u•ra•tion Computers.

tow•hee

town

town house or town•house

town•ship

towns•peo•ple

tow•path n., pl. tow•paths.

tox○e•mi○a

tox○ic

toxic shock syn•drome

tox•ic•i○ty

tox○i•col○o○gist

tox○i•col○o○gy

tox•in (poison: cf. TOC-SIN)

toy v., toyed, toy•ing.

TPI Computers. (tracks per inch)

trace v., traced, trac•ing.

trace•a○ble

trac○er

trac•er○y n., pl. trac•er•ies.

tra•che•a n., pl. tra•che•ae or tra•che○as.

tra•che•al

tra•che•ot○o○my n., pl. tra•che•ot○o•mies.

tra•cho○ma

trac•ing

track v., tracked, track•ing. (parallel rails; path; to pursue a trail: cf. TRACT)

track light•ing

track•a○ble

track•ball Computers.

track○er

track•less

tract (region; pamphlet: cf. TRACK)

trac•ta○ble

trac•tion

trac•tor

tractor feed Computers.

tractor pull

tractor-trail○er

trade v., trad○ed, trad•ing.

trade ac•cept•ance Business.

trade as•so•ci•a•tion Business.

trade bal•ance Business.

trade def○i•cit Business.

trade dis•count *Business.*

trade-in *Business.*

trade name *Business.*

trade-off or trade•off

trade sur•plus *Business.*

trade un•ion *Business.*

trade•craft

trade•mark *v.*, trade•marked, trade•mark•ing. *Business.*

trad○er

trades•man *n., pl.* trades•men. *Business.*

trades•wom○an *n., pl.* trades•wom○en. *Business.*

tra•di•tion

tra•di•tion•al

tra•di•tion•al○ly

tra•duce *v.*, tra•duced, tra•duc•ing.

traf•fic *v.*, traf•ficked, traf•fick•ing.

traffic man•ag○er *Business.*

traf•fick○er

tra•ge•di○an

trag○e○dy *n., pl.* trag○e○dies.

trag○ic

trag○i•cal○ly

trag○i•com○e○dy *n., pl.* trag○i•com○e•dies.

trag○i•com○ic

trail *v.*, trailed, trail•ing. (path; to drag: cf. TRIAL)

trail•blaz○er

trail○er

train *v.*, trained, train•ing.

train○ee

train○er

train•ing

traipse *v.*, traipsed, traips•ing.

trait

trai•tor

trai•tor○ous

tra•jec•to○ry *n., pl.* tra•jec•to•ries.

tram

tram•mel *v.*, tram•meled or tram•melled, tram•mel•ing or tram•mel•ling.

tramp *v.*, tramped, tramp•ing.

tram•ple *v.*, tram•pled, tram•pling.

tram•po•line

tram•way

trance

tran•quil

tran•quil•i○ty

tran•quil•ize or tran•quil•lize *v.*, tran•quil•ized or tran•quil•lized, tran•quil•iz•ing or tran•quil•liz•ing.

tran•quil•iz○er or tran•quil•liz○er

tran•quil•li○ty

tran•quil○ly

trans•act *v.*, trans•act○ed, trans•act•ing.

trans•ac○tion

transaction cost *Business.*

transaction proc•ess•ing *Computers.*

trans•at•lan•tic

trans•ceiv○er

tran•scend *v.*, tran•scend○ed, tran•scend•ing.

tran•scend•ence

tran•scend•ent

tran•scen•den•tal

tran•scen•den•tal•ism

trans•con•ti•nen•tal

tran•scribe *v.*, tran•scribed, tran•scrib•ing.

tran•script

tran•scrip•tion

trans•duc○er

tran•sept

trans•fer *v.*, trans•ferred, trans•fer•ring.

transfer price *Business.*

trans•fer•a○ble

trans•fer○al or trans•fer•ral

trans•fig•u•ra•tion

trans•fig•ure *v.*, trans•fig•ured, trans•fig•ur•ing.

trans•fix *v.*, trans•fixed, transfix•ing.

trans•form *v.*, trans•formed, trans•form•ing.

trans•for•ma•tion

trans•form○er

trans•fuse *v.*, trans•fused, trans•fus•ing.

trans•fu•sion

trans•gen○ic

trans•gress *v.*, trans•gressed, trans•gress•ing.

trans•gres•sion

trans•gres•sor

tran•sient

tran•sis•tor

tran•sit *v.*, tran•sit○ed, tran•sit•ing.

tran•si•tion

tran•si•tion○al

tran•si•tive

tran•si•to○ry

trans•late *v.*, trans•
lat∘ed, trans•lat•
ing.
trans•la•tion
trans•la•tor
trans•lit•er•ate *v.*,
trans•lit•er•at∘ed,
trans•lit•er•at•ing.
trans•lit•er•a•tion
trans•lu•cence
trans•lu•cent
trans•mi•gra•tion
trans•mis•si•ble
trans•mis•sion
trans•mit *v.*, trans•
mit•ted, trans•mit•
ting.
trans•mit•tal
trans•mit•ter
trans•mog•ri•fy *v.*,
trans•mog•ri•fied,
trans•mog•ri•fy•
ing.
trans•mut•a•ble
trans•mu•ta•tion
trans•mute *v.*, trans•
mut∘ed, trans•mut•
ing.
trans•na•tion∘al
trans•o∘ce∘an∘ic
tran•som
trans•pa•cif∘ic
trans•par•en•cy
trans•par•ent
trans•par•ent∘ly
tran•spire *v.*, tran•
spired, tran•spir•
ing.
trans•plant *v.*, trans•
plant∘ed, trans•
plant•ing.
trans•plan•ta•tion
tran•spon•der
trans•port *v.*, trans•
port∘ed, trans•port•
ing.
trans•port•a•ble

com•put∘er *Comput-
ers.*
trans•por•ta•tion
trans•pose *v.*, trans•
posed, trans•pos•
ing.
trans•po•si•tion
trans•sex•u•al
trans•ship or tran•
ship *v.*, trans•
shipped, trans•ship•
ping. *Business.*
trans•ship•ment
tran•sub•stan•ti•a•
tion
trans•verse
trans•verse∘ly
trans•ves•tism
trans•ves•tite
trap *v.*, trapped, trap•
ping.
trap•door
tra•peze
trap∘e•zoid
trap∘e•zoi•dal
trap•per
trap•pings
trap•shoot•er
trap•shoot•ing
trash *v.*, trashed,
trash•ing.
trash∘y *adj.*, trash•
i∘er, trash•i•est.
trau∘ma *n.*, *pl.* trau•
mas or trau•ma∘ta.
trau•mat∘ic
trau•ma•tize *v.*, trau•
ma•tized, trau•ma•
tiz•ing.
tra•vail (toil)
trav•el *v.*, trav•eled
or trav•elled, trav•
el•ing or trav•el•
ling. (to journey)
trav•el∘er or trav•el•
ler
trav•el∘er's check

trav•el•ing sales•
man *Business.*
trav∘e•logue or
trav∘e•log
tra•verse *v.*, tra•
versed, tra•vers•ing.
trav•es∘ty *n.*, *pl.*
trav•es•ties; *v.*,
trav•es•tied, trav•
es•ty•ing.
trawl∘er
tray
treach•er•ous
treach•er•ous∘ly
treach•er∘y *n.*, *pl.*
treach•er•ies.
trea•cle
tread *v.*, trod, trod•
den or trod, tread•
ing.
trea•dle
tread•mill
trea•son
trea•son•a•ble
treas•ure *v.*, treas•
ured, treas•ur•ing.
treas∘ure-trove
treas•ur∘er *Business.*
treas•ur∘y *n.*, *pl.*
treas•ur•ies. *Busi-
ness.*
treasury bill *Business.*
treasury bond *Busi-
ness.*
treasury note *Business.*
treasury stock *Busi-
ness.*
treat *v.*, treat∘ed,
treat•ing.
trea•ties (formal agree-
ments)
trea•tise (written expo-
sition)
treat•ment
trea∘ty *n.*, *pl.* trea•
ties.

tre•ble v., tre•bled, tre•bling.

tree v., treed, tree•ing.

tree•less

tre•foil

trek v., trekked, trek•king.

trel•lis

trem•ble v., trem•bled, trem•bling.

tre•men•dous

tre•men•dous•ly

trem∘o∘lo n., pl. trem∘o∘los.

trem∘or

trem∘u∘lous

trem∘u∘lous•ly

trench

trench•ant

trench∘er•man n., pl. trench∘er•men.

trend

trend∘i•ness

trend∘y adj., trend•i∘er, trend•i•est.

Tren•ton

Tren•to•ni∘an

trep∘i•da•tion

tres•pass v., tres•passed, tres•pass•ing.

tres•pass∘er

tress

tres•tle

tre•tin∘o∘in

trey

tri∘ad

tri•ad∘ic

tri•age

tri∘al (judicial proceeding: cf. TRAIL)

trial bal•ance Busi-ness.

tri•an•gle

tri•an•gu•lar

tri•an•gu•late v., tri•an•gu•lat∘ed, tri•an•gu•lat•ing.

tri•an•gu•la•tion

Tri•as•sic

trib∘al

tribe

trib∘u•la•tion

tri•bu•nal

trib•une

trib∘u•tar∘y n., pl. trib∘u•tar•ies.

trib•ute

trice

tri•cen•ten•ni∘al

tri•ceps n., pl. tri•ceps∘es or tri•ceps.

tri•cer∘a•tops

trich∘i•no•sis or trich∘i•ni•a•sis

tri•chot∘o•my

trick v., tricked, trick•ing.

trick•er∘y

trick•i∘ly

trick∘i•ness

trick∘le v., trick•led, trick•ling.

trick∘le-down the∘o∘ry Business.

trick•ster

trick∘y adj., trick•i∘er, trick•i•est.

tri•col∘or

tri•cy•cle

tri•dent

tried

tried-and-true

tri•en•ni∘al

tri•en•ni•al∘ly

Tri•este

tri•fect∘a n., pl. tri•fect∘as.

tri•fle v., tri•fled, tri•fling.

tri•fo•cal

trig•ger v., trig•gered, trig•ger•ing.

tri•glyc•er•ide

trig∘o∘no•met•ric

trig∘o∘nom•e•try

tri•lat•er∘al

tri•lin•gual

trill v., trilled, trill•ing.

tril•lion n., pl. tril•lions or tril•lion.

tril•lionth

tril•li∘um

tril∘o∘gy n., pl. tril∘o∘gies.

trim v., adj., trimmed, trim•ming; adj., trim•mer, trim•mest.

tri•mes•ter

trim∘ly

trim•mer

trim•mings

trim•ness

tri•month∘ly

trine

Trin∘i•dad and To•ba∘go

trin•i∘ty n., pl. trin•i•ties.

Trin•i∘ty

trin•ket

tri∘o n., pl. tri∘os.

trip v., tripped, trip•ping.

tri•par•tite

trip•ham•mer

tri•ple v., tri•pled, tri•pling.

tri∘ple-tax-free Busi-ness.

tri•ple witch•ing hour Business.

trip•let

tri•plex

trip•li•cate

trip•ly
tri•pod
Trip∘o∘li
trip•per
trip•tych
tri•sect v., tri•sect∘ed, tri•sect•ing.
tri•syl•lab∘ic
tri•syl•la∘ble
trite adj., trit∘er, trit•est.
trite•ness
trit•i∘um
tri•umph v., tri•umphed, tri•umph•ing.
tri•um•phant
tri•um•phant∘ly
tri•um•vi•rate
triv∘et
triv∘i∘a
triv∘i∘al
triv∘i•al•i∘ty
triv∘i•al•ize v., triv∘i•al•ized, triv∘i•al•iz•ing.
tro•cha∘ic (of a trochee)
troche (losenge)
tro•chee (poetic meter)
trod
trod•den
trog•lo•dyte
troi∘ka n., pl. troi•kas.
Tro•jan
troll v., trolled, troll•ing.
trol•ley n., pl. trol•lies.
trol•lop
Trol•lope
trom•bone
troop v., trooped, troop•ing. (company

of soldiers; to flock together: cf. TROUPE)
troop∘er (police officer: cf. TROUPER)
trope
tro•phy n., pl. tro•phies.
trop∘ic
trop∘i•cal
tro•pism
trop∘o∘sphere
trot v., trot•ted, trot•ting.
troth
trot•ter
trou•ba•dour
trou•ble v., trou•bled, trou•bling.
trou∘ble•mak∘er
trou∘ble•shoot∘er
trou∘ble•some
trough
trounce v., trounced, trounc•ing.
troupe (company of actors: cf. TROOP)
troup∘er (actor: cf. TROOPER)
trou•sers
trous•seau n., pl. trous•seaux or trous•seaus.
trout n., pl. trout or trouts.
trow∘el
troy
tru•an∘cy
tru•ant
truce
truck v., trucked, truck•ing.
truck•age
truck∘er
truck∘le
truck•load
truc∘u•lence

truc∘u•lent
trudge v., trudged, trudg•ing.
true v., trued, tru•ing or true•ing; adj., tru∘er, tru•est.
true-blue
truf•fle
tru•ism (cliche: cf. TRUTH)
tru∘ly
Tru•man
trump v., trumped, trump•ing.
trump∘er∘y
trum•pet v., trum•pet∘ed, trum•pet•ing.
trum•pet∘er
trun•cate v., trun•cat∘ed, trun•cat•ing.
trun•ca•tion
trun•cheon
trun•dle bed
trunk
truss v., trussed, truss•ing.
trust v., trust∘ed, trust•ing.
trust com•pa∘ny Business.
trust deed Business.
trust fund
trust ter•ri•tory
trust•bust∘er
trust∘ee (administrator: cf. TRUSTY)
trust∘ee•ship
trust•ful
trust•ful∘ly
trust•wor•thi•ness
trust•wor•thy
trust∘y n., pl. trust•ies; adj., trust•i∘er, trust•i•est. (reliable;

trusted convict: cf.
TRUSTEE)
truth *n.*, *pl.* truths.
(fact: cf. TRUISM)
truth•ful
truth•ful•ly
truth•ful•ness
try *n.*, *pl.* tries; *v.*,
tried, try•ing.
try•out
tryst
tsar (czar)
tset•se
tsp. (teaspoon)
TSR *n.*, *pl.* TSRs or
TSR's. *Computers.* (ter-
minate-and-stay-
resident software pro-
gram)
tsu•na•mi *n.*, *pl.* tsu•
na•mis.
TTL mon•i•tor *Com-
puters.* (transistor-
transistor logic moni-
tor)
tu•ba *n.*, *pl.* tu•bas.
(musical instrument:
cf. TUBER)
tub•by *adj.*, tub•
bi•er, tub•bi•est.
tube•less
tu•ber (underground
stem)
tu•ber•cu•lar
tu•ber•cu•lo•sis
tube•rose
tu•ber•ous
tub•ing
tu•bu•lar
tu•bule
tuck *v.*, tucked, tuck•
ing.
Tuck•er
tuck•ered
Tuc•son
Tues•day
tuft

tuft•ed
tug *v.*, tugged, tug•
ging.
tug•boat
tu•i•tion
tu•la•re•mi•a
tu•lip
tulle (net fabric: cf.
TOOL)
Tul•sa
tum•ble *v.*, tum•bled,
tum•bling.
tum•ble-down
tum•bler
tum•ble•weed
tu•mes•cent
tum•my *n.*, *pl.* tum•
mies.
tu•mor
tu•mor•ous
tu•mult
tu•mul•tu•ous
tu•na *n.*, *pl.* tu•na or
tu•nas.
tun•dra *n.*, *pl.* tun•
dras.
tune *v.*, tuned, tun•
ing.
tune-up
tune•ful
tune•less
tune•less•ly
tun•er
tung•sten
tu•nic
tun•ing fork
Tu•nis
Tu•ni•sia
Tu•ni•sian
tun•nel *v.*, tun•neled
or tun•nelled, tun•
nel•ing or tun•nel•
ling.
tur•ban (headdress)
tur•bid
tur•bine (motor)

tur•bo•fan
tur•bo•jet
tur•bo•prop
tur•bot *n.*, *pl.* tur•bot
or tur•bots.
tur•bu•lence
tur•bu•lent
tur•bu•lent•ly
tu•reen
turf *n.*, *pl.* turfs.
tur•gid
tur•gid•i•ty
tur•gid•ly
Tu•rin
Turk
tur•key *n.*, *pl.* tur•
keys or tur•key.
Turk•ish
tur•mer•ic
tur•moil
turn *v.*, turned, turn•
ing. (to rotate: cf.
TERN)
turn•a•bout
turn•a•round
turn•coat
Tur•ner (last name)
turn•er (one that
turns)
turn•ing point
tur•nip
turn•key *n.*, *pl.* turn•
keys. *Computers.*
turnkey sys•tem
turn•off
turn•out
turn•o•ver
turn•pike
turn•stile
turn•ta•ble
tur•pen•tine
tur•pi•tude
tur•quoise
tur•ret
tur•tle *n.*, *pl.* tur•tles
or tur•tle.

tur○tle•dove
tur○tle•neck
tusk
tusked
tus•sle v., tus•sled, tus•sling.
Tut•ankh○a•men
tu•te•lage
tu•tor v., tu•tored, tu•tor•ing.
tu•to•ri○al
tut○ti-frut○ti
tu○tu n., pl. tu•tus.
tux (tuxedo)
tux○e○do n., pl. tux○e•dos.
TV (television)
TVA (Tennessee Valley Authority)
twad•dle
twain
twang v., twanged, twang•ing.
twas (it was)
tweak v., tweaked, tweak•ing.
tweed○y adj., tweed•i○er, tweed•i•est.
tween (between)
tweet v., tweet○ed, tweet•ing.
tweet○er
tweez•ers
twelfth
twelve
twelve-tone
twen•ti•eth
twen○ty n., pl. twen•ties.
twen•ty-one
twen○ty-twen○ty or 20-20
twerp
twi-night
twi-night○er

twice
twid•dle v., twid•dled, twid•dling.
twi•light
twill
twin
twin-size or twin-sized
twinge
twin•kle v., twin•kled, twin•kling.
twirl v., twirled, twirl•ing.
twist v., twist○ed, twist•ing.
twist○ed-pair ca•ble *Computers.*
twist○er
twit v., twit•ted, twit•ting.
twitch v., twitched, twitch•ing.
twit•ter v., twit•tered, twit•ter•ing.
twit•ter○y
twixt (betwixt)
two n., pl. twos. (the number: cf. TO; TOO)
two-bit
two-by-four
two-faced
two-fist○ed
two-ply
two-tier *Business.*
two-time v., two-timed, two-tim○ing.
two-tim○er
two-way
two•fer
two○fold
two○some
TX (Texas)
ty•coon
ty•ing
tyke or tike

Ty•ler
tym•pa○ni (timpani)
tym•pan○ic mem•brane
tym•pa•nist
tym•pa•num n., pl. tym•pa•nums or tym•pa○na.
type v., typed, typ•ing.
type•cast v., type•cast, type•cast•ing.
type•script
type•set v., type•set, type•set•ting.
type•set•ter
type•writ○er
ty•phoid
ty•phoon
ty•phus
typ○i•cal
typ○i•cal○ly
typ○i•fy v., typ○i•fied, typ○i•fy•ing.
typ•ist
ty○po•graph○ic or ty○po•graph○i•cal
typographical er•ror
ty○po•graph○i•cal○ly
ty•pog•ra•phy (printing: cf. TOPOGRAPHY)
ty•pol○o○gy
ty•ran•ni•cal
ty•ran•ni•cal○ly
tyr•an•nize v., tyr•an•nized, tyr•an•niz•ing.
ty•ran•no•saur
tyr•an•ny n., pl. tyr•an•nies.
ty•rant
ty○ro n., pl. ty•ros.
Ty•rol or Ti•rol
Ty•ro•le○an

U

U-•boat (German submarine)

U-•turn

u•biq•ui•ty

UCC (Uniform Commercial Code)

ud•der (milk gland: cf. UTTER)

UFO n., pl. UFOs or UFO's. (unidentified flying object)

U•gan•da

U•gan•dan

ugh

ug•li n., pl. ug•lis or ug•lies. (citrus fruit)

ug•li•ness

ug•ly adj., ug•li•er, ug•li•est. (unattractive)

uh

UHF (ultrahigh frequency)

U.K. or UK (United Kingdom).

u•kase

U•kraine

U•krain•i•an

u•ku•le•le n., pl. u•ku•le•les.

U•lan Ba•tor

ul•cer

ul•cer•ate v., ul•cer•at•ed, ul•cer•at•ing.

ul•cer•a•tion

ul•na n., pl. ul•nae or ul•nas.

Ul•ster

ul•te•ri•or

ul•ti•mate

ultimate con•sum•er Business.

ul•ti•mate•ly

ul•ti•ma•tum n., pl. ul•ti•ma•tums or ul•ti•ma•ta.

ul•tra n., pl. ul•tras.

ul•tra•con•serv•a•tive

ul•tra•high

ultrahigh fre•quen•cy (UHF)

ul•tra•ma•rine

ul•tra•mod•ern

ul•tra•son•ic

ul•tra•sound

ul•tra•vi•o•let

u•u•late v., u•u•lat•ed, u•u•lat•ing.

u•u•la•tion

U•lys•ses

um•bel

um•ber

um•bil•i•cal

um•bil•i•cus n., pl. um•bil•i•ci.

um•bra n., pl. um•bras or um•brae.

um•brage

um•brel•la n., pl. um•brel•las.

umbrella pol•i•cy Business.

um•laut

ump

um•pire v., um•pired, um•pir•ing. (referee; to referee: cf. EMPIRE)

ump•teen

ump•teenth

UN or U.N. (United Nations).

un•a•ble (not able: cf. ENABLE)

un•a•bridged

un•ac•com•pa•nied

un•ac•count•a•ble

un•ac•count•a•bly

un•ac•cus•tomed

un•af•fect•ed

un-A•mer•i•can

u•na•nim•i•ty

u•nan•i•mous

u•nan•i•mous•ly

un•armed

un•as•sail•a•ble

un•as•sum•ing

un•at•tached

un•a•vail•ing

un•a•vail•ing•ly

un•a•void•a•ble

un•a•void•a•bly

un•a•ware

un•a•wares

un•bal•anced

un•bar v., un•barred, un•bar•ring.

un•bear•a•ble

un•bear•a•bly

un•beat•en

un•be•com•ing

un•be•known or un•be•knownst

un•be•lief

un•be•liev•a•ble

un•be•liev•a•bly

un•be•liev•er

un•bend v., un•bent, un•bend•ing.

un•bend•ing

un•bi•ased

un•bid•den

un•bind v., un•bound, un•bind•ing.

un•blessed or un•blest

un•blush•ing

un•blush•ing•ly

un•bolt *v.*, un•
bolt•ed, un•bolt•
ing.
un•born
un•bos•om *v.*, un•
bos•omed, un•bos•
om•ing.
un•bound•ed
un•bowed
un•bri•dled
un•bro•ken
un•bur•den *v.*, un•
bur•dened, un•bur•
den•ing.
un•but•ton *v.*, un•
but•toned, un•but•
ton•ing.
un•called-for
un•can•ny
un•cap *v.*, un•capped,
un•cap•ping.
un•ceas•ing
un•ceas•ing•ly
un•cer•e•mo•ni•ous
un•cer•e•mo•ni•
ous•ly
un•cer•tain
un•cer•tain•ty
un•char•i•ta•ble
un•char•i•ta•bly
un•chart•ed
un•chris•tian
un•ci•al
un•cir•cum•cised
un•civ•il
un•civ•i•lized
un•clad
un•clasp *v.*, un•
clasped, un•clasp•
ing.
un•cle
un•clean *adj.*, un•
clean•er, un•clean•
est.
un•clean•ly
un•clean•ness
un•cloak *v.*, un•

cloaked, un•cloak•
ing.
un•clog *v.*, un•
clogged, un•clog•
ging.
un•clothed
un•com•fort•a•ble
un•com•fort•a•bly
un•com•mit•ted
un•com•mon
un•com•mu•ni•ca•
tive
un•com•pro•mis•ing
un•con•cern
un•con•cerned
un•con•di•tion•al
un•con•di•tion•al•ly
un•con•scion•a•ble
un•con•scion•a•bly
un•con•scious
un•con•sti•tu•
tion•al
un•con•ven•tion•al
un•cork *v.*, un•
corked, un•cork•ing.
un•count•ed
un•cou•ple *v.*, un•
cou•pled, un•cou•
pling.
un•couth
un•cov•er *v.*, un•
cov•ered, un•cov•
er•ing.
un•cross *v.*, un•
crossed, un•cross•
ing.
unc•tion
unc•tu•ous
unc•tu•ous•ness
un•cut
un•daunt•ed
un•de•cid•ed
un•de•lete *v.*, un•
de•let•ed, un•de•
let•ing. *Computers.*
un•de•mon•stra•tive
un•de•ni•a•ble

un•de•ni•a•bly
un•der
un•der sec•re•tar•y
or un•der-sec•re•
tar•y
un•der-the-count•er
un•der•a•chieve *v.*,
un•der•a•chieved,
un•der•a•chiev•ing.
un•der•a•chiev•er
un•der•act *v.*,
un•der•act•ed,
un•der•act•ing.
un•der•age
un•der•arm
un•der•bel•ly *n., pl.*
un•der•bel•lies.
un•der•bid *v.*,
un•der•bid,
un•der•bid•ding.
un•der•brush
un•der•cap•i•tal•
ized *Business.*
un•der•car•riage
un•der•charge *v.*,
un•der•charged,
un•der•charg•ing.
un•der•class•man *n.*,
pl. un•der•class•
men.
un•der•clothes or
un•der•cloth•ing
un•der•coat
un•der•cov•er
un•der•cur•rent
un•der•cut *v.*,
un•der•cut,
un•der•cut•ting.
un•der•de•vel•oped
un•der•dog
un•der•done
un•der•em•ployed
Business.
un•der•em•ploy•
ment *Business.*
un•der•es•ti•mate *v.*,
un•der•es•ti•

mat∘ed, un∘der∘es∘
ti•mat∘ing.
un∘der∘es∘ti∘ma∘
tion
un∘der∘ex∘pose v.,
un∘der∘ex∘posed,
un∘der∘ex∘pos∘ing.
un∘der∘ex∘po∘sure
un∘der∘flow *Comput-
ers.*
un∘der∘foot
un∘der∘gar∘ment
un∘der∘go v.,
un∘der∘went,
un∘der∘gone,
un∘der∘go∘ing.
un∘der∘grad∘u∘ate
un∘der∘ground
un∘der∘growth
un∘der∘hand
un∘der∘hand∘ed
un∘der∘hand∘ed∘ly
un∘der∘in∘sure v.,
un∘der∘in∘sured,
un∘der∘in∘sur∘ing.
Business.
un∘der∘lie v.,
un∘der∘lay, un∘der∘
lain, un∘der∘ly∘ing.
un∘der∘line v.,
un∘der∘lined,
un∘der∘lin∘ing.
un∘der∘ling
un∘der∘ly∘ing
un∘der∘mine v.,
un∘der∘mined,
un∘der∘min∘ing.
un∘der∘most
un∘der∘neath
un∘der∘nour∘ished
un∘der∘pants
un∘der∘pass
un∘der∘pay v.,
un∘der∘paid,
un∘der∘pay∘ing.
un∘der∘pin∘ning
un∘der∘play v.,

un∘der∘played,
un∘der∘play∘ing.
un∘der∘price v.,
un∘der∘priced,
un∘der∘pric∘ing.
Business.
un∘der∘priv∘i∘leged
un∘der∘pro∘duce v.,
un∘der∘pro∘duced,
un∘der∘pro∘duc∘
ing.
un∘der∘pro∘duc∘tion
Business.
un∘der∘rate v.,
un∘der∘rat∘ed,
un∘der∘rat∘ing.
un∘der∘score v.,
un∘der∘scored,
un∘der∘scor∘ing.
un∘der∘sea
un∘der∘seas
un∘der∘sell v.,
un∘der∘sold,
un∘der∘sell∘ing.
Business.
un∘der∘sexed
un∘der∘shirt
un∘der∘shorts
un∘der∘shot
un∘der∘side
un∘der∘signed
un∘der∘sized
un∘der∘skirt
un∘der∘slung
un∘der∘staffed
un∘der∘stand v.,
un∘der∘stood,
un∘der∘stand∘ing.
un∘der∘stand∘a∘ble
un∘der∘stand∘a∘bly
un∘der∘stand∘ing
un∘der∘state v.,
un∘der∘stat∘ed,
un∘der∘stat∘ing.
un∘der∘state∘ment
un∘der∘stood

un∘der∘stud∘y n., pl.
un∘der∘stud∘ies.
un∘der∘take v.,
un∘der∘took,
un∘der∘tak∘en,
un∘der∘tak∘ing.
un∘der∘tak∘er
un∘der∘tak∘ing
un∘der∘things n., pl.
un∘der∘tone
un∘der∘tow
un∘der∘val∘u∘a∘tion
un∘der∘val∘ue v.,
un∘der∘val∘ued,
un∘der∘val∘u∘ing.
un∘der∘wa∘ter
un∘der∘wear
un∘der∘weight
un∘der∘world
un∘der∘write v.,
un∘der∘wrote,
un∘der∘writ∘ten,
un∘der∘writ •ing.
Business.
un∘der∘writ∘er *Busi-
ness.*
un•de•sir•a•ble
un•dies n., pl.
un∘do v., un•did, un•
done, un•do•ing. (to
reverse: cf. ENDUE; UN-
DUE)
undo com•mand *Com-
puters.*
un•doubt•ed
un•doubt•ed•ly
un•dress v., un•
dressed, un•dress•
ing.
un•due (excessive: cf.
ENDUE; UNDO)
un•du•lant
un•du•late v., un•
du•lat•ed, un•du•
lat•ing.
un•du•la•tion
un•du•ly

un•dy•ing
un•earned
unearned in•cre•ment *Business.*
un•earth *v.,* un•earthed, un•earth•ing.
un•earth•ly
un•eas•i•ly
un•eas•i•ness
un•eas•y *adj.,* un•eas•i•er, un•eas•i•est.
un•em•ploy•a•ble
un•em•ployed
un•em•ploy•ment *Business.*
unemployment ben•e•fit *Business.*
unemployment in•sur•ance *Business.*
un•e•qual
un•e•qualed
un•e•qual•ly
un•e•quiv•o•cal
un•err•ing
UNESCO (United Nations Educational, Scientific, and Cultural Organization)
un•e•ven
un•e•ven•ly
un•e•vent•ful
un•ex•am•pled
un•ex•cep•tion•a•ble
un•ex•cep•tion•a•bly
un•ex•cep•tion•al
un•ex•pect•ed
un•ex•pect•ed•ly
un•fail•ing
un•fail•ing•ly
un•fair
un•fair•ly
un•faith•ful

un•faith•ful•ly
un•fa•mil•iar
un•fas•ten *v.,* un•fas•tened, un•fas•ten•ing.
un•fa•vor•a•ble
un•feel•ing
un•feel•ing•ly
un•feigned
un•fit *v.,* un•fit•ted, un•fit•ting.
un•flap•pa•ble
un•fledged
un•flinch•ing
un•fold *v.,* un•fold•ed, un•fold•ing. (to lay open: cf. ENFOLD)
un•for•get•ta•ble
un•formed
un•for•tu•nate
un•for•tu•nate•ly
un•found•ed
un•friend•li•ness
un•friend•ly *adj.,* un•friend•li•er, un•friend•li•est.
un•frock *v.,* un•frocked, un•frock•ing.
un•furl *v.,* un•furled, un•furl•ing.
un•gain•ly
un•god•li•ness
un•god•ly
un•gov•ern•a•ble
un•gra•cious
un•grate•ful
un•guard•ed
un•guent
un•gu•late
un•hand *v.,* un•hand•ed, un•hand•ing.
un•hap•pi•ly
un•hap•pi•ness

un•hap•py *adj.,* un•hap•pi•er, un•hap•pi•est.
un•har•ness *v.,* un•har•nessed, un•har•ness•ing.
un•health•y *adj.,* un•health•i•er, un•health•i•est.
un•heard
un•heard-of
un•hinge *v.,* un•hinged, un•hing•ing.
un•ho•ly *adj.,* un•ho•li•er, un•ho•li•est.
un•hook *v.,* un•hooked, un•hook•ing.
un•horse *v.,* un•horsed, un•hors•ing.
u•ni•cam•er•al
UNICEF (United Nations International Children's Emergency Fund, now "United Nations Children's Fund")
u•ni•corn
u•ni•cy•cle *v.,* u•ni•cy•cled, u•ni•cy•cling.
u•ni•fi•ca•tion
u•ni•form *v.,* u•ni•formed, u•ni•form•ing.
Uniform Com•mer•cial Code (UCC)
u•ni•form•i•ty
u•ni•form•ly
u•ni•fy *v.,* u•ni•fied, u•ni•fy•ing.
u•ni•lat•er•al
un•im•peach•a•ble
un•in•hib•it•ed

un•in•sur•a•ble risk *Business.*

un•in•tel•li•gent

un•in•ten•tion•al

un•in•ter•est•ed

un•ion

un•ion•ism

un•ion•ize *v.,* un•ion•ized, un•ion•iz•ing.

u•nique

u•nique•ly

u•ni•sex

u•ni•son

u•nit

u•nit trust *Business.*

U•ni•tar•i•an

u•nite *v.,* u•nit•ed, u•nit•ing.

U•nit•ed King•dom (UK)

United Na•tions (UN)

United States (US)

United States Em•ploy•ment Serv•ice (USES)

United States Trade•mark As•so•ci•a•tion (USTA)

u•nit•ize *v.,* u•nit•ized, u•nit•iz•ing.

u•ni•ty *n., pl.* u•ni•ties.

u•ni•va•lent

u•ni•ver•sal

U•ni•ver•sal Prod•uct Code (UPC) *Business.*

u•ni•ver•sal•ist

u•ni•ver•sal•i•ty

u•ni•ver•sal•ly

u•ni•verse

u•ni•ver•si•ty *n., pl.* u•ni•ver•si•ties.

UNIX *Computers.* (the operating system)

un•just

un•just•ly

un•kempt

un•kind *adj.,* un•kind•er, un•kind•est.

un•kind•ly

un•kind•ness

un•know•ing

un•known

un•lace *v.,* un•laced, un•lac•ing.

un•law•ful

un•law•ful•ly

un•law•ful•ness

un•learn *v.,* un•learned, un•learn•ing. (forgot knowledge of)

un•learn•ed (uneducated)

un•leash *v.,* un•leashed, un•leash•ing.

un•less

un•let•tered

un•like

un•like•li•hood

un•like•ly *adj.,* un•like•li•er, un•like•li•est.

un•lim•ber *v.,* un•lim•bered, un•lim•ber•ing.

un•lim•it•ed

un•load *v.,* un•load•ed, un•load•ing.

un•lock *v.,* un•locked, un•lock•ing.

un•looked-for

un•loose *v.,* un•loosed, un•loos•ing.

un•luck•i•ly

un•luck•i•ness

un•luck•y *adj.,* un•luck•i•er, un•luck•i•est.

un•make *v.,* un•made, un•mak•ing.

un•man *v.,* un•manned, un•man•ning.

un•man•ly *adj.,* un•man•li•er, un•man•li•est.

un•manned

un•man•ner•ly

un•mask *v.,* un•masked, un•mask•ing.

un•mean•ing

un•men•tion•a•ble

un•mer•ci•ful

un•mind•ful

un•mis•tak•a•ble

un•mis•tak•a•bly

un•mit•i•gat•ed

un•nat•u•ral

un•nat•u•ral•ly

un•nec•es•sar•i•ly

un•nec•es•sar•y

un•nerve *v.,* un•nerved, un•nerv•ing.

un•num•bered

un•oc•cu•pied

un•or•gan•ized

un•pack *v.,* un•packed, un•pack•ing.

un•par•al•leled

un•per•son

un•pin *v.,* un•pinned, un•pin•ning.

un•pleas•ant

un•pleas•ant•ly

un•pleas•ant•ness

un•plug *v.,* un•plugged, un•plug•ging.

un•plumbed

un•pop•u•lar

un•pop•u•lar•i•ty

un•prec•e•dent•ed

un•pre•dict•a○ble
un•prin•ci•pled
un•print•a○ble
un•pro•fes•sion○al
un•prof•it•a○ble
un•qual○i•fied
un•ques•tion•a○ble
un•quote v., un•quot○ed, un•quot•ing.
un•rav○el v., un•rav•eled or un•rav•elle
d, un•rav•el•ing or un•rav•el •ling.
un•read
un•re○al
un•rea•son•a○ble
un•rea•son•a○ble•ness
un•rea•son•a○bly
un•rea•son○ing
un•re•con•struct○ed
un•re•gen•er•ate
un•re•lent•ing
un•re•mit•ting
un•re•served
un•rest
un•ripe
un•ri•valed
un•roll v., un•rolled, un•roll○ing. (to display: cf. ENROLL)
un•ruf•fled
un•ru•li•ness
un•ru○ly adj., un•ru•li○er, un•ru•li•est.
un•sad○dle v., un•sad•dled, un•sad•dling.
un•sat○u•rat○ed
un•sa•vor○y
un•scathed
un•schooled
un•sci•en•tif○ic
un•scram•ble v., un•

scram•bled, un•scram•bling.
un•screw v., un•screwed, un•screw○ing.
un•scru•pu•lous
un•seal v., un•sealed, un•seal•ing.
un•sealed
un•sea•son•a○ble
un•seat v., un•seat○ed, un•seat•ing.
un•se•cured loan *Business.*
un•seem○ly adj., un•seem•li○er, un•seem•li•est.
un•self•ish
un•set○tle v., un•set•tled, un•set•tling.
un•shack○le v., un•shack•led, un•shack•ling.
un•sheathe v., un•sheathed, un•sheath•ing.
un•sight○ly
un•skilled
un•skill•ful
un•snap v., un•snapped, un•snap•ping.
un•snarl v., un•snarled, un•snarl•ing.
un•so•phis•ti•cat○ed
un•sound adj., un•sound○er, un•sound•est.
un•spar•ing
un•speak•a○ble
un•speak•a•bly
un•sta○ble
un•sta•bly
un•stead•i○ly
un•stead○i•ness

un•stead○y
un•stop v., un•stopped, un•stop•ping.
un•strung
un•stuck
un•stud•ied
un•sub•stan•tial
un•sung
un•tan•gle v., un•tan•gled, un•tan•gling.
un•taught
un•tax•a○ble *Business.*
un•taxed *Business.*
un•think•a○ble
un•think•ing
un•ti○dy adj., un•ti•di○er, un•ti•di•est.
un•tie v., un•tied, un•ty•ing.
un•til
un•time○ly
un○to
un•told
un•touch•a○ble
un•to○ward
un•true adj., un•tru○er, un•tru•est.
un•truth n., pl. un•truths.
un•truth•ful•ness
un•tu•tored
un•used
un•u○su○al
un•u○su•al○ly
un•ut•ter•a○ble
un•ut•ter•a•bly
un•var•nished
un•veil v., un•veiled, un•veil•ing.
un•voiced
un•want○ed (not wanted: cf. UNWONTED)
un•war○y

un•well
un•whole•some
un•whole•some•ness
un•wield•y
un•will•ing
un•will•ing•ly
un•wind v., un•wound, un•wind•ing.
un•wise adj., un•wis•er, un•wis•est.
un•wit•ting
un•wont•ed (rare: cf. UNWANTED)
un•wor•thi•ness
un•wor•thy
un•wrap v., un•wrapped, un•wrap•ping. (to uncover: cf. ENWRAP)
un•writ•ten
un•zip v., un•zipped, un•zip•ping.
up v., upped, up•ping.
up-and-com•ing
up-front
up-to-date
up•beat
up•braid v., up•braid•ed, up•braid•ing.
up•bring•ing
UPC Business. (Universal Product Code)
up•chuck v., up•chucked, up•chuck•ing.
up•com•ing
up•coun•try
up•date v., up•dat•ed, up•dat•ing.
up•draft
up•end v., up•end•ed, up•end•ing.
up•grade v., up•

grad•ed, up•grad•ing.
up•heav•al
up•hill
up•hold v., up•held, up•hold•ing.
up•hol•ster v., up•hol•stered, up•hol•ster•ing.
up•hol•ster•er
up•hol•ster•y
up•keep
up•land
up•lift v., up•lift•ed, up•lift•ing.
up•load v., up•load•ed, up•load•ing. Computers.
up•mar•ket Business.
up•on
up•per
upper man•age•ment Business.
Up•per Vol•ta
up•per•class•man n., pl. up•per•class•men.
up•per•cut v., up•per•cut, up•per•cut•ting.
up•per•most
up•pish
up•pi•ty
up•raise v., up•raised, up•rais•ing.
up•rear v., up•reared, up•rear•ing.
up•right v., up•right•ed, up•right•ing.
up•ris•ing
up•roar
up•roar•i•ous
up•root v., up•root•ed, up•root•ing.

UPS¹ Trademark. (United Postal Service)
UPS² Computers. (uninterruptible power supply)
up•scale Business.
up•set v., up•set, up•set•ting.
upset price Business.
up•shot
up•side
upside down adv., up•side-down adj.
up•si•lon
up•stage v., up•staged, up•stag•ing.
up•stairs
up•stand•ing
up•start
up•state
up•stream
up•stroke
up•surge v., up•surged, up•surg•ing.
up•swing v., up•swung, up•swing•ing.
up•take
up•tick Business.
up•tight
up•town
up•turn v., up•turned, up•turn•ing.
up•ward or up•wards
up•ward-com•pat•i•ble Computers.
up•ward•ly
u•ra•cil
U•ral Moun•tains n.
u•ran•ic
u•ra•ni•um
U•ra•nus
urb
ur•ban (of a city)

ur•bane (sophisticated)
ur•ban•i•ty
ur•ban•oi•za•tion
ur•ban•ize v., ur•ban•ized, ur•ban•iz•ing.
ur•chin
Ur•du
u•re•a
u•re•mi•a
u•re•mic
u•re•ter
u•re•thane
u•re•thra n., pl. u•re•thrae or u•re•thras.
u•re•thral
urge v., urged, urg•ing.
ur•gen•cy
ur•gent
ur•gent•ly
ur•gi•cen•ter
u•ric
u•ri•nal
u•ri•nal•y•sis n., pl. u•ri•nal•y•ses.
u•ri•nar•y
u•ri•nate v., u•ri•nat•ed, u•ri•nat•ing.
u•rine
urn (vase: cf. EARN)
u•ro•gen•i•tal
u•rol•o•gist
u•rol•o•gy
Ur•sa Ma•jor
Ursa Mi•nor
ur•sine
ur•ti•car•i•a

U•ru•guay
U•ru•guay•an
U.S. or US (United States).
us
USA or U.S.A. (United States of America).
us•a•bil•i•ty
us•a•ble or use•able
us•age
use v., used, us•ing.
use tax Business.
use•ful
use•ful•ly
use•ful•ness
use•less
use•less•ly
use•less•ness
us•er
us•er-de•fined Computers.
us•er-friend•ly Computers.
user group Computers.
user in•ter•face Computers.
us•er•name Computers.
USES (United States Employment Service)
ush•er v., ush•ered, ush•er•ing.
ush•er•ette
USTA Business. (United States Trademark Association)
u•su•al
u•su•al•ly
u•su•rer
u•su•ri•ous

u•surp v., u•surped, u•surp•ing.
u•sur•pa•tion
u•surp•er
u•su•ry
UT (Utah)
U•tah (UT)
U•tah•an
u•ten•sil
u•ter•ine
u•ter•us n., pl. u•ter•i or u•ter•us•es.
u•til•i•tar•i•an
u•til•i•ty n., pl. u•til•i•ties.
utility pro•gram Computers.
u•ti•li•za•tion
u•ti•lize v., u•ti•lized, u•ti•liz•ing.
ut•most
U•to•pi•a n., pl. U•to•pi•as.
U•to•pi•an
u•to•pi•an
ut•ter¹ adj. (absolute)
ut•ter² v., ut•tered, ut•ter•ing. (to speak)
ut•ter•ance
ut•ter•ly
ut•ter•most
u•vu•la, n., pl. u•vu•las or u•vu•lae.
u•vu•lar
ux•o•ri•ous
U•zi n., pl. U•zis.

V

V-∘Day (Victory Day)
V-∘necked
VA (Virginia)
va•can∘cy n., pl. va•
can∘cies.
va•cant
va•cate v., va•cat∘ed,
va•cat•ing.
va•ca•tion v., va•ca•
tioned, va•ca•tion•
ing.
va•ca•tion∘er
vac•ci•nate v., vac•
ci•nat∘ed, vac•ci•
nat•ing.
vac•ci•na•tion
vac•cine
vac•il•late v., vac•il•
lat∘ed, vac•il•lat•
ing.
vac•il•la•tion
va•cu•i∘ty
vac∘u•ous
vac∘u•ous∘ly
vac∘u•um n., pl.
vac∘u•ums or
vac∘u•a; v., vac∘u•
umed, vac∘u•um•
ing.
vacuum clean∘er
vac∘u•um-packed
va∘de me•cum n., pl.
va∘de me•cums.
Va•duz
vag∘a•bond
va•gar∘y n., pl. va•
gar•ies.
va•gi•na n., pl. va•
gi•nas or va•gi•nae.
vag∘i•nal
va•gran∘cy
va•grant

vague adj., va•guer,
va•guest.
vague∘ly
vague•ness
vain adj., vain•er,
vain•est. (conceited;
futile: cf. VANE; VEIN)
vain•glo•ri∘ous
vain•glo∘ry
vain∘ly
val•ance (short drape:
cf. VALENCE)
vale (valley: cf. VEIL)
val∘e∘dic•to•ri∘an
val∘e∘dic•to∘ry n., pl.
val∘e∘dic•to•ries.
va•lence (chemical
combining power: cf.
VALANCE)
Va•len•ci∘a
Va•len•ci∘ennes
val•en•tine
val∘et v., val•et∘ed,
val•et•ing.
Val•hal∘la
val•iance
val•iant
val•iant∘ly
val∘id
val∘i•date v., val∘i•
dat∘ed, val∘i•dat•
ing.
val∘i•da•tion
va•lid•i∘ty
val∘id∘ly
va•lise
Val•i∘um Trademark.
Val•kyr∘ie
Val•let∘ta
val•ley n., pl. val•
leys.
val∘or
val•or∘ous

val•or•ous∘ly
val∘u•a•ble
val∘u•a•tion
val∘ue v., val∘ued,
val∘u•ing.
value-add∘ed tax
(VAT) Business.
val∘ue•less
valve
va•moose v., va•
moosed, va•moos•
ing.
vamp v., vamped,
vamp•ing.
vam•pire
van
Van Al•len belt
Van Bu•ren
van Gogh
va•na•di∘um
Van•cou•ver
van•dal
van•dal•ism
van•dal•ize v., van•
dal•ized, van•dal•
iz•ing.
Vandyke beard
vane (blade: cf. VAIN;
VEIN)
van•guard
va•nil∘la
van•ish v., van•ished,
van•ish•ing.
van•i∘ty n., pl. van•
i•ties.
van•quish v., van•
quished, van•quish•
ing.
van•tage
Va•nu•a∘tu
Va•nu•a•tu∘an
vap∘id

va•pid•i•ty or vap•
id•ness
va•por
va•por•i•za•tion
va•por•ize v., va•
por•ized, va•por•
iz•ing.
va•por•ous
va◦por•ware Comput-
ers.
va•que◦ro n., pl. va•
que•ros.
var◦i•a•bil•i•ty
var◦i•a◦ble
var◦i•a◦ble-length
field Computers.
var◦i•a◦ble life Busi-
ness.
var◦i•a◦ble-rate Busi-
ness.
var◦i•a•bly
var◦i•ance
var◦i•ant
var◦i•a◦tion
var◦i•col•ored
var◦i◦cose
var•ied
var◦i•e•gate v.,
var◦i•e•gat◦ed,
var◦i•e•gat•ing.
var◦i•e•gat◦ed
va•ri•e•tal
va•ri•e◦ty n., pl. va•
ri•e•ties.
variety store Business.
var◦i◦ous
var◦i•ous◦ly
var•let
var•mint
var•nish v., var•
nished, var•nish•
ing.
var•si◦ty n., pl. var•
si•ties.
var◦y v., var•ied,
var◦y•ing. (to alter:
cf. VERY)

vas•cu•lar
vase
va•sec•to◦my n., pl.
va•sec•to•mies.
Vas◦e◦line Trademark.
vas◦o•mo•tor
vas•sal (feudal tenant:
cf. VESSEL)
vas•sal•age
vast adj., vast◦er,
vast•est.
vast◦ly
vast•ness
VAT Business. (value-
added tax)
vat
Vat◦i•can
Vatican Cit◦y
vaude•ville
vaude•vil•lian
vault v., vault◦ed,
vault•ing.
vault◦er
vaunt v., vaunt◦ed,
vaunt•ing.
VCR (videocassette re-
corder)
VD (venereal disease)
VDT Computers. (video
display terminal)
veal
vec•tor v., vec•tored,
vec•tor•ing.
vec•tor graph•ics
Computers.
vec•to•ri◦al
Ve◦da n., pl. Ve•das.
Ve•dan◦ta
Ve•dan•tic
Ve◦dic
veep
veer v., veered, veer•
ing.
veg◦e•ta◦ble
veg◦e•tar◦i◦an
veg◦e•tar◦i•an•ism

veg◦e•tate v., veg◦e•
tat◦ed, veg◦e•tat•
ing.
veg◦e•ta•tion
veg◦e•ta•tive
ve•he•mence
ve•he•ment
ve•he•ment◦ly
ve•hi•cle
ve•hic◦u•lar
veil v., veiled, veil•
ing. (something that
conceals; to veil: cf.
VALE)
vein v., veined, vein•
ing. (blood vessel: cf.
VAIN; VANE)
ve•lar
Vel•cro Trademark.
veld or veldt
vel•lum
ve•loc•i◦ty n., pl. ve•
loc•i•ties.
ve•lour or ve•lours
ve•lum n., pl. ve◦la.
vel•vet
vel•vet•een
vel•vet◦y
ve•nal (mercenary: cf.
VENIAL)
ve•nal•i◦ty
vend v., vend◦ed,
vend•ing.
vend◦ee Business.
ven•det◦ta n., pl.
ven•det•tas.
ven•dor Business.
ve•neer
ven•er•a◦ble
ven•er•ate v., ven•
er•at◦ed, ven•er•
at•ing.
ven•er•a•tion
ve•ne•re◦al
venereal dis•ease
Ve•ne•tian

ve•ne•tian blind
Ven•e•zue•la
Ven•e•zue•lan
venge•ance
venge•ful
venge•ful•ly
ve•ni•al (forgivable: cf. VENAL)
Ven•ice
ve•ni•re•man n., pl. ve•ni•re•men.
ven•i•son
ven•om
ven•om•ous
ve•nous
vent v., vent•ed, vent•ing.
ven•ti•late v., ven•ti•lat•ed, ven•ti•lat•ing.
ven•ti•la•tion
ven•ti•la•tor
ven•tral
ven•tri•cle
ven•tric•u•lar
ven•tril•o•quism
ven•tril•o•quist
ven•ture v., ven•tured, ven•tur•ing.
venture cap•i•tal Business.
venture cap•i•tal•ist Business.
ven•ture•some
ven•ue
Ve•nus n., pl. Ve•nus•es.
Ve•nu•si•an
ve•ra•cious (truthful: cf. VORACIOUS)
ve•rac•i•ty n., pl. ve•rac•i•ties.
ve•ran•da or ve•ran•dah n., pl. ve•ran•das or ve•ran•dahs.
verb

ver•bal
ver•bal•oi•za•tion
ver•bal•ize v., ver•bal•ized, ver•bal•iz•ing.
ver•bal•ly
ver•ba•tim
ver•be•na n., pl. ver•be•nas.
ver•bi•age
ver•bose
ver•bos•i•ty
ver•bo•ten
ver•dant
Ver•di
ver•dict
ver•di•gris
ver•dure
verge v., verged, verg•ing.
verg•er
ver•i•est
ver•i•fi•a•ble
ver•i•fi•ca•tion
ver•i•fy v., ver•i•fied, ver•i•fy•ing.
ver•i•ly
ver•i•si•mil•i•tude
ver•i•ta•ble
ver•i•ta•bly
vé•ri•té (cinéma vérité)
ver•i•ty n., pl. ver•i•ties. (truth)
ver•meil
ver•mi•cel•li
ver•mic•u•lite
ver•mi•form
ver•mil•ion
ver•min n., pl. ver•min.
ver•min•ous
Ver•mont (VT)
Ver•mont•er
ver•mouth
ver•nac•u•lar

ver•nal
ver•ni•er
Ver•nier
ve•ron•i•ca n., pl. ve•ron•i•cas.
Ver•sailles
ver•sa•tile
ver•sa•til•i•ty
verse
versed
ver•si•cle
ver•si•fi•ca•tion
ver•si•fi•er
ver•si•fy v., ver•si•fied, ver•si•fy•ing.
ver•sion
ver•so n., pl. ver•sos.
ver•sus
ver•te•bra n., pl. ver•te•brae or ver•te•bras.
ver•te•bral
ver•te•brate
ver•tex n., pl. ver•tex•es or ver•ti•ces.
ver•ti•cal
vertical in•te•gra•tion Business.
vertical jus•ti•fi•ca•tion Computers.
vertical merg•er Business.
vertical scroll•ing Computers.
ver•ti•cal•ly
ver•tig•i•nous
ver•ti•go n., pl. ver•ti•goes or ver•tig•i•nes.
verve
ver•y (extremely: cf. VARY)
very high fre•quen•cy (VHF)
very low fre•quen•cy (VLF)
ves•i•cle

ve•sic•u•lar
ves•per
Ves•puc•ci
ves•sel (ship; container: cf. VASSAL)
vest v., vest•ed, vest•ing.
vest-pock•et
Ves•ta
ves•tal
vest•ed
vested in•ter•est *Business.*
ves•ti•bule
ves•tige
ves•tig•i•al
vest•ing *Business.*
vest•ment
ves•try n., pl. ves•tries.
Ve•su•vi•an
Ve•su•vi•us
vet¹ (animal doctor)
vet² v., vet•ted, vet•ting. *(to appraise)*
vetch
vet•er•an
vet•er•i•nar•i•an
vet•er•i•nar•y n., pl. vet•er•i•nar•ies.
ve•to n., pl. ve•toes; v., ve•toed, ve•to•ing.
vex v., vexed, vex•ing.
vex•a•tion
vex•a•tious
VGA (video graphics array)
VHF (very high frequency)
vi•a
vi•a•bil•i•ty
vi•a•ble
vi•a•duct
Vi•ag•ra *Trademark.*

vi•al (bottle: cf. VILE; VIOL)
vi•and
vibes n., pl.
vi•bra•harp
vi•bran•cy
vi•brant
vi•brant•ly
vi•bra•phone
vi•bra•phon•ist
vi•brate v., vi•brat•ed, vi•brat•ing.
vi•bra•tion
vi•bra•to n., pl. vi•bra•tos.
vi•bra•tor
vi•bur•num
vic•ar
vic•ar•age
vi•car•i•ous
vi•car•i•ous•ly
vice (evil practice: cf. VISE)
vice-ad•mi•ral
vice-ad•mi•ral•ty
vice pres•i•dent or vice-pres•i•dent
vi•ce ver•sa
vice•ge•rent
vice•roy
vi•chys•soise
vi•cin•i•ty n., pl. vi•cin•i•ties.
vi•cious
vicious cir•cle
vi•cious•ly
vi•cious•ness
vi•cis•si•tude
vic•tim
vic•tim•i•za•tion
vic•tim•ize v., vic•tim•ized, vic•tim•iz•ing.
vic•tor
Vic•to•ri•a

Vic•to•ri•an
Vic•to•ri•an•ism
vic•to•ri•ous
vic•to•ry n., pl. vic•to•ries.
vict•ual v., vict•ualed or vict•ualled, vict•ual•ing or vict•ual•ling.
vi•cu•na or vi•cu•ña n., pl. vi•cu•nas or vi•cu•ñas.
vi•de
vid•e•o n., pl. vid•e•os.
video a•dapt•er *Computers.*
video dis•play ter•mi•nal (VDT) *Computers.*
video game
video mode *Computers.*
video stand•ard *Computers.*
vid•e•o•cas•sette
videocassette re•cord•er (VCR)
vid•e•o•disc
vid•e•og•ra•pher
vid•e•o•tape v., vid•e•o•taped, vid•e•o•tap•ing.
vid•e•o•tex or vid•e•o•text *Computers.*
vie v., vied, vy•ing.
Vi•en•na
Vi•en•nese n., pl. Vi•en•nese.
Vien•tiane
Vi•et•nam or Vi•et Nam
Vi•et•nam•ese
view v., viewed, view•ing.
view•er

view•find∘er
view•point
vig∘il
vig∘i•lance
vig∘i•lant
vig∘i•lan∘te n., pl. vig∘i•lan•tes.
vig∘i•lan•tism
vi•gnette
vig∘or
vig∘or•ous
Vi•king
Vi∘la
vile adj., vil∘er, vil•est. (very bad: cf. VIAL; VIOL)
vile•ness
vil∘i•fi•ca•tion
vil∘i∘fy v., vil∘i•fied, vil∘i•fy•ing.
vil∘la n., pl. vil•las.
vil•lage
vil•lag∘er
vil•lain (scoundrel)
vil•lain•ous
vil•lain∘y n., pl. vil•lain•ies.
vil•lein (serf)
vil•lein•age
vim
vin n., pl. vins.
vin•ai•grette
Vin∘ci
vin•di•cate v., vin•di•cat∘ed, vin•di•cat∘ing.
vin•di•ca•tion
vin•dic•ta•tive (justifying)
vin•dic•tive (vengeful)
vin•dic•tive•ly
vin•dic•tive•ness
vine
vin∘e∘gar
vin∘e∘gar∘y
vine•yard

vi∘no
vi•nous
vin•tage
vint•ner
vi•nyl
vi∘ol (string instrument: cf. VIAL; VILE)
vi•o∘la n., pl. vi•o•las. (string instrument; the flower: cf. VOILÀ)
vi•o•late v., vi•o•lat∘ed, vi•o•lat∘ing.
vi•o•la•tion (transgression: cf. VOLITION)
vi•o•lence
vi•o•lent
vi•o•lent∘ly
vi•o•let
vi•o•lin
vi•o•lin•ist
vi•ol•ist
vi•o∘lon•cel•list
vi•o∘lon•cel∘lo n., pl. vi•o∘lon•cel•los.
VIP or V.I.P. (very important person).
vi•per
vi•per•ous
vi•ra∘go n., pl. vi•ra•goes or vi•ra•gos.
vi•ral
vir∘e∘o n., pl. vir•e∘os.
Vir•gil
vir•gin
Vir•gin Mar∘y
vir•gin•al
Vir•gin∘ia (VA)
Vir•gin•ian
vir•gin•i∘ty
Vir∘go
vir•gule
vi•rile
vi•ril•i∘ty
vi•rol∘o•gist
vi•rol∘o∘gy

vir•tu•al
virtual disk Computers.
virtual mem∘o∘ry Computers.
virtual re•al∘i∘ty Computers.
vir•tu•al∘ly
vir•tue
vir•tu•os•i∘ty (skill)
vir•tu•o∘so n., pl. vir•tu•o∘sos or vir•tu•o∘si.
vir•tu•ous
vir•tu•ous∘ly
vir•tu•ous•ness (virtue)
vir∘u•lence
vir∘u•lent
vi•rus n., pl. vi•rus∘es.
vi•rus•oid
vis-à-vis _n., pl._ vis-à-vis _prep phrase_
vi•osa n., pl. vi•sas, vi•saed, vi•sa∘ing.
vis•age
vis•cer∘a n., pl. vis•cus.
vis•cer•al
vis•cid
vis•cose
vis•cos•i∘ty n., pl. vis•cos•i•ties.
vis•count
vis•count•ess
vis•cous
vise (clamp: cf. VICE)
Vish∘nu
vis•i•bil•i∘ty
vis•i•ble
vis•i•bly
vi•sion
vi•sion•ar∘y n., pl. vi•sion•ar•ies.
vis∘it v., vis•it∘ed, vis•it•ing.

vis•it•ant
vis•it•a•tion
vis•oi•tor
vi•sor or vi•zor v., vi•sored or vi•zored, vi•sor•ing or vi•zor•ing.
vis•ta n., pl. vis•tas.
vis•u•al
vis•u•al•i•za•tion
vis•u•al•ize v., vis•u•al•ized, vis•u•al•iz•ing.
vis•u•al•ly
vi•tal
vi•tal•i•ty
vi•tal•ize v., vi•tal•ized, vi•tal•iz•ing.
vi•tal•ly
vi•tals
vi•ta•min
vi•ti•ate v., vi•ti•ated, vi•ti•at•ing.
vit•i•cul•ture
vit•re•ous
vit•ri•ol
vi•tu•per•a•tion
vi•tu•per•a•tive
vi•va
vi•va•ce
vi•va•cious
vi•va•cious•ly
vi•vac•i•ty
viv•id
viv•id•ly
viv•id•ness
viv•oi•fy v., viv•i•fied, viv•i•fy•ing.
vi•vip•a•rous
viv•i•sec•tion
vix•en
vix•en•ish
viz.
vi•zier
VLF or **vlf** (very low frequency).

VLSI Computers. (very large-scale integration)
vo•ca•ble
vo•cab•u•lar•oy n., pl. vo•cab•u•lar•ies.
vo•cal
vo•cal•ic
vo•cal•ist
vo•cal•i•za•tion
vo•cal•ize v., vo•cal•ized, vo•cal•iz•ing.
vo•cal•ly
vo•ca•tion (career: cf. AVOCATION)
vo•ca•tion•al
voc•a•tive
vo•cif•er•ate v., vo•cif•er•at•ed, vo•cif•er•at•ing.
vo•cif•er•a•tion
vo•cif•er•ous
vo•cif•er•ous•ly
vod•ka
vogue
vo•guing
vogu•ish
voice v., voiced, voic•ing.
voice mail Computers.
voice-o•ver
voice rec•og•ni•tion Computers.
voice/•da•ta switch Computers.
voice•less
voice•print
void v., void•ed, void•ing.
void•a•ble
voi•là or voi•la (behold!: cf. VIOLA).
voile
vol. (volume)
vol•a•tile
volatile mem•o•ry Computers.

volatile stock Business.
vol•a•til•i•ty
vol•can•ic
vol•can•ism
vol•ca•no n., pl. vol•ca•noes or vol•ca•nos.
vole
Vol•ga
vo•li•tion (act of willing: cf. VOLITION)
vo•li•tion•al
vol•ley n., pl. vol•leys; v., vol•leyed, vol•ley•ing.
vol•ley•ball
volt
volt•age
vol•ta•ic
Vol•taire
volt•me•ter
vol•u•bil•i•ty
vol•u•ble
vol•u•bly
vol•ume
volume la•bel Computers.
vol•u•met•ric
vo•lu•mi•nous
vo•lu•mi•nous•ly
vol•un•tar•i•ly
vol•un•ta•rism
vol•un•tar•oy
vol•un•teer v., vol•un•teered, vol•un•teer•ing.
vo•lup•tu•ar•oy n., pl. vo•lup•tu•ar•ies.
vo•lup•tu•ous
vo•lup•tu•ous•ness
vom•it v., vom•it•ed, vom•it•ing.
voo•doo n., pl. voo•doos; v., voo•dooed, voo•doo•ing.
voo•doo•ism

vo•ra•cious (greedy: cf. VERACIOUS)

vo•ra•cious•ly

vo•rac•i•ty

vor•tex n., pl. vor•tex•es, vor•ti•ces.

vo•ta•ry n., pl. vo•ta•ries.

vote v., vot•ed, vot•ing.

vot•er

vo•tive

vouch v., vouched, vouch•ing.

vouch•er v., vouch•ered, vouch•er•ing. *Business.*

vouch•safe v., vouch•safed, vouch•saf•ing.

vow v., vowed, vow•ing.

vow•el

vox po•pu•li

voy•age v., voy•aged, voy•ag•ing.

voy•ag•er

vo•ya•geur n., pl. vo•ya•geurs.

voy•eur

voy•eur•ism

voy•eur•is•tic

VRAM (video RAM)

vs. (versus)

VT (Vermont)

Vul•can

vul•can•i•za•tion

vul•can•ize v., vul•can•ized, vul•can•iz•ing.

vul•gar

vul•gar•i•an

vul•gar•ism

vul•gar•i•ty n., pl. vul•gar•i•ties.

vul•gar•i•za•tion

vul•gar•ize v., vul•gar•ized, vul•gar•iz•ing.

vul•gar•ly

Vul•gate

vul•ner•a•bil•i•ty

vul•ner•a•ble

vul•ner•a•bly

vul•pine

vul•ture

vul•tur•ine

vul•va n., pl. vul•vae or vul•vas.

vul•val or vul•var

vul•vi•form

vy•ing

W

WA (Washington)

wab•ble v., wab•bled, wab•bling.

Wac (Women's Army Corps member)

wack•i•ly

wack•i•ness

wack•y adj., wack•i•er, wack•i•est.

wad v., wad•ded, wad•ding.

wad•dle v., wad•dled, wad•dling.

wade v., wad•ed, wad•ing. (to walk through resistant material: cf. WEIGHED)

wad•ers

Waf (Women in the Air Force)

wa•fer

wa•fer•like

waf•fle v., waf•fled, waf•fling.

waft v., waft•ed, waft•ing.

wag v., wagged, wag•ging.

wage v., waged, wag•ing.

wage con•trol *Business.*

wage•less

wa•ger v., wa•gered, wa•ger•ing.

wa•ger•er

wag•ger•y

wag•gish

wag•gish•ly

wag•gish•ness

wag•gle v., wag•gled, wag•gling.

waggle dance

Wag•ner

wag•on

wa•hi•ne n., pl. wa•hi•ne.

wa•hoo n., pl. wa•hoos or wa•hoo.

waif

wail v., wailed, wail•ing. (to cry: cf. WALE; WHALE)

wail•ing•ly

wain•scot•ing

wain•wright

waist (narrowest part of torso: cf. WASTE)

waist•band

waist•coat

waist•line

wait v., wait•ed, wait•ing. (to stay: cf. WEIGHT)

wait state *Computers.*

wait•er

wait•ress
wait•ron
waive v., waived, waiv•ing. (to forgo: cf. WAVE)
waiv•er (relinquishment: cf. WAVER)
wake v., waked or woke, waked or wok○en, wak•ing.
wake•ful
wake•ful•ness
wak○en v., wak•ened, wak•en•ing.
Wal•dorf sal○ad
wale v., waled, wal•ing. (ridge: cf. WAIL; WHALE)
Wales
walk v., walked, walk•ing.
walk-in
walk-on
walk-up
walk•a○way
walk○ie-talk○ie or walk○y-talk○y, n., pl. walk○ie-talk○ies.
walk•out or walk•out
walk•o○ver
walk•way
wall v., walled, wall•ing.
wall-like
wal•la○by n., pl. wal•la•bies or wal•la○by.
wall•board
wal•let
wall•eye n., pl. wall•eyes or wall•eye.
wall•flow○er
Wal•loon
wal•lop v., wal•loped, wal•lop•ing.
wal•lop•ing

wal•low v., wal•lowed, wal•low•ing.
wall•pa•per v., wall•pa•pered, wall•pa•per•ing.
Wall Street Business.
wal•ly•ball
wal•nut
wal•rus n., pl. wal•rus○es or wal•rus.
waltz v., waltzed, waltz•ing.
waltz•like
wam•pum
wan
WAN (wide-area network)
wand
wan•der v., wan•dered, wan•der•ing. (to roam: cf. WONDER)
wan•der○er
wan•der○lust
wand•like
wane v., waned, wan•ing.
wan•gle v., wan•gled, wan•gling.
wan•na○be or wan○na•bee, n., pl. wan○na•bes or wan○na•bees.
wan•ness
want v., want○ed, want•ing. (to desire: cf. WONT; WON'T)
want ad
wan•ton (unjustifiable: cf. WON TON or WON-TON)
wan•ton•ly
wan•ton•ness
wap○i○ti n., pl. wap○i•tis or wap○i○ti.
war v., warred, war•ring. (armed conflict;

to fight a war: cf. WORE)
war-horse
war•ble v., war•bled, war•bling.
war•bler
war bond Business.
war•bon•net or war bon•net
ward v., ward○ed, ward•ing. (division; to avert: cf. WARRED)
war•den
ward○er
ward•robe
ward•room
ware (merchandise: cf. WEAR; WARE)
ware•house n., pl. ware•hous○es; v., ware•housed, ware•hous•ing. Business.
warehouse re•ceipt Business.
wares
war•fare
war•fa•rin
war•head
war•i○ly
war○i•ness
war•like
war•lock
war•lord
warm v., warmed, warm•ing; adj., warm○er, warm•est.
warm-blood○ed or warm•blo od○ed
warm-blood○ed○ness
warm boot Computers.
warm-heart○ed or warm•heart○ed
warm-heart○ed•ly
warm-heart○ed○ness
warmed-o○ver
warm○er
warm○ly

warm•ness
war•mon•ger
war•mon•ger•ing
warmth
warm◦up or warm-up
warn *v.*, warned,
warn•ing.
warn◦er (one who warns)
War•ner (last name)
warn•ing
warn•ing•ly
warp *v.*, warped,
warp•ing.
warp speed
war•path
war•plane
war•rant *v.*, war•
rant◦ed, war•rant•
ing.
war•rant•less
war•ran•tor *Business.*
war•ran•ty *n., pl.*
war•ran•ties; *v.*;
war•ran•tied, war•
ran•ty•ing. *Business.*
warranty deed *Business.*
warred (fought: cf.
WARD)
war•ren
war•ri◦or
War•saw
war•ship
wart
wart•hog
war•time
war◦y *adj.*, war•i◦er,
war•i•est.
was
wash *v.*, washed,
wash•ing.
wash-and-wear
wash•a•bil•i◦ty
wash•a◦ble
wash•board

wash•bowl
wash•cloth *n., pl.*
wash•cloths.
washed-out
washed-up
wash◦er
wash◦er•wom◦an *n.,
pl.* wash◦er•
wom◦en.
wash◦i•ness
wash•ing
washing ma•chine
Wash•ing•ton (WA)
wash•out
wash•room
wash•stand
wash•tub
wash•wom◦an *n., pl.*
wash•wom◦en.
was◦n't (was not)
WASP or Wasp (white
Anglo-Saxon Protes-
tant)
wasp (insect)
wasp-waist◦ed
wasp•ish
was•sail
Was•ser•mann test
wast (archaic "was")
wast•age
waste *v.*, wast◦ed,
wast•ing. (to squan-
der: cf. WAIST)
waste•bas•ket
waste•ful
waste•ful•ly
waste•ful•ness
waste•land
waste•pa◦per
wast•rel
watch *v.*, watched,
watch•ing.
watch•band
watch•dog *v.*, watch•
dogged, watch•
dog•ging.

watch◦er
watch•ful
watch•ful•ly
watch•ful•ness
watch•mak◦er
watch•mak•ing
watch•man *n., pl.*
watch•men.
watch•tow◦er
watch•word
wa•ter *v.*, wa◦tered,
wa•ter•ing.
wa◦ter-cool *v.*,
wa◦ter-cooled,
wa◦ter-cool◦ing.
wa◦ter-re◦pel•lent
wa◦ter-re◦sist◦ant
wa◦ter-ski *v.*, wa◦ter-
skied, wa◦ter-
ski◦ing.
wa◦ter-ski◦er
wa•ter ta•ble or
wa◦ter•ta◦ble
wa◦ter•bed
wa◦ter•borne
Wa◦ter•bur◦y
wa◦ter•col◦or
wa◦ter•col◦or•ist
wa◦ter•course
wa◦ter•craft
wa◦ter•cress
wa•tered stock *Busi-
ness.*
wa◦ter•fall
wa◦ter•fowl *n., pl.*
wa◦ter•fowls or
wa◦ter•fowl.
wa◦ter•front
Wa◦ter•gate
wa◦ter◦i•ness
wa◦ter•less
wa•ter line or
wa◦ter•line
wa◦ter•logged
Wa•ter•loo
wa◦ter•mark

wa∘ter•marked
wa∘ter•mel∘on
wa•ter pow∘er or wa∘ter•pow∘er
wa∘ter•proof v., wa∘ter•proofed, wa∘ter•proof•ing.
wa∘ter•shed
wa∘ter•side
wa∘ter•spout
wa∘ter•tight
wa∘ter•way
wa∘ter•wheel or wa•ter wheel
wa∘ter•works n., pl. wa∘ter•works.
wa•ter∘y
WATS (Wide Area Telecommunications Service)
watt
watt•age
wat•tle
wat•tled
wave v., waved, wav•ing. (surging movement: cf. WAIVE)
wave•length or wave length
wave•like
wa•ver[1] v., wa•vered, wa•ver•ing. (to vacillate: cf. WAIVER)
wav∘er[2] (one who waves)
wa•ver∘er
wa•ver•ing∘ly
wav∘i•ness
wav∘y adj., wav•i∘er, wav•i•est.
wax v., waxed, wax•ing.
wax pa•per
wax∘en
wax∘i•ness
wax•like
wax•wing

wax•works
wax∘y adj., wax•i∘er, wax•i•est.
way (manner: cf. WEIGH; WHEY)
way-out
way•bill Business.
way•far∘er
way•lay v., way•laid, way•lay•ing.
way•side
way•ward
way•ward∘ly
way•ward•ness
way•worn
we, us, our, ours. (plural of "I": cf. WEE)
weak adj., weak∘er, weak•est. (not strong: cf. WEEK)
weak-kneed
weak∘en v., weak•ened, weak•en•ing.
weak•fish n., pl. weak•fish or weak•fish•es.
weak•ling
weak∘ly (sickly: cf. WEEKLY)
weak•ness
weal (well-being: cf. WE'LL; WHEAL; WHEEL)
wealth
wealth∘y adj., wealth•i∘er, wealth•i•est.
wean v., weaned, wean•ing.
weap∘on
weap•oned
weap•on•less
weap•on∘ry
wear v., wore, worn, wear•ing. (have on the body: cf. WARE; WHERE)
wear∘er

wea•ri∘ly
wea•ri•ness
wea•ri•some
wea∘ry v., wea•ried, wea•ry∘ing; adj., wea•ri∘er, wea•ri•est.
wea•ry•ing∘ly
wea•sel n., pl. wea•sels or wea∘sel; v., wea•seled, wea•sel•ing.
wea•sel word
wea∘sel-word∘ed
wea•sel∘ly adj.
weath∘er v., weath•ered, weath•er•ing. (atmospheric condition; to endure: cf. WHETHER)
weath∘er-beat∘en
weath∘er-bound
weath∘er-strip or weath∘er strip[1] n.
weath∘er-strip[2] v., weath∘er-stripped, weath∘er-strip∘ping.
weath∘er vane or weath∘er•vane
weath∘er-wise
weath∘er•board
weath∘er•cock
weath∘er•glass
weath•er•ing
weath•er•ize v., weath•er•ized, weath•er•iz∘ing.
weath∘er•proof v., weath∘er•proofed, weath∘er•proof•ing.
weath∘er•worn
weave v., wove or weaved, wo•ven or wove, weav•ing.
Wea•ver (last name)

weav○er (one who weaves)
web
web-foot○ed
webbed
web•bing
web•foot n., pl. web•feet.
web•like
Web•ster
we'd (we would)
wed v., wed•ded or wed, wed•ding.
wedge v., wedged, wedg○ing.
wedge•like
wed•lock
Wednes•day
wee (tiny: cf. WE)
weed v., weed○ed, weed•ing.
weed○i•ness
weed•less
weed•like
weed○y adj., weed•i○er, weed•i•est.
week (seven successive days: cf. WEAK)
week•day
week•end v., week•end○ed, week•end•ing.
week○ly n., pl. week•lies. (once a week; a weekly publication: cf. WEAKLY)
wee•nie or wie•nie
wee○ny
weep v., wept, weep•ing.
weep○i•ness
weep•ing
weep○y adj., weep•i○er, weep•i•est.
wee•vil
weft
weigh v., weighed,

weigh•ing. (to measure heaviness: cf. WAY; WHEY)
weighed (did weigh: cf. WADE)
weight v., weight○ed, weight•ing. (heaviness; to add weight to: cf. WAIT)
weight•i○ly
weight○i•ness
weight•less
weight•less○ly
weight•less•ness
weight•lift○er
weight•lift•ing
weight○y adj., weight•i○er, weight•i•est.
weir
weird adj., weird○er, weird•est.
weird○ly
weird•ness
weird○o n., pl. weird○os.
welch v., welched, welch•ing.
welch○er
wel•come v., wel•comed, wel•com•ing.
weld v., weld○ed, weld•ing.
weld○er
wel•fare
welfare state
wel•kin
we'll (we will: cf. WEAL; WHEAL; WHEEL)
well v., welled, well•ing;. adj., bet•ter, best.
well-ad○vised
well-ap○point○ed
well-bal○anced
well-be○ing

well-bred
well-de○fined
well-dis○posed
well-done
well-fa○vored
well-fed
well-fixed
well-found○ed
well-groomed
well-ground○ed
well-heeled
well-in○formed
well-in○ten○tioned
well-knit
well-known
well-man○nered
well-mean○ing
well-nigh
well-off
well-or○dered
well-read
well-round○ed
well-spo○ken
well-thought-of
well-timed
well-to-do
well-turned
well-wish○er
well-wish○ing
well-worn
well•born
well•head
Wel•ling•ton
well•ness
well•spring
Welsh
welsh or welch v., welshed or welched, welsh•ing or welch•ing
Welsh cor○gi
Welsh rab•bit
welsh○er
welt
wel•ter v., wel•tered, wel•ter•ing.

wel•ter•weight

wen

wench

wend *v.*, wend○ed, wend•ing.

went

wept

we're

were○n't

were•wolf *n.*, pl. were•wolves.

wert

Wes•ley

west

West Bank

West Virgin○ia (WV)

west•er•li•ness

west•er•ly *n.*, pl. west•er•lies.

west•ern

West•ern○er

west•ern○i•za•tion

west•ern•ize *v.*, west•ern•ized, west•ern•iz•ing.

west•ward

wet *v.*, wet•ted, wet•ting; *adj.*, wet•ter, wet•test. (to moisten; moistened: cf. WHET)

wet nurse *n.*

wet-nurse *v.*, wet-nursed, wet-nurs○ing.

wet•ness

we've

whack *v.*, whacked, whack•ing.

whack○y *adj.*, whack○i•er, whack•i•est.

whale[1] *v.*, whaled, whal•ing. (to thrash)

whale[2] *n.*, pl. whales or whale. (the mammal: cf. WAIL; WALE)

whale•boat

whale•bone

whale•like

whal○er

wham *v.*, whammed, wham•ming.

wham○my *n.*, pl. wham•mies.

wharf *n.*, pl. wharves or wharfs.

wharf•age

what

what-if

what-if a○nal○y•sis *Computers.*

what•ev○er

what•not

what•so•ev○er

wheal (swelling: cf. WEAL; WE'LL; WHEEL)

wheat

whee•dle *v.*, whee•dled, whee•dling.

whee•dler

whee•dling○ly

wheel *v.*, wheeled, wheel•ing. (disk on axis; to wheel: cf. WEAL; WE'LL; WHEAL)

wheel•bar•row

wheel•base

wheel•chair

wheel○er-deal○er

wheel•wright

wheeze *v.*, wheezed, wheez•ing.

wheez○y *adj.*, wheez•i○er, wheez•i•est.

whelk

whelp

when

whence (cf. HENCE; THENCE)

when•ev○er

where (at what place: cf. WARE; WEAR)

where•a•bouts

where○as *n.*, pl. where•as○es.

where○at

where○by

where•fore

where•from

where○in

where○of

where○on

where•so•ev○er

where○to

where•up○on

wher•ev○er

where•with

where•with○al

wher○ry *n.*, pl. wher•ries.

whet *v.*, whet•ted, whet•ting. (to sharpen: cf. WET)

wheth○er (if: cf. WEATHER)

whet•stone

whew

whey (part of milk: cf. WAY; WEIGH)

which (what one: cf. WITCH)

which•ev○er

which•so•ev○er

whiff *v.*, whiffed, whiff•ing.

Whig

Whig•gish

while *n., v.*, whiled, whil•ing. (interval; to spend, as time: cf. WILE)

whiles

whi•lom

whilst

whim

whim•per *v.*, whim•pered, whim•per•ing.

whim•per○er

whim•per•ing○ly

whim•si•cal

whim•si•cal•i•ty
whim•si•cal•ly
whim•sy or whim•sey n., pl. whim•sies or whim•seys
whine v., whined, whin•ing. (complaining sound; to whine: cf. WINE)
whin•er
whin•ing•ly
whin•ny n., pl. whin•nies; v., whin•nied, whin•ny•ing.
whip v., whipped, whip•ping.
whip•cord
whip•lash
whip•like
whip•per•snap•per
whip•pet
whip•ple•tree
whip•poor•will or whip-p oor-will
whip•saw v., whip•sawed, whip•saw•ing.
whir or whirr v., whirred, whir•ring
whirl v., whirled, whirl•ing.
whirl•i•gig
whirl•pool
whirl•wind
whirl•y•bird
whisk v., whisked, whisk•ing.
whisk broom
whisk•er
whisk•ered
whisk•er•y
whis•key or whis•ky n., pl. whis•keys or whis•kies.
whis•per v., whis•pered, whis•per•ing.

whis•per•y
whist
whis•tle v., whis•tled, whis•tling.
whistle stop n.
whis•tle-stop v., whis•tle-stopped, whis•tle-stop•ping.
whis•tle•a•ble
whit (bit: cf. WIT)
white adj., whit•er, whit•est.
white-bread
white-col•lar
white knight Business.
white-shoe
white•board
white•cap
white•fish n., pl. white•fish or white•fish•es.
white•head
White•horse
whit•en v., whit•ened, whit•en•ing.
white space Computers.
white•wall
white•wash v., white•washed, white•wash•ing.
whith•er (where: cf. WITHER)
whith•er•so•ev•er
whit•ish
whit•ish•ness
whit•low
Whit•man
Whit•ney
Whit•sun•day
whit•tle v., whit•tled, whit•tling.
whit•tler
whiz or whizz, v., whizzed, whiz•zing.
WHO (World Health Organization)

who
whoa
who•dun•it
who•ev•er
whole (entire: cf. HOLE)
whole wheat n.
whole-wheat adj.
whole•heart•ed
whole•heart•ed•ly
whole•heart•ed•ness
whole•ness
whole•sale v., whole•saled, whole•sal•ing. Business.
whole•sal•er Business.
whole•some
whole•some•ness
who'll
whol•ly (entirely: cf. HOLEY; HOLY)
whom
whom•ev•er
whom•so
whom•so•ev•er
whoop v., whooped, whoop•ing. (loud shout; to whoop: cf. HOOP)
whoop•ing cough
whoosh v., whooshed, whoosh•ing.
whop•per
whop•ping
who're
whore v., whored, whor•ing. (prostitute; to be a whore: cf. HOAR)
whorl
who's (who is)
whose (belonging to whom)
whose•so•ev•er
whos•ev•er
who•so
who•so•ev•er

WI (Wisconsin)
Wich○i○ta
wick¹
wick² *adj.*, wicked,
 wicking *v.*, (drew off
 by capillary action.)
wick○ed (evil)
wick•ed○ly
wick○er
wick○er•work
wick○et
wide *adj.*, wid○er,
 wid•est.
wide-ar○e○a net•
 work (WAN) *Comput-
 ers.*
wide-a○wake
wide-a○wake○ness
wide-eyed
wide•mouthed
wid○en *v.*, wid•ened,
 wid•en○ing.
wide•ness
wide•spread
widg•eon *n.*, *pl.*
 widg•eons or widg•
 eon.
wid○ow *v.*, wid•
 owed, wid•ow○ing.
wid•ow○er
width
wield *v.*, wield○ed,
 wield•ing.
wield•a○ble
wield○er
wie•ner
Wie•ner
wife *n.*, *pl.* wives.
wife•dom
wife•less
wig *v.*, wigged, wig•
 ging.
wig•gle *v.*, wig•gled,
 wig•gling.
wiggle room
wig•less

wig•let
wig•like
wig•wag *v.*, wig•
 wagged, wig•wag•
 ging.
wig•wam
wild *v.*, wild○ed,
 wild•ing; *adj.*,
 wild○er, wild•est.
wild-eyed
wild-goose chase
wild•cat *n.*, *pl.* wild•
 cats or wild•cat; *v.*,
 wild•cat•ted, wild•
 cat•ting.
wil•de•beest *n.*, *pl.*
 wil•de•beests or
 wil•de•be est.
wil•der•ness
wild•fire
wild•fowl
wild○ing
wild○ly
wild•ness
wile (trick: cf. WHILE)
wiles
wil○i•ness
will *v.*, would or
 willed, willed, will•
 ing.
will-less
will-o'-the-wisp
will•ful or wil•ful
will•ful○ly
will•ful•ness
Wil•liam
wil•lies
will•ing
will•ing○ly
will•ing•ness
wil•low
wil•low○y
will•pow○er or will
 pow○er
wil○ly-nil○ly
Wil•son

wilt *v.*, wilt○ed, wilt•
 ing.
Wil•ton
wil○y *adj.*, wil•i○er,
 wil•i•est.
wimp
wimp○y *adj.*, wimp•
 i○er, wimp•i•est.
win *v.*, won, win•
 ning.
win-win
wince *v.*, winced,
 winc•ing.
winch *v.*, winched,
 winch•ing.
Win•ches•ter drive
 Computers.
wind¹ *v.*, wind○ed,
 wind•ing. (moving
 air; to make short of
 breath)
wind² *v.*, wound,
 wind•ing. *(to mean-
 der)*
wind-bro○ken
wind-swept
wind•age
wind•bag
wind•break
wind•burn
wind•burned
wind•chill fac•tor
wind○ed
wind•fall
wind•flow○er
Wind•hoek
wind○i○ly
wind○i•ness
wind•ing
wind•jam•mer
wind•lass
wind•mill
win•dow
win○dow-shop○per
win•dow○ing *Comput-
 ers.*

win○dow•less
win○dow•pane
win○dow-shop v.,
  win○dow-shopped,
  win○dow-shop○
  ping.
win○dow•sill
wind•pipe
wind•shield
Wind•sor
wind•storm
wind•surf v., wind•
  surfed, wind•surf•
  ing.
wind•surf○er
wind•up
wind•ward
wind○y adj., wind•
  i○er, wind•i•est.
wine v., wined, win•
  ing. (fermented bever-
  age; to supply with
  wine: cf. WHINE)
win•er○y n., pl. win•
  er•ies.
wing v., winged,
  wing•ing.
wing•like
wing•spread
wink v., winked,
  wink•ing.
win•kle v., win•kled,
  win•kling.
win•na○ble
win•ner
win•ning
win•ning○ly
Win•ni•peg
win•now v., win•
  nowed, win•now•
  ing.
win•now○er
win○o n., pl. win○os.
win•some
win•ter v., win•tered,
  win•ter•ing.
win○ter•green

win•ter•ize v., win•
  ter•ized, win•ter•
  iz•ing.
win•ter•kill v.,
  win•ter•killed,
  win•ter•kill•ing.
win•ter•time
win•tri•ness
win•try adj., win•
  tri•er, win•tri•est.
win○y adj., win•i○er,
  win•i•est.
wipe v., wiped, wip•
  ing.
wire v., wired, wir•
  ing.
wire•less
wire•like
Wire•pho○to n., pl.
  Wire•pho•tos.
  Trademark.
wire•pull○er
wire•pull•ing
wire•tap v., wire•
  tapped, wire•tap•
  ping.
wire•tap•per
wir○y adj., wir•i○er,
  wir•i•est.
Wis•con•sin (WI)
Wis•con•sin•ite
wis•dom
wisdom tooth
Wise
wise¹
wise² v., wised, wis•
  ing;. adj., wis○er,
  wis•est.
wise•a○cre
wise•crack v., wise•
  cracked, wise•crack•
  ing.
wise○ly
wish v., wished,
  wish•ing.
wish•bone
wish•ful

wish○y-wash○y
wisp
wis•te•ri○a or wis•
  tar○i○a, n., pl. wis•
  te•ri•as or wis•tar•
  i○as.
wist•ful
wist•ful○ly
wist•ful•ness
wit (cleverness: cf.
  WHIT)
witch (sorceress: cf.
  WHICH)
witch hunt or witch-
  hunt
witch-hunt○ing
witch•er○y
witch•ing
witch•like
witch○y adj., witch•
  i○er, witch•i•est.
with○al
with•draw v., with•
  drew, with•drawn,
  with•draw•ing.
with•draw○al
with•drawn
with○er v., with•ered,
  with•er•ing. (to
  shrivel: cf. WHITHER)
with•er•ing○ly
with•ers
with•hold v., with•
  held, with•hold•ing.
with•hold•ing tax
  Business.
with○in
with○out
with•stand v., with•
  stood, with•stand•
  ing.
wit•less
wit•ness v., wit•
  nessed, wit•ness•
  ing.
wit•ti•cism
wit•ti○ly

wit•ti•ness
wit•ting
wit•ting•ly
wit•ty adj., wit•ti•er,
  wit•ti•est.
wive v., wived, wiv•
  ing.
wives
wiz•ard
wiz•ard•ry
wiz•ened
wob•ble v., wob•
  bled, wob•bling.
wob•bly adj., wob•
  bli•er, wob•bli•est.
woe
woe•be•gone
woe•ful
woe•ful•ly
woe•ful•ness
wok
woke
wok•en
wolf n., pl. wolves; v.,
  wolfed, wolf•ing.
wolf•hound
wolf•like
wolfs•bane
wol•ver•ine
wom○an n., pl.
  wom○en.
wom○an-suf○fra○gist
wom○an•hood
wom○an•ish
wom○an•ish•ness
wom○an•ize v.,
  wom○an•ized,
  wom○an•iz•ing.
wom○an•kind
wom○an•less
wom○an•like
wom○an•li•ness
wom•an○ly
womb
wom•bat
wombed

wom○en
wom○en•folk or
  wom○en•folks
wom○en's lib•er•a•
  tion
wom○yn n. pl.
won¹ (did win: cf. ONE)
won² n., pl. won. (Ko-
  rean monetary unit)
won ton or won•ton,
  (Chinese dumpling: cf.
  WANTON)
won•der v., won•
  dered, won•der•ing.
  (to speculate: cf. WAN-
  DER)
won•der•ful
won•der•ful○ly
won•der•land
won•der•ment
won•drous
won•drous○ly
wont (habit: cf. WANT;
  WON'T)
won't (will not)
wont○ed
woo v., wooed, woo•
  ing.
wood (lumber: cf.
  WOULD)
wood•bine
wood•block
wood•carv○er
wood•carv○ing
wood•chuck
wood•cock n., pl.
  wood•cocks or
  wood•cock.
wood•craft
wood•crafts•man n.,
  pl. wood•crafts•
  men.
wood•cut
wood•cut•ter
wood•cut•ting
wood○ed
wood○en

wood•en○ly
wood•en•ness
wood○en•ware
wood○i•ness
wood•land
wood•man n., pl.
  wood•men.
wood•peck○er
wood•pile
wood•ruff
wood•shed v., wood•
  shed•ded, wood•
  shed•ding.
woods•man n., pl.
  woods•men.
woods○y adj., woods•
  i○er, woods•i•est.
wood•wind
wood•work
wood•work•ing
wood○y¹ adj., wood•
  i○er, wood•i•est.
wood○y or wood○ie,²
  n., pl. wood•ies.
woo○er
woof v., woofed,
  woof•ing.
woof○er
wool
wool○en
wool•gath○er v.,
  wool•gath•ered,
  wool•gath•er•ing.
wool•gath•er•ing
wool•lies or wool•ies
wool•li•ness
wool○ly
wooz○y adj., wooz•
  i○er, wooz•i•est.
Worces•ter
word v., word○ed,
  word•ing.
word proc•ess•ing
  Computers.
word proc•es•sor
  Computers.
word•age

word•book
word•ing
word•play
Words•worth
wore (did wear: cf. WAR)
work v., worked or wrought, working.
work force Business.
work rules Business.
work•a•ble
work•a•day
work•a•hol•ic
work•a•hol•ism
work•bench
work•book
work•day
work•er
work•ers' com•pen•sa•tion Business.
work•horse
work•house n., pl. work•hous•es.
work•ing as•set Business.
working cap•i•tal Business.
working di•rec•to•ry Computers.
work•ing•man n., pl. work•ing•men.
work load or work•load
work•man n., pl. work•men.
work•man•like or work•man•ly
work•man•ship
work•men's com•pen•sa•tion Business.
work•out
work•place
work•room
work•shop
work•sta•tion Computers.

work•ta•ble
work•up
work•week
world
world beat
World War I
World War II
world•beat•er or world-be at•er
world•li•ness
world•ly adj., world•li•er, world•li•est.
world•ly-wise
world•wide or world-wide
WORM Computers. (write-once, read-many optical disc)
worm v., wormed, worm•ing.
worm gear or worm•gear
worm•like
worm•wood
worn
worn-out
wor•ri•er
wor•ri•ment
wor•ri•some
wor•ri•some•ly
wor•ri•some•ness
wor•ry n., pl. wor•ries; v., wor•ried, wor•ry•ing.
wor•ry•ing•ly
wor•ry•wart
worse
wors•en v., wors•ened, wors•en•ing.
wor•ship v., wor•shiped or wor•shipped, wor•ship•ing or wor•ship•ping.
wor•ship•er
wor•ship•ful
worst v., worst•ed,

worst•ing. (most bad: cf. WURST)
worst•ed¹ (defeated)
wor•sted² (fabric)
wort
worth
wor•thi•ly
wor•thi•ness
worth•less
worth•less•ly
worth•less•ness
worth•while
worth•while•ness
wor•thy n., pl. wor•thies; adj., wor•thi•er, wor•thi•est.
would (might: cf. WOOD)
would-be
would•n't (would not)
wouldst
wound v., wound•ed, wound•ing.
wound•ing•ly
wove
wo•ven
wow v., wowed, wow•ing.
WP Computers. (word processing)
wrack v., wracked, wrack•ing.
wraith
wraith•like
wran•gle v., wran•gled, wran•gling.
wrap v., wrapped, wrap•ping. (to en-close: cf. RAP)
wrap-up
wrap•a•round or wrap-a•round Computers.
wrapped (enclosed: cf. RAPPED; RAPT)
wrap•per
wrap•ping

wrath

wreak *v.*, wreaked, wreak•ing. (to inflict: cf. REEK; WRECK)

wreath *n.*, *pl.* wreaths.

wreathe *v.*, wreathed, wreath•ing.

wreath•like

wreck *v.*, wrecked, wreck•ing. (to de-stroy: cf. REEK; WREAK)

wreck•age

wreck∘er

wren

wrench *v.*, wrenched, wrench•ing.

wrench•ing∘ly

wrest *v.*, wrest∘ed, wrest•ing. (to pull away: cf. REST)

wres•tle *v.*, wres•tled, wres•tling.

wres•tler

wres•tling

wretch (unfortunate person: cf. RETCH)

wretch∘ed

wretch•ed∘ly

wretch•ed•ness

wrig•gle *v.*, wrig•gled, wrig•gling.

wright (worker: cf. RIGHT; RITE; WRITE)

wring *v.*, wrung, wring•ing. (to twist: cf. RING)

wring∘er

wrin•kle *v.*, wrin•kled, wrin•kling.

wrin•kly *adj.*, wrin•kli∘er, wrin•kli•est.

wrist

wrist•band

wrist•watch or wrist watch

writ

write *v.*, wrote, writ•ten, writ•ing. (to put words on paper: cf. RIGHT; RITE; WRIGHT)

write-down *Business.*

write-in

write-off *Business.*

write-pro∘tect *v.*, write-pro∘tect∘ed, write-pro∘tect∘ing. *Computers.*

write-up

writ∘er

writhe *v.*, writhed, writh•ing.

writh•ing∘ly

writ•ing

writ•ten

wrong *v.*, wronged, wrong•ing.

wrong•do∘er

wrong•ful

wrong•ful∘ly

wrong•head∘ed or wrong-head∘ed

wrong•head•ed∘ly

wrong•head•ed•ness

wrong•ly

wrong•ness

wrote (did write: cf. ROTE)

wroth

wrought

wrought i∘ron *n.*

wrought-i∘ron *adj.*

wrought-up

wrung (did wring: cf. RUNG)

wry (lopsided: cf. RYE)

wry∘ly

wry•neck

wry•ness

wu shu

wurst (sausage: cf. WORST)

wuss

WV (West Virginia)

WY (Wyoming)

Wy•o•ming **(WY)**

Wy•o•ming•ite

WYSIWYG *Computers.* (what you see is what you get)

X Y Z

X chro•mo•some

x-∘ra∘di∘a∘tion

x-∘ray or X-∘ray, *v.*, x-∘rayed, x-∘ray∘ing.

XD *Business.* (without dividend, "ex divi-dend")

xe•non

xen∘o•pho•bi∘a

xen∘o•pho•bic

xe•ri•scap∘ing

xe•ro•graph∘ic

xe•rog•ra•phy

Xe•rox *Trademark.*

xi

x in *Business.* (without interest, "ex interest")

X∘mas

X∘mo∘dem *Computers.*

xy•lem

xy∘lo•phone

xy∘lo•phon•ist

Y chro•mo•some

yacht

yacht•ing

yachts•man *n., pl.*
yachts•men.

Ya•hoo *n., pl.* Ya•
hoos.

Yah•weh

yak¹ (the animal)

yak² or yack *v.,*
yakked or yacked,
yak•king or yack•
ing. (to chatter idly)

y'all (you all: cf. YAWL;
YOWL)

yam

yam•mer *v.,* yam•
mered, yam•mer•
ing.

yang

Yan•gon

Yang•tze

yank *v.,* yanked,
yank•ing.

Yan•kee

yap *v.,* yapped, yap•
ping.

yard

yard•age

yard•arm

yard•man *n., pl.*
yard•men.

yard•stick

yar•mul•ke *n., pl.*
yar•mul•kes.

yarn *v.,* yarned, yarn•
ing.

yar•row

yaw *v.,* yawed, yaw•
ing.

yawl (sailboat: cf. Y'ALL;
YOWL)

yawn *v.,* yawned,
yawn•ing.

yaws

y•clept

ye

yea

yeah

year

year-round

year•book

year•ling

year•ly *n., pl.* year•
lies.

yearn *v.,* yearned,
yearn•ing.

yeast

yeast•y *adj.,* yeast•
i•er, yeast•i•est.

yegg

yell *v.,* yelled, yell•
ing.

yel•low *v.,* yel•
lowed, yel•low•ing;
adj., yel•low•er,
yel•low•est.

yel•low fe•ver

yel•low rib•bon

yel•low•ish

yelp *v.,* yelped, yelp•
ing.

Yel•tsin

Yem•en

yen¹ *n., pl.* yens. (crav-
ing)

yen² *n., pl.* yen. (Japanese monetary unit)

yeo•man *n., pl.* yeo•
men.

yeo•man•ry

yes *n., pl.* yes•es; *v.,*
yessed, yes•sing.

yes-man *n., pl.* yes-
men.

ye•shi•va *n., pl.* ye•
shi•vas.

yes•ter•day

yes•ter•year

yet

yew (tree: cf. EWE; YOU)

Yid•dish

yield *v.,* yield•ed,
yield•ing.

yin and yang

yip *v.,* yipped, yip•
ping.

yip•pie

Y•mo•dem *Computers.*

yo-yo stock *Business.*

yo•del *v.,* yo•deled or
yo•delled, yo•del•
ing or yo•del•ling.

yo•ga

yo•gi *n., pl.* yo•gis.

yo•gurt or yo•ghurt

yoke *n., pl.* yokes or
yoke; *v.,* yoked,
yok•ing. (frame for
joining animals; to
join)

yo•kel

Yo•ko•ha•ma

yolk (part of egg)

yolked

yolk•y

Yom Kip•pur

yon

yon•der

Yon•kers

yoo-hoo *v.,* yoo-
hooed, yoo-hoo•ing.

yore (time past: cf.
YOUR; YOU'RE)

you you, your, yours.
(person addressed: cf.
EWE; YEW)

you'll (you will: cf.
YULE)

young *adj.,* young•er,
young•est.

young•ish

young•ster

Youngs•town

your (belonging to you:
cf. YORE; YOU'RE)

you're (you are)

yours

yours tru•ly

your•self *n., pl.* your•
selves.

youth *n., pl.* youths or
youth.

youth•ful

youth•ful•ly

youth•ful•ness

yowl v., yowled, yowl•ing. (loud cry; to yowl: cf. Y'ALL; YAWL)

yo-yo n., pl. yo-yos.

yt•ter•bi•um

yt•tri•um

yuc•ca n., pl. yuc•cas.

yuck•y adj., yuck•i•er, yuck•i•est.

Yu•go•sla•vi•a

Yu•go•sla•vi•an

Yu•kon

Yule (Christmas: cf. YOU'LL)

yule•tide

yum•my adj., yum•mi•er, yum•mi•est.

yup or yep

yup•pie n., pl. yup•pies.

zai•ba•tsu n., pl. zai•ba•tsu. Business.

Za•ire or Za•ïre

Zam•bi•a

za•ni•ness

za•ny n., pl. za•nies; adj., za•ni•er, za•ni•est.

Zan•zi•bar

zap v., zapped, zap•ping.

zeal

zeal•ot

zeal•ous (enthusiastic: cf. JEALOUS)

zeal•ous•ly

ze•bra n., pl. ze•bras, ze•bra.

ZEG Business. (zero economic growth)

zeit•ge•ber

Zeit•geist

Zen

ze•nith

zeph•yr

zep•pe•lin

ze•ro n., pl. ze•ros, ze•roes;. v., ze•roed, ze•ro•ing.

ze•ro-based Business.

ze•ro-cou•pon Business.

ze•ro-e•mis•sion ve•hic•le

zero pop•u•la•tion growth

zero wait state

ze•ro-sum Business.

zest

zest•ful

zest•y adj., zest•i•er, zest•i•est.

ze•ta n., pl. ze•tas.

Zeus

zig•zag v., zig•zagged, zig•zag•ging.

zilch

zil•lion n., pl. zil•lions, zil•lion.

Zim•bab•we

Zim•bab•we•an

zinc

zing•er

zing•y adj., zing•i•er, zing•i•est.

zin•ni•a n., pl. zin•ni•as.

Zi•on

Zi•on•ism

Zi•on•ist

zip v., zipped, zip•ping.

ZIP code Trademark. (Zone Improvement Program code for mail)

zip•per v., zip•pered, zip•per•ing.

zip•py adj., zip•pi•er, zip•pi•est.

zir•con

zir•co•ni•um

zit

zith•er

Z•mo•dem Computers.

zo•di•ac

zo•di•a•cal

zom•bie

zon•al

zone v., zoned, zon•ing.

zone pric•ing Business.

zoned-bit re•cord•ing Computers.

zonked

zoo n., pl. zoos.

zo•o•log•i•cal

zo•ol•o•gist

zo•ol•o•gy

zoom v., zoomed, zoom•ing.

zoom box Computers.

zoom lens

zo•o•phyte

zo•o•phyt•ic

Zo•ro•as•ter

Zo•ro•as•tri•an•ism

zouk

zuc•chi•ni n., pl. zuc•chi•ni, zuc•chi•nis.

Zu•lu n., pl. Zu•lus, Zu•lu.

Zu•ni or Zu•ñi n., pl. Zu•nis or Zu•ñis, Zu•ni or Zu•ñi.

Zu•rich

zwie•back

zy•gote

zy•mur•gy

ENGLISH-LANGUAGE
RESOURCES
ON THE NET

ENGLISH-LANGUAGE RESOURCES ON THE NET

This list of Web sites for language buffs was compiled by Jesse Sheidlower, author of *Jesse's Word of the Day*, whose own site is listed below. The list contains invaluable resources for all of us who are interested in spelling, grammar, usage, and whatever other information we can find to make our writing worth reading.

http://www.jessesword.com

Language expert Jesse Sheidlower offers witty and informative answers to the most interesting real-life language questions posed by visitors to his popular site.

alt.usage.english
news:alt.usage.english

The main Usenet group for discussions of English. Enormously high-volume, the quality of information on alt.usage.english varies, but there's always something useful to be found here. Virtually every English-related topic, simple to complex, is discussed here.

alt.usage.english FAQ
http://www.scripps.edu/pub/dem-web/misrael/usage.html

An exceptionally useful FAQ (Frequently Asked Questions) document, written by Mark Israel, covering everything from the etymology of common phrases to advice on reference works to the use of ASCII to represent International Phonetic Alphabet symbols.

Perhaps the best single document on the Net devoted to English. The above address is for Mark Israel's language page, which has links to several versions of the FAQ.

American Dialect Society
http://www.jerrynet.com/ads/index.htm

The American Dialect Society is the premier scholarly organization for the study of the English language in North America. Their Web site provides background about the ADS, an index to its journal, *American Speech*, information about and archives of ADS-L, the Society's very active electronic mailing list, and more.

American Name Society
http://www.wtsn.binghamton.edu/ANS/

A brief description of the American Name Society, devoted to the study of names—both personal and geographical—and naming practices in the U.S. and abroad.

Copy Editor
http://www.copyeditor.com

The Web site for *Copy Editor*, an outstanding newsletter for publishing professionals. Especially good in its coverage of cutting-edge language issues.

Dictionary of American Regional English
http://polyglot.lss.wisc.edu/dare/dare.html

The Dictionary of American Regional English, or DARE, is an ongoing project (three volumes, covering the letters A through O, have been published) to catalogue the regional variations in American English. The

DARE site provides a general introduction to this most important dictionary project.

The Eclectic Company
http://www.lsa.umich.edu/ling/jlawler/
    lingmarks.html

An array of links to sites, resources, and articles on many aspects of English (and other languages) by University of Michigan linguist John Lawler. Includes Lawler's own excellent articles on usage, and the great ChomskyBot, which randomly generates surprisingly believable linguistics articles.

Grammar and Style Notes
http://www.english.upenn.edu/ ~ jlynch/
    Grammar/

A large collection of essays by Jack Lynch, a graduate student in English, covering grammar, usage, and style. Concise and sensible.

The Jargon File
http://www.wins.uva.nl/ ~ mes/jargon/

An extremely comprehensive guide to the language of the on-line world. Has existed in various forms for many years, and has been published in print as (most recently) *The New Hacker's Dictionary*. Detailed, accurate definitions, masses of historical information, zesty writing. Indispensable.

Oxford English Dictionary
http://www.oed.com

Though still under development and not fully accessible to the public, the Oxford English

Dictionary's site has much fascinating material about the greatest historical dictionary ever produced.

The Scots Haunbuik
http://www.umist.ac.uk/UMIST_CAL/Scots/haunbuik.htm

A short introduction to the Scots language. Includes historical background, pronunciation guidelines, grammar, spelling, vocabulary, and references.

The Word Detective
http://www.word-detective.com

The online version of Evan Morris's syndicated newspaper column. Morris's consistently witty and knowledgeable writing shouldn't be missed. As a very rare bonus, this is an exceptionally well-designed Web site.

World Wide Words
http://clever.net/quinion/words/index.htm

A collection of short essays by Michael Quinion on a wide variety of topics. Sections on new words, newsworthy words, old obscure words, and usage notes. Consistently interesting and reliable.